Models for Writers

Short Essays for Composition

TENTH EDITION

Alfred Rosa
Paul Eschholz

University of Vermont

BEDFORD/ST. MARTIN'S
Boston ◆ *New York*

For Bedford/St. Martin's
Developmental Editor: Adam Whitehurst
Production Editor: Ryan Sullivan
Production Supervisor: Jennifer Peterson
Marketing Manager: Molly Parke
Art Director: Lucy Krikorian
Copy Editor: Rosemary Winfield
Indexer: Schroeder Indexing Services
Photo Research: Helane Prottas
Cover Design: Sara Gates
Cover Art: Donna Dennison and Pelle Cass
Composition: Macmillan Publishing Solutions
Printing and Binding: Haddon Craftsmen, Inc., an RR Donnelley & Sons Company

President: Joan E. Feinberg
Editorial Director: Denise B. Wydra
Editor in Chief: Karen S. Henry
Director of Marketing: Karen R. Soeltz
Director of Editing, Design, and Production: Marcia Cohen
Assistant Director of Editing, Design, and Production: Elise S. Kaiser
Managing Editor: Shuli Traub

Library of Congress Control Number: 2008943129

Manufactured in the United States of America.

1 2 3 4 5 6 14 13 12 11 10 09

For information, write: Bedford/St. Martin's, 75 Arlington Street, Boston, MA 02116 (617-399-4000)

ISBN-10: 0-312-53113-3 ISBN-13: 978-0-312-53113-3 (paperback)
ISBN-10: 0-312-56581-X ISBN-13: 978-0-312-56581-7 (hardcover)

Acknowledgments
Acknowledgments and copyrights are continued at the back of the book on pages 633–36, which constitute an extension of the copyright page.

Preface

Models for Writers, now in its tenth edition, continues to offer students and instructors brief, accessible, high-interest essays that model rhetorical elements, principles, and patterns. As important as it is for students to read while they are learning to write college-level essays, *Models for Writers* offers more than just a collection of essays. The abundant study materials that accompany each selection help students master the writing skills they'll need for their college classes. In addition, writing activities and assignments help students stitch the various rhetorical elements together into coherent, forceful essays of their own. This approach, which has helped several million students over the past thirty years to become better writers, remains at the heart of the book.

In this tenth edition, we continue to emphasize the classic features of *Models for Writers* that have won praise from teachers and students alike. In addition, we have strengthened the book by introducing new selections and new voices and by developing key new features that provide students with the tools they need to become better readers and writers.

FAVORITE FEATURES OF *MODELS FOR WRITERS*

• **Brief, Lively Readings That Provide Outstanding Models.** Most of the seventy-five selections in *Models for Writers* are comparable in length (two to three pages) to the essays students will write themselves, and each clearly illustrates a basic rhetorical element, principle, or pattern. Just as important, the essays deal with subjects that we know from our own teaching experience will spark the interest of most college students. With such well-known authors as Sandra Cisneros, Isaac Asimov, Maya Angelou, Steven Pinker, Langston Hughes, and Sarah Vowell, the range of voices, cultural perspectives, styles, and degrees of complexity represented in the essays will resonate with today's students.

• **Introductory Chapters on Reading and Writing.** The chapters in Part One help students understand the writing process and use the essays they read to improve their own writing. Chapter 1 details the steps in the writing process and illustrates them with a student essay in progress. Chapter 2 shows students how to use the reading apparatus in the text, provides them with guidelines for critical reading, and demonstrates with three student essays how they can generate their own writing from reading.

• **More Help with Sentence Grammar.** Chapter 1 now includes help with the editing concerns instructors across the country identified as the most problematic for their students—such as run-on sentences and misplaced modifiers. Brief explanations and hand-edited examples help students find and correct these common errors in their own writing.

• **Expanded Rhetorical Organization.** Each of the nineteen rhetorically based chapters in *Models for Writers* is devoted to a particular element or pattern important to college writing. In Part Two, Chapters 3 through 10 focus on the concepts of thesis, unity, organization, beginnings and endings, paragraphs, transitions, effective sentences, and writing with sources. In Part Three, Chapter 11 illustrates the importance of controlling diction and tone, and Chapter 12, the uses of figurative language. In Part Four, Chapters 13 through 21 explore the types of writing most often required of college students: illustration, narration, description, process analysis, definition, division and classification, comparison and contrast, cause and effect, and argument.

• **Abundant Study Materials.** To help students use the readings to improve their writing, every essay is accompanied by ample study materials.

Reflecting on What You Know activities precede each reading and prompt students to explore their own ideas and experiences regarding the issues presented in the reading.

A *Thinking Critically about This Reading* question follows each essay, and it encourages students to consider the writer's assumptions, make connections not readily apparent, or explore the broader implications of the selection.

Questions for Study and Discussion focus on the selection's content and on the author's purpose and the particular strategy used to achieve that purpose, with at least one question in each series focusing on a writing concern other than the one highlighted in the chapter to remind students that good writing is never one-dimensional.

Classroom Activities provide brief exercises enabling students to work in the classroom (often in groups) on rhetorical elements, techniques, or patterns. These activities range from developing thesis statements to using strong action verbs and building argumentative evidence. Classroom activities help students apply concepts modeled in the readings to their own writing.

Suggested Writing Assignments provide at least two writing assignments for each essay, with one encouraging students to use the reading selection as a direct model and another asking them to respond to the content of the reading.

- **Concise and Helpful Chapter Introductions.** Writing instructors who use *Models for Writers* have continued to be generous in their praise for the brief, student-friendly chapter introductions, which explain the various elements and patterns. In each one, students will find numerous illuminating examples—many written by students—of the feature or principle under discussion.

- **Longer Readings in Each Part.** To provide a greater variety of essays for students and to help them progress to more demanding reading, Parts Two, Three, and Four of *Models for Writers* include at least one longer essay. Selections by Nancy Gibbs, Steven Pinker, George Orwell, and Alexander Petrunkevitch, for example, introduce students to more complex forms of the genre.

- **Flexible Arrangement.** Each chapter is self-contained so that instructors can easily follow their own teaching sequences, omitting or emphasizing certain chapters according to the needs of their students or the requirements of the course.

- **Appendix on Writing a Research Paper.** A brief, helpful appendix offers guidance on conducting research using print and online sources, using keyword searches, evaluating sources, taking notes, and documenting sources using current MLA citation style.

- **Glossary of Useful Terms.** Cross-referenced in many of the questions and writing assignments throughout the book, this helpful list covers rhetorical and literary terms that student writers need to know. Terms that are defined in the Glossary are shown in boldface the first time they appear in the text.

- **"Thematic Clusters" Alternate Table of Contents.** This alternate table of contents features focused clusters of two to nine essays that share common themes. Students and instructors attracted to the theme of one essay in *Models for Writers* can consult these clusters to find other essays in the book that address the same topic or theme.

• **Instructor's Manual.** In the manual that accompanies *Models for Writers,* we offer insights into the rhetorical features of each essay as well as advice on how best to use the materials in class. Suggested answers for critical thinking questions, study questions, and classroom activities are included.

NEW TO THE TENTH EDITION OF *MODELS FOR WRITERS*

• **Engaging, Informative, and Diverse New Readings.** Twenty-eight readings—one-third of this edition's selections—are new and focus on topics of current interest, such as the environment, human genetic engineering, what we can learn about ourselves through our Internet keyword searches, and the resurgence of the family dinner. We chose these essays for their brevity, clarity, and potential for developing critical thinking and writing skills in student writers. Among the new readings included in this edition are essays by popular contemporary writers such as Steven Pinker, Alice Walker, Diane Ackerman, Sanjay Gupta, Henry Louis Gates Jr., and Malcolm Gladwell.

• **New Chapter 10, "Writing with Sources."** One of the biggest challenges student writers face is incorporating support from other writers. This new chapter models for them some effective strategies for using signal phrases, quotations, summary, and paraphrase in order to help them become more confident in joining an academic conversation through their writing.

• **Additional Argument Pairs.** We've increased the number of argument pairs to four on contemporary topics such as solving the organ transplant shortage and managing the overflow of garbage. Each of the paired argument essays features research-based writing suggestions.

• **New Coverage of Academic Language.** A new section in Chapter 1 helps students determine appropriate word choice for their academic papers, covering a wide range of topics from pronoun usage to discipline-specific prose to levels of formality in different kinds of papers.

• **Updated Visual Writing Prompts.** We've included nine new images, paired with professional essays, encouraging students to analyze connections between print and visual texts.

• **Expanded Companion Web Site, bedfordstmartins.com/models.** The companion Web site for the tenth edition of *Models for Writers* features a Customized Learning Plan through *Exercise Central* that provides students additional opportunities to practice grammar and mechanics online, with exercises chosen specifically to work with the text. The *Models for Writers* Web site also features updated self-scoring quizzes for every professional essay in the book.

MORE INSTRUCTOR AND STUDENT RESOURCES

In addition to the Instructor's Manual and companion Web site, a host of additional resources are available to help meet the needs of your classroom:

- *Teaching Central.* Because teaching is central, Bedford/St. Martin's is committed to supporting the work that teachers do. We have something for everyone—from the first-time adjunct to the program director. And all Bedford/St. Martin's professional resources are free to instructors. Visit **bedfordstmartins.com/teachingcentral.**
- *Just-in-Time Teaching.* Looking for last-minute course materials from a source you can trust? We've culled the best handouts, teaching tips, assignment ideas, and more from our print and online resources and put them all in one place. You can easily search, download, and print whatever you need. Go to **bedfordstmartins.com/justintime.**
- *Re:Writing Plus.* This resource neatly gathers our collections of premium digital content into one online library for composition. Check out *i•cite visualizing sources*, tutorials and hands-on source practice; hundreds of model documents; and *Peer Factor*, the first-ever peer review game at **bedfordstmartins.com/rewritingplus.**

ACKNOWLEDGMENTS

In response to the many thoughtful and helpful reviews from instructors who use this book, we have maintained the solid foundation of the previous edition of *Models for Writers* while adding fresh readings and writing topics to stimulate today's student writers.

We are indebted to many people for their advice as we prepared this tenth edition. We are especially grateful to Steven Accardi, Pima Community College; Richard Baker, Adams State College; Nancy R. Beasley, Georgia College and State University; Christy Burns, Jacksonville State University; Deborah Bush, Copiah-Lincoln Community College; Alanna Callaway, San Jose State University;

Jeffrey Foster, Naugatuck Valley Community College; M. Sue Fox, Central New Mexico Community College; Tina Hallquist, Temple University; William J. Hug, Jacksonville State University; Heather Jett, University of Wisconsin–La Crosse; Richard Johnson, Kirkwood Community College; Melissa Korber, Las Positas College; Heather Lozano, El Paso Community College; Laura L. Morris, Francis Marion University; Robbi Nester, Irvine Valley College; Callie A. Palmer, Linn Benton Community College; Sam Pierstorff, Modesto Junior College; Lisa Ragsdale, Central New Mexico Community College; Holly Schoenecker, Milwaukee Area Tech College–South; Georgeanna Sellers, High Point University; Emmanuel Sigauke, Cosumnes River College; Donnie A. Thompson, Defense Language Institute English Language Center; Tondalaya W. VanLear, Dabney S. Lancaster Community College; and Paul Vera, Glendale Community College.

It has been our good fortune to have the editorial guidance and good cheer of Adam Whitehurst, our developmental editor on this book; Ryan Sullivan, our production editor; Nancy Perry, our long-time colleague; and the rest of the excellent team at Bedford/ St. Martin's—Joan Feinberg, Karen Henry, Denise Wydra, Erica Appel, Marcia Cohen, Shuli Traub, Steve Scipione, and Karita dos Santos—as we planned, developed, and wrote this new edition. Our special thanks go to the late Tom Broadbent—our mentor and original editor at St. Martin's Press—who helped us breathe life and soul into *Models for Writers* more than thirty years ago. The lessons that he shared with us during our fifteen-year partnership have stayed with us throughout our careers.

Thanks also to Sarah Federman, who authored the new material for the Instructor's Manual, and to Brian Kent, Cara Simone Bader, Tom Juvan, the late Susan Wanner, Dick Sweterlitsch, and Betsy Eschholz, who have shared their experiences using *Models for Writers* in the classroom. Our greatest debt is, as always, to our students—especially Lisa Driver, Susan Francis, Jake Jamieson, Zoe Ockenga, and Jeffrey Olesky, whose papers appear in this text—for all they have taught us over the years. Finally, we thank each other, partners in this writing and teaching venture for almost four decades.

Alfred Rosa
Paul Eschholz

Contents

part two The Elements of the Essay

part three The Language of the Essay

part four Types of Essays

Thematic Clusters

The thematic clusters of articles that follow focus on themes that students can pursue in their own compositions. The essays themselves provide ideas and information that will stimulate their thinking as well as provide source material for their writing. The clusters—the themes and the essays associated with them—are meant to be suggestive rather than comprehensive and fairly narrow in scope rather than far-ranging. Instructors and students are, of course, free to develop their own thematic groupings on which to base written work and are not limited by our groupings.

Teachers and Students

Parenting

Personal Dilemmas

Peer Pressure

The Natural World

What's in a Name?

The Power of Language

Punishment

The Sensual World

Medical Dilemmas

The Immigrant Experience

Sense of Place

The American Dream

The Obesity Epidemic

Heroes/Role Models

Consumerism

Sense of Self

Family and Friends

Organ Donation

America's Garbage Problem

Race in America

Introduction for Students

Models for Writers is designed to help you learn to write by providing you with a collection of model essays—that is, essays that are examples of good writing. Good writing is direct and purposeful and communicates its message without confusing the reader. It doesn't wander from the topic, and it answers the reader's questions. Although good writing is well developed and detailed, it also accomplishes its task with the fewest possible words and with the simplest language appropriate to the writer's topic and thesis.

We know that one of the best ways to learn to write and to improve our writing is to read. By reading, we can see how other writers have communicated their experiences, ideas, thoughts, and feelings. We can study how they have used the various elements of the essay (words, sentences, paragraphs, organizational patterns, transitions, examples, evidence, and so forth) and thus learn how we might effectively do the same. When we see how a writer like James Lincoln Collier develops his essay "Anxiety: Challenge by Another Name" from a strong thesis statement, for example, we can better appreciate the importance of having a clear thesis statement in our own writing. When we see the way Russell Baker uses transitions in "Becoming a Writer" to link key phrases and important ideas so that readers can recognize how the parts of his essay fit together, we have a better idea of how to write coherently.

But we do not learn only by observing or by reading. We also learn by doing (that is, by writing), and in the best of all situations, we engage in these two activities in conjunction with one another. *Models for Writers* therefore encourages you to practice what you are learning and to move from reading to writing.

Part One of *Models for Writers* provides you with strategies to do just that. Chapter 1, The Writing Process, introduces you to the important steps of the writing process, gives you guidelines for writing, and illustrates the writing process with a student essay. Chapter 2, From Reading to Writing, shows you how to generate your own essays based on what you learn from the essays in this book. You will soon see that an effective essay has a clear purpose, often provides useful information, has an effect on the reader's thoughts and feelings, and is usually a pleasure to read. The essays that you will read in *Models for Writers* were chosen because they are effective essays.

All well-written essays also share a number of structural and stylistic features that are illustrated by the various essays in *Models for Writers*. One good way to learn what these features are and how you can incorporate them into your own writing is to look at each of them in isolation. For this reason, we have divided the readings in *Models for Writers* into three major parts and, within these parts, into nineteen chapters, each with its own particular focus and emphasis.

Part Two, The Elements of the Essay, includes eight chapters on the elements that are essential to a well-written essay, but because the concepts of thesis, unity, and organization underlie all the others, they come first in our sequence. Chapter 3, Thesis, shows how authors put forth or state the main ideas of their essays and how they use such statements to develop and control content. Chapter 4, Unity, shows how authors achieve a sense of wholeness in their essays, and Chapter 5, Organization, illustrates some important patterns that authors use to organize their thinking and writing. Chapter 6, Beginnings and Endings, offers advice on and models of ways to begin and conclude essays, while Chapter 7, Paragraphs, concentrates on the importance of well-developed paragraphs and what is necessary to achieve them. Chapter 8, Transitions, concerns the various devices that writers use to move from one idea or section of an essay to the next, and Chapter 9, Effective Sentences, focuses on techniques to make sentences powerful and to create stylistic variety. Finally, Chapter 10, Writing with Sources, shows how to integrate quotations, paraphrases, and summaries into the text of a paper and how to avoid plagiarism.

Part Three, The Language of the Essay, includes Chapter 11, Diction and Tone, which shows how writers carefully choose words either to convey exact meanings or to be purposely suggestive. In addition, this chapter shows how the words that a writer uses can create a particular tone or relationship between the writer and reader—one of irony, humor, or seriousness, for example. This part also includes Chapter 12, Figurative Language, which concentrates on the usefulness of the special devices of language—such as simile, metaphor, and personification—that add richness and depth to writing.

Part Four of *Models for Writers*, Types of Essays, includes Chapters 13 to 21, which are on the types of writing that are most often required of college writing students—illustration (how to use examples to illustrate a point or idea); narration (how to tell a story or give an account of an event); description (how to present a verbal picture); process analysis (how to explain how something is done or happens); definition (how to explain what something is); division and classification (how to divide a subject into its parts and place items into appropriate categories); comparison and contrast (how to explain the similarities and differences between two or more items); cause and effect (how to explain the causes of an event or the effects of an action); and argument (how to use reason and logic to persuade someone to your way of thinking). These types of writing are referred to as *organizational patterns* or *rhetorical modes.*

Studying and practicing the organizational patterns are important in any effort to broaden one's writing skills. In *Models for Writers*, we look at each pattern separately because we believe this is the simplest and most effective way to introduce them. However, this does not mean that the writer of a well-written essay necessarily chooses a single pattern and sticks to it exclusively and rigidly. Confining oneself to comparison and contrast throughout an entire essay, for instance, might prove impractical and may yield a strained, unnatural piece of writing. In fact, it is often best to use a single pattern to organize your essay and then to use other patterns as your material dictates. As you read the model essays in this text, you will find that a good many of them use one dominant pattern in combination with other patterns.

Combining organizational patterns is not something that you usually think about when you first tackle a writing assignment. Rather, such combinations of patterns develop naturally as you organize, draft, and revise your materials. Combinations of patterns also make your writing more interesting and effective. See Chapter 1 for a discussion of combining patterns.

Chapters 3 to 21 are organized in the same way. Each opens with an explanation of the element or principle under discussion. These introductions are brief, clear, and practical and usually provide one or more short examples of the feature or principle being studied, including examples from students such as yourself. Following the chapter introduction, we present three or four model essays (Chapter 21, with twelve essays, is an exception). Each essay has a brief introduction of its own, providing information about the author and directing your attention to the way that the essay demonstrates the featured technique. A Reflecting on What You Know prompt precedes each reading and invites you to explore your own ideas and experiences regarding some issue presented in the reading. Each essay is followed by four kinds of study materials—Thinking Critically about This Reading, Questions for Study and Discussion, Classroom Activity, and Suggested Writing Assignments. Read Chapter 2 for help on improving your writing by using the materials that accompany the readings.

Models for Writers provides information, instruction, and practice in writing essays. By reading thoughtfully and by applying the writing strategies and techniques you observe other writers using, you will learn to write more expressively and effectively.

part ■ one

On Reading and Writing Well

chapter **1**

The Writing Process

The essays in this book will help you understand the elements of good writing and provide ample opportunity to practice writing in response to the model essays. As you write your own essays, pay attention to your writing process. This chapter focuses on the stages of the writing process—prewriting, writing the first draft, revising, editing, and proofreading. It concludes with a sample student process that you can model your own writing after, from start to finish. The strategies suggested in this chapter for each stage of the writing process will help you overcome many of the problems you may face while writing your own essays.

PREWRITING

Writers rarely rely on inspiration alone to produce an effective piece of writing. Good writers prewrite or plan, write the first draft, revise, edit, and proofread. It is worth remembering, however, that the writing process is not as simple and as straightforward as this. Often the process is recursive, moving back and forth among the five stages. Moreover, writing is personal; no two people go about it exactly the same way. Still, it is possible to learn the steps in the process and thereby have a reassuring and reliable method for undertaking a writing task and producing a good composition.

Your reading can give you ideas and information, of course. But reading also helps expand your knowledge of the organizational patterns available to you, and, consequently, it can help direct all your prewriting activities. In *prewriting,* you select your subject and topic, gather ideas and information, and determine the thesis and organizational pattern or patterns you will use. Once you have worked through the prewriting process, you will be ready to start on your first draft. Let's explore how this works.

Understand Your Assignment

When you first receive an assignment, read it over several times. Focus on each word and each phrase to make sure you understand what you are being asked to do. Try restating the assignment in your own words to make sure you understand it. For example, consider the following assignments:

1. Narrate an experience that taught you that every situation has at least two sides.
2. Explain what is meant by *theoretical modeling* in the social sciences.
3. Write a persuasive essay in which you support or refute the following proposition: "Violence in the media is in large part responsible for an increase in violence in American society today."

Each of these assignments asks you to write in different ways. The first assignment asks you to tell the story of an event that showed you that every situation has more than one perspective. To complete the assignment, you might choose simply to narrate the event, or you might choose to analyze it in depth. In either case, you have to explain to your reader how you came to this new understanding of multiple perspectives and why it was important to you. The second assignment asks you to explain what theoretical modeling is and why it is used. To accomplish this assignment, you first need to read about the concept to gain a thorough understanding of it, and then you'll need to define it in your own words and explain its purpose and usefulness to your readers. You will also want to demonstrate the abstract concept with concrete examples to help your readers understand it. Finally, the third assignment asks you to take a position on a controversial issue for which there are many studies on both sides of the question. You will need to research the studies, consider the evidence they present, and then take a stand of your own. Your argument will necessarily have to draw on the sources and evidence you have researched, and you will need to refute the arguments and evidence presented by those experts who take an opposing position.

If, after reading the assignment several times, you are still unsure about what is being asked of you or about any additional requirements of the assignment, such as length or format, be sure to consult with your instructor. He or she should be willing to clear up any confusion before you start writing.

Choose a Subject Area, and Focus on a Topic

Although you will usually be given specific assignments in your writing course, you may sometimes have the freedom to write on any subject that interests you. In such a case, you may already have a specific idea in mind. For example, if you are interested in sports, you might argue against the use of performance-enhancing drugs by athletes. What happens, however, when you are free to choose your own subject and cannot think of anything to write about? If you find yourself in this situation, begin by determining a broad subject that you like to think about and might enjoy writing about—a general subject like virtual reality, medical ethics, amateur sports, or foreign travel. Also consider what you've recently read—essays in *Models for Writers,* for example—or your career ambitions when choosing a subject. Select several likely subjects, and let your mind explore their potential for interesting topics. Your goal is to arrive at an appropriately narrowed topic.

A topic is the specific part of a subject on which a writer focuses. Subjects such as the environment, literature, and sports are too broad to be dealt with adequately in a single essay. Entire books are written about these and other subjects. Start with your broad subject, and make it more specific. Thus if your subject is sports, you might choose as your topic rule violations in college recruiting, violence in ice hockey, types of fan behavior, the psychology of marathon runners, or the growth of sports medicine.

Suppose, for example, you select farming and advertising as possible subject areas. The examples on the following page illustrate how to narrow these broad subjects into manageable topics. Notice how each successive topic is more narrowed than the one before it. Moving from the general to the specific, the topics become appropriate for essay-length writing.

In moving from a broad subject to a particular topic, you should take into account any assigned constraints on length or format. You will also want to consider the amount of time you have to write. These practical considerations will affect the scope of your topic. For example, you couldn't adequately address subjects such as farming or

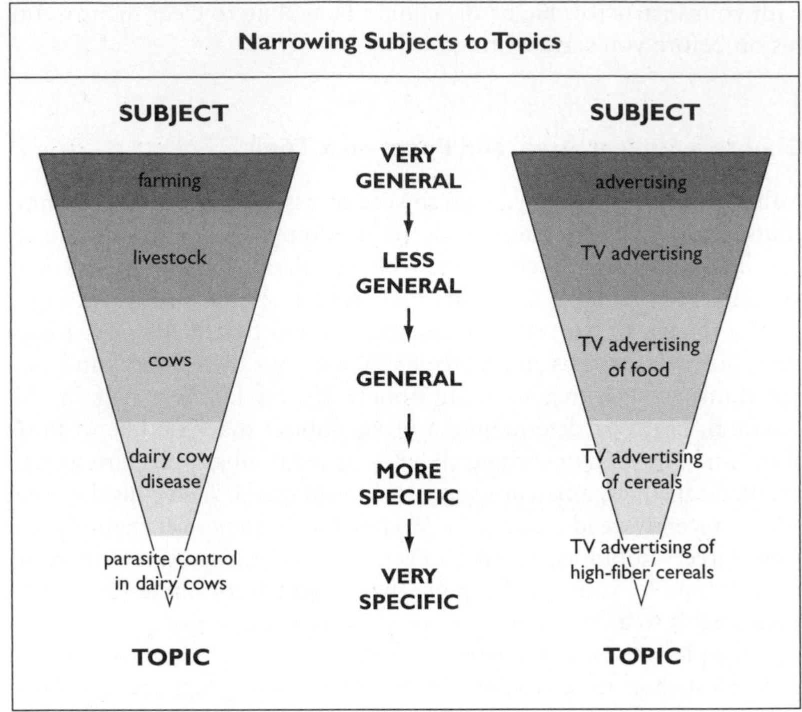

advertising in a five- to ten-page composition. These subjects are usually taken up in book-length publications.

Get Ideas and Collect Information

Once you have found your topic, you will need to determine what you want to say about it. The best way to do this is to gather information. Your ideas about a topic must be supported by information, such as facts and examples. The information you gather about a topic will influence your ideas about the topic and what you want to say. Here are some of the ways you can gather information:

1. *Ask questions about your topic.* If you were assigned the topic of theoretical modeling, for example, you could ask, what is *theoretical modeling*? Why, where, and by whom is theoretical modeling

used? What are the benefits of using it? Is it taught in school? Is it difficult to learn to use? Once the questioning starts, one question will lead to another, and the answers to these questions will be the stuff of your writing. Like a newspaper reporter going after a story, asking questions and getting answers are essential ways to understand a topic before trying to explain it to others.

2. *Brainstorm.* Jot down the things you know about a topic, freely associating ideas and information as a way to explore the topic and its possibilities. (See p. 33 for an example.) Don't censor or edit your notes, and don't worry about spelling or punctuation. Don't write your notes in list form because such an organization will imply a hierarchy of ideas, which may hamper your creativity and the free flow of your thoughts. The objective of *brainstorming* is to free up your thinking before you start to write. You may want to set aside your notes and return to them over several days. Once you generate a substantial amount of brainstormed material, you will want to study the items, attempt to see relationships among them, or sort and group the entries by using different colored highlighters.
3. *Cluster.* Another strategy for stimulating your thinking about a topic is *clustering*. Place your topic in a circle, and draw lines from that circle to other circles in which you write related key words or phrases. Around each of these key words, generate more circles representing the various aspects of the key word that come to mind. (See p. 34 for an example.) The value of clustering over brainstorming is that you are generating ideas and organizing them at the same time. Both techniques work very well, but you may prefer one over the other or may find that one works better with one topic than another.
4. *Research.* You may want to add to what you already know about your topic with research. Research can take many forms beyond formal research carried out in your library. For example, firsthand observations and interviews with people knowledgeable about your topic can provide up-to-date information. Whatever your form of research, take careful notes so you can accurately paraphrase an author or quote an interviewee. The appendix to this book (see pp. 597–621) will help you research a topic.
5. *Think creatively.* To push an idea one step further, to make a connection not easily recognized by others, to step to one side of your topic and see it in a new light, to ask a question no one else would,

or to arrive at a fresh insight is to be creative. Don't be afraid to step outside conventional wisdom and ask a basic or unorthodox question. Take risks. Such bravery adds creativity to your writing.

Establish Your Thesis

Once you have generated ideas and information, you are ready to begin the important task of establishing a controlling idea, or *thesis*. The thesis of an essay is its main idea, the point the writer is trying to make. The thesis is often expressed in one or two sentences called a *thesis statement*. Here's an example:

> The so-called serious news programs are becoming too much like tabloid news shows in both their content and their presentation.

The thesis statement should not be confused with your purpose for writing. While a thesis statement makes an assertion about your topic and actually appears in your essay as such, your purpose is what you are trying to do in the essay—to express, to explain, or to argue. For example, the purpose behind the preceding thesis statement might be expressed as follows:

> By comparing the transcripts of news shows like the *CBS Evening News* and tabloid shows like *Entertainment Tonight*, I will show troubling parallels in what the two genres of programs find "newsworthy."

This type of purpose statement should not appear in your essay. In other words, it's not a good idea to tell your readers what you are going to do in an essay. Just do it.

A thesis statement should be

- The most important point you make about a topic;
- More general than the ideas and facts used to support it; and
- Focused enough to be covered in the space allotted for the essay.

A thesis statement should not be a question but rather an assertion. If you find yourself writing a question for a thesis statement, answer the question first, and then write your statement.

How to Write a Thesis Statement

An effective method for developing a thesis statement is to begin by writing, "What I want to say is that . . ."

> What I want to say is that unless language barriers between patients and healthcare providers are overcome, the lives of many patients in our more culturally diverse cities will be endangered.

Later, when you delete the formulaic opening, you will be left with a thesis statement:

> Unless language barriers between patients and healthcare providers are overcome, many patients' lives in our more culturally diverse cities will be endangered.

A good way to determine whether your thesis is too general or too specific is to consider how easy it will be to present information and examples to support it. If you stray too far in either direction, your task will become much more difficult. A thesis statement that is too general will leave you overwhelmed by the number of issues you must address. For example, the statement, "Malls have ruined the fabric of American life" would lead to the question "How?" To answer it, you would probably have to include information about traffic patterns, urban decay, environmental damage, economic studies, and so on. You would obviously have to take shortcuts, and your paper would be ineffective. On the other hand, too specific a thesis statement will leave you with too little information to present. "The Big City Mall should not have been built because it reduced retail sales at the existing Big City stores by 21.4 percent" does not leave you with many options to develop an argument.

The thesis statement is usually set forth near the beginning of the essay, although writers sometimes begin with a few sentences that establish a context for the piece. One common strategy is to position the thesis as the final sentence of the first paragraph. In the opening paragraph of an essay on the harmful effects of quick weight-loss diets, student Marcie Turple builds a context for her thesis statement, which she presents in her last sentence:

> Americans are obsessed with thinness—even at the risk of dying. In the 1930s, people took dinitrophenol, an industrial poison, to lose weight. It boosted metabolism but caused blindness and some deaths. Since then dieters have used hormone injections, amphetamines, liquid protein diets, and, more recently, the controversial fen-phen. What most dieters need to realize is that there is no magic way to lose weight—no pill, no crash diet plan. *The only way to permanent weight loss is through sensible eating and exercise.*
>
> –Marcie Turple, student

Does Your Thesis Hold Water?

Once you have selected a possible thesis for an essay, ask yourself the following questions:

1. Does my thesis statement take a clear stance on an issue? And if so, what is that stance?
2. Is my thesis too general?
3. Is my thesis too specific?
4. Does my thesis apply to a larger audience than myself? If so, who is that audience?

For a list of guidelines that will help you check the validity of your thesis, see the box above. For more on the various ways to build an effective thesis, see Chapter 3, Thesis.

Know Your Audience

While it is not always possible to know who your readers are, you nevertheless need to consider your intended audience. Your attitude toward your topic, your tone, your sentence structure, and your choice of words are just some of the important considerations that rely on your awareness of audience. For a list of questions to help you determine your audience, see the box below.

Audience Questions

1. Who are my readers?
2. Is my audience specialized (for example, all those in my geology lab) or more general (college students)?
3. What do I know about my audience's age, gender, education, religious affiliation, socioeconomic status, and political attitudes?
4. What do my readers need to know that I can tell them?
5. Will my audience be interested, open-minded, resistant, objective, or hostile to what I am saying?
6. Is there any specialized language that my audience must have to understand my subject or that I should avoid?
7. What do I want my audience to do as a result of reading my essay?

Determine Your Method of Development

Part Four of *Models for Writers* includes chapters on the various types of writing most often required of college students. Often these types of writing are referred to as *methods of development, rhetorical patterns*, or *organizational patterns*.

Studying these organizational patterns and practicing the use of them are important in any effort to broaden your writing skills. In *Models for Writers,* we look at each pattern separately because we believe this is the most effective way to introduce them. However, this does not necessarily mean that a well-written essay adheres exclusively and rigidly to a single pattern of development. Confining yourself exclusively to comparison and contrast throughout an entire essay, for instance, might prove impractical and might yield a strained, unnatural piece of writing. In fact, it is often best to use a single pattern to organize and develop your essay and then use the other patterns as your material dictates. For a description of what each method of development involves, see the box below. As you read the model essays in this text, you will find that many of them utilize a combination of patterns to support the dominant pattern.

Methods of Development	
Illustration	Using examples to illustrate a point or idea
Narration	Telling a story or giving an account of an event
Description	Presenting a picture with words
Process Analysis	Explaining how something is done or happens
Definition	Explaining what something is
Division and Classification	Dividing a subject into its parts and placing them in appropriate categories
Comparison and Contrast	Demonstrating likenesses and differences
Cause and Effect	Explaining the causes of an event or the effects of an action
Argument	Using reason and logic to persuade someone to your way of thinking

Combining organizational patterns is probably not something you want to plan or even think about when you first tackle a writing assignment. Instead, let these patterns develop naturally as you organize, draft, and revise your materials. The combination of patterns will enhance the interest and impact of your writing.

If you're still undecided or concerned about combining patterns, try the following steps:

1. Summarize the point you want to make in a single phrase or sentence.
2. Restate the point as a question (in effect, the question your essay will answer).
3. Look closely at both the summary and the question for key words or concepts that suggest a particular pattern.
4. Consider other strategies that could support your primary pattern.

Here are some examples:

SUMMARY: Venus and Serena Williams are among the best women tennis players in the history of the game.

QUESTION: How do Venus and Serena Williams compare with other tennis players?

PATTERN: Comparison and contrast. The writer must compare the Williams sisters with other women players and provide evidence to support the claim that they are "among the best."

SUPPORTING PATTERNS: Illustration and description. Good evidence includes examples of their superior ability and accomplishments and descriptions of their athletic feats.

SUMMARY: How to build a personal Web site.

QUESTION: How do you build a personal Web site?

PATTERN: Process analysis. The word *how,* especially in the phrase *how to,* implies a procedure that can be explained in steps or stages.

SUPPORTING PATTERNS: Description. It will be necessary to describe the Web site at various points in the process, especially the look and design of the site.

SUMMARY: Petroleum and natural gas prices should be federally controlled.

QUESTION: What should be done about petroleum and natural gas prices?
PATTERN: Argument. The word *should* signals an argument, calling for evidence and reasoning in support of the conclusion.
SUPPORTING PATTERNS: Comparison and contrast and cause-and-effect analysis. The writer should present evidence from a comparison of federally controlled pricing with deregulated pricing as well as from a discussion of the effects of deregulation.

These are just a few examples showing how to decide on a pattern of development and supporting patterns that are suitable for your topic and what you want to say about it. In every case, your reading can guide you in recognizing the best plan to follow.

Map Your Organization

Once you decide what you want to write about and you come up with some ideas about what you might like to say, your next task is to jot down the main ideas for your essay in an order that seems both natural and logical to you. In other words, make a scratch outline. In constructing this outline, if you discover that one of the organizational patterns will help you in generating ideas, you might consider using that as your overall organizing principle.

Whether you write a formal outline, simply set down a rough sequence of the major points of your thesis, or take a middle ground between those two strategies, you need to think about the overall organization of your paper. Some writers make a detailed outline and fill it out point by point, while others follow a general plan and let the writing take them where it will, making any necessary adjustments to the plan when they revise.

Here are some major patterns of organization you may want to use for your outline:

- Chronological (oldest to newest, or the reverse)
- Spatial (top to bottom, left to right, inside to outside, and so forth)
- Least familiar to most familiar
- Easiest to most difficult to comprehend
- Easiest to most difficult to accept
- According to similarities or differences

Notice that some of these organizational patterns correspond to the rhetorical patterns in Part Four of this book. For example, a narrative essay generally follows a chronological organization. If you are having trouble developing or mapping an effective organization, refer to the introduction and readings in Chapter 5, Organization. Once you have settled on an organizational pattern, you are ready to write a first draft.

WRITING THE FIRST DRAFT

Your goal in writing a first draft is to get your ideas down on paper. Write quickly, and let the writing follow your thinking. Do not be overly concerned about spelling, word choice, or grammar because such concerns will break the flow of your ideas. After you have completed your first draft, you will go over your essay to revise and edit it.

As you write your draft, pay attention to your outline, but do not be a slave to it. It is there to help you, not restrict you. Often, when writing, you discover something new about your subject; follow that idea freely. Wherever you deviate from your plan, place an X in the margin to remind yourself of the change. When you revise, you can return to that part of your writing and reconsider the change you made, either developing it further or abandoning it.

It may happen that while writing your first draft, you run into difficulty that prevents you from moving forward. For example, suppose you want to tell the story of something that happened to you, but you aren't certain whether you should be using the pronoun *I* so often. Turn to the essays in Chapters 11 and 14 to see how the authors use diction and tone and how other narrative essays handle this problem. You will find that the frequent use of *I* isn't necessarily a problem at all. For an account of a personal experience, it's perfectly acceptable to use *I* as often as you need to. Or suppose that after writing several pages describing someone you think is quite a character, you find that your draft seems flat and doesn't express how lively and funny the person really is. If you read the introduction to Chapter 13, you will learn that descriptions need lots of factual, concrete detail; the selections in that chapter give further proof of this. You can use those guidelines to add details that are missing from your draft.

If you run into difficulties writing your first draft, don't worry or get upset. Even experienced writers run into problems at the beginning. Just try to keep going, and take the pressure off yourself. Think about your topic, and consider your details and what you want to say. You might even want to go back and look over the ideas and information you've gathered.

Create a Title

What makes a good title? There are no hard-and-fast rules, but most writers would agree that an effective title attracts attention and hooks the reader into reading the essay, either because the title is unusual or colorful and intrigues the reader or because it asks a question and the reader is curious to know the answer. A good title announces your subject and prepares your reader for the approach you take. You can create a title while writing your first draft or after you have seen how your ideas develop. Either way, the important thing is to brainstorm for titles and not simply use the first one that comes to mind. With at least a half dozen to choose from, preferably more, you will have a much better sense of how to pick an effective title, one that does important work explaining your subject to the reader and that is lively and inviting. Spend several minutes reviewing the titles of the essays in *Models for Writers* (see the table of contents, pp. ix–xix). You'll like some better than others, but reflecting on the effectiveness of each one will help you strengthen your own titles.

Focus on Beginnings and Endings

The beginning of your essay is vitally important to its success. Indeed, if your opening doesn't attract and hold your readers' attention, they may be less than enthusiastic about proceeding.

Your ending is almost always as important as your beginning. An effective conclusion does more than end your essay. It wraps up your thoughts and leaves readers satisfied with the presentation of your ideas and information. Your ending should be a natural outgrowth of the development of your ideas. Avoid trick endings, mechanical summaries, and cutesy comments, and never introduce new concepts or information in the ending. Just as with the writing of titles, the writing of beginnings and endings is perhaps best done by generating several alternatives and then selecting from among them. Review the box on page 20 and Chapter 6 for more help developing your beginnings and endings.

Notes on Beginnings and Endings

Beginnings and endings are important to the effectiveness of an essay, but they can be difficult to write. Inexperienced writers often feel that they must write their essays sequentially when, in fact, it is better to write both the beginning and the ending after you have completed most of the rest of your essay. Pay particular attention to both parts during revision. Ask yourself the following questions:

1. Does my introduction grab the reader's attention?
2. Is my introduction confusing in any way? How well does it relate to the rest of the essay?
3. If I state my thesis in the introduction, how effectively is it presented?
4. Does my essay come to a logical conclusion, or does it just stop short?
5. How well does the conclusion relate to the rest of the essay? Am I careful not to introduce new topics or issues that I did not address in the body of the essay?
6. Does the conclusion help to underscore or illuminate important aspects of the body of the essay, or is it just another version of what I wrote earlier?

REVISING

Once you have completed a first draft, set it aside for a few hours or even until the next day. Removed from the process of drafting, you can approach the revision of your draft with a clear mind. When you revise, consider the most important elements of your draft first. You should focus on your thesis, purpose, content, organization, and paragraph structure. You will have a chance to look at grammar, punctuation, and mechanics after you revise. This way you will make sure that your essay is fundamentally solid and says what you want it to say before dealing with the task of editing.

It is helpful to have someone—your roommate or member of your writing class—listen to your essay as you read it aloud. The process of reading aloud allows you to determine if your writing sounds clear and natural. If you have to strain your voice to provide emphasis, try rephrasing the idea to make it clearer. Whether you revise your work on your own or have someone assist you, the questions in the box below will help you focus on the largest, most important elements of your essay early in the revision process.

Questions for Revising

1. Have I focused on my topic?
2. Does my thesis make a clear statement about my topic?
3. Is the organizational pattern I have used the best one, given my purpose?
4. Does the topic sentence of each paragraph relate to my thesis? Does each paragraph support its topic sentence?
5. Do I have enough supporting details, and are my examples the best ones that I can develop?
6. How effective are my beginning and my ending? Can I improve them?
7. Do I have a good title? Does it indicate what my subject is and hint at my thesis?

EDITING

Once you are sure that the large elements of your essay are in place and that you have said what you intended, you are ready to begin editing your essay. At this stage, correct any mistakes in grammar, punctuation, mechanics, and spelling because a series of small errors can add up and distract readers. Such errors can cause readers to doubt the important points you are trying to make.

The following section contains brief editing guidelines for the problems instructors around the country told us trouble their students most. For more guidance with these or other editing or grammar concerns, refer to your grammar handbook or ask your instructor for help. To practice finding and correcting these and many other problems, go to **bedfordstmartins.com/models** and click on "Exercise Central."

Run-ons: Fused Sentences and Comma Splices

Writers can become so absorbed in getting their ideas down on paper that they often combine two independent clauses (complete sentences that can stand alone when punctuated with a period) incorrectly, creating a *run-on sentence*. A run-on sentence fails to show where one thought ends and where another begins and can confuse readers. There are two types of run-on sentences: the fused sentence and the comma splice.

A *fused sentence* occurs when a writer combines two independent clauses with no punctuation at all. To correct a fused sentence, divide the independent clauses into separate sentences, or join them by adding words and/or punctuation.

INCORRECT	Jen loves Harry Potter she was the first in line to buy the latest book.
EDITED	Jen loves Harry Potter ~~she~~ ^. She^ was the first in line to buy the latest book.
EDITED	Jen loves Harry Potter ^; in fact,^ she was the first in line to buy the latest book.

A *comma splice* occurs when writers use only a comma to combine two independent clauses. To correct a comma splice, divide the independent clauses into separate sentences or join them by adding words and/or punctuation.

INCORRECT	The e-mail looked like spam, Marty deleted it.
EDITED	The e-mail looked like spam ^;^ Marty deleted it.
EDITED	The e-mail looked like spam, ^so^ Marty deleted it.

Sentence Fragments

A *sentence fragment* is a word group that cannot stand alone as a complete sentence. Even if a word group begins with a capital letter and ends with punctuation, it is not a sentence unless it has a subject (the person, place, or thing the sentence is about) and a verb (a word that tells what the subject does) and expresses a complete thought. Word groups that do not express complete thoughts often begin with a subordinating conjunction such as *although, because, since,* or *unless*.

To correct a fragment, add a subject or a verb or integrate the fragment into a nearby sentence to complete the thought.

INCORRECT	Divided my time between work and school last semester.
EDITED	~~Divided~~ I divided my time between work and school last semester.
INCORRECT	Terry's essay was really interesting. Because it brought up good points about energy conservation.
EDITED	Terry's essay was really interesting/ ~~Because~~ because it brought up good points about energy conservation.

Creative use of intentional sentence fragments is occasionally acceptable—in narration essays, for example—when writers are trying to establish a particular mood or tone.

> I asked him about his recent trip. He asked me about work. Short questions. One-word answers. Then an awkward pause.
>
> –David P. Bardeen

Subject-Verb Agreement

Subjects and verbs must agree in number—that is, a singular subject (one person, place, or thing) must take a singular verb, and a plural subject (more than one person, place, or thing) must take a plural verb. Most native speakers of English use proper subject-verb agreement in their writing without conscious awareness. Even so, some sentence constructions can be troublesome.

When a prepositional phrase (a phrase that includes a preposition such as *on, of, in, at,* or *between*) falls between a subject and a verb, it can obscure their relationship. To make sure the subject agrees with its verb in a sentence with an intervening prepositional phrase, mentally cross out the phrase (*of basic training* in the following example) to isolate the subject and verb and determine if they agree.

INCORRECT The first three weeks of basic training is the worst.

EDITED The first three weeks of basic training ~~is~~ ^are^ the worst.

Writers often have difficulty with subject-verb agreement in sentences with compound subjects (two or more subjects joined together with the word *and*). As a general rule, compound subjects take plural verbs.

INCORRECT My mother, sister, and cousin is visiting me next month.

EDITED My mother, sister, and cousin ~~is~~ ^are^ visiting me next month.

However, in sentences with subjects joined by *either . . . or*, *neither . . . nor*, or *not only . . . but also*, the verb must agree with the subject closest to it.

INCORRECT Neither the mechanics nor the salesperson know what's wrong with my car.

EDITED Neither the mechanics nor the salesperson ~~know~~ ^knows^ what's wrong with my car.

While editing your essay, be sure to identify the subjects and verbs in your sentences and to check their agreement.

Pronoun-Antecedent Agreement

A *pronoun* is a word that takes the place of a noun in a sentence. To avoid repeating nouns in our speech and writing, we use pronouns as noun substitutes. The noun to which a pronoun refers is called its *antecedent*. A pronoun and its antecedent are said to *agree* when the relationship between them is clear. Pronouns must agree with their antecedents in both *person* and *number*.

There are three types of pronouns: first person (*I* and *we*), second person (*you*), and third person (*he, she, they,* and *it*). First-person pronouns refer to first-person antecedents, second-person pronouns refer to second-person antecedents, and third-person pronouns refer to third-person antecedents.

INCORRECT House hunters should review their finances carefully before you make an offer.

EDITED House hunters should review their finances carefully before ~~you~~ they make an offer.

A pronoun must agree in number with its antecedent; that is, a singular pronoun must refer to a singular antecedent, and a plural pronoun must refer to a plural antecedent. When two or more antecedents are joined by the word *and*, the pronoun must be plural.

INCORRECT Gina, Kim, and Katie took her vacations in August.

EDITED Gina, Kim, and Katie took ~~her~~ their vacations in August.

When the subject of a sentence is an indefinite pronoun such as *everyone, each, everybody, anyone, anybody, everything, either, one, neither, someone,* or *something,* use a singular pronoun to refer to it or recast the sentence to eliminate the agreement problem.

INCORRECT Each of the women submitted their resumé.

EDITED Each of the women submitted ~~their~~ her resumé.

EDITED ~~Each~~ Both of the women submitted their ~~resume~~ resumés.

Verb Tense Shifts

A verb's tense indicates when an action takes place—sometime in the past, right now, or in the future. Using verb tense consistently helps your readers understand time changes in your writing. Inconsistent verb tenses, or *shifts*, within a sentence confuse readers and are especially noticeable in narration and process analysis writing, which are sequence and time oriented. Generally, you should write in the past or present tense and maintain that tense throughout your sentence.

INCORRECT	The painter studied the scene and pulls a fan brush decisively from her cup.
EDITED	The painter studied the scene and ~~pulls~~ pulled a fan brush decisively from her cup.

Misplaced and Dangling Modifiers

A *modifier* is a word or words that describes or gives additional information about other words in a sentence. Always place modifiers as close as possible to the words you want to modify. An error in modifier placement could be unintentionally confusing (or amusing) to your reader. Two common problems arise with modifiers: the misplaced modifier and the dangling modifier.

A *misplaced modifier* unintentionally modifies the wrong word in a sentence because it is placed incorrectly.

INCORRECT	The waiter brought a steak to the man covered with onions.
EDITED	The waiter brought a steak covered with onions to the man. ~~covered with onions.~~

A *dangling modifier* appears at the beginning or end of a sentence and modifies a word that does not appear in the sentence—often an unstated subject.

INCORRECT	Staring into the distance, large rain clouds form.
EDITED	Staring into the distance, Jon saw large rain clouds form.

While editing your essay, make sure that you have positioned your modifiers as close as possible to the words you want to modify and that each sentence has a clear subject that is modified correctly.

Faulty Parallelism

Parallelism means using similar grammatical forms to show that ideas in a sentence are of equal importance. Faulty parallelism can interrupt the flow of your writing and confuse your readers. Writers have trouble with parallelism in three kinds of sentence constructions.

In sentences that include items in a pair or series, make sure the elements of the pair or series are parallel in form. Delete any unnecessary or repeated words.

INCORRECT	Nina likes snowboarding, roller skating, and to hike.
EDITED	Nina likes snowboarding, roller skating, and ~~to hike.~~ ^hiking.^

In sentences that include connecting words such as *both . . . and, either . . . or, neither . . . nor, rather . . . than,* and *not only . . . but also,* make sure the elements being connected are parallel in form. Delete any unnecessary or repeated words.

INCORRECT	The lecture was both enjoyable and it was a form of education.
EDITED	The lecture was both enjoyable and ~~it was a form of education.~~ ^educational.^

In sentences that include the comparison word *as* or *than,* make sure the elements of the comparison are parallel in form. Delete any unnecessary or repeated words.

INCORRECT	It would be better to study now than waiting until the night before the exam.
EDITED	It would be better to study now than ~~waiting~~ ^to wait^ until the night before the exam.

Weak Nouns and Verbs

Inexperienced writers often believe that adjectives and adverbs are the stuff of effective writing. They're right in one sense, but not wholly so. Although strong adjectives and adverbs are crucial, good writing depends on well-chosen, strong nouns and verbs. The noun *vehicle* is not nearly as descriptive as *Jeep, snowmobile, pickup truck,* or *SUV,* for example. Why use the weak verb *look* when your meaning would be conveyed more precisely with *glance, stare, spy, gaze, peek, examine,* or *witness*? Instead of the weak verb *run,* use *fly, gallop, hustle, jog, race, rush, scamper, scoot, scramble,* or *trot.*

While editing your essay, look for instances of weak nouns and verbs. If you can't form a clear picture in your mind of what a noun looks like or what a verb's action is, your nouns and verbs are likely weak. The more specific and strong you make your nouns and verbs, the more lively and descriptive your writing will be.

WEAK The flowers moved toward the bright light of the sun.

EDITED The ~~flowers moved~~ tulips stretched toward the bright light of the sun.

When you have difficulty thinking of strong, specific nouns and verbs, reach for a thesaurus—but only if you are sure you can identify the best word for your purpose. Thesauruses are available free online and in inexpensive paperback editions; most word processing programs include a thesaurus as well. A thesaurus will help you avoid redundancy in your writing and find specific words with just the right meaning.

Academic Diction and Tone

The language that you use in your college courses, known as *American Standard English,* is formal in diction and objective in tone. American Standard English is the language used by educators, civic leaders, the media, and professionals in all fields. Although the standard is fairly narrow in scope, it allows for individual differences in expression and voice so that your writing can retain its personality and appeal.

Tone is the distance that you establish between yourself and your audience and is created by your *diction* (the particular words you choose) and the complexity of your sentences. Formal writing creates a distance between yourself and your audience through the use of third-person pronouns (*he, she, it, they*) and provides the impression of objectivity. Formal writing values logic, evidence, and reason over opinion and bias. Informal writing, on the other hand, uses first-person pronouns (*I*, *we*), is usually found in narratives, and respects feelings, individual tastes, and personal preferences. Similarly, the second-person pronoun (*you*) is used to bring your reader close to you, as is done in this text, but it is too familiar for most academic writing and is best avoided if there is any question about its appropriateness.

INFORMAL	The experiment looked like it was going to be a bust.
FORMAL	After detecting a number of design flaws in the experiment, we concluded that it was going to be a failure.
SUBJECTIVE	The governor said that the shortfall in tax revenues was quite a bit bigger than anyone expected.
OBJECTIVE	The governor reported that tax revenues fell by 9 percent over last year.

When writing in a particular discipline, use discipline-specific language and conventions that reflect your understanding of the discipline. Key resources are your readings and the language you use with your instructors and classmates in each discipline. As you read, note how the writer uses technical language (*point of view* and *denouement*, for example, in literature; *mean distribution* in statistics; *derivatives* in financial analysis; *pan*, *tilt*, and *track* in film study; *exogamy* and *endogamy* in anthropology; and *polyphony* and *atonality* in music) to communicate difficult concepts, recognized phenomena in the discipline, and nuances that are characteristic of the discipline.

Discipline-Specific Prose (Psychology)

> Shyness may be defined experientially as discomfort and/or inhibition in interpersonal situations that interferes with pursuing one's interpersonal or professional goals. It is a form of excessive self-focus, a preoccupation with one's thoughts, feelings, and physical reactions. It may vary from mild social awkwardness to totally inhibiting social phobia. Shyness may be chronic and dispositional, serving as a personality trait that is central in one's self-definition. Situational shyness involves experiencing the symptoms of shyness in specific social performance situations but not incorporating it into

> one's self-concept. Shyness reactions can occur at any or all of the following levels: cognitive, affective, physiological, and behavioral, and may be triggered by a wide variety of arousal cues. Among the most typical are: authorities, one-on-one opposite sex interactions, intimacy, strangers, having to take individuating action in a group setting, and initiating social actions in unstructured, spontaneous behavioral settings. Metaphorically, shyness is a shrinking back from life that weakens the bonds of human connection.
>
> –"Shyness," Lynne Henderson and Philip Zimbardo

If you listen carefully and read closely, you will be able to discern the discipline-specific language cues that make a writer sound more like, say, a historian or an anthropologist than a psychologist. In turn, you will be able to use the language of your own discipline with greater ease and accuracy and achieve the subtleties of language that will allow you to carry out your research, draw sound conclusions, and write effectively and with authority.

ESL Concerns (Articles and Nouns)

Two areas of English grammar that can be especially problematic for nonnative speakers of English are articles and nouns. In English, correct use of articles and nouns is necessary for sentences to make sense.

There are two kinds of articles in English: *indefinite* (*a* and *an*) and *definite* (*the*). Use *a* before words beginning with a consonant sound and *an* before words beginning with a vowel sound. Note, too, that *a* is used before an *h* with a consonant sound (*happy*) and *an* is used before a silent *h* (*hour*).

There are two kinds of nouns in English: count and noncount. *Count nouns* name individual things or units that can be counted or separated out from a whole, such as *students* and *pencils*. *Noncount nouns* name things that cannot be counted because they are considered wholes in themselves and cannot be divided, such as *work* and *furniture*.

Use the indefinite article (*a* or *an*) before a singular count noun when you do not specify which one.

> I would like to borrow *a* colored pencil.

Plural count nouns take *the*.

> I would like to borrow *the* colored pencils.

If a plural count noun is used in a general sense, it does not take an article at all.

> I brought colored pencils to class today.

Noncount nouns are always singular and never take an indefinite article.

> We need new living room furniture.

The is sometimes used with noncount nouns to refer to a specific idea or thing.

> *The* furniture will be delivered tomorrow.

While editing your essay, be sure that you have used articles and nouns correctly.

INCORRECT I love an aroma of freshly baked cookies.

EDITED I love ~~an~~ the aroma of freshly baked cookies.

INCORRECT I have never had the chicken pox.

EDITED I have never had ~~the~~ chicken pox.

Questions for Editing Sentences

1. Do I include any fused sentences or comma splices?
2. Do I include any unintentional sentence fragments?
3. Do my verbs agree with their subjects?
4. Do my pronouns agree with their antecedents?
5. Do I make any unnecessary shifts in verb tense?
6. Do I have any misplaced or dangling modifiers?
7. Are my sentences parallel?
8. Do I use strong nouns and active verbs?
9. Do I pair articles and nouns correctly?

PROOFREADING

Do not assume that because you made edits and corrections to your essay electronically in your word processor that all of your changes were saved or that your essay will print out correctly. Also do not assume that because you used your word processor's spell-check or grammar-check function that you've found and corrected every spelling and grammatical error. In fact, such checkers often allow incorrect or misspelled words to pass while flagging correct grammatical constructions as incorrect. Although your word processor's spell-checker and grammar-checker are a good "first line of defense" against certain types of errors, there is no replacement for a human proofreader—you.

Print out your essay and carefully proofread it manually. Check to make sure you do not use *your* where you intend *you're*, *its* where you mean *it's*, or *to* where you want *too*. Spell-checkers *never* catch these types of errors. If you know that you are prone to certain mistakes, go through your essay looking for those particular problems. For example, if you often have trouble with placing commas or other punctuation marks with quotations, proofread your essay for that specific problem.

Proofread a hard copy of your essay to make sure that all of your electronic changes appear on it and that you have caught and corrected any grammatical problems. (Be sure to refer to the Questions for Editing Sentences box on p. 31 and to the Questions for Proofreading Essays box that follows.) Check to be certain you have followed your instructor's formatting guidelines. Above all, give your hard-copy essay one final read-through before submitting it to your instructor.

Questions for Proofreading Essays

1. Have I printed a hard copy of my essay for proofreading?
2. Have I misspelled or incorrectly typed any words? Has my spell-checker inadvertently approved commonly confused words like *its* and *it's*, or *their*, *there*, and *they're*?
3. Have I checked my essay for errors I make often?
4. Do all of my edits and corrections appear in my hard copy?
5. Have I formatted my essay according to my instructor's directions?
6. Have I given the hard copy of my final draft a thorough review before turning it in?

WRITING AN EXPOSITORY ESSAY: A STUDENT ESSAY IN PROGRESS

While he was a student in a writing class at the University of Vermont, Jeffrey Olesky was asked to write an essay on any topic using a suitable method of development. After making a brief list of the subjects that interested him, he chose to write about golf. Golf had been a part of Olesky's life since he was a youngster, so he figured he would have enough material for an essay.

First, he needed to focus on a specific topic within the broad subject area of golf. Having considered a number of aspects of the game—how it's played, its popularity because of Tiger Woods, the controversies over the exclusion of women and minorities from private clubs—he kept coming back to how much golf meant to him. Focusing on his love of golf, he then established his tentative thesis: Golf has taught me a lot.

Olesky needed to develop a number of examples to support his thesis, so he brainstormed for ideas, examples, and anecdotes—anything that came to mind to help him develop his essay. These are his notes:

Brainstorming Notes

Golf is my life—I can't imagine being who I am without it.

I love to be out on the course early in the morning.

It's been embarrassing and stressful sometimes.

There's so much to know and remember about the game, even before you try to hit the ball.

The story about what my father taught me—felt badly and needed to apologize.

"You know better than that, Jeffrey."

I have pictures of me on the greens with a cut-down golf putter.

All kinds of character building goes on.

It's all about rules and playing fairly.

Wanted to be like my father.

The frustration is awesome, but you can learn to deal with it.

Golf is methodical.

I use golf to clear my head.

Golf teaches life's lessons.

Golf teaches you manners, to be respectful of others.

Golf teaches you to abide by the rules.

Golf is an internal tool.

When he thought that he had gathered enough information, he began to sort it out. He needed an organizational plan, some way to present his information that was not random but rather showed a logical progression. He realized that the character-building benefits of golf that he included in his brainstorming notes clustered around some key subtopics. He decided to do some clustering and drew circles that included his ideas about golf: the physical and mental demands of the game, the social values and morals it teaches, and the reflective benefits of golf. He then sorted out his related ideas and examples and added them, mapping their relationship in this diagram.

Clustering Diagram

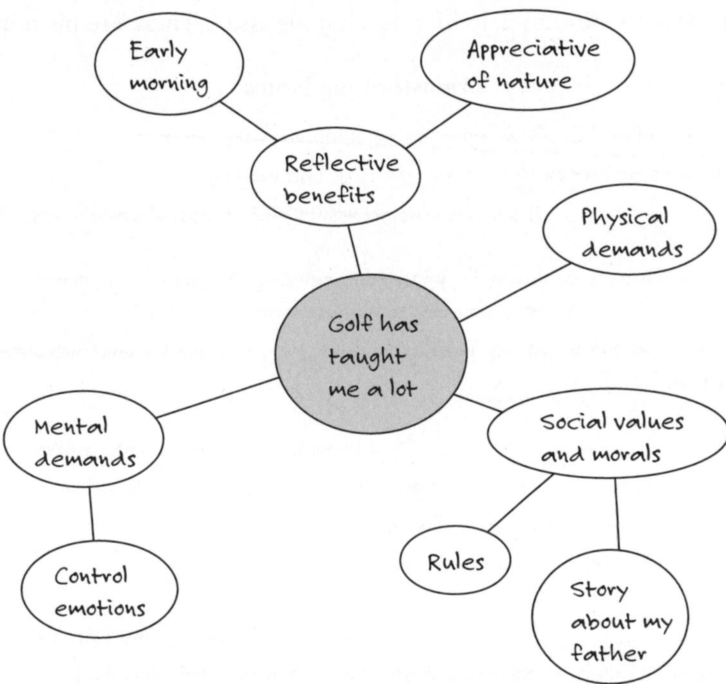

Before beginning to write the first draft of his paper, Olesky thought it would be a good idea to list in an informal outline the major points he wanted to make. Here is his informal outline:

Informal Outline

1. Brief introductory paragraph announcing the topic
2. An expansion of the introductory paragraph and the thesis statement: Golf has taught me a lot
3. A discussion of how, above all, golf teaches one to control one's emotions
4. A discussion of how much one needs to know and remember to play golf well
5. The values that golf teaches
6. A multiparagraph example illustrating a valuable lesson taught through golf
7. Golf provides an opportunity to reflect
8. Reflection, in turn, leads to a deeper appreciation of nature

With his outline before him, Olesky felt ready to try a rough draft of his paper. He wrote quickly, keeping his organizational plan in mind but striving to keep the writing going and get his thoughts down on paper. He knew that once he had a draft, he could determine how to improve it. Olesky wrote some fairly solid paragraphs, but he sensed that they were on different aspects of his topic and that the logical order of the points he was making was not quite right. He needed a stronger organizational plan, some way to present his information that was not random but rather showed a logical progression.

Reviewing his outline, Olesky could see that there was a natural progression from the physical lessons of the sport to the social and moral lessons to the psychological, emotional, and even spiritual benefits that one could derive. He decided therefore to move item 3 ("A discussion of how, above all, golf teaches one to control one's emotions") in his original organization and make it item 6 in the revision. Here is his reordered outline:

Reordered Outline

1. Brief introductory paragraph announcing the topic
2. An expansion of the introductory paragraph and the <u>thesis statement:</u> Golf has taught me a lot
3. A discussion of how much one needs to know and remember to play golf well
4. The social values that golf teaches
5. A multiparagraph example illustrating a valuable lesson taught through golf
6. A discussion of how, above all, golf teaches one to control one's emotions
7. Golf provides an opportunity to reflect
8. Reflection, in turn, leads to a deeper appreciation of nature

Olesky was satisfied that his essay now had a natural and logical organization: it moved from matters of lesser to greater importance to him personally. However, he now needed to revise his thesis to suit the argument he had established. He wanted his revised thesis to be focused and specific and to include the idea that the lessons and values golf taught him could not be learned as easily in other ways. Here is his revised thesis statement:

Revised Thesis Statement

In its simplicity, golf has taught me many lessons and values that other people have trouble learning elsewhere.

After revising the organization, he was now ready to edit his essay and to correct those smaller but equally important errors in word choice, wordiness, punctuation, and mechanics. He had put aside these errors to make sure that his essay had the appropriate content.

Now he needed to make sure that it was grammatically correct. Here are several sample paragraphs showing the editing that Olesky did on his essay:

Edited Paragraphs

Addition for clarity

Elimination of unessential information

Change of period to colon to eliminate sentence fragment and introduce appositive phrase

Correction of it's *to* its

Elimination of wordiness

Addition of specific information for clarity

Ever since I was a little boy, no older than two or three, I have had a golf club in my hand. My mother has pictures of me [as a toddler] with my father on the putting green of the golf course. ~~that my father belonged to.~~ With a cut-down putter, the shaft ~~had been~~ reduced in length so that it would fit me, I would spend hours trying to place the small white ball into the little round hole. I'm sure at first that I took to the game to be like my father: ~~T~~to act like him, play like him, and hit the ball like him. However, it is not what I have learned about the mechanics of the golf swing, or ~~all~~ [about] the facts ~~and figures~~ of the game that have caused golf to mean so much to me, but rather [it is] the things golf has taught me about everyday life [in general]. In it~~'~~s simplicity, golf has taught me many lessons and values other people have trouble learning elsewhere.

~~Along the same lines,~~ [Golf is a good teacher because] there are many variables and aspects to the game. ~~of golf.~~ You ~~are~~ constantly hav~~ing~~[e] to think, analyze, and evaluate [your position and strategy]. ~~That is the difficulty of the game of golf.~~ Unlike many sports ~~once you~~ [that rely on] committ~~ed the~~[ing] actions to muscle memory, [golf requires] ~~there is no guarantee you will still perform well. There is~~ a phenomenal amount of information to think about and keys to remember. Legs shoulder-width apart, knees flexed, fingers interlocked, body loose . . . and you haven't even tried to hit the ball yet. But having to go about things so methodically [in golf] has enabled me to apply ~~the methods of golf~~ [the skills of patience and analysis] to many other parts of my life. I don't believe I would have nearly the same personality if golf had not played such an ~~intricate~~ integral role in my development.

Improved dicton

In addition to editing his revised paper, Olesky reexamined his title, "Character Builder." Olesky considered a half dozen alternatives. He finally settled on the use of "Golf" as a main title because it was such a key word for his topic and thesis; he used "A Character Builder" as his subtitle. He also thought about his conclusion, wondering whether it was forceful enough. After giving it considerable thought and seeking the advice of his classmates, Olesky decided to end with the low-key but meaningful final paragraphs he generated in his original draft. Here is the final version of his essay:

Final Essay

Title: suggests what the essay will be about

Golf: A Character Builder

Jeffrey Olesky

Golf is what I love. It is what I do, and it is who I am. In many respects, it has defined and shaped my character and personality. I couldn't possibly imagine my life without golf and what it has meant for me.

Beginning: effective opening paragraph sets the context for the essay

Ever since I was a little boy, no older than two or three, I have had a golf club in my hand. My mother has pictures of me as a toddler with my father on the putting green of the golf course. With a cut-down putter, the shaft reduced in length so that it would fit me, I would spend hours trying to place the small white ball in the little round hole. I'm sure at first that I took to the game to be like my father: to act like him, play like him, and hit the ball like him. However, it is not what I have learned about the mechanics of the golf swing or about the facts of the game that have caused golf to mean so much to me, but rather it is the things golf has taught me about everyday life in general. In its simplicity, golf has taught me many lessons and values other people have trouble learning elsewhere.

Thesis statement: sets clear expectation in the reader's mind

Transition: discussion moves to how the game influences personality

Golf is a good teacher because there are many variables and aspects to the game. You constantly have to think, analyze, and evaluate your position and strategy. Unlike many sports that rely on committing actions to muscle memory, golf requires a phenomenal amount of information to think about and keys to remember. Legs shoulder-width apart, knees flexed, fingers interlocked, body loose . . . and you haven't even tried to hit the ball yet. But having to go about things so methodically in golf has enabled me to apply the skills of patience and analysis to many other parts of my life. I don't believe I would have nearly the same personality if golf had not played such an integral role in my development.

Golf requires lots of information, both physical and mental.

Golf teaches life lessons.

Golf has also changed and shaped my personality by repeatedly reinforcing many of the lessons of life. You know the ones I'm referring to, the rules you learn in kindergarten: treat others as you would like to be treated; respect other people and their property . . . the list goes on. Golf may not blare them out as obviously as my kindergarten teacher, but in its own subtle, respectful tone, golf has imbued me with many of the values and morals I have today. Simply by learning the rules of such a prestigious, honest, and respected game, you gradually learn the reasoning behind them and the ways that they relate to life.

Illustration: extended example in narrative of some lessons that golf teaches

A good example of such a life lesson comes from the first time my father ever took me out on an actual golf course. I had been waiting for this day for quite some time and was so excited when he finally gave me the chance. He had gone out to play with a few of his friends early one Saturday morning in one of the larger tournaments. I was caddying for my father. Although I was too young to actually carry his bag, I would clean his golf ball, rake the bunkers for him, and do the other minor tasks that caddies do. But the fact that I was actually out "with the big boys," watching them play golf, was enough to make me happy. Besides, none of the other gentlemen my father was playing with seemed to mind that I was along for the ride.

Narrative example continues.

The lesson I learned that day appears rather simple now. It came on the putting green of the second hole. My father had finished putting out, and I was holding the flagstick off to the side of the green while the other players finished. Generally, my father would come stand next to me and give me a hand, but due to circumstances we ended up on opposite sides of the green. During the next player's putt, my father lowered his eyebrows at me and nodded his head to one side a few times. Curious as to what he wanted me to do, I almost let the question slip out of my mouth. But I knew better. I had already learned the rules of not talking or moving while other golfers were hitting. I quietly stood my ground until everyone was finished and then placed the flagstick back in the hole. While walking toward the next tee box, I neared my father. Regardless of what he had wanted me to do, I thought he would commend me for not talking or moving during the ordeal.

Dialogue: "shows rather than tells" and puts the reader in the scene

"You know better than that, Jeffrey," he said.

"What?" I asked curiously, disappointed that he had not praised me on a job well done.

"You never stand so that your shadow is in someone's line."

How could I be so stupid? He had reminded me a thousand times before. You never allow your shadow to fall in the line of someone's putt because it is distracting to the person putting. I rationalized to my father that maybe the man hadn't noticed or that it didn't bother him. Unfortunately, my father wasn't going to take that as an excuse. After explaining to me what I had done wrong, he suggested that I go over and apologize to the gentleman. I was still a young boy, and the figure of the older man was somewhat intimidating. This task was no easy chore because I was obviously very scared, and this is perhaps what made the lesson sink in a little deeper. I remember gradually approaching my father's friend and periodically looking back to my father for help. Once I realized I was on my own, I bashfully gave him my apologies and assured him that it wouldn't happen again. As you can probably guess, the repercussions were not as dramatic as I had envisioned them to be. Once my father had pointed out my mistake, I begged him to reconcile with the gentleman for me. However, in apologizing for myself, I learned a valuable lesson. Golf is important because it has taught me many social values such as this, but it can also be a personal, internal tool.

Transition: golf can also be a personal, internal tool.

Golf has taught me how to deal with frustration and to control myself mentally in difficult and strenuous situations. Golf is about mastering your emotions in stressful times and prevailing with a methodical, calm mind. I have dealt with the disappointment of missing a two-foot putt on the last hole to break eighty and the embarrassment of shanking my drive off the first hole in front of dozens of people. In dealing with these circumstances and continuing with my game, I have learned how to control my emotions. Granted, golf is not the most physically strenuous sport, but it is the mental challenge of complete and utter concentration that makes it difficult. People who are not able to control their temper or to take command of their emotions generally do not end up playing this game for very long.

Organization continues to move from concrete practical concerns to those that are more abstract.

Golf gives me the opportunity to be reflective--time to myself when I can debate and organize the thoughts in my head. There are few places where you can find the peace and tranquility like that of a golf course in the early morning or late afternoon. When I am playing by myself, which I make an effort to do when I need to "get away," I am able to reflect and work out some of the difficulties I am facing. I can think in complete quietness, but at the same time I have something to do while I am thinking. There are few places in the world offering this type of sanctuary that are easily accessible.

Organization: Olesky moves to more philosophic influences.

It is in these morning reflections that I also gain an appreciation of my surroundings. I often like to get up early on a Saturday or Sunday and be the first one on the course. There are many things I love about the scenery of a golf course during the

Organization: Olesky discusses golf's ability to bring him close to nature.

morning hours. I love the smell of the freshly cut grass as the groundskeepers crisscross their patterns onto the fairways and greens. I love looking back on my progress toward the tee box on the first hole to witness my solitary foot tracks in the morning dew. I love the chirp of the yellow finches as they signal the break of dawn. All these conditions help to create the feeling of contentment as I walk down the first fairway. Thinking back to those days on the putting green with my father, I realize how dear golf is to me. Golf has created my values, taught me my lessons, and been my outlet. I love the game for all these reasons.

Ending: a quiet but appropriate conclusion

chapter **2**

From Reading to Writing

To move from reading to writing, you need to read actively, in a thoughtful spirit, and with an alert, inquiring mind. Reading actively means learning how to analyze what you read. You must be able to discover what is going on in an essay, to figure out the writer's reasons for shaping the essay in a particular way, to decide whether the result works well or poorly—and why. At first, such digging may seem odd, and for good reason. After all, we all know how to read. But do we know how to read *actively*?

Active reading is a skill that takes time to acquire. By becoming more familiar with different types of writing, you will sharpen your critical thinking skills and learn how good writers make decisions in their writing. After reading an essay, most people feel more confident talking about the content of the piece than about the writer's style. Content is more tangible than style, which always seems elusive. In large part, this discrepancy results from our schooling. Most of us have been taught to read for ideas. Not many of us, however, have been trained to read actively, to engage a writer and his or her writing, to ask why we like one piece of writing and not another. Similarly, most of us do not ask ourselves why one piece of writing is more convincing than another. When you learn to read actively, you begin to answer these important questions and come to appreciate the craftsmanship involved in writing. Active reading, then, is a skill you need if you are truly to engage and understand the content of a piece of writing as well as the craft that shapes the writer's ideas into a presentable form. Active reading will repay your efforts by helping you read more effectively and grow as a writer.

■ GETTING THE MOST OUT OF YOUR READING

Active reading requires, first of all, that you commit time and effort. Second, try to take a positive interest in what you are reading, even if the subject matter is not immediately appealing. Remember, you are not reading for content alone but also to understand a writer's methods—to see firsthand the kinds of choices writers make while they write.

To get the most out of your reading, follow the five steps of the reading process.

1. Prepare yourself to read the selection.
2. Read the selection.
3. Reread the selection.
4. Annotate the text with marginal notes.
5. Analyze the text with questions.

Step 1: Prepare Yourself to Read the Selection

Instead of diving right into any given selection in *Models for Writers* or any other book, there are a few things that you can do that will prepare you to get the most out of what you will be reading. It's helpful, for example, to get a context for the reading: What's the essay about? What do you know about the writer's background and reputation? Where was the essay first published? Who was the intended audience for the essay? How much do you already know about the subject of the reading selection? We encourage you to review the materials that precede each selection in this book.

Each selection begins with a title, a headnote, and a writing prompt. From the *title,* you often discover the writer's position on an issue or attitude toward the topic. On occasion, the title provides clues about the intended audience and the writer's purpose in writing the piece. The *headnote* contains three essential elements: a *biographical note* about the author, *publication information,* and *rhetorical highlights* of the selection. In addition to information on the person's life and work, you'll find out something about his or her reputation and authority to write on the subject of the piece. The *publication information* tells you when the selection was published and in what book or magazine it appeared. This information gives you insights about the intended audience and the historical context. The *rhetorical highlights* direct your attention to one or more of the model features of the selection. Finally, the *writing prompt,* called "Reflecting on What You Know," encourages you to collect your own thoughts and opinions about the topic or related subjects before you commence reading. This prompt makes it easy for you to keep a record of your own knowledge or thinking about a topic before you see what the writer has to offer in the essay.

To demonstrate how these context-building materials can work for you, carefully review the following materials that accompany Isaac Asimov's "Intelligence." The essay itself appears later in this chapter (pp. 49–51).

Intelligence

Title

Isaac Asimov

Headnote

1. Biographical note

Born in the Soviet Union, Isaac Asimov immigrated to the United States in 1923. His death in 1992 ended a long, prolific career as a science-fiction and nonfiction writer. Asimov was uniquely talented at making a diverse range of topics—from Shakespeare to atomic physics—comprehensible and entertaining to the general reader. Asimov earned three degrees at Columbia University and later taught biochemistry at Boston University. At the time of his death, he had published more than five hundred books. It's Been a Good Life, *published in 2002, was compiled from selections made from Asimov's three previous autobiographical volumes:* In Memory Yet Green *(1979),* In Joy Still Felt *(1980), and* I. Asimov: A Memoir *(1994). Edited by Janet Jeppson Asimov, the book also features "A Way of Thinking," Asimov's four hundredth essay for the* Magazine of Fantasy and Science Fiction.

2. Publication information

In the following essay, which first appeared in Please Explain: The Myriad Mysteries of the Universe Revealed *(1973), Asimov, an intellectually gifted man, ponders the nature of intelligence. His academic brilliance, he concedes, would mean little or nothing if like-minded intellectuals had not established the standards for intelligence in our society. Notice how he uses personal experience and the example of his auto mechanic to develop his definition of intelligence.* **3. Rhetorical highlights**

Reflecting on What You Know

Writing prompt

Our society defines the academically gifted as intelligent, but perhaps *book smart* would be a better term. IQ tests don't take into account common sense or experience, attributes that the academically gifted sometimes lack outside of a scholarly setting. Who's the smartest person you know? Is he or she academically gifted or smart in some way that would not be readily recognized as a form of intelligence?

From these preliminary materials, what expectations do you have for the selection itself? And how does this knowledge equip you to engage the selection before you read it? Asimov's title suggests the question "What is intelligence?" You can reasonably infer that Asimov will discuss the nature of intelligence. His purpose clearly seems to be to explore the subject with his readers. The short biographical note reveals that Asimov, a scientist, teacher, and prolific author, is no longer living, that he enjoyed a reputation as a renaissance man, and that he wrote with an ease and understanding that make difficult subjects readily accessible to the general public. This background material suggests that in the essay you'll get a thoughtful, easy-to-comprehend discussion of intelligence. The publication information indicates that this essay first appeared in a 1973 book in which Asimov explains popular "mysteries of the universe." The rhetorical highlights advise you to pay particular attention to how Asimov uses the examples of himself and his auto mechanic to think about the meaning of intelligence. Finally, the journal prompt asks you to consider how society defines the term *intelligence,* first by identifying the smartest person in your life and then by thinking about whether that person is more academically gifted (book smart) or experientially gifted (street smart). After reading the essay, you can compare your thoughts about the nature of intelligence with Asimov's.

Step 2: Read the Selection

Always read the selection at least twice, no matter how long it is. The first reading gives you a chance to get acquainted with the essay and to form your first impressions of it. With the first reading, you want to get an overall sense of what the writer is saying, keeping in mind the essay's title and the facts that you know about the writer from the essay's headnote. The essay will offer you information, ideas, and arguments—some you may have expected, some you may not have expected. As you read, you may find yourself modifying your sense of the writer's message and purpose. If there are any words that you do not recognize, circle them so that you can look them up later in a dictionary. Put question marks alongside any passages that are not immediately clear. You may, in fact, want to delay most of your annotating until a second reading so that your first reading can be fast and free.

Step 3: Reread the Selection

Your second reading should be quite different from the first. You will know what the essay is about, where it is going, and how it gets there. Now you can relate the parts of the essay more accurately to the whole. Use your second reading to test your first impressions against the words on the page, developing and deepening your sense of how the essay is written and how well. Because you now have a general understanding of the essay, you can pay special attention to the author's purpose and means of achieving that purpose. You can look for features of organization and style that you can learn from and adapt to your own work.

Step 4: Annotate the Text with Marginal Notes

When you annotate a text, you should do more than simply underline or highlight important points to remember. It is easy to underline so much that the notations become almost meaningless because you forget why you underlined the passages in the first place. Instead, as you read, write down your thoughts in the margins or on a separate piece of paper. (See pp. 49–51 for Asimov's "Intelligence" with student annotations.) Mark the selection's main point when you find it stated directly. Look for the pattern or patterns of development the author uses to explore and support that point, and jot the information down. If you disagree with a statement or conclusion, object in the margin: "No!" If you feel skeptical, indicate that response: "Why?" or "Explain." If you are impressed by an argument or turn of phrase, compliment the writer: "Good point!" Place vertical lines or stars in the margin to indicate important points.

Jot down whatever marginal notes come to mind. Most readers combine brief responses written in the margins with underlining, circling, highlighting, stars, or question marks. Here are some suggestions of elements you may want to mark to help you keep a record of your responses as you read:

What to Annotate in a Text

- Memorable statements of important points
- Key terms or concepts
- Central issues or themes
- Examples that support a main point
- Unfamiliar words
- Questions you have about a point or passage
- Your responses to a specific point or passage

Remember that there are no hard-and-fast rules for which elements you should annotate. Choose a method of annotation that works best for you and that will make sense when you go back to recollect your thoughts and responses to the essay. When annotating a text, don't be timid. Mark up your book as much as you like, or jot down as many responses in your notebook as you think will be helpful. Don't let annotating become burdensome. A word or phrase is usually as good as a sentence. One helpful way to focus your annotations is to ask yourself questions as you read the selection a second time.

Step 5: Analyze the Text with Questions

As you read the essay a second time, probe for a deeper understanding of and appreciation for what the writer has done. Focus your attention by asking yourself some basic questions about its content and its form. Here are some questions you may find useful:

Questions to Ask Yourself as You Read

1. What does the writer want to say? What is the writer's main point or thesis?
2. Why does the writer want to make this point? What is the writer's purpose?
3. What pattern or patterns of development does the writer use?
4. How does the writer's pattern of development suit his or her subject and purpose?
5. What, if anything, is noteworthy about the writer's use of this pattern?
6. How effective is the essay? Does the writer make his or her points clearly?

Each essay in *Models for Writers* is followed by study questions that are similar to the ones suggested here but specific to the essay. These questions help you analyze both the content of the essay and the writer's craft. As you read the essay a second time, look for details that will support your answers to these questions, and then answer the questions as fully as you can.

An Example: Annotating Isaac Asimov's "Intelligence"

Notice how one of our students, guided by the six preceding questions, recorded her responses to Asimov's text with marginal notes.

Asks question central to the essay and relates army experience

What is intelligence, anyway? When I was in the army I received a kind of aptitude test that soldiers took and, against a norm of 100, scored 160. No one at the base had ever seen a figure like that, and for two hours they made a big fuss over me. (It didn't mean anything. The next day I was still a buck private with KP as my highest duty.)

All my life I've been registering scores like that, so that I have the complacent feeling that I'm highly intelligent, and I expect other people to think so, too.

Actually, though, don't such scores simply mean that I am very good at answering the type of academic questions that are considered worthy of answers by the people who make up the intelligence tests—people with intellectual bents similar to mine?

Questions the meaning of high test scores. What do I think they mean?

Auto repair example. Any relationship between test scores and ability to fix cars?

For instance, I had an auto-repair man once, who, on these intelligence tests, could not possibly have scored more than 80, by my estimate. I always took it for granted that I was far more intelligent than he was. Yet, when anything went wrong with my car I hastened to him with it, watched him anxiously as he explored its vitals, and listened to his pronouncements as though they were divine oracles—and he always fixed my car.

Well, then, suppose my auto-repair man devised questions for an intelligence test. Or suppose a carpenter did, or a farmer, or, indeed, almost anyone but an academician. By every one of those tests, I'd prove myself a moron. And I'd *be* a moron, too. In a world where I could not use my academic training and my verbal talents but had to do something intricate or hard, working with my hands, I would do poorly. My intelligence, then, is not absolute but is a function of the society I live in and of the fact that a small subsection of that society has managed to foist itself on the rest as an arbiter of such matters.

Sees intelligence as function of roles in society. Good point!

Consider my auto-repair man, again. He had a habit of telling me jokes whenever he saw me. One time he raised his head from under the automobile hood to say, "Doc, a deaf-and-dumb guy went into a hardware store to ask for some nails. He put two fingers together on the counter and made hammering motions with the other hand. The clerk brought him a hammer. He shook his head and pointed to the two fingers he was hammering. The clerk brought him nails. He picked out the sizes he wanted, and left. Well doc, the next guy who came in was a blind man. He wanted scissors. How do you suppose he asked for them?"

Mechanic's joke about "deaf-and-dumb carpenter."

Indulgently, I lifted my right hand and made scissoring motions with my first two fingers. Whereupon my auto-repair man laughed raucously and said, "Why you dumb jerk, he used his *voice* and asked for them." Then he said, smugly, "I've been trying

Traps Asimov with question about blind customer.

What point did mechanic have?

that on all my customers today." "Did you catch many?" I asked. "Quite a few," he said, "but I knew for sure I'd catch *you*." "Why is that?" I asked. "Because you're so goddamned educated, doc, I *knew* you couldn't be very smart."

And I have an uneasy feeling he had something there.

Brings up question, "Are all educated people smart?" Not in my experience!

Practice: Reading and Annotating Rachel Carson's "Fable for Tomorrow"

Before you read the following essay, think about its title, the biographical and rhetorical information in the headnote, and the writing prompt. Make some marginal notes of your expectations for the essay, and write out a response to the prompt. Then, as you read the essay itself for the first time, try not to stop; take it all in as if in one breath. The second time, however, pause to annotate key points in the text, using the marginal fill-in lines provided alongside each paragraph. As you read, remember the six basic questions mentioned earlier:

1. What does Carson want to say? What is her main point or thesis?
2. Why does she want to make this point? What is her purpose?
3. What pattern or patterns of development does Carson use?
4. How does Carson's pattern of development suit her subject and purpose?
5. What, if anything, is noteworthy about Carson's use of this pattern?
6. How effective is Carson's essay? Does Carson make her points clearly?

Fable for Tomorrow

Title:

■ Rachel Carson

Headnote:

1. Biographical note:

Naturalist Rachel Carson (1907–1964) majored in biology at the Pennsylvania College for Women (which later became Chatham College) in the mid-1920s and earned a master's degree in marine zoology from Johns Hopkins University. Later she worked as an aquatic biologist for the U.S. Bureau of Fisheries in Washington, D.C. She wrote Under the Sea Wind *(1941),* The Sea around Us *(1951), and* The Edge of the Sea *(1955)—all sensitive investigations of marine life. But it was* Silent Spring *(1962), her study of herbicides and insecticides, that made Carson a controversial figure. Once denounced as an alarmist, she is now regarded as an early prophet of the ecology movement.*

In the following fable (a short tale teaching a moral) taken from Silent Spring, *Carson uses contrast to show her readers the devastating effects of the indiscriminate use of pesticides.*

2. Publication information:

3. Rhetorical highlights:

Reflecting on What You Know

Hardly a week goes by that we don't hear a news story about the poisoning of the environment. Popular magazines have run cover stories about Americans' growing interest in organic foods. Where do you stand on the issue of using chemical fertilizers, herbicides, and pesticides to grow our nation's food? Do you seek out organic products when you shop? Why or why not?

Writing prompt:

There was once a town in the heart of America where all life seemed to live in harmony with its surroundings. The town lay in the midst of a checkerboard of prosperous farms, with fields of grain and 1

Annotations:

hillsides of orchards where, in spring, white clouds of bloom drifted above the green fields. In autumn, oak and maple and birch set up a blaze of color that flamed and flickered across a backdrop of pines. Then foxes barked in the hills and deer silently crossed the fields, half hidden in the mists of the fall mornings.

2 Along the roads, laurels, viburnum and alder, great ferns and wildflowers delighted the traveler's eye through much of the year. Even in winter the roadsides were places of beauty, where countless birds came to feed on the berries and on the seed heads of the dried weeds rising above the snow. The countryside was, in fact, famous for the abundance and variety of its bird life, and when the flood of migrants was pouring through in spring and fall people traveled from great distances to observe them. Others came to fish the streams, which flowed clear and cold out of the hills and contained shady pools where trout lay. So it had been from the days many years ago when the first settlers raised their houses, sank their wells, and built their barns.

3 Then a strange blight crept over the area and everything began to change. Some evil spell had settled on the community: mysterious maladies swept the flocks of chickens; the cattle and sheep sickened and died. Everywhere was a shadow of death. The farmers spoke of much illness among their families. In the town the doctors had become more and more puzzled by new kinds of sickness appearing among their patients. There had been several sudden and unexplained deaths, not only among adults but even among children, who would be stricken suddenly while at play and die within a few hours.

4 There was a strange stillness. The birds, for example—where had they gone? Many people spoke of them, puzzled and disturbed. The feeding stations in the backyards were deserted. The few birds seen anywhere were moribund; they trembled violently and could not fly. It was a spring without voices. On the

mornings that had once throbbed with the dawn chorus of robins, catbirds, doves, jays, wrens, and scores of other bird voices there was now no sound; only silence lay over the fields and woods and marsh.

5 On the farms the hens brooded, but no chicks hatched. The farmers complained that they were unable to raise any pigs—the litters were small and the young survived only a few days. The apple trees were coming into bloom but no bees droned among the blossoms, so there was no pollination and there would be no fruit.

6 The roadsides, once so attractive, were now lined with browned and withered vegetation as though swept by fire. These, too, were silent, deserted by all living things. Even the streams were now lifeless. Anglers no longer visited them, for all the fish had died.

7 In the gutters under the eaves and between the shingles of the roofs, a white granular powder still showed a few patches; some weeks before it had fallen like snow upon the roofs and the lawns, the fields and streams.

8 No witchcraft, no enemy action had silenced the rebirth of new life in this stricken world. The people had done it themselves.

9 This town does not actually exist, but it might easily have a thousand counterparts in America or elsewhere in the world. I know of no community that has experienced all the misfortunes I describe. Yet every one of these disasters has actually happened somewhere, and many real communities have already suffered a substantial number of them. A grim specter has crept upon us almost unnoticed, and this imagined tragedy may easily become a stark reality we all shall know.

Once you have read and reread Carson's essay and annotated the text, write your own answers to the six basic questions listed on page 51. Then compare your answers with the set of answers that follows.

1. *What does Carson want to say? What is her main point or thesis?* Carson wants to tell her readers a fable, a short narrative

that makes an edifying or cautionary point. Carson draws the "moral" of her fable in the final paragraph. She believes that we have in our power the ability to upset the balance of nature, to turn what is an idyllic countryside into a wasteland. As she states in paragraph 8, "The people had done it [silenced the landscape] themselves." Human beings need to take heed and understand their role in environmental stewardship.

2. *Why does she want to make this point? What is her purpose?* Carson's purpose is to alert us to the clear danger of pesticides (the "white granular powder," paragraph 7) to the environment. Even though the composite environmental disaster she describes has not occurred yet, she feels compelled to inform her readers that each of the individual disasters has happened somewhere in a real community. Although Carson does not make specific recommendations for what each of us can do, her message is clear: to do nothing about pesticides is to invite environmental destruction.

3. *What pattern or patterns of development does Carson use?* Carson's dominant pattern of development is comparison and contrast. In paragraphs 1 and 2, she describes the mythical town before the blight ("all life seemed to live in harmony with its surroundings"); in paragraphs 3–7, she portrays the same town after the blight ("some evil spell had settled on the community"). Carson seems less interested in making specific contrasts than in drawing a total picture of the town before and after the blight. In this way, she makes the change dramatic and powerful. Carson enhances her contrast by using vivid descriptive details that appeal to our senses to paint her pictures of the town before and after the "strange blight." The countryside before the blight is full of life; the countryside after, barren and silent.

4. *How does Carson's pattern of development suit her subject and purpose?* Carson selects comparison and contrast as her method of development because she wants to shock her readers into seeing what happens when humans use pesticides indiscriminately. By contrasting a mythical American town before the blight with the same town after the blight, Carson is able to *show* us the differences, not merely tell us about them. The descriptive details enhance this contrast: for example, "checkerboard of prosperous farms," "white clouds of bloom," "foxes barked," "seed heads of the dried weeds," "cattle and sheep sickened," "they trembled

violently," "no bees droned," and "browned and withered vegetation." Perhaps the most striking detail is the "white granular powder" that "had fallen like snow upon the roofs and the lawns, the fields and streams" (7). The powder is the residue of the pervasive use of insecticides and herbicides in farming. Carson waits to introduce the powder for dramatic impact. Readers absorb the horror of the changing scene, wonder at its cause, and then suddenly realize it is not an unseen, uncontrollable force, but human beings who have caused the devastation.

5. *What, if anything, is noteworthy about Carson's use of this pattern?* In her final paragraph, Carson says, "A grim specter has crept upon us almost unnoticed." And this is exactly what happens in her essay. By starting with a two-paragraph description of "a town in the heart of America where all life seemed to live in harmony with its surroundings," Carson lulls her readers into thinking that all is well. But then at the beginning of paragraph 3, she introduces change: "a strange blight crept over the area." By opting to describe the preblight town in its entirety first and then to contrast it with the blighted town, she makes the change more dramatic and thus enhances its impact on readers.
6. *How effective is Carson's essay? Does Carson make her points clearly?* Instead of writing a strident argument against the indiscriminate use of pesticides, Carson chooses to engage her readers in a fable with an educational message. In reading her story of this American town, we witness what happens when farmers blanket the landscape with pesticides. When we learn in the last paragraph that "this town does not actually exist," we are given cause for hope. In spite of the fact that "every one of these disasters has actually happened somewhere," we are led to believe that there is still time to act before "this imagined tragedy" becomes "a stark reality we all shall know." When she wrote *Silent Spring* in 1962 Carson was considered an alarmist, and now almost daily we read reports of water pollution, oil spills, hazardous waste removal, toxic waste dumps, and global warming. Her warning is as appropriate today as it was when she first wrote it more than four decades ago.

USING YOUR READING IN THE WRITING PROCESS

Reading and writing are the two sides of the same coin. Many people view writing as the making of reading. But the connection does not end there. Active reading is a means to help you become a better writer. We know that one of the best ways to learn to write and to improve our writing is to read. By reading we can begin to see how other writers have communicated their experiences, ideas, thoughts, and feelings in their writing. We can study how they have effectively used the various elements of the essay—thesis, unity, organization, beginnings and endings, paragraphs, transitions, effective sentences, diction and tone, and figurative language—to say what they wanted to say. By studying the style, technique, and rhetorical strategies of other writers, we learn how we might effectively do the same. The more we read and write, the more we begin to read as writers and, in turn, to write knowing what readers expect.

Reading as a Writer

What does it mean to read as a writer? As mentioned earlier, most of us have not been taught to read with a writer's eye, to ask why we like one piece of writing and not another. Similarly, most of us do not ask ourselves why one piece of writing is more convincing than another. When you learn to read with a writer's eye, you begin to answer these important questions. You read beyond the content to see how certain aspects of the writing itself impact you. You come to appreciate what is involved in selecting and focusing a subject as well as the craftsmanship involved in writing—how a writer selects descriptive details, uses an unobtrusive organizational pattern, opts for fresh and lively language, chooses representative and persuasive examples, and emphasizes important points with sentence variety. You come to see writing as a series of choices or decisions the writer makes.

On one level, reading stimulates your thinking by providing you with subjects to write about. For example, after reading Helen Keller's "The Most Important Day," you might take up your pen to write about a turning point in your life. Or by reading Mike Rose's "I Just Wanna Be Average," Carl T. Rowan's "Unforgettable Miss Bessie," and Thomas L. Friedman's "My Favorite Teacher," you might see how each of these writers creates a dominant impression of an influential person in his life and write about an influential person in your own life.

On a second level, reading provides you with information, ideas, and perspectives for developing your own paper. In this way, you respond to what you read, using material from what you've read in your essay. For example, after reading June Tangney's essay "Condemn the Crime, Not the Person," you might want to elaborate on what she has written and either agree with her examples or generate better ones of your own. You could also qualify her argument or take issue against it. Similarly, if you want to write about the effects of new technologies and medical practices on our health and well being, you will find Ronald M. Green's "Building Baby from the Genes Up" and Barbara Huttmann's "A Crime of Compassion" invaluable resources.

On a third level, active reading can increase your awareness of how others' writing affects you, thus making you more sensitive to how your own writing will affect your readers. For example, if you have ever been impressed by an author who uses convincing evidence to support each of his or her claims, you might be more likely to back up your own claims carefully. If you have been impressed by an apt turn of phrase or absorbed by a writer's new idea, you may be less inclined to feed your readers dull, worn-out, and trite phrases.

More to the point, however, the active reading that you are encouraged to do in *Models for Writers* will help you recognize and analyze the essential elements of the essay. When you see, for example, how a writer like Buzz Bissinger uses a strong thesis statement to control the parts of his essay on doing away with the Olympic Games, you can better appreciate what a clear thesis statement is and see the importance of having one in your essay. When you see the way Nancy Gibbs uses transitions to link key phrases and important ideas so that readers can recognize clearly how the parts of her essay are meant to flow together, you have a better idea of how to achieve such coherence in your own writing. And when you see how Martin Luther King Jr. divides the ways in which people characteristically respond to oppression into three distinct categories, you witness a powerful way in which you too can organize an essay using division and classification.

Another important reason, then, to master the skills of active reading is that, for everything you write, you will be your own first reader and critic. How well you are able to scrutinize your own drafts will powerfully affect how well you revise them, and revising well is crucial to writing well. So reading others' writing with a critical eye is a useful and important practice; the more you read, the more practice you will have in sharpening your skills.

Remember, writing is the making of reading. The more sensitive you become to the content and style decisions made by the writers in

Models for Writers, the more skilled you will be at seeing the rhetorical options available to you and making conscious choices in your own writing.

WRITING FROM READING: THREE SAMPLE STUDENT ESSAYS

A Narrative Essay

Reading often triggers memories of experiences that we have had. After reading several personal narratives about growing up—David Raymond's "On Being 17, Bright, and Unable to Read" (p. 196) and Dick Gregory's "Shame" (p. 278), in particular—student Lisa Driver found herself thinking about what it was like growing up in rural Vermont. When her classmates asked her to share with them a childhood experience that they wouldn't be able to forget, Driver told them of an experience that she'd had in the sixth grade. She confided that as a sixth grader the experience felt very traumatic. In retrospect, however, she was able to appreciate the humor in the uncomfortable situation. Encouraged by her classmates, Driver wrote the following narrative in which she tells of her memorable encounter with Mrs. Armstrong, her teacher. Notice that she uses chronological order and descriptive details to capture both the drama and the humor of the incident.

Title: introduces subject and provides focus

The Strong Arm of a Sixth-Grade Teacher

Lisa V. Driver

Point of view: first-person narration

Context: description of self, classroom setting, and another student

Sometimes experiences that we have had in a classroom leave an indelible imprint on our lives. For me, it was one experience that I had with Mrs. Armstrong, a powerful, overbearing teacher. I was a scrawny, sixth-grade girl. I sat in the back of the classroom in the third row behind Todd, the class troublemaker. There was a little bit of safety in sitting behind Todd. Usually Mrs. Armstrong targeted him and not anyone close by. Todd was the type of kid who loved to get into trouble. He had a heart of gold but had absolutely no use for school. He was not at all intimidated by Mrs. Armstrong and her academic credentials, her perfect children, her world travel, and, most of all, her condescending manner to her rural farm students.

Context: description of teacher foreshadows later action

Mrs. Armstrong was a very large, domineering, and commanding figure. She loved jelly donuts, and it showed. Her hands, desk, and papers always had globs of sticky jam on them. She's the only person I've ever known who could make almost a whole donut disappear in one bite. The bright, red jam would ooze out the sides of the donut and get all over her face. My classmates and I all drooled at the thought of having such a treat ourselves. Most days she managed to devour a half-dozen Koffee Kup jelly donuts.

Narrative begins: antonym/synonym drill

Description: dominant impression of teacher as "drill sergeant"

On one particular dull and dreary day, Mrs. Armstrong was droning on about antonyms and synonyms. She loved to use her knowledge to evoke fear and terror in her sixth-grade students, and none of us was immune to her reign of terror. She was the type of teacher who expected the right answer right away. The drill sergeant strutted around the room that day, snapping her pudgy, sticky fingers in our faces and expecting answers on the spot. If a student did not deliver immediately, then she would yell at and humiliate that student in front of his or her classmates. Many of my classmates had suffered her snapping fingers and been left embarrassed and defeated. But I was safe--I was behind Todd.

Organization: chronological sequence of events

Descriptive details

Dramatic short sentence

Climactic moment

The class dragged on as Mrs. Armstrong delighted in her antonym game. She'd march down each aisle and point to two different things, expecting us to quickly state the correct antonyms. For example, if she pointed to the ceiling and the floor, we were supposed to respond "up and down." If she pointed to the classroom and the window, the answer would be "inside and outside." As she neared my desk, I was feeling pretty safe, hidden as I was behind Todd. But then Todd cleverly knocked his pencil to the floor and leaned over to retrieve it. Well, there I was totally exposed to Mrs. Armstrong. I froze. Suddenly, she pointed to herself and then pointed at me and snapped those fingers, demanding an answer. Before I realized what I was saying, I blurted out, "fat and skinny"!

Mrs. Armstrong exploded. She started yelling and then grabbed hold of my shirt, dragged me to the door, and marched me down the hallway, screaming at me all the way. She stormed into the principal's office and deposited me in a hard wooden chair. In a loud voice she told Mr. Alderman, the principal, that I was not to come back to her class for an entire week. She slammed the door on her way out, leaving me with the principal. By now I was shaking and crying because I'd never ever been sent to the principal's office.

Descriptive details

Mr. Alderman sat in his old swivel chair and behind him on the wall hung a wooden paddle with the words "Board of Education" etched in large letters. Todd often bragged that he had firsthand knowledge of the purpose of that paddle. All that kept going through my head was that my parents were going to kill me after I'd been spanked by this man.

Conclusion: realizes mistakes and reflects on the incident

Mr. Alderman was a huge man with a short crew cut. Everyone except Todd was afraid of him. With steely eyes peering out over his glasses straight at me, the principal raised his eyebrows and demanded an explanation for my visit. I choked out the story to him between crying spells. When I told him that I had said "fat and skinny" in response to Mrs. Armstrong's antonym problem, he leaned back in his chair and started laughing as hard as I'd ever seen a person laugh. When he finished laughing and drying his eyes, he told me that the correct response should have been "teacher and student." Slowly it dawned on me that I had mistakenly given the wrong antonym to Mrs. Armstrong, and I started to giggle with the principal. I spent the entire week in Mr. Alderman's office, answering the phone and being his secretary. I think he was afraid of that teacher also.

A Response Essay

For an assignment following James Lincoln Collier's essay "Anxiety: Challenge by Another Name" (p. 82), Zoe Ockenga tackled the topic of anxiety. In her first draft, she explored how anxious she felt the night before her first speech in a public speaking class and how in confronting that anxiety she benefited from the course. Ockenga read her paper aloud in class, and other students had an opportunity to ask her questions and to offer constructive criticism. Several students suggested that she might want to relate her experiences to those that Collier recounts in his essay. Another asked if she could include other examples to bolster the point she wanted to make. At this point in the discussion, Ockenga recalled a phone conversation she had had with her mother regarding her mother's indecision about accepting a new job. The thought of working outside the home for the first time in more than twenty years brought out her mother's worst fears and threatened to keep her from accepting the challenge. Armed with these valuable suggestions and ideas, Ockenga began revising. In subsequent drafts, she worked on the Collier connection, actually citing his essay on several occasions, and developed the example of the anxiety surrounding her mother's decision. What follows is the final draft of her essay, which incorporates the changes she made based on the peer evaluation of her first draft.

Title: indicates main idea of the essay

The Excuse "Not To"

Zoe Ockenga

Beginning: captures reader's attention with personal experience most college students can relate to

I cannot imagine anything worse than the nervous, anxious feeling I got the night before my first speech in public-speaking class last spring semester. The knots in my stomach were so fierce that I racked my brain for an excuse to give the teacher so that I would not have to go through with the dreaded assignment. Once in bed, I lay awake thinking of all the mistakes that I might make while standing alone in front of my classmates. I spent the rest of the night tossing and turning, frustrated that now, on top of my panic, I would have to give my speech with huge bags under my eyes.

Anxiety is an intense emotion that can strike at any time or place, before a simple daily activity or a life-changing decision. For some people, anxiety is only a minor interference in the process of achieving a goal. For others, it can be a force that is impossible to overcome. In these instances, anxiety can prevent the accomplishment of lifelong hopes and dreams. Avoiding the causes of stress or fear can make us feel secure and safe. Avoiding anxiety, however, may mean forfeiting a once-in-a-lifetime opportunity. Confronting anxiety can make for a richer, more fulfilling existence.

Thesis

First example: continues story introduced in opening paragraph to support thesis

The next day I trudged to class and sat on the edge of my seat until I could not stand the tension any longer. At this point, I forced myself to raise my hand to volunteer to go next simply to end my suffering. As I walked to the front of the room and assumed my position at the podium, the faces of the twenty-five classmates I had been sitting beside a minute ago suddenly seemed like fifty. I probably fumbled over a word or two as I discussed the harmful aspects of animal testing, but my mistakes were not nearly as severe as I had imagined the night before. Less than five minutes later the whole nightmare was over, and it had been much less painful than I had anticipated. As I sat down with a huge sigh of relief to listen to the next victim stumble repeatedly over how to milk dairy cows, I realized that I had not been half bad.

Although I still dreaded giving the next series of speeches, I eventually became more accustomed to speaking in front of my peers. I would still have to force myself to volunteer, secretly hoping the teacher would forget about me, but the audience that once seemed large and forbidding eventually became much more human. A speech class is something that I would never have taken if it had not been a requirement, but I can honestly say that I am better off because of it. I was forced to grapple with my anxiety and in the process become a stronger, more self-confident individual. Before this class I had been able to hide out in large lectures, never offering any comments or insights. For the first time at college I was forced to participate, and I realized that I could speak effectively in front of strangers and, more important, that I had something to say.

Second example: cites essay from Models for Writers *to support thesis*

The insomnia-inducing anticipation of giving a speech was a type of anxiety that I had to overcome to meet my distribution requirements for graduation. In the essay "Anxiety: Challenge by Another Name" by James Lincoln Collier, the author tells of his own struggles with anxiety. He tells of one particular event that happened between his sophomore and junior years in college when he was asked to spend a summer in Argentina with a good friend. He writes about how he felt after he made his decision not to go:

> I had turned down something I wanted to do because I was scared, and had ended up feeling depressed. I stayed that way for a long time. And it didn't help when I went back to college in the fall to discover that Ted and his friend had had a terrific time. (83)

The proposition of going to Argentina was an extremely difficult choice for Collier as it meant abandoning the comfortable routine of the past and venturing completely out of his element. Although the idea of the trip was exciting, the author could not bring himself to choose the summer in Argentina because of his uncertainties.

The summer abroad that Collier denied himself in his early twenties left him with such a feeling of regret that he vowed to change his approach to life. From then on, he faced challenges that made him uncomfortable and was able to accomplish feats he would never have dreamed possible--interviewing celebrities, traveling extensively throughout Europe, parachuting, and even learning to ski at age forty. Collier emphasizes that he was able to make his life fulfilling and exciting by adhering to his belief that anxiety cannot be stifled by avoidance; it can be stifled only by confrontation (84).

Third example: introduces mother's dilemma

Anxiety prevents many individuals from accepting life's challenges and changes. My own mother is currently struggling with such a dilemma. At age fifty-three, having never had a career outside the home, my mother has been recommended to manage a new art gallery. The River Gallery, as it will be called, will be opening in our town of Ipswich, Massachusetts, this spring. An avid collector and art lover as well as a budding potter, my mother would, I believe, be exceptional at this job.

Anticipating this new opportunity and responsibility has caused my mother great anxiety. Reentering the workforce after over twenty years is as frightening for my mother as the trip to Argentina was for Collier. When I recently discussed the job prospect with my mother, she was negative and full of doubt. "There's no way I could ever handle such a responsibility," she commented. "I have no business experience. I would look like a fool if I actually tried to pull something like this off. Besides, I'm sure the artists would never take me seriously." Just as my mother focused on all the possible negative aspects of the opportunity in front of her, Collier questioned the value of his opportunity to spend a summer abroad. He describes having second thoughts about just how exciting the trip would be:

Quotation: quotes Collier to help explain mother's indecision

Block quote in MLA style

> I had never been very far from New England, and I had been homesick my first few weeks at college. What would it be like in a strange country? What about the language? And besides, I had promised to teach my younger brother to sail that summer. (82–83)

Focusing on all the possible problems accompanying a new opportunity can arouse such a sense of fear that it can overpower the ability to take a risk. Both my mother and Collier found out that dwelling on possible negative outcomes allowed them to ignore the benefits of a new experience and thus maintain their safe current situations.

Currently my mother is using anxiety as an excuse "not to" act. To confront her anxiety and take an opportunity in which there is a possibility of failure as well as success is a true risk. Regardless of the outcome, to even contemplate a new challenge has changed her life. The summer forgone by Collier roused him to never again pass up an exciting opportunity and thus to live his life to the fullest. Just the thought of taking the gallery position has prompted my mother to contemplate taking evening classes so that if she refuses the offer she may be better prepared for a similar challenge in the future. Although her decision is unresolved, her anxiety has made her realize the possibilities that may be opening for her, whether or not she chooses to take them. If in the end her answer is no, I believe that a lingering "What if?" feeling will cause her to reevaluate her expectations and goals for the future.

Conclusion: includes strong statement about anxiety that echoes optimism of thesis

Anxiety can create confidence and optimism or depression, low self-esteem, and regret. The outcome of anxiety is entirely dependent on whether the individual runs from it or embraces it. Some forms of anxiety can be conquered merely by repeating the activity that causes them, such as giving speeches in a public speaking class. Anxiety brought on by unique opportunities or life-changing decisions, such as a summer in a foreign country or a new career, must be harnessed. Opportunities forgone due to anxiety and fear could be the chances of a lifetime. Although the unpleasant feelings that may accompany anxiety may make it initially easier to do nothing, the road not taken will never be forgotten. Anxiety is essentially a blessing in disguise. It is a physical and emotional trigger that tells us when and where there is an opportunity for us to grow and become stronger human beings.

MLA-style works cited list

Works Cited

Collier, James Lincoln. "Anxiety: Challenge by Another Name." Models for Writers. Ed. Alfred Rosa and Paul Eschholz. 10th ed. Boston: Bedford, 2010. 82–85.

An Analytical Essay

When student Susan Francis wrote an analysis of George Orwell's "A Hanging" (p. 366), her purpose was both to show that she understood the essay and to help her readers increase their understanding of it. She started by thinking about aspects of the work's meaning, structure, and style that are important but not obvious. Her analysis grew directly out of her reading and out of the notes she made during her first and subsequent readings of Orwell's text.

From the start, Francis knew that she had to decide what point she most wanted to make—what her thesis would be. With a little thought, she developed a list of four theses that she could use in her analytical paper:

1. In "A Hanging," George Orwell carefully selects details to persuade readers that capital punishment is wrong.
2. "A Hanging" reveals how thoroughly the British had imposed their laws, customs, and values on colonial Burma.
3. Though "A Hanging" appeals powerfully to the emotions, it does not make a reasoned argument against capital punishment.
4. In "A Hanging," George Orwell employs simile and metaphor, personification, and dialogue to express people's inhumanity to other people.

After considering the merits of each of her four choices, Francis chose thesis 4 to use in her paper. She thought she could support this thesis strongly and effectively using evidence from Orwell's essay.

Following is the final draft of her analytical paper. Her discussion is clear and coherent, and it is firmly based on Orwell's text. She cites many details from the essay that capture Orwell's attitude toward the hanging and toward his imperial colleagues, and she interprets them so that her readers can plainly see how those details contribute to the total effect of "A Hanging."

The Disgrace of Man

Susan Francis

Thesis: statement of central idea

George Orwell's "A Hanging" graphically depicts the execution of a prisoner in a way that expresses a universal tragedy. He artfully employs simile and metaphor, personification, and dialogue to indicate people's inhumanity toward other people regardless of nationality and to prompt readers' sympathy and self-examination.

Point 1: examples of simile and metaphor

Orwell uses simile and metaphor to show that the prisoner is treated more like an animal than like a human being. The cells of the condemned men, "a row of sheds . . . quite bare within," are "like small animal cages" (366). The warders grip the prisoner "like men handling a fish" (367). Though they refer to the prisoner as "this man" (368) or "our friend" (370), the other characters view him as less than human. Even his cry resounds like "the tolling of a bell" rather than a human "prayer or a cry for help" (369), and after he is dead, the superintendent pokes at the body with a stick. These details direct readers' attention to the lack of human concern for the condemned prisoner.

Documentation: parenthetical citations in MLA style

Point 2: examples of personification—prisoner's body parts

In contrast, Orwell emphasizes the "wrongness of cutting a life short" (368) by representing the parts of the prisoner's body as taking on human behavior. He describes how "the lock of hair . . . danced" on the man's scalp, how "his feet printed themselves on the wet gravel," and how all his organs were "toiling away" (368) like a team of laborers at some collective project. In personifying these bodily features, Orwell forces readers to confront the prisoner's vitality, his humanity. Readers, in turn, associate each body part with themselves; they become highly aware of the fragility of life. As the author focuses on how easily these actions can be stopped in any human being "with a sudden snap" (368), readers feel the "unspeakable wrongness" of the hanging as if their own lives were threatened.

Personification: example of dog

In addition to creating this sense of unmistakable life, Orwell uses the dog as a standard for evaluating the characters' appreciation of human life. The dog loves people--he is "wild with glee at finding so many human beings together" (367)--and the person he loves the most is the prisoner, who has been treated as less than human by the jail attendants. When the prisoner starts to pray, the other people are silent, but the dog "answer[s] . . . with a whine" (369). Even after the hanging, the dog runs directly to the gallows to see the prisoner again. Readers are forced to reflect on their own reactions: which is more shocking, the dog's actions or the observers' cold response?

Point 3: insensitive dialogue regardless of nationality

Finally, Orwell refers to the characters' nationalities to stress that this insensitivity extends to all nationalities and races. The hanging takes place in Burma in a jail run by a European army doctor and a native of southern India. The warders are also Indians, and the hangman is actually a fellow prisoner. The author calls attention to each of these participants and implies that each one of them might have halted the brutal proceeding. He was there, too, and could have intervened when he suddenly realized that killing the prisoner would be wrong. Yet the formality of the hanging goes on.

As he reflects on the meaning of suddenly destroying human life, Orwell emphasizes the similarities among all men, regardless of nationality. Before the hanging, they are "seeing, hearing, feeling, understanding the same world," and afterward there would be "one mind less, one world less" (368). Such insights do not affect the other characters, who think of the hanging not as a killing but as a job to be done, a job made unpleasant by those reminders (the incident of the dog, the prisoner's praying) that they are dealing with a human being. Orwell uses dialogue to show how selfish and callous the observers are. Though they have different accents--the superintendent's "for God's sake hurry up" (367), the Dravidian's "all hass passed off with the utmost satisfactoriness" (370)--they think and feel the same. Their words, such as "He's all right" (369), show that they are more concerned about their own lives than the one they are destroying.

Conclusion: value of human life stressed

Although George Orwell sets his story in Burma, his point is universal; although he deals with capital punishment, he implies other questions about life and death. We are all faced with issues such as capital punishment, abortion, and euthanasia, and sometimes we find ourselves directly involved, as Orwell was in

Burma. "A Hanging" confronts us with a situation that won't go away and urges us to take very seriously the value of human life.

MLA-style works cited list

Works Cited

Orwell, George. "A Hanging." Models for Writers. Ed. Alfred Rosa and Paul Eschholz. 10th ed. Boston: Bedford, 2010. 366–71.

part ■ two

The Elements of the Essay

chapter **3**

Thesis

The **thesis** of an essay is its main or controlling idea, the point the writer is trying to make. The thesis is often expressed in a one- or two-sentence statement, although sometimes it is implied or suggested rather than stated directly. The thesis statement determines the content of the essay: everything the writer says must be logically related to the thesis statement.

Because everything you say in your composition must be logically related to your thesis, the thesis statement controls and directs the choices you make about the content of your essay. This does not mean that your thesis statement is a straitjacket. As your essay develops, you may want to modify your thesis statement to accommodate your new thinking. This urge is not only acceptable; it is normal.

One way to develop a working thesis is to determine a question that you are trying to answer in your essay. A one- or two-sentence answer to this question often produces a tentative thesis statement. For example, a student wanted to answer the following question in her essay:

> Do men and women have different conversational speaking styles?

Her preliminary answer to this question was this:

> Men and women appear to have different objectives when they converse.

After writing two drafts, she modified her thesis to better fit the examples she had gathered:

> Very often, conversations between men and women become situations in which the man gives a mini-lecture and the woman unwittingly turns into a captive audience.

A thesis statement should be

- The most important point you make about your topic,
- More general than the ideas and facts used to support it, and
- Appropriately focused for the length of your paper.

A thesis statement is not a question but an assertion—a claim made about a debatable issue that can be supported with evidence.

Another effective strategy for developing a thesis statement is to begin by writing "What I want to say is that. . . ."

> What I want to say is that unless the university administration enforces its strong anti-hazing policy, the well-being of many of its student-athletes will be endangered.

Later, when you delete the formulaic opening, you will be left with a thesis statement:

> Unless the university administration enforces its strong anti-hazing policy, the well-being of many of its student-athletes will be endangered.

Usually the thesis is presented early in the essay, sometimes in the first sentence. Here are some thesis statements that begin essays:

> One of the most potent elements in body language is eye behavior.
>
> –Flora Davis

> Americans can be divided into three groups—smokers, nonsmokers, and that expanding pack of us who have quit.
>
> –Franklin E. Zimring

> Over the past ten to fifteen years it has become apparent that eating disorders have reached epidemic proportions among adolescents.
>
> –Helen A. Guthrie

> Clutter is the disease of American writing. We are a society strangling in unnecessary words, circular constructions, pompous frills, and meaningless jargon.
>
> –William Zinsser

Each of these sentences does what a good thesis statement should do: it identifies the topic and makes an assertion about it.

Often writers prepare readers for the thesis statement with one or several sentences that establish a context. Notice in the following example how the author eases the reader into his thesis about television instead of presenting it abruptly in the first sentence:

> With the advent of television, for the first time in history, all aspects of animal and human life and death, of societal and individual behavior have been condensed on the average to a 19-inch diagonal screen and a 30-minute time slot. Television, a unique medium, claiming to be neither a reality nor art, has become reality for many of us, particularly for our children who are growing up in front of it.
>
> –Jerzy Kosinski

On occasion a writer may even purposely delay the presentation of a thesis until the middle or the end of an essay. If the thesis is controversial or needs extended discussion and illustration, the writer might present it later to make it easier for the reader to understand and accept it. Appearing near or at the end of an essay, a thesis also gains prominence. For example, after an involved discussion about why various groups put pressure on school libraries to ban books, a student ended an essay with her thesis:

> The effort to censor what our children are reading can turn into a potentially explosive situation and cause misunderstanding and hurt feelings within our schools and communities. If we can gain an understanding of why people have sought to censor children's books, we will be better prepared to respond in a sensitive and reasonable manner. More importantly, we will be able to provide the best educational opportunity for our children through a sensible approach, one that neither overly restricts the range of their reading nor allows them to read all books, no matter how inappropriate. *Thesis*
>
> –Tara Ketch, student

Some kinds of writing do not need thesis statements. These include descriptions, narratives, and personal writing such as letters and diaries. But any essay that seeks to explain or prove a point has a thesis that is usually set forth in a formal thesis statement.

The Most Important Day

■ Helen Keller

Helen Keller (1880–1968) was afflicted by a disease that left her blind and deaf at the age of eighteen months. With the aid of her teacher, Anne Mansfield Sullivan, she was able to overcome her severe handicaps, to graduate from Radcliffe College, and to lead a productive and challenging adult life. In the following selection from her autobiography, The Story of My Life *(1902), Keller tells of the day she first met Anne Sullivan, a day she regarded as the most important in her life.*

As you read, note that Keller states her thesis in the first paragraph and that the remaining paragraphs maintain unity by emphasizing the importance of the day her teacher arrived, even though they deal with the days and weeks following.

Reflecting on What You Know

Reflect on the events of what you consider "the most important day" of your life. Briefly describe what happened. Why was that particular day so significant?

The most important day I remember in all my life is the one on which my teacher, Anne Mansfield Sullivan, came to me. I am filled with wonder when I consider the immeasurable contrast between the two lives which it connects. It was the third of March, 1887, three months before I was seven years old. 1

On the afternoon of that eventful day, I stood on the porch, dumb,[1] expectant. I guessed vaguely from my mother's signs and from the hurrying to and fro in the house that something unusual was about to happen, so I went to the door and waited on the steps. The afternoon sun penetrated the mass of honeysuckle that covered the porch and fell on my upturned face. My fingers lingered almost unconsciously on the familiar leaves and blossoms which had just come forth to greet the sweet southern spring. I did not know what the future held of marvel or 2

[1] *dumb:* unable to speak; mute.

surprise for me. Anger and bitterness had preyed upon me continually for weeks and a deep languor[2] had succeeded this passionate struggle.

Have you ever been at sea in a dense fog, when it seemed as if a 3
tangible white darkness shut you in, and the great ship, tense and anxious, groped her way toward the shore with plummet and sounding-line,[3] and you waited with beating heart for something to happen? I was like that ship before my education began, only I was without compass or sounding-line, and had no way of knowing how near the harbor was. "Light! Give me light!" was the wordless cry of my soul, and the light of love shone on me in that very hour.

I felt approaching footsteps. I stretched out my hand as I supposed 4
to my mother. Someone took it, and I was caught up and held close in the arms of her who had come to reveal all things to me, and, more than all things else, to love me.

The morning after my teacher came she led me into her room and 5
gave me a doll. The little blind children at the Perkins Institution[4] had sent it and Laura Bridgman[5] had dressed it; but I did not know this until afterward. When I had played with it a little while, Miss Sullivan slowly spelled into my hand the word "d-o-l-l." I was at once interested in this finger play and tried to imitate it. When I finally succeeded in making the letters correctly I was flushed with childish pleasure and pride. Running downstairs to my mother I held up my hand and made the letters for doll. I did not know that I was spelling a word or even that words existed; I was simply making my fingers go in monkeylike imitation. In the days that followed I learned to spell in this uncomprehending way a great many words, among them *pin, hat, cup* and a few verbs like *sit, stand,* and *walk*. But my teacher had been with me several weeks before I understood that everything has a name.

One day, while I was playing with my new doll, Miss Sullivan put 6
my big rag doll into my lap also, spelled "d-o-l-l" and tried to make me understand that "d-o-l-l" applied to both. Earlier in the day we had had a tussle over the words "m-u-g" and "w-a-t-e-r." Miss Sullivan had tried to impress it upon me that "m-u-g" is *mug* and

---

[2]*languor:* sluggishness.

[3]*plummet . . . line:* a weight tied to a line that is used to measure the depth of the ocean.

[4]*Perkins Institution:* the first school for blind children in the United States, opened in 1932 and located in South Boston during her time there. The school moved to Watertown, Massachusetts, in 1912.

[5]*Laura Bridgman* (1829–1889): a deaf-blind girl who was educated at the Perkins Institution in the 1840s.

that "w-a-t-e-r" is *water,* but I persisted in confounding the two. In despair she had dropped the subject for the time, only to renew it at the first opportunity. I became impatient at her repeated attempts and, seizing the new doll, I dashed it upon the floor. I was keenly delighted when I felt the fragments of the broken doll at my feet. Neither sorrow nor regret followed my passionate outburst. I had not loved the doll. In the still, dark world in which I lived there was no strong sentiment or tenderness. I felt my teacher sweep the fragments to one side of the hearth, and I had a sense of satisfaction that the cause of my discomfort was removed. She brought me my hat, and I knew I was going out into the warm sunshine. This thought, if a wordless sensation may be called a thought, made me hop and skip with pleasure.

We walked down the path to the well-house, attracted by the fragrance of the honeysuckle with which it was covered. Someone was drawing water and my teacher placed my hand under the spout. As the cool stream gushed over one hand she spelled into the other the word *water,* first slowly, then rapidly. I stood still, my whole attention fixed upon the motions of her fingers. Suddenly I felt a misty consciousness as of something forgotten—a thrill of returning thought; and somehow the mystery of language was revealed to me. I knew then that "w-a-t-e-r" meant the wonderful cool something that was flowing over my hand. The living word awakened my soul, gave it light, hope, joy, set it free! There were barriers still, it is true, but barriers that could in time be swept away. 7

I left the well-house eager to learn. Everything had a name, and each name gave birth to a new thought. As we returned to the house every object which I touched seemed to quiver with life. That was because I saw everything with the strange, new sight that had come to me. On entering the door I remembered the doll I had broken. I felt my way to the hearth and picked up the pieces. I tried vainly to put them together. Then my eyes filled with tears; for I realized what I had done, and for the first time I felt repentance and sorrow. 8

I learned a great many new words that day. I do not remember what they all were; but I do know that *mother, father, sister, teacher* were among them—words that were to make the world blossom for me, "like Aaron's rod,[6] with flowers." It would have been difficult to find a happier child than I was as I lay in my crib at the close of that 9

[6]*Aaron's rod:* in Jewish and Christian traditions, a rod similar to Moses's staff that, in the high priest Aaron's hands, had miraculous power.

eventful day and lived over the joys it had brought me, and for the first time longed for a new day to come.

Thinking Critically about This Reading

Keller writes that "'Light! Give me light!' was the wordless cry of [her] soul" (paragraph 3). What was the "light" Keller longed for, and how did receiving it change her life?

Questions for Study and Discussion

1. What is Keller's thesis? What question do you think Keller is trying to answer? Does her thesis answer her question?
2. What is Keller's purpose? (Glossary: *Purpose*)
3. What was Keller's state of mind before Anne Sullivan arrived to help her? To what does she compare herself? (Glossary: *Analogy*) How effective is this comparison? Explain.
4. Why was the realization that everything has a name important to Keller?
5. How was the "mystery of language" (7) revealed to Keller? What were the consequences for her of this new understanding of the nature of language?
6. Keller narrates the events of the day Sullivan arrived (2–4), the morning after she arrived (5), and one day several weeks after her arrival (6–9). (Glossary: *Narration*) Describe what happens on each day, and explain how these separate incidents support Keller's thesis.

Classroom Activity Using Thesis

One effective way of focusing on your subject is to develop a list of specific questions about it at the start. This strategy has a number of advantages. Each question narrows the general subject area, suggesting a more manageable essay. Also, simply phrasing your topic as a question gives you a starting point; your work has focus and direction from the outset. Finally, a one- or two-sentence answer to your question often provides you with a preliminary thesis statement.

To test this strategy, develop a list of five questions about the subject "recycling paper waste on campus." To get you started, here is one possible question: should students be required to recycle paper waste?

1. ______________________________
2. ______________________________
3. ______________________________
4. ______________________________
5. ______________________________

Suggested Writing Assignments

1. Think about an important day in your own life. Using the thesis statement "The most important day of my life was __________," write an essay in which you show the significance of that day by recounting and explaining the events that took place, as Keller does in her essay. Before you write, you might find it helpful to reflect on your journal entry for this reading.
2. For many people around the world, the life of Helen Keller symbolizes what a person can achieve despite seemingly insurmountable obstacles. Her achievements have inspired people with and without disabilities, leading them to believe they can accomplish more than they ever thought possible. Consider the role of people with disabilities in our society, develop an appropriate thesis, and write an essay on the topic.
3. Keller was visually and hearing impaired from the age of eighteen months, which meant she could neither read nor hear people speak. She was eventually able to read and write using braille, a system of "touchable symbols" invented by Louis Braille. In the accompanying photograph taken at the Sorbonne in Paris, France, upon the one-hundredth anniversary of Braille's death, Keller demonstrates how to use the system. Write an essay in which you put forth the thesis that the invention of braille has liberated countless numbers of people who have shared Keller's impairment.

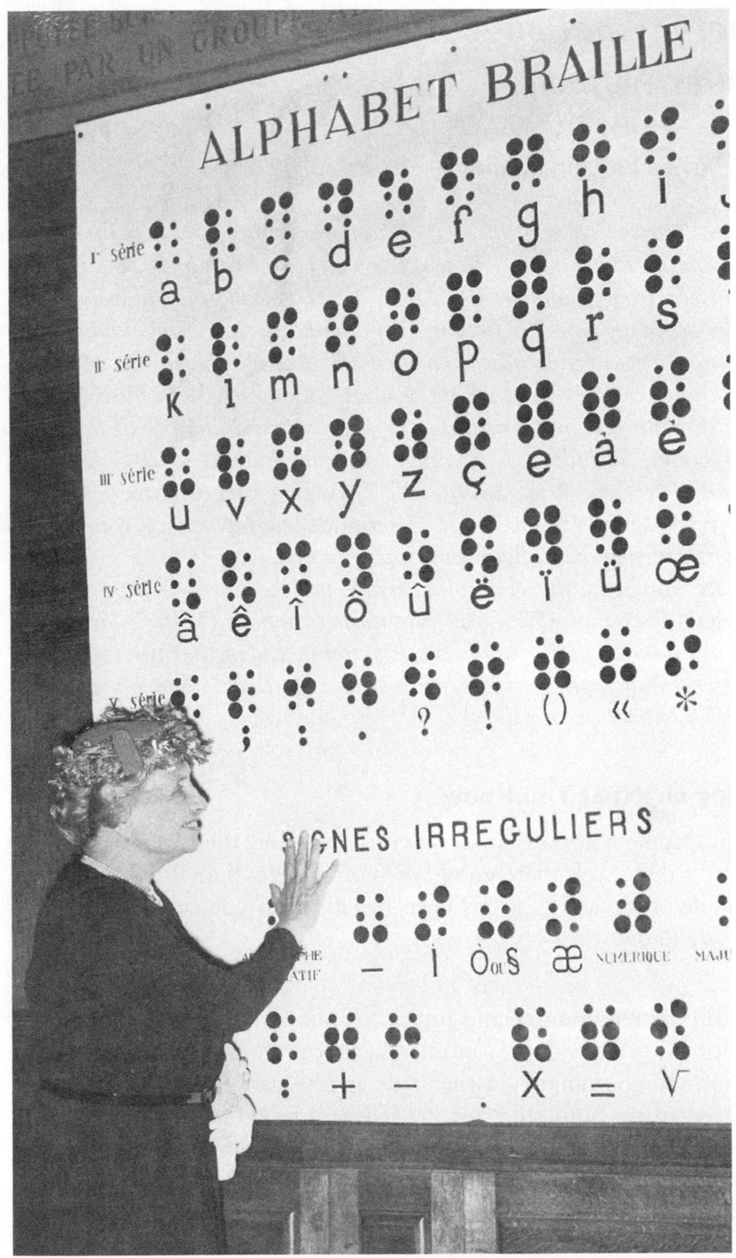
ALPHABET BRAILLE
Ire série
a b c d e f g h i
IIe série
k l m n o p q r s
IIIe série
u v x y z ç é à è
IVe série
â ê î ô û ë ï ü œ
V^e série
; : . ? ! ( ) « *
SIGNES IRREGULIERS
— ì ò ou § æ NUMERIQUE
: + — X = √

Anxiety: Challenge by Another Name

■ James Lincoln Collier

James Lincoln Collier is a freelance writer with more than six hundred articles to his credit. He was born in New York in 1928 and graduated from Hamilton College in 1950. Among his published books are many works of fiction, including novels for young adults. His nonfiction writing has often focused on American music. His best-known book is The Making of Jazz: A Comprehensive History *(1978). With his son Christopher he has written a number of history books, including* A Century of Immigration: 1820–1924 *(2000),* The Civil War *(2000),* The Changing Face of American Society: 1945–2000 *(2001), and a series of biographies for young readers covering major figures in American history.*

As you read the following essay, which first appeared in Reader's Digest *in 1986, pay attention to where Collier places his thesis. Note also how his thesis statement identifies the topic (anxiety) and makes an assertion about it (that it can have a positive impact on our lives).*

Reflecting on What You Know

Many people associate anxiety with stress and think of it as a negative thing. Are there good kinds of anxiety, too? Provide an example of anxiety that has been beneficial to you or to someone you know.

Between my sophomore and junior years at college, a chance came up for me to spend the summer vacation working on a ranch in Argentina. My roommate's father was in the cattle business, and he wanted Ted to see something of it. Ted said he would go if he could take a friend, and he chose me. 1

The idea of spending two months on the fabled Argentine Pampas[1] was exciting. Then I began having second thoughts. I had 2

[1]*Pampas:* a vast plain in central Argentina.

never been very far from New England, and I had been homesick my first few weeks at college. What would it be like in a strange country? What about the language? And besides, I had promised to teach my younger brother to sail that summer. The more I thought about it, the more the prospect daunted[2] me. I began waking up nights in a sweat.

In the end I turned down the proposition. As soon as Ted asked somebody else to go, I began kicking myself. A couple of weeks later I went home to my old summer job, unpacking cartons at the local supermarket, feeling very low. I had turned down something I wanted to do because I was scared, and had ended up feeling depressed. I stayed that way for a long time. And it didn't help when I went back to college in the fall to discover that Ted and his friend had had a terrific time. 3

In the long run that unhappy summer taught me a valuable lesson out of which I developed a rule for myself: *do what makes you anxious; don't do what makes you depressed.* 4

I am not, of course, talking about severe states of anxiety or depression, which require medical attention. What I mean is that kind of anxiety we call stage fright, butterflies in the stomach, a case of nerves—the feelings we have at a job interview, when we're giving a big party, when we have to make an important presentation at the office. And the kind of depression I am referring to is that downhearted feeling of the blues, when we don't seem to be interested in anything, when we can't get going and seem to have no energy. 5

I was confronted by this sort of situation toward the end of my senior year. As graduation approached, I began to think about taking a crack at making my living as a writer. But one of my professors was urging me to apply to graduate school and aim at a teaching career. 6

I wavered. The idea of trying to live by writing was scary—a lot more scary than spending a summer on the Pampas, I thought. Back and forth I went, making my decision, unmaking it. Suddenly, I realized that every time I gave up the idea of writing, that sinking feeling went through me; it gave me the blues. 7

The thought of graduate school wasn't what depressed me. It was giving up on what deep in my gut I really wanted to do. Right then I learned another lesson. To avoid that kind of depression meant, inevitably, having to endure a certain amount of worry and concern. 8

The great Danish philosopher Søren Kierkegaard believed that anxiety always arises when we confront the possibility of our own 9

[2]*daunted:* discouraged.

development. It seems to be a rule of life that you can't advance without getting that old, familiar, jittery feeling.

Even as children we discover this when we try to expand ourselves by, say, learning to ride a bike or going out for the school play. Later in life we get butterflies when we think about having that first child, or uprooting the family from the old hometown to find a better opportunity halfway across the country. Any time, it seems, that we set out aggressively to get something we want, we meet up with anxiety. And it's going to be our traveling companion, at least part of the way, into any new venture. 10

When I first began writing magazine articles, I was frequently required to interview big names—people like Richard Burton,[3] Joan Rivers,[4] sex authority William Masters, baseball-great Dizzy Dean. Before each interview I would get butterflies and my hands would shake. 11

At the time, I was doing some writing about music. And one person I particularly admired was the great composer Duke Ellington. Onstage and on television, he seemed the very model of the confident, sophisticated man of the world. Then I learned that Ellington still got stage fright. If the highly honored Duke Ellington, who had appeared on the bandstand some 10,000 times over thirty years, had anxiety attacks, who was I to think I could avoid them? 12

I went on doing those frightening interviews, and one day, as I was getting onto a plane for Washington to interview columnist Joseph Alsop, I suddenly realized to my astonishment that I was looking forward to the meeting. What had happened to those butterflies? 13

Well, in truth, they were still there, but there were fewer of them. I had benefited, I discovered, from a process psychologists call "extinction." If you put an individual in an anxiety-provoking situation often enough, he will eventually learn that there isn't anything to be worried about. 14

Which brings us to a corollary[5] to my basic rule: *you'll never eliminate anxiety by avoiding the things that caused it.* I remember how my son Jeff was when I first began to teach him to swim at the lake cottage where we spent our summer vacations. He resisted, and when I got him into the water he sank and sputtered and wanted to 15

---

[3]*Richard Burton* (1925–1984): a well-known British stage and Hollywood movie actor.
[4]*Joan Rivers* (b. 1933): a stand-up comedian and talk-show host.
[5]*corollary:* analogy; another example.

quit. But I was insistent. And by summer's end he was splashing around like a puppy. He had "extinguished" his anxiety the only way he could—by confronting it.

The problem, of course, is that it is one thing to urge somebody else to take on those anxiety-producing challenges; it is quite another to get ourselves to do it. 16

Some years ago I was offered a writing assignment that would require three months of travel through Europe. I had been abroad a couple of times on the usual "If it's Tuesday this must be Belgium" trips, but I hardly could claim to know my way around the continent. Moreover, my knowledge of foreign languages was limited to a little college French. 17

I hesitated. How would I, unable to speak the language, totally unfamiliar with local geography or transportation systems, set up interviews and do research? It seemed impossible, and with considerable regret I sat down to write a letter begging off. Halfway through, a thought—which I subsequently made into another corollary to my basic rule—ran through my mind: *you can't learn if you don't try.* So I accepted the assignment. 18

There were some bad moments. But by the time I had finished the trip I was an experienced traveler. And ever since, I have never hesitated to head for even the most exotic of places, without guides or even advanced bookings, confident that somehow I will manage. 19

The point is that the new, the different, is almost by definition scary. But each time you try something, you learn, and as the learning piles up, the world opens to you. 20

I've made parachute jumps, learned to ski at forty, flown up the Rhine[6] in a balloon. And I know I'm going to go on doing such things. It's not because I'm braver or more daring than others. I'm not. But I don't let the butterflies stop me from doing what I want. Accept anxiety as another name for challenge and you can accomplish wonders. 21

Thinking Critically about This Reading

Collier writes that "Kierkegaard believed that anxiety always arises when we confront the possibility of our own development" (paragraph 9). How do Collier's own experiences and growth substantiate Kierkegaard's belief in the value of anxiety?

---

[6]*Rhine:* a major river and waterway of western Europe.

Questions for Study and Discussion

1. What is Collier's thesis? Based on your own experiences, do you think Collier's thesis is valid? Explain.
2. What is the process known to psychologists as "extinction"?
3. What causes Collier to come up with his basic rule for himself: "Do what makes you anxious; don't do what makes you depressed" (4)? (Glossary: *Cause and Effect*) How does he develop the two corollaries to his basic rule? How do the basic rule and the two corollaries prepare you for his thesis?
4. What is Collier's purpose? (Glossary: *Purpose*)
5. What figure of speech does Collier use toward the end of paragraph 10? (Glossary: *Figure of Speech*)
6. What function do paragraphs 17–19 serve in Collier's essay?

Classroom Activity Using Thesis

A good thesis statement identifies the topic and makes an assertion about it. Evaluate each of the following sentences, and explain why each one either works or doesn't work as a thesis statement.

1. Americans are suffering from overwork.
2. Life is indeed precious, and I believe the death penalty helps to affirm this fact.
3. Birthday parties are loads of fun.
4. New York is a city of sounds: muted sounds and shrill sounds, shattering sounds and soothing sounds, urgent sounds and aimless sounds.
5. Everyone is talking about the level of violence in American society.
6. Neighborhoods are often assigned human characteristics, one of which is a life cycle: they have a birth, a youth, a middle age, and an old age.

Suggested Writing Assignments

1. Building on your own experiences and the reading you have done, write an essay in which you use as your thesis either Collier's basic rule or one of his corollaries to that basic rule.

2. Write an essay in which you use any one of the following as your thesis:

   Good manners are a thing of the past.
   We need rituals in our lives.
   To tell a joke well is an art.
   We are a drug-dependent society.
   A regular low-dosage regimen of aspirin can be therapeutic.
   Regular exercise offers many benefits.

Faster, Higher, Stronger, No Longer

■ Buzz Bissinger

H. G. "Buzz" Bissinger is a journalist, screenwriter, television writer, and nonfiction author. Born in New York City in 1954, Bissinger was educated at Phillips Academy in Massachusetts, the University of Pennsylvania, and Harvard University. After beginning his newspaper career at the Ledger-Star *in Norfolk, Virginia, Bissinger moved to the* St. Paul Pioneer Press *and the* Philadelphia Inquirer, *where, with two colleagues, he won the Pulitzer Prize for investigative reporting for a six-part series on the Philadelphia court system. Bissinger moved to Odessa, Texas, where he wrote* Friday Night Lights *(1997), a book about how football influences Texas small-town life. The book was a* New York Times *bestseller and was made into a popular movie. Bissinger followed* Friday Night Lights *with two other books,* A Prayer for the City *(2003) and* Three Nights in August *(2005), a book on baseball. Now a contributing editor for* Vanity Fair *magazine, Bissinger divides his time between homes in Philadelphia and the Pacific Northwest.*

In the following essay, which first appeared in the New York Times *on April 13, 2008, Bissinger puts forth a provocative thesis regarding the Olympics. Writing as the world awaited the beginning of the 2008 Summer Games in Beijing amid a swirl of protests, Bissinger supports his thesis with examples that remind us that the Olympics have never been free of controversy.*

Reflecting on What You Know

What do you think about the Olympics? Are they just another televised sporting event? Do the games represent lofty ideals such as honesty, goodwill, and physical and moral achievements?

In 1894, Baron Pierre de Coubertin, having refused the military and political careers typical of a French aristocrat, settled upon the revival of the Olympic Games as his life's work. He saw sport as a higher 1 calling, a religion. And he saw the Olympics as an event that would enhance and heighten moral virtue: "May joy and good fellowship reign, and in this manner, may the Olympic torch pursue its way through ages, increasing friendly understanding among nations, for the good of a humanity always more enthusiastic, more courageous, and more pure."

He is considered by many the father of the modern Games, first held in 1896 in Athens. But if he were alive today and witness to the Olympics over the past forty years, he would almost surely come to the conclusion that his grand idea had failed, that idealism is no match for the troika of politics, money, and sports. 2

The Summer Games in Beijing are four months away and already a predictable mess. The running of the Olympic torch resulted in arrests and nasty confrontations with the police last week in London and Paris amid protests against China's recent crackdown in Tibet and other human rights abuses. In San Francisco, the only North American stop, the torch-bearers played literal hide-and-seek with protesters when the route was suddenly changed for security reasons. There have been repeated calls for heads of state to boycott the opening ceremonies. But protests and boycotts are no longer effective remedies. There is only one way left to improve the Olympics: to permanently end them. 3

True, in the world of sports, any plan that puts morality over money is unlikely to happen. Commissions are formed only once the problem is over (see Major League Baseball), and the cheaters will always find another angle—you can bet that some lab somewhere is working on the design of a new steroid undetectable to testing (see every professional sport and many "amateur" ones). The loftier the rose-colored rhetoric, which in the Olympics has become an Olympian growth industry, the worse the underlying stink. And this is an institution that is rotted in so many different ways. 4

A short history: in 1968, in what became known as the Tlatelolco massacre, government troops fired on thousands of student protesters in Mexico City ten days before the Summer Games. Nobody knows exactly how many were killed, but the best estimate is two hundred to three hundred. 5

Four years later in 1972, members of the pro-Palestinian group Black September took members of the Israeli team hostage from its quarters in the Olympic village in Munich; eleven died. 6

In 1976, the East German women's swim team won eleven of 7
thirteen gold medals, a performance that was stunning—too stunning, since it was later revealed that hundreds of East German athletes had been using steroids for years to enhance performance.

In 1980, the United States and roughly sixty other nations boy- 8
cotted the Games in Moscow because of the Soviet Union's invasion of Afghanistan.

In 1984, although nation-by-nation medal counts are supposed 9
to be against the very spirit of the Games, the performance of the United States in Los Angeles was ballyhooed. Such chest-beating only reinforced the inherent jingoism of the Games, since the Soviet Union and East Germany boycotted of course in retaliation for the American snub of Moscow. More important, 1984 became the first Olympics in which corporate sponsors got their hooks in deep, making the Games too often seem like one running advertisement.

As for the 1988 Games, in arguably the premier track event of the 10
Olympics, the men's 100 meters, the Canadian Ben Johnson was ultimately stripped of his gold medal after testing positive for performance-enhancing drugs. In addition, the host nation, South Korea, displaced 720,000 residents to build facilities. (According to an advocacy group, the Center on Housing Rights and Evictions, China has now more than doubled that figure to an estimated 1.5 million for its Games.)

In 1996, the Olympics in Atlanta were marred by a bombing that 11
resulted in two deaths.

In 2000, the American track star Marion Jones won five medals, 12
three gold, while taking performance-enhancing drugs, lied about it for seven years, and is now in prison for perjury. In addition, forty of China's three hundred athletes withdrew after seven rowers failed blood tests.

Before the 2002 Winter Olympics in Salt Lake City, it was 13
revealed that backers, in trying to get the Games, had bribed officials of the International Olympic Committee with college scholarships, plastic surgery, and free guns and skis. At those Games, one of the judges in the pairs skating competition admitted that she voted to ensure victory for the Russian team.

In 2004, the Greek government spent as much as $12 billion on the 14
Summer Games in Athens, 5 percent of the country's economy. Yes, part of that money went to the building of a new rail system and airport, but the Greek government also admitted it had no plan for what to do afterward with many of the lavish facilities it was required to build for the Games.

At the 2006 Winter Games in Turin, Italy, policemen raided the Olympic residences of the Austrian ski federation for possible illegal use of performance-enhancing drugs; two members fled the country. 15

With the Summer Games approaching in August, one event has already started, the who-is-in-who-is-out opening ceremonies boycott over China's record on human rights (as of the last tally, President Bush was in, Chancellor Angela Merkel of Germany and Prime Minister Gordon Brown of Britain were out, and President Nicolas Sarkozy of France was on the fence). 16

But lest we as Americans feel too righteous, we should consider this: if the host country this summer were the United States, every visiting nation would have to consider either boycotting the opening ceremonies or withdrawing given a disturbing record of our own, which includes the occupation of Iraq and the abuses at Abu Ghraib and Guantánamo Bay. 17

It is, of course, unfair to make a sweeping condemnation of all the athletes who participate. "This is their chance to march into the Olympic stadium," says Bob Costas, who will have his seventh turn as the prime-time Olympics host for NBC in Beijing. "It is the culmination of all their time and effort. Many of them come out of impoverished circumstances, and they are exposed to more in two weeks than they might be in two years." 18

It is the single best argument for the Olympics. But still not enough to overcome the sordid history. 19

A permanent end to the Olympics might actually not be that difficult. All it would really take is a single act of courage and morality by the United States to pull out of the Games forever on the basis that the mission is not coming close to being served. An American departure would severely dilute the Games since it would no longer be a world competition of anything. 20

But a far stronger factor in the exit of the American team would be the likelihood that American corporations would stop backing the Olympics with their megamillions. It would also severely diminish the willingness of American networks to continue to pay mind-boggling sums for the broadcast rights to the Olympics, which in the case of NBC was about $2.2 billion for the Games in 2010 and 2012. If Americans aren't playing, Americans won't watch. 21

In place of the Olympics, world championships would still be held in individual sports as they are now, but perhaps at permanent venues designed for optimum performance. This would be a good thing for athletes. For all the hype, the Games often don't provide the greatest performances. In Athens, for example, there was not enough 22 time to build a roof for the pool because of the huge construction project that the Olympics had become, exposing swimmers to hideous summer heat and the backstrokers to blinding sunlight.

Would some athletes become innocent victims with the loss of the Olympics? Yes. But it would be nothing close to the number of innocent victims killed in Darfur with Chinese-supplied weapons, or in Iraq during the American occupation. 23

The world would carry on without the Games. The ideals set forth by Coubertin when he revived them, instead of being routinely mocked as they are now, would be honored by the admission that the Olympics have simply failed. 24

Thinking Critically about This Reading

In your opinion, has Bissinger been unfair to the athletes who have participated in the Olympics? Does he condemn them all by criticizing the actions of a few?

Questions for Study and Discussion

1. What is Bissinger's thesis? Where does he state it?
2. What does Bissinger say are the recent activities that undermine Coubertin's idealism in reviving the ancient games?
3. What evidence does Bissinger provide for believing that the goals of the Olympics have been undermined? (Glossary: *Evidence*)
4. In paragraph 19, what does Bissinger say is "the single best argument for the Olympics"? Why does he think that the argument is "not enough to overcome the sordid history" of the games?
5. Why does Bissinger think that it's difficult to combat the influence of drugs in sports?
6. What suggestions does Bissinger have for an alternative to the Olympics? Are you in favor of that alternative? Explain.

Classroom Activity Using Thesis

Based on your reading of Bissinger's essay, write at least one thesis statement for each of the following questions:

1. What is the importance of sports?
2. How do we pay for the costs of large sports events if governments and corporations are banned from providing the necessary funds?

3. Is it possible to be too idealistic about the value of sports and especially the Olympics?
4. Have we overestimated the goodwill that has been the result of the Olympics?
5. If the modern Olympic games came to an end, would they be missed?

Suggested Writing Assignments

1. Write an essay with the following thesis: We must support the Olympic games despite problems that threaten to undermine their lofty ideals. Be sure to address the problems that Bissinger emphasizes—money, drugs, and politics and their negative influence on the games.
2. "Winning isn't everything, it's the only thing," said legendary National Football League coach Vince Lombardi of the Green Bay Packers. He meant that coming in second doesn't count for much, it is not well remembered by anyone, and we should strive to be the best. Does the statement also implicitly encourage actions that are not positive? Write an essay arguing against Lombardi's statement as embodying and perhaps encouraging victory at any cost and by any means. Might the rampant use of performance-enhancing drugs in sports, for example, be to some extent a result of the thinking illustrated by Lombardi's statement?

chapter **4**

Unity

Unity is an essential quality in a well-written essay. The principle of **unity** requires that every element in a piece of writing—whether a paragraph or an essay—be related to the main idea. Sentences that stray from the subject, even though they might be related to it or provide additional information, can weaken an otherwise strong piece of writing. Note how the italicized segments in the following paragraph undermine its unity and divert our attention from its main idea:

> When I was growing up, one of the places I enjoyed most was the cherry tree in the backyard. *Behind the yard was an alley and then more houses.* Every summer when the cherries began to ripen, I used to spend hours high up in the tree, picking and eating the sweet, sun-warmed cherries. *My mother always worried about my falling out of the tree, but I never did.* But I had some competition for the cherries—flocks of birds that enjoyed them as much as I did and would perch all over the tree, devouring the fruit whenever I wasn't there. I used to wonder why the grown-ups never ate any of the cherries—*my father loved all kinds of fruit*—but actually, when the birds and I had finished, there weren't many left.
>
> –Betty Burns, student

When the italicized sentences are eliminated, the paragraph is unified and reads smoothly.

Now consider another paragraph, this one from an essay about family photographs and how they allow the author to learn about her past and to stay connected with her family in the present:

> Photographs have taken me to places I have never been and have shown me people alive before I was born. I can visit my grandmother's childhood home in Vienna, Austria, and walk down the high-ceilinged, iron staircase by looking through the small,

white album my grandma treasures. I also know of the tomboy she once was, wearing lederhosen instead of the dirndls worn by her friends. And I have seen her as a beautiful young woman who traveled with the Red Cross during the war, uncertain of her future. The photograph that rests in a red leather frame on my grandma's nightstand has allowed me to meet the man she would later marry. He died before I was born. I have been told that I would have loved his calm manner, and I can see for myself his gentle smile and tranquil expression.

–Carrie White, student

Did you notice that the first sentence gives focus and direction to the paragraph and that all of the subsequent sentences are directly related to it?

A well-written essay should be unified both within and between paragraphs; that is, everything in it should be related to its **thesis,** the main idea of the essay. The first requirement for unity is that the thesis itself be clear, either through a direct statement, called the *thesis statement,* or by implication. The second requirement is that there be no digressions—no discussion or information that is not shown to be logically related to the thesis. A unified essay stays within the limits of its thesis.

Here, for example, is a short essay by Stuart Chase about the dangers of making generalizations. As you read, notice how carefully Chase sticks to his point.

Overgeneralizing

One swallow does not make a summer, nor can two or three cases often support a dependable generalization. Yet all of us, including the most polished eggheads, are constantly falling into this mental peopletrap. It is the most common, probably the most seductive, and potentially the most dangerous, of all the fallacies. 1

You drive through a town and see a drunken man on the sidewalk. A few blocks further on you see another. You turn to your companion: "Nothing but drunks in this town!" Soon you are out in the country, bowling along at fifty. A car passes you as if you were parked. On a curve a second whizzes by. Your companion turns to you: "All the drivers in this state are crazy!" Two thumping generalizations, each built on two cases. If we stop to think, we 2 usually recognize the exaggeration and the unfairness of such generalizations. Trouble comes when we do not stop to think—or when we build them on a prejudice.

This kind of reasoning has been around for a long time. Aristotle was aware of its dangers and called it "reasoning by example," meaning too few examples. What it boils down to is failing to count your swallows before announcing that summer is here. Driving from my home to New Haven the other day, a distance of about forty miles, I caught myself saying: "Every time I look around I see a new ranch-type house going up." So on the return trip I counted them; there were exactly five under construction. And how many times had I "looked around"? I suppose I had glanced to right and left—as one must at side roads and so forth in driving—several hundred times. 3

In this fallacy, we do not make the error of neglecting facts altogether and rushing immediately to the level of opinion. We start at the fact level properly enough, but *we do not stay there*. A case of two and up we go to a rousing oversimplification about drunks, speeders, ranch-style houses—or, more seriously, about foreigners, African Americans, labor leaders, teenagers. 4

Why do we overgeneralize so often and sometimes so disastrously? One reason is that the human mind is a generalizing machine. We would not be people without this power. The old academic crack: "All generalizations are false, including this one," is only a play on words. We *must* generalize to communicate and to live. But we should beware of beating the gun; of not waiting until enough facts are in to say something useful. Meanwhile it is a plain waste of time to listen to arguments based on a few handpicked examples. 5

–Stuart Chase

Everything in the essay relates to Chase's thesis statement, which is included in the essay's first sentence: "nor can two or three cases often support a dependable generalization." Paragraphs 2 and 3 document the thesis with examples; paragraph 4 explains how overgeneralizing occurs; paragraph 5 analyzes why people overgeneralize; and, for a conclusion, Chase restates his thesis in different words. An essay may be longer, more complex, and more wide-ranging than this one, but to be effective it must also avoid digressions and remain close to the author's main idea.

A good way to check that your essay is indeed unified is to underline your thesis and then to explain to yourself how each paragraph in your essay is related to the thesis. If you find a paragraph that does not appear to be logically connected, you can revise it so that the relationship is clear. Similarly, it is useful to make sure that each sentence in a paragraph is related to the topic sentence. (See pp. 169–71 for a discussion of topic sentences.)

My Name

■ Sandra Cisneros

Sandra Cisneros was born in Chicago in 1954. After graduating from Loyola University in Chicago and attending the Iowa Writers' Workshop in the late 1970s, she moved to the Southwest and now lives in San Antonio, Texas. Cisneros has had numerous occupations within the fields of education and the arts and has been a visiting writer at various universities. Although she has written two well-received books of poetry, My Wicked, Wicked Ways *(1987) and* Loose Woman *(1994), she is better known for the autobiographical fiction of* The House on Mango Street *(1984)—from which the following selection is taken—and for* Woman Hollering Creek and Other Stories *(1991). In 1995, she was awarded a grant from the prestigious MacArthur Foundation. In 2002, she published a novel,* Caramelo. *She is currently working on a collection of fiction titled* Infinito.

As you read "My Name," pay attention to how tightly Cisneros unifies her paragraphs by intertwining the meanings of her name (originally Esperanza) and her feelings about the great-grandmother with whom she shares that name.

Reflecting on What You Know

Who chose your name, and why was it given to you? Does your name have a special meaning for the person who gave it to you? Are you happy with your name?

In English my name means hope. In Spanish it means too many letters. It means sadness, it means waiting. It is like the number nine. A muddy color. It is the Mexican records my father plays on Sunday mornings when he is shaving, songs like sobbing. 1

It was my great-grandmother's name and now it is mine. She was a horse woman too, born like me in the Chinese year of the horse—which is supposed to be bad luck if you're born female—but I think this is a Chinese lie because the Chinese, like the Mexicans, don't like their women strong. 2

My great-grandmother. I would've liked to have known her, a wild horse of a woman, so wild she wouldn't marry until my great-grandfather threw a sack over her head and carried her off. Just like that, as if she were a fancy chandelier. That's the way he did it. 3

And the story goes she never forgave him. She looked out the window all her life, the way so many women sit their sadness on an elbow. I wonder if she made the best with what she got or was she sorry because she couldn't be all the things she wanted to be. Esperanza. I have inherited her name, but I don't want to inherit her place by the window. 4

At school they say my name funny as if the syllables were made out of tin and hurt the roof of your mouth. But in Spanish my name is made out of a softer something like silver, not quite as thick as my sister's name Magdalena which is uglier than mine. Magdalena who at least can come home and become Nenny. But I am always Esperanza. 5

I would like to baptize[1] myself under a new name, a name more like the real me, the one nobody sees. Esperanza as Lisandra or Maritza or Zeze the X. Yes. Something like Zeze the X will do. 6

Thinking Critically about This Reading

What does Cisneros mean when she says of her great-grandmother, "I have inherited her name, but I don't want to inherit her place by the window" (paragraph 4)? What about her great-grandmother does she admire and respect?

Questions for Study and Discussion

1. What is Cisneros's thesis? (Glossary: *Thesis*)
2. Are there any digressions, discussions, or information in this essay that do not logically connect to Cisneros's thesis? (Glossary: *Thesis*) Explain how each paragraph in the essay relates to her thesis.
3. What is Cisneros's purpose? (Glossary: *Purpose*)
4. In what way do you think a name can be "like the number nine"? Like "a muddy color" (1)? What is your impression of the author's name, based on these similes? (Glossary: *Figure of Speech*)

---

[1]*baptize:* to give a first or Christian name to.

5. What is Cisneros's tone? (Glossary: *Tone*) How does she establish the tone? What does it tell the reader about how she feels about her name?
6. Why do you think Cisneros waits until the end of paragraph 4 to reveal her given name?
7. Why do you think Cisneros chose "Zeze the X" as a name that better represents her inner self?

Classroom Activity Using Unity

Take a paragraph from a draft of an essay you have been working on, and test it for unity. Be prepared to read the paragraph in class and explain why it is unified, or why it is not, and what you need to do to make it unified.

Suggested Writing Assignments

1. If you, like Cisneros, wished to choose a different name for yourself, what would it be? Write an essay that reveals your choice of a new name and explains why you like it or why it might be particularly appropriate for you. Make sure the essay is unified and that every paragraph directly supports your name choice.
2. Choose a grandparent or other relative at least two generations older than you about whom you know an interesting story. What impact has the relative, or the stories about him or her, had on your life? Write a unified narrative essay about the relative and what is interesting about him or her. (Glossary: *Narration*)

No Mercy

■ **Malcolm Gladwell**

Malcolm Gladwell was born in 1963 in England and grew up in Elmira, Ontario, Canada. He graduated from the University of Toronto in 1984 with a major in history. After a short stint as an advertising copywriter, he worked for the American Spectator *before becoming a reporter for the* Washington Post *in 1987. In 1996, he moved to the* New Yorker, *where his essays on the unexplained phenomena of everyday life soon attracted a large following. Gladwell is the author of two books. His first,* The Tipping Point: How Little Things Can Make a Big Difference *(2000), grew out of an early* New Yorker *article. In it, Gladwell explains how certain products, ideas, and trends catch on with the public and take on a life of their own. In the second,* Blink: The Power of Thinking without Thinking *(2005), he explores the world of snap decisions and the ways that our subconscious beliefs or feelings influence them. In 2005,* Time *magazine named Gladwell to its list of 100 most influential people.*

In the following essay, first published in the September 4, 2006, issue of the New Yorker, *Gladwell voices his concern about zero-tolerance programs and argues for a return to "discretionary justice" in America's schools when disciplining the young. Notice how he uses his examples to support this central idea and bring unity to his essay.*

Reflecting on What You Know

Many schools have adopted "zero-tolerance" programs to combat fighting, cheating, and drug and alcohol use. What do you think of such programs? Do they curb undesirable behaviors? Do you think there are better ways to address bad behavior?

In 1925, a young American physicist was doing graduate work at Cambridge University, in England. He was depressed. He was fighting with his mother and had just broken up with his girlfriend. His 1 strength was in theoretical physics, but he was being forced to sit in a laboratory making thin films of beryllium. In the fall of that year, he dosed an apple with noxious chemicals from the lab and put it on the desk of his tutor, Patrick Blackett. Blackett, luckily, didn't eat the apple. But school officials found out what happened and arrived at a punishment: the student was to be put on probation and ordered to go to London for regular sessions with a psychiatrist.

Probation? These days, we routinely suspend or expel high school students for doing infinitely less harmful things, like fighting or drinking or taking drugs—that is, for doing the kinds of things that teenagers do. This past summer, Rhett Bomar, the starting quarterback for the University of Oklahoma Sooners, was cut from the team when he was found to have been "overpaid" (receiving wages for more hours than he worked, with the apparent complicity of his boss) at his job at a car dealership. Even in Oklahoma, people seemed to think that kicking someone off a football team for having cut a few corners on his job made perfect sense. This is the age of zero tolerance. Rules are rules. Students have to be held accountable for their actions. Institutions must signal their expectations firmly and unambiguously: every school principal and every college president, these days, reads from exactly the same script. What, then, of a student who gives his teacher a poisoned apple? Surely he ought to be expelled from school and sent before a judge. 2

Suppose you cared about the student, though, and had some idea of his situation and his potential. Would you feel the same way? You might. Trying to poison your tutor is no small infraction. Then again, you might decide, as the dons at Cambridge clearly did, that what had happened called for a measure of leniency. They knew that the student had never done anything like this before, and that he wasn't well. And they knew that to file charges would almost certainly ruin his career. Cambridge wasn't sure that the benefits of enforcing the law, in this case, were greater than the benefits of allowing the offender an unimpeded future. 3

Schools, historically, have been home to this kind of discretionary justice. You let the principal or the teacher decide what to do about cheating because you know that every case of cheating is different—and, more to the point, that every cheater is different. Jimmy is incorrigible, and needs the shock of expulsion. But Bobby just needs a talking to, because he's a decent kid, and Mary and Jane cheated because the teacher foolishly stepped out of the classroom in the middle of the test, and the temptation was simply too much. A 4

Tennessee study found that after zero-tolerance programs were adopted by the state's public schools the frequency of targeted offenses soared: the firm and unambiguous punishments weren't deterring bad behavior at all. Is that really a surprise? If you're a teenager, the announcement that an act will be sternly punished doesn't always sink in, and it isn't always obvious when you're doing the thing you aren't supposed to be doing. Why? Because you're a teenager.

Somewhere along the way—perhaps in response to Columbine— 5
we forgot the value of discretion in disciplining the young. "Ultimately, they have to make right decisions," the Oklahoma football coach, Bob Stoops, said of his players, after jettisoning his quarterback. "When they do not, the consequences are serious." Open and shut: he sounded as if he were talking about a senior executive of Enron, rather than a college sophomore whose primary obligation at Oklahoma was to throw a football in the direction of young men in helmets. You might think that if the University of Oklahoma was so touchy about its quarterback being "overpaid" it ought to have kept closer track of his work habits with an on-campus job. But making a fetish of personal accountability conveniently removes the need for institutional accountability. (We court-martial the grunts who abuse prisoners, not the commanding officers who let the abuse happen.) To acknowledge that the causes of our actions are complex and muddy seems permissive, and permissiveness is the hallmark of an ideology now firmly in disgrace. That conservative patron saint Whittaker Chambers once defined liberalism as Christ without the Crucifixion. But punishment without the possibility of redemption is worse: it is the Crucifixion without Christ.

As for the student whose career Cambridge saved? He left at the 6
end of the academic year and went to study at the University of Göttingen, where he made important contributions to quantum theory. Later, after a brilliant academic career, he was entrusted with leading one of the most critical and morally charged projects in the history of science. His name was Robert Oppenheimer.[1]

Thinking Critically about This Reading

In your opinion, what place does "discretion" have when it comes to disciplining people in high school or college? According to Gladwell,

[1]*Robert Oppenheimer* (1904–1967): American theoretical physicist, director of the Manhattan Project during World War II, and "the father of the atomic bomb."

how well should teachers know their students to be able to determine when discretion is appropriate? Do you think your teachers know you?

Questions for Study and Discussion

1. Gladwell begins and ends his essay with the example of theoretical physicist Robert Oppenheimer. In what ways does this example illustrate Gladwell's main point? What, if anything, does Oppenheimer's fame or importance contribute to the power of this example? Explain.
2. Gladwell's essay is a plea for a return of what he calls "discretionary justice" in our nation's schools. For you, what is his strongest argument for the use of discretion in doling out punishment?
3. On at least three occasions, Gladwell dismisses immature or inappropriate behavior by arguing that teenagers will be teenagers and should be treated leniently, at least for first-time infractions. What do you think of this argument: teenagers should be less accountable than adults are for their behavior? Explain.
4. Identify the transitional expressions and repeated key words and ideas that Gladwell uses to maintain continuity from one paragraph to the next in his essay. (Glossary: *Transition*) Explain how each works to ensure unity in the context of this essay.
5. Do you agree with Gladwell when he says that "making a fetish of personal accountability conveniently removes the need for institutional accountability" (paragraph 5)? Explain why or why not.
6. What does Gladwell mean when he responds to a comment by Whittaker Chambers by saying that "punishment without the possibility of redemption is worse: it is the Crucifixion without Christ" (5)? Do you agree with his thinking? Why?

Classroom Activity Using Unity

Mark Wanner, a student, wrote the following paragraphs for an essay using this thesis statement:

> In order to provide a good learning environment in school, the teachers and administrators need to be strong leaders.

Unfortunately, some of the sentences disrupt the unity of the essay. Find these sentences, eliminate them, and reread the essay.

Strong School Leaders

School administrators and teachers must do more than simply supply students with information and a school building. They must also provide students with an atmosphere that allows them to focus on learning within the walls of the school. Whether the walls are brick, steel, or cement, they are only walls, and they do not help to create an appropriate atmosphere. Strong leadership both inside and outside the classroom yields a school in which students are able to excel in their studies because they know how to conduct themselves in their relationships with their teachers and fellow students. 1

A recent change in the administration of Eastside High School demonstrated how important strong leadership is to learning. Under the previous administration, parents and students complained that not enough emphasis was placed on studies. Most of the students lived in an impoverished neighborhood that had only one park for several thousand residents. Students were allowed to leave school at any time of the day, and little was done to curb the growing substance abuse problem. "What's the point of trying to teach algebra to students who are just going to get jobs as part-time sales clerks, anyway?" Vice Principal Iggy Norant said when questioned about his school's poor academic standards. Mr. Norant was known to students as Twiggy Iggy because of his tall, thin frame. Standardized test scores at the school lagged well behind the state average, and only 16% of the graduates attended college within two years. 2

Five years ago, the school board hired Mary Peña, former chair of the state educational standards committee, as principal. A cheerleader in college, Ms. Peña got her B.A. in recreation science before getting her masters in education. She immediately emphasized the importance of learning, replacing any faculty members who did not share her high expectations of the students. Among those she fired was Mr. Norant; she also replaced two social studies teachers, one math teacher, four English teachers, and a lab instructor who let students play Gameboy in lab. She also established a code of conduct, which clearly stated the rules all students had to follow. Students were allowed second chances, but those who continued to conduct themselves in a way that interfered with the other students' ability to learn were dealt 3 with quickly and severely. "The attitude at Eastside has changed so much since Mary Peña arrived," said math teacher Jeremy Rifkin after Peña's second year. "Students come to class much more relaxed and ready to learn. I feel like I can teach again." Test scores at Eastside are now well above state averages, and 68% of the most recent graduating class went straight to college.

–Mark Wanner, student

Suggested Writing Assignments

1. In paragraph 2, Gladwell states, "This is the age of zero tolerance. Rules are rules. Students have to be held accountable for their actions. Institutions must signal their expectations firmly and unambiguously." Write an essay in which you argue your position on the issue of zero tolerance. What experience, if any, have you had with zero-tolerance programs? Are such programs appropriate for all types of misbehavior, or should zero tolerance be reserved for only the most serious wrongdoing?
2. Identify several current problems at your college or university involving violations of campus rules for cheating on exams, plagiarizing papers, using drugs and alcohol, or vandalizing school or community property. How does your school currently punish violators? Do the punishments seem to be working, or do you think they are either too harsh or too lenient? Select one problem, and write a proposal in which you either support your school's current policy or argue for an alternative approach. Before you start to write, read or review June Tangney's "Condemn the Crime, Not the Person" (566–69) and Dan M. Kahan's "Shame Is Worth a Try" (571–73).
3. What statement does the following cartoon make about punishment? How do you think Gladwell would respond to the cartoon? Why? Using Gladwell's essay, the cartoon, and your own experience, write an argumentative essay in which you take a position on how people—especially school-age children—should be held accountable for bad behavior.

"What do I think is an appropriate punishment? I think an appropriate punishment would be to make me live with my guilt."

The Meanings of a Word

■ Gloria Naylor

American novelist, essayist, and screenwriter Gloria Naylor was born in 1950 in New York City, where she lives today. She worked first as a missionary for the Jehovah's Witnesses in 1967–1975 and then as a telephone operator until 1981. That year she graduated from Brooklyn College of the City University of New York. She also holds a graduate degree in African American studies from Yale University. Naylor has taught writing and literature at George Washington University, New York University, and Cornell University, in addition to publishing several novels: The Women of Brewster Place *(1982),* Linden Hills *(1985),* Mama Day *(1988),* Bailey's Cafe *(1992), and* The Men of Brewster Place *(1998). Naylor's most recent novel is* 1996 *(2005), a book that has been described as a "fictionalized memoir."*

The following essay first appeared in the New York Times *in 1986. In it Naylor examines the ways in which words can take on meaning, depending on who uses them and for what purpose. Notice how the paragraphs describing her experiences with the word* nigger *relate back to a clearly stated thesis at the end of paragraph 2.*

Reflecting on What You Know

Have you ever been called a derogatory name? What was the name, and how did you feel about it?

Language is the subject. It is the written form with which I've managed to keep the wolf away from the door and, in diaries, to keep my sanity. In spite of this, I consider the written word inferior to the spoken, and much of the frustration experienced by novelists is the awareness that whatever we manage to capture in even the most transcendent[1] passages falls far short of the richness of life. Dialogue achieves its power in the dynamics of a fleeting moment of sight, sound, smell, and touch. 1

[1]*transcendent:* preeminent; above all others.

I'm not going to enter the debate here about whether it is language that shapes reality or vice versa. That battle is doomed to be waged whenever we seek intermittent reprieve from the chicken and egg dispute. I will simply take the position that the spoken word, like the written word, amounts to a nonsensical arrangement of sounds or letters without a consensus that assigns "meaning." And building from the meanings of what we hear, we order reality. Words themselves are innocuous;[2] it is the consensus that gives them true power. 2

I remember the first time I heard the word *nigger*. In my third-grade class, our math tests were being passed down the rows, and as I handed the papers to a little boy in back of me, I remarked that once again he had received a much lower mark than I did. He snatched his test from me and spit out that word. Had he called me a nymphomaniac or a necrophiliac, I couldn't have been more puzzled. I didn't know what a nigger was, but I knew that whatever it meant, it was something he shouldn't have called me. This was verified when I raised my hand, and in a loud voice repeated what he had said and watched the teacher scold him for using a "bad" word. I was later to go home and ask the inevitable question that every black parent must face—"Mommy, what does *nigger* mean?" 3

And what exactly did it mean? Thinking back, I realize that this could not have been the first time the word was used in my presence. I was part of a large extended family that had migrated from the rural South after World War II and formed a close-knit network that gravitated around my maternal grandparents. Their ground-floor apartment in one of the buildings they owned in Harlem[3] was a weekend mecca for my immediate family, along with countless aunts, uncles, and cousins who brought along assorted friends. It was a bustling and open house with assorted neighbors and tenants popping in and out to exchange bits of gossip, pick up an old quarrel, or referee the ongoing checkers game in which my grandmother cheated shamelessly. They were all there to let down their hair and put up their feet after a week of labor in the factories, laundries, and shipyards of New York. 4

Amid the clamor, which could reach deafening proportions—two or three conversations going on simultaneously, punctuated by the sound of a baby's crying somewhere in the back rooms or out on the street—there was still a rigid set of rules about what was said and how. Older children were sent out of the living room when it was time 5

---

[2]*innocuous:* harmless; lacking significance or impact.

[3]*Harlem:* a predominantly African American neighborhood located in New York City.

to get into the juicy details about "you-know-who" up on the third floor who had gone and gotten herself "p-r-e-g-n-a-n-t!" But my parents, knowing that I could spell well beyond my years, always demanded that I follow the others out to play. Beyond sexual misconduct and death, everything else was considered harmless for our young ears. And so among the anecdotes[4] of the triumphs and disappointments in the various workings of their lives, the word *nigger* was used in my presence, but it was set within contexts and inflections[5] that caused it to register in my mind as something else.

In the singular, the word was always applied to a man who had distinguished himself in some situation that brought their approval for his strength, intelligence, or drive: 6

"Did Johnny *really* do that?" 7

"I'm telling you, that nigger pulled in $6,000 of overtime last year. Said he got enough for a down payment on a house." 8

When used with a possessive adjective by a woman—"my nigger"—it became a term of endearment for her husband or boyfriend. But it could be more than just a term applied to a man. In their mouths it became the pure essence of manhood—a disembodied force that channeled their past history of struggle and present survival against the odds into a victorious statement of being: "Yeah, that old foreman found out quick enough—you don't mess with a nigger." 9

In the plural, it became a description of some group within the community that had overstepped the bounds of decency as my family defined it. Parents who neglected their children, a drunken couple who fought in public, people who simply refused to look for work, those with excessively dirty mouths or unkempt households were all "trifling niggers." This particular circle could forgive hard times, unemployment, the occasional bout of depression—they had gone through all of that themselves—but the unforgivable sin was a lack of self-respect. 10

A woman could never be a "nigger" in the singular, with its connotation of confirming worth. The noun *girl* was its closest equivalent in that sense, but only when used in direct address and regardless of the gender doing the addressing. *Girl* was a token of respect for a woman. The one-syllable word was drawn out to sound like three in recognition of the extra ounce of wit, nerve, or daring that the woman had shown in the situation under discussion. 11

---

[4]*anecdotes:* short accounts or stories of life experiences.

[5]*inflections:* alterations in pitch or tone of voice.

"G-i-r-l, stop. You mean you said that to his face?" 12

But if the word was used in a third-person reference or shortened 13
so that it almost snapped out of the mouth, it always involved some element of communal disapproval. And age became an important factor in these exchanges. It was only between individuals of the same generation, or from any older person to a younger (but never the other way around), that *girl* would be considered a compliment.

I don't agree with the argument that use of the word *nigger* at this 14
social stratum of the black community was an internalization of racism. The dynamics were the exact opposite: the people in my grandmother's living room took a word that whites used to signify worthlessness or degradation and rendered it impotent.[6] Gathering there together, they transformed *nigger* to signify the varied and complex human beings they knew themselves to be. If the word was to disappear totally from the mouths of even the most liberal of white society, no one in that room was naive enough to believe it would disappear from white minds. Meeting the word head-on, they proved it had absolutely nothing to do with the way they were determined to live their lives.

So there must have been dozens of times that *nigger* was spoken 15
in front of me before I reached the third grade. But I didn't "hear" it until it was said by a small pair of lips that had already learned it could be a way to humiliate me. That was the word I went home and asked my mother about. And since she knew that I had to grow up in America, she took me in her lap and explained.

Thinking Critically about This Reading

What does Naylor mean when she states that "words themselves are innocuous; it is the consensus that gives them true power" (paragraph 2)? How does she use the two meanings of the word *nigger* to illustrate her point?

Questions for Study and Discussion

1. Naylor states her thesis in the last sentence of paragraph 2. (Glossary: *Thesis*) How does what she says in the first two paragraphs build unity by connecting to her thesis statement?

[6]*impotent:* weak; powerless.

2. What are the two meanings of the word *nigger* as Naylor uses it in her essay? Where is the clearest definition of each use of the word presented? (Glossary: *Definition*)
3. Naylor says she must have heard the word *nigger* many times while she was growing up; yet she "heard" it for the first time when she was in the third grade. How does she explain this seeming contradiction?
4. Naylor gives a detailed narration of her family and its lifestyle in paragraphs 4 and 5. (Glossary: *Narration*) What kinds of details does she include in her brief story? (Glossary: *Details*) How does this narration contribute to your understanding of the word *nigger* as used by her family? Why do you suppose she offers so little in the way of a definition of the other use of the word *nigger*? (Glossary: *Definition*) Explain.
5. Would you characterize Naylor's tone as angry, objective, cynical, or something else? (Glossary: *Tone*) Cite examples of her diction to support your answer. (Glossary: *Diction*)
6. What is the meaning of Naylor's last sentence? How well does it work as an ending for her essay? (Glossary: *Beginnings and Endings*)

Classroom Activity Using Unity

Carefully read the following five-paragraph sequence, paying special attention to how each paragraph relates to the writer's thesis. Identify the paragraph that disrupts the unity of the sequence, and explain why it doesn't belong.

How to Build a Fire in a Fireplace

Though "experts" differ as to the best technique to follow when building a fire, one generally accepted method consists of first laying a generous amount of crumpled newspaper on the hearth between the andirons. Kindling wood is then spread generously over this layer of newspaper and one of the thickest logs is placed across the back of the andirons. This should be as close to the back of the fireplace as possible, but not quite touching it. A second log is then placed an inch or so in front of this, and a few additional sticks of kindling are laid across these two. A third log 1 is then placed on top to form a sort of pyramid with air space between all logs so that flames can lick freely up between them.

Roaring fireplace fires are particularly welcome during the winter months, especially after hearty outdoor activities. To avoid any mid-winter tragedies, care should be taken to have a professional inspect and clean the chimney before starting to use the fireplace in the fall. Also, be sure to clean out the fireplace after each use. 2

A mistake frequently made is building the fire too far forward so that the rear wall of the fireplace does not get properly heated. A heated back wall helps increase the draft and tends to suck smoke and flames rearward with less chance of sparks or smoke spurting out into the room. 3

Another common mistake often made by the inexperienced fire-tender is to try to build a fire with only one or two logs, instead of using at least three. A single log is difficult to ignite properly, and even two logs do not provide an efficient bed with adequate fuel-burning capacity. 4

Use of too many logs, on the other hand, is also a common fault and can prove hazardous. Building too big a fire can create more smoke and draft than the chimney can safely handle, increasing the possibility of sparks or smoke being thrown out into the room. For best results, the homeowner should start with three medium-size logs as described above, then add additional logs as needed if the fire is to be kept burning. 5

The five paragraphs on "How to Build a Fire in a Fireplace" are taken from Bernard Gladstone's book *The New York Times Complete Manual of Home Repair*.

Suggested Writing Assignments

1. Naylor disagrees with the notion that use of the word *nigger* in the African American community can be taken as an "internalization of racism" (14). Reexamine her essay, and discuss in what ways her definition of the word *nigger* affirms or denies her position. (Glossary: *Definition*) Draw on your own experiences, observations, and reading to support your answer.
2. Write a short essay in which you define a word—for example, *wife, macho, liberal, success,* or *marriage*—that has more than one meaning, depending on one's point of view.

chapter **5**

Organization

In an essay, ideas and information cannot be presented all at once; they have to be arranged in some order. That order is the essay's **organization.**

The pattern of organization in an essay should be suited to the writer's subject and **purpose.** For example, if you are writing about your experience working in a fast-food restaurant and your purpose is to tell about the activities of a typical day, you might present those activities in chronological order. If, on the other hand, you wish to argue that working in a bank is an ideal summer job, you might proceed from the least rewarding to the most rewarding aspect of this job; this is called *climactic order.*

Some common patterns of organization are time order, space order, and logical order. Time order, or chronological order, is used to present a sequence of events as they occurred. A personal narrative, a report of a campus incident, or an account of a historical event can be most naturally and easily related in chronological order. In the following paragraph, the author uses chronological order to recount a disturbing childhood memory:

> I clearly remember my sixth birthday because Dad was in the hospital with pneumonia. He was working so hard he paid very little attention to his health. As a result, he spent almost the entire summer before I entered the first grade in the hospital. Mom visited him nightly. On my birthday I was allowed to see him. I have memories of sitting happily in the lobby of the hospital talking to the nurses, telling them with a big smile that I was going to see my dad because it was my birthday. I couldn't wait to see him because children under twelve were not allowed to visit patients, so I had not seen him in a long time. When I entered the hospital room, I saw tubes inserted into his nose and needles stuck in his arm. He was very, very thin. I was frightened and wanted to cry, but I was determined to

have a good visit. So I stayed for a while, and he wished me a happy birthday. When it was time to go, I kissed him good-bye and waited until I left his room to cry.

–Grace Ming-Yee Wai

Of course, the order of events can sometimes be rearranged for special effect. For example, an account of an auto accident may begin with the collision itself and then flash back in time to the events leading up to it. The description of a process—such as framing a poster, constructing a bookcase with cinder blocks and boards, or serving a tennis ball—almost always calls for a chronological organization.

When analyzing a causally related series of events, writers often use a chronological organization to clarify for readers the exact sequence of events. In the following example, the writer examines sequentially the series of malfunctions that led to the near disaster at the Three Mile Island nuclear facility in Harrisburg, Pennsylvania, showing clearly how each one led to the next:

On March 28, 1979, at 3:53 a.m., a pump at the Harrisburg plant failed. Because the pump failed, the reactor's heat was not drawn off in the heat exchanger and the very hot water in the primary loop overheated. The pressure in the loop increased, opening a release valve that was supposed to counteract such an event. But the valve stuck open and the primary loop system lost so much water (which ended up as a highly radioactive pool, six feet deep, on the floor of the reactor building) that it was unable to carry off all the heat generated within the reactor core. Under these circumstances, the intense heat held within the reactor could, in theory, melt its fuel rods, and the resulting "meltdown" could then carry a hugely radioactive mass through the floor of the reactor. The reactor's emergency cooling system, which is designed to prevent this disaster, was then automatically activated, but when it was, apparently, turned off too soon, some of the fuel rods overheated. This produced a bubble of hydrogen gas at the top of the reactor. (The hydrogen is dissolved in the water in order to react with oxygen that is produced when the intense reactor radiation splits water molecules into their atomic constituents. When heated, the dissolved hydrogen bubbles out of the solution.) This bubble blocked the flow of cooling water so that despite the action of the emergency cooling system the reactor core was again in danger of melting down. Another danger was that the gas might contain enough oxygen to cause an explosion that could rupture the huge containers that surround the reactor and release a

> deadly cloud of radioactive material into the surrounding country-side. Working desperately, technicians were able to gradually reduce the size of the gas bubble using a special apparatus brought in from the atomic laboratory at Oak Ridge, Tennessee, and the danger of a catastrophic release of radioactive materials subsided. But the sealed-off plant was now so radioactive that no one could enter it for many months—or, according to some observers, for years—without being exposed to a lethal dose of radiation.
>
> –Barry Commoner

Space order is used when describing a person, place, or thing. This organizational pattern begins at a particular point and moves in some direction, such as left to right, top to bottom, east to west, outside to inside, front to back, near to far, around, or over. In describing a house, for example, a writer could move from top to bottom, from outside to inside, or in a circle around the outside.

In the following paragraph, the subject is a baseball, and the writer describes it from the inside out, moving from its "composition-cork nucleus" to the print on its stitched cowhide cover:

> It weighs just over five ounces and measures between 2.86 and 2.94 inches in diameter. It is made of a composition-cork nucleus encased in two thin layers of rubber, one black and one red, surrounded by 121 yards of tightly wrapped blue-gray wool yarn, 45 yards of white wool yarn, 54 more yards of blue-gray wool yarn, 150 yards of fine cotton yarn, a coat of rubber cement, and a cowhide (formerly horsehide) exterior, which is held together with 216 slightly raised red cotton stitches. Printed certifications, endorsements, and outdoor advertising spherically attest to its authenticity.
>
> –Roger Angell

Logical order can take many forms, depending on the writer's purpose. Often used patterns include general to specific, most familiar to least familiar, and smallest to biggest. Perhaps the most common type of logical order is order of importance. Notice how the writer uses this order in the following paragraph:

> The Egyptians have taught us many things. They were excellent farmers. They knew all about irrigation. They built temples which were afterwards copied by the Greeks and which served as the earliest models for the churches in which we worship nowadays. They invented a calendar which proved such a useful instrument for the

> purpose of measuring time that it has survived with few changes until today. But most important of all, the Egyptians learned how to preserve speech for the benefit of future generations. They invented the art of writing.

By organizing the material according to the order of increasing importance, the writer places special emphasis on the final sentence.

A student essay on outdoor education provides another example of logical order. In the paragraph that follows, the writer describes some of the special problems students have during the traditionally difficult high school years. She then explains the benefits of involving such students in an outdoor education curriculum as a possible remedy, offers a quotation from a noteworthy text on outdoor education to support her views, and presents her thesis statement in the final sentence of the paragraph—all logical steps in her writing.

Statement of the problem

> For many students, the normally difficult time of high school is especially troublesome. These students may have learning disabilities, emotional-behavioral disorders, or low self-esteem, or they may be labeled "at-risk" because of socioeconomic background, delinquency, or drug and alcohol abuse. Any combination of these factors contributes negatively to students' success in school. Often the traditional public or private high school may not be the ideal environment in which these students can thrive and live up to their highest potential. Outdoor Education can benefit these high schoolers and provide them with the means necessary to overcome their personal issues and develop skills, knowledge, and self-esteem that will enable them to become successful, self-aware, emotionally stable, and functional adults. In their book *Outdoor Education,* authors Smith, Carlson, Donaldson, and Masters state poignantly that outdoor education "can be one of the most effective forces in the community to prevent human erosion as well as land erosion; it can be one of the means of saving youngsters from the education scrap heap" (49). Outdoor education builds a relationship between students and the natural environment that might not be formed otherwise and gives students a respect for the world in which they live.

A possible remedy is offered and explained.

Authorities are quoted to support the suggested solution.

The thesis is given after a preliminary discussion to increase its acceptability.

> Aspects of outdoor education should be implemented in the curriculums of high schools in order to achieve these results in all students.
>
> –Jinsie Ward, student

Although logical order can take many different forms, the exact rationale always depends on the topic of the writing. For example, in writing a descriptive essay about a place you visited, you can move from the least striking to the most striking detail to keep your readers interested and involved in the description. In an essay explaining how to pick individual stocks for investment, you can start with the point that readers will find least difficult to understand and move on to the most difficult. (That's how teachers organize many courses.) Or in writing an essay arguing for more internships and service learning courses, you can move from your least controversial point to the most controversial, preparing your reader gradually to accept your argument.

A simple way to check the organization of an essay is to outline it once you have a draft. Does the outline represent the organizational pattern—chronological, spatial, or logical—that you set out to use? Problems in outlining will naturally indicate sections that you need to revise.

A View from the Bridge

■ Cherokee Paul McDonald

A fiction writer, memoirist, and journalist, Cherokee Paul McDonald was raised and schooled in Fort Lauderdale, Florida. In 1970 he returned home from a tour of duty in Vietnam and joined the Fort Lauderdale Police Department, where he rose to the rank of sergeant. In 1980, after receiving a degree in criminal science from Broward Community College, McDonald left the police department to become a writer. He worked a number of odd jobs before publishing his first book, The Patch, *in 1986. In 1991, he published* Blue Truth, *a memoir. His novel,* Summer's Reason, *was released in 1994, and his most recent book, a memoir of the Vietnam War titled* Into the Green: A Reconnaissance by Fire, *was published in 2001. "A View from the Bridge" was originally published in* Sunshine *magazine in 1990.*

As you read, notice how McDonald organizes his narrative. He tells us what the narrator and the boy are doing, but he also relies heavily on their dialogue to structure his story, which unfolds as the two talk. McDonald makes the story come alive by showing us, rather than by simply telling us, what happens.

Reflecting on What You Know

Make a list of your interests, focusing on those to which you devote a significant amount of time. Do you share any of these interests with people you know? What does a shared interest do for a relationship between two people?

I was coming up on the little bridge in the Rio Vista neighborhood of Fort Lauderdale, deepening my stride and my breathing to negotiate the slight incline without altering my pace. And then, as I neared the crest, I saw the kid. 1

He was a lumpy little guy with baggy shorts, a faded T-shirt and heavy sweat socks falling down over old sneakers. 2

Partially covering his shaggy blond hair was one of those blue baseball caps with gold braid on the bill and a sailfish patch sewn 3 onto the peak. Covering his eyes and part of his face was a pair of those stupid-looking '50s-style wrap-around sunglasses.

He was fumbling with a beat-up rod and reel, and he had a little bait bucket by his feet. I puffed on by, glancing down into the empty bucket as I passed. 4

"Hey mister! Would you help me, please?" 5

The shrill voice penetrated my jogger's concentration, and I was determined to ignore it. But for some reason, I stopped. 6

With my hands on my hips and the sweat dripping from my nose I asked, "What do you want, kid?" 7

"Would you please help me find my shrimp? It's my last one and I've been getting bites and I know I can catch a fish if I can just find that shrimp. He jumped outta my hand as I was getting him from the bucket." 8

Exasperated, I walked slowly back to the kid, and pointed. 9

"There's the damn shrimp by your left foot. You stopped me for *that*?" 10

As I said it, the kid reached down and trapped the shrimp. 11

"Thanks a lot, mister," he said. 12

I watched as the kid dropped the baited hook down into the canal. Then I turned to start back down the bridge. 13

That's when the kid let out a "Hey! Hey!" and the prettiest tarpon[1] I'd ever seen came almost six feet out of the water, twisting and turning as he fell through the air. 14

"I got one!" the kid yelled as the fish hit the water with a loud splash and took off down the canal. 15

I watched the line being burned off the reel at an alarming rate. The kid's left hand held the crank while the extended fingers felt for the drag setting. 16

"No, kid!" I shouted. "Leave the drag alone . . . just keep that damn rod tip up!" 17

Then I glanced at the reel and saw there were just a few loops of line left on the spool. 18

"Why don't you get yourself some decent equipment?" I said, but before the kid could answer I saw the line go slack. 19

"Ohhh, I lost him," the kid said. I saw the flash of silver as the fish turned. 20

[1]*tarpon:* a large silvery fish.

"Crank, kid, crank! You didn't lose him. He's coming back toward you. Bring in the slack!" 21

The kid cranked like mad, and a beautiful grin spread across his face. 22

"He's heading in for the pilings,"[2] I said. "Keep him out of those pilings!" 23

The kid played it perfectly. When the fish made its play for the pilings, he kept just enough pressure on to force the fish out. When the water exploded and the silver missile hurled into the air, the kid kept the rod tip up and the line tight. 24

As the fish came to the surface and began a slow circle in the middle of the canal, I said, "Whooee, is that a nice fish or what?" 25

The kid didn't say anything, so I said, "Okay, move to the edge of the bridge and I'll climb down to the seawall and pull him out." 26

When I reached the seawall I pulled in the leader, leaving the fish lying on its side in the water. 27

"How's that?" I said. 28

"Hey, mister, tell me what it looks like." 29

"Look down here and check him out," I said. "He's beautiful." 30

But then I looked up into those stupid-looking sunglasses and it hit me. The kid was blind. 31

"Could you tell me what he looks like, mister?" he said again. 32

"Well, he's just under three, uh, he's about as long as one of your arms," I said. "I'd guess he goes about 15, 20 pounds. He's mostly silver, but the silver is somehow made up of *all* the colors, if you know what I mean." I stopped. "Do you know what I mean by colors?" 33

The kid nodded. 34

"Okay. He has all these big scales, like armor all over his body. They're silver too, and when he moves they sparkle. He has a strong body and a large powerful tail. He has big round eyes, bigger than a quarter, and a lower jaw that sticks out past the upper one and is very tough. His belly is almost white and his back is a gunmetal gray. When he jumped he came out of the water about six feet, and his scales caught the sun and flashed it all over the place." 35

By now the fish had righted itself, and I could see the bright-red gills as the gill plates opened and closed. I explained this to the kid, and then said, more to myself, "He's a beauty." 36

---

[2]*pilings:* support columns driven vertically into the ground or ocean floor.

"Can you get him off the hook?" the kid asked. "I don't want to 37
kill him."

I watched as the tarpon began to slowly swim away, tired but 38
still alive.

By the time I got back up to the top of the bridge the kid had his 39
line secured and his bait bucket in one hand.

He grinned and said, "Just in time. My mom drops me off here, 40
and she'll be back to pick me up any minute."

He used the back of one hand to wipe his nose. 41

"Thanks for helping me catch that tarpon," he said, "and for 42
helping me to see it."

I looked at him, shook my head, and said, "No, my friend, thank 43
you for letting *me* see that fish."

I took off, but before I got far the kid yelled again. 44

"Hey, mister!" 45

I stopped. 46

"Someday I'm gonna catch a sailfish and a blue marlin and a 47
giant tuna and *all* those big sportfish!"

As I looked into those sunglasses I knew he probably would. I 48
wished I could be there when it happened.

Thinking Critically about This Reading

Near the end of the story, why does the narrator say to the boy, "No, my friend, thank you for letting *me* see that fish" (paragraph 43)? What happens to the narrator's attitude as a result of his encounter with the boy? What lesson do you think the narrator learns?

Questions for Study and Discussion

1. How does McDonald organize his essay? What period of time would you estimate is covered in this essay?
2. What clues lead up to the revelation that the boy is blind? Why does it take McDonald so long to realize it?
3. Notice the way McDonald chooses and adjusts some of the words he uses to describe the fish to the boy in paragraphs 33–36. Why does he do this? How does he organize his description of the fish so that the boy can visualize it better?

4. By the end of the essay, we know much more about the boy than the fact that he is blind, but after the initial description, McDonald characterizes him only indirectly. As the essay unfolds, what do we learn about the boy, and how does the author convey this knowledge?
5. McDonald tells much of his experience through dialogue. (Glossary: *Dialogue*) What does this dialogue add to the narration? (Glossary: *Narration*) What would have been lost had McDonald not used dialogue?
6. What is the connotation of the word *view* in the title? (Glossary: *Connotation/Denotation*) Of the word *bridge?*

Classroom Activity Using Organization

Consider the ways in which you might organize a discussion of the seven states listed below. For each state, we have provided some basic information: the date it entered the Union, population (2000 census), land area, and number of electoral votes in a presidential election.

ALASKA
January 3, 1959
626,932 people
570,374 square miles
3 electoral votes

ARIZONA
February 14, 1912
5,130,632 people
113,642 square miles
10 electoral votes

FLORIDA
March 3, 1845
16,396,515 people
53,937 square miles
27 electoral votes

MAINE
March 15, 1820
1,274,923 people
30,865 square miles
4 electoral votes

MISSOURI
August 10, 1821
5,595,211 people
69,709 square miles
11 electoral votes

MONTANA
November 8, 1889
902,195 people
145,556 square miles
3 electoral votes

OREGON
February 14, 1859
3,472,867 people
98,386 square miles
7 electoral votes

Suggested Writing Assignments

1. In groups of two or three, take turns describing a specific beautiful or remarkable thing to the others as if they were blind. You may want to actually bring an object to observe while your classmates cover their eyes. Help each other find the best words to create a vivid verbal picture. Using McDonald's paragraphs 33–36 as a model, write a brief description of your object, retaining the informal style of your speaking voice.
2. Recall a time when you and one other person held a conversation that helped you see something more clearly—visually, in terms of understanding, or both. Using McDonald's narrative as an organizational model, tell the story of that moment, re-creating the dialogue exactly as you remember it.
3. McDonald's "A View from the Bridge" and the *Calvin and Hobbes* cartoon on page 125 are just two "fish stories" in the long and rich tradition of that genre. In their own ways, both the essay and the cartoon play on the ironic notion that fishing is a quiet sport but one in which participants come to expect the unexpected. (Glossary: *Irony*) For the narrator in McDonald's story, there is a lesson in not merely looking but truly seeing, in describing the fish so that the blind boy can "see" it. For Calvin, there is the story of "latchin' on to the big one." It is interesting that a sport in which "nothing happens" can be the source of so much storytelling. Write an essay in which you tell a "fish story" of your own, one that reveals a larger, significant truth or life lesson. Pay particular attention to the pattern of organization you choose, and be sure to revise your essay to tighten up your use of that pattern. If possible, incorporate some elements of surprise as well.

FISHING IS THE MOST BORING SPORT IN THE WORLD.
©1986 Universal Press Syndicate

WE'VE BEEN SITTING HERE FOR TWENTY MINUTES AND NOT ONE THING HAS HAPPENED!

WAAUGHH
WATTERSON
8-26

Two Ways to Belong in America

■ Bharati Mukherjee

The prominent Indian American writer and university professor Bharati Mukherjee was born into an aristocratic family in Calcutta (now Kolkata), India, in 1940. After her family relocated to England because of her father's work, she earned both her bachelor's and master's degrees from the University of Calcutta. In 1961, she pursued her long-held desire to become a writer by earning a master of fine arts degree at the University of Iowa and eventually a doctorate in English and comparative literature. After marrying the American Clark Blaise, she and her husband moved to Canada, where they lived for fourteen years until legislation against South Asians led them to move back to the United States. Mukherjee now teaches at the University of California, Berkeley, where her work centers on writing and the themes of immigration, particularly concerning women, immigration policy, and cultural alienation. Her published works include The Tiger's Daughter *(1971),* Wife *(1975),* Darkness *(1985),* Jasmine *(1989),* The Holder of the World *(1993), and* The Tree Bride *(2004).*

The following essay was first published in the New York Times *in 1996 in response to new legislation championed by the then-vice president, Al Gore, that gave expedited citizenship for legal immigrants living in the United States. As you read Mukherjee's essay, notice the way that she has organized her presentation of the different views that she and her sister have toward the various aspects of living as either a legal immigrant or a citizen.*

Reflecting on What You Know

Has a member of your family or a friend faced the decision of whether to become a citizen of the United States? What issues have they expressed concerning this decision? What do you think such a decision would be like?

This is a tale of two sisters from Calcutta, Mira and Bharati, who have lived in the United States for some thirty-five years, but who find themselves on different sides in the current debate over the status of immigrants. I am an American citizen and she is not. I am moved that thousands of long-term residents are finally taking the oath of citizenship. She is not. 1

Mira arrived in Detroit in 1960 to study child psychology and preschool education. I followed her a year later to study creative writing at the University of Iowa. When we left India, we were almost identical in appearance and attitude. We dressed alike, in saris; we expressed identical views on politics, social issues, love and marriage in the same Calcutta convent-school accent. We would endure our two years in America, secure our degrees, then return to India to marry the grooms of our father's choosing. 2

Instead, Mira married an Indian student in 1962 who was getting his business administration degree at Wayne State University. They soon acquired the labor certifications necessary for the green card of hassle-free residence and employment. 3

Mira still lives in Detroit, works in the Southfield, Michigan, school system, and has become nationally recognized for her contributions in the fields of preschool education and parent-teacher relationships. After thirty-six years as a legal immigrant in this country, she clings passionately to her Indian citizenship and hopes to go home to India when she retires. 4

In Iowa City in 1963, I married a fellow student, an American of Canadian parentage. Because of the accident of his North Dakota birth, I bypassed labor-certification requirements and the race-related "quota" system that favored the applicant's country of origin over his or her merit. I was prepared for (and even welcomed) the emotional strain that came with marrying outside my ethnic community. In thirty-three years of marriage, we have lived in every part of North America. By choosing a husband who was not my father's selection, I was opting for fluidity, self-invention, blue jeans and T-shirts, and renouncing three thousand years (at least) of caste-observant, "pure culture" marriage in the Mukherjee family. My books have often been read as unapologetic (and in some quarters overenthusiastic) texts for cultural and psychological "mongrelization." It's a word I celebrate. 5

Mira and I have stayed sisterly close by phone. In our regular Sunday morning conversations, we are unguardedly affectionate. I am her only blood relative on this continent. We expect to see each 6 other through the looming crises of aging and ill health without being asked. Long before Vice President Gore's "Citizenship USA" drive, we'd had our polite arguments over the ethics of retaining an overseas citizenship while expecting the permanent protection and economic benefits that come with living and working in America.

Like well-raised sisters, we never said what was really on our 7
minds, but we probably pitied one another. She, for the lack of structure in my life, the erasure of Indianness, the absence of an unvarying daily core. I, for the narrowness of her perspective, her uninvolvement with the mythic depths or the superficial pop culture of this society. But, now, with the scapegoating of "aliens" (documented or illegal) on the increase, and the targeting of long-term legal immigrants like Mira for new scrutiny and new self-consciousness, she and I find ourselves unable to maintain the same polite discretion. We were always unacknowledged adversaries, and we are now, more than ever, sisters.

"I feel used," Mira raged on the phone the other night. "I feel 8
manipulated and discarded. This is such an unfair way to treat a person who was invited to stay and work here because of her talent. My employer went to the INS and petitioned for the labor certification. For over thirty years, I've invested my creativity and professional skills into the improvement of *this* country's preschool system. I've obeyed all the rules, I've paid my taxes, I love my work, I love my students, I love the friends I've made. How dare America now change its rules in midstream? If America wants to make new rules curtailing benefits of legal immigrants, they should apply only to immigrants who arrive after those rules are already in place."

To my ears, it sounded like the description of a long-enduring, 9
comfortable yet loveless marriage, without risk or recklessness. Have we the right to demand, and to expect, that we be loved? (That, to me, is the subtext of the arguments by immigration advocates.) My sister is an expatriate, professionally generous and creative, socially courteous and gracious, and that's as far as her Americanization can go. She is here to maintain an identity, not to transform it.

I asked her if she would follow the example of others who have 10
decided to become citizens because of the anti-immigration bills in Congress. And here, she surprised me. "If America wants to play the manipulative game, I'll play it too," she snapped. "I'll become a U.S. citizen for now, then change back to Indian when I'm ready to go

home. I feel some kind of irrational attachment to India that I don't to America. Until all this hysteria against legal immigrants, I was totally happy. Having my green card meant I could visit any place in the world I wanted to and then come back to a job that's satisfying and that I do very well."

In one family, from two sisters alike as peas in a pod, there could not be a wider divergence of immigrant experience. America spoke to me—I married it—I embraced the demotion from expatriate aristocrat to immigrant nobody, surrendering those thousands of years of "pure culture," the saris, the delightfully accented English. She retained them all. Which of us is the freak? 11

Mira's voice, I realize, is the voice not just of the immigrant South Asian community but of an immigrant community of the millions who have stayed rooted in one job, one city, one house, one ancestral culture, one cuisine, for the entirety of their productive years. She speaks for greater numbers than I possibly can. Only the fluency of her English and the anger, rather than fear, born of confidence from her education, differentiate her from the seamstresses, the domestics, the technicians, the shop owners, the millions of hardworking but effectively silenced documented immigrants as well as their less fortunate "illegal" brothers and sisters. 12

Nearly twenty years ago, when I was living in my husband's ancestral homeland of Canada, I was always well-employed but never allowed to feel part of the local Quebec or larger Canadian society. Then, through a Green Paper that invited a national referendum on the unwanted side effects of "nontraditional" immigration, the Government officially turned against its immigrant communities, particularly those from South Asia. 13

I felt then the same sense of betrayal that Mira feels now. I will never forget the pain of that sudden turning, and the casual racist outbursts the Green Paper elicited. That sense of betrayal had its desired effect and drove me, and thousands like me, from the country. 14

Mira and I differ, however, in the ways in which we hope to interact with the country that we have chosen to live in. She is happier to live in America as an expatriate Indian than as an immigrant American. I need to feel like a part of the community I have adopted (as I tried to feel in Canada as well). I need to put roots down, to vote and make the difference that I can. The price that the immigrant willingly pays, and that the exile avoids, is the trauma of self-transformation. 15

Thinking Critically about This Reading

What does Mukherjee's sister mean when she says in paragraph 10, "If America wants to play the manipulative game, I'll play it, too"? What do you think of her decision and her possible plans if and when she eventually returns to India?

Questions for Study and Discussion

1. What is Mukherjee's thesis? (Glossary: *Thesis*)
2. Mukherjee has used comparison and contrast as her organizing principle. What type of comparison and contrast has she used? (Glossary: *Comparison and Contrast*)
3. Why is the pattern of organization that Mukherjee used appropriate for her subject and her purpose?
4. Why might Mukherjee have ordered her points of discussion in the way that she has? Explain.
5. What arguments does Mukherjee make for becoming an American citizen? What arguments does her sister make for retaining her Indian citizenship?
6. Why does Mukherjee's sister feel "used" by attempts to change American laws regarding social security benefits for noncitizens?
7. What does Mukherjee mean when she says in paragraph 15, "The price that the immigrant willingly pays, and that the exile avoids, is the trauma of self-transformation"?

Classroom Activity Using Organization

While cleaning out the center drawer of his desk, a student found the following items:

2 no. 2 pencils	2 pairs of scissors
3 rubber bands	1 book mailing bag
1 roll of adhesive tape	1 mechanical pencil
1 plastic comb	3 first-class postage stamps
25 3 × 5-inch cards	5 postcards
3 ballpoint pens	2 clasps
1 eraser	2 8 × 10-inch manila envelopes
6 paper clips	7 thumbtacks

1 nail clipper	1 bottle of correction fluid
1 highlighting marker	1 nail file
1 bottle of glue	1 toothbrush
3 business envelopes	1 felt-tip pen
6 postcard stamps	2 airmail stamps

To organize the student's drawer, into what categories would you divide these items? Explain which items you would place in each category, and suggest an order you might use to discuss the categories in an essay. (Glossary: *Division and Classification*)

Suggested Writing Assignments

1. Mukherjee presents her sister's reasons for not becoming a citizen and supports them with statements that her sister has made. Imagine that you are Mira Mukherjee. Write a counterargument to the one presented by your sister that gives your reasons for remaining an Indian citizen. Consider that you have already broken with tradition by marrying a man not of your father's choosing but also that the "trauma of self-transformation" that your sister raises in the conclusion of her essay is much deeper and more complicated than she has represented it. Can you say that you are holding to tradition when you are not? Can you engage in a challenging self-transformation if it is not genuinely motivated?
2. Mukherjee writes about the relationship that she had with her sister in paragraph 7 by saying that "we never said what was really on our minds, but we probably pitied one another." These types of differences are played out on a larger scale when immigrants who have transformed themselves into Americans are confronted by those who have chosen to retain their ethnic identity, and these tensions often lead to name-calling and aggressive prejudice. Similar situations also exist within the Latino, African American, and Southeast Asian American communities and perhaps among all immigrant groups. Write an essay comparing and contrasting the choices of lifestyle that members of an ethnic or cultural community you are familiar with make as they try to find a comfortable place in American society.

The Ways of Meeting Oppression

■ Martin Luther King Jr.

Martin Luther King Jr. (1929–1968) was the leading spokesman for the rights of African Americans during the 1950s and 1960s before his assassination in 1968. He established the Southern Christian Leadership Conference, organized many civil rights demonstrations, and opposed the Vietnam War and the draft. In 1964, he was awarded the Nobel Peace Prize.

In the following essay, taken from his book Strive toward Freedom *(1958), King classifies the three ways that oppressed people throughout history have reacted to their oppressors. As you read, pay particular attention to how King orders his discussions of the three types of oppression to support his argument and the conclusion he presents in paragraph 8.*

Reflecting on What You Know

Isaac Asimov once said, "Violence is the last resort of the incompetent." What are your thoughts on the reasons for violent behavior on either a personal or a national level? Is violence ever justified? If so, under what circumstances?

1 Oppressed people deal with their oppression in three characteristic ways. One way is acquiescence: the oppressed resign themselves to their doom. They tacitly adjust themselves to oppression, and thereby become conditioned to it. In every movement toward freedom some of the oppressed prefer to remain oppressed. Almost 2800 years ago Moses[1] set out to lead the children of Israel from the slavery of Egypt to the freedom of the promised land. He soon discovered that slaves do not always welcome their deliverers. They become accustomed to being slaves. They would rather bear those ills they have, as Shakespeare

[1]*Moses:* a Hebrew prophet, teacher, and leader of the fourteenth to thirteenth centuries B.C.E.

pointed out, than flee to others that they know not of. They prefer the "fleshpots of Egypt" to the ordeals of emancipation.

There is such a thing as the freedom of exhaustion. Some people 2 are so worn down by the yoke of oppression that they give up. A few years ago in the slum areas of Atlanta, a Negro guitarist used to sing almost daily: "Been down so long that down don't bother me."[2] This is the type of negative freedom and resignation that often engulfs the life of the oppressed.

But this is not the way out. To accept passively an unjust system 3 is to cooperate with that system; thereby the oppressed become as evil as the oppressor. Noncooperation with evil is as much a moral obligation as is cooperation with good. The oppressed must never allow the conscience of the oppressor to slumber. Religion reminds every man that he is his brother's keeper. To accept injustice or segregation passively is to say to the oppressor that his actions are morally right. It is a way of allowing his conscience to fall asleep. At this moment the oppressed fails to be his brother's keeper. So acquiescence—while often the easier way—is not the moral way. It is the way of the coward. The Negro cannot win the respect of his oppressor by acquiescing; he merely increases the oppressor's arrogance and contempt. Acquiescence is interpreted as proof of the Negro's inferiority. The Negro cannot win the respect of the white people of the South or the peoples of the world if he is willing to sell the future of his children for his personal and immediate comfort and safety.

A second way that oppressed people sometimes deal with oppres- 4 sion is to resort to physical violence and corroding hatred. Violence often brings about momentary results. Nations have frequently won their independence in battle. But in spite of temporary victories, violence never brings permanent peace. It solves no social problem; it merely creates new and more complicated ones.

Violence as a way of achieving racial justice is both impractical 5 and immoral. It is impractical because it is a descending spiral ending in destruction for all. The old law of an eye for an eye leaves everybody blind. It is immoral because it seeks to humiliate the opponent rather than win his understanding; it seeks to annihilate rather than to convert. Violence is immoral because it thrives on hatred rather than love. It destroys community and makes brotherhood impossible.

---

[2]*"Been down . . . bother me"*: lyric possibly adapted from "Stormy Blues" by the American jazz singer Billie Holiday (1915–1959).

It leaves society in monologue rather than dialogue. Violence ends by defeating itself. It creates bitterness in the survivors and brutality in the destroyers. A voice echoes through time saying to every potential Peter, "Put up your sword."[3] History is cluttered with the wreckage of nations that failed to follow this command.

If the American Negro and other victims of oppression succumb 6
to the temptation of using violence in the struggle for freedom, future generations will be the recipients of a desolate night of bitterness, and our chief legacy to them will be an endless reign of meaningless chaos. Violence is not the way.

The third way open to oppressed people in their quest for freedom 7
is the way of nonviolent resistance. Like the synthesis in Hegelian[4] philosophy, the principle of nonviolent resistance seeks to reconcile the truths of two opposites—acquiescence and violence—while avoiding the extremes and immoralities of both. The nonviolent resister agrees with the person who acquiesces that one should not be physically aggressive toward his opponent; but he balances the equation by agreeing with the person of violence that evil must be resisted. He avoids the nonresistance of the former and the violent resistance of the latter. With nonviolent resistance, no individual or group need submit to any wrong, nor need anyone resort to violence in order to right a wrong.

It seems to me that this is the method that must guide the actions 8
of the Negro in the present crisis in race relations. Through nonviolent resistance the Negro will be able to rise to the noble height of opposing the unjust system while loving the perpetrators of the system. The Negro must work passionately and unrelentingly for full stature as a citizen, but he must not use inferior methods to gain it. He must never come to terms with falsehood, malice, hate, or destruction.

Nonviolent resistance makes it possible for the Negro to remain 9
in the South and struggle for his rights. The Negro's problem will not be solved by running away. He cannot listen to the glib suggestion of those who would urge him to migrate en masse to other sections of the country. By grasping his great opportunity in the South he can make a lasting contribution to the moral strength of the nation and set a sublime example of courage for generations yet unborn.

---

[3]*"Put up your sword":* the apostle Peter had drawn his sword to defend Christ from arrest; the voice was Christ's, who surrendered himself for trial and crucifixion (John 18:11).

[4]*Georg Wilhelm Friedrich Hegel* (1770–1831): German philosopher.

By nonviolent resistance, the Negro can also enlist all men of good 10
will in his struggle for equality. The problem is not a purely racial one, with Negroes set against whites. In the end, it is not a struggle between people at all, but a tension between justice and injustice. Nonviolent resistance is not aimed against oppressors but against oppression. Under its banner consciences, not racial groups, are enlisted.

Thinking Critically about This Reading

King states that "there is such a thing as the freedom of exhaustion" (paragraph 2). Why, according to King, is this type of freedom "negative"?

Questions for Study and Discussion

1. What is King's thesis? (Glossary: *Thesis*)
2. How does classifying the three types of resistance to oppression help him to develop his thesis?
3. Why do you suppose King discusses acquiescence, violence, and nonviolent resistance in that order? What organizational principle does he use to rank them?
4. How does King's organizational pattern help him build his argument and support his thesis? Would his argument work as well if he changed the order of his discussion? Why or why not?
5. King states that he favors nonviolent resistance over the other two ways of meeting oppression. What disadvantages does he see in meeting oppression with acquiescence or with violence?

Classroom Activity Using Organization

The best ways to conserve energy in a home might be organized according to space, time, and logic, as follows:

1. From the basement to the attic
2. From the least expensive to the most expensive
3. From the inside of the home to the outside
4. From the simplest to the most difficult
5. From the quickest to the longest

6. From the longest payback to the quickest payback
7. From the easiest to the most difficult
8. From the most general to the most specific
9. From the first to the last
10. From what you can do to what you need help with

How might you organize an essay on one of the following topics using space, time, and logical patterns?

1. What to do when a tornado threatens
2. What we can do about the homeless
3. What we mean by freedom of speech
4. A description of a painting
5. How a digital camera works
6. Why we need a flat income tax
7. What happened at your friend's birthday party
8. Why we can't let languages become extinct
9. The case for the legalization of drugs

Suggested Writing Assignments

1. Using King's essay as a model, write an essay on various solutions to a current social or personal problem. Organize your ideas according to some rational scheme, such as increasing effectiveness, easiest to most difficult to bring about, increasing importance, least dramatic to most dramatic, least enduring to most enduring, and so forth. Be sure that you have a clear thesis statement and that the organizational pattern you use helps to convince your reader of your beliefs.
2. King's pattern of organization in "The Ways of Meeting Oppression" is simple, logical, and natural. He knows that the oppressed can't give in to their oppressors, can't answer violence with violence, and therefore must take a third path of nonviolent resistance to rise above their enemies. Using his essay as a model, write an essay in which you discuss how to respond to prejudice, hatred, competition, greed, aggression, or some other social force that you find difficult to overcome.

chapter **6**

Beginnings and Endings

"Begin at the beginning and go on till you come to the end: then stop," advised the King of Hearts in *Alice in Wonderland.* "Good advice, but more easily said than done," you might be tempted to reply. Certainly, no part of writing essays can be more daunting than coming up with effective **beginnings and endings.** In fact, many writers feel these are the most important parts of any piece of writing regardless of its length. Even before coming to your introduction, your readers will usually know something about your intentions from your title. Titles such as "The Case against Euthanasia," "How to Buy a Used Car," and "What Is a Migraine Headache?" indicate both your subject and approach and prepare your readers for what follows.

BEGINNINGS

What makes for an effective beginning? Not unlike a personal greeting, a good beginning should catch a reader's interest and then hold it. The experienced writer realizes that many readers would rather do almost anything than make a commitment to read, so the opening or *lead,* as journalists refer to it, requires a lot of thought and much revising to make it right and to keep the reader's attention from straying. The inexperienced writer, on the other hand, knows that the beginning is important but tries to write it first and to perfect it before moving on to the rest of the essay. Although there are no "rules" for writing introductions, we can offer one bit of general advice: wait until the writing process is well under way or almost completed before focusing on your lead. Following this advice will keep you from spending too much time on an introduction that you will undoubtedly revise. More important, once you actually see how your essay develops, you will know better how to introduce it to your reader.

In addition to capturing your reader's attention, a good beginning usually introduces your thesis and either suggests or actually reveals the structure of the composition. Keep in mind that the best beginning is not necessarily the most catchy or the most shocking but the one most appropriate for the job you are trying to do.

There are many effective ways of beginning an essay. Consider using one of the following.

Anecdote

Introducing your essay with an anecdote—a brief narrative drawn from current news events, history, or your personal experience—can be an effective way to capture your reader's interest. In the following example, the writer introduces an essay on becoming a man by recounting an encounter he witnessed between two boys.

> Two nine-year-old boys, neighbors and friends, were walking home from school. The one in the bright blue windbreaker was laughing and swinging a heavy-looking book bag toward the head of his friend, who kept ducking and stepping back. "What's the matter?" asked the kid with the bag, whooshing it over his head. "You chicken?"
>
> His friend stopped, stood still, and braced himself. The bag slammed into the side of his face, the thump audible all the way across the street where I stood watching. The impact knocked him to the ground, where he lay mildly stunned for a second. Then he struggled up, rubbing the side of his head. "See?" he said proudly. "I'm no chicken."
>
> No. A chicken would probably have had the sense to get out of the way. This boy was already well on the road to becoming a *man*, having learned one of the central ethics of his gender: experience pain rather than show fear.
>
> –Jon Katz

Analogy and Comparison

An analogy or comparison can be useful in getting readers to contemplate a topic they might otherwise reject as unfamiliar or uninteresting. In the following multiparagraph example, Roger Garrison introduces a subject few would consider engrossing—writing—with an analogy to stone wall building. By pairing these two seemingly unrelated concepts, he both introduces and vividly illustrates the idea he will develop in his essay: that writing is a difficult, demanding craft with specific skills to be learned.

> In northern New England, where I live, stone walls mark boundaries, border meadows, and march through the woods that grew up around them long ago. Flank-high, the walls are made of granite rocks stripped from fields when pastures were cleared and are used to fence in cattle. These are dry walls, made without mortar, and the stones in them, all shapes and sizes, are fitted to one another with such care that a wall, built a hundred years ago, still runs as straight and solid as it did when people cleared the land.
>
> Writing is much like wall building. The writer fits together separate chunks of meaning to make an understandable statement. Like the old Yankee wall builders, anyone who wants to write well must learn some basic skills, one at a time, to build soundly. This [essay] describes these skills and shows you how to develop them and put them together. You can learn them.
>
> Building a stone wall is not easy: It is gut-wrenching labor. Writing is not easy either. It is a complex skill, mainly because it demands a commitment of our own complicated selves. But it is worth learning how to do well—something true of any skill. Solid walls do get built, and good writing does get done. We will clear away some underbrush and get at the job.
>
> –Roger Garrison

Dialogue/Quotation

Although relying heavily on the ideas of others can weaken an effective introduction, opening your essay with a quotation or a brief dialogue can attract a reader's attention and can succinctly illustrate a particular attitude or point that you want to discuss. In the following example, the writer introduces an essay about the three main types of stress in our lives by recounting a brief dialogue with one of her roommates.

> My roommate, Megan, pushes open the front door, throws her keys on the counter, and flops down on the couch.
>
> "Hey, Megan, how are you?" I yell from the kitchen.
>
> "I don't know what's wrong with me. I sleep all the time, but I'm still tired. No matter what I do, I just don't feel well."
>
> "What did the doctor say?"
>
> "She said it sounds like chronic fatigue syndrome."
>
> "Do you think it might be caused by stress?" I ask.
>
> "Nah, stress doesn't affect me very much. I like keeping busy and running around. This must be something else."

Like most Americans, Megan doesn't recognize the numerous factors in her life that cause her stress.

–Sarah Federman

Facts and Statistics

For the most part, you should use facts and statistics to support your argument rather than let them speak for you, but presenting brief and startling facts or statistics can be an effective way to engage readers in your essay.

One out of every five new recruits in the United States military is female.

The Marines gave the Combat Action Ribbon for service in the Persian Gulf to twenty-three women.

Two female soldiers were killed in the bombing of the USS *Cole*.

The Selective Service registers for the draft all male citizens between the ages of eighteen and twenty-five.

What's wrong with this picture?

–Anna Quindlen

Irony or Humor

It is often effective to introduce an essay with irony or humor. Humor signals to the reader that your essay will be entertaining to read, and irony can indicate an unexpected approach to a topic. In his essay "Shooting an Elephant," George Orwell begins by simultaneously establishing a wry tone and indicating to the reader that he, the narrator, occupies the position of outsider in the events he is about to relate.

In Moulmein, in lower Burma, I was hated by large numbers of people—the only time in my life that I have been important enough for this to happen to me.

–George Orwell

In his essay "I Led the Pigeons to the Flag," language commentator William Safire uses humorous examples to introduce his discussion of what happens when we creatively reproduce what we think we hear.

The most saluted man in America is Richard Stans. Legions of schoolchildren place their hands over their hearts to pledge allegiance to the flag, "and to the republic for Richard Stans."

With all due patriotic fervor, the same kids salute "one nation, under guard." Some begin with "I pledge a legion to the flag," others with "I led the pigeons to the flag."

This is not a new phenomenon. When they come to "one nation, indivisible," this generation is likely to say, "One naked individual," as a previous generation was to murmur, "One nation in a dirigible," or "One nation and a vegetable."

–William Safire

There are several other good ways to begin an essay; the following opening paragraphs illustrate each approach.

Short Generalization

Washington is a wonderful city. The scale seems right, more humane than other places. I like all the white marble and green trees, the ideals celebrated by the great monuments and memorials. I like the climate, the slow shift of the seasons here. Spring, so southern in feeling, comes early, and the long, sweet autumns can last into December. Summers are murder, equatorial—no question; the compensation is that Congress adjourns, the city empties out, eases off. Winter evenings in Georgetown with the snow falling and the lights just coming on are as beautiful as any I've known.

–David McCullough

Startling Claim

I've finally figured out the difference between neat and sloppy people. The distinction is, as always, moral. Neat people are lazier and meaner than sloppy people.

–Suzanne Britt

Strong Proposition

Everyone agrees that we've got to improve academic achievement in America's public schools. So why is it that districts distract students from core academics with a barrage of activities—everything from field hockey to music, drama, debating, and chess teams? And there's more: Drug education and fundraising eat away at classroom time. All manner of holidays, including Valentine's Day, get celebrated during the school day, as well as children's birthdays. These diversions are costly. They consume money and time.

Here's a bold proposition: privatize school sports and other extracurricular activities, and remove all but basic academic studies from the classroom. Sound like sacrilege? Look at what these extras really cost.

–Etta Kralovec

Rhetorical Questions

> Is a girl called Gloria apt to be better-looking than one called Bertha? Are criminals more likely to be dark than blond? Can you tell a good deal about someone's personality from hearing his voice briefly over the phone? Can a person's nationality be pretty accurately guessed from his photograph? Does the fact that someone wears glasses imply that he is intelligent?
>
> The answer to all these questions is obviously, "No."
>
> Yet, from all the evidence at hand, most of us believe these things. Ask any college boy if he'd rather take his chances with a Gloria or a Bertha, or ask a college girl if she'd rather blind-date a Richard or a Cuthbert. . . .
>
> –Robert L. Heilbroner

Following are some examples of how *not* to begin an essay. You should always *avoid* using beginnings such as these in your writing.

Beginnings to Avoid

Apology
I am a college student and do not consider myself an expert on intellectual property, but I think file sharing and MP3 downloads should be legal.

Complaint
I'd rather write about a topic of my own choice than the one that is assigned, but here goes.

Webster's Dictionary
Webster's New Collegiate Dictionary defines the verb *to snore* as follows: "to breathe during sleep with a rough hoarse noise due to vibration of the soft palate."

Platitude
America is the land of opportunity, and no one knows that better than Martha Stewart.

Reference to Title
As you can see from my title, this essay is about why we should continue to experiment with embryonic stem cells.

ENDINGS

An effective ending does more than simply indicate where the writer stopped writing. A conclusion may summarize; may inspire the reader to further thought or even action; may return to the beginning by repeating key words, phrases, or ideas; or may surprise the reader by providing a particularly convincing example to support a thesis. Indeed, there are many ways to write a conclusion, but the effectiveness of any choice must be measured by how appropriately it fits what comes before it. You might consider concluding with a restatement of your thesis, with a prediction, or with a recommendation.

In an essay contrasting the traditional Hispanic understanding of the word *macho* with the meaning it has developed in mainstream American culture, Rose Del Castillo Guilbault begins her essay with a succinct, two-sentence paragraph offering her thesis:

> What is macho? That depends which side of the border you come from.

She concludes her essay by restating her thesis, but in a manner that reflects the detailed examination she has given the concept of macho in her essay:

> The impact of language in our society is undeniable. And the misuse of macho hints at a deeper cultural misunderstanding that extends beyond mere word definitions.
>
> –Rose Del Castillo Guilbault

In the following conclusion to a long chapter on weasel words, a form of deceptive advertising language, the writer summarizes the points that he has made, ending with a recommendation to the reader:

> A weasel word is a word that's used to imply a meaning that cannot be truthfully stated. Some weasels imply meanings that are not the same as their actual definition, such as "help," "like," or "fortified." They can act as qualifiers and/or comparatives. Other weasels, such as "taste" and "flavor," have no definite meanings, and are simply subjective opinions offered by the manufacturer. A weasel of omission is one that implies a claim so strongly that it forces you to supply the bogus fact. Adjectives are weasels used to convey feelings and emotions to a greater extent than the product itself can.
>
> In dealing with weasels, you must strip away the innuendos and try to ascertain the facts, if any. To do this, you need to ask

> questions such as: How? Why? How many? How much? Stick to basic definitions of words. Look them up if you have to. Then, apply the strict definition to the text of the advertisement or commercial. "Like" means similar to, but not the same as. "Virtually" means the same in essence, but not in fact.
>
> Above all, never underestimate the devious qualities of a weasel. Weasels twist and turn and hide in dark shadows. You must come to grips with them, or advertising will rule you forever.
>
> My advice to you is: Beware of weasels. They are nasty and untrainable, and they attack pocketbooks.
>
> –Paul Stevens

In the following conclusion to a composition titled "Title IX Just Makes Sense," the writer offers an overview of her argument and concludes by predicting the outcome of the solution she advocates:

> There have undeniably been major improvements in the treatment of female college athletes since the enactment of Title IX. But most colleges and universities still don't measure up to the actual regulation standards, and many have quite a ways to go. The Title IX fight for equality is not a radical feminist movement, nor is it intended to take away the privileges of male athletes. It is, rather, a demand for fairness, for women to receive the same opportunities that men have always had. When colleges and universities stop viewing Title IX budget requirements as an inconvenience and start complying with the spirit and not merely the letter of the law, collegiate female athletes will finally reach the parity they deserve.
>
> –Jen Jarjosa, student

If you are having trouble with your conclusion—and this is not an uncommon occurrence—it may be because of problems with your essay itself. Frequently, writers do not know when to end because they are not sure about their overall purpose. For example, if you are taking a trip and your purpose is to go to Chicago, you'll know when you get there and will stop. But if you don't really know where you are going, it's very difficult to know when to stop.

It's usually a good idea in your conclusion to avoid such overworked expressions as "In conclusion," "In summary," "I hope I have shown," or "Finally." Your conclusion should also do more than simply repeat what you've said in your opening paragraph. The most satisfying essays are those in which the conclusion provides an interesting way of wrapping up ideas introduced in the beginning and developed throughout so that your reader has the feeling of coming full circle.

You might find it revealing as your course progresses to read with special attention the beginnings and endings of the essays throughout *Models for Writers.* Take special note of the varieties of beginnings and endings, the possible relationship between a beginning and an ending, and the general appropriateness of these elements to the writer's subject and purpose.

Of My Friend Hector and My Achilles Heel

■ **Michael T. Kaufman**

The former writer of the "About New York" column for the New York Times, *Michael T. Kaufman was born in 1938 in Paris and grew up in the United States. He studied at the Bronx High School of Science, City College of New York, and Columbia University. He began his career at the* New York Times *as a reporter and feature writer, and he served as bureau chief in Ottawa and Warsaw before assuming his position as columnist. The experience in Warsaw is evident in his book about Poland,* Mad Dreams, Saving Graces, *published in 1989. Kaufman is also a past winner of the George Polk Award for International Reporting. His most recent book is* Soros: The Life and Times of a Messianic Billionaire *(2002).*

In the following selection, which appeared in the New York Times *in 1992, Kaufman uses the story of his childhood friend Hector Elizondo to reflect on his own "prejudice and stupidity." Take note of how the two brief sentences at the beginning establish the chronological and narrative structure of what follows.*

Reflecting on What You Know

Many schools "track" students by intellectual ability into such categories as "honors," "college bound," "vocational," "remedial," or "terminal." Did you go to a high school that tracked its students? How did you feel about your placement? What did you think about classmates who were on tracks higher or lower than yours?

This story is about prejudice and stupidity. My own. 1

It begins in 1945 when I was a 7-year-old living on the fifth floor of a tenement walkup on 107th Street between Columbus and Manhattan Avenues in New York City. The block was almost entirely Irish and Italian, and I believe my family was the only Jewish one around. 2

One day a Spanish-speaking family moved into one of the four apartments on our landing. They were the first Puerto Ricans I had met. They had a son who was about my age named Hector, and the two of us became friends. We played with toy soldiers and I particularly remember how, using rubber bands and wood from orange crates, we made toy pistols that shot off little squares we cut from old linoleum. 3

We visited each other's homes and I know that at the time I liked Hector and I think he liked me. I may even have eaten my first avocado at his house. 4

About a year after we met, my family moved to another part of Manhattan's West Side and I did not see Hector again until I entered Booker T. Washington Junior High School as an 11-year-old. 5

The Special Class

The class I was in was called 7SP-1; the SP was for special. Earlier, I recall, I had been in the IGC class, for "intellectually gifted children." The SP class was to complete the seventh, eighth and ninth grades in two years and almost all of us would then go to schools like Bronx Science, Stuyvesant or Music and Art, where admission was based on competitive exams. I knew I was in the SP class and the IGC class. I guess I also knew that other people were not. 6

Hector was not. He was in some other class, maybe even 7-2, the class that was held to be the next-brightest, or maybe 7-8. I remember I was happy to see him whenever we would meet, and sometimes we played punchball during lunch period. Mostly, of course, I stayed with my own classmates, with other Intellectually Gifted Children. 7

Sometimes children from other classes, those presumably not so intellectually gifted, would tease and taunt us. At such times I was particularly proud to have Hector as a friend. I assumed that he was tougher than I and my classmates and I guess I thought that if necessary he would come to my defense. 8

Different High Schools

For high school, I went uptown to Bronx Science. Hector, I think, went downtown to Commerce. Sometimes I would see him in Riverside 9

Park, where I played basketball and he worked out on the parallel bars. We would acknowledge each other, but by this time the conversations we held were perfunctory[1]—sports, families, weather.

After I finished college, I would see him around the neighborhood pushing a baby carriage. He was the first of my contemporaries to marry and to have a child. 10

A few years later, in the 60's, married and with children of my own, I was once more living on the West Side, working until late at night as a reporter. Some nights as I took the train home I would see Hector in the car. A few times we exchanged nods, but more often I would pretend that I didn't see him, and maybe he also pretended he didn't see me. Usually he would be wearing a knitted watch cap, and from that I deduced that he was probably working on the docks as a longshoreman. 11

I remember quite distinctly how I would sit on the train and think about how strange and unfair fate had been with regard to the two of us who had once been playmates. Just because I had become an intellectually gifted adult or whatever and he had become a longshoreman or whatever, was that any reason for us to have been left with nothing to say to each other? I thought it was wrong and unfair, but I also thought that conversation would be a chore or a burden. That is pretty much what I thought about Hector, if I thought about him at all, until one Sunday in the mid-70's, when I read in the drama section of this newspaper that my childhood friend, Hector Elizondo, was replacing Peter Falk[2] in the leading role in *The Prisoner of Second Avenue*.[3] 12

Since then, every time I have seen this versatile and acclaimed actor in movies or on television I have blushed for my assumptions. I have replayed the subway rides in my head and tried to fathom why my thoughts had led me where they did. 13

In retrospect it seems far more logical that the man I saw on the train, the man who had been my friend as a boy, was coming home from an Off Broadway theater or perhaps from a job as a waiter 14

---

[1]*perfunctory:* a routine act done with little interest or care.

[2]*Peter Falk* (b. 1927): a well-known stage, television, and movie actor who starred as the rumpled television detective Columbo.

[3]*The Prisoner of Second Avenue:* a play by Neil Simon, which premiered at the Eugene O'Neill Theatre in New York City in 1971. The Broadway hit was made into a movie released in 1975.

while taking acting classes. So why did I think he was a longshoreman? Was it just the cap? Could it be that his being Puerto Rican had something to do with it? Maybe that reinforced the stereotype I concocted, but it wasn't the root of it.

When It Got Started

No, the foundation was laid when I was 11, when I was in 7SP-1 and he was not, when I was in the IGC class and he was not. 15

I have not seen him since I recognized how I had idiotically kept tracking him for years and decades after the school system had tracked both of us. I wonder now if my experience was that unusual, whether social categories conveyed and absorbed before puberty do not generally tend to linger beyond middle age. And I wonder, too, that if they affected the behavior of someone like myself who had been placed on the upper track, how much more damaging it must have been for someone consigned to the lower. 16

I have at times thought of calling him, but kept from doing it because how exactly does one apologize for thoughts that were never expressed? And there was still the problem of what to say. "What have you been up to for the last 40 years?" Or "Wow, was I wrong about you!" Or maybe just, "Want to come over and help me make a linoleum gun?" 17

Thinking Critically about This Reading

What "thoughts that were never expressed" (paragraph 17) does Kaufman feel the need to apologize for? In retrospect, how do you suppose Kaufman feels about his treatment of Hector?

Questions for Study and Discussion

1. How do Kaufman's first two sentences affect how the reader views the rest of the essay? Did they catch your attention? Why or why not?
2. If you are unfamiliar with the Greek myth of Hector and Achilles, look it up in a book on mythology. Why does Kaufman allude to Hector and Achilles in his title? (Glossary: *Allusion*)

3. How does Kaufman organize his essay? (Glossary: *Organization*)
4. What is Kaufman's purpose? (Glossary: *Purpose*) How does his organization help him express his purpose?
5. Why did Kaufman ignore Hector after graduating from college? What does this tell him about society in general?
6. Why is Kaufman's ending effective? What point does he emphasize with his ending?

Classroom Activity Using Beginnings and Endings

Carefully read the following three possible beginnings for an essay on the world's most famous practical joker, Hugh Troy. What are the advantages and disadvantages of each? Which one would you select as an opening paragraph? Why?

> Whether questioning the values of American society or simply relieving the monotony of daily life, Hugh Troy always managed to put a little of himself into each of his stunts. One day he attached a plaster hand to his shirt sleeve and took a trip through the Holland Tunnel. As he approached the tollbooth, with his toll ticket between the fingers of the artificial hand, Troy left both ticket and hand in the grasp of the stunned tollbooth attendant and sped away.

> Nothing seemed unusual. In fact, it was a rather common occurrence in New York City. Five men dressed in overalls roped off a section of busy Fifth Avenue in front of the old Rockefeller residence, hung out MEN WORKING signs, and began ripping up the pavement. By the time they stopped for lunch, they had dug quite a hole in the street. This crew was different, however, from all the others that had descended upon the streets of the city. It was led by Hugh Troy—the world's greatest practical joker.

> Hugh Troy was born in Ithaca, New York, where his father was a professor at Cornell University. After graduating from Cornell, Troy left for New York City, where he became a successful illustrator of children's books. When World War II broke out, he went into the army and eventually became a captain in the 21st Bomber Command, 20th Air Force, under General Curtis LeMay. After the war he made his home in Garrison, New York, for a short while before finally settling in Washington, D.C., where he lived until his death.

Suggested Writing Assignments

1. Kaufman's essay is a deeply personal one. Use it as a model to write an essay about a time or an action in your life that you are not proud of. What happened? Why did it happen? What would you do differently if you could? Be sure to catch the reader's attention in the beginning and to end your essay with a thought-provoking conclusion.
2. Everyone has childhood friends that we either have lost track of or don't communicate with as often as we would like. Choose an old friend whom you have lost track of and would like to see again. Write an essay about your relationship. What made your friend special to you as a child? Why did you lose touch? What does the future hold? Organize your essay chronologically.

How I Got Smart

■ Steve Brody

Steve Brody is a retired high school English teacher who enjoys writing about the lighter side of teaching. He was born in Chicago in 1915 and received his bachelor's degree in English from Columbia University. In addition to his articles in educational publications, Brody has published many newspaper articles on travel and a humorous book about golf, How to Break Ninety before You Reach It *(1979).*

As you read his account of how love made him smart, an essay that first appeared in the New York Times *in September 1986, notice his well-chosen and thoughtfully emphasized details.*

Reflecting on What You Know

Motivation is a difficult topic about which to generalize. What motivates one person to act often will not work on another person. How do you get motivated to work, to join extracurricular activities, or to take care of yourself? Are you able to motivate yourself, or do you need someone else to give you a push?

A common misconception among youngsters attending school is that their teachers were child prodigies.[1] Who else but a bookworm, prowling the libraries and disdaining the normal youngster's propensity for play rather than study, would grow up to be a teacher anyway? 1

I tried desperately to explain to my students that the image they had of me as an ardent devotee of books and homework during my adolescence was a bit out of focus. Au contraire! I hated compulsory education with a passion. I could never quite accept the notion of having to go to school while the fish were biting. 2

Consequently, my grades were somewhat bearish.[2] That's how my father, who dabbled in the stock market, described them. Presenting 3

[1]*prodigies:* people with exceptional talents.
[2]*bearish:* trending downward; a term used to describe the stock market.

my report card for my father to sign was like serving him a subpoena. At midterm and other sensitive periods, my father kept a low profile.

But in my sophomore year, something beautiful and exciting happened. Cupid aimed his arrow and struck me squarely in the heart. All at once, I enjoyed going to school, if only to gaze at the lovely face beneath the raven tresses in English II. My princess sat near the pencil sharpener, and that year I ground up enough pencils to fuel a campfire. 4

Alas, Debbie was far beyond my wildest dreams. We were separated not only by five rows of desks, but by about 50 I.Q. points. She was the top student in English II, the apple of Mrs. Larrivee's eye. I envisioned how eagerly Debbie's father awaited her report card. 5

Occasionally, Debbie would catch me staring at her, and she would flash a smile—an angelic smile that radiated enlightenment and quickened my heartbeat. It was a smile that signaled hope and made me temporarily forget the intellectual gulf that separated us. 6

I schemed desperately to bridge that gulf. And one day, as I was passing the supermarket, an idea came to me. 7

A sign in the window announced that the store was offering the first volume of a set of encyclopedias at the introductory price of 29 cents. The remaining volumes would cost $2.49 each, but it was no time to be cynical. 8

I purchased Volume I—Aardvark to Asteroid—and began my venture into the world of knowledge. I would henceforth become a seeker of facts. I would become chief egghead in English II and sweep the princess off her feet with a surge of erudition.[3] I had it all planned. 9

My first opportunity came one day in the cafeteria line. I looked behind me and there she was. 10

"Hi," she said. 11

After a pause, I wet my lips and said, "Know where anchovies come from?" 12

She seemed surprised. "No, I don't." 13

I breathed a sigh of relief. "The anchovy lives in salt water and is rarely found in fresh water." I had to talk fast, so that I could get all the facts in before we reached the cash register. "Fishermen catch anchovies in the Mediterranean Sea and along the Atlantic coast near Spain and Portugal." 14

"How fascinating," said Debbie. 15

[3]*erudition:* extensive knowledge gained from books.

"The anchovy is closely related to the herring. It is thin and silvery in color. It has a long snout and a very large mouth." 16

"Incredible." 17

"Anchovies are good in salads, mixed with eggs, and are often used as appetizers before dinner, but they are salty and cannot be digested too rapidly." 18

Debbie shook her head in disbelief. It was obvious that I had made quite an impression. 19

A few days later, during a fire drill, I sidled[4] up to her and asked, "Ever been to the Aleutian Islands?" 20

"Never have," she replied. 21

"Might be a nice place to visit, but I certainly wouldn't want to live there," I said. 22

"Why not?" said Debbie, playing right into my hands. 23

"Well, the climate is forbidding. There are no trees on any of the 100 or more islands in the group. The ground is rocky and very little plant life can grow on it." 24

"I don't think I'd even care to visit," she said. 25

The fire drill was over and we began to file into the building, so I had to step it up to get the natives in. "The Aleuts are short and sturdy and have dark skin and black hair. They subsist on fish, and they trap blue fox, seal, and otter for their valuable fur." 26

Debbie's hazel eyes widened in amazement. She was undoubtedly beginning to realize that she wasn't dealing with an ordinary lunkhead. She was gaining new and valuable insights instead of engaging in the routine small talk one would expect from most sophomores. 27

Luck was on my side, too. One day I was browsing through the library during my study period. I spotted Debbie sitting at a table, absorbed in a crossword puzzle. She was frowning, apparently stumped on a word. I leaned over and asked if I could help. 28

"Four-letter word for Oriental female servant," Debbie said. 29

"Try *amah*," I said, quick as a flash. 30

Debbie filled in the blanks, then turned to stare at me in amazement. "I don't believe it," she said. "I just don't believe it." 31

And so it went, that glorious, amorous, joyous sophomore year. Debbie seemed to relish our little conversations and hung on my every word. Naturally, the more I read, the more my confidence 32

---

[4]*sidled:* approached sideways or in a stealthy manner.

grew. I expatiated[5] freely on such topics as adenoids,[6] air brakes, and arthritis.

In the classroom, too, I was gradually making my presence felt. Among my classmates, I was developing a reputation as a wheeler-dealer in data. One day, during a discussion of Coleridge's "The Ancient Mariner," we came across the word *albatross*. 33

"Can anyone tell us what an albatross is?" asked Mrs. Larrivee. 34

My hand shot up. "The albatross is a large bird that lives mostly in the ocean regions below the equator, but may be found in the north Pacific as well. The albatross measures as long as four feet and has the greatest wingspread of any bird. It feeds on the surface of the ocean, where it catches shellfish. The albatross is a very voracious[7] eater. When it is full it has trouble getting into the air again." 35

There was a long silence in the room. Mrs. Larrivee couldn't quite believe what she had just heard. I sneaked a peek at Debbie and gave her a big wink. She beamed proudly and winked back. 36

It was a great feeling, having Debbie and Mrs. Larrivee and my peers according me respect and paying attention when I spoke. 37

My grades edged upward and my father no longer tried to avoid me when I brought home my report card. I continued reading the encyclopedia diligently, packing more and more into my brain. 38

What I failed to perceive was that Debbie all this while was going steady with a junior from a neighboring school—a hockey player with a C+ average. The revelation hit me hard, and for a while I felt like disgorging[8] and forgetting everything I had learned. I had saved enough money to buy Volume II—Asthma to Bullfinch—but was strongly tempted to invest in a hockey stick instead. 39

How could she lead me on like that—smiling and concurring and giving me the impression that I was important? 40

I felt not only hurt, but betrayed. Like Agamemnon, but with less dire consequences, thank God. 41

In time I recovered from my wounds. The next year Debbie moved from the neighborhood and transferred to another school. Soon she became no more than a fleeting memory. 42

---

[5]*expatiated:* to speak or write at length.
[6]*adenoids:* masses of tissue that obstruct nasal and ear passages into the throat.
[7]*voracious:* excessively eager.
[8]*disgorging:* discharging violently; vomiting.

Although the original incentive was gone, I continued poring over the encyclopedias, as well as an increasing number of other books. Having savored the heady wine of knowledge, I could not now alter my course. For: 43

> "A little knowledge is a dangerous thing:
> Drink deep, or taste not the Pierian spring."

So wrote Alexander Pope, Volume XIV, Paprika to Pterodactyl. 44

Thinking Critically about This Reading

In paragraph 43 Brody states, "Although the original incentive was gone, I continued poring over the encyclopedias, as well as an increasing number of other books." What was Brody's "original incentive"? What other incentive did he have to continue his quest to learn?

Questions for Study and Discussion

1. How are paragraphs 2 and 3, 3 and 4, 5 and 6, 31 and 32, and 43 and 44 linked? (Glossary: *Transitions*)
2. Brody uses dialogue to tell his story in paragraphs 10–35. (Glossary: *Dialogue*) What would have been lost had he simply told his readers what happened?
3. Why didn't Brody stop reading the encyclopedia when he discovered that Debbie had a steady boyfriend?
4. If you find Brody's narrative humorous, try to explain the sources of his humor. For example, what humor resides in the choice of examples Brody uses?
5. Comment on the effectiveness of the beginning and ending of Brody's essay. (Glossary: *Beginnings and Endings*)

Classroom Activity Using Beginnings and Endings

Brody, a teacher himself, opens his essay with an interesting question about teachers: "Who else but a bookworm, prowling the libraries and disdaining the normal youngster's propensity for play rather than study, would grow up to be a teacher anyway?" The surprising answer that Brody gave his own students serves to introduce his story about young love and getting smart. After rereading Brody's essay, write an alternate beginning and then share your beginning with your classmates. What kinds of changes, if any, would you have to make to Brody's essay to accommodate your beginning?

Suggested Writing Assignments

1. One serious thought that Brody raises is that we learn best when we are sufficiently motivated. Once we are motivated, the desire to learn seems to feed on itself: "Having savored the heady wine of knowledge, I could not now alter my course" (43). Write an essay in which you explore this subject using your own experiences.
2. Brody's essay and the cartoon below illustrate the lengths to which two boys will go to impress girls. What do you remember about your own first crush or experience with "puppy love"? What did you do to "impress" the other person? Did the other person do anything that particularly impressed you? Do you think boys and girls behave differently when it comes to impressing a potential love? If so, how? Using Brody's essay as a model, write an essay in which you narrate the story of one of your first loves.

"If I want to impress a woman online, what font should I use? Aristocrat Bold so she'll think I'm rich or Comic Sans so she'll think I'm funny?"

The Wounds That Can't Be Stitched Up

■ Ruth Russell

Ruth Russell was born in Greenfield, Massachusetts, in 1959, and graduated from Greenfield Community College. When we selected Russell's essay for inclusion in Models for Writers, *we had no idea that she had used the sixth edition as the textbook as a student in a college composition course. Russell said of her experience with* Models for Writers, *"The book was tremendously helpful to me in learning to write. I would do a lot of the exercises at the end of the essays, even when they were not assigned, as a way of deconstructing them, of finding out how they were written, what their essential parts were. I was really interested in improving my writing." After writing the following essay for her course, she submitted it to the "My Turn" column in* Newsweek, *where it appeared in December 1999 without much editing by the column's editor, Pam Hammer. "Her suggestions helped to make it a little shorter and stronger," recalls Russell. "At one point, I had entitled the piece 'Full Circle,' but I much prefer the present title. I often think how amazing it is that the incident that caused me to write the essay occurred on about the twentieth anniversary of my mother's accident."*

As you read, notice how Russell ties her ending to her beginning, bringing the essay full circle. Although the first sentence of her final paragraph harkens back to her opening sentence, it in no way prepares you for the painfully ironic conclusion.

Reflecting on What You Know

Everyone has childhood fears that are often associated with a particular event or experience and that can last for years. What particular fear or fears did you have as a child? Were they caused by a specific incident that you can recall? How have they affected your life as a teenager and young adult?

It was a mild December night. Christmas was only two weeks away. The evening sky was overcast, but the roads were dry. All was quiet in our small town as I drove to my grandmother's house. 1

I heard the sirens first. Red lights and blue lights strobed in tandem. Ambulances with their interiors lit like television screens in a dark room flew by, escorted by police cruisers on the way to the hospital. 2

When I arrived at my gram's, she was on the porch steps struggling to put on her coat. "Come on," she said breathlessly, "your mother has been in an accident." I was seventeen then, and it would take a long time before sirens lost their power to reduce me to tears. 3

Twenty-three years have passed, but only recently have I realized how deeply affected I was by events caused by a drunk driver so long ago. 4

When the accident occurred, my youngest brother was eight. He was sitting in the back seat of our family's large, sturdy sedan. The force of the crash sent him flying headlong into the back of the front seat, leaving him with a grossly swollen black eye. He was admitted to the hospital for observation. He didn't talk much when I visited him that night. He just sat in the bed, a lonely little figure in a darkened hospital room. 5

My sister, who was twelve, was sitting in the front seat. She confided to me later how much she missed the beautiful blue coat she'd been wearing at the time. It was an early Christmas present, and it was destroyed beyond repair by the medical personnel who cut it off her body as they worked to save her life. She had a severely fractured skull that required immediate surgery. The resulting facial scar became for our family a permanent reminder of how close she came to dying that night. 6

My mother was admitted to the intensive-care unit to be stabilized before her multiple facial cuts could be stitched up. Dad tried to prepare me before we went in to see her by telling me that she looked and sounded worse than she was. One eye was temporarily held in place by a bandage wrapped around her head. Her lower lip hideously gaped,[1] exposing a mouthful of broken teeth. Delirious, she cried out for her children and apologized for an accident she neither caused nor could have avoided. An accident that happened when her car was hit head-on by a drunk driver speeding down the wrong side of the road in a half-ton truck with no headlights. 7

[1]*gaped:* opened wide.

My dad, my brothers, my sister, and I spent Christmas at the hospital visiting my mother. Sometimes she was so out of it from medication that she barely recognized us. We celebrated two of my brothers' birthdays—one only days after Christmas and the other in early January—there too. 8

I remember watching the police escort the drunk driver out of the hospital the night of the accident. He looked about thirty-five years old, but his face was so distorted by rage and alcohol that I could only guess. A bandaged wrist was his only visible injury. He kept repeating that he'd done nothing wrong as several officers tried to get him into the cruiser waiting outside the emergency-room exit. 9

The man was jailed over the weekend and lost his license for thirty days for driving while intoxicated. I don't know if that was his first alcohol-related traffic violation, but I know it wasn't the last. Now and then I'd see his name in the court log of our local paper for another DWI, and wonder how he could still be behind the wheel. 10

Sometimes when I tell this story, I'd be asked in an accusatory[2] tone if my mom and siblings were wearing seat belts. I think that's a lot like asking a rape victim how she was dressed. The answer is no. This all happened before seat-belt-awareness campaigns began. In fact, if they had been in a smaller car, seat belts or not, I believe my mother and sister would have died. 11

Many local people who know the driver are surprised when they hear about the accident, and they are quick to defend him. They tell me he was a war hero. His parents aren't well. He's an alcoholic. Or my favorite: "He's a good guy when he doesn't drink." 12

Two years ago I discovered this man had moved into my apartment building. I felt vaguely apprehensive, but I believed the accident was ancient history. Nothing could have prepared me for what happened next. 13

It was a mild afternoon, just a few days before Christmas. I had started down the back staircase of the building, on my way to visit my son, when I recognized my neighbor's new pickup truck as it roared down the street. The driver missed the entrance to our shared parking lot. He reversed crookedly in the road, slammed the transmission into forward, then quickly pulled into his parking space. Gravel and sand flew as he stomped on the brakes to halt his truck 14

[2]*accusatory:* implying error or misdeed.

just inches from where I stood frozen on the staircase. As he staggered from his vehicle, he looked at me and asked drunkenly, "Did I scare you?"

Thinking Critically about This Reading

In paragraph 11 Russell relates a story about how people asked whether her family members were wearing seat belts at the time of the accident, and in paragraph 12 she tells of how people who knew the drunk driver responsible for the accident were quick to defend or make excuses for him. What is Russell's point in mentioning these incidents?

Questions for Study and Discussion

1. Russell begins her essay with a somewhat generic description—season, weather, road conditions—of the day of her mother's accident. Why are such details important in her memory? How does her first paragraph work with her title to draw the reader in?
2. Russell provides the reader with an image of her little brother—the least injured of the three in the car—before discussing her sister and mother. What is the image? Why is it an effective introduction to the scene at the hospital?
3. What is Russell's tone in her essay? (Glossary: *Tone*) How does she establish it? Cite specific examples from the text.
4. Russell ironically describes the platitude " 'He's a good guy when he doesn't drink' " as her "favorite" (12). Why is the statement ironic? (Glossary: *Irony*) Why do you think Russell emphasizes it as her favorite excuse for the man's behavior?
5. Russell's ending does not offer a neat conclusion to her situation and makes no concrete statement about her own feelings. Why does she leave the interaction between the drunk driver and herself so open-ended? How does her ending tie in with her purpose for writing the essay? (Glossary: *Purpose*)

Classroom Activity Using Beginnings and Endings

Choose one of the essays you have been writing for your course, and write at least two different beginnings for it. If you are having trouble coming up with two, check to see whether one of the paragraphs in the body of your essay would be appropriate, or consult the list of effective beginnings in the introduction to this chapter. After you have finished, have several classmates read your beginnings and select their favorite. Do any of your new beginnings suggest ways that you can improve the focus, the organization, or the ending of your essay? Explain these revision possibilities to your partners.

Suggested Writing Assignments

1. Russell's essay says a lot about how our society reacts to drunk drivers, but she never directly argues a point. Her experiences alone speak to the problem very clearly. Write an essay in which you present an indirect argument about a topic that is important to you, using your experiences and observations to lead the reader to the desired conclusion. (Glossary: *Argumentation*) Construct your beginning and ending with care so that the reader immediately understands how your experiences are relevant to the issue and is left with a strong image or statement that supports your point of view.
2. Write a short essay about an ongoing conflict or situation that you are either working to resolve or hoping will be resolved in the near future. For example, you can use a test you are studying for, an up-and-down relationship, or a search for employment. Have a clear purpose in mind regarding how you want the reader to react—with anger, sympathy, amusement, and so on—and craft your essay to accomplish your goal. Pay particular attention to the conclusion, which will be open-ended but should clearly communicate your purpose to the reader.

Unforgettable Miss Bessie

■ Carl T. Rowan

In addition to being a popular syndicated newspaper columnist, Carl T. Rowan (1925–2000) was an ambassador to Finland and director of the U.S. Information Agency. Born in Ravenscroft, Tennessee, he received degrees from Oberlin College and the University of Minnesota. He worked as a columnist for the Minneapolis Tribune *and the* Chicago Sun-Times *before moving to Washington, D.C. In 1996, Washington College awarded Rowan an honorary doctor of letters degree in recognition of his achievements as a writer and his contributions to minority youth, most notably through the organization he founded in 1987, Project Excellence. In 1991, Rowan published* Breaking Barriers: A Memoir. *He is also the author of two biographies, one of baseball great Jackie Robinson and the other of former Supreme Court Justice Thurgood Marshall. His last book,* The Coming Race War in America, *was published in 1996.*

In the following essay, first published in the March 1985 issue of Reader's Digest, *Rowan describes one of his high school teachers whose lessons went far beyond the subjects she taught. Through telling details about Miss Bessie's background, behavior, and appearance, Rowan creates a dominant impression of her—the one he wants to leave readers with. Notice how he begins with some factual information about Miss Bessie and concludes by showing why she was "so vital to the minds, hearts, and souls" of her students.*

Reflecting on What You Know

Perhaps you have at some time taught a friend or younger brother or sister how to do something—tie a shoe, hit a ball, read, solve a puzzle, drive a car—but you never thought of yourself as a teacher. Did you enjoy the experience of sharing what you know with someone else? Would you consider becoming a teacher someday?

She was only about five feet tall and probably never weighed more than 110 pounds, but Miss Bessie was a towering presence in the classroom. She was the only woman tough enough to make me read *Beowulf*[1] and think for a few foolish days that I liked it. From 1938 to 1942, when I attended Bernard High School in McMinnville, Tennessee, she taught me English, history, civics—and a lot more than I realized. 1

I shall never forget the day she scolded me into reading *Beowulf*. 2

"But Miss Bessie," I complained, "I ain't much interested in it." 3

Her large brown eyes became daggerish slits. "Boy," she said, "how dare you say 'ain't' to me! I've taught you better than that." 4

"Miss Bessie," I pleaded, "I'm trying to make first-string end on the football team, and if I go around saying 'it isn't' and 'they aren't,' the guys are gonna laugh me off the squad." 5

"Boy," she responded, "you'll play football because you have guts. But do you know what *really* takes guts? Refusing to lower your standards to those of the crowd. It takes guts to say you've got to live and be somebody fifty years after all the football games are over." 6

I started saying "it isn't" and "they aren't," and I still made first-string end—and class valedictorian—without losing my buddies' respect. 7

During her remarkable 44-year career, Mrs. Bessie Taylor Gwynn taught hundreds of economically deprived black youngsters—including my mother, my brother, my sisters, and me. I remember her now with gratitude and affection—especially in this era when Americans are so wrought-up about a "rising tide of mediocrity"[2] in public education and the problems of finding competent, caring teachers. Miss Bessie was an example of an informed, dedicated teacher, a blessing to children, and an asset to the nation. 8

Born in 1895, in poverty, she grew up in Athens, Alabama, where there was no public school for blacks. She attended Trinity School, a private institution for blacks run by the American Missionary Association, and in 1911 graduated from the Normal School (a "super" high school) at Fisk University in Nashville. Mrs. Gwynn, the essence of pride and privacy, never talked about her years in Athens; only in the months before her death did she reveal that she had never attended Fisk University itself because she could not afford the four-year course. 9

---

[1]*Beowulf:* an epic poem written in Old English by an anonymous author in the early eighth century.

[2]*mediocrity:* state of being second-rate; not outstanding.

At Normal School she learned a lot about Shakespeare, but most of all about the profound importance of education—especially, for a people trying to move up from slavery. "What you put in your head, boy," she once said, "can never be pulled out by the Ku Klux Klan,[3] the Congress, or anybody." 10

Miss Bessie's bearing of dignity told anyone who met her that she was "educated" in the best sense of the word. There was never a discipline problem in her classes. We didn't dare mess with a woman who knew about the Battle of Hastings, the Magna Carta, and the Bill of Rights—and who could also play the piano. 11

This frail-looking woman could make sense of Shakespeare, Milton, Voltaire, and bring to life Booker T. Washington and W. E. B. Du Bois. Believing that it was important to know who the officials were that spent taxpayers' money and made public policy, she made us memorize the names of everyone on the Supreme Court and in the President's Cabinet. It could be embarrassing to be unprepared when Miss Bessie said, "Get up and tell the class who Frances Perkins[4] is and what you think about her." 12

Miss Bessie knew that my family, like so many others during the Depression,[5] couldn't afford to subscribe to a newspaper. She knew we didn't even own a radio. Still, she prodded me to "look out for your future and find some way to keep up with what's going on in the world." So I became a delivery boy for the Chattanooga *Times*. I rarely made a dollar a week, but I got to read a newspaper every day. 13

Miss Bessie noticed things that had nothing to do with schoolwork, but were vital to a youngster's development. Once a few classmates made fun of my frayed, hand-me-down overcoat, calling me "Strings." As I was leaving school, Miss Bessie patted me on the back of that old overcoat and said, "Carl, never fret about what you *don't* have. Just make the most of what you *do* have—a brain." 14

Among the things that I did not have was electricity in the little frame house that my father had built for $400 with his World War I bonus. But because of her inspiration, I spent many hours squinting 15

[3]*Ku Klux Klan:* a secret organization in the United States hostile toward African Americans (eventually other groups as well), founded in 1915 and continuing to the present.

[4]*Frances Perkins:* the U.S. secretary of labor during the presidency of Franklin D. Roosevelt and the first woman appointed to a cabinet post.

[5]*Depression:* the longest and most severe economic slump in North America, Europe, and other industrialized areas of the world, which began in 1929 and ended around 1939. Also called the *Great Depression.*

beside a kerosene lamp reading Shakespeare and Thoreau, Samuel Pepys and William Cullen Bryant.

No one in my family had ever graduated from high school, so there was no tradition of commitment to learning for me to lean on. Like millions of youngsters in today's ghettos and barrios, I needed the push and stimulation of a teacher who truly cared. Miss Bessie gave plenty of both, as she immersed me in a wonderful world of similes, metaphors and even onomatopoeia. She led me to believe that I could write sonnets as well as Shakespeare, or iambic-pentameter verse to put Alexander Pope to shame. 16

In those days the McMinnville school system was rigidly "Jim Crow,"[6] and poor black children had to struggle to put anything in their heads. Our high school was only slightly larger than the once-typical little red schoolhouse, and its library was outrageously inadequate—so small, I like to say, that if two students were in it and one wanted to turn a page, the other one had to step outside. 17

Negroes, as we were called then, were not allowed in the town library, except to mop floors or dust tables. But through one of those secret Old South arrangements between whites of conscience and blacks of stature, Miss Bessie kept getting books smuggled out of the white library. That is how she introduced me to the Brontës, Byron, Coleridge, Keats and Tennyson. "If you don't read, you can't write, and if you can't write, you might as well stop dreaming," Miss Bessie once told me. 18

So I read whatever Miss Bessie told me to, and tried to remember the things she insisted that I store away. Forty-five years later, I can still recite her "truths to live by," such as Henry Wadsworth Longfellow's lines from "The Ladder of St. Augustine": 19

> The heights by great men reached and kept
> Were not attained by sudden flight.
> But they, while their companions slept,
> Were toiling upward in the night.

Years later, her inspiration, prodding, anger, cajoling, and almost osmotic infusion of learning finally led to that lovely day when Miss Bessie dropped me a note saying, "I'm so proud to read your column in the Nashville *Tennessean*." 20

[6]"*Jim Crow*": a term referring to the racial segregation laws in the U.S. South between the late 1800s and the mid-1900s.

Miss Bessie was a spry 80 when I went back to McMinnville and visited her in a senior citizens' apartment building. Pointing out proudly that her building was racially integrated, she reached for two glasses and a pint of bourbon. I was momentarily shocked, because it would have been scandalous in the 1930s and '40s for word to get out that a teacher drank, and nobody had ever raised a rumor that Miss Bessie did. 21

I felt a new sense of equality as she lifted her glass to mine. Then she revealed a softness and compassion that I had never known as a student. 22

"I've never forgotten that examination day," she said, "when Buster Martin held up seven fingers, obviously asking you for help with question number seven, 'Name a common carrier.' I can still picture you looking at your exam paper and humming a few bars of 'Chattanooga Choo Choo.' I was so tickled, I couldn't punish either of you." 23

Miss Bessie was telling me, with bourbon-laced grace, that I never fooled her for a moment. 24

When Miss Bessie died in 1980, at age 85, hundreds of her former students mourned. They knew the measure of a great teacher: love and motivation. Her wisdom and influence had rippled out across generations. 25

Some of her students who might normally have been doomed to poverty went on to become doctors, dentists, and college professors. Many, guided by Miss Bessie's example, became public-school teachers. 26

"The memory of Miss Bessie and how she conducted her classroom did more for me than anything I learned in college," recalls Gladys Wood of Knoxville, Tennessee, a highly respected English teacher who spent 43 years in the state's school system. "So many times, when I faced a difficult classroom problem, I asked myself, *How would Miss Bessie deal with this?* And I'd remember that she would handle it with laughter and love." 27

No child can get all the necessary support at home, and millions of poor children get *no* support at all. This is what makes a wise, educated, warm-hearted teacher like Miss Bessie so vital to the minds, hearts, and souls of this country's children. 28

Thinking Critically about This Reading

Rowan states that Miss Bessie "taught me English, history, civics—and a lot more than I realized" (paragraph 1). Aside from the standard school subjects, what did Miss Bessie teach Rowan? What role did she play in his life?

Questions for Study and Discussion

1. Do you think Rowan's first few paragraphs make for an effective introduction? Explain.
2. At what point in the essay does Rowan give us the details of Miss Bessie's background? Why do you suppose he delays giving us this important information?
3. Throughout the essay Rowan offers details of Miss Bessie's physical appearance. What specific details does he give, and in what context does he give them? (Glossary: *Details*) Do Miss Bessie's physical characteristics match the quality of her character? Explain.
4. Does Miss Bessie's drinking influence your opinion of her? Why or why not? Why do you think Rowan includes this part of her behavior in his essay?
5. How does dialogue serve Rowan's purpose? (Glossary: *Dialogue; Purpose*)
6. How would you sum up the character of Miss Bessie? Make a list of the key words that Rowan uses that you feel best describe her.

Classroom Activity Using Beginnings and Endings

Rowan uses a series of facts about his teacher, the "unforgettable" Miss Bessie, to begin his essay. Pick two from among the seven other methods for beginning essays discussed in the introduction to this chapter, and use them to write alternative openings for Rowan's essay. Share your beginnings with others in the class, and discuss their effectiveness.

Suggested Writing Assignments

1. In paragraph 18, Rowan writes the following: "'If you don't read, you can't write, and if you can't write, you might as well stop dreaming,' Miss Bessie once told me." Write an essay in which you explore this theme (which, in essence, is also the theme of *Models for Writers*).
2. Think of all the teachers you have had, and write a description of the one who has had the greatest influence on you. (Glossary: *Description*) Remember to give some consideration to the balance you want to achieve between physical attributes and personality traits.

chapter **7**

Paragraphs

Within an essay, the **paragraph** is the most important unit of thought. Like the essay, it has its own main idea, often stated directly in a topic sentence. Like a good essay, a good paragraph is unified: it avoids digressions and develops its main idea. Paragraphs use many of the rhetorical strategies that essays use—strategies like classification, comparison and contrast, and cause and effect. As you read the following three paragraphs, notice how each writer develops his or her topic sentence with explanations, concrete details and statistics, or vivid examples. The topic sentence in each paragraph is italicized.

> *I've learned from experience that good friendships are based on a delicate balance.* When friends are on a par, professionally and personally, it's easier for them to root for one another. It's taken me a long time to realize that not all my "friends" wish me well. Someone who wants what you have may not be able to handle your good fortune: If you find yourself apologizing for your hard-earned raise or soft-pedaling your long-awaited promotion, it's a sure sign that the friendship is off balance. Real friends are secure enough in their own lives to share each other's successes—not begrudge them.
>
> –Stephanie Mansfield

> The problem of substance abuse is far more complex and far more pervasive than any of us really knows or is willing to admit. *Most stories of illegal drugs overshadow Americans' struggles with alcohol, tobacco, food, and nonprescription drugs—our so-called legal addictions.* In 2000, for example, 17,000 deaths were attributed to cocaine and heroin. In that same year, 435,000 deaths were attributed to tobacco and 85,000 to alcohol. It's not surprising, then, that many sociologists believe we are a nation of substance abusers—drinkers, smokers, overeaters, and pill poppers. Although the statistics are alarming, they do not begin to suggest the heavy

toll of substance abuse on Americans and their families. Loved ones die, relationships are fractured, children are abandoned, job productivity falters, and the dreams of young people are extinguished.

–Alfred Rosa and Paul Eschholz

Photographs have let me know my parents before I was born, as the carefree college students they were, in love and awaiting the rest of their lives. I have seen the light blue Volkswagen van my dad used to take surfing down the coast of California and the silver dress my mom wore to her senior prom. Through pictures I was able to witness their wedding, which showed me that there is much in their relationship that goes beyond their children. I saw the look in their eyes as they held their first, newborn daughter, as well as the jealous expressions of my sister when I was born a few years later. There is something almost magical about viewing images of yourself and your family that you were too young to remember.

–Carrie White, student

Many writers find it helpful to think of the paragraph as a very small, compact essay. Here is a paragraph from an essay on testing:

Multiple-choice questions distort the purposes of education. Picking one answer among four is very different from thinking a question through to an answer of one's own, and far less useful in life. Recognition of vocabulary and isolated facts makes the best kind of multiple-choice questions, so these dominate the tests, rather than questions that test the use of knowledge. Because schools want their children to perform well, they are often tempted to teach the limited sorts of knowledge most useful on the tests.

This paragraph, like all well-written paragraphs, has several distinguishing characteristics. It is unified, coherent, and adequately developed. It is unified in that every sentence and every idea relates to the main idea, stated in the topic sentence, "Multiple-choice questions distort the purposes of education." It is coherent in that the sentences and ideas are arranged logically and the relationships among them are made clear by the use of effective transitions. Finally, the paragraph is adequately developed in that it presents a short but persuasive argument supporting its main idea.

How much development is "adequate" development? The answer depends on many things—how complicated or controversial the main idea is, what readers already know and believe, how much space the writer is permitted. Nearly everyone agrees that the earth circles around the sun; a single sentence would be enough to make that point. A writer arguing that affirmative action has outlived its usefulness, however, would need many sentences—indeed, many paragraphs—to develop that idea convincingly.

Here is another model of an effective paragraph. As you read this paragraph about the resourcefulness of pigeons in evading attempts to control them, pay attention to its main idea, unity, development, and coherence.

> Pigeons (and their human friends) have proved remarkably resourceful in evading nearly all the controls, from birth-control pellets to carbide shells to pigeon apartment complexes, that pigeon-haters have devised. One of New York's leading museums once put large black rubber owls on its wide ledges to discourage the large number of pigeons that roosted there. Within the day the pigeons had gotten over their fear of owls and were back perched on the owls' heads. A few years ago San Francisco put a sticky coating on the ledges of some public buildings, but the pigeons got used to the goop and came back to roost. The city then tried trapping, using electric owls, and periodically exploding carbide shells outside a city building, hoping the noise would scare the pigeons away. It did, but not for long, and the program was abandoned. More frequent explosions probably would have distressed the humans in the area more than the birds. Philadelphia tried a feed that makes pigeons vomit, and then, they hoped, go away. A New York firm claimed it had a feed that made a pigeon's nervous system send "danger signals" to the other members of its flock.

The main idea is stated at the beginning in a topic sentence. Other sentences in the paragraph support this idea with examples. Because all the separate examples illustrate how pigeons have evaded attempts to control them, the paragraph is unified. Because there are enough examples to convince the reader of the truth of the topic statement, the paragraph is adequately developed. Finally, the regular use of transitional words and phrases like *once, within the day, a few years ago,* and *then* lends the paragraph coherence.

How long should a paragraph be? In modern essays, most paragraphs range from 50 to 250 words, but some run a full page or more, and others may be only a few words long. The best answer is that a paragraph should be long enough to develop its main idea adequately.

When some writers find a paragraph running very long, they break it into two or more paragraphs so that readers can pause and catch their breath. Other writers forge ahead, relying on the unity and coherence of their paragraph to keep their readers from getting lost.

Articles and essays that appear in magazines and newspapers often have relatively short paragraphs, some of only one or two sentences. Short paragraphs are a convention in journalism because of the narrow columns, which make paragraphs of average length appear very long. But often you will find that these journalistic "paragraphs" could be joined together into a few longer paragraphs. Longer, adequately developed paragraphs are the kind you should use in all but journalistic writing.

Simplicity

■ **William Zinsser**

William Zinsser was born in New York City in 1922. After graduating from Princeton University, he worked for the New York Herald Tribune, *first as a feature writer and later as its drama editor and film critic. During the 1970s he taught writing at Yale University. A former executive editor of the Book-of-the-Month Club, Zinsser has also served on the Usage Panel of the* American Heritage Dictionary. *Currently, he is the series editor for the Writer's Craft Series, which publishes talks by writers, and teaches writing at the New School University in New York. Zinsser's own published works cover many aspects of contemporary American culture, but he is best known as the author of lucid and accessible books about writing, including* Writing to Learn *(1988),* Inventing the Truth: The Art and Craft of Memoir *(1998, with Russell Baker and Jill Ker Conway),* Writing about Your Life: A Journey into the Past *(2005), and* On Writing Well, *a perennial favorite for college writing courses, published in a thirtieth anniversary edition in 2006.*

In the following piece from On Writing Well, *Zinsser reminds us, as did Henry David Thoreau before him, to "simplify, simplify." As you read each paragraph, notice the clarity with which Zinsser presents its main idea, and observe how he develops that idea with adequate and logically related supporting information. You should also note that he follows his own advice about simplicity.*

Reflecting on What You Know

Sometimes we get so caught up in what's going on around us that we start to feel frantic, and we lose sight of what is really important or meaningful to us. At such times, it's a good idea to take stock of what we are doing and to simplify our lives by dropping activities that are no longer rewarding. Write about a time when you've felt the need to simplify your life.

Clutter is the disease of American writing. We are a society strangling in unnecessary words, circular constructions, pompous frills, and meaningless jargon. 1

Who can understand the clotted language of everyday American commerce: the memo, the corporation report, the business letter, the notice from the bank explaining its latest "simplified" statement? What member of an insurance or medical plan can decipher the brochure explaining his costs and benefits? What father or mother can put together a child's toy from the instructions on the box? Our national tendency is to inflate and thereby sound important. The airline pilot who announces that he is presently anticipating experiencing considerable precipitation wouldn't think of saying it may rain. The sentence is too simple—there must be something wrong with it. 2

But the secret of good writing is to strip every sentence to its cleanest components. Every word that serves no function, every long word that could be a short word, every adverb that carries the same meaning that's already in the verb, every passive construction that leaves the reader unsure of who is doing what—these are the thousand and one adulterants[1] that weaken the strength of a sentence. And they usually occur in proportion to education and rank. 3

During the 1960s the president of my university wrote a letter to mollify[2] the alumni after a spell of campus unrest. "You are probably aware," he began, "that we have been experiencing very considerable potentially explosive expressions of dissatisfaction on issues only partially related." He meant the students had been hassling them about different things. I was far more upset by the president's English than by the students' potentially explosive expressions of dissatisfaction. I would have preferred the presidential approach taken by Franklin D. Roosevelt when he tried to convert into English his own government's memos, such as this blackout order of 1942: 4

> Such preparations shall be made as will completely obscure all Federal buildings and non-Federal buildings occupied by the Federal government during an air raid for any period of time from visibility by reason of internal or external illumination.

"Tell them," Roosevelt said, "that in buildings where they have to keep the work going to put something across the windows." 5

[1]*adulterants:* unnecessary ingredients that taint the purity of something.
[2]*mollify:* to soothe in temper; appease.

Simplify, simplify. Thoreau[3] said it, as we are so often reminded, and no American writer more consistently practiced what he preached. Open *Walden* to any page and you will find a man saying in a plain and orderly way what is on his mind: 6

> I went to the woods because I wished to live deliberately, to front only the essential facts of life, and see if I could not learn what it had to teach, and not, when I came to die, discover that I had not lived.

How can the rest of us achieve such enviable freedom from clutter? The answer is to clear our heads of clutter. Clear thinking becomes clear writing; one can't exist without the other. It's impossible for a muddy thinker to write good English. He may get away with it for a paragraph or two, but soon the reader will be lost, and there's no sin so grave, for the reader will not easily be lured back. 7

Who is this elusive creature, the reader? The reader is someone with an attention span of about 30 seconds—a person assailed by many forces competing for attention. At one time those forces were relatively few: newspapers, magazines, radio, spouse, children, pets. Today they also include a galaxy of electronic devices for receiving entertainment and information—television, VCRs, DVDs, CDs, video games, the Internet, e-mail, cell phones, BlackBerries, iPods—as well as a fitness program, a pool, a lawn, and that most potent of competitors, sleep. The man or woman snoozing in a chair with a magazine or a book is a person who was being given too much unnecessary trouble by the writer. 8

It won't do to say that the reader is too dumb or too lazy to keep pace with the train of thought. If the reader is lost, it's usually because the writer hasn't been careful enough. The carelessness can take any number of forms. Perhaps a sentence is so excessively cluttered that the reader, hacking through the verbiage, simply doesn't know what it means. Perhaps a sentence has been so shoddily constructed that the reader could read it in several ways. Perhaps the writer has switched pronouns in midsentence, or has switched tenses, so the reader loses track of who is talking or when the action took place. Perhaps Sentence B is not a logical sequel to Sentence A; the writer, in whose 9

[3]*Henry David Thoreau* (1817–1862): American essayist, poet, and philosopher activist. *Walden,* his masterwork, was published in 1854.

head the connection is clear, hasn't bothered to provide the missing link. Perhaps the writer has used a word incorrectly by not taking the trouble to look it up.

Faced with such obstacles, readers are at first tenacious. They blame themselves—they obviously missed something, and they go back over the mystifying sentence, or over the whole paragraph, piecing it out like an ancient rune, making guesses and moving on. But they won't do that for long. The writer is making them work too hard, and they will look for one who is better at the craft. 10

Writers must therefore constantly ask: what am I trying to say? Surprisingly often they don't know. Then they must look at what they have written and ask: have I said it? Is it clear to someone encountering the subject for the first time? If it's not, some fuzz has worked its way into the machinery. The clear writer is someone clearheaded enough to see this stuff for what it is: fuzz. 11

I don't mean that some people are born clearheaded and are therefore natural writers, whereas others are naturally fuzzy and will never write well. Thinking clearly is a conscious act that writers must force on themselves, as if they were working on any other project that requires logic: making a shopping list or doing an algebra problem. Good writing doesn't come naturally, though most people seem to think it does. Professional writers are constantly bearded[4] by people who say they'd like to "try a little writing sometime"—meaning when they retire from their real profession, like insurance or real estate, which is hard. Or they say, "I could write a book about that." I doubt it. 12

Writing is hard work. A clear sentence is no accident. Very few sentences come out right the first time, or even the third time. Remember this in moments of despair. If you find that writing is hard, it's because it *is* hard. 13

Thinking Critically about This Reading

How does Zinsser support his claim that "we are a society strangling in unnecessary words, circular constructions, pompous frills, and meaningless jargon" (paragraph 1)? What are the implications of his claim for writers in general and for you in particular?

[4]*bearded:* confronted boldly.

Questions for Study and Discussion

1. What exactly does Zinsser mean by "clutter" (1)? How does he believe we can free ourselves of clutter?
2. Identify the main idea in each of the thirteen paragraphs. How is each paragraph related to Zinsser's topic and purpose?
3. In what ways do paragraphs 4–6 serve to illustrate the main idea of paragraph 3? (Glossary: *Illustration*)
4. In paragraph 11, Zinsser says that writers must constantly ask themselves some questions. What are these questions, and why are they important?
5. How do Zinsser's first and last paragraphs serve to introduce and conclude his essay? (Glossary: *Beginnings and Endings*)
6. What is the relationship between thinking and writing for Zinsser?

Classroom Activity Using Paragraphs

Below you will find a passage from Zinsser's final manuscript of this chapter from the first edition of *On Writing Well.* Zinsser has included these manuscript pages showing his editing for clutter in every edition of his book because he believes they are instructive. He says, "Although they look like a first draft, they had already been rewritten and retyped—like almost every other page—four or five times. With each rewrite I try to make what I have written tighter, stronger, and more precise, eliminating every element that's not doing useful work. Then I go over it once more, reading it aloud, and am always amazed at how much clutter can still be cut. (In later editions I eliminated the sexist pronoun 'he' denoting 'the writer' and 'the reader.')"

Carefully study these manuscript pages and Zinsser's editing, and be prepared to discuss how the changes enhance his paragraphs' unity, coherence, and logical development.

is too dumb or too lazy to keep pace with the ~~writer's~~ train of thought. My sympathies are ~~entirely~~ with him. ~~He's not so dumb.~~ If the reader is lost, it is generally because the writer ~~of the article~~ has not been careful enough to keep him on the ~~proper~~ path.

This carelessness can take any number of ~~different~~ forms. Perhaps a sentence is so excessively ~~long and~~ cluttered that the reader, hacking his way through ~~all~~ the verbiage, simply doesn't know what it ~~the writer~~ means. Perhaps a sentence has been so shoddily constructed that the reader could read it in any of several ~~two or three different~~ ways. ~~He thinks he knows what the writer is trying to say, but he's not sure.~~ Perhaps the writer has switched pronouns in midsentence, or ~~perhaps he~~ has switched tenses, so the reader loses track of who is talking ~~to whom~~ or ~~exactly~~ when the action took place. Perhaps Sentence B is not a logical sequel to Sentence A -- the writer, in whose head the connection is ~~perfectly~~ clear, has not bothered to provide ~~given enough thought to providing~~ the missing link. Perhaps the writer has used an important word incorrectly by not taking the trouble to look it up. ~~and make sure.~~ He may think that "sanguine" and "sanguinary" mean the same thing, but ~~I can assure you that~~ the difference is a bloody big one. ~~to the reader.~~ The reader ~~He~~ can only ~~try to~~ infer ~~xxxx~~ (speaking of big differences) what the writer is trying to imply.

Faced with these ~~such a variety of~~ obstacles, the reader is at first a remarkably tenacious bird. He ~~tends to~~ blames himself. He obviously missed something, ~~he thinks,~~ and he goes back over the mystifying sentence, or over the whole paragraph, piecing it out like an ancient rune, making guesses and moving on. But he won't do this for long. ~~He will soon run out of patience.~~ The writer is making him work too hard, ~~-- harder than he should have to work --~~ and the reader will look for one ~~a writer~~ who is better at his craft.

The writer must therefore constantly ask himself: What am I trying to say? ~~in this sentence?~~ Surprisingly often, he doesn't know. ~~And~~ Then he must look at what he has ~~just~~ written and ask: Have I said it? Is it clear to someone encountering ~~who is coming upon~~ the subject for the first time? If it's not, ~~clear,~~ it is because some fuzz has worked its way into the machinery. The clear writer is a person ~~who is~~ clear-headed enough to see this stuff for what it is: fuzz.

I don't mean ~~to suggest~~ that some people are born clear-headed and are therefore natural writers, whereas others ~~other people~~ are naturally fuzzy and will ~~therefore~~ never write well. Thinking clearly is a ~~an entirely~~ conscious act that the writer must force ~~keep forcing~~ upon himself, just as if he were embarking ~~starting out~~ on any other ~~kind of~~ project that requires ~~calls for~~ logic: adding up a laundry list or doing an algebra problem. ~~or playing chess.~~ Good writing doesn't ~~just~~ come naturally, though most people obviously think it does. ~~it's as easy as walking.~~

Suggested Writing Assignments

1. If what Zinsser writes about clutter is an accurate assessment, we should easily be able to find numerous examples of clutter all around us. During the next few days, make a point of looking for clutter in the written materials you come across. Choose one example that you find—an article, an essay, a form letter, or a section from a textbook, for example—and write an extended analysis explaining how it might have been written more simply. Develop your paragraphs well, make sure they are coherent, and try not to "clutter" your own writing.
2. Using some of the ideas you explored in your journal entry for this selection, write a brief essay analyzing your need to simplify some aspect of your life. For example, are you involved in too many extracurricular activities, taking too many courses, working too many hours at an off-campus job, or not making sensible choices with regard to your social life?

Once Unique, Soon a Place Like Any Other

■ Abe Whaley

Abe Whaley was born John Abraham Whaley in Sevierville, Tennessee, in 1981. He received his BS degree in logistics in 2003 and his master's of public administration in 2007, both from the University of Tennessee. He is currently a doctoral student in public administration at the University of Tennessee. He has written a number of articles on environmental issues for regional magazines and newspapers. An avid outdoorsman, Whaley is interested in conservation and participates in a variety of recreational sports activities as well.

In the following essay, which first appeared in Newsweek *on November 14, 2005, Whaley laments the loss of natural beauty caused by poorly planned subdivisions built where generations of his family have lived. The essay was published three weeks after he submitted it with only a few words changed at the request of his* Newsweek *editors. "I need to lay some praise on my writing teachers for that," he says. As you read, notice how he has crafted his paragraphs and unified the sentences in them. Whaley's essay has generated a lot of discussion in his part of Tennessee, and he has been invited to a number of community forums that are trying to check "reckless development" in the area. "People are fed up, so things are beginning to change. It's happening all too slowly, however," he reports.*

Reflecting on What You Know

How well do you know the zoning laws in the area where you live? How easy is it for developers to build housing subdivisions in your town? Has the real estate development in your area always been in the best interests of the community in providing jobs and housing and also preserving its natural beauty?

I grew up in the mountains of East Tennessee, on a modest farm where we raised a lot of what we ate, watched sunsets on the porch, and had supper together every night. For nine generations, mine included, both 1 sides of my family have lived and died in the shadows of the surrounding peaks.

My formative years were spent listening to Papaw (my grandfather) saw away on an old fiddle and Dad flat-pick his six-string guitar as they taught me the songs of Southern Appalachia and handed down a centuries-old musical tradition. A great-great-great-great-great-grandfather of mine was baptized into the Forks of the Pigeon River Baptist Church in 1796, which he later pastored for thirty-one years—we are still faithful members, though the name has changed. No one ever really moves away from here, and no one ever used to move in. Lately, though, they've been coming in droves. 2

The Great Smoky Mountains National Park, where my family lived before 1933, and Dollywood, Dolly Parton's theme park, draw year-round crowds. New home construction has been climbing steadily for years, and the rental housing market, mostly overnight log-cabin outfits, has exploded. It seems that no ridge is too steep, no mountaintop too high, no creek too pristine to bulldoze and build on. 3

I haven't been home much since I graduated from high school six years ago. College, a "real" job, extended international travel, the Tennessee Air National Guard, and work on a master's degree have kept me pretty busy. As much as I love visiting, I hate the trip back. Every time I drive the road into town I see more ridges in the distance that have fallen to construction. 4

Do not misunderstand me, it is not the simple single-family homes that are so irritating; I have framed up quite a few of those over my summer breaks from school. What bothers me is the way developers feel the need to put a subdivision on the most beautiful piece of mountain farmland they can find. Of course, the farmers cannot be blamed much—a million-dollar buyout sounds a lot better than trying to make ends meet for another twenty harvests and then losing it all to the bank during their retirement years. But the land magnates, most of whom are from out of town, have no excuse. They wreak wholesale destruction on the surrounding mountaintops and ridge-lines as they build their rental cabins and condominiums. They ruin the views that make our piece of Southern Appalachia so enviable in the first place. 5

I traveled extensively in New Zealand last year, and I was amazed by the environmental ethos that seems to be shared by its government and citizens. I rarely saw mass development that went higher than halfway up the mountains that surrounded any given 6 town. The locals I talked to told me that most places had laws that limited construction. What a novel idea—to zone in such a way as to minimize the environmental havoc that developers can impose. Our planners and decision makers could use a lesson in that kind of logic. But so often government officials seem more interested in privately investing in land deals than publicly regulating them.

Those of us seeking to preserve the countryside in Tennessee 7 were dealt another blow by the Supreme Court's recent decision in *Kelo v. City of New London.* The court upheld the government's power of eminent domain, which allows it to take private land for public purpose. Unfortunately, the court ruled that public purpose can be interpreted as economic growth. The chairman of the Tennessee Valley Authority, which acquired most of its waterfront property through eminent domain years ago, has already stated that the fate of 181,000 acres of wild land set aside for natural-resource conservation is negotiable. This has developers licking their lips in anticipation as they dream of building houses on top of hiking trails. It is obvious that nothing is sacred. It scares me. It scares me a lot.

Though native Appalachians like me are gradually being outnum- 8 bered by newcomers, we remain tied to the land in a way outsiders will never understand. It provides for us physically, socially, spiritually, and emotionally. Without it, we lose our cultural identity and, ultimately, ourselves. This is not a new fight; it has raged in these mountains for generations as our land has been exploited again and again. For too long, we have suffered the effects of clear-cutting, strip mining, and unscrupulous land grabs by timber companies, coal companies, and even the federal government. Developers are simply the latest to try their hand at making a buck.

My home is fast becoming a place like many others in this coun- 9 try, homogenized and prepackaged. My roots are neither of those things, and the land I grew up on deserves something better than the reckless development now disgracing its rugged beauty.

Thinking Critically about This Reading

What relationship does Whaley see between reckless real estate development in his area and the loss of the cultural identity that he and his family have enjoyed since the eighteenth century? What exactly does he mean by "cultural identity"?

Questions for Study and Discussion

1. What is Whaley arguing for in this essay? (Glossary: *Argument*)
2. Choose any two of Whaley's paragraphs, and examine each one for paragraph integrity by asking the following questions (consult the Glossary for definitions of any unfamiliar terms):
   - Does the paragraph have a clear topic sentence?
   - Does the author develop the paragraph clearly and effectively?
   - Is the paragraph unified?
   - Is the paragraph coherent?

   Be prepared to discuss your evaluation of the two paragraphs.
3. What other activities, in addition to the building of subdivisions, have ruined the land in Whaley's part of Tennessee?
4. What did Whaley learn about land development in his travels to New Zealand?
5. Explain the importance of the U.S. Supreme Court decision in *Kelo v. City of New London* (paragraph 7) for Whaley's argument. (Glossary: *Evidence*)

Classroom Activity Using Paragraphs

Rearrange the following sentences to create an effective paragraph. Be ready to explain why you chose the order that you did.

1. PGA golfer Fred Divot learned the hard way what overtraining could do.
2. Divot's case is typical, and most researchers believe that too much repetition makes it difficult for the athlete to reduce left-hemisphere brain activity.
3. Athletes who overtrain find it very difficult to get in the flow.
4. "Two weeks later, all I could think about was mechanics, and I couldn't hit a fairway to save my life!"
5. Athletes think about mechanics (left hemisphere) rather than feel (right hemisphere), and they lose the ability to achieve peak performance.
6. "I was playing well, so I thought with a bit more practice, I could start winning on tour," Divot recalled.

Suggested Writing Assignments

1. The boom in new construction in the mountains of East Tennessee concerns Whaley because his hometown is beginning to feel "homogenized and prepackaged" (9) by "overnight log-cabin outfits" (3) and unscrupulous land developers. Construction like this is not unique to East Tennessee. The photograph on page 185, for example, shows the kind of new construction that dots our once remote mountaintops. In New Zealand, Whaley learned that land use needs to be regulated and zoned to control aggressive building. Write an essay in which you argue against land exploitation and reckless development and for the preservation of a ruggedly beautiful natural landscape. Argue for greater control of the land through stricter zoning laws and education of the public. What are the costs to a community when farmland disappears and mountaintops are developed recklessly? How can developers continue to earn profits while being sensitive to the needs of the people they are trying to serve? Pay attention to how the topic sentences in your paragraphs develop your thesis.
2. Whaley argues that America is being homogenized and that everywhere is beginning to look like everywhere else. Cities and towns throughout America are beginning to look alike because of an influx of malls and chain stores with similar appearance. Do we want to live in a country that is dotted with large cities surrounded by suburbs and towns that are interchangeable? Write an essay in which you argue against such homogenization as a threat to regional and cultural identities and, as Whaley says, ourselves. Build your essay on a strong thesis, and be sure your paragraphs are solidly constructed, linked by strong transitions, and clearly related to your thesis. (Glossary: *Transitions; Thesis*)

© Philip Wegener/Beateworks/Corbis.

"I Just Wanna Be Average"

■ Mike Rose

Born in Altoona, Pennsylvania, in 1944 to Italian American parents, Mike Rose moved to California in the early 1950s. A graduate of Loyola University in Los Angeles, Rose is now a professor at the UCLA Graduate School of Education and Information Studies. He has written a number of books and articles on language and literacy. His best-known book, Lives on the Boundary: The Struggles and Achievements of America's Underprepared, *was recognized by the National Council of Teachers of English with its highest award in 1989. More recently, he published* Possible Lives: The Promise of Public Education *(1995),* The Mind at Work: Valuing the Intelligence of the American Worker *(2004), and* An Open Language: Selected Writing on Literacy, Learning, and Opportunity *(2006).*

In the following selection from Lives on the Boundary, *Rose explains how his high school English teacher, Jack MacFarland, picked him up out of the doldrums of "scholastic indifference." As you read, notice that although his paragraphs are fairly lengthy, Rose never digresses from the main point of each.*

Reflecting on What You Know

Often our desire to get more out of high school and to go on to college can be traced back to the influence of a single teacher. Which teacher turned you on to learning? Describe what that person did to stimulate change in you.

Jack MacFarland couldn't have come into my life at a better time. My father was dead, and I had logged up too many years of scholastic indifference. Mr. MacFarland had a master's degree from Columbia and decided, at twenty-six, to find a little school and teach his heart out. He never took any credentialing courses, couldn't bear to, he said, so he had to find employment in a private system. He ended up at Our Lady of Mercy teaching five sections of senior English. He was a beatnik[1] who was born too late. His teeth were stained, he tucked his sorry 1

[1]*beatnik:* a person whose behavior, views, and style of dress are unconventional.

tie in between the third and fourth buttons of his shirt, and his pants were chronically wrinkled. At first, we couldn't believe this guy, thought he slept in his car. But within no time, he had us so startled with work that we didn't much worry about where he slept or if he slept at all. We wrote three or four essays a month. We read a book every two to three weeks, starting with the *Iliad*[2] and ending up with Hemingway. He gave us a quiz on the reading every other day. He brought a prep school curriculum to Mercy High.

MacFarland's lectures were crafted, and as he delivered them he would pace the room jiggling a piece of chalk in his cupped hand, using it to scribble on the board the names of all the writers and philosophers and plays and novels he was weaving into his discussion. He asked questions often, raised everything from Zeno's paradox to the repeated last line of Frost's "Stopping by Woods on a Snowy Evening." He slowly and carefully built up our knowledge of Western intellectual history—with facts, with connections, with speculations. We learned about Greek philosophy, about Dante, the Elizabethan world view, the Age of Reason, existentialism. He analyzed poems with us, had us reading sections from John Ciardi's *How Does a Poem Mean?*, making a potentially difficult book accessible with his own explanations. We gave oral reports on poems Ciardi didn't cover. We imitated the styles of Conrad, Hemingway, and *Time* magazine. We wrote and talked, wrote and talked. The man immersed us in language. 2

Even MacFarland's barbs were literary. If Jim Fitzsimmons, hung over and irritable, tried to smart-ass him, he'd rejoin[3] with a flourish that would spark the indomitable[4] Skip Madison—who'd lost his front teeth in a hapless tackle—to flick his tongue through the gap and opine, "good chop," drawing out the single "o" in stinging indictment. Jack MacFarland, this tobacco-stained intellectual, brandished linguistic weapons of a kind I hadn't encountered before. Here was this *egghead*, for God's sake, keeping some pretty difficult people in line. And from what I heard, Mike Dweetz and Steve Fusco and all the notorious Voc. Ed.[5] crowd settled down as well when MacFarland took the podium. Though a lot of guys groused in the schoolyard, it just seemed that giving trouble to this particular teacher was a silly thing to do. 3

[2]*Iliad:* an ancient Greek epic poem attributed to Homer.
[3]*rejoin:* respond sharply; counterattack.
[4]*indomitable:* impossible to subdue.
[5]*Voc. Ed.:* vocational education, training for a specific industry or trade.

Tomfoolery, not to mention assault, had no place in the world he was trying to create for us, and instinctively everyone knew that. If nothing else, we all recognized MacFarland's considerable intelligence and respected the hours he put into his work. It came to this: The troublemaker would look foolish rather than daring. Even Jim Fitzsimmons was reading *On the Road* and turning his incipient[6] alcoholism to literary ends.

There were some lives that were already beyond Jack MacFarland's ministrations,[7] but mine was not. I started reading again as I hadn't since elementary school. I would go into our gloomy little bedroom or sit at the dinner table while, on the television, Danny McShane was paralyzing Mr. Moto with the atomic drop, and work slowly back through *Heart of Darkness,* trying to catch the words in Conrad's sentences. I certainly was not MacFarland's best student; most of the other guys in College Prep, even my fellow slackers, had better backgrounds than I did. But I worked very hard, for MacFarland had hooked me. He tapped my old interest in reading and creating stories. He gave me a way to feel special by using my mind. And he provided a role model that wasn't shaped on physical prowess alone, and something inside me that I wasn't quite aware of responded to that. Jack MacFarland established a literacy club, to borrow a phrase of Frank Smith's, and invited me—invited all of us—to join. 4

There's been a good deal of research and speculation suggesting that the acknowledgment of school performance with extrinsic rewards—smiling faces, stars, numbers, grades—diminishes the intrinsic satisfaction children experience by engaging in reading or writing or problem solving. While it's certainly true that we've created an educational system that encourages our best and brightest to become cynical grade collectors and, in general, have developed an obsession with evaluation and assessment, I must tell you that venal[8] though it may have been, I loved getting good grades from MacFarland. I now know how subjective grades can be, but then they came tucked in the back of essays like bits of scientific data, some sort of spectroscopic readout that said, objectively and publicly, that I had made something of value. I suppose I'd been mediocre for too long and 5

[6]*incipient:* developing; starting to appear.
[7]*ministrations:* help; service.
[8]*venal:* unprincipled.

enjoyed a public redefinition. And I suppose the workings of my mind, such as they were, had been private for too long. My linguistic play moved into the world; like the intergalactic stories I told years before on Frank's berry-splattered truck bed, these papers with their circled, red B-pluses and A-minuses linked my mind to something outside it. I carried them around like a club emblem.

One day in the December of my senior year, Mr. MacFarland asked me where I was going to go to college. I hadn't thought much about it. Many of the students I teach today spent their last year in high school with a physics text in one hand and the Stanford catalog in the other, but I wasn't even aware of what "entrance requirements" were. My folks would say that they wanted me to go to college and be a doctor, but I don't know how seriously I ever took that; it seemed a sweet thing to say, a bit of supportive family chatter, like telling a gangly[9] daughter she's graceful. The reality of higher education wasn't in my scheme of things: No one in the family had gone to college; only two of my uncles had completed high school. I figured I'd get a night job and go to the local junior college because I knew that Snyder and Company were going there to play ball. But I hadn't even prepared for that. When I finally said, "I don't know," MacFarland looked down at me—I was seated in his office—and said, "Listen, you can write." 6

My grades stank. I had A's in biology and a handful of B's in a few English and social science classes. All the rest were C's—or worse. MacFarland said I would do well in his class and laid down the law about doing well in the others. Still, the record for my first three years wouldn't have been acceptable to any four-year school. To nobody's surprise, I was turned down flat by USC and UCLA. But Jack MacFarland was on the case. He had received his bachelor's degree from Loyola University, so he made calls to old professors and talked to somebody in admissions and wrote me a strong letter. Loyola finally accepted me as a probationary student. I would be on trial for the first year, and if I did okay, I would be granted regular status. MacFarland also intervened to get me a loan, for I could never have afforded a private college without it. Four more years of religion classes and four more years of boys at one school, girls at another. But at least I was going to college. Amazing. 7

[9]*gangly:* ungracefully tall and thin.

Thinking Critically about This Reading

Rose writes, "While it's certainly true that we've created an educational system that encourages our best and brightest to become cynical grade collectors and, in general, have developed an obsession with evaluation and assessment, I must tell you that venal though it may have been, I loved getting good grades from MacFarland" (paragraph 5). Why did Rose love getting good grades from his English teacher? Why did those grades mean something different coming from MacFarland?

Questions for Study and Discussion

1. Why do you think Rose chose the title "I Just Wanna Be Average"? (Glossary: *Title*) How does it relate to the essay?
2. Describe Jack MacFarland. How does his appearance contrast with his ability as a teacher?
3. Rose's paragraphs are long and full of information, but they are very coherent. Summarize the topic of each of the seven paragraphs in separate sentences.
4. How does Rose organize paragraph 2? How does he prepare the reader for the concluding sentence: "The man [MacFarland] immersed us in language"?
5. Analyze the transitions between paragraphs 2 and 3 and between paragraphs 3 and 4. (Glossary: *Transition*) What techniques does Rose use to smoothly introduce the reader to different aspects of his relationship with MacFarland?
6. Rose introduces the reader to some of his classmates, quickly establishes their personalities, and names them in full: Jim Fitzsimmons, Skip Madison, Mike Dweetz, Steve Fusco (3). Why does he do this? How does it help him describe MacFarland?
7. Why does Rose have difficulty getting into college? How does he finally make it?

Classroom Activity Using Paragraphs

Write a unified, coherent, and adequately developed paragraph using one of the following topic sentences. Be sure to select details that clearly demonstrate or support the general statement you choose. In a classroom discussion students should compare and discuss those paragraphs developed from the same topic sentences as a way to understand the potential for variety in developing a topic sentence.

1. It was the noisiest place I had ever visited.
2. I was terribly frightened.
3. Signs of the sanitation strike were evident everywhere.
4. It was the best meal I've ever eaten.
5. Even though we lost, our team earned an "A" for effort.

Suggested Writing Assignments

1. Describe how one of your teachers has influenced your life. Write an essay about the teacher using Rose's essay as a model. Make sure that each paragraph accomplishes a specific purpose and is coherent enough to be readily summarized.
2. Write an essay about the process you went through to get into college. Did you visit different schools? Did a parent or relative pressure you to go? Had you always wanted to go to college, or did you make the decision in high school, like Rose, or after high school? Did a particular teacher help you? Make sure to develop your paragraphs fully and to include effective transitions between paragraphs.

chapter **8**

Transitions

Transitions are words and phrases that are used to signal the relationships among ideas in an essay and to join the various parts of an essay together. Writers use transitions to relate ideas within sentences, between sentences, and between paragraphs. Perhaps the most common type of transition is the so-called transitional expression. Following is a list of transitional expressions categorized according to their functions.

Transitional Expressions
Addition and, again, too, also, in addition, further, furthermore, moreover, besides
Cause and Effect therefore, consequently, thus, accordingly, as a result, hence, then, so
Comparison similarly, likewise, by comparison
Concession to be sure, granted, of course, it is true, to tell the truth, certainly, with the exception of, although this may be true, even though, naturally
Contrast but, however, in contrast, on the contrary, on the other hand, yet, nevertheless, after all, in spite of
Example for example, for instance

Place
elsewhere, here, above, below, farther on, there, beyond, nearby, opposite to, around

Restatement
that is, as I have said, in other words, in simpler terms, to put it differently, simply stated

Sequence
first, second, third, next, finally

Summary
in conclusion, to conclude, to summarize, in brief, in short

Time
afterward, later, earlier, subsequently, at the same time, simultaneously, immediately, this time, until now, before, meanwhile, shortly, soon, currently, when, lately, in the meantime, formerly

Besides transitional expressions, there are two other important ways to make transitions: by using pronoun references and by repeating key words, phrases, and ideas. This paragraph begins with the phrase "Besides transitional expressions," which contains the transitional word *besides* and also repeats wording from the last sentence of the previous paragraph. Thus the reader knows that this discussion is moving toward a new but related idea. Repetition can also give a word or idea emphasis: "Foreigners look to America as a land of freedom. Freedom, however, is not something all Americans enjoy."

Pronoun references avoid monotonous repetition of nouns and phrases. Without pronouns, these two sentences are wordy and tiring to read: "Jim went to the concert, where he heard Beethoven's Ninth Symphony. Afterward, Jim bought a recording of the Ninth Symphony." A more graceful and readable passage results if two pronouns are substituted in the second sentence: "Afterward, he bought a recording of it." The second version has another advantage in that it is now more tightly related to the first sentence. The transition between the two sentences is smoother.

In the following example, notice how Rachel Carson uses transitional expressions, repetition of words and ideas, and pronoun references:

> Under primitive agricultural conditions the farmer had few insect problems. *These* arose with the intensification of agriculture—the devotion of immense acreages to a single crop. *Such a system* set the stage for explosive increases in specific insect populations. Single-crop farming does not take advantage of the principles by which nature works; *it* is agriculture as an engineer might conceive it to be. Nature has introduced great variety into the landscape, but man has displayed a passion for simplifying *it. Thus he* undoes the built-in checks and balances by which nature holds the species within bounds. One important natural *check* is a limit on the amount of suitable habitat for each species. *Obviously then,* an insect that lives on wheat can build up its population to much higher levels on a farm devoted to wheat than on one in which wheat is intermingled with other crops to which the insect is not adapted.
>
> *The same thing* happens in other situations. A generation or more ago, the towns of large areas of the United States lined their streets with the noble elm tree. *Now* the beauty *they* hopefully created is threatened with complete destruction as disease sweeps through the elms, carried by a beetle that would have only limited chance to build up large populations and to spread from tree to tree if the elms were only occasional trees in a richly diversified planting.
>
> –Rachel Carson

Pronoun reference (These) · *Repeated key idea* (Such a system) · *Pronoun reference* (it) · *Transitional expression; pronoun reference* (Thus he) · *Pronoun reference* (it) · *Repeated key word* (check) · *Transitional expression* (Obviously then) · *Repeated key idea* (The same thing) · *Transitional expression; pronoun reference* (Now, they)

Carson's transitions in this passage enhance its **coherence**—that quality of good writing that results when all sentences and paragraphs of an essay are effectively and naturally connected.

In the following four-paragraph sequence about a vegetarian's ordeal with her family at Thanksgiving each year, the writer uses transitions effectively to link one paragraph to another.

> The holiday that I dread the most is fast approaching. The relatives will gather to gossip and

bicker, the house will be filled with the smells of turkey, onions, giblets, and allspice, and I will be pursuing trivial conversations in the hope of avoiding any commentaries upon the state of my plate.

Reference to key idea in previous paragraph

Do not misunderstand me: I am not a scrooge. I enjoy the idea of Thanksgiving—the giving of thanks for blessings received in the past year and the opportunity to share an unhurried day with family and friends. The problem for me is that I am one of those freaky, misunderstood people who—as my family jokingly reminds me—eats "rabbit food." Because all traditional Western holidays revolve around food and more specifically around ham, turkey, lamb, or roast beef and their respective starchy accompaniments, it is no picnic for us vegetarians.

Repeated key word

The mention of the word *vegetarian* has, at various family get-togethers, caused my Great-Aunt Bertha to rant and rave for what seems like hours about those "liberal conspirators." Other relations cough or groan or simply stare, change the subject or reminisce about somebody they used to know who was "into that," and some proceed either to demand that I defend my position or try to talk me out of it. That is why I try to avoid the subject, but especially during the holidays.

Transitional time reference

Repeated key idea

In years past I have had about as many *successes as failures in steering comments about my food toward other topics.* Politics and religion are the easiest outs, guaranteed to immerse the family in a heated debate lasting until the loudest shouter has been abandoned amidst empty pie plates, wine corks, and rumpled linen napkins. I prefer, however, to use this tactic as a last resort. Holidays are supposed to be for relaxing.

–Mundy Wilson-Libby, student

On Being 17, Bright, and Unable to Read

■ **David Raymond**

David Raymond was born in 1959 in Connecticut. When the following article appeared in the New York Times *in 1976, Raymond was a junior in high school. In 1981, Raymond graduated from Curry College outside of Boston, one of the few colleges with learning-disability programs at the time. He and his family now live in Fairfield, Connecticut, where he works as a builder.*

In his essay, Raymond poignantly discusses the great difficulties he had with reading because of his dyslexia and the many problems he experienced in school as a result. As you read, pay attention to the simple and unassuming quality of the words he uses to convey his ideas and the way that naturalness of diction contributes to the essay's informal yet sincere tone. Notice how he transitions from one paragraph to the next with repeated words, repeated key ideas, and pronoun references.

Reflecting on What You Know

One of the fundamental skills that we are supposed to learn in school is how to read. How would you rate yourself as a reader? Would you like to be able to read better? How important is reading in your everyday life?

One day a substitute teacher picked me to read aloud from the textbook. When I told her "No, thank you," she came unhinged. She thought I was acting smart, and told me so. I kept calm, and that got her madder and madder. We must have spent 10 minutes trying to solve the problem, and finally she got so red in the face I thought she'd blow up. She told me she'd see me after class. 1

Maybe someone like me was a new thing for that teacher. But she wasn't new to me. I've been through scenes like that all my life. You see, 2 even though I'm 17 and a junior in high school, I can't read because I have dyslexia.[1] I'm told I read "at a fourth-grade level," but from where I sit, that's not reading. You can't know what that means unless you've been there. It's not easy to tell how it feels when you can't read your homework assignments or the newspaper or a menu in a restaurant or even notes from your own friends.

My family began to suspect I was having problems almost from the first day I started school. My father says my early years in school were the worst years of his life. They weren't so good for me, either. As I look back on it now, I can't find the words to express how bad it really was. I wanted to die. I'd come home from school screaming, "I'm dumb. I'm dumb—I wish I were dead!" 3

I guess I couldn't read anything at all then—not even my own name—and they tell me I didn't talk as good as other kids. But what I remember about those days is that I couldn't throw a ball where it was supposed to go, I couldn't learn to swim, and I wouldn't learn to ride a bike, because no matter what anyone told me, I knew I'd fail. 4

Sometimes my teachers would try to be encouraging. When I couldn't read the words on the board they'd say, "Come on, David, you know that word." Only I didn't. And it was embarrassing. I just felt dumb. And dumb was how the kids treated me. They'd make fun of me every chance they got, asking me to spell "cat" or something like that. Even if I knew how to spell it, I wouldn't; they'd only give me another word. Anyway, it was awful, because more than anything I wanted friends. On my birthday when I blew out the candles I didn't wish I could learn to read; what I wished for was that the kids would like me. 5

With the bad reports coming from school, and with me moaning about wanting to die and how everybody hated me, my parents began looking for help. That's when the testing started. The school tested me, the child-guidance center tested me, private psychiatrists tested me. Everybody knew something was wrong—especially me. 6

It didn't help much when they stuck a fancy name onto it. I couldn't pronounce it then—I was only in second grade—and I was ashamed to talk about it. Now it rolls off my tongue, because I've been living with it for a lot of years—dyslexia. 7

All through elementary school it wasn't easy. I was always having to do things that were "different," things the other kids didn't have to do. I had to go to a child psychiatrist, for instance. 8

[1]*dyslexia:* a learning disorder that impairs the ability to read.

One summer my family forced me to go to a camp for children with reading problems. I hated the idea, but the camp turned out pretty good, and I had a good time. I met a lot of kids who couldn't read and somehow that helped. The director of the camp said I had a higher I.Q. than 90 percent of the population. I didn't believe him. 9

About the worst thing I had to do in fifth and sixth grade was go to a special education class in another school in our town. A bus picked me up, and I didn't like that at all. The bus also picked up emotionally disturbed kids and retarded kids. It was like going to a school for the retarded. I always worried that someone I knew would see me on that bus. It was a relief to go to the regular junior high school. 10

Life began to change a little for me then, because I began to feel better about myself. I found the teachers cared; they had meetings about me and I worked harder for them for a while. I began to work on the potter's wheel, making vases and pots that the teachers said were pretty good. Also, I got a letter for being on the track team. I could always run pretty fast. 11

At high school the teachers are good and everyone is trying to help me. I've gotten honors some marking periods and I've won a letter on the cross-country team. Next quarter I think the school might hold a show of my pottery. I've got some friends. But there are still some embarrassing times. For instance, every time there is writing in the class, I get up and go to the special education room. Kids ask me where I go all the time. Sometimes I say, "to Mars." 12

Homework is a real problem. During free periods in school I go into the special ed room and staff members read assignments to me. When I get home my mother reads to me. Sometimes she reads an assignment into a tape recorder, and then I go into my room and listen to it. If we have a novel or something like that to read, she reads it out loud to me. Then I sit down with her and we do the assignment. She'll write, while I talk my answers to her. Lately I've taken to dictating into a tape recorder, and then someone—my father, a private tutor or my mother—types up what I've dictated. Whatever homework I do takes someone else's time, too. That makes me feel bad. 13

We had a big meeting in school the other day—eight of us, four from the guidance department, my private tutor, my parents and me. The subject was me. I said I wanted to go to college, and they told me about colleges that have facilities and staff to handle people like me. That's nice to hear. 14

As for what happens after college, I don't know and I'm worried 15
about that. How can I make a living if I can't read? Who will hire me? How will I fill out the application form? The only thing that gives me any courage is the fact that I've learned about well-known people who couldn't read or had other problems and still made it. Like Albert Einstein,[2] who didn't talk until he was 4 and flunked math. Like Leonardo da Vinci,[3] who everyone seems to think had dyslexia.

I've told this story because maybe some teacher will read it and go 16
easy on a kid in the classroom who has what I've got. Or maybe some parent will stop nagging his kid, and stop calling him lazy. Maybe he's not lazy or dumb. Maybe he just can't read and doesn't know what's wrong. Maybe he's scared, like I was.

Thinking Critically about This Reading

Raymond writes about having to take a bus to another school in his town in order to attend special education classes: "I always worried that someone I knew would see me on that bus" (paragraph 10). Why doesn't Raymond want his classmates to know that he attends special education classes? What does he do to keep his learning disability a secret?

Questions for Study and Discussion

1. Writers often use repeated words and phrases, transitional expressions, pronouns that refer to a specific antecedent, and repeated key ideas to connect one paragraph to another. What types of transitional devices does Raymond use in his essay? Cite specific examples.
2. Raymond uses many colloquial and idiomatic expressions, such as "she came unhinged" and "she got so red in the face I thought she'd blow up" (1). (Glossary: *Colloquial Expression*) Identify other examples of such diction, and tell how they affect your reaction to the essay.
3. How would you describe Raymond's tone?

---

[2]*Albert Einstein* (1879–1955): German-American physicist.

[3]*Leonardo da Vinci* (1452–1519): Italian painter, draftsman, sculptor, architect, and engineer.

4. What is dyslexia? Is it essential for an understanding of the essay that we know more about dyslexia than Raymond tells us? Explain.
5. What is Raymond's purpose? (Glossary: *Purpose*)
6. What does Raymond's story tell us about the importance of our early childhood experiences?

Classroom Activity Using Transitions

In *The New York Times Complete Manual of Home Repair,* Bernard Gladstone gives directions for applying blacktop sealer to a driveway. His directions appear below in scrambled order. First read all of Gladstone's twelve sentences carefully. Next, arrange the sentences in what seems to you to be the logical sequence. Finally, identify places where Gladstone has used transitional expressions, the repetition of words and ideas, and pronoun reference to give coherence to his paragraph.

1. A long-handled pushbroom or roofing brush is used to spread the coating evenly over the entire area.
2. Care should be taken to make certain the entire surface is uniformly wet, though puddles should be swept away if water collects in low spots.
3. Greasy areas and oil slicks should be scraped up, then scrubbed thoroughly with a detergent solution.
4. With most brands there are just three steps to follow.
5. In most cases one coat of sealer will be sufficient.
6. The application of blacktop sealer is best done on a day when the weather is dry and warm, preferably while the sun is shining on the surface.
7. This should not be applied until the first coat is completely dry.
8. First sweep the surface absolutely clean to remove all dust, dirt, and foreign material.
9. To simplify spreading and to ensure a good bond, the surface of the driveway should be wet down thoroughly by sprinkling with a hose.
10. However, for surfaces in poor condition a second coat may be required.
11. The blacktop sealer is next stirred thoroughly and poured on while the surface is still damp.

12. The sealer should be allowed to dry overnight (or longer if recommended by the manufacturer) before normal traffic is resumed.

Suggested Writing Assignments

1. After explaining his learning disability and how he plans to deal with it in college, Raymond goes on to say, "As for what happens after college, I don't know and I'm worried about that" (15). Write an essay in which you explain what worries you about life after college. Are you concerned about finding a job, paying off student loans, or moving away from friends and family, for example? Are you looking forward to living in "the real world," as so many college students call the postgraduation world? Why or why not?
2. Imagine that you and your friends have plans to go to a concert next weekend. However, you will not be able to attend because you have a research paper due the following Monday, and you haven't even chosen a topic yet. Write an e-mail in which you apologize to your friends and explain how you procrastinated. Make sure your e-mail is coherent and flows well by using transitional expressions to help readers follow what you did instead of working on your paper.

Becoming a Writer

■ Russell Baker

Russell Baker has had a long and distinguished career as a newspaper reporter and columnist. He was born in Morrisonville, Virginia, in 1925 and graduated from Johns Hopkins University in 1947. He got his first newspaper job with the Baltimore Sun *and moved to the* New York Times *in 1954, where he wrote the "Observer" column from 1962 to 1998. His columns have been collected in numerous books over the years. In 1979, he was awarded the Pulitzer Prize, journalism's highest award, as well as the George Polk Award for commentary. Baker's memoir,* Growing Up *(1983), also received a Pulitzer. His autobiographical follow-up,* The Good Times, *appeared in 1989. His other works include* Russell Baker's Book of American Humor *(1993);* Inventing the Truth: The Art and Craft of Memoir *(1998, with William Zinsser and Jill Ker Conway); and* Looking Back *(2002), a collection of Baker's essays for the* New York Review of Books. *From 1992 to 2004, he hosted the PBS television series* Exxon-Mobil Masterpiece Theater.

The following selection is from Growing Up. *As you read Baker's account of how he discovered his abilities as a writer, note how effectively he uses repetition of key words and ideas to achieve coherence and to emphasize his emotional responses to the events he describes.*

Reflecting on What You Know

Life is full of moments that change us, for better or worse, in major and minor ways. We decide what hobbies we like and dislike, whom we want to date and perhaps eventually marry, what we want to study in school, what career we eventually pursue. Identify an event that changed your life or helped you make an important decision. How did it clarify your situation? How might your life be different if the event had never happened?

The notion of becoming a writer had flickered off and on in my head . . . but it wasn't until my third year in high school that the possibility took hold. Until then I'd been bored by everything associated with English courses. I found English grammar dull and baffling. I hated the assignments to turn out "compositions," and went at them like heavy labor, turning out laden, lackluster paragraphs that were agonies for teachers to read and for me to write. The classics thrust on me to read seemed as deadening as chloroform.[1] 1

When our class was assigned to Mr. Fleagle for third-year English I anticipated another grim year in that dreariest of subjects. Mr. Fleagle was notorious among City students for dullness and inability to inspire. He was said to be stuffy, dull, and hopelessly out of date. To me he looked to be sixty or seventy and prim to a fault. He wore primly severe eyeglasses, his wavy hair was primly cut and primly combed. He wore prim vested suits with neckties blocked primly against the collar buttons of his primly starched white shirts. He had a primly pointed jaw, a primly straight nose, and a prim manner of speaking that was so correct, so gentlemanly, that he seemed a comic antique. 2

I anticipated a listless, unfruitful year with Mr. Fleagle and for a long time was not disappointed. We read *Macbeth*. Mr. Fleagle loved *Macbeth* and wanted us to love it too, but he lacked the gift of infecting others with his own passion. He tried to convey the murderous ferocity of Lady Macbeth one day by reading aloud the passage that concludes 3

> . . . I have given suck, and know
> How tender 'tis to love the babe that milks me.
> I would, while it was smiling in my face,
> Have plucked my nipple from his boneless gums . . .

The idea of prim Mr. Fleagle plucking his nipple from boneless gums was too much for the class. We burst into gasps of irrepressible[2] snickering. Mr. Fleagle stopped.

"There is nothing funny, boys, about giving suck to a babe. It is the—the very essence of motherhood, don't you see." 4

He constantly sprinkled his sentences with "don't you see." It wasn't a question but an exclamation of mild surprise at our ignorance. "Your pronoun needs an antecedent, don't you see," he would say, 5

---

[1]*chloroform:* a chemical that puts one to sleep.
[2]*irrepressible:* unable to be restrained or controlled.

very primly. "The purpose of the Porter's scene, boys, is to provide comic relief from the horror, don't you see."

Late in the year we tackled the informal essay. "The essay, don't you see, is the . . ." My mind went numb. Of all forms of writing, none seemed so boring as the essay. Naturally we would have to write informal essays. Mr. Fleagle distributed a homework sheet offering us a choice of topics. None was quite so simpleminded as "What I Did on My Summer Vacation," but most seemed to be almost as dull. I took the list home and dawdled until the night before the essay was due. Sprawled on the sofa, I finally faced up to the grim task, took the list out of my notebook, and scanned it. The topic on which my eye stopped was "The Art of Eating Spaghetti." 6

This title produced an extraordinary sequence of mental images. Surging up from the depths of memory came a vivid recollection of a night in Belleville when all of us were seated around the supper table—Uncle Allen, my mother, Uncle Charlie, Doris, Uncle Hal—and Aunt Pat served spaghetti for supper. Spaghetti was an exotic treat in those days. Neither Doris nor I had ever eaten spaghetti, and none of the adults had enough experience to be good at it. All the good humor of Uncle Allen's house reawoke in my mind as I recalled the laughing arguments we had that night about the socially respectable method for moving spaghetti from plate to mouth. 7

Suddenly I wanted to write about that, about the warmth and good feeling of it, but I wanted to put it down simply for my own joy, not for Mr. Fleagle. It was a moment I wanted to recapture and hold for myself. I wanted to relive the pleasure of an evening at New Street. To write it as I wanted, however, would violate all the rules of formal composition I'd learned in school, and Mr. Fleagle would surely give it a failing grade. Never mind. I would write something else for Mr. Fleagle after I had written this thing for myself. 8

When I finished it the night was half gone and there was no time left to compose a proper, respectable essay for Mr. Fleagle. There was no choice next morning but to turn in my private reminiscence of Belleville. Two days passed before Mr. Fleagle returned the graded papers, and he returned everyone's but mine. I was bracing myself for a command to report to Mr. Fleagle immediately after school for discipline when I saw him lift my paper from his desk and rap for the class's attention. 9

"Now, boys," he said, "I want to read you an essay. This is titled 'The Art of Eating Spaghetti.' " 10

And he started to read. My words! He was reading *my words* out loud to the entire class. What's more, the entire class was listening. Listening attentively. Then somebody laughed, then the entire class was laughing, and not in contempt and ridicule, but with open-hearted enjoyment. Even Mr. Fleagle stopped two or three times to repress a small prim smile. 11

I did my best to avoid showing pleasure, but what I was feeling was pure ecstasy at this startling demonstration that my words had the power to make people laugh. In the eleventh grade, at the eleventh hour as it were, I had discovered a calling. It was the happiest moment of my entire school career. When Mr. Fleagle finished he put the final seal on my happiness by saying, "Now that, boys, is an essay, don't you see. It's—don't you see—it's of the very essence of the essay, don't you see. Congratulations, Mr. Baker." 12

For the first time, light shone on a possibility. It wasn't a very heartening possibility, to be sure. Writing couldn't lead to a job after high school, and it was hardly honest work, but Mr. Fleagle had opened a door for me. After that I ranked Mr. Fleagle among the finest teachers in the school. 13

Thinking Critically about This Reading

In paragraph 11 Baker states, "And he started to read. My words! He was reading *my words* out loud to the entire class. What's more, the entire class was listening. Listening attentively." Why was this episode so key to Baker's decision to become a writer? Why did it lead him to rank "Mr. Fleagle among the finest teachers in the school" (13)?

Questions for Study and Discussion

1. Baker makes good use of transitional expressions, repetition of words and ideas, and pronoun references in paragraphs 1 and 2. Carefully reread the paragraphs, and identify where he employs these techniques, using the analysis of Carson's essay in the introduction to this chapter as a model.
2. Examine the transitions Baker uses between paragraphs from paragraph 4 to the end of the essay. Explain how these transitions work to make the paragraphs flow smoothly from one to another.

3. How does Baker describe his English teacher, Mr. Fleagle, in the second paragraph? (Glossary: *Description*) Why does he repeat the word *prim* throughout the paragraph? Why is the vivid description important to the essay as a whole? (Glossary: *Dominant Impression*)
4. Baker gives Mr. Fleagle an identifiable voice. What is ironic about what Mr. Fleagle says? (Glossary: *Irony*) In what way does this irony contribute to Baker's purpose? (Glossary: *Purpose*)
5. What does Baker write about in his informal essay for Mr. Fleagle? Why does he write about this subject? Why doesn't he want to turn the essay in?
6. What door does Mr. Fleagle open for Baker? Why is Baker reluctant to pursue the opportunity?

Classroom Activity Using Transitions

Read the following three paragraphs. Provide transitions between paragraphs so that the narrative flows smoothly.

> In the late 1950s, I got lost on a camping trip in the Canadian wilderness. My only thought was to head south, toward warmth and civilization. My perilous journey was exhausting: the cold sapped my strength, and there were few places to find shelter and rest.
>
> There I found friendly faces and a warm fire. As I built my strength, I tried to communicate with the villagers, but they did not understand me. I came to the conclusion that I could stay in the village and wait—perhaps forever—for help to come, or I could strike out on my own again.
>
> I heard a gurgling sound. It was running water. Running water! Spring was here at last. Perhaps I would survive after all. I picked up my pack, squared my shoulders, and marched, the afternoon sun a beautiful sight, still ahead, but starting to drift to my right.

Suggested Writing Assignments

1. Using as a model Baker's effort to write about eating spaghetti, write something from your own experience that you would like to record for yourself, not necessarily for the teacher. Don't worry about writing a formal essay. Simply use language with which

you are comfortable to convey why the event or experience is important to you.

2. Write an essay in which you describe how your perception of someone important in your life changed. How did you feel about the person at first? How do you feel now? What brought about the change? What impact did the transition have on you? Make sure your essay is coherent and flows well: use transitional expressions to help the reader follow the story of *your* transition.

The Magic of the Family Meal

■ **Nancy Gibbs**

Born in 1960 in New York City, Nancy Gibbs graduated with honors in history from Yale University in 1982. She continued her studies at Oxford University as a Marshall scholar, earning a master's degree in politics and philosophy in 1984. She went to work at Time *magazine in 1985 and became a feature writer in 1988. In 1991, she was named a senior editor and later became chief political writer. In that capacity, she wrote more than twenty cover stories about the 1996 and 2000 presidential campaigns and elections. In 2002,* Time *appointed her editor-at-large. In her years at* Time, *she has authored more than one hundred cover stories, including the one on 9/11 for which she received the National Magazine Award in 2002 and another entitled "Faith, God, and the Oval Office" about the role of religion in the 2004 George Bush–John Kerry presidential campaign. Most recently, Gibbs coauthored* Preacher and the Presidents: Billy Graham in the White House *(2007) with Michael Duffy.*

In "The Magic of the Family Meal," an essay first published in the June 12, 2006, issue of Time, *Gibbs reports on the current status of family dining in America and the ways that this dying tradition has shown a resurgence in recent years. Because research shows that children who eat with their parents are healthier, happier, and better students, Gibbs advises that families should "make meals together a priority." As you read Gibbs's essay, notice how she achieves unity and coherence by using repeated words and phrases, transitional expressions, pronouns with specific antecedents, and repeated key ideas to connect one paragraph to another.*

Reflecting on What You Know

What was dinnertime like in your house while you were growing up? How many times a week did you eat with your family? What activities and obligations made it difficult to eat together as a family? For you, what is the value of the so-called family meal?

Close your eyes and picture Family Dinner. June Cleaver is in an apron and pearls, Ward in a sweater and tie. The napkins are linen, the children are scrubbed, steam rises from the greenbean casserole, and even the dog listens intently to what is being said. This is where the tribe comes to transmit wisdom, embed expectations, confess, conspire, forgive, repair. The idealized version is as close to a regular worship service, with its litanies and lessons and blessings, as a family gets outside a sanctuary. 1

That ideal runs so strong and so deep in our culture and psyche that when experts talk about the value of family dinners, they may leave aside the clutter of contradictions. Just because we eat together does not mean we eat right: Domino's alone delivers a million pizzas on an average day. Just because we are sitting together doesn't mean we have anything to say: children bicker and fidget and daydream; parents stew over the remains of the day. Often the richest conversations, the moments of genuine intimacy, take place somewhere else, in the car, say, on the way back from soccer at dusk, when the low light and lack of eye contact allow secrets to surface. 2

Yet for all that, there is something about a shared meal—not some holiday blowout, not once in a while but regularly, reliably—that anchors a family even on nights when the food is fast and the talk cheap and everyone has someplace else they'd rather be. And on those evenings when the mood is right and the family lingers, caught up in an idea or an argument explored in a shared safe place where no one is stupid or shy or ashamed, you get a glimpse of the power of this habit and why social scientists say such communion acts as a kind of vaccine, protecting kids from all manner of harm. 3

In fact, it's the experts in adolescent development who wax most emphatic about the value of family meals, for it's in the teenage years that this daily investment pays some of its biggest dividends. Studies show that the more often families eat together, the less likely kids are to smoke, drink, do drugs, get depressed, develop eating disorders, and consider suicide, and the more likely they are to do well in school, delay having sex, eat their vegetables, learn big words, and know which fork to use. "If it were just about food, we would squirt it into their mouths with a tube," says Robin Fox, an anthropologist who teaches at Rutgers University in New Jersey, about the mysterious way that family dinner engraves our souls. "A meal is about civilizing children. It's about teaching them to be a member of their culture." 4

The most probing study of family eating patterns was published last year by the National Center on Addiction and Substance Abuse (CASA) at Columbia University and reflects nearly a decade's worth of data gathering. The researchers found essentially that family dinner gets better with practice; the less often a family eats together, the worse the experience is likely to be, the less healthy the food, and the more meager the talk. Among those who eat together three or fewer times a week, 45 percent say the TV is on during meals (as opposed to 37 percent of all households), and nearly one-third say there isn't much conversation. Such kids are also more than twice as likely as those who have frequent family meals to say there is a great deal of tension among family members, and they are much less likely to think their parents are proud of them. 5

The older that kids are, the more they may need this protected time together, but the less likely they are to get it. Although a majority of twelve-year-olds in the CASA study said they had dinner with a parent seven nights a week, only a quarter of seventeen-year-olds did. Researchers have found all kinds of intriguing educational and ethnic patterns. The families with the least educated parents, for example, eat together the most; parents with less than a high school education share more meals with their kids than do parents with high school diplomas or college degrees. That may end up acting as a generational corrective; kids who eat most often with their parents are 40 percent more likely to say they get mainly A's and B's in school than kids who have two or fewer family dinners a week. Foreign-born kids are much more likely to eat with their parents. When researchers looked at ethnic and racial breakdowns, they found that more than half of Hispanic teens ate with a parent at least six times a week, in contrast to 40 percent of black teens and 39 percent of whites. 6

Back in the really olden days, dinner was seldom a ceremonial event for U.S. families. Only the very wealthy had a separate dining room. For most, meals were informal, a kind of rolling refueling; often only the men sat down. Not until the mid-nineteenth century did the day acquire its middle-class rhythms and rituals; a proper dining room became a Victorian aspiration. When children were eight or nine, they were allowed to join the adults at the table for instruction in proper etiquette. By the turn of the century, restaurants had appeared to cater to clerical workers, and in time, eating out became a recreational sport. Family dinner in the Norman Rockwell mode 7 had taken hold by the 1950s: Mom cooked, Dad carved, son cleared, daughter did the dishes.

All kinds of social and economic and technological factors then conspired to shred that tidy picture to the point that the frequency of family dining fell about a third over the next thirty years. With both parents working and the kids shuttling between sports practices or attached to their screens at home, finding a time for everyone to sit around the same table, eating the same food and listening to one another, became a quaint kind of luxury. Meanwhile, the message embedded in the microwave was that time spent standing in front of a stove was time wasted. 8

But something precious was lost, anthropologist Fox argues, when cooking came to be cast as drudgery and meals as discretionary. "Making food is a sacred event," he says. "It's so absolutely central—far more central than sex. You can keep a population going by having sex once a year, but you have to eat three times a day." Food comes so easily to us now, he says, that we have lost a sense of its significance. When we had to grow the corn and fight off predators, meals included a serving of gratitude. "It's like the American Indians. When they killed a deer, they said a prayer over it," says Fox. "That is civilization. It is an act of politeness over food. Fast food has killed this. We have reduced eating to sitting alone and shoveling it in. There is no ceremony in it." 9

Or at least there wasn't for many families until researchers in the 1980s began looking at the data and doing all kinds of regression analyses that showed how a shared pot roast could contribute to kids' success and health. What the studies could not prove was what is cause and what is effect. Researchers speculate that maybe kids who eat a lot of family meals have less unsupervised time and thus less chance to get into trouble. Families who make meals a priority also tend to spend more time on reading for pleasure and homework. A whole basket of values and habits, of which a common mealtime is only one, may work together to ground kids. But it's a bellwether, and baby boomers who won't listen to their instincts will often listen to the experts: the 2005 CASA study found that the number of adolescents eating with their family most nights has increased 23 percent since 1998. 10

That rise may also reflect a deliberate public-education campaign, including public-service announcements on TV Land and Nick at Nite that are designed to convince families that it's worth some 11 inconvenience or compromise to make meals together a priority. The enemies here are laziness and leniency: "We're talking about a contemporary style of parenting, particularly in the middle class, that is overindulgent of children," argues William Doherty, a professor of family social science at the University of Minnesota at Minneapolis and author of *The Intentional Family: Simple Rituals to Strengthen Family Ties.* "It treats them as customers who need to be pleased." By that, he means the willingness of parents to let dinner be an individual improvisation—no routine, no rules, leave the television on, everyone eats what they want, teenagers take a plate to their room so they can keep IMing their friends.

The food-court mentality—Johnny eats a burrito, Dad has a burger, and Mom picks pasta—comes at a cost. Little humans often resist new tastes; they need some nudging away from the salt and fat and toward the fruits and fiber. A study in the *Archives of Family Medicine* found that more family meals tends to mean less soda and fried food and far more fruits and vegetables. 12

Beyond promoting balance and variety in kids' diets, meals together send the message that citizenship in a family entails certain standards beyond individual whims. This is where a family builds its identity and culture. Legends are passed down, jokes rendered, eventually the wider world examined through the lens of a family's values. In addition, younger kids pick up vocabulary and a sense of how conversation is structured. They hear how a problem is solved, learn to listen to other people's concerns, and respect their tastes. "A meal is about sharing," says Doherty. "I see this trend where parents are preparing different meals for each kid, and it takes away from that. The sharing is the compromise. Not everyone gets their ideal menu every night." 13

Doherty heard from a YMCA camp counselor about the number of kids who arrive with a list of foods they won't eat and who require basic instruction from counselors on how to share a meal. "They have to teach them how to pass food around and serve each other. The kids have to learn how to eat what's there. And they have to learn how to remain seated until everyone else is done." The University of Kansas and Michigan State offer students coaching on how to handle a business lunch, including what to do about food they don't like ("Eat it anyway") and how to pass the salt and pepper ("They're married. They never take separate vacations"). 14

When parents say their older kids are too busy or resistant to come to the table the way they did when they were seven, the dinner 15 evangelists produce evidence to the contrary. The CASA study found that a majority of teens who ate three or fewer meals a week with their families wished they did so more often. Parents sometimes seem a little too eager to be rejected by their teenage sons and daughters, suggests Miriam Weinstein, a freelance journalist who wrote *The Surprising Power of Family Meals.* "We've sold ourselves on the idea that teenagers are obviously sick of their families, that they're bonded to their peer group," she says. "We've taken it to an extreme. We've taken it to mean that a teenager has no need for his family. And that's just not true." She scolds parents who blame their kids for undermining mealtime when the adults are coconspirators. "It's become a badge of honor to say, 'I have no time. I am so busy,'" she says. "But we make a lot of choices, and we have a lot more discretion than we give ourselves credit for," she says. Parents may be undervaluing themselves when they conclude that sending kids off to every conceivable extracurricular activity is a better use of time than an hour spent around a table, just talking to Mom and Dad.

The family-meal crusaders offer lots of advice to parents seeking 16
to recenter their household on the dinner table. Groups like Ready, Set, Relax!, based in Ridgewood, New Jersey, have dispensed hundreds of kits to towns from Kentucky to California, coaching communities on how to fight overscheduling and carve out family downtime. More schools are offering basic cooking instruction. It turns out that when kids help prepare a meal, they are much more likely to eat it, and it's a useful skill that seems to build self-esteem. Research on family meals does not explore whether it makes a difference if dinner is with two parents or one or even whether the meal needs to be dinner. For families whose schedules make evenings together a challenge, breakfast or lunch may have the same value. So pull up some chairs. Lose the TV. Let the phone go unanswered. And see where the moment takes you.

Thinking Critically about This Reading

In paragraph 6, Gibbs states that "researchers have found [that] all kinds of intriguing educational and ethnic patterns" surround family dining. Did any of the statistical patterns cited in that paragraph surprise you? How well do these statistical findings fit your own experiences and observations? What conclusions, if any, can you draw from them?

Questions for Study and Discussion

1. According to Gibbs, what happens at the "idealized" family dinner? What do you think she means when she says, "The idealized version is as close to a regular worship service, with its litanies and lessons and blessings, as a family gets outside a sanctuary" (paragraph 1)?
2. What are the dividends for teenagers who grow up in a family that eats together? In what ways do family dinners act "as a kind of vaccine, protecting kids from all manner of harm"?
3. Do you agree with Gibbs when she says, "The older that kids are, the more they may need this protected time [family meals] together" (6)? Explain why or why not.
4. Gibbs cites a number of surveys, studies, and experts in her essay to both explain and support the points she makes. Which information did you find most interesting? Most convincing?
5. Identify the strategies that Gibbs uses to transition between paragraphs 1 and 2, 7 and 8, 8 and 9, 10 and 11, 11 and 12, and 12 and 13. How does each strategy work? Explain.
6. What cultural factors during the 1960s, 1970s, and 1980s undermined and helped destroy the ritual of family dining? According to Gibbs, what has happened since then to reinvigorate the idea of family meals?
7. According to Robin Fox, with the advent of fast food "we have reduced eating to sitting alone and shoveling it in. There is no ceremony in it" (9). What nutritional, social, and family values does a "shared pot roast" offer children? Do you think "it's worth some inconvenience or compromise to make meals together a priority" (11)? Explain.

Classroom Activity Using Transitions

The following sentences, which make up the first paragraph of E. B. White's essay "Once More to the Lake," have been rearranged. Place the sentences in what seems to you to be a coherent sequence by relying on language signals like transitions, repeated words, pronouns, and temporal references. Be prepared to explain your reasons for the placement of each sentence.

1. I have since become a salt-water man, but sometimes in summer there are days when the restlessness of the tides and the fearful cold of the sea water and the incessant wind which blows across the afternoon and into the evening make me wish for the placidity of a lake in the woods.
2. We all got ringworm from some kittens and had to rub Pond's Extract on our arms and legs night and morning, and my father rolled over in a canoe with all his clothes on; but outside of that the vacation was a success and from then on none of us ever thought there was any place in the world like that lake in Maine.
3. A few weeks ago this feeling got so strong I bought myself a couple of bass hooks and a spinner and returned to the lake where we used to go for a week's fishing and to revisit old haunts.
4. One summer, along about 1904, my father rented a camp on a lake in Maine and took us all there for the month of August.
5. We returned there summer after summer—always on August 1st for one month.

Suggested Writing Assignments

1. In paragraph 4, Gibbs quotes anthropologist Robin Fox: "A meal is about civilizing children. It's about teaching them to be a member of their culture." What exactly is Fox claiming here? What do children learn from eating meals with their family on a regular basis? Write an essay in which you agree or disagree with Fox's claim. Be sure to use examples from your own family experiences or observations of other families to illustrate and support your position.
2. Looking back on your own childhood and adolescence, how would you assess your family's mealtime experiences? Was mealtime in your house a family time, or did a "food-court mentality" prevail? Was mealtime a place where your family built "its identity and culture"? What did your parents do really well? What could they have done better? Based on your own experiences and observations, write an essay in which you offer advice to today's young parents. What insights can you offer parents to help them "recenter their household on the dinner table"?
3. From February 20 to March 13, 1943, during the height of World War II, the *Saturday Evening Post* published Norman

Rockwell's now famous "The Four Freedoms" series of paintings, which were inspired by President Franklin D. Roosevelt's speech of the same name. When Gibbs states that "family dinner in the Norman Rockwell mode had taken hold by the 1950s" (7), she's undoubtedly referring to Rockwell's *Freedom from Want* painting, also popularly known as *Thanksgiving Dinner*, that captured the standard for family dining in the postwar era. After viewing Rockwell's painting at www.normanrockwellvt.com/NewsletterIssues/FreedomfromWant.htm, consider the following photograph by Michael Elins that accompanied Gibbs's essay in *Time* magazine. What were your first impressions of each picture? What feelings or ideas about family meals do you think that Rockwell and Elins are trying to convey to viewers? Do these two pictures evoke feelings of a past era for you, or do you think they have something to offer us today? Write an essay in which you compare and contrast Rockwell's painting with Elin's photograph and discuss any insights into the value of family meals you gain from them.

chapter **9**

Effective Sentences

Each of the following paragraphs describes the city of Vancouver. Although the content of both paragraphs is essentially the same, the first paragraph is written in sentences of nearly the same length and pattern, and the second paragraph in sentences of varying length and pattern.

Unvaried Sentences

Water surrounds Vancouver on three sides. The snow-crowned Coast Mountains ring the city on the northeast. Vancouver has a floating quality of natural loveliness. There is a curved beach at English Bay. This beach is in the shape of a half moon. Residential high rises stand behind the beach. They are in pale tones of beige, blue, and ice-cream pink. Turn-of-the-century houses of painted wood frown upward at the glitter of office towers. Any urban glare is softened by folds of green lawns, flowers, fountains, and trees. Such landscaping appears to be unplanned. It links Vancouver to her ultimate treasure of greenness. That treasure is thousand-acre Stanley Park. Surrounding stretches of water dominate. They have image-evoking names like False Creek and Lost Lagoon. Sailboats and pleasure craft skim blithely across Burrard Inlet. Foreign freighters are out in English Bay. They await their turn to take on cargoes of grain.

Varied Sentences

Surrounded by water on three sides and ringed to the northeast by the snow-crowned Coast Mountains, Vancouver has a floating quality of natural loveliness. At English Bay, the half-moon curve of beach is backed by high rises in pale tones of beige, blue, and ice-cream pink. Turn-of-the-century houses of painted wood frown upward at the glitter of office towers. Yet any urban glare is quickly softened by folds of green lawns, flowers, fountains, and trees that

> in a seemingly unplanned fashion link Vancouver to her ultimate treasure of greenness—thousand-acre Stanley Park. And always it is the surrounding stretches of water that dominate, with their image-evoking names like False Creek and Lost Lagoon. Sailboats and pleasure craft skim blithely across Burrard Inlet, while out in English Bay foreign freighters await their turn to take on cargoes of grain.

The difference between these two paragraphs is dramatic. The first is monotonous because of the sameness of the sentences and because the ideas are not related to one another in a meaningful way. The second paragraph is much more interesting and readable; its sentences vary in length and are structured to clarify the relationships among the ideas. Sentence variety, an important aspect of all good writing, should not be used for its own sake but should express ideas precisely and emphasize the most important ideas within each sentence. Sentence variety includes the use of subordination, periodic and loose sentences, dramatically short sentences, active and passive voice, coordination, and parallelism.

SENTENCE VARIETY

Subordination

Subordination, the process of giving one idea less emphasis than another in a sentence, is one of the most important characteristics of an effective sentence and a mature prose style. Writers subordinate ideas by introducing them either with subordinating conjunctions (*because, if, as though, while, when, after, in order that*) or with relative pronouns (*that, which, who, whomever, what*). Subordination not only deemphasizes some ideas, but also highlights others that the writer feels are more important.

There is nothing about an idea—*any* idea—that automatically makes it primary or secondary in importance. The writer decides what to emphasize, and he or she may choose to emphasize the less profound or noteworthy of two ideas. Consider, for example, the following sentence: "Melissa was reading a detective story while the national election results were televised." Everyone, including the author of the sentence, knows that the national election is a more noteworthy event than Melissa's reading the detective story. But the sentence concerns Melissa, not the election, and so the fact that she was reading is stated in the main clause, while the election news is subordinated in a dependent clause.

Generally, writers place the ideas they consider important in main clauses, and other ideas go into dependent clauses. For example:

> When she was thirty years old, she made her first solo flight across the Atlantic.

> When she made her first solo flight across the Atlantic, she was thirty years old.

The first sentence emphasizes the solo flight; in the second, the emphasis is on the pilot's age.

Periodic and Loose Sentences

Another way to achieve emphasis is to place the most important words, phrases, and clauses at the beginning or end of a sentence. The ending is the most emphatic part of a sentence, the beginning is less emphatic, and the middle is the least emphatic of all. The two sentences about the pilot put the main clause at the end, achieving special emphasis. The same thing occurs in a much longer kind of sentence, called a *periodic sentence,* in which the main idea is placed at the end, closest to the period. Here is an example:

> On the afternoon of the first day of spring, when the gutters were still heaped high with Monday's snow but the sky itself had been swept clean, we put on our galoshes and walked up the sunny side of Fifth Avenue to Central Park.
>
> –John Updike

By holding the main clause back, Updike keeps his readers in suspense and so puts the most emphasis possible on his main idea.

A *loose sentence,* on the other hand, states its main idea at the beginning and then adds details in subsequent phrases and clauses. Rewritten as a loose sentence, Updike's sentence might read like this:

> We put on our galoshes and walked up the sunny side of Fifth Avenue to Central Park on the afternoon of the first day of spring, when the gutters were still heaped high with Monday's snow but the sky itself had been swept clean.

The main idea still gets plenty of emphasis, since it is contained in a main clause at the beginning of the sentence. A loose sentence resembles the way people talk: it flows naturally and is easy to understand.

Dramatically Short Sentences

Another way to create emphasis is to use a *dramatically short sentence*. Especially following a long and involved sentence, a short declarative sentence helps drive a point home. Here are two examples:

> The qualities that Barbie promotes (slimness, youth, and beauty) allow no tolerance of gray hair, wrinkles, sloping posture, or failing eyesight and hearing. Barbie's perfect body is eternal.
>
> –Danielle Kuykendall, student

> The executive suite on the thirty-fifth floor of the Columbia Broadcasting System skyscraper in Manhattan is a tasteful blend of dark wood paneling, expensive abstract paintings, thick carpets, and pleasing colors. It has the quiet look of power.
>
> –David Wise

Active and Passive Voice

Finally, since the subject of a sentence is automatically emphasized, writers may choose to use the *active voice* when they want to emphasize the doer of an action and the *passive voice* when they want to downplay or omit the doer completely. Here are two examples:

> High winds pushed our sailboat onto the rocks, where the force of the waves tore it to pieces.

> Our sailboat was pushed by high winds onto the rocks, where it was torn to pieces by the force of the waves.
>
> –Liz Coughlan, student

The first sentence emphasizes the natural forces that destroyed the boat, while the second sentence focuses attention on the boat itself. The passive voice may be useful in placing emphasis, but it has important disadvantages. As the examples show, and as the terms suggest, active-voice verbs are more vigorous and vivid than the same verbs in the passive voice. Then, too, some writers use the passive voice to hide or evade responsibility. "It has been decided" conceals who did the deciding, whereas "I have decided" makes all clear. So the passive voice should be used only when necessary—as it is in this sentence.

SENTENCE EMPHASIS

Coordination

Often a writer wants to place equal emphasis on several facts or ideas. One way to do this is to give each its own sentence. For example, consider these three sentences about golfer Lorena Ochoa.

> Lorena Ochoa selected her club. She lined up her shot. She chipped the ball to within a foot of the pin.

But a long series of short, simple sentences quickly becomes tedious. Many writers would combine these three sentences by using **coordination.** The coordinating conjunctions *and, but, or, nor, for, so,* and *yet* connect words, phrases, and clauses of equal importance:

> Lorena Ochoa selected her club, lined up her shot, *and* chipped the ball to within a foot of the pin.
>
> –Will Briggs, student

By coordinating three sentences into one, the writer makes the same words easier to read and also shows that Lopez's three actions are equally important parts of a single process.

Parallelism

When parts of a sentence are not only coordinated but also grammatically the same, they are parallel. **Parallelism** in a sentence is created by balancing a word with a word, a phrase with a phrase, or a clause with a clause. Here is a humorous example from the beginning of Mark Twain's *Adventures of Huckleberry Finn:*

> Persons attempting to find a motive in this narrative will be prosecuted; persons attempting to find a moral in it will be banished; persons attempting to find a plot in it will be shot.
>
> –Mark Twain

Parallelism is also often found in speeches. For example, in the last sentence of the Gettysburg Address, Lincoln proclaims his hope that "government of the people, by the people, for the people, shall not perish from the earth."

Childhood

■ Alice Walker

Alice Walker is a prolific writer of poetry, essays, and fiction and won the Pulitzer Prize for her novel The Color Purple. *She was born in Georgia in 1944, the youngest of eight children in a sharecropping family. She escaped a life of poverty and servitude by attending Spelman College in Georgia and then graduating from Sarah Lawrence College in New York. An African American activist and feminist, Walker has dealt with controversial subjects in her novels,* The Color Purple *(1982) and* Possessing the Secret of Joy *(1992) and in the nonfiction* Warrior Marks *(1993). Other widely acclaimed works by Walker include her collected poems,* Her Blue Body Everything We Know: Earthling Poems, 1965–1990 *(1991); a memoir entitled* The Same River Twice: Honoring the Difficult *(1996); a collection of essays,* Anything We Love Can Be Saved: A Writer's Activism *(1997); and a collection of stories,* The Way Forward Is with a Broken Heart *(2000). Walker's most recent work includes* Sent by Earth: A Message from the Grandmother Spirit after the Bombing of the World Trade Center and the Pentagon *(2001) and* Absolute Trust in the Goodness of the Earth: New Poems *(2003).*

In the following essay, Walker uses her considerable craft to build sentences about how she was introduced to the wonders of planting and harvesting when she was a little girl and how she passed on her love of the earth and her people to her daughter.

Reflecting on What You Know

Think about your childhood memories. Which pleasant memory recurs often and leads you to believe that it has a significance greater than your other memories? What might be the significance of that memory?

One evening my daughter came to pick me up from the country; I had been expecting her for several hours. Almost as soon as she came through the door I asked if she knew how potatoes look before 1 they are dug out of the ground. She wasn't sure. Then I will show you in the morning before we head back to the city, I told her.

I had begun to harvest my potato crop the day before. In the spring I planted five varieties: my favorite, Yellow Finn; Yukon Gold; Peruvian Purple; Irish white; and red new. Even though the summer had been chilly and there was morning shade from the large oak at the front of the garden, the potatoes came up quickly and developed into healthy plants. Jose, who helps me in the garden, had shoveled an extra collar of humus around each plant, and I was delighted as each of them began to bloom. It had been years since I planted potatoes. I planted them in the garden I'd previously devoted to corn, because I have a schedule that often means I am far away from my garden at just the time my corn becomes ripe. Having sped home to my garden three years in a row to a plot of overmatured, tasteless corn, I decided to plant potatoes instead, thinking the worst that could happen, if I was delayed elsewhere, would be a handful of potatoes nibbled by gophers or moles. 2

I had been dreading going back to the city, where I had more things to do than I cared to think about; I sat in the swing on the deck thinking hard about what would be my last supper in the country. I had bought some green peas from the roadside stand a few miles from my house, chard and kale were flourishing a few steps from my door, and I had brought up corn from a small hopeful planting in a lower garden. Tasting the corn, however, I discovered it had, as I'd feared, given up its sweetness and turned into starch. Then I remembered my potatoes! Grabbing a shovel, I went out to the garden and began to dig. The experience I had had digging the potatoes, before turning them into half of a delicious meal, was one I wanted my daughter to know. 3

After boiling, I ate my newly dug potatoes, several small Yellow Finns and two larger Peruvian Purples, with only a dressing of butter. Organic butter with a dash of sea salt—that reminded me of the butter my mother and grandmother used to make. As I ate the mouthwatering meal, I remembered them sitting patiently beside the brown or creamy white churn, moving the dasher up and down in a steady rhythmic motion until flecks of butter appeared at the top of the milk. These flecks grew until eventually there was enough butter to make a small mound. We owned a beautiful handcrafted butter press. It was sometimes my job to press its wooden carving of flowers into the hardening butter, making a cheerful and elegant design. 4

In the morning, just before packing the car for the ride to the city, I harvested an abundance of Chardonnay grapes, greenish silver and refreshingly sweet, a bucket of glistening eggplants, an armful of collards and chard and kale, some dark green and snake-like cucumbers, plus a small sack of figs and half a dozen late-summer peaches. Then I took my daughter out to the neat rows of potatoes, all beginning to turn brown. Using the shovel to scrape aside the dirt, I began to reveal, very slowly and carefully, the golden and purple potatoes that rested just beneath the plants. She was enchanted. It's just like . . . it's just like . . . she said. It's just like finding gold, I completed her thought. Yes! she said, her eyes wide. 5

Though my daughter is now thirty-one, her enthusiasm reminded me of my own when I was probably no more than three. My parents, exemplary farmers and producers of fine produce in garden and field, had enchanted me early in just this same way. As I scraped dirt aside from another potato plant and watched as my daughter began to fill her skirt with our treasure, I was taken back to a time when I was very young, perhaps too young even to speak. The very first memory I have is certainly preverbal; I was lifted up by my father or an older brother, very large and dark and shining men, and encouraged to pick red plums from a heavily bearing tree. The next is of going with my parents, in a farm wagon, to a watermelon patch that in memory seems to have been planted underneath pine trees. A farmer myself now, I realize this couldn't have been true. It is likely that to get to the watermelon patch we had to go through the pines. In any case, and perhaps this was preverbal as well, I remember the absolute wonder of rolling along in a creaky wooden wagon that was pulled by obedient if indifferent mules, arriving at a vast field, and being taken down and placed out of the way as my brothers and parents began to find watermelon after watermelon and to bring them back, apparently, as gifts for me! In a short time the wagon was filled with large green watermelons. And there were still dozens more left to grow larger, in the field! How had this happened? What miracle was this? 6

As soon as they finished filling the wagon, my father broke open a gigantic melon right on the spot. The "spot" being a handy boulder as broad as a table that happened to reside there, underneath the shady pines, beside the field. We were all given pieces of its delicious red and thirst-quenching heart. He then carefully, from my piece, removed all the glossy black seeds. If you eat one of these, he joked, poking at my protruding tummy, a watermelon just like this will grow inside you. 7

It will? My eyes were probably enormous. I must have looked shocked. 8

Everyone laughed. 9

If you put the seed into the ground, it will grow, said an older brother, who could never bear to see me deceived. That's how all of these watermelons came to be here. We planted them. 10

It seemed too wonderful for words. *Too incredible to be believed.* One thing seemed as astonishing as another. That a watermelon could grow inside me if I ate a seed, and that watermelons grew from seeds put in the ground! 11

When I think of my childhood at its best, it is of this magic that I think. Of having a family that daily worked with nature to produce the extraordinary, and yet they were all so casual about it, and never failed to find my wonderment amusing. Years later I would write poems and essays about the way growing up in the country seemed the best of all possible worlds, regardless of the hardships that made getting by year to year, especially for a family of color in the South half a century ago, a heroic affair. 12

Thinking Critically about This Reading

Walker places a lot of value on the "magic" of growing up in the country, particularly the ability of her family to "produce the extraordinary" and do it casually. If you grew up in the country, do you agree with Walker? If you grew up in a city or suburb, what form of magic did you encounter?

Questions for Study and Discussion

1. What is Walker's thesis in this essay? (Glossary: *Thesis*) Where does she give her thesis statement?
2. Analyze the sentences in the first four paragraphs. How would you describe Walker's use of sentence variety? Identify her very short sentences—those with eight or fewer words. What does each contribute to the essay?
3. Walker uses a very long sentence to begin paragraph 5. How effective is that sentence? Is it difficult to read? Explain.
4. Reread paragraph 12, noting Walker's sentence constructions. In what way does their construction reinforce Walker's content? Explain.

5. Why did Walker want to share with her daughter the experience of harvesting potatoes?
6. What does the similarity of Walker's and her daughter's responses to digging potatoes reveal about the significance of that activity for them?
7. How does Walker reveal that she is an experienced farmer?

Classroom Activity Using Effective Sentences

Rewrite the following paragraph, presenting the information in any order you choose. Use sentence variety and subordination, as discussed in the chapter introduction, to make the paragraph more interesting to read.

> When Billy saw the crime, he was in a grocery store buying hot dog buns for the barbecue he had scheduled for the next weekend. The crime was a burglary, and the criminal was someone you would never expect to see commit a crime. His basketball shoes squeaked as he ran away, and he looked no more than fifteen years old with a fresh, eager face that was the picture of innocence. Billy watched the youth steal a purse right off a woman's shoulder, and the bright sun reflected off the thief's forehead as he ran away, although the weather was quite chilly and had been for a week. The police officer who caught the thief tripped him and handcuffed him as Billy paid for the hot dog buns, got in his car, and drove away.

Suggested Writing Assignments

1. Alice Walker shares with her daughter the surprise and joy of harvesting the potatoes she has planted. The experience is a dual sharing—of each other's company and of nature's bounty through the harvest. In addition, the act of writing also allows Walker to share her experiences with readers. Write an essay about a similar experience—whether with a friend, a sibling, an aunt or uncle, or a parent—that brought you some new awareness or insight and also taught you something about the friendship and guidance offered to you. Perhaps someone taught you to swim, read to you, brought you to a special sporting event, consoled you, or celebrated one of your achievements. Think about the quality of your sentences as you draft your essay, and pay attention to their effectiveness and variety when you revise and edit.

2. Write a brief essay using one of the following sentences to focus and control the descriptive details you select. Place the sentence in the essay wherever it will have the greatest emphasis.
   a. I couldn't believe what I had just seen.
   b. The music stopped.
   c. It was broken glass.
   d. I started to sweat.
   e. She had convinced me.
   f. It was my turn to step forward.
   g. Now I understand.

Salvation

■ Langston Hughes

Born in Joplin, Missouri, Langston Hughes (1902–1967) became an important figure in the African American cultural movement of the 1920s known as the Harlem Renaissance. He wrote poetry, fiction, and plays and contributed columns to the New York Post *and an African American weekly, the* Chicago Defender. *He is best known for* The Weary Blues *(1926) and other books of poetry that express his racial pride, his familiarity with African American traditions, and his understanding of blues and jazz rhythms. In his memory, New York City designated his residence at 20 East 127th Street in Harlem as a landmark, and his street was renamed "Langston Hughes Place."*

In the following selection from his autobiography, The Big Sea *(1940), note how, for the sake of emphasis, Hughes varies the length and types of sentences he uses. The impact of the dramatically short sentence in paragraph 12, for instance, derives from the variety of sentences preceding it.*

Reflecting on What You Know

What role does religion play in your family? Do you consider yourself a religious person? Have you ever felt pressure from others to participate in religious activities? How did that make you feel?

I was saved from sin when I was going on thirteen. But not really saved. It happened like this. There was a big revival at my Auntie Reed's church. Every night for weeks there had been much preaching, singing, praying, and shouting, and some very hardened sinners had been brought to Christ, and the membership of the church had grown by leaps and bounds. Then just before the revival ended, they held a special meeting for children, "to bring the young lambs to the fold." My aunt spoke of it for days ahead. That night I was escorted to the front row and placed on the mourners' bench with all the other young sinners, who had not yet been brought to Jesus. 1

My aunt told me that when you were saved you saw a light, and something happened to you inside! And Jesus came into your life! And God was with you from then on! She said you could see and hear and feel Jesus in your soul. I believed her. I had heard a great many old people say the same thing and it seemed to me they ought to know. So I sat there calmly in the hot, crowded church, waiting for Jesus to come to me. 2

The preacher preached a wonderful rhythmical sermon, all moans and shouts and lonely cries and dire pictures of hell, and then he sang a song about the ninety and nine safe in the fold, but one little lamb was left out in the cold. Then he said: "Won't you come? Won't you come to Jesus? Young lambs, won't you come?" And he held out his arms to all us young sinners there on the mourners' bench. And the little girls cried. And some of them jumped up and went to Jesus right away. But most of us just sat there. 3

A great many old people came and knelt around us and prayed, old women with jet-black faces and braided hair, old men with work-gnarled hands. And the church sang a song about the lower lights are burning, some poor sinners to be saved. And the whole building rocked with prayer and song. 4

Still I kept waiting to *see* Jesus. 5

Finally all the young people had gone to the altar and were saved, but one boy and me. He was a rounder's son named Westley. Westley and I were surrounded by sisters and deacons praying. It was very hot in the church, and getting late now. Finally Westley said to me in a whisper: "God damn! I'm tired o' sitting here. Let's get up and be saved." So he got up and was saved. 6

Then I was left all alone on the mourners' bench. My aunt came and knelt at my knees and cried, while prayers and songs swirled all around me in the little church. The whole congregation prayed for me alone, in a mighty wail of moans and voices. And I kept waiting serenely for Jesus, waiting, waiting—but he didn't come. I wanted to see him, but nothing happened to me. Nothing! I wanted something to happen to me, but nothing happened. 7

I heard the songs and the minister saying: "Why don't you come? My dear child, why don't you come to Jesus? Jesus is waiting for you. He wants you. Why don't you come? Sister Reed, what is this child's name?" 8

"Langston," my aunt sobbed. 9

"Langston, why don't you come? Why don't you come and be saved? Oh, Lamb of God! Why don't you come?" 10

Now it was really getting late. I began to be ashamed of myself, holding everything up so long. I began to wonder what God thought about Westley, who certainly hadn't seen Jesus either, but who was now sitting proudly on the platform, swinging his knickerbockered legs and grinning down at me, surrounded by deacons and old women on their knees praying. God had not struck Westley dead for taking his name in vain or for lying in the temple. So I decided that maybe to save further trouble, I'd better lie, too, and say that Jesus had come, and get up and be saved. 11

So I got up. 12

Suddenly the whole room broke into a sea of shouting, as they saw me rise. Waves of rejoicing swept the place. Women leaped in the air. My aunt threw her arms around me. The minister took me by the hand and led me to the platform. 13

When things quieted down, in a hushed silence, punctuated by a few ecstatic "Amens," all the new young lambs were blessed in the name of God. Then joyous singing filled the room. 14

That night, for the last time in my life but one—for I was a big boy twelve years old—I cried. I cried, in bed alone, and couldn't stop. I buried my head under the quilts, but my aunt heard me. She woke up and told my uncle I was crying because the Holy Ghost had come into my life, and because I had seen Jesus. But I was really crying because I couldn't bear to tell her that I had lied, that I had deceived everybody in the church, that I hadn't seen Jesus, and that now I didn't believe there was a Jesus any more, since he didn't come to help me. 15

Thinking Critically about This Reading

Why does Hughes cry on the night of his being "saved"? What makes the story of his being saved so ironic?

Questions for Study and Discussion

1. What is salvation? Is it important to young Hughes that he be saved? Why does he expect to be saved at the revival meeting?
2. Hughes varies the length and structure of his sentences throughout the essay. How does this variety capture and reinforce the rhythms and drama of the evening's events? Explain.

3. What would be gained or lost if the essay began with the first two sentences combined as follows: "I was saved from sin when I was going on thirteen, but I was not really saved"?
4. Identify the coordinating conjunctions in paragraph 3. (Glossary: *Coordination*) Rewrite the paragraph without them. Compare your paragraph with the original, and explain what Hughes gains by using coordinating conjunctions.
5. Identify the subordinating conjunctions in paragraph 15. (Glossary: *Subordination*) What is it about the ideas in this last paragraph that makes it necessary for Hughes to use subordinating conjunctions?
6. How does Hughes's choice of words, or diction, help to establish a realistic atmosphere for a religious revival meeting? (Glossary: *Diction*)

Classroom Activity Using Effective Sentences

Using coordination or subordination, rewrite each set of short sentences as a single sentence. Here is an example:

ORIGINAL: This snow is good for Colorado's economy. Tourists are now flocking to ski resorts.

REVISED: This snow is good for Colorado's economy because tourists are now flocking to ski resorts.

1. I can take the 6:30 express train. I can catch the 7:00 bus.
2. Miriam worked on her research paper. She interviewed five people for the paper. She worked all weekend. She was tired.
3. Juan's new job kept him busy every day. He did not have time to work out at the gym for over a month.
4. The Statue of Liberty welcomes newcomers to America. It was a gift of the French government. It was completely restored for the nation's two hundredth birthday. It is over 120 years old.
5. Carla is tall. She is strong. She is a team player. She was the starting center on the basketball team.
6. Betsy loves Bach's music. She also likes Scott Joplin.

Suggested Writing Assignments

1. Like the young Hughes, we sometimes find ourselves in situations in which, for the sake of conformity, we do things we do not believe in. Consider one such experience you have had, and write an essay about it. What in human nature makes us act occasionally in ways that contradict our inner feelings? As you write, pay attention to your sentence variety.
2. Reread the introduction to this chapter. Then review one of the essays that you have written, paying attention to sentence structure. Recast sentences as necessary to make your writing more interesting and effective.

My House: Plain and Fantasy

■ Meghan Daum

Meghan Daum was born in California in 1970. She graduated from Vassar College and earned her MFA degree from Columbia University's School of the Arts. After living in New York for a few years, she moved to southeastern Nebraska in 1999 and wrote My Misspent Youth *(2001), a collection of essays, and the novel* The Quality of Life Report *(2003), a* New York Times *notable book in 2003. She has also written with verve, humor, and cultural insight many articles and essays that have been published in a variety of magazines, including the* New Yorker, Vogue, Self, Harper's Bazaar, *the* Village Voice, *and the* New York Times Book Review. *She has been called "one of the most celebrated nonfiction writers of her generation," and her entry into the literary world has reminded some of the appearance of noted essayist Joan Didion forty years earlier.*

In the following essay, which first appeared in the September/October 2001 issue of Metropolitan Home, *Daum describes her first home, its meaning for her, and the fantasies that it conjures for her. In the essay, she displays a dazzling variety of sentences, some very short and some quite long, but none as long as the opening sentence in* The Quality of Life Report, *which runs to a staggering 201 words with no loss of clarity or punch.*

Reflecting on What You Know

If you have lived in a number of places, which home is the one that has the most meaning for you and why? Perhaps its meaning relates to its presence as a physical structure, the memories of it that you still hold, the views it offered you, or its interior decoration.

This house is only the beginning. There will be others, and as much as I love this house, a hundred-year-old bungalow on a small farm in southeastern Nebraska, the future houses are what I see when 1

I close my eyes. They are fantasies that consume me, dwellings so real that I can actually spend hours solving hypothetical problems—what if the house couldn't sustain additional phone lines? What if the bed can't fit through the door? What if there's a body in the attic? I imagine a plantation style house reminiscent of Isaak Dineson's farm in Africa. I imagine a Stick Style house with a wrap-around verandah, a late Queen Anne with a molded brick chimney and polygonal turrets. It's as if my little bungalow created a monster, turned me from a humble apartment dweller into a person who will not rest until she finds Villa Exactly-What-I-Want, which, after all these other styles have been exhausted, is a stately High Victorian Italianate with bay windows and a cupola that looks out over the vast prairie (of which I will own no less than twenty acres).

The rooms of my fantasy house will be furnished sparsely yet impeccably. In the living room, nothing but a Victorian sofa, a turn-of-the-century Persian rug, and a single orchid in a vase. In the bedrooms nothing but antique iron beds with Egyptian cotton sheets. The walls are interrupted only by the occasional piece of original art. The woodwork is gleamingly preserved. The pine floors stretch into the bathrooms and the kitchen, where all the appliances date from the 1930s, though they're in perfect working condition. The cupola, with its widow's walk and towering windows on all sides, is where I will write. I will see twenty miles in every direction. I will have nothing in that room but a simple desk and a laptop computer. When no one else is home and I'm working late at night, the desk lamp and the glow from computer screen will make the cupola glow like a low, harvest moon over the prairie. Coyotes will howl at it. Biplanes bringing visitors will use it as a beacon. I will wear a crepe-de-chine robe and velvet mules and drink gin sours from an Old Fashioned glass. Everything I write in this room will win the Pulitzer Prize. 2

But back to my bungalow, since it's where I live now. It's one story, about one thousand square feet, has two bedrooms, a sagging porch, and old telephone cables that won't support more than two phone lines. The basement has a dirt floor and ever since the telephone man told me that mice had chewed through all the wires I've refused to go down there. (My greatest fear is that I'll be sucked up by a tornado because I'm scared of the basement.) The oven, which is circa 1967, broke down in the middle of cooking Thanksgiving turkey. Plywood has been glued over the crumbling plaster walls in the dining room, and some idiot has painted over the woodwork. 3

Still, it's a great first step. All things considered, my house is a showplace. Before moving in, I painted the dining room Barrister White and then Cool Sausalito before settling on Riverboat Cruise, a washed out turquoise that, when covering the plywood, creates a sort of rococo effect. A long-horned cow's skull (found, not bought) is mounted above the archway in the living room. Long white, sheer cotton curtains hang from the windows. Large pieces of stained glass cover the tops of two windows. On the front porch there's a rocking chair and a porch swing, where you can sit and drink coffee and watch the cows moseying in the pasture across the road. But this activity requires caution, because sitting on the swing carries with it the remote but not implausible possibility that the porch roof will collapse. 4

My house is kind of like an average looking woman in a spectacular designer outfit. It is upstaged by its scenery. With the miles of rolling hills to the north, the seven acres of horse pasture to the east, the five acres of natural grassland to the west, and the indescribably huge, frequently Biblical-looking sky that looms above it, the house doesn't have a prayer. In the designer outfit that is this homestead, the house is an undergarment, barely visible beneath the fine fabrics of the nature surrounding it. Which is as it should be. To live on this farm is to live in the sky and the grass as well as the house. It is to live in the barn, which has seven horse stalls and is actually bigger than the house. The barn is home to the horses, the dogs, the cat, and the barn swallows. When it's cold, the barn is where I go three times a day to break the ice that's formed in the water bowls and the stock tanks. This activity, which is only performed after putting on four layers of clothing, including a pair of Reebok acetate warm-up pants that I bought for $55 back when I lived in New York, is exactly the kind of thing that makes you not care about the fact that your porch is sagging because you are so glad that you have heat. And being glad for things like heat is exactly what living on a farm is all about. 5

Not only does this house have the distinction of being the first actual house I've occupied since I was a kid, it's the first place I've ever lived in with another person, not including the revolving door of actors and graduate students that shared my apartment in New York. I live on this farm with my significant other. And the fact that the house is the result of a joint effort, a comingling of tastes and chores and foods in the refrigerator, elevates it from mere house status to 6 being a real home. He is responsible for the cow's skull and the stained glass. He is responsible for mending the fences and mowing the lawn, which requires a tractor mower. He is the one who goes outside before dawn to feed the animals, which leaves me no right to complain about the midday ice-breaking sessions.

I am responsible for the room that serves as my office, which is 7
the low point of the entire spread. At least three quarters of the entire contents of my apartment in New York are crammed into this ten-by-twelve-foot room. My office is where this farm stops being a farm and begins to look like a cross between a college dorm room and the foreclosure auction of a bankrupt publishing company. My office is where the ugly things are kept, the computer and the stereo and stacks of bills and old sweatshirts for which there is no room in the bedroom closet. My office is home to no less than fifteen used FedEx envelopes that comprise my "filing system" since there is no room for filing cabinets. My office is where I spent 75 percent of my time, the other twenty-five being evenly divided between outdoor chores and the preparation of meals, which are eaten at the dining room table in front of the huge picture window that looks out onto miles of prairie grass and cattle pasture. Since my chair faces away from the window I have a habit during dinner of turning my head around and looking outside, as if the view were a member of the family. I don't want to miss anything it has to say.

That's why I want my cupola. I want to be able to see in every di- 8
rection, all the time, and not have to wear four layers of clothing while I'm doing it. That's why this house is just step one, the gateway drug to what is sure to be a lifelong addiction to old farmhouses in need of paint jobs and new support beams for the porch. But even though every drive in the country serves as a secret mission to find my next house—it could be around any curve, huge and dilapidated and crying out for a Victorian sofa and a single orchid, plus $30,000 of renovations—I'm not in any hurry to leave this house. I never really understood what it meant to come home until I experienced the particular joy of driving down my dark, gravel road at night and seeing the glow of my little house in the distance. No matter where I move, this will always be my first house. When I'm old and sitting in that cupola, I'll close my eyes and see the sagging porch, the turquoise painted plywood, the barn swallows dipping in and out of the rafters. No fantasy, no matter how splendidly realized, can take the place of your first love. No Italianate mansion will be like this place, the first place, the house that made me fall in love with houses.

Thinking Critically about This Reading

Do you think that Daum's excitement about owning her first home is what most homeowners feel, or is it overly romanticized? Assuming that you do not yet own a home, do you see yourself one day responding to a house as Daum has?

Questions for Study and Discussion

1. What is Daum's thesis? (Glossary: *Thesis*) Where does she present her thesis?
2. Identify several examples of parallelism in paragraphs 1 and 7. (Glossary: *Parallelism*) What is she emphasizing by using parallelism? (Glossary: *Emphasis*)
3. Identify several sentence fragments in paragraph 2. Why are they fragments? What does the author achieve by using them rather than complete sentences?
4. Identify Daum's use of the passive voice in paragraph 2. How does the passive voice serve her purpose?
5. In paragraph 5, Daum's third sentence is a periodic sentence. Why does that construction make sense given the construction of the first two sentences in the paragraph?
6. Where has Daum used subordination, and where has she used coordination? (Glossary: *Subordination; Coordination*). Give an example of each construction, and explain how it works.

Classroom Activity Using Effective Sentences

Rewrite the following sets of sentences to combine short, simple sentences and to reduce repetition wherever possible. Here is an example:

ORIGINAL: Angelo's team won the championship. He pitched a two-hitter. He struck out ten batters. He hit a home run.

REVISED: Angelo's team won the championship because he pitched a two-hitter, struck out ten batters, and hit a home run.

1. Bonnie wore shorts. The shorts were red. The shorts had pockets.
2. The deer hunter awoke at 5 a.m. He ate a quick breakfast. The breakfast consisted of coffee, juice, and cereal. He was in the woods before the sun came up.

3. My grandparents played golf every weekend for years. Last year they stopped playing. They miss the game now.
4. Fly over any major city. Look out the airplane's window. You will be appalled at the number of tall smokestacks you will see.
5. It did not rain for over three months. Most crops in the region failed. Some farmers were on the brink of declaring bankruptcy.
6. Every weekday I go to work. I exercise. I shower and relax. I eat a light, low-fat dinner.

Suggested Writing Assignments

1. Most writers have a particular place in their homes where they write. It's usually a quiet place that is away from normal household activities and is comfortable enough to allow them to think, create, and do their best work. That place might be a dining room table, an alcove under a stairway, a room over a garage, or a bedroom. For these artists, trying to write in another location simply doesn't work. Daum describes her office in detail because she spends 75 percent of her time there and it's important to her as a writer. If you have a certain place where you usually write, describe it, and share with your readers why it works best for you. Have a clear purpose for your description, and use a variety of sentences to make your writing lively.
2. Have you ever dreamed of owning something only to be disappointed when you followed through on that dream? For example, have you ever fantasized about taking a trip someplace only to be disappointed when you actually visited that place? Write a brief essay about how reality can sometimes fall short of our dreams. What if you dreamed of attending a particular college or university and it turned out to be unlike what you hoped it would be? Write an essay about an experience in which reality overpowers a dream. Be sure to use a variety of sentences—passive and active, subordinated and coordinated, loose and periodic—as well as sentences demonstrating parallelism to create an essay written with a lively and varied style.

Thirty-Eight Who Saw Murder Didn't Call Police

■ **Martin Gansberg**

Reporter Martin Gansberg (1920–1995) was born in Brooklyn, New York, and graduated from St. John's University. Gansberg was an experienced copy editor completing one of his first reporting assignments when he wrote the following essay for the New York Times *in 1964, two weeks after the events he poignantly narrates. Once you've finished reading the essay, you will understand why it has been reprinted often and why the name Kitty Genovese is still invoked whenever questions of public apathy arise.*

Notice how Gansberg uses dialogue effectively in this essay to emphasize his point. Pay attention to how he constructs the sentences that incorporate dialogue and to how subordination and coordination often determine where quoted material appears.

Reflecting on What You Know

Have you ever witnessed an accident or a crime? How did you react to the situation: did you come forward and testify, or did you choose not to get involved? Why do you think you reacted the way you did? How do you feel about your behavior?

For more than half an hour thirty-eight respectable, law-abiding citizens in Queens[1] watched a killer stalk and stab a woman in three separate attacks in Kew Gardens. 1

Twice their chatter and the sudden glow of their bedroom lights interrupted him and frightened him off. Each time he returned, sought her out, and stabbed her again. Not one person telephoned the police during the assault; one witness called after the woman was dead. 2

That was two weeks ago today. 3

Still shocked is Assistant Chief Inspector Frederick M. Lussen, in charge of the borough's detectives and a veteran of twenty-five years of 4

[1]*Queens:* one of New York City's five boroughs.

homicide investigations. He can give a matter-of-fact recitation on many murders. But the Kew Gardens slaying baffles him—not because it is a murder, but because the "good people" failed to call the police.

"As we have reconstructed the crime," he said, "the assailant had 5
three chances to kill this woman during a thirty-five-minute period. He returned twice to complete the job. If we had been called when he first attacked, the woman might not be dead now."

This is what the police say happened beginning at 3:20 a.m. in 6
the staid, middle-class, tree-lined Austin Street area:

Twenty-eight-year-old Catherine Genovese, who was called Kitty 7
by almost everyone in the neighborhood, was returning home from her job as manager of a bar in Hollis. She parked her red Fiat in a lot adjacent to the Kew Gardens Long Island Rail Road Station, facing Mowbray Place. Like many residents of the neighborhood, she had parked there day after day since her arrival from Connecticut a year ago, although the railroad frowns on the practice.

She turned off the lights of her car, locked the door, and started to 8
walk the one hundred feet to the entrance of her apartment at 82-70 Austin Street, which is in a Tudor building, with stores in the first floor and apartments on the second.

The entrance to the apartment is in the rear of the building because 9
the front is rented to retail stores. At night the quiet neighborhood is shrouded in the slumbering darkness that marks most residential areas.

Miss Genovese noticed a man at the far end of the lot, near a 10
seven-story apartment house at 82-40 Austin Street. She halted. Then, nervously, she headed up Austin Street toward Lefferts Boulevard, where there is a call box to the 102nd Police Precinct in nearby Richmond Hill.

She got as far as a street light in front of a bookstore before 11
the man grabbed her. She screamed. Lights went on in the ten-story apartment house at 82-67 Austin Street, which faces the bookstore. Windows slid open and voices punctuated the early-morning stillness.

Miss Genovese screamed: "Oh, my God, he stabbed me! Please 12
help me! Please help me!"

From one of the upper windows in the apartment house, a man 13
called down: "Let that girl alone!"

The assailant looked up at him, shrugged, and walked down Austin 14
Street toward a white sedan parked a short distance away. Miss Genovese struggled to her feet.

Lights went out. The killer returned to Miss Genovese, now trying to make her way around the side of the building by the parking lot to get to her apartment. The assailant stabbed her again. 15

"I'm dying!" she shrieked. "I'm dying!" 16

Windows were opened again, and lights went on in many apartments. The assailant got into his car and drove away. Miss Genovese staggered to her feet. A city bus, Q-10, the Lefferts Boulevard line to Kennedy International Airport, passed. It was 3:35 a.m. 17

The assailant returned. By then, Miss Genovese had crawled to the back of the building, where the freshly painted brown doors to the apartment house held out hope for safety. The killer tried the first door; she wasn't there. At the second door, 82-62 Austin Street, he saw her slumped on the floor at the foot of the stairs. He stabbed her a third time—fatally. 18

It was 3:50 by the time the police received their first call, from a man who was a neighbor of Miss Genovese. In two minutes they were at the scene. The neighbor, a seventy-year-old woman, and another woman were the only persons on the street. Nobody else came forward. 19

The man explained that he had called the police after much deliberation. He had phoned a friend in Nassau County for advice and then he had crossed the roof of the building to the apartment of the elderly woman to get her to make the call. 20

"I didn't want to get involved," he sheepishly told the police. 21

Six days later, the police arrested Winston Moseley, a twenty-nine-year-old business-machine operator, and charged him with homicide. Moseley had no previous record. He is married, has two children and owns a home at 133-19 Sutter Avenue, South Ozone Park, Queens. On Wednesday, a court committed him to Kings County Hospital for psychiatric observation. 22

When questioned by the police, Moseley also said that he had slain Mrs. Annie May Johnson, twenty-four, of 146-12 133d Avenue, Jamaica, on February 29 and Barbara Kralik, fifteen, of 174-17 140th Avenue, Springfield Gardens, last July. In the Kralik case, the police are holding Alvin L. Mitchell, who is said to have confessed to that slaying. 23

The police stressed how simple it would have been to have gotten in touch with them. "A phone call," said one of the detectives, "would have done it." The police may be reached by dialing "O" for operator or SPring 7-3100.[2] 24

---

[2]*SPring 7-3100:* a mid-twentieth century phone number that used a combination of both letters (the *SP* of *spring*) and numbers.

Today witnesses from the neighborhood, which is made up of one-family homes in the $35,000 to $60,000 range with the exception of the two apartment houses near the railroad station, find it difficult to explain why they didn't call the police. 25

A housewife, knowingly if quite casually, said, "We thought it was a lovers' quarrel." A husband and wife both said, "Frankly, we were afraid." They seemed aware of the fact that events might have been different. A distraught woman, wiping her hands in her apron, said, "I didn't want my husband to get involved." 26

One couple, now willing to talk about that night, said they heard the first screams. The husband looked thoughtfully at the bookstore where the killer first grabbed Miss Genovese. 27

"We went to the window to see what was happening," he said, "but the light from our bedroom made it difficult to see the street." The wife, still apprehensive, added: "I put out the light and we were able to see better." 28

Asked why they hadn't called the police, she shrugged and replied: "I don't know." 29

A man peeked out from a slight opening in the doorway to his apartment and rattled off an account of the killer's second attack. Why hadn't he called the police at the time? "I was tired," he said without emotion. "I went back to bed." 30

It was 4:25 a.m. when the ambulance arrived to take the body of Miss Genovese. It drove off. "Then," a solemn police detective said, "the people came out." 31

Thinking Critically about This Reading

How does Gansberg reveal his attitude about the lack of response to the attack on Kitty Genovese, even though he writes in the third-person point of view and interjects no opinions of his own?

Questions for Study and Discussion

1. What is Gansberg's purpose? (Glossary: *Purpose*) What are the advantages or disadvantages in using narration to accomplish this purpose? Explain.
2. Where does the narrative actually begin? What is the function of the material that precedes the beginning of the narrative?

3. Analyze Gansberg's sentences in paragraphs 7–9. How does he use subordination to highlight what he believes is essential information? (Glossary: *Subordination*)
4. Gansberg uses a number of two- and three-word sentences in his narrative. Identify several of these sentences, and explain how they serve to punctuate and add drama to this story. Which short sentences have the greatest impact on you? Why?
5. Gansberg uses dialogue throughout his essay. (Glossary: *Dialogue*) How many people does he quote? What does he accomplish by using dialogue?
6. How would you describe Gansberg's tone? (Glossary: *Tone*) Is it appropriate for the story he narrates? Explain.
7. Reflect on Gansberg's ending. (Glossary: *Beginnings and Endings*) What would be lost or gained by adding a paragraph that analyzes the meaning of the narrative for readers?

Classroom Activity Using Effective Sentences

Repetition can be an effective writing device to emphasize important points and to enhance coherence. Unless it is handled carefully, however, it can often result in a tedious piece of writing. Rewrite the following paragraph, either eliminating repetition or reworking the repetitions to improve coherence and to emphasize important information.

> Daycare centers should be available to all women who work and have no one to care for their children. Daycare centers should not be available only to women who are raising their children alone or to families whose income is below the poverty level. All women who work should have available to them care for their children that is reliable, responsible, convenient, and does not cost an exorbitant amount. Women who work need and must demand more daycare centers. No woman should be prevented from working because of the lack of convenient and reliable facilities for child care.

Suggested Writing Assignments

1. Gansberg's essay is about public apathy and fear. What reasons did Kitty Genovese's neighbors give for not calling the police when they first heard her calls for help? How do these reasons reflect on human nature, particularly as it manifests itself in contemporary American society? Modeling your essay after Gansberg's, narrate another event or series of events you know about that

demonstrates either public involvement or public apathy. (Glossary: *Narration*)

2. It is common when using narration to tell about firsthand experience and to tell the story in the first person. (Glossary: *Narration; Point of View*) It is good practice, however, to try writing a narrative essay on something you don't know about firsthand but must learn about, much as a newspaper reporter gathers information for a story. For several days, be attentive to events occurring around you—in your neighborhood, school, community, region—events that would be appropriate for a narrative essay. Interview the principal characters involved in your story, take detailed notes, and then write your narration.
3. Both Gansberg's essay and the following cartoon illustrate how people often choose to let someone else take care of a situation instead of taking action themselves. Reflect on the essay and the cartoon, and write an essay in which you explore the reasons some people in dangerous or life-threatening situations choose to act while so many others do not. In your opinion, when should bystanders involve themselves in a situation such as the attack on Kitty Genovese? How involved should a bystander become? What advice do you think Gansberg would give? Why?

chapter **10**

Writing with Sources

Some of the writing that you do in college will be experiential (that is, based on your personal experiences), but many of your college assignments will ask you to do some research—to write with sources. Although most of us can do basic research—locate and evaluate print and online sources, take notes from those sources, and document those sources—we have not learned how to integrate these sources effectively and purposefully into our papers. (For more information on basic research and documentation practices, see the appendix, Writing a Research Paper, pp. 597–621.) Your purpose in writing with sources is not to present quotations that report what others have said about your topic. Your goal is to take ownership of your topic by analyzing, evaluating, and synthesizing the materials you have researched. By learning how to view the results of research from your own perspective, you can arrive at an informed opinion of your topic. In short, you become a participant in a conversation with your sources about your topic.

Each time that you introduce an outside source into your paper, be sure that you are using that source in a purposeful way. Outside sources can be used to

- support your thesis,
- support your points with statements from noted authorities,
- offer memorable wording of key terms or ideas,
- extend your ideas by introducing new information, and
- articulate opposing positions for you to argue against.

In this chapter, you will learn how to (1) integrate quotations, paraphrases, and summaries smoothly into the text of your paper using signal phrases and (2) avoid plagiarism when writing with sources.

INTEGRATE BORROWED MATERIAL INTO YOUR TEXT

Whenever you want to use borrowed material (such as a quotation, a paraphrase, or summary), your goal is to integrate these sources smoothly and logically and not disrupt the flow of your paper or confuse your readers. It is best to introduce borrowed material with a *signal phrase*, which alerts readers that borrowed information is about to be presented.

A signal phrase consists of at least the author's name and a verb (such as "Stephen King contends"). Signal phrases help readers follow your train of thought. When you integrate a quote, paraphrase, or summary into your paper, vary your signal phrases and choose verbs for the signal phrases that accurately convey the tone and intent of the writer you are citing. If a writer is arguing, use the verb *argues* (or *asserts, claims,* or *contends*); if a writer is contesting a particular position or fact, use the verb *contests* (or *denies, disputes, refutes,* or *rejects*). Verbs that are specific to the situation in your paper will bring your readers into the intellectual debate (and avoid the monotony of all-purpose verbs like *says* or *writes*). The following examples show how you can vary signal phrases to add precision to your paper:

Ellen Goodman asserts that . . .

To summarize Judith Viorst's observations on friends, . . .

Social activist and nutrition guru Dick Gregory demonstrates that . . .

Mary Sherry explains . . .

George Orwell rejects the widely held belief that . . .

Oscar Hijuelos exposes . . .

Other verbs that you should keep in mind when constructing signal phrases include the following:

acknowledges	compares	grants	reasons
adds	confirms	implies	reports
admits	declares	insists	responds
believes	endorses	points out	suggests

Well-chosen signal phrases help you integrate quotations, paraphrases, and summaries into the flow of your paper. Besides, signal phrases let your reader know who is speaking and, in the case of summaries and paraphrases, exactly where your ideas end and someone else's begin. Never confuse your reader with a quotation that appears suddenly without introduction. Unannounced quotations leave your reader wondering how the quoted material relates to the point you are trying to make. Look at the following student example. The quotation is from Ruth Russell's "The Wounds That Can't Be Stitched Up," which appears on pages 158–61 in this text.

Unannounced Quotation

America has a problem with drinking and driving. In 2004 drunk drivers killed almost 17,000 people and injured 500,000 others. While many are quick to condemn drinking and driving, they are also quick to defend or offer excuses for such behavior, especially when the offender is a friend. "Many local people who know the driver are surprised when they hear about the accident, and they are quick to defend him. They tell me he was a war hero. His parents aren't well. He's an alcoholic. Or my favorite: 'He's a good guy when he doesn't drink'" (Russell 160). When are we going to get tough with drunk drivers?

In the following revision, the student integrates the quotation into the text by means of a signal phrase and in a number of other ways as well. By giving the name of the writer being quoted, referring to her authority on the subject, and noting that the writer is speaking from experience, the student provides more context so that the reader can better understand how this quotation fits into the discussion.

Integrated Quotation

America has a problem with drinking and driving. In 2004 drunk drivers killed almost 17,000 people and injured 500,000 others. While many are quick to condemn drinking and driving, they are also quick to defend or offer excuses for such behavior, especially when the offender is a friend. Ruth Russell, whose family was shattered by a drunk driver, recalls that "many local people who know the driver are surprised when they hear about the accident, and they are quick to defend him. They tell me he was a war hero. His parents aren't well. He's an alcoholic. Or my favorite: 'He's a good guy when he doesn't drink'" (160). When are we going to get tough with drunk drivers?

AVOID PLAGIARISM

Honesty and accuracy with sources are essential. Any material that you have borrowed word for word must be placed within quotation marks and be properly cited. Any idea, explanation, or argument that you have paraphrased or summarized must be documented, and you must show clearly where the paraphrased or summarized material begins and ends. In short, to use someone else's idea—whether in its original form or in an altered form—without proper acknowledgment is to be guilty of *plagiarism*.

You must acknowledge and document the source of your information whenever you do any of the following:

- quote a source word for word;
- refer to information and ideas from another source that you present in your own words as either a paraphrase or summary; or
- cite statistics, tables, charts, graphs, or other visuals.

You do not need to document the following types of information:

- your own observations, experiences, ideas, and opinions;
- factual information available in many sources (information known as *common knowledge*); or
- proverbs, sayings, or familiar quotations.

For a discussion of MLA style for in-text documentation practices, see pages 614–15.

The Council of Writing Program Administrators offers the following helpful definition of *plagiarism* in academic settings for administrators, faculty, and students: "In an instructional setting, plagiarism occurs when a writer deliberately uses someone else's language, ideas, or other (not common-knowledge) material without acknowledging its source." Accusations of plagiarism can be substantiated even if plagiarism is accidental. A little attention and effort at the note-taking stage can go a long way toward eliminating inadvertent plagiarism. Check all direct quotations against the wording of the original, and double-check your paraphrases to be sure that you have not used the writer's wording or sentence structure. It is easy to forget to put quotation marks around material taken verbatim or to use the same sentence structure and most of the same words—substituting a synonym here and there—and treat it as a paraphrase. In working closely with the ideas and words of others, intellectual honesty demands that we distinguish between what we borrow—acknowledging it in a citation—and what is our own.

While writing your paper, be careful whenever you incorporate one of your notes into your paper. Make sure that you put quotation marks around material taken verbatim, and double-check your text against your note card—or, better yet, against the original if you have it on hand—to make sure that your quotation is accurate. When paraphrasing or summarizing, make sure you do not inadvertently borrow key words or sentence structures from the original.

For additional guidance, go to the St. Martin's Tutorial on Avoiding Plagiarism at **bedfordstmartins.com/plagiarismtutorial.**

Using Quotation Marks for Language Borrowed Directly

When you use another person's exact words or sentences, you must enclose the borrowed language in quotation marks. Without quotation marks, you give your reader the impression that the wording is your own. Even if you cite the source, you are guilty of plagiarism if you fail to use quotation marks. The following examples demonstrate both plagiarism and a correct citation for a direct quotation.

Original Source

So Grant and Lee were in complete contrast, representing two diametrically opposed elements in American life. Grant was the modern man emerging; beyond him, ready to come on the stage, was the great age of steel and machinery, of crowded cities and a restless burgeoning vitality.

–Bruce Catton, "Grant and Lee: A Study in Contrasts," page 492

Plagiarism

So Grant and Lee were in complete contrast, according to Civil War historian Bruce Catton, representing two diametrically opposed elements in American life. Grant was the modern man emerging; beyond him, ready to come on the stage, was the great age of steel and machinery, of crowded cities and a restless burgeoning vitality (492).

Correct Citation of Borrowed Words in Quotation Marks

"So Grant and Lee were in complete contrast," according to Civil War historian Bruce Catton, "representing two diametrically opposed elements in American life. Grant was the modern man emerging; beyond him, ready to come on the stage, was the great age of steel and machinery, of crowded cities and a restless burgeoning vitality" (492).

Using Your Own Words and Word Order When Summarizing and Paraphrasing

When summarizing or paraphrasing a source, you must use your own language. Pay attention to word choice and word order, especially if you are paraphrasing. Remember, it is not enough simply to use a synonym here or there and think you have paraphrased the source; you *must* restate the original idea in your own words, using your own style and sentence structure. In the following examples, notice how plagiarism can occur when care is not taken in the wording or sentence structure of a paraphrase. Notice that in the acceptable paraphrase, the student writer uses her own language and sentence structure.

Original Source

Worse, this absence of moral authority in the realm of food leaves children—everyone, really—vulnerable to the one force in American life that has no problem making absolute claims: food advertisers, who spend billions teaching kids how to bug their parents into feeding them high-fat, high-sugar foods. Combine that with the lingering (albeit debunked) 1980s dogma—that "kids know when kids are full"—and you get, as one nutritionist-parent forcefully told me, the idea that "kids have the right to make bad nutritional decisions."

–Greg Critser, "Don't Eat the Flan," page 559

Unacceptably Close Wording

According to Critser, when there is no moral authority guiding what we eat, children are left unprotected to the strong claims of food advertisers. Each year billions of dollars are spent persuading kids to persuade their parents into serving foods that are high-fat and high-sugar. When this is taken together with the 1980s belief that children know when children are full, the result is children not only make but they actually have the right to make unhealthy nutritional decisions, according to one informed parent (559).

Unacceptably Close Sentence Structure

Critser believes that without any objective directives when it comes to food all of us—especially children—are left defenseless to the one economic power free to make unquestioned assertions: food producers who spend huge dollars convincing children they need unhealthy foods loaded with fats and sugars. Blend that thinking with the still heard (but false) 1980s mantra—children stop eating when they're full—and the result is, as one informed adult argued, anything goes when children make their own diet choices (559).

Acceptable Paraphrase

Critser believes that Americans, especially our children, have no public directives to follow about food choices. Large advertising campaigns, costing billions of dollars, push unhealthy foods that are high in fat and sugar. Much of this advertising is aimed at impressionable children who, in turn, beg their parents to buy the advertised products. When coupled with the 1980s belief that children know their limits when it comes to food, the result is a formula for disaster—children somehow have the right to make unhealthy dietary choices (559).

Review the Avoiding Plagiarism box below as you proofread your final draft and check your citations one last time. If at any time while you are taking notes or writing your paper you have a question about plagiarism, consult your instructor for clarification and guidance before proceeding.

Avoiding Plagiarism

Questions to Ask about Direct Quotations

- Do quotation marks clearly indicate the language that I borrowed verbatim?
- Is the language of the quotation accurate, with no missing or misquoted words or phrases?
- Do the brackets or ellipsis marks clearly indicate any changes or omissions I have introduced?
- Does a signal phrase naming the author introduce each quotation?
- Does the verb in the signal phrase help establish a context for each quotation?
- Does a parenthetical page citation follow each quotation?

Questions to Ask about Summaries and Paraphrases

- Is each summary or paraphrase written in my own words and style?
- Does each summary or paraphrase accurately represent the opinion, position, or reasoning of the original writer?
- Does each summary or paraphrase start with a signal phrase so that readers know where my borrowed material begins?
- Does each summary or paraphrase conclude with a parenthetical page citation?

Questions to Ask about Facts and Statistics

- Do I use a signal phrase or some other marker to introduce each fact or statistic that is not common knowledge so that readers know where the borrowed material begins?
- Is each fact or statistic that is not common knowledge clearly documented with a parenthetical page citation?

Praise the Humble Dung Beetle

■ Sharon Begley

Award-winning science journalist Sharon Begley was born in Englewood, New Jersey, in 1956. After graduating from Yale University in 1977, she became an editorial assistant in science at Newsweek *and was named senior science editor at the magazine in 1996. Her many cover stories on a variety of cutting-edge science topics have demonstrated her ability to write about complex scientific ideas, theories, and laboratory studies in clear, accessible prose. Begley teamed up with Collette Dowling and Anne Marie Cunningham to write* The Techno/Peasant Survival Manual *(1980), a book that describes new technologies, explains the principles behind them, and speculates on the impact their use could have on society. In 2002, Begley published* The Mind and the Brain *with psychiatrist Jeffrey Schwartz. She regularly serves as a science consultant for radio and television shows like* Imus in the Morning, Today Weekend, CBS's The Early Show, *and* The Charlie Rose Show. *Since 2002, Begley has been science editor at the* Wall Street Journal, *where her column "Science Journal" appears every Friday.*

In "Praise the Humble Dung Beetle," an essay first published in the June 9, 2008, issue of Newsweek, *Begley champions the cause of bugs and other creepy-crawly invertebrates that should be protected by the Endangered Species Act. As you read, pay attention to how Begley integrates her sources into the discussion smoothly with clear signal phrases.*

Reflecting on What You Know

Make a list of any endangered wildlife that you've heard about. Are any of these plants and animals from your region of the country? How did you first hear about the endangered species on your list?

Nothing against polar bears, which Sacha Spector loves as much as the next biologist, but to really get him going you need to ask about beetles. Specifically, dung beetles, whose disappearance would 1 undoubtedly leave less of a void in our collective heart than the polar bear's but would rip a bigger hole in the web of life. Without the dung beetles that roam America's rangelands and pastures, animal droppings would not get rolled up and buried. Seeds in the droppings would not get dispersed. Populations of parasites and disease-carrying pest species such as flies, to which the raw droppings on the ground are like condos with MOVE RIGHT IN! signs, would explode. Nutrients in the waste would be washed away rather than returned to the ground. Spector, who runs the invertebrate program at the Center for Biodiversity and Conservation at the American Museum of Natural History, could go on, but you can tell from his voice that he knows he's fighting a losing battle. Getting people to care about the 238 species of spiders, clams, moths, snails, isopods, and other invertebrates on the list of endangered species is about as likely as a magazine putting a photo of a dung beetle rather than a polar bear on its cover.

Of all creatures great and small, it is the charismatic megafauna— 2
tigers and rhinos and gorillas and pandas and other soulful-eyed, warm, and fuzzy animals—that personify endangered species. That's both a shame and a dangerous bias. "Plants and invertebrates are the silent majority which feed the entire planet, stabilize the soil, and make all life possible," says Kiernan Suckling, cofounder of the Center for Biological Diversity. They pollinate crops and decompose carcasses, filter water, and, lacking weapons like teeth and claws, brew up molecules to defend themselves that turn out to be remarkably potent medicines: the breast-cancer compound taxol comes from a yew tree, and a leukemia drug from the rosy periwinkle. Those are tricks that, Suckling dryly notes, "polar bears and blue whales haven't mastered yet."

Since the lesser beasts of the field can't just muscle their way to sur- 3
vival, they tend to have talents that higher ones—with more brains as well as brawn to draw on—don't. As a result, they're loaded with gizmos that human engineers are tapping for inspiration. The Namibian beetle, for instance, has tips on the bumpy scales of its wings that pull water from fog, a design that has inspired a fog-harvesting net (it's used in cooling towers, industrial condensers, and dry farming regions). The spiral in mollusk shells, which fluids flow through especially smoothly and efficiently, has inspired a rotor that draws up to 85 percent less energy than standard fans and is finding its way into computers and air conditioners. Biologists are cloning mussel proteins to produce an epoxy, mimicking the bivalves' ability to stick to rocks, that is expected to

rival any superglue on the market. The American burying beetle, which feeds on carrion, can smell death from afar. "It can find a dead mouse [which it eats and feeds, regurgitated, to its offspring] within an hour of its demise from two miles away," says Quentin Wheeler, director of the International Institute for Species Exploration at Arizona State University. "Think of the potential if we could mimic that for finding earthquake victims."

Biologists draw an analogy between ecosystems and airplanes. 4
The latter can fly without some of their rivets, and the former can survive without some of their species. But in neither case can you tell how many, or which ones, are dispensable until the thing crashes. "Some 99.99 percent of species that ever existed have disappeared, and nature moves on," notes Wheeler. "But you can never predict what the consequences will be in the short term, especially for humans who rely on the services that invertebrates provide." But after a species' numbers plummet, the effects haven't been pretty. For instance, as freshwater mussels have declined (70 percent of their species are threatened or endangered), taking with them their filtration services, water quality in streams, rivers, and lakes has deteriorated badly. In the Chesapeake Bay, each adult oyster once filtered 60 gallons of water a day, packaging sediment and pollutants into blobs that fell harmlessly to the bay floor. Before the population crashed in the 1990s, oysters filtered 19 trillion gallons—an entire bay's worth—once a week. The survivors struggle to do that in a year. The result is cloudy, more polluted water, and a loss of fisheries and baymen's livelihoods.

The value of creepy-crawlies is not reflected in which creatures 5
are protected by the Endangered Species Act, and this one isn't the Bush administration's fault. Like the rest of us, scientists gravitate toward the huggable. The upshot is that much less is known about invertebrates, including whether they're in danger of extinction, than about mammals. "With 57 insect species on the endangered list, out of 90,000 in the United States, either there's something unbelievably resilient about insects or we're off by an order of magnitude in how many are in trouble," says Spector.

If Earth's species are a living library, then polar bears and other 6
cuddly mammals are the best-selling beach reads. Everything else is the volumes of history and literature and other scholarship, written in the alphabet of DNA: 99 percent of all animals are invertebrates. To understand the history and the majesty of life requires reading, and thus preserving, those volumes.

Thinking Critically about This Reading

What is Begley's purpose in this essay? (Glossary: *Purpose)* Does she simply want to inform us about beetles and other invertebrates? Is she arguing that more plants and invertebrates should be included on the list of endangered species? Is she asking us to become better informed about invertebrates, which account for 99 percent of all animals? Or all three? Explain.

Questions for Study and Discussion

1. According to Begley, what would happen to "the web of life" (paragraph 1) if the dung beetle were to become extinct? How does Begley use Sacha Spector's expertise and perspective to help her make this point?
2. Begley acknowledges that "it is the charismatic megafauna . . . that personify endangered species" (2). In what ways is this "both a shame and a dangerous bias"? How does Begley use the opinions of Kiernan Suckling of the Center for Biological Diversity to answer this question?
3. Identify the signal phrases that Begley uses to introduce her sources. How do these signal phrases help you as a reader? Besides giving the name of each source, what other information does Begley provide?
4. Begley claims that lesser beasts are "loaded with gizmos that human engineers are tapping for inspiration" (3). What examples does she use to support this claim? To what end does she quote Quentin Wheeler in paragraph 3? Explain.
5. Explain the analogy "between ecosystems and airplanes" (4) that biologists use. How does it inform Begley's discussion of unappreciated invertebrates?
6. What point does Begley make with her "if Earth's species are a living library" analogy in the final paragraph?

Classroom Activity Using Writing with Sources

Use the examples of signal phrases and parenthetical citations on pages 246–47 as models for integrating the quotation into the flow of the discussion in each of the following two paragraphs. The quotation in the first example comes from page 100 of William L. Rathje's article entitled "Rubbish!" in the *Atlantic Monthly.* Rathje teaches at the University of Arizona, where he directs the Garbage Project.

> Most Americans think that we are producing more trash per person than ever, that plastic is a huge problem, and that paper biodegrades quickly in landfills. "The biggest challenge we will face is to recognize that the conventional wisdom about garbage is often wrong."

The quotation in the second example comes from page 99 of Rita Dove's essay "Loose Ends" from her 1995 book *The Poet's World.* Dove is a former poet laureate of the United States and teaches at the University of Virginia.

> Television, it could be argued, presents life in tidy almost predictable thirty- and sixty-minute packages. As any episode of *Friends, House,* or *Law and Order* demonstrates, life on television, though exciting, is relatively easy to follow. Humor, simultaneous action, and special effects cannot overshadow the fact that each show has a beginning, a middle, and an end. "Life . . . is ragged. Loose ends rule." For many Americans, television provides an escape from their disjointed day-to-day lives.

Compare your signal phrases with those of your classmates, and discuss how smoothly each integrates the quotation into the passage.

Suggested Writing Assignments

1. Visit the U.S. Fish and Wildlife Service Web site at www.fws.gov/Endangered/wildlife.html#Species to learn about its Endangered Species Program and the Endangered Species Act. Find the Service's list of endangered vertebrate and invertebrate animals and flowering and nonflowering plants in the United States. From these lists, adopt an endangered species that is found in your region of the country, and write a report about it. In your report, include a description of your plant or "critter," an explanation of where it is found and what it does, and an argument for why it should be protected.
2. Begley says that "getting people to care about the 238 species of spiders, clams, moths, snails, isopods, and other invertebrates on the list of endangered species is about as likely as a magazine putting a photo of a dung beetle rather than a polar bear on its cover" (1). Consider the pair of photographs—one of the dung beetle and the other, a polar bear—on page 257.

Were you drawn to the picture of the polar bear? Why or why not? Write an essay in which you argue that because "lowly bugs, spiders,

© Mark Moffett/Minden Pictures/Getty Images, Inc.

Photo by Alfred Rosa.

and mollusks are more critical to ecology than larger, more glamorous mammals are," we all should learn more about unglamorous invertebrates instead of focusing our attention and dollars on cuddly and huggable mammals.

Be Specific

■ Natalie Goldberg

Born in 1948, Natalie Goldberg has made a specialty of writing about writing. Her first and best-known work, Writing Down the Bones: Freeing the Writer Within, *was published in 1986. Goldberg's advice to would-be writers is, on the one hand, practical and pithy; on the other, it is almost mystical in its call to know and appreciate the world. Her other books about writing include* Wild Mind: Living the Writer's Life *(1990),* Living Color *(1996),* Thunder and Lightning: Cracking Open the Writer's Craft *(2000), and* Old Friend from Far Away: The Practice of Writing Memoir *(2008). Goldberg has also written fiction. Her first novel,* Banana Rose, *was published in 1994. She is also a painter whose work is exhibited in Taos, New Mexico.* Living Color: A Writer Paints Her World *(1997) is about painting as her second art form, and* Top of My Lungs *(2002) is a collection of poetry and paintings.*

In "Be Specific," a chapter from Writing Down the Bones, *notice how Goldberg demonstrates her advice to be specific.*

Reflecting on What You Know

Suppose someone says to you, "I walked in the woods." What do you envision? Write down what you see in your mind's eye. Now suppose someone says, "I walked in the redwood forest." Again, write what you see. How are the two descriptions different, and why?

Be specific. Don't say "fruit." Tell what kind of fruit—"It is a pomegranate." Give things the dignity of their names. Just as with human beings, it is rude to say, "Hey, girl, get in line." That "girl" has a name. (As a matter of fact, if she's at least twenty years old, she's a woman, not a "girl" at all.) Things, too, have names. It is much better to say "the geranium in the window" than "the flower in the window." "Geranium"—that one word gives us a much more specific picture. It penetrates more deeply into the beingness of that flower. It immediately gives us the scene by the window—red petals, green circular leaves, all straining toward sunlight. 1

About ten years ago I decided I had to learn the names of plants and flowers in my environment. I bought a book on them and walked down the tree-lined streets of Boulder,[1] examining leaf, bark, and seed, trying to match them up with their descriptions and names in the book. Maple, elm, oak, locust. I usually tried to cheat by asking people working in their yards the names of the flowers and trees growing there. I was amazed how few people had any idea of the names of the live beings inhabiting their little plot of land. 2

When we know the name of something, it brings us closer to the ground. It takes the blur out of our mind; it connects us to the earth. If I walk down the street and see "dogwood," "forsythia," I feel more friendly toward the environment. I am noticing what is around me and can name it. It makes me more awake. 3

If you read the poems of William Carlos Williams,[2] you will see how specific he is about plants, trees, flowers—chicory, daisy, locust, poplar, quince, primrose, black-eyed Susan, lilacs—each has its own integrity. Williams says, "Write what's in front of your nose." It's good for us to know what is in front of our nose. Not just "daisy," but how the flower is in the season we are looking at it—"The dayseye hugging the earth / in August . . . brownedged, / green and pointed scales / armor his yellow."* Continue to hone your awareness: to the name, to the month, to the day, and finally to the moment. 4

Williams also says: "No idea, but in things." Study what is "in front of your nose." By saying "geranium" instead of "flower," you are penetrating more deeply into the present and being there. The closer we can get to what's in front of our nose, the more it can teach us everything. "To see the World in a Grain of Sand, and a heaven in a Wild Flower . . ."** 5

In writing groups and classes too, it is good to quickly learn the names of all the other group members. It helps to ground you in the group and make you more attentive to each other's work. 6

Learn the names of everything: birds, cheese, tractors, cars, buildings. A writer is all at once everything—an architect, French cook, farmer—and at the same time, a writer is none of these things. 7

[1] *Boulder:* a city in Colorado.
[2] *William Carlos Williams* (1883–1963): American poet.
* William Carlos Williams, "Daisy," in *The Collected Earlier Poems* (New York: New Directions, 1938). [Goldberg's note]
** William Blake, "The Auguries of Innocence." [Goldberg's note]

Thinking Critically about This Reading

What does Goldberg mean when she states, "Give things the dignity of their names" (paragraph 1)? Why, according to Goldberg, should writers refer to things by their specific names?

Questions for Study and Discussion

1. How does Goldberg "specifically" follow the advice she gives writers in this essay?
2. Goldberg makes several lists of the names of things. What purpose do these lists serve? (Glossary: *Purpose*)
3. In paragraph 4, Goldberg paraphrases and quotes the poet William Carlos Williams. How does Goldberg signal where the paraphrase begins? For what purpose does Goldberg bring Williams into a discussion of being specific? Explain.
4. In the context of paragraph 5, what purpose does the quotation from William Blake's poem "The Auguries of Innocence" serve?
5. In what ways do the Williams and Blake sources enrich and support Goldberg's personal experience and advice to be specific?
6. In paragraphs 3, 5, and 6, Goldberg cites a number of advantages to be gained by knowing the names of things. What are these advantages? Do they ring true to you?
7. What specific audience does Goldberg address here? (Glossary: *Audience*) How do you know?

Classroom Activity Using Writing with Sources

Using the examples on pages 250–51 as a model, write a paraphrase for each of the following paragraphs—that is, restate the original ideas in your own words, using your own style and sentence structure.

> Stereotypes are a kind of gossip about the world, a gossip that makes us prejudge people before we ever lay eyes on them. Hence it is not surprising that stereotypes have something to do with the dark world of prejudice. Explore most prejudices (note that the word means prejudgment) and you will find a cruel stereotype at the core of each one.
>
> –Robert L. Heilbroner, "Don't Let Stereotypes Warp Your Judgments"

The history of a nation is more often the result of the unexpected than of the planned. In many cases it turns on momentous events. In 1968, American history was determined by a garbage men's strike. As Martin Luther King Jr. and the members of the SCLC commenced planning the Poor Peoples' March on Washington, the garbage men of Memphis, Tennessee, were embroiled in a wage dispute with Mayor Henry Loeb. On February 12th, the garbage men, most of whom were black, went on strike. What began as a simple dispute over wages soon developed into a full-fledged racial battle between the predominantly black union, local 1733, and the white power structure of the City of Memphis.

–Robert L. Walsh and Leon F. Burrell, *The Other America*

Compare your paraphrases with those of your classmates.

Suggested Writing Assignments

1. Goldberg likes William Carlos Williams's statement, "No idea, but in things" (5). Using this line as both a title and a thesis, write your own argument for the use of the specific over the general in a certain field—news reporting, poetry, or baking, for example. (Glossary: *Argumentation*) Be sure to support your argument with examples.
2. Write a brief essay advising your readers of something they should do. Title your essay, as Goldberg does, with a directive ("Be Specific"). Tell your readers how they can improve their lives by taking your advice, and give strong examples of the behavior you are recommending.

The English-Only Movement: Can America Proscribe Language with a Clear Conscience?

■ Jake Jamieson

An eighth-generation Vermonter, Jake Jamieson was born in Berlin, Vermont, and grew up in nearby Waterbury, home of Ben & Jerry's ice cream. He graduated from the University of Vermont in 1996 with a degree in elementary education and a focus in English. After graduation, he "bounced around" California and Colorado before landing in the Boston area, where he directs the product innovation and training department at iProspect, a search-engine marketing company.

Jamieson wrote the following essay while he was a student at the University of Vermont and has updated it for inclusion in this book. As a believer in the old axiom "If it isn't broken, don't fix it," Jamieson feels that the official-English crowd wants to fix a system that seems to be working just fine. In this essay, he tackles the issue of legislating English as the official language for the United States. As you read, notice how he uses outside sources to present various pieces of the English-only position. He then tries to undercut that position by using his own thinking and examples as well as the opinions of experts who support him. Throughout his essay, Jamieson uses MLA style for his in-text citations and his list of works cited.

Reflecting on What You Know

It is now possible to visit many countries and be understood in English, regardless of the other languages that are spoken in the host country. If you were to emigrate, how hard would you work to learn the predominant language of your chosen country? What advantages would you gain by learning that language, even if you could get by in English? How would you feel if the country had a law that required you to use its language in its schools and businesses? Write down your thoughts about these questions.

Many people think of the United States as a giant cultural "melting pot" where people from other countries come together and bathe in the warm waters of assimilation. In this scenario, the newly arrived immigrants readily adopt American cultural ways and learn to speak English. For others, however, this serene picture of the melting pot analogy does not ring true. These people see the melting pot as a giant cauldron into which immigrants are tossed; here their cultures, values, and backgrounds are boiled away in the scalding waters of discrimination. At the center of the discussion about immigrants and assimilation is language: should immigrants be required to learn English, or should accommodations be made so they can continue to use their native languages? 1

Those who argue that the melting pot analogy is valid believe that immigrants who come to America do so willingly and should be expected to become a part of its culture instead of hanging on to their past. For them, the expectation that immigrants will celebrate this country's holidays, dress as Americans dress, embrace American values, and most importantly speak English is not unreasonable. They believe that assimilation offers the only way for everyone in this country to live together in harmony and the only way to dissipate the tensions that inevitably arise when cultures clash. A major problem with this argument, however, is that there is no agreement on what exactly constitutes the "American way" of doing things. 2

Not everyone in America is of the same religious persuasion or has the same set of values, and different people affect vastly different styles of dress. There are so many sets of variables that it would be hard to defend the argument that there is only one culture in the United States. Currently, the one common denominator in America is that the majority of us speak English, and because of this a major movement is being staged in favor of making English the country's "official" language while it is still the country's national and common language. Making English America's "official" language would change the ground rules and expectations surrounding immigrant assimilation. According to the columnist and social commentator Charles Krauthammer, making English the "official" language has important implications: 3

> "Official" means the language of the government and its institutions. "Official" makes clear our expectations of acculturation. "Official" means that every citizen, upon entering America's most sacred political space, the voting booth, should minimally be able

> to identify the words *president* and *vice president* and *county commissioner* and *judge*. The immigrant, of course, has the right to speak whatever he wants. But he must understand that when he comes to the United States, swears allegiance, and accepts its bounty, he undertakes to join its civic culture. In English. (112)

Many reasons are given to support the notion that making English the official language of the land is a good idea and that it is exactly what this country needs, especially in the face of the growing diversity of languages in metropolitan areas. Indeed, in a recent survey one Los Angeles school reported sixty different languages spoken in the homes of its students (National Education Association, par. 4).

Supporters of English-only contend that all government communication must be in English. Because communication is absolutely necessary for democracy to survive, they believe that the only way to ensure the existence of our nation is to make sure a common language exists. Making English official would ensure that all government business, from ballots to official forms to judicial hearings, would have to be conducted in English. According to former senator and presidential candidate Bob Dole, "Promoting English as our national language is not an act of hostility but a welcoming act of inclusion." He goes on to state that while immigrants are encouraged to continue speaking their native languages, "thousands of children [are] failing to learn the language, English, that is the ticket to the 'American Dream'" (qtd. in Donegan 51). Political and cultural commentator Greg Lewis echoes Dole's sentiments when he boldly states, "To succeed in America . . . it's important to speak, read, and understand English as most Americans speak it. There's nothing cruel or unfair in that; it's just the way it is" (par. 5). 4

For those who do not subscribe to this way of thinking, however, this type of legislation is anything but the "welcoming act of inclusion" that it is described to be. Many of them, like Myriam Marquez, readily acknowledge the importance of English but fear that "talking in Spanish—or any other language, for that matter—is some sort of litmus test used to gauge American patriotism" ("Why and When" 512). Others suggest that anyone attempting to regulate language is treading dangerously close to the First Amendment and must have a hidden agenda of some type. Why, it is asked, make a language official when it is already firmly entrenched and widely used in this country without legislation to mandate it? According to language diversity advocate James Crawford, the answer is plain and simple: "discrimination." He 5 states that "it is certainly more respectable to discriminate by language than by race" or ethnicity. He points out that "most people are not sensitive to language discrimination in this nation, so it is easy to argue that you're doing someone a favor by making them speak English" (qtd. in Donegan 51). English-only legislation has been criticized as bigoted, anti-immigrant, mean-spirited, and steeped in nativism by those who oppose it, and some go so far as to say that this type of legislation will not foster better communication, as is the claim, but will instead encourage a "fear of being subsumed by a growing 'foreignness' in our midst" (Underwood 65).

For example, when a judge in Texas ruled that a mother was abusing her five-year-old girl by speaking to her only in Spanish, an uproar ensued. This ruling was accompanied by the statement that by talking to her daughter in a language other than English, the mother was "abusing that child and . . . relegating her to the position of house maid." The National Association for Bilingual Education (NABE) condemned this statement for "labeling the Spanish language as abuse." The judge, Samuel C. Kiser, subsequently apologized to the housekeepers of the country, adding that he held them "in the highest esteem," but stood firm on his ruling (qtd. in Donegan 51). One might notice that he went out of his way to apologize to the housekeepers he might have offended but saw no need to apologize to the millions of Spanish speakers whose language had just been belittled in a nationally publicized case. 6

This tendency of official-English proponents to put down other languages is one that shows up again and again, even though they maintain that they have nothing against other languages or the people who speak them. If there is no malice intended toward other languages, why is the use of any language other than English tantamount to lunacy according to an almost constant barrage of literature and editorial opinion? In a recent listing of the "New Year's Resolutions" of various conservative organizations, a group called U.S. English, Inc., stated that the U.S. government was not doing its job of convincing immigrants that they "must learn English to succeed in this country." Instead, according to Stephen Moore and his associates, "in a bewildering display of irrationality, the U.S. government makes it possible to vote, file a tax return, get married, obtain a driver's license, and become a U.S. citizen in many languages" (46). 7

Now, according to this mindset, not only is speaking any language other than English abusive, but it is also irrational and bewildering. What is this world coming to when people want to speak and make transactions in their native language? Why do they refuse to change 8 and become more like us? Why can't immigrants see that speaking English is quite simply the right way to go? These and many other questions like them are implied by official-English proponents when they discuss the issue.

Conservative attorney David Price argues that official-English legislation is a good idea because most English-speaking Americans prefer "out of pride and convenience to speak their native language on the job" (A13). This statement implies not only that the pride and convenience of non-English-speaking Americans is unimportant but that their native tongues are not as important as English. The scariest prospect of all is that this opinion is quickly gaining popularity all around the country. It appears to be most prevalent in areas with high concentrations of Spanish-speaking residents. 9

To date, a number of official-English bills and one amendment to the Constitution have been proposed in the House and Senate. There are more than twenty-seven states—including Missouri, North Dakota, Florida, Massachusetts, California, Virginia, and New Hampshire—that have made English their official language, and more are debating the issue every day. An especially disturbing fact about this debate—and it was front and center in 2007 during the discussions and protests about what to do with America's 12.5 million illegal immigrants—is that official-English laws always seem to be linked to anti-immigration legislation, such as proposals to limit immigration or to restrict government benefits to immigrants. 10

Although official-English proponents maintain that their bid for language legislation is in the best interest of immigrants, the facts tend to show otherwise. University of Texas Professor Robert D. King strongly believes that "language does not threaten American unity." He recommends that "we relax and luxuriate in our linguistic richness and our traditional tolerance of language differences" (64). A decision has to be made in this country about what kind of message we will send to the rest of the world. Do we plan to allow everyone in this country the freedom of speech that we profess to cherish, or will we decide to reserve it only for those who speak English? Will we hold firm to our belief that everyone is deserving of life, liberty, and the pursuit of happiness in this country? Or will we show the world that we believe in these things only when they pertain to ourselves and people like us? "The irony," as Hispanic columnist Myriam Marquez observes, "is that English-only laws directed at government have done little to change the inevitable multicultural flavor of America" ("English-Only Laws" A10). 11

Works Cited

Donegan, Craig. "Debate over Bilingualism: Should English Be the Nation's Official Language?" *CQ Researcher* 19 Jan. 1996: 51–71. Print.

King, Robert D. "Should English Be the Law?" *The Atlantic Monthly* Apr. 1997: 55–64. Print.

Krauthammer, Charles. "In Plain English: Let's Make It Official." *Time* 12 June 2006: 112. Print.

Lewis, Greg. "An Open Letter to Diversity's Victims." WashingtonDispatch .com. 12 Aug. 2003. Web. 15 May 2008.

Marquez, Myriam. "English-Only Laws Serve to Appease Those Who Fear the Inevitable." *Orlando Sentinel* 10 July 2000: A10. Print.

______. "Why and When We Speak Spanish in Public." *Models for Writers.* 10th ed. Ed. Alfred Rosa and Paul Eschholz. Boston: Bedford, 2010. 511–13. Print.

Moore, Stephen, et al. "New Year's Resolutions." *National Review* 29 Jan. 1996: 46–48. Print.

National Education Association. "NEA Statement on the Debate over English Only." Teacher's College, U of Nebraska, Lincoln. 27 Sept. 1999. Web. 15 May 2008.

Underwood, Robert L. "At Issue: Should English Be the Official Language of the United States?" *CQ Researcher* 19 Jan. 1996: 65. Print.

Thinking Critically about This Reading

Jamieson claims that "there are so many sets of variables that it would be hard to defend the argument that there is only one culture in the United States" (paragraph 3). Do you agree with him, or do you see a dominant American culture with many regional variations? Explain.

Questions for Study and Discussion

1. What question does Jamieson seek to answer in his paper? How does he answer this question?
2. How does Jamieson respond to the people who argue that the melting pot analogy is valid? Do you agree with his counterargument?
3. Former senator Bob Dole believes that English "is the ticket to the 'American Dream'" (4). In what ways can it be considered the ticket?
4. For what purpose does Jamieson quote Greg Lewis in paragraph 4? What would have been lost had he dropped the Lewis quotation? Explain.

5. James Crawford believes that official-English legislation is motivated by "discrimination" (5). What do you think he means? Do you think Crawford would consider Bob Dole's remarks in paragraph 4 discriminatory? Explain.
6. In paragraph 6, Jamieson presents the example of the Texas judge who ruled that speaking to a child only in Spanish constituted abuse. What point does this example help Jamieson to make?
7. Jamieson is careful to use signal phrases to introduce each of his quotations and paraphrases. How do these signal phrases help readers follow the flow of the argument in his essay?
8. In his concluding paragraph, Jamieson leaves his readers with three important questions. How do you think he would answer each one? How would you answer them?

Classroom Activity Using Writing with Sources

For each of the following quotations, write an acceptable paraphrase and then a paraphrase including a partial quotation that avoids plagiarism (see pp. 249–51). Pay attention to the word choice and sentence structure of the original.

> The sperm whale is the largest of the toothed whales. Moby Dick was a sperm whale. Generally, male toothed whales are larger than the females. Female sperm whales may grow thirty-five to forty feet in length, while the males may reach sixty feet.
>
> –Richard Hendrick, *The Voyage of the Mimi*

> Astronauts from over twenty nations have gone into space, and they all come back, amazingly enough, saying the very same thing: the earth is a small, blue place of profound beauty that we must take care of. For each, the journey into space, whatever its original intents and purposes, became above all a spiritual one.
>
> –Al Reinhert, *For All Mankind*

> One of the usual things about education in mathematics in the United States is its relatively impoverished vocabulary. Whereas the student completing elementary school will already have a vocabulary for most disciplines of many hundreds, even thousands of words, the typical student will have a mathematics vocabulary of only a couple of dozen words.
>
> –Marvin Minsky, *The Society of Mind*

Suggested Writing Assignments

1. It's no secret that English is the common language of the United States, but few of us know that our country has been cautious about promoting a government-mandated official language. Why do you suppose the federal government has chosen to take a hands-off position on the language issue? If it has not been necessary to mandate English in the past, why do you think that people now feel a need to declare English the "official language" of the United States? Do you think that this need is real? Write an essay in which you articulate your position on the English-only issue. Support your position with your own experiences and observations as well as several outside sources.
2. Before writing an essay about assimilating non-English-speaking immigrants into American society, consider the following three statements:

   a. At this time, it is highly unlikely that Congress will pass a law saying that English is the official language of the United States.
   b. Immigrants should learn English as quickly as possible after arriving in the United States.
   c. The culture and languages of immigrants should be respected and valued to reduce bitterness and resentment as immigrants are assimilated into American society.

   In your opinion, what is the best way to assimilate non-English-speaking immigrants into our society? Write an essay in which you propose how the United States, as a nation, can make statements (b) and (c) above a reality without resorting to an English-only solution. How can we help immigrants become Americans without provoking ill will?
3. Is the English-only debate a political issue, a social issue, an economic issue, or some combination of the three? In this context, what do you see as the relationship between language and power? Write an essay in which you explore the relationship between language and power as it pertains to the non-English-speaking immigrants living and functioning within an English-speaking culture.

part ■ three

The Language of the Essay

chapter **11**

Diction and Tone

DICTION

Diction refers to a writer's choice and use of words. Good diction is precise and appropriate: the words mean exactly what the writer intends, and the words are well suited to the writer's subject, purpose, and intended audience.

Careful writers do not merely come close to saying what they want to say; they select words that convey their exact meaning. Perhaps Mark Twain put this best when he said, "The difference between the right word and the almost right word is the difference between lightning and the lightning bug." Inaccurate, imprecise, or inappropriate diction fails to convey the writer's intended meaning and also may cause confusion and misunderstanding for the reader.

Connotation and Denotation

Both **connotation** and **denotation** refer to the meanings of words. Denotation is the dictionary meaning of a word, the literal meaning. Connotative meanings are the associations or emotional overtones that words have acquired. For example, the word *home* denotes a place where someone lives, but it connotes warmth, security, family, comfort, affection, and other more private thoughts and images. The word *residence* also denotes a place where someone lives, but its connotations are colder and more formal.

Many words in English have synonyms, words with very similar denotations—for example, *mob, crowd, multitude,* and *bunch.* Deciding which to use depends largely on the connotations that each synonym has and the context in which the word is to be used. For example, you might say, "There was a crowd at the lecture," but not "There was a mob at the lecture." Good writers are sensitive to both the denotations and the connotations of words.

Abstract and Concrete Words

Abstract words name ideas, conditions, emotions—things nobody can touch, see, or hear. Some abstract words are *love, wisdom, cowardice, beauty, fear,* and *liberty.* People often disagree about abstract things. You may find a forest beautiful, while someone else might find it frightening, and neither of you would be wrong. Beauty and fear are abstract ideas; they exist in your mind, not in the forest along with the trees and the owls. **Concrete** words refer to things we can touch, see, hear, smell, and taste, such as *sandpaper, soda, birch tree, smog, cow, sailboat, rocking chair,* and *pancake.* If you disagree with someone on a concrete issue—say, you claim that the forest is mostly birch trees, while the other person says it is mostly pine—only one of you can be right, and both of you can be wrong; the kinds of trees that grow in the forest is a concrete fact, not an abstract idea.

Good writing balances ideas and facts, and it also balances abstract and concrete diction. If the writing is too abstract and has too few concrete facts and details, it will be unconvincing and tiresome. If the writing is too concrete and is devoid of abstract ideas and emotions, it can seem mundane and dry.

General and Specific Words

General and **specific** do not necessarily refer to opposites. The same word can often be either general or specific, depending on the context: *dessert* is more specific than *food* but more general than *chocolate cream pie.* Being specific is like being concrete: chocolate cream pie is something you can see and taste. Being general, on the other hand, is like being abstract. Food, dessert, and even pie are large classes of things that bring to mind only general tastes or images.

Good writing moves back and forth from the general to the specific. Without specific words, generalities can be unconvincing and even confusing: the writer's idea of "good food" may be very different from the reader's. But writing that does not relate specifics to each other by generalization often lacks focus and direction.

Clichés

Words, phrases, and expressions that have become trite through overuse are called **clichés.** Let's assume your roommate has just returned from an evening out. You ask her, "How was the concert?" She responds, "The concert was okay, but they had us *packed in* there *like sardines.*

How was your evening?" And you reply, "Well, I finished my term paper, but the noise here is enough to *drive me crazy*. The dorm is a real *zoo*." At one time the italicized expressions were vivid and colorful, but through constant use they have grown stale and ineffective. Experienced writers always try to avoid such clichés as *believe it or not, doomed to failure, hit the spot, let's face it, sneaking suspicion, step in the right direction*, and *went to great lengths*. They strive to use fresh language.

Jargon

Jargon, or technical language, is the special vocabulary of a trade or profession. Writers use jargon with an awareness of their audience. If their audience is a group of coworkers or professionals, jargon may be used freely. If the audience is general, jargon should be used sparingly and carefully so that readers can understand it. Jargon becomes inappropriate when it is overused, used out of context, or used pretentiously. For example, computer terms like *input, output,* and *feedback* are sometimes used in place of *contribution, result,* and *response* in other fields, especially in business. If you think about it, these terms suggest that people are machines that receive and process information according to a program imposed by someone else.

Formal and Informal Diction

Diction is appropriate when it suits the occasion for which it is intended. If the situation is informal—a friendly letter, for example—the writing may be colloquial; that is, its words may be chosen to suggest the way people talk with each other. If, on the other hand, the situation is formal—an academic paper or a research report, for example—then the words should reflect this formality. Informal writing tends to be characterized by slang, contractions, references to the reader, and concrete nouns. Formal writing tends to be impersonal, abstract, and free of contractions and references to the reader. Formal writing and informal writing are the extremes. Most writing falls between these two extremes and is a blend of those formal and informal elements that best fit the context.

TONE

Tone is the attitude that a writer takes toward the subject and the audience. The tone may be friendly or hostile, serious or humorous, intimate or distant, enthusiastic or skeptical.

As you read the following paragraphs, notice how each writer creates a different tone and how that tone is supported by the diction—the writer's particular choice and use of words.

Nostalgic

When I was six years old, I thought I knew a lot. How to jump rope, how to skip a rock across a pond, and how to color and stay between the lines—these were all things I took great pride in. Nothing was difficult, and my days were carefree. That is, until the summer when everything became complicated and I suddenly realized I didn't know that much.

–Heather C. Blue, student

Angry

Cans. Beer cans. Glinting on the verges of a million miles of roadways, lying in scrub, grass, dirt, leaves, sand, mud, but never hidden. Piels, Rheingold, Ballantine, Schaefer, Schlitz, shining in the sun or picked by moon or the beams of headlights at night; washed by rain or flattened by wheels, but never dulled, never buried, never destroyed. Here is the mark of savages, the testament of wasters, the stain of prosperity.

–Marya Mannes

Humorous

In perpetrating a revolution, there are two requirements: someone or something to revolt against and someone to actually show up and do the revolting. Dress is usually casual and both parties may be flexible about time and place but if either faction fails to attend the whole enterprise is likely to come off badly. In the Chinese Revolution of 1650 neither party showed up and the deposit on the hall was forfeited.

–Woody Allen

Resigned

I make my living humping cargo for Seaboard World Airlines, one of the big international airlines at Kennedy Airport. They handle strictly all cargo. I was once told that one of the Rockefellers is the major stockholder for the airline, but I don't really think about that too much. I don't get paid to think. The big thing is to beat that race with the time clock every morning of your life so the airline will be happy. The worst thing a man could ever do is to make suggestions about building a better airline. They pay people $40,000 a year to come up with better ideas. It doesn't matter that these ideas never work; it's just that they get nervous when a guy from South Brooklyn or Ozone Park acts like he has a brain.

–Patrick Fenton

Ironic

Once upon a time there was a small, beautiful, green and graceful country called Vietnam. It needed to be saved. (In later years no one could remember exactly what it needed to be saved from, but that is another story.) For many years Vietnam was in the process of being saved by France, but the French eventually tired of their labors and left. Then America took on the job. America was well equipped for country-saving. It was the richest and most powerful nation on earth. It had, for example, nuclear explosives on hand and ready to use equal to six tons of TNT for every man, woman, and child in the world. It had huge and very efficient factories, brilliant and dedicated scientists, and most (but not everybody) would agree, it had good intentions. Sadly, America had one fatal flaw—its inhabitants were in love with technology and thought it could do no wrong. A visitor to America during the time of this story would probably have guessed its outcome after seeing how its inhabitants were treating their own country. The air was mostly foul, the water putrid, and most of the land was either covered with concrete or garbage. But Americans were never much on introspection, and they didn't foresee the result of their loving embrace on the small country. They set out to save Vietnam with the same enthusiasm and determination their forefathers had displayed in conquering the frontier.

–The Sierra Club

The diction and tone of an essay are subtle forces, but they exert a tremendous influence on readers. They are instrumental in determining how we will feel while reading the essay and what attitude we will have toward its argument or the points that it makes. Readers react in a variety of ways. An essay written informally but with a largely angry tone may make one reader defensive and unsympathetic; another may feel that the author is being unusually honest and courageous and may admire these qualities and feel moved by them. Either way, the diction and tone of the piece have made a strong emotional impression. As you read the essays in this chapter and throughout this book, see if you can analyze how the diction and tone shape your reactions.

Shame

■ Dick Gregory

Dick Gregory, activist, comedian, and nutrition expert, was born in St. Louis, Missouri, in 1932. While attending Southern Illinois University on an athletic scholarship, Gregory excelled in track, winning the university's Outstanding Athlete Award in 1953. In 1954, he was drafted into the army. After his discharge, he immediately became active in the civil rights movement led by Martin Luther King Jr. In the 1960s, Gregory was an outspoken critic of America's involvement in Vietnam. This in turn led to his run for the presidency in 1968 as a write-in candidate for the Freedom and Peace Party. Two of his books from this era are No More Lies: The Myth and Reality of American History *(1971) and* Dick Gregory's Political Primer *(1972). Throughout his life he has crusaded for economic reforms, antidrug issues, and minority rights. In 2000, he published* Callus on My Soul, *the second volume of his autobiography. In recent years, Gregory has been active in the diet and health food industry.*

In the following episode from Nigger *(1964), the first volume of his autobiography, Gregory narrates the story of a childhood experience that taught him the meaning of shame. Through his use of dialogue, he dramatically re-creates the experience for readers. Notice how he uses concrete nouns and strong action verbs to describe his experiences and his emotional responses to them.*

Reflecting on What You Know

We all learn many things in school beyond the lessons we study formally. Some of the extracurricular truths we learn stay with us for the rest of our lives. Write about something you learned in school—something that has made life easier or more understandable for you—that you still find useful.

I never learned hate at home, or shame. I had to go to school for that. 1
I was about seven years old when I got my first big lesson. I was in love with a little girl named Helene Tucker, a light-complexioned little

girl with pigtails and nice manners. She was always clean and she was smart in school. I think I went to school then mostly to look at her. I brushed my hair and even got me a little old handkerchief. It was a lady's handkerchief, but I didn't want Helene to see me wipe my nose on my hand. The pipes were frozen again, there was no water in the house, but I washed my socks and shirt every night. I'd get a pot, and go over to Mister Ben's grocery store, and stick my pot down into his soda machine. Scoop out some chopped ice. By evening the ice melted to water for washing. I got sick a lot that winter because the fire would go out at night before the clothes were dry. In the morning I'd put them on, wet or dry, because they were the only clothes I had.

Everybody's got a Helene Tucker, a symbol of everything you 2
want. I loved her for her goodness, her cleanness, her popularity. She'd walk down my street and my brothers and sisters would yell, "Here comes Helene," and I'd rub my tennis sneakers on the back of my pants and wish my hair wasn't so nappy[1] and the white folks' shirt fit me better. I'd run out on the street. If I knew my place and didn't come too close, she'd wink at me and say hello. That was a good feeling. Sometimes I'd follow her all the way home, and shovel the snow off her walk and try to make friends with her Momma and her aunts. I'd drop money on her stoop late at night on my way back from shining shoes in the taverns. And she had a Daddy, and he had a good job. He was a paper hanger.

I guess I would have gotten over Helene by summertime, but 3
something happened in that classroom that made her face hang in front of me for the next twenty-two years. When I played the drums in high school it was for Helene and when I broke track records in college it was for Helene and when I started standing behind microphones and heard applause I wished Helene could hear it, too. It wasn't until I was twenty-nine years old and married and making money that I finally got her out of my system. Helene was sitting in that classroom when I learned to be ashamed of myself.

It was on a Thursday. I was sitting in the back of the room, in a 4
seat with a chalk circle drawn around it. The idiot's seat, the trouble-maker's seat.

The teacher thought I was stupid. Couldn't spell, couldn't read, 5
couldn't do arithmetic. Just stupid. Teachers were never interested in finding out that you couldn't concentrate because you were so hungry,

---

[1]*nappy:* shaggy or fuzzy.

because you hadn't had any breakfast. All you could think about was noontime, would it ever come? Maybe you could sneak into the cloakroom and steal a bite of some kid's lunch out of a coat pocket. A bite of something. Paste. You can't really make a meal of paste, or put it on bread for a sandwich, but sometimes I'd scoop a few spoonfuls out of the paste jar in the back of the room. Pregnant people get strange tastes. I was pregnant with poverty. Pregnant with dirt and pregnant with smells that made people turn away, pregnant with cold and pregnant with shoes that were never bought for me, pregnant with five other people in my bed and no Daddy in the next room, and pregnant with hunger. Paste doesn't taste too bad when you're hungry.

The teacher thought I was a troublemaker. All she saw from the front of the room was a little black boy who squirmed in his idiot's seat and made noises and poked the kids around him. I guess she couldn't see a kid who made noises because he wanted someone to know he was there. 6

It was on a Thursday, the day before the Negro payday. The eagle always flew on Friday. The teacher was asking each student how much his father would give to the Community Chest. On Friday night, each kid would get the money from his father, and on Monday he would bring it to the school. I decided I was going to buy me a Daddy right then. I had money in my pocket from shining shoes and selling papers, and whatever Helene Tucker pledged for her Daddy I was going to top it. And I'd hand the money right in. I wasn't going to wait until Monday to buy me a Daddy. 7

I was shaking, scared to death. The teacher opened her book and started calling out names alphabetically. 8

"Helene Tucker?" 9

"My daddy said he'd give two dollars and fifty cents." 10

"That's very nice, Helene. Very, very nice indeed." 11

That made me feel pretty good. It wouldn't take too much to top that. I had almost three dollars in dimes and quarters in my pocket. I stuck my hand in my pocket and held onto the money, waiting for her to call my name. But the teacher closed her book after she called everybody else in the class. 12

I stood up and raised my hand. 13

"What is it now?" 14

"You forgot me." 15

She turned toward the blackboard. "I don't have time to be playing with you, Richard." 16

"My Daddy said he'd . . ." 17

"Sit down, Richard, you're disturbing the class." 18

"My Daddy said he'd give . . . fifteen dollars." 19

She turned around and looked mad. "We are collecting this 20 money for you and your kind, Richard Gregory. If your Daddy can give fifteen dollars you have no business being on relief."

"I got it right now, I got it right now, my Daddy gave it to me to 21 turn in today, my Daddy said . . ."

"And furthermore," she said, looking right at me, her nostrils 22 getting big and her lips getting thin and her eyes opening wide, "we know you don't have a Daddy."

Helene Tucker turned around, her eyes full of tears. She felt sorry 23 for me. Then I couldn't see her too well because I was crying, too.

"Sit down, Richard." 24

And I always thought the teacher kind of liked me. She always 25 picked me to wash the blackboard on Friday, after school. That was a big thrill, it made me feel important. If I didn't wash it, come Monday the school might not function right.

"Where are you going, Richard?" 26

I walked out of school that day, and for a long time I didn't go 27 back very often. There was shame there.

Now there was shame everywhere. It seemed like the whole world 28 had been inside that classroom, everyone had heard what the teacher had said, everyone had turned around and felt sorry for me. There was shame in going to the Worthy Boys Annual Christmas Dinner for you and your kind, because everybody knew what a worthy boy was. Why couldn't they just call it the Boys Annual Dinner; why'd they have to give it a name? There was shame in wearing the brown and orange and white plaid mackinaw[2] the welfare gave to three thousand boys. Why'd it have to be the same for everybody so when you walked down the street the people could see you were on relief? It was a nice warm mackinaw and it had a hood, and my Momma beat me and called me a little rat when she found out I stuffed it in the bottom of a pail full of garbage way over on Cottage Street. There was shame in running over to Mister Ben's at the end of the day and asking for his rotten peaches, there was shame in asking Mrs. Simmons for a spoonful of sugar, there was shame in running out to meet the relief truck.

---

[2]*mackinaw:* a short, double-breasted wool coat.

I hated that truck, full of food for you and your kind. I ran into the house and hid when it came. And then I started to sneak through alleys, to take the long way home so the people going into White's Eat Shop wouldn't see me. Yeah, the whole world heard the teacher that day, we all know you don't have a Daddy.

Thinking Critically about This Reading

In paragraph 28 Gregory states, "Now there was shame everywhere. It seemed like the whole world had been inside that classroom, everyone had heard what the teacher had said, everyone had turned around and felt sorry for me." What did Gregory's teacher say, and why did it hurt him so greatly?

Questions for Study and Discussion

1. How do the first three paragraphs of the essay help to establish a context for the narrative that follows? (Glossary: *Narration*)
2. What does Gregory mean by "shame"? What precisely was he ashamed of, and what in particular did he learn from the incident? (Glossary: *Definition*)
3. In a word or phrase, how would you describe Gregory's tone? What specific words or phrases in his essay lead you to this conclusion?
4. What is the teacher's attitude toward Gregory? In arriving at your answer, consider her own words and actions as well as Gregory's opinion.
5. What role does money play in Gregory's experience? How does money relate to his sense of shame?
6. Specific details can enhance the reader's understanding and appreciation of a subject. (Glossary: *Details*) Gregory's description of Helene Tucker's manners or the plaid of his mackinaw, for example, makes his account vivid and interesting. Cite several other specific details he gives, and consider how the essay would be different without them.
7. Reread this essay's first and last paragraphs, and compare how much each one emphasizes shame. (Glossary: *Beginnings and Endings*) Which emotion other than shame does Gregory reveal in the first paragraph, and does it play a role in the last one? Is the last paragraph an effective ending? Explain.

Classroom Activity Using Diction and Tone

Good writers rely on strong verbs—verbs that contribute significantly to what is being said. Because they must repeatedly describe similar situations, sportswriters, for example, are acutely aware of the need for strong action verbs. It is not enough for them to say that a team wins or loses; they must describe the type of win or loss more precisely. As a result, such verbs as *beat, bury, edge, shock,* and *trounce* are common in the headlines on the sports page. In addition to describing the act of winning, each of these verbs makes a statement about the quality of the victory. Like sportswriters, all of us write about actions that are performed daily. If we were restricted only to the verbs *eat, drink, sleep,* and *work* for each of these activities, our writing would be repetitious, monotonous, and most likely wordy. List as many verbs as you can that you could use in place of these four. What connotative differences do you find in your lists of alternatives? What is the importance of these connotative differences for you as a writer?

Suggested Writing Assignments

1. Using Gregory's essay as a model, write an essay narrating an experience that made you feel especially afraid, angry, surprised, embarrassed, or proud. Include details that allow your readers to know exactly what happened. Pay attention to how you use your first and last paragraphs to present the emotion your essay focuses on.
2. Most of us grow up with some sense of the socioeconomic class that our family belongs to, and often we are aware of how we are, or believe we are, different from people of other classes. Write an essay in which you describe a possession or activity that you thought revealed your socioeconomic standing and made you self-conscious about how you were different from others. Be sure to recount an experience that seemed to confirm your belief, and discuss why it did. Pay attention to your essay's first and last paragraphs so that they serve your purpose.

The Case for Short Words

■ **Richard Lederer**

Born in 1938, Richard Lederer holds degrees from Haverford College, Harvard, and the University of New Hampshire. He has been a prolific and popular writer about language. A former high school English teacher, he is vice president of SPELL, the Society for the Preservation of English Language and Literature. Lederer has written numerous books about how Americans use language, including Anguished English *(1987),* Crazy English: The Ultimate Joy Ride through Our Language *(1989),* The Play of Words *(1990),* The Miracle of Language *(1991),* More Anguished English *(1993),* Adventures of a Verbivore *(1994),* Fractured English *(1996), and* A Man of My Words: Reflections on the English Language *(2003). In addition to writing books, Lederer pens a weekly column called "Looking at Language" for newspapers and magazines across the United States. He is also the Grammar Grappler for* Writer's Digest, *the language commentator for National Public Radio, and an award-winning public speaker who makes approximately two hundred appearances each year.*

In the following essay, taken from The Miracle of Language, *pay attention to the different ways Lederer uses examples to illustrate his central point. Notice also that Lederer's diction demonstrates the versatility and strength of everyday words, thus helping him make the case for short words.*

Reflecting on What You Know

We all carry with us a vocabulary of short, simple-looking words that possess a special personal meaning. For example, to some the word *rose* represents not just a flower but a whole array of gardens, ceremonies, and romantic occasions. What little words have special meaning for you? What images do they bring to mind?

When you speak and write, there is no law that says you have to use big words. Short words are as good as long ones, and short, old words—like *sun* and *grass* and *home*—are best of all. A lot of small 1 words, more than you might think, can meet your needs with a strength, grace, and charm that large words do not have.

Big words can make the way dark for those who read what you write and hear what you say. Small words cast their clear light on big things—night and day, love and hate, war and peace, and life and death. Big words at times seem strange to the eye and the ear and the mind and the heart. Small words are the ones we seem to have known from the time we were born, like the hearth fire that warms the home. 2

Short words are bright like sparks that glow in the night, prompt like the dawn that greets the day, sharp like the blade of a knife, hot like salt tears that scald the cheek, quick like moths that flit from flame to flame, and terse like the dart and sting of a bee. 3

Here is a sound rule: Use small, old words where you can. If a long word says just what you want to say, do not fear to use it. But know that our tongue is rich in crisp, brisk, swift, short words. Make them the spine and the heart of what you speak and write. Short words are like fast friends. They will not let you down. 4

The title of this [essay] and the four paragraphs that you have just read are wrought entirely of words of one syllable. In setting myself this task, I did not feel especially cabined, cribbed, or confined. In fact, the structure helped me to focus on the power of the message I was trying to put across. 5

One study shows that twenty words account for twenty-five percent of all spoken English words, and all twenty are monosyllabic. In order of frequency they are: *I, you, the, a, to, is, it, that, of, and, in, what, he, this, have, do, she, not, on,* and *they*. Other studies indicate that the fifty most common words in written English are each made of a single syllable. 6

For centuries our finest poets and orators have recognized and employed the power of small words to make a straight point between two minds. A great many of our proverbs punch home their points with pithy monosyllables: "Where there's a will, there's a way," "A stitch in time saves nine," "Spare the rod and spoil the child," "A bird in the hand is worth two in the bush." 7

Nobody used the short word more skillfully than William Shakespeare, whose dying King Lear laments: 8

And my poor fool is hang'd! No, no, no life!
Why should a dog, a horse, a rat have life,
And thou no breath at all? . . .
Do you see this? Look on her, look, her lips.
Look there, look there!

Shakespeare's contemporaries made the King James Bible a centerpiece of short words—"And God said, Let there be light: and there was light. And God saw the light, that it was good." The descendants of such mighty lines live on in the twentieth century. When asked to explain his policy to Parliament, Winston Churchill[1] responded with these ringing monosyllables: "I will say: it is to wage war, by sea, land, and air, with all our might and with all the strength that God can give us." In his "Death of the Hired Man" Robert Frost[2] observes that "Home is the place where, when you have to go there, / They have to take you in." And William H. Johnson[3] uses ten two-letter words to explain his secret of success: "If it is to be, / It is up to me." 9

You don't have to be a great author, statesman, or philosopher to tap the energy and eloquence of small words. Each winter I ask my ninth graders at St. Paul's School to write a composition composed entirely of one-syllable words. My students greet my request with obligatory moans and groans, but, when they return to class with their essays, most feel that, with the pressure to produce high-sounding polysyllables relieved, they have created some of their most powerful and luminous prose. Here are submissions from two of my ninth graders: 10

> What can you say to a boy who has left home? You can say that he has done wrong, but he does not care. He has left home so that he will not have to deal with what you say. He wants to go as far as he can. He will do what he wants to do.
>
> This boy does not want to be forced to go to church, to comb his hair, or to be on time. A good time for this boy does not lie in your reach, for what you have he does not want. He dreams of ripped jeans, shorts with no starch, and old socks.
>
> So now this boy is on a bus to a place he dreams of, a place with no rules. This boy now walks a strange street, his long hair blown back by the wind. He wears no coat or tie, just jeans and an old shirt. He hates your world, and he has left it.
>
> –Charles Shaffer

> For a long time we cruised by the coast and at last came to a wide bay past the curve of a hill, at the end of which lay a small

[1]*Sir Winston Churchill* (1874–1965): British orator, author, and statesman.
[2]*Robert Frost* (1874–1963): American poet.
[3]*William H. Johnson* (1771–1834): associate justice of the U.S. Supreme Court, 1804–1834.

> town. Our long boat ride at an end, we all stretched and stood up to watch as the boat nosed its way in.
>
> The town climbed up the hill that rose from the shore, a space in front of it left bare for the port. Each house was a clean white with sky blue or gray trim; in front of each one was a small yard, edged by a white stone wall strewn with green vines.
>
> As the town basked in the heat of noon, not a thing stirred in the streets or by the shore. The sun beat down on the sea, the land, and the back of our necks, so that, in spite of the breeze that made the vines sway, we all wished we could hide from the glare in a cool, white house. But, as there was no one to help dock the boat, we had to stand and wait.
>
> At last the head of the crew leaped from the side and strode to a large house on the right. He shoved the door wide, poked his head through the gloom, and roared with a fierce voice. Five or six men came out, and soon the port was loud with the clank of chains and creak of planks as the men caught ropes thrown by the crew, pulled them taut, and tied them to posts. Then they set up a rough plank so we could cross from the deck to the shore. We all made for the large house while the crew watched, glad to be rid of us.
>
> –Celia Wren

You too can tap into the vitality and vigor of compact expression. Take a suggestion from the highway department. At the boundaries of your speech and prose place a sign that reads "Caution: Small Words at Work." 11

Thinking Critically about This Reading

Lederer states that "short, old words—like *sun* and *grass* and *home*—are best of all" (paragraph 1). What attributes make these words the "best"? Why are they superior to short, new words?

Questions for Study and Discussion

1. In this essay, written to encourage the use of short words, Lederer himself employs many polysyllabic words, especially in paragraphs 5–9. What is his purpose in doing so? (Glossary: *Purpose*)
2. Lederer quotes a wide variety of passages to illustrate the effectiveness of short words. For example, he quotes from famous, universally familiar sources such as Shakespeare and the King

James Bible, and from unknown contemporary sources such as his own ninth-grade students. How does the variety of his illustrations serve to inform his readers? How does each example gain impact from the inclusion of the others?

3. To make clear to the reader why short words are effective, Lederer relies heavily on metaphors and similes, especially in the first four paragraphs. (Glossary: *Figure of Speech*) Choose at least one metaphor and one simile from these paragraphs, and explain the comparison implicit in each.
4. In paragraph 10, Lederer refers to the relief his students feel when released from "the pressure to produce high-sounding polysyllables." Where does this pressure come from? How does it relate to the central purpose of this essay?
5. How does the final paragraph serve to close the essay effectively? (Glossary: *Beginnings and Endings*)
6. This essay abounds with examples of striking sentences and passages consisting entirely of words of one syllable. Choose four of the single-sentence examples or a section of several sentences from one of the longer examples, and rewrite them, using primarily words of two or more syllables. Notice how the revision differs from the original.

Classroom Activity Using Diction and Tone

Writers create and control tone in their writing in part through the words they choose. For example, the words *laugh, cheery, dance,* and *melody* help create a tone of celebration. Make a list of the words that come to mind for each of the following tones:

humorous	authoritative	tentative
angry	triumphant	repentant

Compare your lists of words with those of others in the class. What generalizations can you make about the connotations associated with each of these tones?

Suggested Writing Assignments

1. Follow the assignment Lederer gives his own students, and write a composition composed entirely of one-syllable words. Make your

piece about the length of his student examples or of his own four-paragraph opening.

2. A chief strength of Lederer's essay is his use of a broad variety of examples to illustrate his thesis that short words are the most effective. Choose a subject about which you are knowledgeable, and find as wide a range of examples as you can to illustrate its appeal. For example, if you are enthusiastic about water, you could explore the relative attractions of puddles, ponds, lakes, and oceans; if you are a music lover, you might consider why Bach or the Beatles remain popular today.

Me Talk Pretty One Day

■ **David Sedaris**

David Sedaris was born in 1956 in Johnson City, New York, and grew up in North Carolina. He attended Kent State University but ultimately graduated from the Art Institute of Chicago in 1987. Before becoming a writer, Sedaris worked as a mover, an office temp, a housekeeper, and an elf in a department store Christmas display, an experience he wrote about in his celebrated essay "Santaland Diaries." He is a regular contributor to National Public Radio, Harper's, Details, *the* New Yorker, *and* Esquire *and has won several awards, including the James Thurber Prize for American Humor. Sedaris often writes about his quirky Greek family and his travels with his partner Hugh, with whom he currently lives in London. His essays and stories have been collected in several best-selling books, including* Barrel Fever *(1994),* Holidays on Ice *(1997),* Naked *(1997),* Dress Your Family in Corduroy and Denim *(2004), and most recently,* When You Are Engulfed in Flames *(2008).*

The following essay about taking French language lessons in Paris first appeared in Esquire *in March 1999 and later became the title piece for Sedaris's fourth book,* Me Talk Pretty One Day *(2000). As you read, pay attention to how he uses his words to play with the ideas of language, understanding, and belonging.*

Reflecting on What You Know

Have you ever been in a situation where you did not speak the prevalent language—for example, in a foreign country, a language class, or a group of people who spoke a language other than yours? How did you feel about not being able to communicate? How, if at all, did you get your thoughts across to others?

At the age of forty-one, I am returning to school and having to think of myself as what my French textbook calls "a true debutant." 1
After paying my tuition, I was issued a student ID, which allows me a discounted entry fee at movie theaters, puppet shows, and Festyland, a

far-flung amusement park that advertises with billboards picturing a cartoon stegosaurus sitting in a canoe and eating what appears to be a ham sandwich.

I've moved to Paris in order to learn the language. My school is the Alliance Française, and on the first day of class, I arrived early, watching as the returning students greeted one another in the school lobby. Vacations were recounted, and questions were raised concerning mutual friends with names like Kang and Vlatnya. Regardless of their nationalities, everyone spoke what sounded to me like excellent French. Some accents were better than others, but the students exhibited an ease and confidence I found intimidating. As an added discomfort, they were all young, attractive, and well dressed, causing me to feel not unlike Pa Kettle[1] trapped backstage after a fashion show. 2

I remind myself that I am now a full-grown man. No one will ever again card me for a drink or demand that I weave a floor mat out of newspapers. At my age, a reasonable person should have completed his sentence in the prison of the nervous and the insecure—isn't that the great promise of adulthood? I can't help but think that, somewhere along the way, I made a wrong turn. My fears have not vanished. Rather, they have seasoned and multiplied with age. I am now twice as frightened as I was when, at the age of twenty, I allowed a failed nursing student to inject me with a horse tranquilizer, and eight times more anxious than I was the day my kindergarten teacher pried my fingers off my mother's ankle and led me screaming toward my desk. "You'll get used to it," the woman had said. 3

I'm still waiting. 4

The first day of class was nerve-racking because I knew I'd be expected to perform. That's the way they do it here—everyone into the language pool, sink or swim. The teacher marched in, deeply tanned from a recent vacation, and rattled off a series of administrative announcements. I've spent some time in Normandy,[2] and I took a monthlong French class last summer in New York. I'm not completely in the dark, yet I understood only half of what this teacher was saying. 5

"If you have not *meismslsxp* by this time, you should not be in this room. Has everybody *apzkiubjxow*? Everyone? Good, we shall 6

[1]*Pa Kettle:* someone who is simple or unsophisticated; the name of a character in a series of comic movies popular in the 1950s.
[2]*Normandy:* a province in northwestern France.

proceed." She spread out her lesson plan and sighed, saying, "All right, then, who knows the alphabet?"

It was startling because a) I hadn't been asked that question in a while, and b) I realized, while laughing, that I myself did not know the alphabet. They're the same letters, but they're pronounced differently. 7

"Ahh." The teacher went to the board and sketched the letter *A*. "Do we have anyone in the room whose first name commences with an ahh?" 8

Two Polish Annas raised their hands, and the teacher instructed them to present themselves, giving their names, nationalities, occupations, and a list of things they liked and disliked in this world. The first Anna hailed from an industrial town outside of Warsaw and had front teeth the size of tombstones. She worked as a seamstress, enjoyed quiet times with friends, and hated the mosquito. 9

"Oh, really," the teacher said. "How very interesting. I thought that everyone loved the mosquito, but here, in front of all the world, you claim to detest him. How is it that we've been blessed with someone as unique and original as you? Tell us, please." 10

The seamstress did not understand what was being said, but she knew that this was an occasion for shame. Her rabbity mouth huffed for breath, and she stared down at her lap as though the appropriate comeback were stitched somewhere alongside the zipper of her slacks. 11

The second Anna learned from the first and claimed to love sunshine and detest lies. It sounded like a translation of one of those Playmate of the Month data sheets, the answers always written in the same loopy handwriting: "Turn-ons: Mom's famous five-alarm chili! Turnoffs: Insincerity and guys who come on too strong!!!" 12

The two Polish women surely had clear notions of what they liked and disliked, but, like the rest of us, they were limited in terms of vocabulary, and this made them appear less than sophisticated. The teacher forged on, and we learned that Carlos, the Argentine bandoneon[3] player, loved wine, music, and, in his words, "Making sex with the women of the world." Next came a beautiful young Yugoslavian who identified herself as an optimist, saying that she loved everything life had to offer. 13

The teacher licked her lips, revealing a hint of the sadist[4] we would later come to know. She crouched low for her attack, placed her hands 14

[3]*bandoneon:* a small accordion popular in Latin America.
[4]*sadist:* one who finds pleasure in being cruel to others.

on the young woman's desk, and said, "Oh, yeah? And do you love your little war?"[5]

While the optimist struggled to defend herself, I scrambled to 15
think of an answer to what had obviously become a trick question. How often are you asked what you love in this world? More important, how often are you asked and then publicly ridiculed for your answer? I recalled my mother, flushed with wine, pounding the table late one night, saying, "Love? I love a good steak cooked rare. I love my cat, and I love . . ." My sisters and I leaned forward, waiting to hear our names. "Tums," our mother said. "I love Tums." The teacher killed some time accusing the Yugoslavian girl of masterminding a program of genocide, and I jotted frantic notes in the margins of my pad. While I can honestly say that I love leafing through medical textbooks devoted to severe dermatological conditions, it is beyond the reach of my French vocabulary, and acting it out would only have invited unwanted attention.

When called upon, I delivered an effortless list of things I detest: 16
blood sausage, intestinal paté, brain pudding. I'd learned these words the hard way. Having given it some thought, I then declared my love for IBM typewriters, the French word for "bruise," and my electric floor waxer. It was a short list, but still I managed to mispronounce IBM and afford the wrong gender to both the floor waxer and the typewriter. Her reaction led me to believe that these mistakes were capital crimes in the country of France.

"Were you always this *palicmkrexjs?*" she asked. "Even a 17
fiuscrzsws tociwegixp knows that a typewriter is feminine."

I absorbed as much of her abuse as I could understand, thinking, 18
but not saying, that I find it ridiculous to assign a gender to an inanimate object incapable of disrobing and making an occasional fool of itself. Why refer to Lady Flesh Wound or Good Sir Dishrag when these things could never deliver in the sack?

The teacher proceeded to belittle everyone from German Eva, 19
who hated laziness, to Japanese Yukari, who loved paintbrushes and soap. Italian, Thai, Dutch, Korean, Chinese—we all left class foolishly believing that the worst was over. We didn't know it then, but the coming months would teach us what it is like to spend time in the presence

---

[5] *". . . your little war":* the Balkan War (1991–2001), armed conflict and genocide in the territory of the former Yugoslavia.

of a wild animal. We soon learned to dodge chalk and to cover our heads and stomachs whenever she approached us with a question. She hadn't yet punched anyone, but it seemed wise to prepare ourselves against the inevitable.

Though we were forbidden to speak anything but French, the teacher would occasionally use us to practice any of her five fluent languages. 20

"I hate you," she said to me one afternoon. Her English was flawless. "I really, really hate you." Call me sensitive, but I couldn't help taking it personally. 21

Learning French is a lot like joining a gang in that it involves a long and intensive period of hazing. And it wasn't just my teacher; the entire population seemed to be in on it. Following brutal encounters with my local butcher and the concierge[6] of my building, I'd head off to class, where the teacher would hold my corrected paperwork high above her head, shouting, "Here's proof that *David* is an ignorant and uninspired *ensigiejsokhjx*." 22

Refusing to stand convicted on the teacher's charges of laziness, I'd spend four hours a night on my homework, working even longer whenever we were assigned an essay. I suppose I could have gotten by with less, but I was determined to create some sort of an identity for myself. We'd have one of those "complete the sentence" exercises, and I'd fool with the thing for hours, invariably settling on something like, "A quick run around the lake? I'd love to. Just give me a minute to strap on my wooden leg." The teacher, through word and action, conveyed the message that, if this was my idea of an identity, she wanted nothing to do with it. 23

My fear and discomfort crept beyond the borders of my classroom and accompanied me out onto the wide boulevards, where, no matter how hard I tried, there was no escaping the feeling of terror I felt whenever anyone asked me a question. I was safe in any kind of a store, as, at least in my neighborhood, one can stand beside the cash register for hours on end without being asked something so trivial as, "May I help you?" or "How would you like to pay for that?" 24

My only comfort was the knowledge that I was not alone. Huddled in the smoky hallways and making the most of our pathetic French, my fellow students and I engaged in the sort of conversation commonly overheard in refugee camps. 25

---

[6]*concierge:* a doorman in a French apartment building.

"Sometimes me cry alone at night." 26

"That is common for me also, but be more strong, you. Much work, and someday you talk pretty. People stop hate you soon. Maybe tomorrow, okay?" 27

Unlike other classes I have taken, here there was no sense of competition. When the teacher poked a shy Korean woman in the eyelid with a freshly sharpened pencil, we took no comfort in the fact that, unlike Hyeyoon Cho, we all knew the irregular past tense of the verb "to defeat." In all fairness, the teacher hadn't meant to hurt the woman, but neither did she spend much time apologizing, saying only, "Well, you should have been paying more attention." 28

Over time, it became impossible to believe that any of us would ever improve. Fall arrived, and it rained every day. It was mid-October when the teacher singled me out, saying, "Every day spent with you is like having a cesarean section." And it struck me that, for the first time since arriving in France, I could understand every word that someone was saying. 29

Understanding doesn't mean that you can suddenly speak the language. Far from it. It's a small step, nothing more, yet its rewards are intoxicating and deceptive. The teacher continued her diatribe, and I settled back, bathing in the subtle beauty of each new curse and insult. 30

"You exhaust me with your foolishness and reward my efforts with nothing but pain, do you understand me?" 31

The world opened up, and it was with great joy that I responded, "I know the thing what you speak exact now. Talk me more, plus, please, plus." 32

Thinking Critically about This Reading

Sedaris's French teacher tells him that "every day spent with you is like having a cesarean section" (paragraph 29). Why is Sedaris's ability to recount this insult significant? What does the teacher's "cesarean section" metaphor mean?

Questions for Study and Discussion

1. Sedaris's tone is humorous. (Glossary: *Tone*) What words in particular help him create this tone? Did you find yourself smiling or

laughing out loud as you read his essay? If so, what specific passages affected you this way?

2. What is your impression of Sedaris and his classmates? What words and phrases does he use to describe himself and them?
3. Why do you think Sedaris uses nonsense jumbles of letters—*meismslsxp* and *palicmkrexjs,* for example—in several places? How would his essay be different had he used the real words instead?
4. What does Sedaris realize in the final three paragraphs? What evidence does he provide of his realization?

Classroom Activity Using Diction and Tone

Many restaurant menus use connotative language in an attempt to persuade patrons that they are about to have an exceptional dining experience: "skillfully seasoned," "festive and spicy," "fresh from the garden," "grilled to perfection," "freshly ground." Imagine that you are charged with the task of creating such a menu. Use connotative language to describe the following basic foods, making them sound as attractive and inviting as possible.

tomato juice	peas	pasta
onion soup	potatoes	ice cream
ground beef	salad	tea
chicken	bread and butter	cake

Suggested Writing Assignments

1. Write a narrative essay recounting a humorous incident in your life. (Glossary: *Narration*) Use the following questions to start thinking about the incident: Where were you? What happened? Who witnessed the incident? Did you think it was humorous at the time? Do you view it differently now? Why or why not? Choose words and phrases for your narrative that convey a humorous tone. (Glossary: *Tone*)
2. "Refusing to stand convicted on the teacher's charge of laziness," Sedaris explains, "I'd spend four hours a night on my homework, working even longer whenever we were assigned an essay" (23). Write an essay in which you evaluate Sedaris's teacher. Given that

she inspired Sedaris to apply himself to his work, do you think she was an effective teacher? Would her methods have the same effect on you? Why or why not? (Glossary: *Cause and Effect*)

3. As Sedaris's essay and the following cartoon illustrate, fitting in often depends on our ability to communicate with authenticity—using the appropriate pronunciation, terminology, or slang—to a particular audience. (Glossary: *Audience; Slang*) Have you ever felt alienated by a group because you didn't use its lingo appropriately, or have you ever alienated someone else for the same reason? Write a narrative essay in which you recount one such event. (Glossary: *Narration*) Be sure to use diction and tone creatively to convey your meaning. Before you begin, you might find it helpful to refer to your prereading prompt response for this selection.

Pop-A-Shot

■ **Sarah Vowell**

Author and cultural observer, Sarah Vowell was born in Oklahoma in 1969. She graduated from Montana State University in 1993 and earned her MA from the Art Institute of Chicago in 1996. She is perhaps best known for the witty and sometimes quirky monologues and documentaries that she's done for National Public Radio's This American Life *since 1996. Vowell has performed her comic routines at the Aspen Comedy Festival, Amsterdam's Crossing Borders Festival, and Seattle's Foolproof Comedy Festival. Vowell's essays have appeared in* Esquire, *the* Los Angeles Times, *the* Village Voice, Spin, *and* Salon. *Her books include* Radio On: A Listener's Diary *(1997),* Take the Cannoli: Stories from the New World *(2000),* The Partly Cloudy Patriot *(2002),* Assassination Vacation *(2005), and* The Wordy Shipmates *(2008). In 2004, she voiced the character Violet for the animated movie* The Incredibles.

In the following essay, taken from The Partly Cloudy Patriot, *Vowell reflects on her own fascination with the arcade game Pop-A-Shot. As you read, notice how she uses her humorous, offbeat perspective to make a point about what she does to find happiness.*

Reflecting on What You Know

What does it mean to "goof off"? What kinds of things do you and your friends do when goofing off? For example, do you play arcade games or video games when you want to escape the stresses of everyday life? What, for you, are the benefits of goofing off?

Along with voting, jury duty, and paying taxes, goofing off is one of the central obligations of American citizenship. So when my friends Joel and Stephen and I play hooky from our jobs in the middle of the afternoon to play Pop-A-Shot in a room full of children, I like to think we are not procrastinators;[1] we are patriots pursuing happiness. 1

[1] *procrastinators:* people who delay doing something unpleasant or burdensome.

Pop-A-Shot is not a video game. It involves shooting real, if miniature, basketballs for forty seconds. It's embarrassing how giddy the three of us get when it's our turn to put money into the machine. (Often, we have to stand behind some six-year-old girl who bogarts[2] the game and whose father keeps dropping in quarters even though the kid makes only about 4 points if she's lucky and we are forced to glare at the back of her pigtailed head, waiting just long enough to start questioning our adulthood and how by the time our parents were our age they were beholden to mortgages and PTA meetings and here we are, stuck in an episode of *Friends*.) 2

Finally it's my turn. A wave of balls slide toward me and I shoot, making my first basket. I'm good at this. I'm not great. The machine I usually play on has a high score of 72, and my highest score is 56. But considering that I am five foot four, that I used to get C's in gym, and that I campaigned for Dukakis,[3] the fact that I am capable of scoring 56 points in forty seconds is a source of no small amount of pride. Plus, even though these modern men won't admit it, it really bugs Joel and Steve to get topped by a girl. 3

There are two reasons I can shoot a basketball: black-eyed peas and Uncle Hoy. I was a forward on my elementary school team. This was in Oklahoma, back when girls played half-court basketball, which meant I never crossed over to the other team's side, which meant all I ever had to do was shoot, a bonus considering that I cannot run, pass, or dribble. Blessed with one solitary athletic skill, I was going to make the most of it. I shot baskets in the backyard every night after dinner. We lived out in the country, and my backboard was nailed to an oak tree that grew on top of a hill. If I missed a shot, the ball would roll downhill into the drainage ditch for the kitchen sink, a muddy rivulet[4] flecked with corn and black-eyed peas. So if the ball bounced willy-nilly off the rim, I had to run after it, retrieve it from the gross black-eyed pea mud, then hose it off. So I learned not to miss. 4

My mother's brother, Hoy, was a girls' basketball coach. Once he saw I had a knack for shooting, he used to drill me on free throws, standing under the hoop at my grandmother's house, where he himself learned to play. And Hoy, who was also a math teacher—he had 5

[2]*bogarts:* is selfish; takes more than one's share of something.

[3]*Michael Dukakis* (b. 1933): former governor of Massachusetts who lost the 1988 presidential election.

[4]*rivulet:* a brook or little stream.

gone to college on a dual math-basketball scholarship—revered the geometrical arc of the swish. Hoy hated the backboard, and thought players who used it to make anything other than layups lacked elegance. And so, if I made a free throw that bounced off the backboard before gliding through the basket, he'd yell, "Doesn't count." Sometimes, trash-talking at Pop-A-Shot, I bark that at Joel and Stephen when they score their messy bank shots. "Doesn't count!" The electronic scoreboard, unfortunately, makes no distinction for grace and beauty.

I watch the NBA. I lived in Chicago during the heyday of the Bulls. 6
And I have noticed that in, as I like to call it, the moving-around-basketball, the players spend the whole game trying to shoot. There's all that wasted running and throwing and falling down on cameramen in between baskets. But Pop-A-Shot is basketball concentrate. I've made 56 points in forty seconds. Michael Jordan never did that. When Michael Jordan would make even 40 points in a game it was the lead in the eleven o'clock news. It takes a couple of hours to play a moving-around-basketball game. Pop-A-Shot distills this down to less than a minute. It is the crack cocaine of basketball. I can make twenty-eight baskets at a rate of less than two seconds per.

Joel, an excellent shot, also appreciates this about Pop-A-Shot. 7
He likes the way it feels, but he's embarrassed by how it sounds stupid when he describes it to other people. (He spent part of last year working in Canada, and I think it rubbed off on him, diminishing his innate American ability to celebrate the civic virtue of idiocy.) Joel plays in a fairly serious adult basketball league in New York. One night, he left Stephen and me in the arcade and rushed off to a—this hurt my feelings—"real" game. That night, he missed a foul shot by two feet and made the mistake of admitting to the other players that his arms were tired from throwing miniature balls at a shortened hoop all afternoon. They laughed and laughed. "In the second overtime," Joel told me, "when the opposing team fouled me with four seconds left and gave me the opportunity to shoot from the line for the game, they looked mighty smug as they took their positions along the key. Oh, Pop-A-Shot guy, I could hear them thinking to their smug selves. He'll never make a foul shot. He plays baby games. Wa-wa-wa, little Pop-A-Shot baby, would you like a zwieback biscuit? But you know what? I made those shots, and those sons of bitches had to wipe their smug grins off their smug faces and go home thinking that maybe Pop-A-Shot wasn't just a baby game after all."

I think Pop-A-Shot's a baby game. That's why I love it. Unlike the game of basketball itself, Pop-A-Shot has no standard socially redeeming value whatsoever. Pop-A-Shot is not about teamwork or getting along or working together. Pop-A-Shot is not about getting exercise or fresh air. It takes place in fluorescent-lit bowling alleys or darkened bars. It costs money. At the end of a game, one does not swig Gatorade. One sips bourbon or margaritas or munches cupcakes. Unless one is playing the Super Shot version at the ESPN Zone in Times Square,[5] in which case, one orders the greatest appetizer ever invented on this continent—a plate of cheeseburgers. 8

In other words, Pop-A-Shot has no point at all. And that, for me, is the point. My life is full of points—the deadlines and bills and recycling and phone calls. I have come to appreciate, to depend on, this one dumb-ass little passion. Because every time a basketball slides off my fingertips and drops perfectly, flawlessly, into that hole, well, swish, happiness found. 9

Thinking Critically about This Reading

At various points in her essay Vowell compares and contrasts the arcade game Pop-A-Shot to the game of basketball. How are the two games similar? How are they different? What conclusions about Pop-A-Shot does this comparison enable Vowell to draw?

Questions for Study and Discussion

1. In the opening paragraph, Vowell announces that "goofing off is one of the central obligations of American citizenship." How serious do you think she is in making this claim? How does she support this claim?
2. How does Vowell account for her success at Pop-A-Shot?
3. How would you describe Vowell's tone in this essay? How does her choice of words lead you to this conclusion?
4. What does Vowell mean when she says that "Pop-A-Shot is basketball concentrate" (paragraph 6)?

[5]*Times Square:* a major entertainment district in New York City.

5. In paragraph 7, Vowell relates a story about her friend Joel's experience in a "real" basketball game. How is this paragraph about Joel related to Vowell's main idea, or is this paragraph a digression in the essay? (Glossary: *Unity*)
6. What do you know about the writer as a result of reading this essay? How would you describe her?
7. What, for Vowell, is the point of Pop-A-Shot? Why does she love this game?

Classroom Activity Using Diction and Tone

Writers use different levels of diction to communicate with different audiences of readers. For example, a writer might use the formal label *police officer* in an article for law enforcement professionals and the more informal word *cop* in a humorous piece for a general audience. Recall a fairground activity, an amusement park ride, or a video game that you have enjoyed. Write a paragraph in which you describe this activity, ride, or game to an older relative. Then rewrite the paragraph to appeal to a ten-year-old.

Suggested Writing Assignments

1. Vowell states that Americans like her friend Joel have the "innate . . . ability to celebrate the civic virtue of idiocy" (7). What do you think? Has the world gotten so serious and stressful that we all need "one dumb-ass little passion" (9) like Pop-A-Shot to make life tolerable? Write an essay in which you present your views on mindless or pointless games in our culture.
2. What makes you happy? For example, do you find happiness when you are with other people or while you are doing a particular activity? Write an essay in which you explain what makes you happy.

chapter **12**

Figurative Language

Figurative language is language used in an imaginative rather than a literal sense. Although it is most often associated with poetry, figurative language is used widely in our daily speech and in our writing. Prose writers have long known that figurative language brings freshness and color to writing and also helps to clarify ideas. For example, when asked by his teacher to explain the concept of brainstorming, one student replied, "Well, brainstorming is like having a tornado in your head." This figurative language helps others imagine the whirl of ideas in this young writer's head as he brainstorms a topic for writing.

The two most common **figures of speech** are the simile and the metaphor. A **simile** compares two essentially different ideas or things and uses the word *like* or *as* to link them.

> Canada geese sweep across the hills and valleys like a formation of strategic bombers.
>
> –Benjamin B. Bachman

> I walked toward her and hailed her as a visitor to the moon might salute a survivor of a previous expedition.
>
> –John Updike

A **metaphor** compares dissimilar ideas or things without using *like* or *as.*

> She was very old and small and she walked slowly in the dark pine shadows, moving a little from side to side in her steps, with the balanced heaviness and lightness of a pendulum in a grandfather clock.
>
> –Eudora Welty

> Charm is the ultimate weapon, the supreme seduction, against which there are few defenses.
>
> –Laurie Lee

To expand the richness of a particular comparison, writers sometimes use several sentences or even a whole paragraph to develop a metaphor. Such a comparison is called an *extended metaphor*.

> The point is that you have to strip down your writing before you can build it back up. You must know what the essential tools are and what job they were designed to do. If I may belabor the metaphor on carpentry, it is first necessary to be able to saw wood neatly and to drive nails. Later you can bevel the edges or add elegant finials, if that is your taste. But you can never forget that you are practicing a craft that is based on certain principles. If the nails are weak, your house will collapse. If your verbs are weak and your syntax is rickety, your sentences will fall apart.
>
> –William Zinsser

Another frequently used figure of speech is **personification**. In personification, the writer attributes human qualities to ideas or objects.

> The moon bathed the valley in a soft, golden light.
>
> –Corey Davis, student

> Blond October comes striding over the hills wearing a crimson shirt and faded green trousers.
>
> –Hal Borland

> Indeed, haste can be the assassin of elegance.
>
> –T. H. White

In all of the preceding examples, note how the writers' use of figurative language enlivens their prose and emphasizes their ideas. Each vividly communicates an idea or the essence of an object by comparing it to something concrete and familiar. In each case, too, the figurative language grows out of the writer's thinking, reflecting the way he or she sees the material. Be similarly honest in your use of figurative language, keeping in mind that figures of speech should never be used merely to "dress up" writing. Above all, use them to develop your ideas and clarify your meaning for the reader.

The Barrio

■ **Robert Ramirez**

Robert Ramirez was born in Edinburg, Texas, in 1949. After graduating from the University of Texas–Pan American, he taught writing and worked as a cameraman, reporter, anchor, and producer for the local news on KGBT-TV, the CBS affiliate in Harlingen, Texas. He currently works as an alumni fundraiser for the University of Texas–Pan American.

The following essay first appeared in Pain and Promise: The Chicano Today *(1972), edited by Edward Simmens. Notice how Ramirez uses figurative language, particularly metaphors, to awaken the reader's senses to the sights, sounds, and smells that are the essence of the barrio.*

Reflecting on What You Know

Where did you grow up? What do you remember most about your childhood neighborhood? How did it feel as a young person to live in this world? Do you still call this neighborhood "home"? Explain.

The train, its metal wheels squealing as they spin along the silvery tracks, rolls slower now. Through the gaps between the cars blinks a streetlamp, and this pulsing light on a barrio streetcorner beats slower, like a weary heartbeat, until the train shudders to a halt, the light goes out, and the barrio is deep asleep. 1

Throughout Aztlán[1] (the Nahuatl term meaning "land to the north"), trains grumble along the edges of a sleeping people. From Lower California, through the blistering Southwest, down the Rio Grande[2] to the muddy Gulf, the darkness and mystery of dreams engulf communities fenced off by railroads, canals, and expressways. Paradoxical[3] 2

[1]*Aztlán:* the mythical place of origin of the Aztec peoples.
[2]*Rio Grande:* a river flowing from southwest Colorado to Texas and Mexico and into the Gulf of Mexico.
[3]*paradoxical:* seemingly contradictory.

communities, isolated from the rest of the town by concrete columned monuments of progress, and yet stranded in the past. They are surrounded by change. It eludes their reach, in their own backyards, and the people, unable and unwilling to see the future, or even touch the present, perpetuate the past.

Leaning from the expressway or jolting across the tracks, one enters a different physical world permeated by a different attitude. The physical dimensions are impressive. It is a large section of town which extends for fifteen blocks north and south along the tracks, and then advances eastward, thinning into nothingness beyond the city limits. Within the invisible (yet sensible) walls of the barrio are many, many people living in too few houses. The homes, however, are much more numerous than on the outside. 3

Members of the barrio describe the entire area as their home. It is a home, but it is more than this. The barrio is a refuge from the harshness and the coldness of the Anglo world. It is a forced refuge. The leprous people are isolated from the rest of the community and contained in their section of town. The stoical pariahs of the barrio accept their fate, and from the angry seeds of rejection grow the flowers of closeness between outcasts, not the thorns of bitterness and the mad desire to flee. There is no want to escape, for the feeling of the barrio is known only to its inhabitants, and the material needs of life can also be found here. 4

The *tortillería* [tortilla factory] fires up its machinery three times a day, producing steaming, round, flat slices of barrio bread. In the winter, the warmth of the tortilla factory is a wool *sarape* [blanket] in the chilly morning hours, but in the summer, it unbearably toasts every noontime customer. 5

The *panadería* [bakery] sends its sweet messenger aroma down the dimly lit street, announcing the arrival of fresh, hot sugary *pan dulce* [sweet rolls]. 6

The small corner grocery serves the meal-to-meal needs of customers, and the owner, a part of the neighborhood, willingly gives credit to people unable to pay cash for foodstuffs. 7

The barbershop is a living room with hydraulic chairs, radio, and television, where old friends meet and speak of life as their salted hair falls aimlessly about them. 8

The pool hall is a junior level country club where *'chucos* [young men], strangers in their own land, get together to shoot pool and rap, while veterans, unaware of the cracking, popping balls on the 9 green felt, complacently play dominoes beneath rudely hung *Playboy* foldouts.

The *cantina* [canteen or snackbar] is the night spot of the barrio. 10
It is the country club and the den where the rites of puberty are enacted. Here the young become men. It is in the taverns that a young dude shows his *machismo* through the quantity of beer he can hold, the stories of *rucas* [women] he has had, and his willingness and ability to defend his image against hardened and scarred old lions.

No, there is no frantic wish to flee. It would be absurd to leave 11
the familiar and nervously step into the strange and cold Anglo community when the needs of the Chicano[4] can be met in the barrio.

The barrio is closeness. From the family living unit, familial rela- 12
tionships stretch out to immediate neighbors, down the block, around the corner, and to all parts of the barrio. The feeling of family, a rare and treasurable sentiment, pervades and accounts for the inability of the people to leave. The barrio is this attitude manifested on the countenances[5] of the people, on the faces of their homes, and in the gaiety of their gardens.

The color-splashed homes arrest your eyes, arouse your curiosity, 13
and make you wonder what life scenes are being played out in them. The flimsy, brightly colored, wood-frame houses ignore no neon-brilliant color. Houses trimmed in orange, chartreuse, lime-green, yellow, and mixtures of these and other hues beckon the beholder to reflect on the peculiarity of each home. Passing through this land is refreshing like Brubeck,[6] not narcoticizing like revolting rows of similar houses, which neither offend nor please.

In the evenings, the porches and front yards are occupied with 14
men calmly talking over the noise of children playing baseball in the unpaved extension of the living room, while the women cook supper or gossip with female neighbors as they water the *jardines* [gardens]. The gardens mutely echo the expressive verses of the colorful houses. The denseness of multicolored plants and trees gives the house the appearance of an oasis or a tropical island hideaway, sheltered from the rest of the world.

Fences are common in the barrio, but they are fences and not the 15
walls of the Anglo community. On the western side of town, the high

[4]*Chicano:* an American of Mexican descent.

[5]*countenances:* facial expressions that indicate mood or character.

[6]*Dave Brubeck* (b. 1920): pianist, composer, and conductor of "cool" modern jazz.

wooden fences between houses are thick, impenetrable walls, built to keep the neighbors at bay. In the barrio, the fences may be rusty, wire contraptions or thick green shrubs. In either case you can see through them and feel no sense of intrusion when you cross them.

Many lower-income families of the barrio manage to maintain a comfortable standard of living through the communal action of family members who contribute their wages to the head of the family. Economic need creates interdependence and closeness. Small barefooted boys sell papers on cool, dark Sunday mornings, deny themselves pleasantries, and give their earnings to *mamá*. The older the child, the greater the responsibility to help the head of the household provide for the rest of the family. 16

There are those, too, who for a number of reasons have not achieved a relative sense of financial security. Perhaps it results from too many children too soon, but it is the homes of these people and their situation that numbs rather than charms. Their houses, aged and bent, oozing children, are fissures[7] in the horn of plenty. Their wooden homes may have brick-pattern asbestos tile on the outer walls, but the tile is not convincing. 17

Unable to pay city taxes or incapable of influencing the city to live up to its duty to serve all the citizens, the poorer barrio families remain trapped in the nineteenth century and survive as best they can. The backyards have well-worn paths to the outhouses, which sit near the alley. Running water is considered a luxury in some parts of the barrio. Decent drainage is usually unknown, and when it rains, the water stands for days, an incubator of health hazards and an avoidable nuisance. Streets, costly to pave, remain rough, rocky trails. Tires do not last long, and the constant rattling and shaking grind away a car's life and spread dust through screen windows. 18

The houses and their *jardines,* the jollity of the people in an adverse world, the brightly feathered alarm clock pecking away at supper and cautiously eyeing the children playing nearby, produce a mystifying sensation at finding the noble savage[8] alive in the twentieth century. It is easy to look at the positive qualities of life in the barrio, and look at them with a distantly envious feeling. One wishes to experience the feelings of the barrio and not the hardships. Remembering the illness, the hunger, the feeling of time running out on you, the walls, both 19

[7]*fissures:* narrow openings or cracks.

[8]*noble savage:* in literature, an idealized concept of uncivilized man.

real and imagined, reflecting on living in the past, one finds his envy becoming more elusive, until it has vanished altogether.

Back now beyond the tracks, the train creaks and groans, the cars 20
jostle each other down the track, and as the light begins its pulsing, the barrio, with all its meanings, greets a new dawn with yawns and restless stretchings.

Thinking Critically about This Reading

What evidence does Ramirez give to support the following claim: "Members of the barrio describe the whole area as their home. It is a home, but it is more than this" (paragraph 4)?

Questions for Study and Discussion

1. What is the barrio? Where is it? What does Ramirez mean when he states, "There is no want to escape, for the feeling of the barrio is known only to its inhabitants, and the material needs of life can also be found here" (4)?
2. Ramirez uses Spanish phrases throughout his essay. Why do you suppose he uses them? What is their effect on the reader? He also uses the words *home, refuge, family*, and *closeness*. What do they connote in the context of this essay? (Glossary: *Connotation/Denotation*) In what ways, if any, are they essential to the writer's purpose? (Glossary: *Purpose*)
3. Identify several metaphors and similes that Ramirez uses in his essay, and explain why they are particularly appropriate.
4. In paragraph 6, Ramirez uses personification when he calls the aroma of freshly baked sweet rolls a "messenger" who announces the arrival of the baked goods. Cite other words or phrases that Ramirez uses to give human characteristics to the barrio.
5. Explain Ramirez's use of the imagery of walls and fences to describe a sense of cultural isolation. What might this imagery symbolize? (Glossary: *Symbol*)
6. Ramirez begins with a relatively positive picture of the barrio, but ends on a more disheartening note. (Glossary: *Beginnings and Endings*) Why does he organize his essay in this way? What might the effect have been if he had reversed these images?

Classroom Activity Using Figurative Language

Create a metaphor or simile that would be helpful in describing each item in the following list. The first one has been completed for you to illustrate the process.

1. Skyscraper: The skyscraper sparkled like a huge glass needle.
2. Sound of an explosion
3. Intelligent student
4. Crowded bus
5. Slow-moving car
6. Pillow
7. Narrow alley
8. Greasy french fries
9. Hot sun
10. Dull knife

Compare your metaphors and similes with those written by other members of your class. Which metaphors and similes for each item on the list seem to work best? Why? Do any seem tired or clichéd?

Suggested Writing Assignments

1. In paragraph 19 Ramirez states, "One wishes to experience the feelings of the barrio and not the hardships." Explore his meaning in light of what you have just read and of other experience or knowledge you may have of "ghetto" living. In what way can it be said that the hardships of such living are a necessary part of its "feelings"? How might barrio life change, for better or for worse, if the city were to "live up to its duty to serve all the citizens" (18)?
2. Write a brief essay in which you describe your own neighborhood. (Glossary: *Description*) You may find it helpful to review what you wrote in response to the journal prompt for this selection.
3. The photograph on page 311 shows a Hispanic woman in San Diego, California, carrying her groceries past a striking mural honoring Hispanic heroes and revolutionaries. Prominently featured are such figures as Cesar Chavez, an American who led migrant farmworkers' protests against poor working conditions in California in the 1950s to 1970s, and Che Guevara, a Cuban revolutionary leader

who helped Fidel Castro come to power in the late 1950s. What details about the San Diego community can you glean from the mural? Which details tell you about the neighborhood? About the socioeconomic struggles of the barrio? Write an essay about life in the barrio as it is depicted in the mural, incorporating the visual details you see and inferences you draw from them. Be creative: use as many figures of speech as you can in your essay.

The Jacket

■ **Gary Soto**

*Born in Fresno, California, in 1952 to working-class Mexican American parents, Gary Soto is an award-winning author of poetry and fiction for readers of all ages, as well as an opera librettist and film producer. After laboring as a migrant farmworker in the San Joaquin Valley during the 1960s, he studied geography at California State University–Fresno and at the University of California–Irvine before turning his hand to poetry. In his first two collections of poetry—*The Elements of San Joaquin *(1977) and* The Tale of Sunlight *(1978)—Soto draws heavily on his childhood experiences as a Mexican American growing up in the central valley of California. He has published four other volumes of poetry, a collection of short stories, and four works of nonfiction, including* Living up the Street: Narrative Recollections *(1985) and* A Summer Life *(1991). In May 2008, he published his first book for young adult readers,* Facts of Life: Stories.

"The Jacket" is taken from Soto's popular collection of essays, The Effects of Knut Hamsun on a Fresno Boy *(2000). As you read, notice how Soto makes the intensity of his feelings for his jacket known through his extensive use of figurative language—simile, personification, and metaphor.*

Reflecting on What You Know

Do you remember an article of clothing that took on special significance for you as you were growing up? It might have been a pair of beautiful cowboy boots, a dress that made you feel like a princess, or a T-shirt you couldn't bear to be without. Recall the emotions that arose when you wore that special article of clothing. Reflect on the relationship between clothes and one's identity.

My clothes have failed me. I remember the green coat that I wore in fifth and sixth grades when you either danced like a champ or pressed yourself against a greasy wall, bitter as a penny toward the happy couples. 1

When I needed a new jacket and my mother asked what kind I wanted, I described something like bikers wear: black leather and silver studs with enough belts to hold down a small town. We were in the kitchen, steam on the windows from her cooking. She listened so long while stirring dinner that I thought she understood for sure the kind I wanted. The next day when I got home from school, I discovered draped on my bedpost a jacket the color of day-old guacamole. I threw my books on the bed and approached the jacket slowly, as if it were a stranger whose hand I had to shake. I touched the vinyl sleeve, the collar, and peeked at the mustard-colored lining. 2

From the kitchen mother yelled that my jacket was in the closet. I closed the door to her voice and pulled at the rack of clothes in the closet, hoping the jacket on the bedpost wasn't for me but my mean brother. No luck. I gave up. From my bed, I stared at the jacket. I wanted to cry because it was so ugly and so big that I knew I'd have to wear it a long time. I was a small kid, thin as a young tree, and it would be years before I'd have a new one. I stared at the jacket, like an enemy, thinking bad things before I took off my old jacket whose sleeves climbed halfway to my elbow. 3

I put the big jacket on. I zipped it up and down several times, and rolled the cuffs up so they didn't cover my hands. I put my hands in the pockets and flapped the jacket like a bird's wings. I stood in front of the mirror, full face, then profile, and then looked over my shoulder as if someone had called me. I sat on the bed, stood against the bed, and combed my hair to see what I would look like doing something natural. I looked ugly. I threw it on my brother's bed and looked at it for a long time before I slipped it on and went out to the backyard, smiling a "thank you" to my mom as I passed her in the kitchen. With my hands in my pockets I kicked a ball against the fence, and then climbed it to sit looking into the alley. I hurled orange peels at the mouth of an open garbage can and when the peels were gone I watched the white puffs of my breath thin to nothing. 4

I jumped down, hands in my pockets, and in the backyard on my knees I teased my dog, Brownie, by swooping my arms while making bird calls. He jumped at me and missed. He jumped again and again, until a tooth sunk deep, ripping an L-shaped tear on my left sleeve. I pushed Brownie away to study the tear as I would a cut on my arm. There was no blood, only a few loose pieces of fuzz. Damn dog, I thought, and pushed him away hard when he tried to bite again. I got 5 up from my knees and went to my bedroom to sit with my jacket on my lap, with the lights out.

That was the first afternoon with my new jacket. The next day I wore it to sixth grade and got a D on a math quiz. During the morning recess Frankie T., the playground terrorist, pushed me to the ground and told me to stay there until recess was over. My best friend, Steve Negrete, ate an apple while looking at me, and the girls turned away to whisper on the monkey bars. The teachers were no help: they looked my way and talked about how foolish I looked in my new jacket. I saw their heads bob with laughter, their hands half-covering their mouths. 6

Even though it was cold, I took off the jacket during lunch and played kickball in a thin shirt, my arm feeling like braille[1] from the goose bumps. But when I returned to class I slipped the jacket on and shivered until I was warm. I sat on my hands, heating them up, while my teeth chattered like a cup of crooked dice. Finally warm, I slid out of the jacket but a few minutes later put it back on when the fire bell rang. We paraded out into the yard where we, the sixth graders, walked past all the other grades to stand against the back fence. Everybody saw me. Although they didn't say out loud, "Man, that's ugly," I heard the buzz-buzz of gossip and even laughter that I knew was meant for me. 7

And so I went, in my guacamole-colored jacket. So embarrassed, so hurt, I couldn't even do my homework. I received Cs on quizzes, and forgot the state capitals and rivers of South America, our friendly neighbor. Even the girls who had been friendly blew away like loose flowers to follow the boys in neat jackets. 8

I wore that thing for three years until the sleeves grew short and my forearms stuck out like the necks of turtles. All during that time no love came to me—no little dark girl in a Sunday dress she wore on Monday. At lunchtime I stayed with the ugly boys who leaned against the chainlink fence and looked around with propellers of grass spinning in our mouths. We saw girls walk by alone, saw couples, hand in hand, their heads like bookends pressing air together. We saw them and spun our propellers so fast our faces were blurs. 9

I blame that jacket for those bad years. I blame my mother for her bad taste and her cheap ways. It was a sad time for the heart. With a friend I spent my sixth-grade year in a tree in the alley, waiting for something good to happen to me in that jacket, which had become 10

[1]*braille:* a system of writing for the blind in which characters are formed with patterns of raised dots that can be felt with the fingers.

the ugly brother who tagged along wherever I went. And it was about that time that I began to grow. My chest puffed up with muscle and, strangely, a few more ribs. Even my hands, those fleshy hammers, showed bravely through the cuffs, the fingers already hardening for the coming fights. But that L-shaped rip on the left sleeve got bigger, bits of stuffing coughed out from its wound after a hard day of play. I finally Scotch-taped it closed, but in rain or cold weather the tape peeled off like a scab and more stuffing fell out until that sleeve shriveled into a palsied arm. That winter the elbows began to crack and whole chunks of green began to fall off. I showed the cracks to my mother, who always seemed to be at the stove with steamed-up glasses, and she said that there were children in Mexico who would love that jacket. I told her that this was America and yelled that Debbie, my sister, didn't have a jacket like mine. I ran outside, ready to cry, and climbed the tree by the alley to think bad thoughts and watch my breath puff white and disappear.

But whole pieces still casually flew off my jacket when I played hard, read quietly, or took vicious spelling tests at school. When it became so spotted that my brother began to call me "camouflage," I flung it over the fence into the alley. Later, however, I swiped the jacket off the ground and went inside to drape it across my lap and mope. 11

I was called to dinner: steam silvered my mother's glasses as she said grace; my brother and sister with their heads bowed made ugly faces at their glasses of powdered milk. I gagged too, but eagerly ate big rips of buttered tortilla that held scooped-up beans. Finished, I went outside with my jacket across my arm. It was a cold sky. The faces of clouds were piled up, hurting. I climbed the fence, jumping down with a grunt. I started up the alley and soon slipped into my jacket, that green ugly brother who breathed over my shoulder that day and ever since. 12

Thinking Critically about This Reading

Does Soto's embarrassment come from what people around him say about his jacket or from another source? Would his sense of embarrassment have been relieved if his mother had bought him the leather jacket he wanted? Explain.

Questions for Study and Discussion

1. Explain the relationship between Soto and the jacket. What does the jacket symbolize for him? (Glossary: *Symbol*) In what sense

might the jacket be something more than the cause of his failures and embarrassments? What is the jacket's role in Soto's essay? Explain.

2. What does the tree in the backyard symbolize? (Glossary: *Symbol*)
3. Why do you suppose that Soto's mother did not buy him the black leather jacket he wanted so badly? Was she trying to embarrass him or punish him in some way? What other reason might explain her decision to buy a jacket that was the color of "day-old guacamole" (paragraph 2)?
4. Soto includes a rich range of figurative language in his narrative. Identify at least six figures of speech. What purpose does each one serve? What effect does each one have on you as a reader? Would his story have been as effective had he not used these figures of speech? Explain.
5. Soto refers to his brother when explaining how much he disliked the new jacket. What is the relationship between the new jacket and the brother?
6. Did Soto's new jacket cause his grades to suffer? Explain. (Glossary: *Cause and Effect*) Did the jacket cause Soto to miss out on any friendships with girls? Explain.

Classroom Activity Using Figurative Language

Soto makes use of a variety of figures of speech, including personification. For example, the essay begins with "My clothes have failed me" (1), and it ends with Soto referring to his jacket as "that green ugly brother who breathed over my shoulder that day and ever since" (12). Select an article of your own clothing, and personify it in a brief description or narrative.

Suggested Writing Assignments

1. It might be argued that in times of crisis everything becomes symbolic. So it is with this essay. Soto is going through a rough period in his life as he tries to negotiate the stresses of approaching adolescence. The jacket becomes symbolic of all the difficulties he is having, or perceives himself to be having, with his circumstances and everyone around him. (Glossary: *Symbol*) His situation

is not unlike our own at times. That Soto is able to make us understand and feel for the narrator is the product of his expertise as a writer. Write an essay about a dilemma or crisis, real or perceived, in your life that is similar to what the narrator experiences in "The Jacket." Try to include as many figures of speech as you can but only if they are natural and occasioned by the context of your narrative.

2. In an interview in *Esquire* magazine, Hollywood producer Bob Evans said the following: "Background makes foreground. This goes for the movies, it goes for dressing, it goes for living. Here's an example: If I go to a party and eight different people come over and say, 'Gee, that's a great-looking tie,' as soon as I get home, I take the tie off and put it in the shredder. Screw the tie! I'm not there to make the *tie* look good. The tie is there to make *me* look good. That's what I mean by background makes foreground." Write an essay on the relationship between people and clothes. Do clothes make the person? If not, why are so many people clothes-conscious? Use as many types of figurative language as you can to enliven your prose and make your point.

Watching a Night Launch of the Space Shuttle

■ Diane Ackerman

Diane Ackerman was born in Waukegan, Illinois, in 1948. She received her BA from Pennsylvania State University and her MFA and PhD from Cornell University. Ackerman has worked as a writer-in-residence at several major universities, has directed the writers' program at Washington University in St. Louis, and has been a staff writer at the New Yorker. *She has written several books of poetry and several collections of essays, among them* The Moon by Whale Light, and Other Adventures among Bats, Penguins, Crocodilians, and Whales *(1991);* A Natural History of Love *(1994);* The Rarest of the Rare: Vanishing Animals, Timeless Worlds *(1995);* The Curious Naturalist *(1998); and* A Natural History of My Garden *(2002).*

As you read the following selection from her A Natural History of the Senses *(1990), notice the lush figurative language that Ackerman uses to describe the effects of 7 million pounds of thrust defying gravity by pushing 4.5 million pounds of rockets and shuttle into orbit 184 miles up above earth's atmosphere.*

Reflecting on What You Know

Have you ever seen a rocket or space shuttle launch from the Kennedy Space Center, whether in person or on television? What were your sensory impressions of the event? What do you remember most vividly?

A huge glittering tower sparkles across the Florida marshlands. 1
Floodlights reach into the heavens all around it, rolling out carpets of light. Helicopters and jets blink around the launch pad like insects drawn to flame. Oz never filled the sky with such diamond-studded improbability. Inside the cascading lights, a giant trellis holds a slender rocket to its heart, on each side a tall thermos bottle filled with solid fuel the color and feel of a hard eraser, and on its back a sharp-nosed space

shuttle, clinging like the young of some exotic mammal. A full moon bulges low in the sky, its face turned toward the launch pad, its mouth open.

On the sober consoles of launch control, numbers count backward toward zero. When numbers vanish, and reverse time ends, something will disappear. Not the shuttle—that will stay with us through eyesight and radar, and be on the minds of dozens of tracking dishes worldwide, rolling their heads as if to relieve the anguish. For hours we have been standing on these Floridian bogs, longing for the blazing rapture of the moment ahead, longing to be jettisoned free from routine, and lifted, like the obelisk we launch, that much nearer the infinite. On the fog-wreathed banks of the Banana River, and by the roadside lookouts, we are waiting: 55,000 people are expected at the Space Center alone. 2

When floodlights die on the launch pad, camera shutters and mental shutters all open in the same instant. The air feels loose and damp. A hundred thousand eyes rush to one spot, where a glint below the booster rocket flares into a pinwheel of fire, a sparkler held by hand on the Fourth of July. White clouds shoot out in all directions, in a dust storm of flame, a gritty, swirling Sahara, burning from gray-white to an incandescent platinum so raw it makes your eyes squint, to a radiant gold so narcotic you forget how to blink. The air is full of bee stings, prickly and electric. Your pores start to itch. Hair stands up stiff on the back of your neck. It used to be that the launch pad would melt at lift-off, but now 300,000 gallons of water crash from aloft, burst from below. Steam clouds scent the air with a mineral ash. Crazed by reflection, the waterways turn the color of pounded brass. Thick cumulus clouds shimmy and build at ground level, where you don't expect to see thunderheads. 3

Seconds into the launch, an apricot *whoosh* pours out in spasms, like the rippling quarters of a palomino, and now outbleaches the sun, as clouds rise and pile like a Creation scene. Birds leap into the air along with moths and dragonflies and gnats and other winged creatures, all driven to panic by the clamor: booming, crackling, howling downwind. What is flight, that it can take place in the fragile wings of a moth, whose power station is a heart small as a computer chip? What is flight, that it can groan upward through 4.5 million pounds of dead weight on a colossal gantry? Close your eyes, and you hear the deafening *rat-a-tat-tat* of firecrackers, feel them arcing against your chest. Open your eyes, and you see a huge steel muscle 4 dripping fire, as 7 million pounds of thrust pauses a moment on a silver haunch, and then the bedlam clouds let rip. Iron struts blow over the launch pad like newspapers, and shock waves roll out, pounding their giant fists, pounding the marshes where birds shriek and fly, pounding against your chest, where a heart already rapid begins running clean away from you. The air feels tight as a drum, the molecules bouncing. Suddenly the space shuttle leaps high over the marshlands, away from the now frantic laughter of the loons, away from the reedy delirium of the insects and the open-mouthed awe of the spectators, many of whom are crying, as it rises on a waterfall of flame 700 feet long, shooting colossal sparks as it climbs in a golden halo that burns deep into memory.

5 Only ten minutes from lift-off, it will leave the security blanket of our atmosphere, and enter an orbit 184 miles up. This is not miraculous. After all, we humans began in an early tantrum of the universe, when our chemical makeup first took form. We evolved through accidents, happenstance, near misses, and good luck. We developed language, forged cities, mustered nations. Now we change the course of rivers and move mountains; we hold back trillions of tons of water with cement dams. We break into human chests and heads; operate on beating hearts and thinking brains. What is defying gravity compared to that? In orbit, there will be no night and day, no up and down. No one will have their "feet on the ground." No joke will be "earthy." No point will be "timely." No thrill will be "out of this world." In orbit, the sun will rise every hour and a half, and there will be 112 days to each week. But then time has always been one of our boldest and most ingenious inventions, and, when you think about it, one of the least plausible of our fictions.

6 Lunging to the east out over the water, the shuttle rolls slowly onto its back, climbing at three g's, an upshooting torch, twisting an umbilical of white cloud beneath it. When the two solid rockets fall free, they hover to one side like bright red quotation marks, beginning an utterance it will take four days to finish. For over six minutes of seismic wonder it is still visible, this star we hurl up at the star-studded sky. What is a neighborhood? One wonders. Is it the clump of wild daisies beside the Banana River, in which moths hover and dive without the aid of rockets? For large minds, the earth is a small place. Not small enough to exhaust in one lifetime, but a compact home, cozy, buoyant, a place to cherish, the spectral center of our life. But how could we stay at home forever?

Thinking Critically about This Reading

Near the end of her description of the shuttle launch, Ackerman asks the question, "What is a neighborhood?" What's the point of her question? How does she answer her own question?

Questions for Study and Discussion

1. Identify the figures of speech that Ackerman uses in her first paragraph. What kinds of figures does she employ? What is their effect?
2. What is the dominant impression of Ackerman's description of the launch of the space shuttle? (Glossary: *Dominant Impression*)
3. In which statement or passage does Ackerman come closest to labeling the dominant impression that she tries to create?
4. Where in the text does Ackerman use nature to help her describe what is, after all, an unnatural event?
5. Review the essay, and identify several instances where Ackerman abandons her poetic style for straightforward reporting. What effect do those instances have on the reader? Explain.

Classroom Activity Using Figurative Language

What is the most unusual event you have witnessed? Using the figures of speech you have learned (simile, metaphor, and personification), write a half dozen sentences that describe the event so that your readers can appreciate it. First state what the event was, and then present your sentences in either a connected paragraph or a series of separate sentences. Share your description with your classmates to determine how effectively you have conveyed the dominant impression you wished to create.

Suggested Writing Assignments

1. When you are asked to use more figures of speech in your writing, you may respond in any of the following ways:
    - I really can't see that figures of speech add very much to my writing.
    - It's too much work to think of better ways to say something.

- I usually don't have the time to think of clever ways of expressing myself.
- I've never been very imaginative, so I try to keep things simple.

Everyday speech is actually filled with similes, metaphors, and personifications. Indeed, it's difficult to talk without using them. For example, when we say that "She was as cute as a button," "The path runs around the pond," or "His caress took my breath away," we're using simile, metaphor, and personification. The goal is to find fresh ways to describe, share experiences, and make our writing vibrant and memorable. Review one of your essays, and find opportunities to sharpen your language with figures of speech. Make sure that the figures of speech are fresh and not simply clichés. (Glossary: *Cliché*)

2. As the shuttle prepares to enter orbit around the earth, Ackerman writes in paragraph 5, "This is not miraculous." Indeed, considering what human beings have accomplished, perhaps space shuttles are not spectacular achievements. Has the extraordinary become ordinary? Write an essay in which you discuss whether we have become so accustomed to spectacular events and developments that we view them as commonplace and not as a cause for wonder. As you write, try to employ fresh figures of speech that enliven and brighten your prose.

part ■ four

Types of Essays

chapter **13**

Illustration

Illustration is the use of **examples**—facts, opinions, samples, and anecdotes or stories—to make ideas more concrete and to make generalizations more specific and detailed. Examples enable writers not just to tell but also to show what they mean. The more specific the example, the more effective it is. For instance, in an essay about alternative sources of energy, a writer might offer an example of how a local architecture firm designed a home heated by solar collectors instead of a conventional oil, gas, or electric system.

A writer uses examples to clarify or support the thesis in an essay and the main ideas in paragraphs. Sometimes a single striking example suffices; at other times a whole series of related examples is necessary. The following paragraph presents a single extended example—an anecdote that illustrates the writer's point about cultural differences:

> Whenever there is a great cultural distance between two people, there are bound to be problems arising from differences in behavior and expectations. An example is the American couple who consulted a psychiatrist about their marital problems. The husband was from New England and had been brought up by reserved parents who taught him to control his emotions and to respect the need for privacy. His wife was from an Italian family and had been brought up in close contact with all the members of her large family, who were extremely warm, volatile, and demonstrative. When the husband came home after a hard day at the office, dragging his feet and longing for peace and quiet, his wife would rush to him and smother him. Clasping his hands, rubbing his brow, crooning over his weary head, she never left him alone. But when the wife was upset or anxious about her day, the husband's response was to withdraw completely and leave her alone. No comforting, no affectionate embrace, no attention—just solitude. The woman became convinced her husband didn't love her and, in desperation,

> she consulted a psychiatrist. Their problem wasn't basically psychological but cultural.
>
> –Edward T. Hall

This single example is effective because it is *representative*—that is, essentially similar to other such problems Hall might have described and familiar to many readers. Hall tells the story with enough detail that readers can understand the couple's feelings and so better understand the point he is trying to make.

In contrast, another writer supports his topic sentence about superstitions with ten examples:

> In the folklore of the country, numerous superstitions relate to winter weather. Back-country farmers examine their corn husks—the thicker the husk, the colder the winter. They watch the acorn crop—the more acorns, the more severe the season. They observe where white-faced hornets place their paper nests—the higher they are, the deeper will be the snow. They examine the size and shape and color of the spleens of butchered hogs for clues to the severity of the season. They keep track of the blooming of dogwood in the spring—the more abundant the blooms, the more bitter the cold in January. When chipmunks carry their tails high and squirrels have heavier fur and mice come into country houses early in the fall, the superstitious gird themselves for a long, hard winter. Without any scientific basis, a wider-than-usual black band on a woolly-bear caterpillar is accepted as a sign that winter will arrive early and stay late. Even the way a cat sits beside the stove carries its message to the credulous. According to a belief once widely held in the Ozarks, a cat sitting with its tail to the fire indicates very cold weather is on the way.
>
> –Edwin Way Teale

Teale uses numerous examples because he is writing about various superstitions. Also, putting all those strange beliefs side by side in a kind of catalog makes the paragraph fun to read as well as convincing and informative.

To use illustration effectively, begin by thinking of ideas and generalizations about your topic that you can make clearer and more persuasive by illustrating them with facts, anecdotes, or specific details. You should focus primarily on your main point, the central generalization that you will develop in your essay. Also be alert for other statements or references that may benefit from illustration. Points that are already clear and uncontroversial and that your readers will understand and immediately agree with can stand on their own as you pass along quickly to your next idea; belaboring the obvious wastes your time and energy, as well as your reader's. Often, however, you will find that examples add clarity, color, and weight to what you say.

Consider the following generalization:

> Americans are a pain-conscious people who would rather get rid of pain than seek and cure its root causes.

This assertion is broad and general; it raises the following questions: How so? What does this mean exactly? Why does the writer think so? The statement could be the topic sentence of a paragraph or perhaps even the thesis of an essay or of an entire book. As a writer, you could make the generalization stronger and more meaningful through illustrations. You might support this statement by citing specific situations or specific cases in which Americans have gone to the drugstore instead of to a doctor, as well as by supplying sales figures per capita of painkillers in the United States as compared with other countries.

Illustration is so useful and versatile a strategy that it is found in all kinds of writing. It is essential, for example, in writing a successful argument essay. In an essay arguing that non-English-speaking students starting school in the United States should be taught English as a second language, one writer supports her argument with the following illustration, drawn from her own experience as a Spanish-speaking child in an English-only school:

> Without the use of Spanish, unable to communicate with the teacher or students, for six long weeks we guessed at everything we did. When we lined up to go anywhere, neither my sister nor I knew what to expect. Once, the teacher took the class on a bathroom break, and I mistakenly thought we were on our way to the cafeteria for lunch. Before we left, I grabbed our lunch money, and one of the girls in line began sneering and pointing. Somehow she figured out my mistake before I did. When I realized why she was laughing, I became embarrassed and threw the money into my sister's desk as we walked out of the classroom.
>
> –Hilda Alvarado, student

Alvarado could have summarized her point in the preceding paragraph in fewer words:

> Not only are non-English-speaking students in English-only schools unable to understand the information they are supposed to be learning, but they are also subject to frequent embarrassment and teasing from their classmates.

By offering an illustration, however, Alvarado makes her point more vividly and effectively.

A Crime of Compassion

■ Barbara Huttmann

Barbara Huttmann, who lives in the San Francisco Bay Area, received her nursing degree in 1976. After obtaining a master's degree in nursing administration, she cofounded a healthcare consulting firm for hospitals, nursing organizations, and consumers. Her interest in patients' rights is clearly evident in her two books, The Patient's Advocate *(1981) and* Code Blue *(1982).*

In the following essay, which first appeared in Newsweek *in 1983, Huttmann narrates the final months of the life of Mac, one of her favorite patients. By using emotional and graphic details, Huttmann hopes that Mac's example will convince her audience of the need for new legislation that would permit terminally ill patients to choose to die rather than suffer great pain and indignity. As you read about Mac, consider the degree to which his experience seems representative of what patients often endure because medical technology is now able to keep them alive longer than they would be able to survive on their own.*

Reflecting on What You Know

For most people, being sick is at best an unpleasant experience. Reflect on an illness you have had, whether a simple common cold or an affliction that required you to be hospitalized. What were your concerns and fears? For what were you most thankful?

"Murderer," a man shouted. "God help patients who get *you* for a nurse." 1

"What gives you the right to play God?" another one asked. 2

It was the *Phil Donahue Show*[1] where the guest is a fatted calf and the audience a 200-strong flock of vultures hungering to pick at the bones. I had told them about Mac, one of my favorite cancer 3

[1]*Phil Donahue Show:* the first daytime TV talk show that involved the audience. It aired from 1970 to 1996.

patients. "We resuscitated him fifty-two times in just one month. I refused to resuscitate him again. I simply sat there and held his hand while he died."

There wasn't time to explain that Mac was a young, witty, macho cop who walked into the hospital with thirty-two pounds of attack equipment, looking as if he could single-handedly protect the whole city, if not the entire state. "Can't get rid of this cough," he said. Otherwise, he felt great. 4

Before the day was over, tests confirmed that he had lung cancer. And before the year was over, I loved him, his wife, Maura, and their three kids as if they were my own. All the nurses loved him. And we all battled his disease for six months without ever giving death a thought. Six months isn't such a long time in the whole scheme of things, but it was long enough to see him lose his youth, his wit, his macho, his hair, his bowel and bladder control, his sense of taste and smell, and his ability to do the slightest thing for himself. It was also long enough to watch Maura's transformation from a young woman into a haggard, beaten old lady. 5

When Mac had wasted away to a sixty-pound skeleton kept alive by liquid food we poured down a tube, IV solutions we dripped into his veins, and oxygen we piped to a mask on his face, he begged us: "Mercy . . . for God's sake, please just let me go." 6

The first time he stopped breathing, the nurse pushed the button that calls a "code blue" throughout the hospital and sends a team rushing to resuscitate the patient. Each time he stopped breathing, sometimes two or three times in one day, the code team came again. The doctors and technicians worked their miracles and walked away. The nurses stayed to wipe the saliva that drooled from his mouth, irrigate the big craters of bedsores that covered his hips, suction the lung fluids that threatened to drown him, clean the feces that burned his skin like lye,[2] pour the liquid food down the tube attached to his stomach, put pillows between his knees to ease the bone-on-bone pain, turn him every hour to keep the bedsores from getting worse, and change his gown and linen every two hours to keep him from being soaked in perspiration. 7

At night I went home and tried to scrub away the smell of decaying flesh that seemed woven into the fabric of my uniform. It was in my hair, the upholstery of my car—there was no washing it away. 8

---

[2]*lye:* a chemical that is used in cleaning products and that can burn skin.

And every night I prayed that Mac would die, that his agonized eyes would never again plead with me to let him die.

Every morning I asked his doctor for a "no-code" order. Without that order, we had to resuscitate every patient who stopped breathing. His doctor was one of several who believe we must extend life as long as we have the means and knowledge to do it. To not do it is to be liable for negligence, at least in the eyes of many people, including some nurses. I thought about what it would be like to stand before a judge, accused of murder, if Mac stopped breathing and I didn't call a code. 9

And after the fifty-second code, when Mac was still lucid enough to beg for death again, and Maura was crumbled in my arms again, and when no amount of pain medication stilled his moaning and agony, I wondered about a spiritual judge. Was all this misery and suffering supposed to be building character or infusing us all with the sense of humility that comes from impotence? 10

Had we, the whole medical community, become so arrogant that we believed in the illusion of salvation through science? Had we become so self-righteous that we thought meddling in God's work was our duty, our moral imperative, and our legal obligation? Did we really believe that we had the right to force "life" on a suffering man who had begged for the right to die? 11

Such questions haunted me more than ever early one morning when Maura went home to change her clothes and I was bathing Mac. He had been still for so long, I thought he at last had the blessed relief of coma. Then he opened his eyes and moaned, "Pain . . . no more . . . Barbara . . . do something . . . God, let me go." 12

The desperation in his eyes and voice riddled me with guilt. "I'll stop," I told him as I injected the pain medication. 13

I sat on the bed and held Mac's hands in mine. He pressed his bony fingers against my hand and muttered, "Thanks." Then there was one soft sigh and I felt his hands go cold in mine. "Mac?" I whispered, as I waited for his chest to rise and fall again. 14

A clutch of panic banded my chest, drew my finger to the code button, urged me to do something, anything . . . but sit there alone with death. I kept one finger on the button, without pressing it, as a waxen pallor[3] slowly transformed his face from person to empty shell. Nothing I've ever done in my forty-seven years has taken so much effort as it took *not* to press that code button. 15

---

[3]*pallor:* extreme paleness.

Eventually, when I was as sure as I could be that the code team would fail to bring him back, I entered the legal twilight zone and pushed the button. The team tried. And while they were trying, Maura walked into the room and shrieked, "No . . . don't let them do this to him . . . for God's sake . . . please, no more." 16

Cradling her in my arms was like cradling myself, Mac, and all those patients and nurses who had been in this place before, who do the best they can in a death-denying society. 17

So a TV audience accused me of murder. Perhaps I am guilty. If a doctor had written a no-code order, which is the only *legal* alternative, would he have felt any less guilty? Until there is legislation making it a criminal act to code a patient who has requested the right to die, we will all of us risk the same fate as Mac. For whatever reason, we developed the means to prolong life, and now we are forced to use it. We do not have the right to die. 18

Thinking Critically about This Reading

In the rhetorical question "Did we really believe that we had the right to force 'life' on a suffering man who had begged for the right to die?" (paragraph 11), why do you think Huttmann places the word *life* in quotation marks?

Questions for Study and Discussion

1. Why do people in the audience of the *Phil Donahue Show* call Huttmann a "murderer"? Is their accusation justified? In what ways do you think Huttmann might agree with them?
2. In paragraph 15, Huttmann states, "Nothing I've ever done in my forty-seven years has taken so much effort as it took *not* to press that code button." How effectively does she describe her struggle against pressing the button? What steps led to her ultimate decision not to press the code button?
3. What, according to Huttmann, is "the only *legal* alternative" (18) to her action? What does she find hypocritical about that choice?
4. Huttmann makes a powerfully emotional appeal for a patient's right to die. Some readers might find some of her story shocking or offensive. Cite examples of some of the graphic scenes Huttmann

describes, and discuss their impact on you as a reader. (Glossary: *Example*) Do they help persuade you to Huttmann's point of view, or do you find them overly unnerving? What would have been gained or lost had she left them out?

5. Huttmann's story covers a period of six months. In paragraphs 4–6, she describes the first five months of Mac's illness; in paragraphs 7–10, the sixth month; and in paragraphs 12–17, the final morning. What important point about narration does her use of time in this sequence demonstrate? (Glossary: *Narration*)
6. Huttmann concludes her essay with the statement "We do not have the right to die" (18). What does she mean by this? In your opinion, is she exaggerating or simply stating the facts? Does her example of Mac adequately illustrate her concluding point? Explain.

Classroom Activity Using Illustration

Huttmann illustrates her thesis by using the single example of Mac's experience in the hospital. Using the first statement as a model, find a single example that might be used to best illustrate each of the following potential thesis statements:

- Seat belts save lives. (*Possible answer:* an automobile accident in which a relative's life was saved because she was wearing her seat belt)
- Friends can be very handy.
- Having good study skills can improve a student's grades.
- Loud music can damage your hearing.
- Reading the directions for a new product you have just purchased can save time and aggravation.
- Humor can often make a bad situation more tolerable.
- American manufacturers can make their products safer.

Suggested Writing Assignments

1. Write a letter to the editor of *Newsweek* in response to Huttmann's essay. Are you for or against legislation that would give terminally ill patients the right to die? Give examples from your personal experience or from your reading to support your opinion.

2. Using one of the following sentences as your thesis statement, write an essay giving examples from your personal experience or from your reading to support your opinion.

- Consumers have more power than they realize.
- Most products do (or do not) measure up to the claims of their advertisements.
- Religion is (or is not) alive and well in America.
- Our government works far better than its critics claim.
- Being able to write well is more than a basic skill.
- The seasons for professional sports are too long.
- Today's college students are (or are not) serious-minded when it comes to academics.

Let's Think Outside the Box of Bad Clichés

■ **Gregory Pence**

Born in 1949, Gregory Pence is an internationally known expert in the field of bioethics. He is a cum laude graduate of the College of William and Mary and earned his doctorate in philosophy at New York University, writing his dissertation under the direction of the Australian bioethicist Peter Singer. A longtime professor of philosophy at the Medical School of the University of Alabama in Birmingham, Pence has published a number of books in the field of cloning and medical ethics, including Classic Works in Medical Ethics *(1995),* Who's Afraid of Human Cloning? *(1998),* Flesh of My Flesh: The Ethics of Human Cloning *(1998),* Re-Creating Medicine: Ethical Issues at the Frontiers of Medicine *(2000),* Designer Food: Mutant Harvest or Breadbasket of the World? *(2001),* The Ethics of Food: A Reader for the Twenty-first Century *(2002),* The Elements of Bioethics *(2007), and* Classic Cases in Medical Ethics *(2008).*

In "Let's Think Outside the Box of Bad Clichés," an essay first published in Newsweek *on August 6, 2007, Pence argues that sloppy writing leads to sloppy thinking. Notice how he uses examples of trite expressions and inaccurate phrases from his students' papers to prove his point.*

Reflecting on What You Know

Make a list of six or more clichés that you hear used around you. Why do you think writing instructors discourage their students from using clichés in their writing? What do you think is bad about clichés?

As a professor of bioethics, I strive to teach my students that clear writing fosters clear thinking. But as I was grading a stack of blue books today, I discovered so many clichés that I couldn't help writing them down. Before I knew it, I had spent the afternoon not grading essays but cataloging the many trite or inaccurate phrases my students rely on to express themselves. 1

When I grade written work by students, one of the phrases I hate most is "It goes without saying," in response to which I scribble on their essays, "Then why write it?" Another favorite of undergraduates is "It's not for me to say," to which I jot in their blue books, "Then why continue writing?" 2

I also despise the phrase "Who can say?" to which I reply, "You! That's who! That's the point of writing an essay!" 3

In teaching bioethics, I constantly hear about "playing God," as in "To allow couples to choose X is to play God." Undergraduates use the phrase constantly as a rhetorical hammer, as if saying it ends all discussion. And I don't even want to get into "opening Pandora's box" or "sliding down the slippery slope." 4

Sometimes the clichés are simply redundant, as when my students write of a "mass exodus." Can there be a "small" exodus? "Exodus" implies a mass of people. 5

Other times the expressions defy the rules of logic. A student in a philosophy class writes that philosophy "bores me to tears." But if something brings him to tears, it's certainly not boring. 6

I also fear that most students don't know what they are saying when they write that a question "boggles the mind." Does every problem in bioethics really boggle the mind? What does this mean? 7

My students aren't the only ones guilty of cliché abuse. The language of medicine confuses patients' families when physicians write, "On Tuesday the patient was declared brain dead, and on Wednesday life support was removed." So when did the patient really die? Can people die in two ways, once when they are declared brain dead and second when their respirators are removed? Better to write, "Physicians declared the patient dead by neurological criteria and the next day removed his respirator." 8

All of us repeat trite expressions without thinking. My TV weatherman sometimes says, "It's raining cats and dogs." Should I call the Humane Society? Where did this silly expression come from? 9

Another common mistake involves "literally." I often hear people on election night say, "He literally won by a landslide." If so, should geologists help us understand how? 10

Then, of course, there's the criminal who was caught in "broad daylight." I guess he could not have been caught in "narrow" daylight. And are we sure that the sun shone on the day he was caught? I sometimes read about a "bone of contention." I imagine two animals fighting over a bone from a carcass (and not, as students write, from "a dead carcass"). But do writers want to convey that image? 11

And how can we forget about the "foreseeable future" (versus the "unforeseeable future"?) and the "foregone conclusion" (versus the "non-foregone conclusion"?). 12

Spare me jargon from sports, such as being "on the bubble" for something. I'd also rather do without other jargon, such as "pushing the [edge of the] envelope." And has writing that we should "think outside the box" become such a cliché that it's now inside the box? 13

Some of the worst phrases come from the business world. Because of my profession, I read a lot of essays on medicine, ethics, and money. So I must endure endless strings of nouns acting as adjectival phrases, such as "health care finance administration official business." Even authors of textbooks on business and hospital administration use such phrases; no wonder that students use them, too. 14

And in these fields and others, can we do away with "take a leadership role"? These days, can't anyone just lead? 15

Can we also hear more about the short arm of the law (versus its "long" one), about things that sell well besides "hotcakes" and about a quick tour other than a "whirlwind" one? 16

Beyond the shadow of a doubt, I'd like to leave no stone unturned in grinding such writing to a halt, saving each and every student's essay in the nick of time. But I have a sneaking suspicion that, from time immemorial, that has been an errand of mercy and easier said than done. 17

Thinking Critically about This Reading

In his well-known essay "Politics and the English Language," George Orwell argues that writers should avoid using meaningless language. He writes, "Prose consists less and less of words chosen for the sake of their meaning, and more and more of phrases tacked together like the sections of a prefabricated henhouse." Would Pence agree with Orwell?

Questions for Study and Discussion

1. What is Pence's thesis in this essay? How well does he make his case as far as you are concerned?
2. What types of clichés does Pence discuss? Are they equally bad, or are some more annoying than others? Are there good clichés? Explain.
3. In paragraph 8, Pence gives an example of confusing medical language. Explain how the example he uses contains clichés that are in conflict with each other. Does his rewrite of the example solve the problem that he sees? Explain.

4. Pence does not offer any suggestions for avoiding clichés in writing. How do you avoid such usage? How would you advise others to avoid clichés?
5. One way to determine whether an expression is a cliché is to take part of the expression and see if the missing part comes readily to mind. For example, how would you complete the following incomplete expressions?

   when push comes to ______ paying lip ______

   fall between ______ ______ put the ______ before the ______

   scratch the ______ patience of a ______

   If you correctly filled in each of the above examples, you have a good sense of what constitutes a cliché and will be able to detect and eliminate them in your own writing.
6. How effective did you find Pence's conclusion? (Glossary: *Beginnings and Endings*) How else could he have ended his essay? Explain.

Classroom Activity Using Illustration

A useful exercise in learning to be specific is to see the words we use for people, places, things, and ideas as being positioned somewhere on a "ladder of abstraction." In the following chart, notice how the words progress from more general to more specific.

More General	*General*	*Specific*	*More Specific*
Organism	Plant	Flower	Alstrumaria
Vehicle	Car	Chevrolet	1958 Chevrolet Impala

Try to fill in the missing parts of the following ladder of abstraction:

More General	*General*	*Specific*	*More Specific*
Writing instrument	______	Fountain pen	Waterman fountain pen
______	Sandwich	Corned beef sandwich	Reuben
American	______	Navaho	Laguna Pueblo
Book	Reference book	Dictionary	______
Medicine	Oral medicine	Gel capsule	______

Suggested Writing Assignments

1. Pence claims that "Some of the worst phrases come from the business world" (14). To test his statement, find a recent article in a business magazine such as *Forbes, Fortune, Money,* or *Harvard Business Review* and/or three or four print advertisements, and look for clichés, empty or inaccurate phrases, and unnecessary jargon. Write a report of your findings. Is Pence's statement justified in your opinion?
2. The following cartoon by Goddard depicts a frightened patient begging his doctor for a truthful diagnosis. What is your reaction to the cartoon? What insights, if any, does the cartoon give you into Pence's essay about the nature of clichés and how we use them? Write an essay in which you explore the presence of clichés in the language of sports figures, doctors, educators, lawyers, or fashion designers. You may find it helpful to think about the following questions before beginning to write. What are the most common clichés used by the people in the area you chose? Why do you think these people use so many clichés? What is actually being communicated when people use these clichés? What do you think would happen if clichés were no longer used? Use as support examples from Pence's essay and Goddard's cartoon, as well as your own experiences and observations.

Burdens of the Modern Beast

■ Linton Weeks

Linton Weeks was born in 1955 and grew up in Memphis, Tennessee. In 1976, he graduated from Rhodes College in Memphis with a major in English. In 1982, he published Memphis: A Folk History, *a book that explores the artistic and cultural history of his hometown. His interest in preserving Southern culture led him to start* Southern Magazine *in 1986. When the magazine was bought by Time Warner in 1990, Weeks joined the* Washington Post, *first as editor of the paper's weekly magazine and in 1993 as the first director of the* Post's *online service Washingtonpost.com. Until his early retirement in May 2008, Weeks was a staff writer for the* Post, *where his articles on the American scene drew a large readership.*

In "Burdens of the Modern Beast," an essay that first appeared in the February 8, 2006, issue of Washingtonpost.com, Weeks reflects on all the "stuff" that we carry around with us daily and wonders what it all means. His many examples remind us just how "burdened by our belongings" we truly are.

Reflecting on What You Know

When you head out in the morning, what "stuff" do you carry with you—knapsack, iPod, cell phone, computer, water bottle, coffee cup? How much of your stuff do you really need with you? What would it feel like to leave all your stuff at home? Explain.

Slogging around with a backpack, a notebook, and a bottle of water, you stop for a while and stare at the historic black-and-white photographs in the National Museum of American History. You know, the ones depicting Americans going about their everyday lives: folks waiting for District trolley cars circa 1900, for instance, or people crisscrossing Pennsylvania Avenue in 1905. 1

Notice something missing? That's right: stuff. 2

The people—all ages, all colors, all genders—are not carrying any backpacks or water bottles. They are not schlepping cell phones, cradling coffee cups, or lugging laptops. They have no bags—shopping, 3 tote, or diaper. Besides a small purse here or a walking cane or umbrella there, they are unburdened: footloose and fingers free.

Now walk outside and take a look around. People on the same city streets are loaded down. They are laden with books, newspapers, Gatorade jugs, personal stereos, knapsacks, briefcases, and canvas totes with high-heel shoes inside. They have iPods strapped to upper arms, fanny packs buckled around waists, and house keys Velcroed to shoelaces. 4

Perhaps it's because we are multitaskers. Or because we're insecure. Maybe we are becoming more independent. Whatever the reasons, we are more and more burdened by our belongings. 5

Take Shey Moye, for instance, who is walking down Wisconsin Avenue in Bethesda toward Maurice Villency, a furniture store where he works. Moye, twenty-eight, has a swanky brown leather messenger bag full of books and things over one shoulder. He has two large notebooks in his left arm and a paper-wrapped breakfast sandwich—sausage-and-egg biscuit—and a venti caramel macchiato in his right hand. He just feels more comfortable carrying a lot of things. "I can't help it," he says. 6

Then there's Cheryl Douglass, fifty-nine, a special-education teacher at Tuckahoe Elementary School in Arlington. School is out and she's on her way to her car. In her left hand she carries a black Lancôme sack containing lots of file folders packed with papers, and, for some reason, an empty plastic bag. In her right hand: a *pink* Lancôme sack holding more file folders, a notebook, a tennis ball, contact lens paraphernalia, and a bag of Jolly Ranchers. Over her left shoulder, she carries a long-strapped purse that rests on her right hip. And also on her left shoulder, a Dunlop tennis racket in its black case that hangs by her left side. 7

She is a suburban Sherpa. 8

Asked why people in the past didn't carry so much, she says, "They must have segmented their lives, done their work at work and not at home." 9

She says she carries a different set of things when she goes to the gym—shoes, workout clothes, a compact disc player to listen to while she exercises. And, when she was younger, she carried still another bunch of items—diapers, bottles, blankets. 10

Contemporary life is so fluid. Work bleeds into leisure activity, which oozes over into family time. We never know what we are going to need or when we are going to need it. A book when we get mired on 11 the Metro; a juice box when we are trapped in traffic; cookies for low blood sugar moments; a flashlight in case we have a flat tire at night.

"It's sort of like a safety net," Douglass says of the things we carry. 12

Cultural historian Thomas Hine, author of *I Want That! How We All Became Shoppers,* says he has noticed that we are carting around more things than ever. 13

"Just last weekend," says Hine, who lives in Philadelphia, "I helped a friend pick out a rather elaborate laptop case that also included special compartments for cell phone, personal organizer, MP3 player, and other devices nobody had heard of a dozen years ago." 14

The increased quantity of carry-on items for our flight through life, he says, reflects "the tendency of our society to dispense with sources of shared stability—the long-term job, neighborhoods, unions, family dinners—and transform us into autonomous free agents." 15

The Walkman, introduced in 1979, Hine says in an e-mail, "probably set the precedent; it allowed people to be physically in a space, but mentally detached. The plethora of 'communications' devices we carry are also tools of isolation from the immediate environment. And, in the words of the recruiting ad, we each become 'an army of one' carrying all our tools of survival through a presumably hostile world." 16

It's the perfect posture for the Age of Insecurity. We fret about our jobs, families, country, manhood or womanhood, ability to be a good parent. We believe someone is out to get us. And to get our things. So, like the homeless, we carry our stuff with us. Just in case something, or anything, happens. 17

If wealth is judged by freedom and freedom is the state of being unencumbered, then we are a poor and burdened people. 18

"We are carrying more stuff," says Celeste Niebergall of California-based JanSport, makers of backpacks. "Especially in school." Reams of stories have been written about children being injured by heavy backpacks. Now they tow large suitcases on wheels. They look like so many little flight attendants. Or weekend golfers with pull carts. Can motorized backpack carts be far behind? 19

Backpacks for all ages have been enlarged, Niebergall says: "We have increased capacity." 20

Larger knapsacks, multipocketed cargo pants, nylon slings, commuter bags, purses of all kinds—shoppers, flaps, totes. Gap even makes a purse called a hobo for the urban nomad. PurseBrite was designed with a light inside to help you paw through your pile of possessions. 21

"I always carry lots of stuff with me wherever I roam, always weighted down with books, with cassettes, with pens and paper, just 22 in case I get the urge to sit down somewhere, and oh, I don't know, read something or write my masterpiece," Elizabeth Wurtzel writes in *Prozac Nation.* "I want all my important possessions, my worldly goods, with me at all times. I want to hold what little sense of home I have left with me always. I feel so heavy all the time, so burdened. This must be a little bit like what it's like to be a bag lady, to drag your feet here, there, and everywhere, nowhere at all."

The bag lady does carry a lot of stuff. Traditionally, so does the 23 soldier, a one-man band, the Avon Lady. And now all of us have increased our portable effects, if not our effectiveness.

Douglass seems pretty effective. She has been teaching for twenty- 24 five years. As she loads her things into her Honda, which is parked on the street behind the school, she takes inventory. "Everyone else has a Palm Pilot," she says, laughing. "I still have a calendar."

Piece by piece she removes bags from her arms and hands. The 25 files and the contact lens equipment and even the Jolly Ranchers we understand. But why does she carry a tennis racket? Is she going to play a match?

No, she says. She is not. But when life becomes too overwhelm- 26 ing, she takes the racket from the case and the ball from the pink Lancôme sack and she bangs the ball against a wall. Again and again.

The mindless activity serves two purposes. For one thing, it clears 27 her head. For another, it forces her to set down everything else she has been carrying.

Thinking Critically about This Reading

From all accounts, Americans are carting around more stuff than ever. What does Weeks think about this phenomenon? Is it a good thing? A bad thing? What do you think this phenomenon says about Americans and their common culture?

Questions for Study and Discussion

1. Weeks begins his essay by contrasting the people in two old photographs with people of today. What point is he making with this contrast?
2. What do the examples of Shey Moye, Cheryl Douglass, and Elizabeth Wurtzel reveal about people and contemporary lifestyles? Why do these people feel the need to cart their belongings around with them?

3. In paragraph 4, Weeks describes people on a city street who "are laden with books, newspapers, Gatorade jugs, personal stereos, knapsacks, briefcases, and canvas totes with high-heel shoes inside. They have iPods strapped to upper arms, fanny packs buckled around waists, and house keys Velcroed to shoelaces." He provides several other lists in his essay. What do these lists of things that we carry around at one time or another do for you as a reader? Explain.
4. According to Weeks, what are some of the possible reasons that people today carry large amounts of stuff with them? Which of these reasons is most plausible to you? Least plausible? Explain why.
5. Weeks cites cultural historian Thomas Hine and JanSport executive Celeste Niebergall. What does each of these people bring to the conversation about Americans and their portable gadgets? In what ways do they strengthen Weeks's position on the topic?

Classroom Activity Using Illustration

Suppose that you are writing an essay about trends in the career choices made by members of your extended family. Using your great-grandparents, grandparents, parents, aunts and uncles, cousins, and siblings as potential material, make several lists of examples. For instance, one list could be for family members who worked in agriculture, one for people in the trades, another for those in education, a fourth for those in one of the professions, and a fifth for those in the service sector. Once you have established your examples, you need to decide how to organize them. Here are some major patterns of organization you may want to consider:

- Chronological (oldest to the newest or the reverse)
- Most familiar to least familiar or the reverse
- Easiest to most difficult to comprehend
- Easiest to most difficult to accept or carry out
- Most important to least important or the reverse

Use one of these patterns to organize the lists of examples of career choices you generated above.

Suggested Writing Assignments

1. Using your response to the Thinking Critically about This Reading questions on page 343 as a starting point, write an essay about the

effect of our many gadgets on American life and culture. Have we been transformed, as cultural historian Thomas Hine suggests, "into autonomous free agents" (15)? Has the world become so hostile that each of us has "become 'an army of one' carrying all our tools of survival through a presumably hostile world" (16)? What might be the individual and societal costs of continuing to burden ourselves with more and more material baggage?

2. Linton Weeks examines the problem of people becoming overwhelmed and rendered less effective by the "stuff" in our lives. What do you think? Have Americans become slaves to the so-called labor-saving devices that we just can't seem to be without? Have we, as Weeks suggests, surrendered our freedom and become "a poor and burdened people" (18)? Write an essay in which you present your position on the issue of stuff in our lives, and support it with examples from Weeks's essay and your own experiences and observations.

In Defense of Dangerous Ideas

■ Steven Pinker

Internationally recognized language and cognition scholar and researcher Stephen Pinker was born in Montreal, Quebec, Canada, in 1954. He immigrated to the United States shortly after receiving his BA from McGill University in 1976. After earning a doctorate from Harvard University in 1979, Pinker taught psychology at Stanford University and the Massachusetts Institute of Technology, where he directed the Center for Cognitive Neuroscience. Currently, he is professor of psychology at Harvard University. Pinker has written extensively on language development in children, starting with Language Learnability and Language Development *(1984). He has what one critic writing in the* New York Times Book Review *calls "that facility, so rare among scientists, of making the most difficult material . . . accessible to the average reader." Pinker's books* The Language Instinct *(1994),* How the Mind Works *(1997),* Words and Rules: The Ingredients of Language *(1999),* The Blank Slate: The Modern Denial of Human Nature *(2002), and* The Stuff of Thought: Language as a Window into Human Nature *(2007) all attest to the public's interest in human language and the world of ideas.*

The following article was first published as the preface to What Is Your Dangerous Idea? Today's Leading Thinkers on the Unthinkable *(2006, edited by John Brockman) and later posted at* Edge *(www.edge.com). In this essay Steven Pinker explores what makes an idea "dangerous" and argues that "important ideas need to be aired," especially in academia, no matter how discomfiting people find them. Notice how Pinker uses a number of examples from a wide range of academic disciplines to illustrate his points about dangerous ideas and the need to discuss them.*

Reflecting on What You Know

What did you think when you first read the title to Pinker's essay? For you, what would make an idea dangerous? Do any issues or questions make you uncomfortable or unwilling to discuss them? Explain.

In every age, taboo questions raise our blood pressure and threaten 1
moral panic. But we cannot be afraid to answer them.

Do women, on average, have a different profile of aptitudes and 2
emotions than men?

Were the events in the Bible fictitious—not just the miracles, but 3
those involving kings and empires?

Has the state of the environment improved in the last fifty years? 4

Do most victims of sexual abuse suffer no lifelong damage? 5

Did Native Americans engage in genocide and despoil the 6
landscape?

Do men have an innate tendency to rape? 7

Did the crime rate go down in the 1990s because two decades 8
earlier poor women aborted children who would have been prone to violence?

Are suicide terrorists well-educated, mentally healthy, and morally 9
driven?

Would the incidence of rape go down if prostitution were legalized? 10

Do African American men have higher levels of testosterone, on 11
average, than white men?

Is morality just a product of the evolution of our brains, with no 12
inherent reality?

Would society be better off if heroin and cocaine were legalized? 13

Is homosexuality the symptom of an infectious disease? 14

Would it be consistent with our moral principles to give parents 15
the option of euthanizing newborns with birth defects that would consign them to a life of pain and disability?

Do parents have any effect on the character or intelligence of 16
their children?

Have religions killed a greater proportion of people than Nazism? 17

Would damage from terrorism be reduced if the police could 18
torture suspects in special circumstances?

Would Africa have a better chance of rising out of poverty if it 19
hosted more polluting industries or accepted Europe's nuclear waste?

Is the average intelligence of Western nations declining because 20
duller people are having more children than smarter people?

Would unwanted children be better off if there were a market in 21
adoption rights, with babies going to the highest bidder?

Would lives be saved if we instituted a free market in organs for 22
transplantation?

Should people have the right to clone themselves, or enhance the 23
genetic traits of their children?

Perhaps you can feel your blood pressure rise as you read these questions. Perhaps you are appalled that people can so much as think such things. Perhaps you think less of me for bringing them up. These are dangerous ideas—ideas that are denounced not because they are self-evidently false, nor because they advocate harmful action, but because they are thought to corrode the prevailing moral order. 24

Think about It

By "dangerous ideas" I don't have in mind harmful technologies, like those behind weapons of mass destruction, or evil ideologies, like those of racist, fascist, or other fanatical cults. I have in mind statements of fact or policy that are defended with evidence and argument by serious scientists and thinkers but which are felt to challenge the collective decency of an age. The ideas listed above, and the moral panic that each one of them has incited during the past quarter century, are examples. Writers who have raised ideas like these have been vilified, censored, fired, threatened, and in some cases physically assaulted. 25

Every era has its dangerous ideas. For millennia, the monotheistic religions have persecuted countless heresies, together with nuisances from science such as geocentrism, biblical archeology, and the theory of evolution. We can be thankful that the punishments have changed from torture and mutilation to the canceling of grants and the writing of vituperative reviews. But intellectual intimidation, whether by sword or by pen, inevitably shapes the ideas that are taken seriously in a given era, and the rear-view mirror of history presents us with a warning. 26

Time and again, people have invested factual claims with ethical implications that today look ludicrous. The fear that the structure of our solar system has grave moral consequences is a venerable example, and the foisting of "intelligent design" on biology students is a contemporary one. These travesties should lead us to ask whether the contemporary intellectual mainstream might be entertaining similar moral delusions. Are we enraged by our own infidels and heretics whom history may some day vindicate? 27

Unsettling Possibilities

Dangerous ideas are likely to confront us at an increasing rate, and we are ill-equipped to deal with them. When done right, science (together 28 with other truth-seeking institutions, such as history and journalism) characterizes the world as it is, without regard to whose feelings get hurt. Science in particular has always been a source of heresy, and today the galloping advances in touchy areas like genetics, evolution, and the environment sciences are bound to throw unsettling possibilities at us. Moreover, the rise of globalization and the Internet are allowing heretics to find one another and work around the barriers of traditional media and academic journals. I also suspect that a change in generational sensibilities will hasten the process. The term "political correctness" captures the 1960s conception of moral rectitude that we baby boomers brought with us as we took over academia, journalism, and government. In my experience, today's students—black and white, male and female—are bewildered by the idea, common among their parents, that certain scientific opinions are immoral or certain questions too hot to handle.

What makes an idea "dangerous"? One factor is an imaginable train of events in which acceptance of the idea could lead to an outcome recognized as harmful. In religious societies, the fear is that if people ever stopped believing in the literal truth of the Bible they would also stop believing in the authority of its moral commandments. That is, if today people dismiss the part about God creating the earth in six days, tomorrow they'll dismiss the part about "Thou shalt not kill." In progressive circles, the fear is that if people ever were to acknowledge any differences between races, sexes, or individuals, they would feel justified in discrimination or oppression. Other dangerous ideas set off fears that people will neglect or abuse their children, become indifferent to the environment, devalue human life, accept violence, and prematurely resign themselves to social problems that could be solved with sufficient commitment and optimism. 29

All these outcomes, needless to say, would be deplorable. But none of them actually follows from the supposedly dangerous idea. Even if it turns out, for instance, that groups of people are different in their averages, the overlap is certainly so great that it would be irrational and unfair to discriminate against individuals on that basis. Likewise, even if it turns out that parents don't have the power to shape their children's personalities, it would be wrong on grounds of simple human decency to abuse or neglect one's children. And if currently popular ideas about how to improve the environment are shown to be ineffective, it only highlights the need to know what would be effective. 30

Another contributor to the perception of dangerousness is the 31
intellectual blinkers that humans tend to don when they split into factions. People have a nasty habit of clustering in coalitions, professing certain beliefs as badges of their commitment to the coalition and treating rival coalitions as intellectually unfit and morally depraved. Debates between members of the coalitions can make things even worse, because when the other side fails to capitulate to one's devastating arguments, it only proves they are immune to reason. In this regard, it's disconcerting to see the two institutions that ought to have the greatest stake in ascertaining the truth—academia and government—often blinkered by morally tinged ideologies. One ideology is that humans are blank slates and that social problems can be handled only through government programs that especially redress the perfidy of European males. Its opposite number is that morality inheres in patriotism and Christian faith and that social problems may be handled only by government policies that punish the sins of individual evildoers. New ideas, nuanced ideas, hybrid ideas—and sometimes dangerous ideas—often have trouble getting a hearing against these group-bonding convictions.

The conviction that honest opinions can be dangerous may even 32
arise from a feature of human nature. Philip Tetlock and Alan Fiske have argued that certain human relationships are constituted on a basis of unshakable convictions. We love our children and parents, are faithful to our spouses, stand by our friends, contribute to our communities, and are loyal to our coalitions not because we continually question and evaluate the merits of these commitments but because we feel them in our bones. A person who spends too much time pondering whether logic and fact really justify a commitment to one of these relationships is seen as just not "getting it." Decent people don't carefully weigh the advantages and disadvantages of selling their children or selling out their friends or their spouses or their colleagues or their country. They reject these possibilities outright; they "don't go there." So the taboo on questioning sacred values makes sense in the context of personal relationships. It makes far less sense in the context of discovering how the world works or running a country.

Explore All Relevant Ideas

Should we treat some ideas as dangerous? Let's exclude outright lies, 33
deceptive propaganda, incendiary conspiracy theories from malevolent

crackpots, and technological recipes for wanton destruction. Consider only ideas about the truth of empirical claims or the effectiveness of policies that, if they turned out to be true, would require a significant rethinking of our moral sensibilities. And consider ideas that, if they turn out to be false, could lead to harm if people believed them to be true. In either case, we don't know whether they are true or false a priori, so only by examining and debating them can we find out. Finally, let's assume that we're not talking about burning people at the stake or cutting out their tongues but about discouraging their research and giving their ideas as little publicity as possible. There is a good case for exploring all ideas relevant to our current concerns, no matter where they lead. The idea that ideas should be discouraged a priori is inherently self-refuting. Indeed, it is the ultimate arrogance, as it assumes that one can be so certain about the goodness and truth of one's own ideas that one is entitled to discourage other people's opinions from even being examined.

Also, it's hard to imagine any aspect of public life where ignorance or delusion is better than an awareness of the truth, even an unpleasant one. Only children and madmen engage in "magical thinking," the fallacy that good things can come true by believing in them or bad things will disappear by ignoring them or wishing them away. Rational adults want to know the truth, because any action based on false premises will not have the effects they desire. Worse, logicians tell us that a system of ideas containing a contradiction can be used to deduce any statement whatsoever, no matter how absurd. Since ideas are connected to other ideas, sometimes in circuitous and unpredictable ways, choosing to believe something that may not be true, or even maintaining walls of ignorance around some topic, can corrupt all of intellectual life, proliferating error far and wide. In our everyday lives, would we want to be lied to, or kept in the dark by paternalistic "protectors," when it comes to our health or finances or even the weather? In public life, imagine someone saying that we should not do research into global warming or energy shortages because if it found that they were serious the consequences for the economy would be extremely unpleasant. Today's leaders who tacitly take this position are rightly condemned by intellectually responsible people. But why should other unpleasant ideas be treated differently? 34

There is another argument against treating ideas as dangerous. Many of our moral and political policies are designed to preempt what we know to be the worst features of human nature. The checks 35 and balances in a democracy, for instance, were invented in explicit recognition of the fact that human leaders will always be tempted to arrogate power to themselves. Likewise, our sensitivity to racism comes from an awareness that groups of humans, left to their own devices, are apt to discriminate and oppress other groups, often in ugly ways. History also tells us that a desire to enforce dogma and suppress heretics is a recurring human weakness, one that has led to recurring waves of gruesome oppression and violence. A recognition that there is a bit of Torquemada[1] in everyone should make us wary of any attempt to enforce a consensus or demonize those who challenge it.

"Sunlight is the best disinfectant," according to Justice Louis 36
Brandeis's famous case for freedom of thought and expression. If an idea really is false, only by examining it openly can we determine that it is false. At that point we will be in a better position to convince others that it is false than if we had let it fester in private, since our very avoidance of the issue serves as a tacit acknowledgment that it may be true. And if an idea is true, we had better accommodate our moral sensibilities to it, since no good can come from sanctifying a delusion. This might even be easier than the ideaphobes fear. The moral order did not collapse when the earth was shown not to be at the center of the solar system, and so it will survive other revisions of our understanding of how the world works.

Dangerous to Air Dangerous Ideas?

In the best Talmudic tradition of arguing a position as forcefully as 37
possible and then switching sides, let me now present the case for discouraging certain lines of intellectual inquiry. . . . [Alison] Gopnik and [W. Daniel] Hillis offer as their "dangerous idea" the exact opposite of [Daniel] Gilbert's: they say that it's a dangerous idea for thinkers to air their dangerous ideas. How might such an argument play out?

First, one can remind people that we are all responsible for the 38
foreseeable consequences of our actions, and that includes the consequences of our public statements. Freedom of inquiry may be an important value, according to this argument, but it is not an absolute value, one that overrides all others. We know that the world is full of malevolent and callous people who will use any pretext to justify their

[1]*Torquemada:* Tomás de Torquemada (1420–1498), Spanish grand inquisitor.

bigotry or destructiveness. We must expect that they will seize on the broaching of a topic that seems in sympathy with their beliefs as a vindication of their agenda.

Not only can the imprimatur of scientific debate add legitimacy to toxic ideas, but the mere act of making an idea common knowledge can change its effects. Individuals, for instance, may harbor a private opinion on differences between genders or among ethnic groups but keep it to themselves because of its opprobrium. But once the opinion is aired in public, they may be emboldened to act on their prejudice—not just because it has been publicly ratified but because they must anticipate that everyone else will act on the information. Some people, for example, might discriminate against the members of an ethnic group despite having no pejorative opinion about them, in the expectation that their customers or colleagues will have such opinions and that defying them would be costly. And then there are the effects of these debates on the confidence of the members of the stigmatized groups themselves. 39

Of course, academics can warn against these abuses, but the qualifications and nitpicking they do for a living may not catch up with the simpler formulations that run on swifter legs. Even if they did, their qualifications might be lost on the masses. We shouldn't count on ordinary people to engage in the clear thinking—some would say the hair-splitting—that would be needed to accept a dangerous idea but not its terrible consequence. Our overriding precept, in intellectual life as in medicine, should be "First, do no harm." 40

We must be especially suspicious when the danger in a dangerous idea is to someone other than its advocate. Scientists, scholars, and writers are members of a privileged elite. They may have an interest in promulgating ideas that justify their privileges, that blame or make light of society's victims, or that earn them attention for cleverness and iconoclasm. Even if one has little sympathy for the cynical Marxist argument that ideas are always advanced to serve the interest of the ruling class, the ordinary skepticism of a tough-minded intellectual should make one wary of "dangerous" hypotheses that are no skin off the nose of their hypothesizers. (The mindset that leads us to blind review, open debate, and statements of possible conflicts of interest.) 41

But don't the demands of rationality always compel us to seek the complete truth? Not necessarily. Rational agents often choose to be ignorant. They may decide not to be in a position where they can receive a threat or be exposed to a sensitive secret. They may choose to 42 avoid being asked an incriminating question, where one answer is damaging, another is dishonest, and a failure to answer is grounds for the questioner to assume the worst (hence the Fifth Amendment protection against being forced to testify against oneself). Scientists test drugs in double-blind studies in which they keep themselves from knowing who got the drug and who got the placebo, and they referee manuscripts anonymously for the same reason. Many people rationally choose not to know the gender of their unborn child, or whether they carry a gene for Huntington's disease, or whether their nominal father is genetically related to them. Perhaps a similar logic would call for keeping socially harmful information out of the public sphere.

Intolerance of Unpopular Ideas

As for restrictions on inquiry, every scientist already lives with them. 43
They accede, for example, to the decisions of committees for the protection of human subjects and to policies on the confidentiality of personal information. In 1975, biologists imposed a moratorium on research on recombinant DNA pending the development of safeguards against the release of dangerous microorganisms. The notion that intellectuals have carte blanche in conducting their inquiry is a myth.

Though I am more sympathetic to the argument that important 44
ideas be aired than to the argument that they should sometimes be suppressed, I think it is a debate we need to have. Whether we like it or not, science has a habit of turning up discomfiting thoughts, and the Internet has a habit of blowing their cover.

Tragically, there are few signs that the debates will happen in the 45
place where we might most expect it: academia. Though academics owe the extraordinary perquisite of tenure to the ideal of encouraging free inquiry and the evaluation of unpopular ideas, all too often academics are the first to try to quash them. The most famous recent example is the outburst of fury and disinformation that resulted when Harvard president Lawrence Summers gave a measured analysis of the multiple causes of women's underrepresentation in science and math departments in elite universities and tentatively broached the possibility that discrimination and hidden barriers were not the only cause.

But intolerance of unpopular ideas among academics is an old 46
story. Books like Morton Hunt's *The New Know-Nothings* and Alan Kors and Harvey Silverglate's *The Shadow University* have depressingly shown that universities cannot be counted on to defend the rights of

their own heretics and that it's often the court system or the press that has to drag them into policies of tolerance. In government, the intolerance is even more frightening, because the ideas considered there are not just matters of intellectual sport but have immediate and sweeping consequences. Chris Mooney, in *The Republican War on Science,* joins Hunt in showing how corrupt and demagogic legislators are increasingly stifling research findings they find inconvenient to their interests.

Thinking Critically about This Reading

What do you think is Pinker's purpose in defending dangerous ideas? What does he want his readers to do after reading this essay? Did he achieve his purpose with you? Explain.

Questions for Study and Discussion

1. Pinker starts his essay with a list of twenty-two questions, each an example of a dangerous idea. What were you thinking as you read Pinker's list? Which questions touched a sensitive nerve for you? Explain.
2. How does Pinker define "dangerous idea"? Do you agree with his definition?
3. According to Pinker, fear is one of the main factors that contributes to the perception of dangerousness. What examples of fears does Pinker use to illustrate this claim? What other factors contribute to the perception of dangerousness?
4. Do you believe that "the taboo on questioning sacred values makes sense in the context of personal relationships" (paragraph 32)? Why or why not? Why do you think that Pinker believes that "It makes far less sense in the context of discovering how the world works or running a country" (32)?
5. What does Pinker mean when he says, "The idea that ideas should be discouraged a priori is inherently self-refuting" (33)?
6. According to Pinker, what is the "case for discouraging certain lines of intellectual inquiry" (37)? What evidence does he present to support this side of the issue?
7. How does Pinker support his claim that "intolerance of unpopular ideas among academics is an old story" (46)?

Classroom Activity Using Illustration

Consider the following paragraph from the rough draft of a student paper on Americans' obsession with losing weight. The student writer wanted to show the extreme actions that people sometimes take to improve their appearance.

> Americans have long been obsessed with thinness—even at the risk of dying. In the 1930s, people took di-nitrophenol, an industrial poison, to lose weight. It boosted metabolism but caused blindness and some deaths. Since that time, dieters have experimented with any number of bizarre schemes that seem to work wonders in the short term but often end in disappointment or disaster in the long term. Some weight-loss strategies have even led to life-threatening eating disorders.

Try your hand at revising this paragraph, supplying specific examples of "bizarre schemes" or "weight-loss strategies" that you have tried, observed, or read about. Share your examples with others in your class. Which examples best illustrate and support the central idea contained in the writer's topic sentence?

Suggested Writing Assignments

1. Reread the list of twenty-two questions at the beginning of Pinker's essay. After giving them some thought, select one to use as a central example in an essay about the need to debate important ideas no matter how uncomfortable those ideas might make us. Before you start writing, consider the following questions: What about the question I've chosen makes me or others uncomfortable? What are some of the idea's implications if we find it to be true? False? What would happen if we simply ignore this question?
2. In a case involving freedom of thought and expression, Justice Louis Brandeis said, "Sunlight is the best disinfectant" (36). What do you think he meant? How do you think Justice Brandeis would respond to the proposition that "it's a dangerous idea for thinkers to air their dangerous ideas"? How do you respond to this proposition? Write an essay in which you present your position, and support that position with clear examples from your own experiences or reading.

chapter **14**

Narration

To *narrate* is to tell a story or to recount a series of events. Whenever you relate an incident or use an **anecdote** (a very brief story) to make a point, you use narration. In its broadest sense, **narration** is any account of any event or series of events. We all love to hear stories; some people believe that sharing stories is a part of what defines us as human beings. Good stories are interesting, sometimes suspenseful, and always instructive because they give us insights into the human condition. Although most often associated with fiction, narration is effective and useful in all kinds of writing. For example, in "The Jacket" (pp. 312–15) Gary Soto tells the story of what happens when his mother buys him a new jacket that he hates and thinks is responsible for all kinds of misfortune. In "A Crime of Compassion" (pp. 329–32), nurse Barbara Huttmann tells how she brought one of her patient's long suffering to an end as she argues against repeatedly using extraordinary measures to revive dying patients against their wishes.

Good narration has five essential features—a clear context; well-chosen and thoughtfully emphasized details; a logical, often chronological organization; an appropriate and consistent point of view; and a meaningful point or purpose. Consider, for example, the following narrative, titled "Is Your Jar Full?"

> One day, an expert in time management was speaking to a group of business students and, to drive home a point, used an illustration those students will never forget. As he stood in front of the group of high-powered overachievers he said, "Okay, time for a quiz," and he pulled out a one-gallon mason jar and set it on the table in front of him. He also produced about a dozen fist-sized rocks and carefully placed them, one at a time, into the jar. When the jar was filled to the top and no more rocks would fit inside, he asked, "Is this jar full?"
>
> Everyone in the class yelled, "Yes."

The time management expert replied, "Really?" He reached under the table and pulled out a bucket of gravel. He dumped some gravel in and shook the jar causing pieces of gravel to work themselves down into the spaces between the big rocks. He then asked the group once more, "Is the jar full?" By this time the class was on to him.

"Probably not," one of them answered.

"Good!" he replied. He reached under the table and brought out a bucket of sand. He started dumping the sand in the jar and it went into all of the spaces left between the rocks and the gravel.

Once more he asked the question, "Is this jar full?"

"No!" the class shouted.

Once again he said, "Good." Then he grabbed a pitcher of water and began to pour it in until the jar was filled to the brim. Then he looked at the class and asked, "What is the point of this illustration?"

One eager beaver raised his hand and said, "The point is, no matter how full your schedule is, if you try really hard you can always fit some more things in it!"

"No," the speaker replied, "that's not the point. The truth this illustration teaches us is: If you don't put the big rocks in first, you'll never get them in at all. What are the 'big rocks' in your life—time with your loved ones, your faith, your education, your dreams, a worthy cause, teaching or mentoring others? Remember to put these BIG ROCKS in first or you'll never get them in at all."

So, tonight, or in the morning, when you are reflecting on this short story, ask yourself this question: What are the "big rocks" in my life? Then, put those in your jar first.

This story contains all the elements of good narration. The writer begins by establishing a clear context for her narrative by telling when, where, and to whom the action happened. She has chosen details well, including enough details so that we know what is happening but not so many that we become overwhelmed, confused, or bored. The writer organizes her narration logically with a beginning that sets the scene, a middle that relates the exchange between the time-management expert and the students, and an end that makes her point, all arranged chronologically. She tells the story from the third-person point of view. Finally, she reveals the point of her narration: people need to think about what's important in their lives and put these activities first.

The writer could have told her story from the first-person point of view. In this point of view, the narrator is a participant in the action and uses the pronoun *I*. In the following example, Willie Morris tells a story of how the comfortably well-off respond coolly to the tragedies of the ghetto. We experience the event directly through the writer's eyes and ears, as if we too had been on the scene of the action.

> One afternoon in late August, as the summer's sun streamed into the [railroad] car and made little jumping shadows on the windows, I sat gazing out at the tenement-dwellers, who were themselves looking out of their windows from the gray crumbling buildings along the tracks of upper Manhattan. As we crossed into the Bronx, the train unexpectedly slowed down for a few miles. Suddenly from out of my window I saw a large crowd near the tracks, held back by two policemen. Then, on the other side from my window, I saw a sight I would never be able to forget: a little boy almost severed in halves, lying at an incredible angle near the track. The ground was covered with blood, and the boy's eyes were opened wide, strained and disbelieving in his sudden oblivion. A policeman stood next to him, his arms folded, staring straight ahead at the windows of our train. In the orange glow of late afternoon the policemen, the crowd, the corpse of the boy were for a brief moment immobile, motionless, a small tableau to violence and death in the city. Behind me, in the next row of seats, there was a game of bridge. I heard one of the four men say as he looked out at the sight, "God, that's horrible." Another said, in a whisper, "Terrible, terrible." There was a momentary silence, punctuated only by the clicking of the wheels on the track. Then, after the pause, I heard the first man say: "Two hearts."
>
> –Willie Morris

As you begin to write your own narration, take time to ask yourself why you are telling your story. Your purpose in writing will influence which events and details you include and which you leave out. You should include enough details about the action and its context so that your readers can understand what's going on. You should not get so carried away with details that your readers become confused or bored by an excess of information, however. In good storytelling, deciding what to leave out is as important as deciding what to include.

Be sure to give some thought to the organization of your narrative. Chronological organization is natural in narration because it is a reconstruction of the original order of events, but it is not always the most interesting. To add interest to your storytelling, try using a technique common in the movies and theater called *flashback*. Begin your narration midway through the story with an important or exciting event, and then use flashback to fill in what happened earlier. Notice how one of our students uses this very technique. She disrupts the chronological organization of her narrative by beginning in the recent past and then uses a flashback to take us back to when she was a youngster:

> It was a Monday afternoon, and I was finally home from track practice. The coach had just told me that I had a negative attitude and should contemplate why I was on the team. My father greeted me in the living room.
>
> *Essay opens in recent past*
>
> "Hi, honey. How was practice?"
>
> *Dialogue creates historical present*
>
> "Not good, Dad. Listen, I don't want to do this anymore. I hate the track team."
>
> "What do you mean *hate*?"
>
> "The constant pressure is making me crazy."
>
> "How so?"
>
> "It's just not fun anymore."
>
> "Well, I'll have to talk to the coach—"
>
> "No! You're supposed to be my father, not my coach."
>
> "I am your father, but I'm sure . . ."
>
> "Just let me do what I want. You've had your turn."
>
> He just let out a sigh and left the room. Later he told me that I was wasting my "God-given abilities." The funny part was that none of my father's anger hit me at first. All I knew was that I was free.
>
> *Essay returns in time to when troubles began*
>
> My troubles began the summer I was five years old. It was late June. . . .
>
> –Trena Isley, student

What's in a Name?

■ Henry Louis Gates Jr.

The preeminent African American scholar of our time, Henry Louis Gates Jr. is the Alphonse Fletcher University Professor and director of the W. E. B. Du Bois Institute for African and African American Research at Harvard University. Among his impressive list of publications are Figures in Black: Words, Signs, and the "Racial" Self *(1987),* The Signifying Monkey: A Theory of Afro-American Literary Criticism *(1988),* Loose Canons: Notes on Culture Wars *(1992),* The Future of the Race *(1997), and* Thirteen Ways of Looking at a Black Man *(1999). His most recent books are* Mr. Jefferson and Miss Wheatley *(2003) and* Finding Oprah's Roots: Finding Your Own *(2007). His* Colored People: A Memoir *(1994) recollects in a wonderful prose style his youth growing up in Piedmont, West Virginia, and his emerging sexual and racial awareness. Gates first enrolled at Potomac State College and later transferred to Yale, where he studied history. With the assistance of an Andrew W. Mellon Foundation Fellowship and a Ford Foundation Fellowship, he pursued advanced degrees in English at Clare College at the University of Cambridge. He has been honored with a MacArthur Foundation Fellowship, inclusion on* Time *magazine's "25 Most Influential Americans" list, a National Humanities Medal, and election to the American Academy of Arts and Letters.*

In "What's in a Name?," excerpted from a longer article published in the fall 1989 issue of Dissent *magazine, Gates tells the story of an early encounter with the language of prejudice. In learning how one of the "bynames" used by white people to define African Americans robs them of their identity, he feels the sting of racism first hand. Notice how Gates's use of dialogue gives immediacy and poignancy to his narration.*

Reflecting on What You Know

Reflect on the use of racially charged language. For example, has anyone ever used a racial epithet or name to refer to you? When did you first become aware that such names existed?

How do you feel about being characterized by your race? If you yourself have ever used such names, what was your intent in using them? What was the response of others?

The question of color takes up much space in these pages, but the question of color, especially in this country, operates to hide the graver questions of the self.

–James Baldwin, 1961

. . . blood, darky, Tar Baby, Kaffir, shine . . . moor, blackamoor, Jim Crow, spook . . . quadroon, meriney, red bone, high yellow . . . Mammy, porch monkey, home, homeboy, George . . . spearchucker, schwarze, Leroy, Smokey . . . mouli, buck, Ethiopian, brother, sistah. . . .

–Trey Ellis, 1989

I had forgotten the incident completely, until I read Trey Ellis's essay, "Remember My Name," in a recent issue of the *Village Voice*[1] (June 13, 1989). But there, in the middle of an extended italicized list of the bynames of "the race" ("the race" or "our people" being the terms my parents used in polite or reverential discourse, "jigaboo" or "nigger" more commonly used in anger, jest, or pure disgust), it was: "George." Now the events of that very brief exchange return to mind so vividly that I wonder why I had forgotten it. 1

My father and I were walking home at dusk from his second job. He "moonlighted" as a janitor in the evenings for the telephone company. Every day but Saturday, he would come home at 3:30 from his regular job at the paper mill, wash up, eat supper, then at 4:30 head downtown to his second job. He used to make jokes frequently about a union official who moonlighted. I never got the joke, but he and his friends thought it was hilarious. All I knew was that my family always ate well, that my brother and I had new clothes to wear, and that all of the white people in Piedmont, West Virginia, treated my parents with an odd mixture of resentment and respect that even we understood at the time had something directly to do with a small but certain measure of financial security. 2

He had left a little early that evening because I was with him and I had to be in bed early. I could not have been more than five or six, and we had stopped off at the Cut-Rate Drug Store (where no black person in town but my father could sit down to eat, and eat off real 3

[1]*Village Voice:* a nationally distributed weekly newspaper published in New York City.

plates with real silverware) so that I could buy some caramel ice cream, two scoops in a wafer cone, please, which I was busy licking when Mr. Wilson walked by.

Mr. Wilson was a very quiet man, whose stony, brooding, silent manner seemed designed to scare off any overtures of friendship, even from white people. He was Irish, as was one-third of our village (another third being Italian), the more affluent among whom sent their children to "Catholic School" across the bridge in Maryland. He had white straight hair, like my Uncle Joe, whom he uncannily resembled, and he carried a black worn metal lunch pail, the kind that Riley[2] carried on the television show. My father always spoke to him, and for reasons that we never did understand, he always spoke to my father. 4

"Hello, Mr. Wilson," I heard my father say. 5

"Hello, George." 6

I stopped licking my ice cream cone, and asked my Dad in a loud voice why Mr. Wilson had called him "George." 7

"Doesn't he know your name, Daddy? Why don't you tell him your name? Your name isn't George." 8

For a moment I tried to think of who Mr. Wilson was mixing Pop up with. But we didn't have any Georges among the colored people in Piedmont; nor were there colored Georges living in the neighboring towns and working at the mill. 9

"Tell him your name, Daddy." 10

"He knows my name, boy," my father said after a long pause. "He calls all colored people George." 11

A long silence ensued. It was "one of those things," as my Mom would put it. Even then, that early, I knew when I was in the presence of "one of those things," one of those things that provided a glimpse, through a rent[3] curtain, at another world that we could not affect but that affected us. There would be a painful moment of silence, and you would wait for it to give way to a discussion of a black superstar such as Sugar Ray[4] or Jackie Robinson.[5] 12

---

[2]*Riley:* Chester A. Riley, the lead character on the U.S. television show *The Life of Riley,* a blue-collar, ethnic sitcom popular in the 1950s.

[3]*rent:* torn.

[4]*Sugar Ray:* Walker Smith Jr. (1921–1989), American professional boxer and six-time world champion.

[5]*Jackie Robinson:* Jack Roosevelt Robinson (1919–1972), the first black baseball player in the major leagues in the modern era.

"Nobody hits better in a clutch than Jackie Robinson." 13

"That's right. Nobody." 14

I never again looked Mr. Wilson in the eye. 15

Thinking Critically about This Reading

What is "one of those things," as Gates's mom put it (paragraph 12)? In what ways is "one of those things" really Gates's purpose in telling this story?

Questions for Study and Discussion

1. Gates prefaces his essay with two quotations. What is the meaning of each quotation? Why do you suppose Gates uses both quotations? How does each relate to his purpose? (Glossary: *Purpose*)
2. Gates begins by explaining where he got the idea for his essay. How well does this approach work? Is it an approach that you could see yourself using often? Explain.
3. Gates sets the context for his narrative in his first paragraph. He also reveals that his parents used terms of racial abuse among themselves. Why does Gates make so much of Mr. Wilson's use of *George* when his own parents used words so much more obviously offensive?
4. Gates describes and provides some background information about Mr. Wilson in paragraph 4. (Glossary: *Description*) What is Gates's purpose in providing this information? (Glossary: *Purpose*)

Classroom Activity Using Narration

Beginning at the beginning and ending at the end is not the only way to tell a story. Think of the events in a story that you would like to tell. Don't write the story, but simply list the events that need to be included. Be sure to include at least ten major events in your story. Now play with the arrangement of those events so as to avoid the chronological sequencing of them that would naturally come to mind. Try to develop as many patterns as you can, but be careful that you have a purpose in developing each sequence and that you create nothing that might confuse a listener or reader. Discuss your results with your classmates.

Suggested Writing Assignments

1. Using Gates's essay as a model, identify something that you have recently read that triggers in you a story from the past. Perhaps a newspaper article about how local high school students helped the community reminds you of a community project you and your classmates were involved in. Or perhaps reading about some act of heroism reminds you of a situation in which you performed (or failed to perform) a similar deed. Make sure that you have a purpose in telling the story, that you establish a clear context for it, and that you have enough supporting details to enrich your story. (Glossary: *Purpose*; *Details*) Think, as well, about how to begin and end your story and which narrative sequence you will use. (Glossary: *Beginnings and Endings*)
2. How do you feel about your name? Do you like it? Does it sound pleasant? Do you think your name shapes your self-identity in a positive or negative way, or do you think it has no effect on your sense of who you are? Write an essay about your name and the way it helps or fails to help you present yourself to the world. Be sure to develop your essay using narration by including several anecdotes or a longer story involving your name. (Glossary: *Anecdote*)

A Hanging

■ George Orwell

Although probably best known for his novels Animal Farm *(1945) and* 1984 *(1949), George Orwell (1903–1950) was also a renowned essayist on language and politics. Two of his most famous essays, "Shooting an Elephant" and "Politics and the English Language," are among the most frequently reprinted. Orwell was born in Bengal, India, and was educated in England. He traveled a great deal during his life and spent five years serving with the British colonial police in Burma.*

The following essay is a product of his experience in Burma, and first appeared in Shooting an Elephant and Other Essays *(1950). Notice how Orwell's narrative emphasizes his attitude toward events in which he is both an observer and a participant and brings his readers to some provocative insights.*

Reflecting on What You Know

Throughout history, people have gone out of their way to witness events in which someone was certain to be killed, such as fights between gladiators, jousting tournaments, and public executions. Why do you think such events fascinate people?

It was in Burma,[1] a sodden morning of the rains. A sickly light, like yel- 1
low tinfoil, was slanting over the high walls into the jail yard. We were waiting outside the condemned cells, a row of sheds fronted with double bars, like small animal cages. Each cell measured about ten feet by ten and was quite bare within except for a plank bed and a pot of drinking water. In some of them brown silent men were squatting at the inner bars, with their blankets draped round them. These were the condemned men, due to be hanged within the next week or two.

One prisoner had been brought out of his cell. He was a Hindu,[2] 2
a puny wisp of a man, with a shaven head and vague liquid eyes. He

[1]*Burma:* a country in Southeast Asia, formerly part of Britain's Indian empire, now known as Myanmar.

[2]*Hindu:* a person whose beliefs and practices are rooted in the philosophical and religious tenets of Hinduism, which originated in India.

had a thick, sprouting moustache, absurdly too big for his body, rather like the moustache of a comic man in the films. Six tall Indian warders were guarding him and getting him ready for the gallows. Two of them stood by with rifles with fixed bayonets, while the others handcuffed him, passed a chain through his handcuffs and fixed it to their belts, and lashed his arms tight to his sides. They crowded very close about him, with their hands always on him in a careful, caressing grip, as though all the while feeling him to make sure he was there. It was like men handling a fish which is still alive and may jump back into the water. But he stood quite unresisting, yielding his arms limply to the ropes, as though he hardly noticed what was happening.

Eight o'clock struck and a bugle call, desolately thin in the wet air, floated from the distant barracks. The superintendent of the jail, who was standing apart from the rest of us, moodily prodding the gravel with his stick, raised his head at the sound. He was an army doctor, with a gray toothbrush moustache and a gruff voice. "For God's sake hurry up, Francis," he said irritably. "The man ought to have been dead by this time. Aren't you ready yet?" 3

Francis, the head jailer, a fat Dravidian[3] in a white drill suit and gold spectacles, waved his black hand. "Yes sir, yes sir," he bubbled. "All iss satisfactorily prepared. The hangman iss waiting. We shall proceed." 4

"Well, quick march, then. The prisoners can't get their breakfast till this job's over." 5

We set out for the gallows. Two warders marched on either side of the prisoner, with their rifles at the slope; two others marched close against him, gripping him by arm and shoulder, as though at once pushing and supporting him. The rest of us, magistrates and the like, followed behind. Suddenly, when we had gone ten yards, the procession stopped short without any order or warning. A dreadful thing had happened—a dog, come goodness knows whence, had appeared in the yard. It came bounding among us with a loud volley of barks, and leapt round us wagging its whole body, wild with glee at finding so many human beings together. It was a large woolly dog, half Airedale, half pariah.[4] For a moment it pranced round us, and then, before anyone could stop it, it had made a dash for the prisoner, and jumping up tried to lick his face. Everyone stood aghast, too taken aback even to grab at the dog. 6

[3]*Dravidian:* someone who speaks one of the twenty-three languages belonging to the family of languages known as Dravidian, which is spoken in South Asia.
[4]*pariah:* a social outcast.

"Who let that bloody brute in here?" said the superintendent angrily. "Catch it, someone!" 7

A warder, detached from the escort, charged clumsily after the dog, but it danced and gamboled[5] just out of his reach, taking everything as part of the game. A young Eurasian jailer picked up a handful of gravel and tried to stone the dog away, but it dodged the stones and came after us again. Its yaps echoed from the jail walls. The prisoner, in the grasp of the two warders, looked on incuriously, as though this was another formality of the hanging. It was several minutes before someone managed to catch the dog. Then we put my handkerchief through its collar and moved off once more, with the dog still straining and whimpering. 8

It was about forty yards to the gallows. I watched the bare brown back of the prisoner marching in front of me. He walked clumsily with his bound arms, but quite steadily, with that bobbing gait of the Indian who never straightens his knees. At each step his muscles slid neatly into place, the lock of hair on his scalp danced up and down, his feet printed themselves on the wet gravel. And once, in spite of the men who gripped him by each shoulder, he stepped slightly aside to avoid a puddle on the path. 9

It is curious, but till that moment I had never realized what it means to destroy a healthy, conscious man. When I saw the prisoner step aside to avoid the puddle, I saw the mystery, the unspeakable wrongness, of cutting a life short when it is in full tide. This man was not dying, he was alive just as we were alive. All the organs of his body were working—bowels digesting food, skin renewing itself, nails growing, tissues forming—all toiling away in solemn foolery. His nails would still be growing when he stood on the drop, when he was falling through the air with a tenth of a second to live. His eyes saw the yellow gravel and the gray walls, and his brain still remembered, foresaw, reasoned—reasoned even about puddles. He and we were a party of men walking together, seeing, hearing, feeling, understanding the same world; and in two minutes, with a sudden snap, one of us would be gone—one mind less, one world less. 10

The gallows stood in a small yard, separate from the main grounds of the prison, and overgrown with tall prickly weeds. It was a brick erection like three sides of a shed, with planking on top, and above that two beams and a crossbar with the rope dangling. The hangman, a gray-haired convict in the white uniform of the prison, was waiting beside his machine. He greeted us with a servile crouch as we entered. 11

---

[5]*gamboled:* leaped about playfully; frolicked.

At a word from Francis the two warders, gripping the prisoner more closely than ever, half led, half pushed him to the gallows and helped him clumsily up the ladder. Then the hangman climbed up and fixed the rope round the prisoner's neck.

We stood waiting, five yards away. The warders had formed in a rough circle round the gallows. And then, when the noose was fixed, the prisoner began crying out to his god. It was a high, reiterated cry of "Ram! Ram! Ram! Ram!," not urgent and fearful like a prayer or a cry for help, but steady, rhythmical, almost like the tolling of a bell. The dog answered the sound with a whine. The hangman, still standing on the gallows, produced a small cotton bag like a flour bag and drew it down over the prisoner's face. But the sound, muffled by the cloth, still persisted, over and over again: "Ram! Ram! Ram! Ram! Ram!" 12

The hangman climbed down and stood ready, holding the lever. Minutes seemed to pass. The steady, muffled crying from the prisoner went on and on, "Ram! Ram! Ram!" never faltering for an instant. The superintendent, his head on his chest, was slowly poking the ground with his stick; perhaps he was counting the cries, allowing the prisoner a fixed number—fifty, perhaps, or a hundred. Everyone had changed color. The Indians had gone gray like bad coffee, and one or two of the bayonets were wavering. We looked at the lashed, hooded man on the drop, and listened to his cries—each cry another second of life; the same thought was in all our minds: oh, kill him quickly, get it over, stop that abominable noise! 13

Suddenly the superintendent made up his mind. Throwing up his head he made a swift motion with his stick. "Chalo!" he shouted almost fiercely. 14

There was a clanking noise, and then dead silence. The prisoner had vanished, and the rope was twisting on itself. I let go of the dog, and it galloped immediately to the back of the gallows; but when it got there it stopped short, barked, and then retreated into the corner of the yard, where it stood among the weeds, looking timorously[6] out at us. We went round the gallows to inspect the prisoner's body. He was dangling with his toes pointed straight downwards, very slowly revolving, as dead as a stone. 15

The superintendent reached out with his stick and poked the bare body; it oscillated,[7] slightly. "*He's* all right," said the superintendent. He backed out from under the gallows, and blew out a deep breath. 16

---

[6]*timorously:* timidly; fearfully.

[7]*oscillated:* swung back and forth.

The moody look had gone out of his face quite suddenly. He glanced at his wristwatch. "Eight minutes past eight. Well, that's all for this morning, thank God."

The warders unfixed bayonets and marched away. The dog, sobered and conscious of having misbehaved itself, slipped after them. We walked out of the gallows yard, past the condemned cells with their waiting prisoners, into the big central yard of the prison. The convicts, under the command of warders armed with lathis,[8] were already receiving their breakfast. They squatted in long rows, each man holding a tin pannikin, while two warders with buckets marched round ladling out rice; it seemed quite a homely, jolly scene, after the hanging. An enormous relief had come upon us now that the job was done. One felt an impulse to sing, to break into a run, to snigger. All at once everyone began chattering gaily. 17

The Eurasian boy walking beside me nodded towards the way we had come, with a knowing smile: "Do you know, sir, our friend (he meant the dead man), when he heard his appeal had been dismissed, he pissed on the floor of his cell. From fright.—Kindly take one of my cigarettes, sir. Do you not admire my new silver case, sir? From the boxwallah,[9] two rupees eight annas. Classy European style." 18

Several people laughed—at what, nobody seemed certain. 19

Francis was walking by the superintendent, talking garrulously[10]: "Well, sir, all hass passed off with the utmost satisfactoriness. It wass all finished—flick! like that. It iss not always so—oah, no! I have known cases where the doctor wass obliged to go beneath the gallows and pull the prisoner's legs to ensure decease. Most disagreeable!" 20

"Wriggling about, eh? That's bad," said the superintendent. 21

"Ach, sir, it iss worse when they become refractory![11] One man, I recall, clung to the bars of hiss cage when we went to take him out. You will scarcely credit, sir, that it took six warders to dislodge him, three pulling at each leg. We reasoned with him. 'My dear fellow,' we said, 'think of all the pain and trouble you are causing to us!' But no, he would not listen! Ach, he wass very troublesome!" 22

I found that I was laughing quite loudly. Everyone was laughing. Even the superintendent grinned in a tolerant way. "You'd better all come out and have a drink," he said quite genially. "I've got a bottle of whisky in the car. We could do with it." 23

---

[8]*lathis:* a wooden or metal baton.

[9]*boxwallah:* a trader or peddler.

[10]*garrulously:* annoyingly talkative and loud.

[11]*refractory:* resistant to authority; unruly.

We went through the big double gates of the prison, into the road. "Pulling at his legs!" exclaimed a Burmese magistrate suddenly, and burst into a loud chuckling. We all began laughing again. At that moment Francis's anecdote seemed extraordinarily funny. We all had a drink together, native and European alike, quite amicably. The dead man was a hundred yards away. 24

Thinking Critically about This Reading

Orwell goes to some pains to identify the multicultural nature—Hindu, Dravidian, Eurasian, European, Burmese—of the group participating in the hanging scene. Why is the variety of the participants' backgrounds important to the central idea of the essay?

Questions for Study and Discussion

1. In paragraph 6, why is the appearance of the dog "a dreadful thing"? From whose point of view is it dreadful?
2. The role of the narrator of this essay is never clearly defined, nor is the nature of the prisoner's transgression. Why does Orwell deliberately withhold this information?
3. In paragraphs 9 and 10, the prisoner steps aside to avoid a puddle, and Orwell considers the implications of this action. What understanding does he reach? In paragraph 10, what is the meaning of the phrase "one mind less, one world less"?
4. In paragraph 22, what is ironic about Francis's story of the "troublesome" prisoner? (Glossary: *Irony*)
5. Throughout this essay, Orwell uses figurative language, primarily similes, to bring a foreign experience closer to the reader's understanding. Find and explain three or four similes that clarify the event for a modern American reader.
6. What words would you use to describe the mood of the group that observed the hanging before the event? Afterward? Cite specific details to support your word choice. Why are the moods extreme?

Classroom Activity Using Narration

The number of words or paragraphs a writer devotes to the retelling of an event does not usually correspond to the number of minutes or hours the event took to happen. A writer may require multiple paragraphs to recount an important or complex 10–15 minute encounter, but then pass over several hours, days, or even years in several sentences.

In narration, length has less to do with chronological time than with the amount of detail the writer includes, and that's a function of the amount of emphasis the writer wants to give to a particular incident. Identify several passages in Orwell's essay where he uses multiple paragraphs to retell a relatively brief encounter and where he uses only a paragraph or two to cover a long period of time. Why do you suppose Orwell chose to tell his story in this manner?

Suggested Writing Assignments

1. Are the men who carry out the hanging in Orwell's essay cruel? Are they justified in their actions, following orders from others better able to judge? Or should they question their assigned roles as executioners? Who has the right to take the life of another? In this context, consider the message in the cartoon below, which highlights the great irony that is inherent in capital punishment. Write an essay in which you either condemn or support Orwell's role in the hanging. Was it appropriate for him to have participated, even as a spectator? What, if anything, should or could he have done when he "saw the mystery, the unspeakable wrongness, of cutting a life short when it is in full tide" (10)?
2. Recall and narrate an event in your life when you or someone you know underwent some sort of punishment. You may have been a participant or a spectator in the event. How did you react when you learned what the punishment was to be? When it was administered? After it was over?

"MAYBE THIS WILL TEACH YOU THAT IT'S MORALLY WRONG TO KILL PEOPLE!"

Momma, the Dentist, and Me

■ **Maya Angelou**

Best-selling author and poet Maya Angelou was born in 1928. She is an educator, historian, actress, playwright, civil rights activist, producer, and director. She is best known as the author of I Know Why the Caged Bird Sings *(1970), the first book in a series that constitutes her recently completed autobiography, and for "On the Pulse of the Morning," a characteristically optimistic poem on the need for personal and national renewal that she read at President Bill Clinton's inauguration in 1993. Starting with her beginnings in St. Louis in 1928, Angelou's autobiography presents a life of joyful triumph over hardships that test her courage and threaten her spirit. It includes the titles* All God's Children Need Traveling Shoes *(1986),* Wouldn't Take Nothing for My Journey Now *(1993), and* Heart of a Woman *(1997). The sixth and final book in the series,* A Song Flung Up to Heaven, *was published in 2002. Several volumes of her poetry were collected in* Complete Collected Poems of Maya Angelou *in 1994.*

In the following excerpt from I Know Why the Caged Bird Sings, *Angelou narrates what happened, and what might have happened, when her grandmother, the "Momma" of the story, took her to the local dentist. As you read, consider how vital first-person narration is to the essay's success, particularly as you gauge the effect of the italicized paragraphs.*

Reflecting on What You Know

When you were growing up, were you ever present when one or both of your parents were arguing with another adult about a matter concerning you? What were the circumstances? Narrate the events that brought about the controversy, and show how it was resolved. Were you embarrassed by your parents' actions or happy that they stood up for you?

The angel of the candy counter had found me out at last, and was exacting excruciating penance for all the stolen Milky Ways, 1

Mounds, Mr. Goodbars, and Hersheys with Almonds. I had two cavities that were rotten to the gums. The pain was beyond the bailiwick[1] of crushed aspirins or oil of cloves. Only one thing could help me, so I prayed earnestly that I'd be allowed to sit under the house and have the building collapse on my left jaw. Since there was no Negro dentist in Stamps, nor doctor either, for that matter, Momma had dealt with previous toothaches by pulling them out (a string tied to the tooth with the other end looped over her fist), pain killers, and prayer. In this particular instance the medicine had proved ineffective; there wasn't enough enamel left to hook a string on, and the prayers were being ignored because the Balancing Angel was blocking their passage.

I lived a few days and nights in blinding pain, not so much toying 2
with as seriously considering the idea of jumping in the well, and Momma decided I had to be taken to a dentist. The nearest Negro dentist was in Texarkana, twenty-five miles away, and I was certain that I'd be dead long before we reached half the distance. Momma said we'd go to Dr. Lincoln, right in Stamps, and he'd take care of me. She said he owed her a favor.

I knew there were a number of whitefolks in town that owed her 3
favors. Bailey and I had seen the books which showed how she had lent money to Blacks and whites alike during the Depression, and most still owed her. But I couldn't aptly remember seeing Dr. Lincoln's name, nor had I ever heard of a Negro's going to him as a patient. However, Momma said we were going, and put water on the stove for our baths. I had never been to a doctor, so she told me that after the bath (which would make my mouth feel better) I had to put on freshly starched and ironed underclothes from inside out. The ache failed to respond to the bath, and I knew then that the pain was more serious than that which anyone had ever suffered.

Before we left the Store, she ordered me to brush my teeth and 4
then wash my mouth with Listerine. The idea of even opening my clamped jaws increased the pain, but upon her explanation that when you go to a doctor you have to clean yourself all over, but most especially the part that's to be examined, I screwed up my courage and unlocked my teeth. The cool air in my mouth and the jarring of my molars dislodged what little remained of my reason. I had frozen to the pain, my family nearly had to tie me down to take the toothbrush away. It was

[1]*bailiwick:* a specific area of interest, skill, or authority.

no small effort to get me started on the road to the dentist. Momma spoke to all the passers-by, but didn't stop to chat. She explained over her shoulder that we were going to the doctor and she'd "pass the time of day" on our way home.

5 Until we reached the pond the pain was my world, an aura that haloed me for three feet around. Crossing the bridge into whitefolks' country, pieces of sanity pushed themselves forward. I had to stop moaning and start walking straight. The white towel, which was drawn under my chin and tied over my head, had to be arranged. If one was dying, it had to be done in style if the dying took place in whitefolks' part of town.

6 On the other side of the bridge the ache seemed to lessen as if a whitebreeze blew off the whitefolks and cushioned everything in their neighborhood—including my jaw. The gravel road was smoother, the stones smaller, and the tree branches hung down around the path and nearly covered us. If the pain didn't diminish then, the familiar yet strange sights hypnotized me into believing that it had.

7 But my head continued to throb with the measured insistence of a bass drum, and how could a toothache pass the calaboose,[2] hear the songs of the prisoners, their blues and laughter, and not be changed? How could one or two or even a mouthful of angry tooth roots meet a wagonload of powhitetrash children, endure their idiotic snobbery, and not feel less important?

8 Behind the building which housed the dentist's office ran a small path used by servants and those tradespeople who catered to the butcher and Stamps's one restaurant. Momma and I followed that lane to the backstairs of Dentist Lincoln's office. The sun was bright and gave the day a hard reality as we climbed up the steps to the second floor.

9 Momma knocked on the back door and a young white girl opened it to show surprise at seeing us there. Momma said she wanted to see Dentist Lincoln and to tell him Annie was there. The girl closed the door firmly. Now the humiliation of hearing Momma describe herself as if she had no last name to the young white girl was equal to the physical pain. It seemed terribly unfair to have a toothache and a headache and have to bear at the same time the heavy burden of Blackness.

[2]*calaboose:* a jail.

It was always possible that the teeth would quiet down and maybe drop out of their own accord. Momma said we would wait. We leaned in the harsh sunlight on the shaky railings of the dentist's back porch for over an hour. 10

He opened the door and looked at Momma. "Well, Annie, what can I do for you?" 11

He didn't see the towel around my jaw or notice my swollen face. 12

Momma said, "Dentist Lincoln. It's my grandbaby here. She got two rotten teeth that's giving her a fit." 13

She waited for him to acknowledge the truth of her statement. He made no comment, orally or facially. 14

"She had this toothache purt' near four days now, and today I said, 'Young lady, you going to the Dentist.'" 15

"Annie?" 16

"Yes, sir, Dentist Lincoln." 17

He was choosing words the way people hunt for shells. "Annie, you know I don't treat nigra, colored people." 18

"I know, Dentist Lincoln. But this here is just my little grandbaby, and she ain't gone be no trouble to you . . ." 19

"Annie, everybody has a policy. In this world you have to have a policy. Now, my policy is I don't treat colored people." 20

The sun had baked the oil out of Momma's skin and melted the Vaseline in her hair. She shone greasily as she leaned out of the dentist's shadow. 21

"Seem like to me, Dentist Lincoln, you might look after her, she ain't nothing but a little mite.[3] And seems like maybe you owe me a favor or two." 22

He reddened slightly. "Favor or no favor. The money has all been repaid to you and that's the end of it. Sorry, Annie." He had his hand on the doorknob. "Sorry." His voice was a bit kinder on the second "Sorry," as if he really was. 23

Momma said, "I wouldn't press on you like this for myself but I can't take No. Not for my grandbaby. When you come to borrow my money you didn't have to beg. You asked me, and I lent it. Now, it wasn't my policy. I ain't no moneylender, but you stood to lose this building and I tried to help you out." 24

---

[3]*mite:* a very small creature.

"It's been paid, and raising your voice won't make me change my mind. My policy . . ." He let go of the door and stepped nearer Momma. The three of us were crowded on the small landing. "Annie, my policy is I'd rather stick my hand in a dog's mouth than in a nigger's." 25

He had never once looked at me. He turned his back and went through the door into the cool beyond. Momma backed up inside herself for a few minutes. I forgot everything except her face which was almost a new one to me. She leaned over and took the doorknob, and in her everyday soft voice she said, "Sister, go on downstairs. Wait for me. I'll be there directly." 26

Under the most common of circumstances I knew it did no good to argue with Momma. So I walked down the steep stairs, afraid to look back and afraid not to do so. I turned as the door slammed, and she was gone. 27

Momma walked in that room as if she owned it. She shoved that silly nurse aside with one hand and strode into the dentist's office. He was sitting in his chair, sharpening his mean instruments and putting extra sting into his medicines. Her eyes were blazing like live coals and her arms had doubled themselves in length. He looked up at her just before she caught him by the collar of his white jacket. 28

"Stand up when you see a lady, you contemptuous scoundrel." Her tongue had thinned and the words rolled off well enunciated. Enunciated and sharp like little claps of thunder. 29

The dentist had no choice but to stand at R.O.T.C.[4] *attention. His head dropped after a minute and his voice was humble. "Yes, ma'am, Mrs. Henderson."* 30

"You knave, do you think you acted like a gentleman, speaking to me like that in front of my granddaughter?" She didn't shake him, although she had the power. She simply held him upright. 31

"No, ma'am, Mrs. Henderson." 32

"No, ma'am, Mrs. Henderson, what?" Then she did give him the tiniest of shakes, but because of her strength the action set his head and arms to shaking loose on the ends of his body. He stuttered much worse than Uncle Willie. "No, ma'am, Mrs. Henderson, I'm sorry." 33

With just an edge of her disgust showing, Momma slung him back in his dentist's chair. "Sorry is as sorry does, and you're about the sorriest 34

---

[4]*R.O.T.C.:* Reserve Officers Training Corps of the U.S. military.

dentist I ever laid my eyes on." (She could afford to slip into the vernacular[5] *because she had such eloquent command of English.)*

"I didn't ask you to apologize in front of Marguerite, because I don't want her to know my power, but I order you, now and herewith. Leave Stamps by sundown." 35

"Mrs. Henderson, I can't get my equipment . . ." He was shaking terribly now. 36

"Now, that brings me to my second order. You will never again practice dentistry. Never! When you get settled in your next place, you will be a veterinarian caring for dogs with the mange, cats with the cholera, and cows with the epizootic. Is that clear?" 37

The saliva ran down his chin and his eyes filled with tears. "Yes, ma'am. Thank you for not killing me. Thank you, Mrs. Henderson." 38

Momma pulled herself back from being ten feet tall with eight-foot arms and said, "You're welcome for nothing, you varlet,[6] *I wouldn't waste a killing on the likes of you."* 39

On her way out she waved her handkerchief at the nurse and turned her into a crocus sack of chicken feed. 40

Momma looked tired when she came down the stairs, but who wouldn't be tired if they had gone through what she had. She came close to me and adjusted the towel under my jaw (I had forgotten the toothache; I only knew that she made her hands gentle in order not to awaken the pain). She took my hand. Her voice never changed. "Come on, Sister." 41

I reckoned we were going home where she would concoct a brew to eliminate the pain and maybe give me new teeth too. New teeth that would grow overnight out of my gums. She led me toward the drugstore, which was in the opposite direction from the Store. "I'm taking you to Dentist Baker in Texarkana." 42

I was glad after all that I had bathed and put on Mum[7] and Cashmere Bouquet talcum powder. It was a wonderful surprise. My toothache had quieted to solemn pain, Momma had obliterated the evil white man, and we were going on a trip to Texarkana, just the two of us. 43

On the Greyhound she took an inside seat in the back, and I sat beside her. I was so proud of being her granddaughter and sure that some of her magic must have come down to me. She asked if I was 44

[5]*vernacular:* the everyday language spoken by people of a particular country or region.
[6]*varlet:* a rascal; lowlife.
[7]*Mum:* a brand of deodorant.

scared. I only shook my head and leaned over on her cool brown upper arm. There was no chance that a dentist, especially a Negro dentist, would dare hurt me then. Not with Momma there. The trip was uneventful, except that she put her arm around me, which was very unusual for Momma to do.

The dentist showed me the medicine and the needle before he deadened my gums, but if he hadn't I wouldn't have worried. Momma stood right behind him. Her arms were folded and she checked on everything he did. The teeth were extracted and she bought me an ice cream cone from the side window of a drug counter. The trip back to Stamps was quiet, except that I had to spit into a very small empty snuff can which she had gotten for me and it was difficult with the bus humping and jerking on our country roads. 45

At home, I was given a warm salt solution, and when I washed out my mouth I showed Bailey the empty holes, where the clotted blood sat like filling in a pie crust. He said I was quite brave, and that was my cue to reveal our confrontation with the peckerwood dentist and Momma's incredible powers. 46

I had to admit that I didn't hear the conversation, but what else could she have said than what I said she said? What else done? He agreed with my analysis in a lukewarm way, and I happily (after all, I'd been sick) flounced into the Store. Momma was preparing our evening meal and Uncle Willie leaned on the door sill. She gave her version. 47

"Dentist Lincoln got right uppity. Said he'd rather put his hand in a dog's mouth. And when I reminded him of the favor, he brushed it off like a piece of lint. Well, I sent Sister downstairs and went inside. I hadn't never been in his office before, but I found the door to where he takes out teeth, and him and the nurse was in there thick as thieves. I just stood there till he caught sight of me." Crash bang the pots on the stove. "He jumped just like he was sitting on a pin. He said, 'Annie, I done tole you, I ain't gonna mess around in no niggah's mouth.' I said, 'Somebody's got to do it then,' and he said, 'Take her to Texarkana to the colored dentist' and that's when I said, 'If you paid me my money I could afford to take her.' He said, 'It's all been paid.' I tole him everything but the interest been paid. He said, ''Twasn't no interest.' I said, ''Tis now. I'll take ten dollars as payment in full.' You know, Willie, it wasn't no right thing to do, 'cause I lent that money without thinking about it. 48

"He tole that little snippety nurse of his'n to give me ten dollars and make me sign a 'paid in full' receipt. She gave it to me and I 49 signed the papers. Even though by rights he was paid up before, I figger, he gonna be that kind of nasty, he gonna have to pay for it."

Momma and her son laughed and laughed over the white man's evilness and her retributive[8] sin. 50

I preferred, much preferred, my version. 51

Thinking Critically about This Reading

What does Angelou mean when she states, "On the other side of the bridge the ache seemed to lessen as if a whitebreeze blew off the white-folks and cushioned everything in their neighborhood—including my jaw" (paragraph 6)? How long did Angelou's pain relief last? Why?

Questions for Study and Discussion

1. What is Angelou's purpose? (Glossary: *Purpose*)
2. Compare and contrast the content and style of the interaction between Momma and the dentist that is given in italics with the one given at the end of the narrative. (Glossary: *Comparison and Contrast*)
3. Angelou tells her story chronologically and in the first person. (Glossary: *Point of View*) What are the advantages of first-person narration?
4. Identify three similes that Angelou uses in her narrative. (Glossary: *Figure of Speech*) Explain how each simile serves her purpose. (Glossary: *Purpose*)
5. Why do you suppose Angelou says she prefers her own version of the episode to that of her grandmother?
6. This is a story of pain—and not just the pain of a toothache. How does Angelou describe the pain of the toothache? What other pain does she tell of in this autobiographical piece?

Classroom Activity Using Narration

One of Angelou's themes in "Momma, the Dentist, and Me" is that cruelty, whether racial, social, professional, or personal, is difficult to

[8]*retributive:* demanding something in repayment, especially punishment.

endure and leaves a lasting impression on a person. As a way of practicing chronological order, consider a situation in which an unthinking or insensitive person made you feel inferior. Rather than write a draft of an essay at this point, simply list the sequence of events that occurred, in chronological order. Once you have completed this step, consider whether there is a more dramatic order you might use if you were actually to write an essay.

Suggested Writing Assignments

1. Using Angelou's essay as a model, give two versions of an actual event—one the way you thought or wished it had happened and the other the way events actually took place. You may want to refer to your journal entry for this reading before you begin writing.
2. Every person who tells a story puts his or her signature on it in some way—by the sequencing of events, the amount and type of details used, and the tone the teller of the story employs. (Glossary: *Tone*) If you and a relative or friend experienced the same interesting sequence of events, try telling the story of those events from your unique perspective. (Glossary: *Point of View*) Once you have done so, try telling the story from what you imagine the other person's perspective to be. Perhaps you even heard the other person actually tell the story. What is the same in both versions? How do the renditions differ?

The Story of an Hour

■ Kate Chopin

Kate Chopin (1851–1904) was born in St. Louis of Creole Irish descent. After her marriage, she lived in Louisiana, where she acquired the intimate knowledge of Creole Cajun culture that provided the impetus for much of her work and earned her a reputation as a writer who captured the ambience of the bayou region. When her first novel, The Awakening *(1899), was published, however, it generated scorn and outrage for its explicit depiction of a southern woman's sexual awakening. Only recently has Chopin been recognized for her literary talent and originality. Besides* The Awakening, *her works include two collections of short fiction,* Bayou Folk *(1894) and* A Night in Acadie *(1897). In 1969,* The Complete Works of Kate Chopin *was published by Louisiana State University Press, and the Library of America published* Kate Chopin: Complete Novels and Stories *in 2002.*

As you read the following story, first published as "The Dream of an Hour" in Vogue *magazine in 1894, try to gauge how your reactions to Mrs. Mallard are influenced by Chopin's use of third-person narration.*

Reflecting on What You Know

How do you react to the idea of marriage—committing to someone for life? What are the advantages of such a union? What are the disadvantages?

Knowing that Mrs. Mallard was afflicted with a heart trouble, great care was taken to break to her as gently as possible the news of her husband's death. 1

It was her sister Josephine who told her, in broken sentences; veiled hints that revealed in half concealing. Her husband's friend Richards was there, too, near her. It was he who had been in the newspaper office when intelligence of the railroad disaster was received, with Brently Mallard's name leading the list of "killed." He 2 had only taken the time to assure himself of its truth by a second telegram, and had hastened to forestall any less careful, less tender friend in bearing the sad message.

She did not hear the story as many women have heard the same, 3
with a paralyzed inability to accept its significance. She wept at once, with sudden, wild abandonment, in her sister's arms. When the storm of grief had spent itself she went away to her room alone. She would have no one follow her.

There stood, facing the open window, a comfortable, roomy 4
armchair. Into this she sank, pressed down by a physical exhaustion that haunted her body and seemed to reach into her soul.

She could see in the open square before her house the tops of trees 5
that were all aquiver with the new spring life. The delicious breath of rain was in the air. In the street below a peddler was crying his wares. The notes of a distant song which someone was singing reached her faintly, and countless sparrows were twittering in the eaves.

There were patches of blue sky showing here and there through 6
the clouds that had met and piled one above the other in the west facing her window.

She sat with her head thrown back upon the cushion of the chair, 7
quite motionless, except when a sob came up into her throat and shook her, as a child who has cried itself to sleep continues to sob in its dreams.

She was young, with a fair, calm face, whose lines bespoke re- 8
pression and even a certain strength. But now there was a dull stare in her eyes, whose gaze was fixed away off yonder on one of those patches of blue sky. It was not a glance of reflection, but rather indicated a suspension of intelligent thought.

There was something coming to her and she was waiting for it, 9
fearfully. What was it? She did not know; it was too subtle and elusive to name. But she felt it, creeping out of the sky, reaching toward her through the sounds, the scents, the color that filled the air.

Now her bosom rose and fell tumultuously. She was beginning to 10
recognize this thing that was approaching to possess her, and she was striving to beat it back with her will—as powerless as her two white slender hands would have been.

When she abandoned herself a little whispered word escaped her 11
slightly parted lips. She said it over and over under her breath: "free, free, free!" The vacant stare and the look of terror that had followed it went from her eyes. They stayed keen and bright. Her pulses beat

fast, and the coursing blood warmed and relaxed every inch of her body.

She did not stop to ask if it were or were not a monstrous joy that held her. A clear and exalted perception enabled her to dismiss the suggestion as trivial. 12

She knew that she would weep again when she saw the kind, tender hands folded in death; the face that had never looked save with love upon her, fixed and gray and dead. But she saw beyond that bitter moment a long procession of years to come that would belong to her absolutely. And she opened and spread her arms out to them in welcome. 13

There would be no one to live for her during those coming years; she would live for herself. There would be no powerful will bending hers in that blind persistence with which men and women believe they have a right to impose a private will upon a fellow-creature. A kind intention or a cruel intention made the act seem no less a crime as she looked upon it in that brief moment of illumination. 14

And yet she had loved him—sometimes. Often she had not. What did it matter! What could love, the unsolved mystery, count for in face of this possession of self-assertion which she suddenly recognized as the strongest impulse of her being! 15

"Free! Body and soul free!" she kept whispering. 16

Josephine was kneeling before the closed door with her lips to the keyhole, imploring for admission. "Louise, open the door! I beg; open the door—you will make yourself ill. What are you doing, Louise? For heaven's sake open the door." 17

"Go away. I am not making myself ill." No; she was drinking in a very elixir of life through that open window. 18

Her fancy was running riot along those days ahead of her. Spring days, and summer days, and all sorts of days that would be her own. She breathed a quick prayer that life might be long. It was only yesterday she had thought with a shudder that life might be long. 19

She arose at length and opened the door to her sister's importunities.[1] There was a feverish triumph in her eyes, and she carried herself unwittingly like a goddess of Victory. She clasped her sister's waist, and together they descended the stairs. Richards stood waiting for them at the bottom. 20

---

[1]*importunities:* urgent requests or demands.

Some one was opening the front door with a latchkey. It was Brently Mallard who entered, a little travel-stained, composedly carrying his grip-sack and umbrella. He had been far from the scene of the accident, and did not even know there had been one. He stood amazed at Josephine's piercing cry; at Richards' quick motion to screen him from the view of his wife. 21

But Richards was too late. 22

When the doctors came they said she had died of heart disease— of joy that kills. 23

Thinking Critically about This Reading

Chopin describes Mrs. Mallard as "beginning to recognize this thing that was approaching to possess her, and she was striving to beat it back with her will—as powerless as her two white slender hands would have been" (paragraph 10). Why does Mrs. Mallard fight her feeling of freedom, however briefly? How does she come to accept it?

Questions for Study and Discussion

1. What assumptions do Mrs. Mallard's relatives and friends make about her feelings toward her husband? What are her true feelings?
2. Reread paragraphs 5–9. What is Chopin's purpose in this section? (Glossary: *Purpose*) Do these paragraphs add to the story's effectiveness? Explain.
3. All of the events of Chopin's story take place in an hour. Would the story be as poignant if they had taken place over the course of a day or even several days? Explain. Why do you suppose the author selected the time frame as a title for her story? (Glossary: *Title*)
4. Chopin could have written an essay detailing the oppression of women in marriage, but she chose instead to write a fictional narrative. This allows her to show readers the type of situation that can arise in an outwardly happy marriage rather than tell them about it. Why else do you think she chose to write a fictional narrative? What other advantages does it give her over nonfiction?
5. Why does Chopin narrate her story in the third person? (Glossary: *Point of View*)

Classroom Activity Using Narration

Using cues in the following sentences, rearrange them in chronological order.

1. The sky was gray and gloomy for as far as she could see, and sleet hissed off the glass.
2. "Oh, hi. I'm glad you called," she said happily, but her smile dimmed when she looked outside.
3. As Betty crossed the room, the phone rang, startling her.
4. "No, the weather's awful, so I don't think I'll get out to visit you today," she sighed.
5. "Hello," she said, and she wandered over to the window, dragging the phone cord behind her.

Write five sentences of your own that cover a progression of events. Try to include dialogue. (Glossary: *Dialogue*) Then scramble them, and see if a classmate can put them back in the correct order.

Suggested Writing Assignments

1. Using Chopin's story as a model, write a short piece of narrative fiction in which your main character reacts to a specific, dramatic event. Portray the character's emotional response, as well as how the character perceives his or her surroundings. What does the character sec, hear, touch? How are these senses affected by the situation?
2. Write a narrative essay in which you describe your reaction to a piece of news that you once received—good or bad—that provoked a strong emotional response. What were your emotions? What did you do in the couple of hours after you received the news? How did your perceptions of the world around you change? What made the experience memorable?

chapter **15**

Description

To describe is to create a verbal picture. A person, a place, a thing—even an idea or a state of mind—can be made vividly concrete through **description.** Here, for example, is a brief description of a delicatessen:

> It was a narrow room, with a rather high ceiling, and crowded from floor to ceiling with goodies. There were rows and rows of hams and sausages of all shapes and colors—white, yellow, red, and black; fat and lean and round and long—rows of canned preserves, cocoa and tea, bright translucent glass bottles of honey, marmalade, and jam; round bottles and slender bottles, filled with liqueurs and punch—all these things crowded every inch of the shelves from top to bottom.
>
> –Thomas Mann

Writing any description requires, first of all, that the writer gather many details about a subject, relying not only on what the eyes see but on the other sense impressions—touch, taste, smell, hearing—as well. From this catalog of details, the writer selects those that will most effectively create a **dominant impression**—the single quality, mood, or atmosphere that the writer wishes to emphasize. Consider, for example, the details that Mary McCarthy uses to evoke the dominant impression in the following passage, and contrast them with those in the subsequent example by student Dan Bubany:

> Whenever we children came to stay at my grandmother's house, we were put to sleep in the sewing room, a bleak, shabby, utilitarian rectangle, more office than bedroom, more attic than office, that played to the hierarchy of chambers the role of poor relation. It was a room without pride: the old sewing machine, some cast-off chairs, a shadeless lamp, rolls of wrapping paper, piles of cardboard boxes that might someday come in handy, papers of pins,

and remnants of a material united with the iron folding cots put out for our use and the bare floor boards to give an impression of intense and ruthless temporality. Thin white spreads, of the kind used in hospitals and charity institutions, and naked blinds at the windows reminded us of our orphaned condition and of the ephemeral character of our visit; there was nothing here to encourage us to consider this our home.

–Mary McCarthy

For this particular Thursday game against Stanford, Fleming wears white gloves, a maroon sport coat with brass buttons, and gray slacks. Shiny silver-framed bifocals match the whistle pressed between the lips on his slightly wrinkled face, and he wears freshly polished black shoes so glossy that they reflect the grass he stands on. He is not fat, but his coat neatly conceals a small, round pot belly.

–Dan Bubany, student

The dominant impression that McCarthy creates is one of clutter, bleakness, and shabbiness. There is nothing in the sewing room that suggests permanence or warmth. Bubany, on the other hand, creates a dominant impression of a neat, polished, kindly man.

Writers must also carefully plan the order in which to present their descriptive details. The pattern of organization must fit the subject of the description logically and naturally and must be easy to follow. For example, visual details can be arranged spatially—from left to right, top to bottom, near to far, or in any other logical order. Other patterns include smallest to largest, softest to loudest, least significant to most significant, most unusual to least unusual. McCarthy, for example, suggests a jumble of junk not only by her choice of details but by the apparently random order in which she presents them.

How much detail is enough? There is no fixed answer. A good description includes enough vivid details to create a dominant impression and to bring a scene to life but not so many that readers are distracted, confused, or bored. In an essay that is purely descriptive, there is room for much detail. Usually, however, writers use description to create the setting for a story, to illustrate ideas, to help clarify a definition or a comparison, or to make the complexities of a process more understandable. Such descriptions should be kept short and should include just enough detail to make them clear and helpful.

Subway Station

■ Gilbert Highet

Gilbert Highet (1906–1978) was born in Scotland and became a naturalized U.S. citizen in 1951. A prolific writer and translator, distinguished scholar, and critic, Highet was for many years a professor of classics at Columbia University, as well as a popular radio essayist. His Art of Teaching *(1950), a classic in education, was reissued in paperback and is still available. Another of his books,* The Classical Tradition: Greek and Roman Influences on Western Literature, *was reissued in paperback in 1992.*

The following selection is from his book Talents and Geniuses *(1957). Take note of Highet's keen eye for detail as you read. Concrete and vivid images help him re-create the unseemly world of a subway station.*

Reflecting on What You Know

Try to remember what it is like to be in a subway station, airport, or bus station. What are the sights, sounds, and smells you recall? What do you remember most about any of these crowded, transient places? What was your overall impression of the place?

Standing in a subway station, I began to appreciate the place— 1
almost to enjoy it. First of all, I looked at the lighting: a row of meager electric bulbs, unscreened, yellow, and coated with filth, stretched toward the black mouth of the tunnel, as though it were a bolt hole in an abandoned coal mine. Then I lingered, with zest, on the walls and ceiling: lavatory tiles which had been white about fifty years ago, and were now encrusted with soot, coated with the remains of a dirty liquid which might be either atmospheric humidity mingled with smog or the result of a perfunctory[1] attempt to clean them with cold water; and, above them, gloomy vaulting from which dingy paint was peeling off like scabs from an old wound, sick black paint leaving a leprous white undersurface. Beneath my feet, the floor was

[1]*perfunctory:* hasty and without attention to detail.

a nauseating dark brown with black stains upon it which might be stale oil or dry chewing gum or some worse defilement; it looked like the hallway of a condemned slum building. Then my eye traveled to the tracks, where two lines of glittering steel—the only positively clean objects in the whole place—ran out of darkness into darkness above an unspeakable mass of congealed oil, puddles of dubious[2] liquid, and a mishmash of old cigarette packets, mutilated and filthy newspapers, and the débris that filtered down from the street above through a barred grating in the roof. As I looked up toward the sunlight, I could see more débris sifting slowly downward, and making an abominable pattern in the slanting beam of dirt-laden sunlight. I was going on to relish more features of this unique scene: such as the advertisement posters on the walls—here a text from the Bible, there a half-naked girl, here a woman wearing a hat consisting of a hen sitting on a nest full of eggs, and there a pair of girl's legs walking up the keys of a cash register—all scribbled over with unknown names and well-known obscenities in black crayon and red lipstick; but then my train came in at last, I boarded it, and began to read. The experience was over for the time.

Thinking Critically about This Reading

In his opening sentence, Highet reveals that he "began to appreciate the place—almost enjoy it." What does he mean by "appreciate"? Explain.

Questions for Study and Discussion

1. What dominant impression does Highet create in his description? (Glossary: *Dominant Impression*) List the details that help Highet create his dominant impression.
2. Why do you think Highet observes the subway station with "zest" and "relish"? What does he find appealing about the experience?
3. What similes and metaphors can you find in Highet's description? (Glossary: *Figure of Speech*) How do they help make the description vivid?

---

[2]*dubious:* of uncertain or questionable content.

4. What mix of advertisements does Highet observe? Based on Highet's description of what they depict, their current appearance, and the atmosphere of their surroundings, suggest what product each poster might be advertising. Explain your suggestions.
5. Highet has an eye for detail that is usually displayed by those who are seeing something for the first time. Do you think it is his first time in a subway station, or is he a regular rider who is taking time out to "relish" his physical surroundings? What in the essay leads you to your conclusion?

Classroom Activity Using Description

Make a long list of the objects and people in your classroom as well as the physical features of the room—desks, windows, chalkboard, students, professor, dirty walls, burned-out lightbulb, a clock that is always ten minutes fast, and so on. Determine a dominant impression that you would like to create in describing the classroom. Now choose from your list those items that would best illustrate the dominant impression you have chosen. Your instructor may wish to have students compare their responses.

Suggested Writing Assignments

1. Using Highet's essay as a model, write an extended one-paragraph description of a room in your house or apartment where you do not spend much time. Take your time observing the details in the room. Before you write, decide on the dominant impression you wish to communicate to the reader. (Glossary: *Dominant Impression*)
2. Write a short essay in which you describe one of the following places (or another place of your choice). Arrange the details of your description from top to bottom, left to right, near to far, or according to some other spatial organization.

closet	barbershop or beauty salon
pizza parlor	bookstore
locker room	campus dining hall

3. Consider the photograph on page 392 of historic London Paddington station, a major National Rail and London Underground station complex near central London, England. What is your dominant

impression of Paddington station? (Glossary: *Dominant Impression*) What details in the photograph come together to create this dominant impression for you? How does the subway station that Highet describes compare to the one in the photograph? Using Highet's essay as a model, write a description of Paddington station that captures the dominant impression you identified above.

Photo by Alfred Rosa.

Memories of New York City Snow

■ Oscar Hijuelos

The son of Cuban immigrant parents, Oscar Hijuelos was born in New York City in 1951. He graduated from the City University of New York in 1975 and earned an MA in creative writing from the same institution the following year. During what might be called his apprentice period from 1977 through 1984, Hijuelos worked at an advertising agency during the day and wrote fiction at night. His efforts resulted in the publication of Our House in the Last World *(1983), a novel praised for its richly detailed descriptions of Cuban American life. Hijuelos received the Pulitzer Prize for fiction, the first Hispanic so honored, for* The Mambo Kings Play Songs of Love *(1989). This novel was made into a film in 1992 and a Broadway musical in 2005. His other novels include* The Fourteen Sisters of Emilio Montez O'Brien *(1993),* Mr. Ives' Christmas *(1995),* Empress of the Splendid Season *(1999),* A Simple Habana Melody *(2002), and* Dark Dude *(2008). Since 1989, Hijuelos has taught English at Hofstra University.*

"Memories of New York City Snow" first appeared in Metropolis Found *(2003), an anthology of essays published on the twenty-fifth anniversary of the New York Is Book Country festival in the city. In his essay, Hijuelos describes his parents' New York in the wintertime. Notice how his strong details and active verbs bring the description to life.*

Reflecting on What You Know

What is your earliest memory of snow? Did you grow up in a region where it regularly snowed during the winter, or was snow a rare occurrence? What do you remember doing when it snowed?

For immigrants of my parents' generation, who had first come to New York City from the much warmer climate of Cuba in the mid-1940s, the very existence of snow was a source of fascination. A black-and-white photograph that I have always loved, circa 1948, its surface cracked like that of a thawing ice-covered pond, features my 1 father, Pascual, and my godfather, Horacio, fresh up from Oriente Province, posing in a snow-covered meadow in Central Park. Decked out in long coats, scarves, and black-brimmed hats, they are holding, in their be-gloved hands, a huge chunk of hardened snow. Trees and their straggly witch's hair branches, glimmering with ice and frost, recede into the distance behind them. They stand on a field of whiteness, the two men seemingly afloat in midair, as if they were being held aloft by the magical substance itself.

That they bothered to have this photograph taken—I suppose to send back to family in Cuba—has always been a source of enchantment for me. That something so common to winters in New York would strike them as an object of exotic admiration has always spoken volumes about the newness—and innocence—of their immigrants' experience. How thrilling it all must have seemed to them, for their New York was so very different from the small town surrounded by farms in eastern Cuba that they hailed from. Their New York was a fanciful and bustling city of endless sidewalks and unimaginably high buildings; of great bridges and twisting outdoor elevated train trestles; of walkup tenement houses with mysteriously dark basements, and subways that burrowed through an underworld of girded tunnels; of dancehalls, burlesque houses, and palatial department stores with their complement of Christmastime Salvation Army Santa Clauses on every street corner. Delightful and perilous, their New York was a city of incredibly loud noises, of police and air raid sirens and factory whistles and subway rumble; a city where people sometimes shushed you for speaking Spanish in a public place, or could be unforgiving if you did not speak English well or seemed to be of a different ethnic background. (My father was once nearly hit by a garbage can that had been thrown off the rooftop of a building as he was walking along La Salle Street in upper Manhattan.) 2

Even so, New York represented the future. The city meant jobs and money. Newly arrived, an aunt of mine went to work for Pan Am; another aunt, as a Macy's saleslady. My own mother, speaking nary a word of English, did a stint in the garment district as a seamstress. During the war some family friends, like my godfather, were eventually drafted, while others ended up as factory laborers. Landing a job at the Biltmore Men's Bar, my father joined the hotel and restaurant workers' union, paid his first weekly dues, and came home one day with a brand new white chef's toque in hand. Just about everybody found work, often for low pay and ridiculously long hours. And 3 while the men of that generation worked a lot of overtime, or a second job, they always had their day or two off. Dressed to the hilt, they'd leave their uptown neighborhoods and make an excursion to another part of the city—perhaps to one of the grand movie palaces of Times Square or to beautiful Central Park, as my father and godfather, and their ladies, had once done, in the aftermath of a snowfall.

Snow, such as it can only fall in New York City, was not just about the cold and wintry differences that mark the weather of the north. It was about a purity that would descend upon the grayness of its streets like a heaven of silence, the city's complexity and bustle abruptly subdued. But as beautiful as it could be, it was also something that provoked nostalgia; I am certain that my father would miss Cuba on some bitterly cold days. I remember that whenever we were out on a walk and it began to snow, my father would stop and look up at the sky, with wonderment—what he was seeing I don't know. Perhaps that's why to this day my own associations with a New York City snowfall have a mystical connotation, as if the presence of snow really meant that some kind of inaccessible divinity had settled his breath upon us. 4

Thinking Critically about This Reading

Hijuelos claims that snow "was not just about the cold and wintry differences that mark the weather of the north" (paragraph 4). What is snow about for Hijuelos?

Questions for Study and Discussion

1. Hijuelos states that "snow was a source of fascination" (1) for his parents and other immigrants of their generation. Why do you suppose that they found snow fascinating?
2. Identify one simile and one metaphor in paragraph 1. (Glossary: *Figure of Speech*) What does each figure add to Hijuelos's description of the family photograph?
3. Hijuelos confesses that he is enchanted by the photograph of his father and godfather standing in a snow-covered field in Central Park. What exactly does this old photograph represent for Hijuelos?
4. What dominant impression of his parents' New York does Hijuelos create with the sights and sounds he catalogues in paragraph 2?

5. What do we learn about immigrant life in America in the 1940s from Hijuelos's description of his parents' experience? In what ways did New York represent "the future" (3)?

Classroom Activity Using Description

One of the best ways to make a description of a person memorable is to use a simile (making a comparison using *like* or *as,* such as "Her feet floated like a feather in a breeze") or a metaphor (making a comparison without the use of *like* or *as,* such as "His fists were iron"). Think of a time when you were one of a group of people assembled to do something most or all of you didn't really want to do. People in such a situation behave in various ways, showing their discomfort. One might stare steadily at the ground, for example. A writer describing the scene could use a metaphor to make it more vivid for the reader: "With his gaze he drilled a hole in the ground between his feet." Other people in an uncomfortable situation might fidget, lace their fingers together, breathe rapidly, squirm, or tap an object, such as a pen or key. Create a simile or a metaphor to describe each of these behaviors. Compare your metaphors and similes with those of your classmates. Discuss which ones work best for each behavior.

Suggested Writing Assignments

1. What is your favorite city, and what are your favorite places in that city? For example, if Washington, D.C., is your favorite city, the White House, U.S. Capitol building, Washington Monument, Lincoln Memorial, Vietnam Veterans Memorial, Smithsonian Institution, National Gallery of Art, and National Zoo might be among your favorite places. Write an essay in which you describe the city you love. Be sure to include specific places within the city in your description.
2. As Hijuelos has done with the snow in New York City, write a short essay describing a common weather phenomenon in your area. For example, does your region of the country get more than its share of droughts, flooding, hurricanes, thunderstorms, blizzards, or ice storms? What does this weather phenomenon mean to you? What memories, if any, do you associate with it? Include details in your description that will appeal to your readers' senses of sight, sound, and smell.

The Corner Store

■ **Eudora Welty**

One of the most honored and respected writers of the twentieth century, Eudora Welty was born in 1909 in Jackson, Mississippi, where she lived most of her life and where she died in 2001. Her first book, A Curtain of Green *(1941), is a collection of short stories. Although she went on to become a successful writer of novels, essays, and book reviews, among other genres (as well as a published photographer), she is most often remembered as a master of the short story.* The Collected Stories of Eudora Welty *was published in 1980. Her other best-known works include a collection of essays,* The Eye of the Story *(1975); her autobiography,* One Writer's Beginnings *(1984); and a collection of book reviews and essays,* The Writer's Eye *(1994). Welty's novel* The Optimist's Daughter *won the Pulitzer Prize for fiction in 1973, and in 1999 the Library of Congress published two collections of her work:* Welty: Collected Novels *and* Welty: Collected Essays and Memoirs.

Welty's description of the corner store, taken from an essay in The Eye of the Story *about growing up in Jackson, recalls for many readers the neighborhood store in the town or city where they grew up. As you read, pay attention to the effect Welty's spatial arrangement of descriptive details has on the dominant impression of the store.*

Reflecting on What You Know

Write about a store you frequented as a child. Maybe it was the local supermarket, the hardware store, or the corner convenience store. Using your five senses (sight, smell, taste, touch, and hearing), describe what you remember about the place.

Our Little Store rose right up from the sidewalk; standing in a street of family houses, it alone hadn't any yard in front, any tree or flower bed. It was a plain frame building covered over with brick. Above the door, a little railed porch ran across on an upstairs 1 level and four windows with shades were looking out. But I didn't catch on to those.

Running in out of the sun, you met what seemed total obscurity inside. There were almost tangible smells—licorice recently sucked in a child's cheek, dill pickle brine[1] that had leaked through a paper sack in a fresh trail across the wooden floor, ammonia-loaded ice that had been hoisted from wet croker sacks[2] and slammed into the icebox[3] with its sweet butter at the door, and perhaps the smell of still untrapped mice. 2

Then through the motes of cracker dust, cornmeal dust, the Gold Dust of the Gold Dust Twins that the floor had been swept out with, the realities emerged. Shelves climbed to high reach all the way around, set out with not too much of any one thing but a lot of things—lard, molasses, vinegar, starch, matches, kerosene, Octagon soap (about a year's worth of octagon-shaped coupons cut out and saved brought a signet ring[4] addressed to you in the mail). It was up to you to remember what you came for, while your eye traveled from cans of sardines to tin whistles to ice-cream salt to harmonicas to fly-paper (over your head, batting around on a thread beneath the blades of the ceiling fan, stuck with its testimonial catch). 3

Its confusion may have been in the eye of its beholder. Enchantment is cast upon you by all those things you weren't supposed to have need for, to lure you close to wooden tops you'd outgrown, boys' marbles and agates in little net pouches, small rubber balls that wouldn't bounce straight, frail, frazzly kite string, clay bubble pipes that would snap off in your teeth, the stiffest scissors. You could contemplate those long narrow boxes of sparklers gathering dust while you waited for it to be the Fourth of July or Christmas, and noisemakers in the shape of tin frogs for somebody's birthday party you hadn't been invited to yet, and see that they were all marvelous. 4

You might not have even looked for Mr. Sessions when he came around his store cheese (as big as a doll's house) and in front of the counter looking for you. When you'd finally asked him for, and received from him in its paper bag, whatever single thing it was that 5

[1]*brine:* salty water used to preserve or pickle food.
[2]*croker sacks:* sacks or bags made of burlap, a coarse woven fabric.
[3]*icebox:* a wooden box or cupboard that held ice in a lower compartment to cool a second compartment above it, which was used for storing perishable food.
[4]*signet ring:* a ring bearing an official-looking seal.

you had been sent for, the nickel that was left over was yours to spend.

6 Down at a child's eye level, inside those glass jars with mouths in their sides through which the grocer could run his scoop or a child's hand might be invited to reach for a choice, were wineballs, all-day suckers, gumdrops, peppermints. Making a row under the glass of a counter were the Tootsie Rolls, Hershey bars, Goo Goo Clusters, Baby Ruths. And whatever was the name of those pastilles that came stacked in a cardboard cylinder with a cardboard lid? They were thin and dry, about the size of tiddledy-winks,[5] and in the shape of twisted rosettes. A kind of chocolate dust came out with them when you shook them out in your hand. Were they chocolate? I'd say, rather, they were brown. They didn't taste of anything at all, unless it was wood. Their attraction was the number you got for a nickel.

7 Making up your mind, you circled the store around and around, around the pickle barrel, around the tower of Crackerjack boxes; Mr. Sessions had built it for us himself on top of a packing case like a house of cards.

8 If it seemed too hot for Crackerjacks, I might get a cold drink. Mr. Sessions might have already stationed himself by the cold-drinks barrel, like a mind reader. Deep in ice water that looked black as ink, murky shapes—that would come up as Coca-Colas, Orange Crushes, and various flavors of pop—were all swimming around together. When you gave the word, Mr. Sessions plunged his bare arm in to the elbow and fished out your choice, first try. I favored a locally bottled concoction called Lake's Celery. (What else could it be called? It was made by a Mr. Lake out of celery. It was a popular drink here for years but was not known universally, as I found out when I arrived in New York and ordered one in the Astor bar.) You drank on the premises, with feet set wide apart to miss the drip, and gave him back his bottle and your nickel.

9 But he didn't hurry you off. A standing scale was by the door, with a stack of iron weights and a brass slide on the balance arm, that would weigh you up to three hundred pounds. Mr. Sessions, whose hands were gentle and smelled of carbolic,[6] would lift you up and set your feet on the platform, hold your loaf of bread for you,

[5]*tiddledy-winks:* playing pieces from the game Tiddledy-Winks, flat and round in shape, the size of quarters (tiddledies) and dimes (winks).

[6]*carbolic:* a sweet, musky-smelling chemical once used in soap.

and taking his time while you stood still for him, he would make certain of what you weighed today. He could even remember what you weighed the last time, so you could subtract and announce how much you'd gained. That was goodbye.

Thinking Critically about This Reading

What does Mr. Sessions himself contribute to the overall experience of Welty's store? What does Welty's store contribute to the community?

Questions for Study and Discussion

1. Which of the three patterns of organization does Welty use in this essay—chronological, spatial, or logical? If she uses more than one, where precisely does she use each type?
2. In paragraph 2, Welty describes the smells that a person encountered when entering the corner store. Why do you think she presents these smells before giving any visual details of the inside of the store?
3. What dominant impression does Welty create in her description of the corner store? (Glossary: *Dominant Impression*) How does she create this dominant impression?
4. What impression of Mr. Sessions does Welty create? What details contribute to this impression? (Glossary: *Details*)
5. Why does Welty place certain pieces of information in parentheses? What, if anything, does this information add to your understanding of the corner store? Might this information be left out? Explain.
6. Comment on Welty's ending. (Glossary: *Beginnings and Endings*) Is it too abrupt? Why or why not?

Classroom Activity Using Description

The verbs you use in writing a description can themselves convey much descriptive information. Take, for example, the verb *walk*. This word actually tells us little more than "to move on foot," in the most general sense. Using more precise and descriptive alternatives—*hike*, *slink*, *saunter*, *stalk*, *step*, *stride*, *stroll*, *tramp*, *wander*—enhances your descriptive powers and enlivens your writing. For each of the following verbs, make a list of at least four descriptive alternatives. Then compare your list of descriptive alternatives with those of others in the class.

go	throw	exercise
see	take	study
say	drink	sleep

Suggested Writing Assignments

1. Using Welty's essay as a model, describe your neighborhood store or supermarket. Gather a large quantity of detailed information from memory and from an actual visit to the store if that is still possible. You may find it helpful to reread what you wrote in response to the journal prompt. Once you have gathered your information, try to select those details that will help you create a dominant impression of the store. Finally, organize your examples and illustrations according to some clear organizational pattern.
2. Describe a familiar inanimate object in a way that brings out its character and makes it interesting to the reader. First, determine your purpose in describing the object. Suppose, for example, your family has had the same dining table for as long as you can remember. Think of what that table has been a part of over the years—the birthday parties, the fights, the holiday meals, the long hours of studying and doing homework. A description of such a table would give your reader a sense of the history of your family. Next, make an exhaustive list of the object's physical features, and include in your descriptive essay the features that contribute to your dominant impression and support your purpose. (Glossary: *Dominant Impression*)

My Favorite Teacher

■ Thomas L. Friedman

New York Times *foreign affairs columnist Thomas L. Friedman was born in Minneapolis, Minnesota, in 1953. He graduated from Brandeis University in 1975 and received a Marshall Scholarship to study modern Middle East studies at St. Antony's College, Oxford University, where he earned a master's degree. He has worked for the* New York Times *since 1981, first in Lebanon, then in Israel, and since 1989 in Washington, D.C. He has won three Pulitzer Prizes. His 1989 bestseller,* From Beirut to Jerusalem, *received the National Book Award for nonfiction. Friedman's most recent books are* The Lexus and the Olive Tree: Understanding Globalization *(2000),* Longitudes and Attitudes: Exploring the World after September 11 *(2002),* The World Is Flat: A Brief History of the Twenty-First Century *(2005), and* Hot, Flat, and Crowded: Why We Need a Green Revolution—and How It Can Renew America *(2008).*

In the following essay, which first appeared in the New York Times *on January 9, 2001, Friedman pays tribute to his tenth-grade journalism teacher. As you read Friedman's profile of Hattie M. Steinberg, note the descriptive detail he selects to create the dominant impression of "a woman of clarity in an age of uncertainty."*

Reflecting on What You Know

If you had to name your three favorite teachers to date, who would be on your list? Why do you consider each of the teachers a favorite? Which one, if any, are you likely to remember twenty-five years from now? Why?

Last Sunday's *New York Times Magazine* published its annual review of people who died last year who left a particular mark on the world. I am sure all readers have their own such list. I certainly do. Indeed, someone who made the most important difference in my life died last year—my high school journalism teacher, Hattie M. Steinberg. 1

I grew up in a small suburb of Minneapolis, and Hattie was the legendary journalism teacher at St. Louis Park High School, Room 313. I took her intro to journalism course in 10th grade, back in 1969, and have never needed, or taken, another course in journalism since. She was that good. 2

Hattie was a woman who believed that the secret for success in life was getting the fundamentals right. And boy, she pounded the fundamentals of journalism into her students—not simply how to write a lead or accurately transcribe a quote, but, more important, how to comport yourself in a professional way and to always do quality work. To this day, when I forget to wear a tie on assignment, I think of Hattie scolding me. I once interviewed an ad exec for our high school paper who used a four-letter word. We debated whether to run it. Hattie ruled yes. That ad man almost lost his job when it appeared. She wanted to teach us about consequences. 3

Hattie was the toughest teacher I ever had. After you took her journalism course in 10th grade, you tried out for the paper, *The Echo,* which she supervised. Competition was fierce. In 11th grade, I didn't quite come up to her writing standards, so she made me business manager, selling ads to the local pizza parlors. That year, though, she let me write one story. It was about an Israeli general who had been a hero in the Six-Day War,[1] who was giving a lecture at the University of Minnesota. I covered his lecture and interviewed him briefly. His name was Ariel Sharon.[2] First story I ever got published. 4

Those of us on the paper, and the yearbook that she also supervised, lived in Hattie's classroom. We hung out there before and after school. Now, you have to understand, Hattie was a single woman, nearing 60 at the time, and this was the 1960s. She was the polar opposite of "cool," but we hung around her classroom like it was a malt shop and she was Wolfman Jack.[3] None of us could have articulated it then, but it was because we enjoyed being harangued[4] by her, disciplined by her, and taught by her. She was a woman of clarity in an age of uncertainty. 5

[1]*Six-Day War:* the short but pivotal war in June 1967 between Israel and the allied countries of Egypt, Syria, and Jordan.

[2]*Ariel Sharon* (b. 1928): Israeli general and politician, elected prime minister of Israel in 2001.

[3]*Wolfman Jack:* pseudonym of Robert Weston Smith (1938–1995), a famous American rock-and-roll radio disc jockey.

[4]*harangued:* given a long, scolding lecture.

We remained friends for 30 years, and she followed, bragged about, and critiqued every twist in my career. After she died, her friends sent me a pile of my stories that she had saved over the years. Indeed, her students were her family—only closer. Judy Harrington, one of Hattie's former students, remarked about other friends who were on Hattie's newspapers and yearbooks: "We all graduated 41 years ago; and yet nearly each day in our lives something comes up—some mental image, some admonition[5] that makes us think of Hattie." 6

Judy also told the story of one of Hattie's last birthday parties, when one man said he had to leave early to take his daughter somewhere. "Sit down," said Hattie. "You're not leaving yet. She can just be a little late." 7

That was my teacher! I sit up straight just thinkin' about her. 8

Among the fundamentals Hattie introduced me to was *The New York Times*. Every morning it was delivered to Room 313. I had never seen it before then. Real journalists, she taught us, start their day by reading *The Times* and columnists like Anthony Lewis and James Reston. 9

I have been thinking about Hattie a lot this year, not just because she died on July 31, but because the lessons she imparted seem so relevant now. We've just gone through this huge dot-com-Internet-globalization bubble—during which a lot of smart people got carried away and forgot the fundamentals of how you build a profitable company, a lasting portfolio, a nation state, or a thriving student. It turns out that the real secret of success in the information age is what it always was: fundamentals—reading, writing, and arithmetic; church, synagogue, and mosque; the rule of law; and good governance. 10

The Internet can make you smarter, but it can't make you smart. It can extend your reach, but it will never tell you what to say at a P.T.A. meeting. These fundamentals cannot be downloaded. You can only upload them, the old-fashioned way, one by one, in places like Room 313 at St. Louis Park High. I only regret that I didn't write this column when the woman who taught me all that was still alive. 11

Thinking Critically about This Reading

What do you think Friedman means when he states, "The Internet can make you smarter, but it can't make you smart" (paragraph 11)?

---

[5] *admonition:* a cautionary advice or warning.

Questions for Study and Discussion

1. Friedman claims that his high school journalism teacher, Hattie M. Steinberg, was "someone who made the most important difference in my life" (1). What descriptive details does Friedman use to support this thesis? (Glossary: *Thesis*)
2. Hattie Steinberg taught her students the fundamentals of journalism—"not simply how to write a lead or accurately transcribe a quote, but, more important, how to comport yourself in a professional way and to always do quality work" (3). According to Friedman, what other fundamentals did she introduce to her students? Why do you think he values these fundamentals so much?
3. Friedman punctuates his description of Steinberg's teaching with short, pithy sentences. For example, he ends paragraph 2 with the sentence "She was that good" and paragraph 3 with "She wanted to teach us about consequences." Identify several other short sentences Friedman uses. What do these sentences have in common? How do short sentences like these affect you as a reader? Explain.
4. Why do you think Friedman tells us three times that Hattie's classroom was number 313 at St. Louis Park High School?
5. What details in Friedman's portrait of his teacher stand out for you? Why do you suppose Friedman chose the details that he did? What dominant impression of Hattie M. Steinberg do they collectively create? (Glossary: *Dominant Impression*)
6. According to Friedman, what went wrong when the "huge dot-com-Internet-globalization bubble" (10) of the late 1990s burst? Do you agree?

Classroom Activity Using Description

Important advice for writing well is to show rather than tell. Let's assume that your task is to reveal a person's character. What activities might you show the person doing to give your readers the correct impression of his or her character? For example, to indicate that someone is concerned about current events without coming out and saying so, you might show her reading the morning newspaper. Or you might show a character's degree of formality by including his typical greeting: *How ya doing?* In other words, the things a person says and does are often important indicators of personality. Choose one of the following traits, and make a list of at least four ways to show that someone possesses that trait. Share your list with the class, and discuss the "show-not-tell" strategies you have used.

simple but good	thoughtful	independent
reckless	politically involved	quick-witted
sensitive to the arts	irresponsible	public spirited
a sports lover		

Suggested Writing Assignments

1. Friedman believes that "the real secret of success in the information age is what it always was: fundamentals—reading, writing, and arithmetic; church, synagogue, and mosque; the rule of law; and good governance" (10). Do you agree? What are the fundamentals that you value most? Write an essay in which you discuss what you believe to be the secret of success today.
2. Who are your favorite teachers? What important differences did these people make in your life? What characteristics do these teachers share with Hattie M. Steinberg in this essay, Miss Bessie in Carl T. Rowan's "Unforgettable Miss Bessie" (pp. 163–67), or Anne Mansfield Sullivan in Helen Keller's "The Most Important Day" (pp. 76–79)? Using examples from your own school experience as well as from one or more of the essays above, write an essay in which you explore what makes a great teacher. Be sure to choose examples that clearly illustrate each of your points.

chapter **16**

Process Analysis

When you give someone directions to your home, tell how to make ice cream, or explain how a president is elected, you are using **process analysis.** Process analysis usually arranges a series of events in order and relates them to one another, as narration and cause and effect do, but process analysis has a different emphasis. Whereas narration tells mainly *what* happens and cause and effect focuses on *why* it happens, process analysis tries to explain—in detail—*how* it happens.

There are two types of process analysis—directional and informational. The *directional* type provides instructions on how to do something. These instructions can be as brief as the directions for making instant coffee printed on the label or as complex as the directions in a manual for assembling a new gas grill. The purpose of directional process analysis is to give the reader directions to follow that will lead to the desired results.

Consider these directions for sharpening a knife:

> If you have never done any whittling or wood carving before, the first skill to learn is how to sharpen your knife. You may be surprised to learn that even a brand-new knife needs sharpening. Knives are never sold honed (finely sharpened), although some gouges and chisels are. It is essential to learn the firm stroke on the stone that will keep your blades sharp. The sharpening stone must be fixed in place on the table, so that it will not move around. You can do this by placing a piece of rubber inner tube or a thin piece of foam rubber under it. Or you can tack four strips of wood, if you have a rough worktable, to frame the stone and hold it in place. Put a generous puddle of oil on the stone—this will soon disappear into the surface of a new stone, and you will need to keep adding more oil. Press the knife blade flat against the stone in the puddle of oil, using your index finger. Whichever way the cutting edge of the knife faces is the side of the blade that should get a little more

> pressure. Move the blade around three or four times in a narrow oval about the size of your fingernail, going *counterclockwise* when the sharp edge is facing right. Now turn the blade over in the same spot on the stone, press hard, and move it around the small oval *clockwise,* with more pressure on the cutting edge that faces left. Repeat the ovals, flipping the knife blade over six or seven times, and applying lighter pressure to the blade the last two times. Wipe the blade clean with a piece of rag or tissue and rub it flat on the piece of leather strop at least twice on each side. Stroke *away* from the cutting edge to remove the little burr of metal that may be left on the blade.
>
> –Florence H. Pettit

After first establishing her context and purpose, Pettit presents step-by-step directions for sharpening a knife, selecting details that a novice would understand.

After explaining in two previous paragraphs the first two steps in his article on juggling, a student writer moves to the important third step. Notice here how he explains the third step, offers advice on what to do if things go wrong, and encourages your efforts—all useful in directional process writing:

> Step three is merely a continuum of "the exchange" with the addition of the third ball. Don't worry if you are confused—I will explain. Hold two balls in your right hand and one in your left. Make a perfect toss with one of your balls in your right hand and then an exchange with the one in your left hand. The ball coming from your left hand should now be exchanged with the, as of now, unused ball in your right hand. This process should be continued until you find yourself reaching under nearby chairs for bouncing tennis balls. It is true that many persons' backs and legs become sore when learning how to juggle because they've been picking up balls that they've inadvertently tossed around the room. Try practicing over a bed; you won't have to reach down so far. Don't get too upset if things aren't going well; you're probably keeping the same pace as everyone else at this stage.
>
> –William Peterson, student

The *informational* type of process analysis, on the other hand, tells how something works, how something is made, or how something occurs. You would use informational process analysis if you wanted to explain how the human heart functions, how an atomic bomb

Graphic by Nigel Holmes.

works, how hailstones are formed, how you selected the college you are attending, or how the polio vaccine was developed. Rather than giving specific directions, informational process analysis explains and informs.

In the illustration by Nigel Holmes on page 409, Jim Collins uses informational process analysis to explain a basic legislative procedure—how a bill becomes a law.

Clarity is crucial for successful process analysis. The most effective way to explain a process is to divide it into steps and to present those steps in a clear (usually chronological) sequence. Transitional words and phrases such as *first, next, after,* and *before* help to connect steps to one another. Naturally, you must be sure that no step is omitted or given out of order. Also, you may sometimes have to explain *why* a certain step is necessary, especially if it is not obvious. With intricate, abstract, or particularly difficult steps, you might use analogy or comparison to clarify the steps for your reader.

The Principles of Poor Writing

■ **Paul W. Merrill**

Paul Willard Merrill (1887–1961) was a noted astronomer whose specialty was spectroscopy—the measurement of a quantity as a function of either wavelength or frequency. Merrill earned his AB at Stanford University in 1908 and his PhD at the University of California in 1913. After spending three years at the University of Michigan, Merrill went on to work at the National Bureau of Standards concentrating on aerial photography in the visible and infrared. He was the first to propose doing infrared astronomy from airplanes. In 1919, he joined the Mt. Wilson Observatory, located in Mt. Wilson, California, where he spent more than three decades researching peculiar stars, especially long-period variables. He is the recipient of the Bruce Medal and the Henry Draper Medal, has an asteroid and a lunar crater named after him, and is the author of four books: The Nature of Variable Stars *(1938),* Spectra of Long-Period Variable Stars *(1940),* Lines of the Chemical Elements in Astronomical Spectra *(1956), and* Space Chemistry *(1963).*

As Merrill writes in the beginning of his essay, "Poor writing is so common that every educated person ought to know something about it." As a scientist, he thinks that other scientists write poorly but more by ear than by a set of principles, which he freely offers in his essay. This first appeared in the January 1947 issue of the Scientific Monthly.

Reflecting on What You Know

Describe your three most serious failings when it comes to writing. What do you think you can do to remedy each one?

Books and articles on good writing are numerous, but where can you find sound, practical advice on how to write poorly? Poor writing is so common that every educated person ought to know something about it. Many scientists actually do write poorly, but they probably perform by ear without perceiving clearly how their results 1 are achieved. An article on the principles of poor writing might help. The author considers himself well qualified to prepare such an article; he can write poorly without half trying.

The average student finds it surprisingly easy to acquire the usual tricks of poor writing. To do a consistently poor job, however, one must grasp a few essential principles: 2

1. Ignore the reader.
2. Be verbose, vague, and pompous.
3. Do not revise.

Ignore the Reader

The world is divided into two great camps: yourself and others. A little obscurity or indirection in writing will keep the others at a safe distance. Write as if for a diary. Keep your mind on a direct course between yourself and the subject; don't think of the reader—he makes a bad triangle. This is fundamental. Constant and alert consideration of the probable reaction of the reader is a serious menace to poor writing; moreover, it requires mental effort. A logical argument is that if you write poorly enough, your readers will be too few to merit any attention whatever. 3

Ignore the reader wherever possible. If the proposed title, for example, means something to you, stop right there; think no further. If the title baffles or misleads the reader, you have won the first round. Similarly, all the way through you must write for yourself, not for the reader. Practice a dead-pan technique, keeping your facts and ideas all on the same level of emphasis with no telltale hints of relative importance or logical sequence. Use long sentences containing many ideas loosely strung together. *And* is the connective most frequently employed in poor writing because it does not indicate cause and effect, nor does it distinguish major ideas from subordinate ones. *Because* seldom appears in poor writing, nor does the semicolon—both are replaced by *and*. 4

Camouflage transitions in thought. Avoid such connectives as *moreover, nevertheless, on the other hand*. If unable to resist the temptation to give some signal for a change in thought, use *however*. A poor sentence may well begin with *however* because to the reader, with no idea what comes next, *however* is too vague to be useful. A good sentence begins with the subject or with a phrase that needs emphasis. 5

The "hidden antecedent" is a common trick of poor writing. Use a pronoun to refer to a noun a long way back, or to one decidedly 6 subordinate in thought or syntax; or the pronoun may refer to something not directly expressed. If you wish to play a little game with the reader, offer him the wrong antecedent as bait; you may be astonished how easy it is to catch the poor fish.

In ignoring the reader, avoid parallel constructions which give the thought away too easily. I need not elaborate, for you probably employ inversion frequently. It must have been a naive soul who said, "When the thought is parallel, let the phrases be parallel." 7

In every technical paper omit a few items that most readers need to know. You had to discover these things the hard way; why make it easy for the reader? Avoid defining symbols: never specify the units in which data are presented. Of course it will be beneath your dignity to give numerical values of constants in formulae. With these omissions, some papers may be too short; lengthen them by explaining things that do not need explaining. In describing tables, give special attention to self-explanatory headings; let the reader hunt for the meaning of *Pr*. 8

Be Verbose, Vague, and Pompous

The cardinal sin of poor writing is to be concise and simple. Avoid being specific: it ties you down. Use plenty of deadwood: include many superfluous words and phrases. Wishful thinking suggests to a writer that verbosity somehow serves as a cloak or even as a mystic halo by which an idea may be glorified. A cloud of words may conceal defects in observation or analysis, either by opacity or by diverting the reader's attention. Introduce abstract nouns at the drop of a hat—even in those cases where the magnitude of the motion in a downward direction is inconsiderable. Make frequent use of the words *case, character, condition, former* and *latter, nature, such, very*. 9

Poor writing, like good football, is strong on razzle-dazzle, weak on information. Adjectives are frequently used to bewilder the reader. It isn't much trouble to make them gaudy or hyperbolic; at least they can be flowery and inexact. 10

BIBLE: Render to Caesar the things that are Caesar's.

POOR: In the case of Caesar it might well be considered appropriate from a moral or ethical point of view to render to that potentate all of those goods and materials of whatever character or quality which can be shown to have had their original source in any portion of the domain of the latter.

SHAKESPEARE: I am no orator as Brutus is.

POOR: The speaker is not, what might be termed as adept in the profession of public speaking, as might be properly stated of Mr. Brutus. (Example from P. W. Swain. *Amer. J. Physics,* 13, 318, 1945.)

CONCISE: The dates of several observations are in doubt.

POOR: It should be mentioned that in the case of several observations there is room for considerable doubt concerning the correctness of the dates on which they were made.

REASONABLE: Exceptionally rapid changes occur in the spectrum.

POOR: There occur in the spectrum changes which are quite exceptional in respect to the rapidity of their advent.

REASONABLE: Formidable difficulties, both mathematical and observational, stand in the way.

POOR: There are formidable difficulties of both a mathematical and an observational nature that stand in the way.

Case

REASONABLE: Two sunspots changed rapidly.

POOR: There are two cases where sunspots changed with considerable rapidity.

REASONABLE: Three stars are red.

POOR: In three cases the stars are red in color.

Razzle-Dazzle

Immaculate precision of observation and extremely delicate calculations . . .

It would prove at once a world imponderable, etherealized. Our actions would grow gradific.

Well for us that the pulsing energy of the great life giving dynamo in the sky never ceases. Well, too, that we are at a safe distance from the flame-licked whirlpools into which our earth might drop like a pellet of waste fluff shaken into the live coals of a grate fire.

Do Not Revise

Write hurriedly, preferably when tired. Have no plan; write down items as they occur to you. The article will thus be spontaneous and poor. Hand in your manuscript the moment it is finished. Rereading a few days later might lead to revision—which seldom, if ever, makes the writing worse. If you submit your manuscript to colleagues (a bad practice), pay no attention to their criticisms or comments. Later, resist firmly any editorial suggestion. Be strong and infallible; don't let anyone break down your personality. The critic may be trying to help you or he may have an ulterior motive, but the chance of his causing improvement in your writing is so great that you must be on guard. 11

Thinking Critically about This Reading

Why do you think Merrill might have written "The Principles of Poor Writing"? What special motivation do you think his career as a scientist might have provided him? Explain.

Questions for Study and Discussion

1. *Irony* is the use of words to suggest something different from their meaning. At what point in the essay did you realize that Merrill is being ironic? (Glossary: *Irony*) Did his title, introduction, or actual advice tip you off? Explain.
2. Is the author's process analysis the directional type or the informational type? What leads you to this conclusion?
3. Why has Merrill ordered his three process steps in this particular way? Could he have used a different order? (Glossary: *Organization*) Explain.
4. How helpful are the author's examples in helping you understand his principles? Do you agree with all his examples? (Glossary: *Examples*) Explain.
5. Why do you suppose that Merrill used irony to show his readers that they needed to improve their writing? (Glossary: *Irony*) What

do you see as the potential advantages and disadvantages to such a strategy?

6. In what types of writing situations is irony especially useful?

Classroom Activity Using Process Analysis

Most do-it-yourself jobs require that you follow a set process to achieve results. Make a list of the steps involved in doing one of the following household activities:

cleaning windows
repotting a plant
making burritos
changing a flat tire
unclogging a drain
doing laundry

Suggested Writing Assignments

1. Try writing a process analysis essay in which you are ironic about the steps that need to be followed. For example, in an essay on how to lose weight by changing your diet or increasing your exercise, you might cast in a positive light all the things that absolutely should not be done. These might include parking as close as you can to your destination to avoid walking or buying a half gallon of your favorite ice cream instead of a pint because the half gallons are on sale.
2. Write a process analysis in which you explain the steps you usually follow when deciding to make a purchase of some importance or expense to you. Hint: It's best to analyze your process with a specific product in mind. Do you compare brands, store prices, and so on? What are your priorities—that the item be stylish or durable, offer good overall value, or give high performance?

Young Love

■ Tiffany Sharples

Tiffany Sharples was born in 1981 in New Haven, Connecticut. She earned a bachelor of arts degree from Colgate University and a master of science degree in journalism from the Medill School of Journalism at Northwestern University. As a head reporter for Time *magazine and Time.com, Sharples specializes in family, health and social science issues and has also been published on CNN.com and in* Arthur Frommer's Budget Travel, *the* Santiago Times *(Chile), and* Chicago Parent. *When asked if she had any advice for young writers, she offered, "Don't expect to get everything right the first time. That's what revision is for."*

In the following article, which first appeared on Time.com on January 17, 2008, Sharples writes, "Most Western romance research involves Western cultures, where things may move at a very different pace from that of, say, the Far East or the Muslim world. While not all of the studies yield universal truths, they all suggest that people are wired to pick up their love skills in very specific stages."

Reflecting on What You Know

Do you remember the first time you fell in love? What was it like? Were you exhilarated? Frightened? Intrigued? Bewildered?

There's a very thin line between being thrilled and being terrified, and Candice Feiring saw both emotions on her son's face. The sixth-grader had just gotten off the phone with a girl in his class who called to ask if he'd like to go to the movies—just the two of them. It sounded a whole lot like a date to him. "Don't I have something to do tomorrow?" he asked his mother. A psychologist and an editor of *The Development of Romantic Relationships in Adolescence,* Feiring was uniquely prepared to field that question and give her son the answer that, for now, he needed. "I think you're too young to go out one-on-one," she said. His face broke into a relieved grin. 1

A year later, even a month later, Feiring's adolescent son might have reacted very differently to being told he was not ready to date. That 2 moment-to-moment mutability of his interest in—never mind his readiness for—courtship is only one tiny part of the exhilarating, exhausting, confounding path all humans travel as they make their halting way into the world of love. From the moment we're born—when the world is mostly sensation, and nothing much matters beyond a full belly, a warm embrace, and a clean diaper—until we finally emerge into adulthood and understand the rich mix of tactile, sexual, and emotional experiences that come with loving another adult, we are in a constant state of learning and rehearsing. Along with language, romance may be one of the hardest skills we'll ever be called on to acquire. But while we're more or less fluent in speech by the time we're five, romance takes a lot longer. Most Western romance research involves Western cultures, where things may move at a very different pace from that of, say, the Far East or the Muslim world. While not all of the studies yield universal truths, they all suggest that people are wired to pick up their love skills in very specific stages.

Infancy and Babyhood

Babies may not have much to do right after they're born, but the stakes are vitally high that they do it right. One of the first skills newborns must learn is how to woo the adults in their world. "For a baby literally you're going to be dead without love, so getting people around you to love you is a really good strategy," says Alison Gopnik, a cognitive psychologist at the University of California, Berkeley. 3

Babies do this much the way adults do: by flirting. Within a couple of months, infants may move and coo, bob, and blink in concert with anyone who's paying attention to them. Smiling is a critical and cleverly timed part of this phase. Babies usually manage a first smile by the time they're six weeks old, which, coincidentally or not, is about the time the novelty of a newborn has worn off and sleep-deprived parents are craving some peace. A smile can be a powerful way to win them back. 4

Even before we know how to turn on the charm, touch and chemistry are bonding us firmly to our parents—and bonding them to us. Oxytocin—a hormone sometimes called the cuddle chemical—surges in new mothers and, to a lesser extent, in new fathers, making their baby instantly irresistible to them. One thing grown-ups particularly can't resist doing is picking a baby up, and that too is a key to survival. "Babies need physical contact with human hands to grow and thrive," says Lisa Diamond, a psychologist at the University of Utah. Years of 5 data have shown that premature babies who are regularly touched fare much better than those who aren't.

As babies seduce and adults respond, a sophisticated dynamic develops. Mothers learn to synch their behavior with their newborn's, so that they offer a smile when their baby smiles, food when their baby's hungry. That's a pleasingly reciprocal deal, and while adults are already aware that when you give pleasure and comfort, you get it in return, it's news for the baby. "Babies are building up ideas about how close relationships work," says Gopnik. 6

Toddlerhood and Preschool

When kids reach two, mom and dad aren't paying quite the same attention they used to. You feed yourself, you play on your own, you get held less often. That's not to say you need your parents less—and you're not shy about letting them know it. Children from ages two to five have yet to develop what's known as a theory of mind—the understanding that other people have hidden thoughts that are different from yours and that you can conceal your thoughts too. Without that knowledge, kids conceal nothing. "They love you," says Gopnik, "and they really, really express it." 7

At the same time, kids are learning something about sensual pleasures. They explore their bodies more, discovering that certain areas yield more electrifying feelings than others. This simultaneous emotional development and physical experience can lead to surprising behavior. "Three- and four-year-olds are very sexual beings," says Gopnik, "and a lot of that is directed at their parents." Some of this can get generalized to other adults too, as when a small child develops a crush on a teacher or seems to flirt with an aunt or uncle. While a number of things are at work when this happens, the most important is playacting and the valuable rehearsal for later life it provides. "Kids are trying to play out a set of roles and be more like adults," says psychologist Andrew Collins of the University of Minnesota's Institute of Child Development. 8

The same kind of training behavior can show up with playmates and friends, often accompanied by unexpectedly powerful feelings. Social psychologist Elaine Hatfield of the University of Hawaii is best known for cocreating the Passionate Love Scale, a questionnaire with which she can gauge feelings of romantic connectedness in adults. She has modified the test to elicit similar information from children. In early work, she studied 114 boys and 122 girls, some as young as 9 four, presenting them with statements like "I am always thinking about _______" or "I would rather be with _______ than anybody else." The kids filled in the name of someone they loved, and Hatfield asked them to rate the intensity of feelings with stacks of checkers: the higher the stack, the more they felt. In some instances, the kids became overwhelmed with emotion, as in the case of a five-year-old girl who wept at the thought of a boy she would never see again. "Little kids fall in love too," Hatfield says plainly.

School Age and Puberty

As with so much else in childhood, things get more complicated once kids reach the social incubator of elementary school. Nowhere near sexually mature, they nonetheless become sexually active—in their own fashion. The opposite-sex teasing and chasing that are rife on playgrounds may give teachers headaches, but they teach boys and girls a lot. The games, after all, are about pursuit and emotional arousal, two critical elements of sex. "There are a lot of erotic forms of play," says Barrie Thorne, a sociologist at the University of California, Berkeley, and the author of *Gender Play: Boys and Girls in School.* "It can be titillating, and it may involve sexual meaning, but it comes and goes." 10

More enduring—for a while at least—is the gender segregation that begins at this age. Boys and girls who once played in mixed groups at school begin to drift apart into single-sex camps, drawing social boundaries that will stay in place for years. In her 1986 study that is still cited today, Thorne looked at 802 elementary-school students from California and Massachusetts to determine just what goes on behind these gender fortifications and why they're established in the first place. 11

To no one's surprise, both groups spend a lot of time talking and thinking about the opposite sex, but they do it in very different ways. Boys experiment more with sexually explicit vocabulary and, later, sexual fantasies. Girls focus more heavily—but hardly exclusively—on romantic fantasies. The two-gender world they'll eventually reenter will be a lot more complex than that, but for now, the boys are simply practicing being boys—albeit in a very rudimentary way—and the girls are practicing being girls. "Among the boys, for example, there's a lot of bragging talk," says Thorne. "You're supposed to be powerful and not vulnerable." 12

When puberty hits, the wall between the worlds begins to crumble—a bit. Surging hormones make the opposite sex irresistible, but the rapprochement happens collectively, with single-gender groups beginning to merge into co-ed social circles within which individual boys and girls can flirt and experiment. Generally, kids who pair off with a love interest and begin dating will hold onto a return ticket to the mixed-gender group. Jennifer Connolly, a psychologist at York University in Toronto, studied 174 high school students in grades nine to eleven and found that when things go awry with couples, the kids are quickly absorbed back into the co-ed circle, with the old single-sex group increasingly eclipsed. "Once the progression has started," Connolly says, "we don't see kids retreating back into only same-gender interaction." 13

Almost all of these early relationships are, not surprisingly, short-lived—and a good thing too. If the purpose is to pick a mate for life, you're hardly likely to find a suitable one on your very first go. What's more, even if you did get lucky, you'd almost certainly not have the emotional wherewithal to keep the relationship going. Adults often lament the love they had and lost in high school and wonder what would have happened if they had met just a few years later. But the only way to acquire the skills to conduct a lifetime relationship is to practice on ones you may destroy in the process. "Kids don't really have a sense of working to preserve a relationship," Connolly says. "Adolescence is a time for experimentation." 14

Sexual experimentation is a big part of that—and it's a part that's especially fraught. Pregnancy and sexually transmitted diseases are just two of the things that make sex perilous. There are also emotional conflicts kids bring into their early experiences with intimacy. Psychologists have long warned that children who grow up in a hostile home or one in which warmth is withheld are likelier to start having sex earlier and engage in it more frequently. In a study that will be published in March, Trish Williams, a neuropsychology fellow at Alberta Children's Hospital, studied a group of 1,959 kids ages eleven to thirteen and did find a striking correlation between a volatile home and earlier sexual behavior. A few of the children had had intercourse at as young an age as twelve, and while the number of sexually active kids wasn't high—just 2 percent of the total—the cause was clear. "Hostile parenting is highly associated with problem behavior," says Williams. 15

Even kids without such emotional scarring can be pretty undiscriminating in their sexual choices. Two studies conducted by sociologist Wendy Manning in 2005 and 2006 showed that while 75 percent of 16 kids have their first sexual experience with a partner they're dating—a figure that may bring at least some comfort to worried parents—more than 60 percent will eventually have sex with someone with whom they're not in any kind of meaningful dating relationship. Hooking up—very informal sex between two people with no intent of pursuing a deeper relationship—takes this casualness even further. A 2004 study Manning worked on showed that the overwhelming majority of hookups involve alcohol use—an impairer of sexual judgment if ever there was one—and according to the work of other researchers, more than half the times kids hook up, they do not use a condom. Manning's studies suggest that hooking up prevents kids from practicing the interpersonal skills they'll need in a permanent relationship and may lead to lowered expectations of what those relationships should be like—and a greater willingness to settle for less.

For all these perils, the fact is, most people manage to shake off 17
even such high-stakes behavior and find a satisfying life partner, and that says something about the resilience of humans as romantic creatures. In the United States, by the time we're eighteen, about 80 percent of us have had at least one meaningful romantic relationship. As adults, up to 75 percent of us marry. Certainly, nature doesn't make things easy. From babyhood on, it equips us with the tools we'll need for the hardest social role we'll ever play—the role of romantic—and then chooses the moment when we're drunk on the hormones of adolescence and least confident in ourselves to push us on stage to perform. That we go on at all is a mark of our courage. That we learn the part so well is a mark of how much is at stake.

Thinking Critically about This Reading

In your own words, support Sharples's statement in paragraph 2 that "romance may be one of the hardest skills we'll ever be called on to acquire." If you disagree with the statement, explain why.

Questions for Study and Discussion

1. On what principle has Sharples organized her explanation of the process that we use to learn to love? (Glossary: *Organization*)
2. How effective is the beginning of Sharples's essay? Explain. (Glossary: *Beginnings and Endings*)

3. What role does flirting play in all stages of human development? Why is it important?
4. Why does the author say about relationships in puberty that "Almost all of these early relationships are, not surprisingly, short-lived—and a good thing too" (14)?
5. Comment on the way that Sharples uses research. Where and how has she used outside authorities to support her claims? (Glossary: *Evidence*) How have those outside sources enhanced her essay?
6. Men and women who "hook up" often use alcohol and fail to use condoms, according to researchers. What does hooking up also prevent kids from doing, according to Sharples?

Classroom Activity Using Process Analysis

An airfoil is a device that provides reactive force (e.g., lift) when in motion relative to the surrounding air. Carefully read the directions on page 424 for constructing an astro tube—a cylindrical airfoil made from a sheet of heavy writing paper. Now construct your own astro tube, and fly it. How far, if at all, did your astro tube fly? How helpful did you find the illustrations that accompany the written instructions? Based on your results, what revisions to the instructions would you make? Why?

Suggested Writing Assignments

1. Using the illustration on page 409 as a preliminary outline of how a bill becomes law, research the topic more thoroughly through reading. If possible, discuss the process with a political science instructor at your school. The illustration ends with the question, "Does it *ever* go as smoothly as this?" and the answer, "Nope." What kinds of situations can and often do alter the process?
2. Think about a familiar process that you believe needs improvement. After choosing your topic, do some background research in the library. In your own words, write a process analysis in which you argue for a revision of the existing process. (Glossary: *Argumentation*) For example, are you happy with the process for dealing with recyclables where you live, the process for registering for classes, or the way dorm rooms are assigned on campus?

Making an Astro Tube

Start with an 8.5-inch by 11-inch sheet of heavy writing paper. (Never use newspaper in making paper models because it isn't strongly bonded and can't hold a crease.) Follow these numbered steps, corresponding to the illustrations.

1. With the long side of the sheet toward you, fold up one third of the paper.
2. Fold the doubled section in half.
3. Fold the section in half once more and crease well.
4. Unfold preceding crease.
5. Curve the ends together to form a tube, as shown in the illustration.
6. Insert the right end inside the left end between the single outer layer and the doubled layers. Overlap the ends about an inch and a half. (This makes a tube for right-handers, to be used with an underhand throw. For an overhand tube, or an underhand version to be thrown by a lefty, reverse the directions, and insert the left end inside the right end at this step.)
7. Hold the tube at the seam with one hand, where shown by the dot in the illustration, and turn the rim inward along the crease made in step 3. Start turning in at the seam and roll the rim under, moving around the circumference in a circular manner. Then round out the rim.
8. Fold the fin to the left, as shown, then raise it so that it's perpendicular to the tube. Be careful not to tear the paper at the front.
9. Hold the tube from above, near the rim. Hold it between the thumb and fingers. The rim end should be forward, with the fin on the bottom. Throw the tube underhanded, with a motion like throwing a bowling ball, letting it spin off the fingers as it is released. The tube will float through the air, spinning as it goes. Indoor flights of 30 feet or more are easy. With practice you can achieve remarkable accuracy.

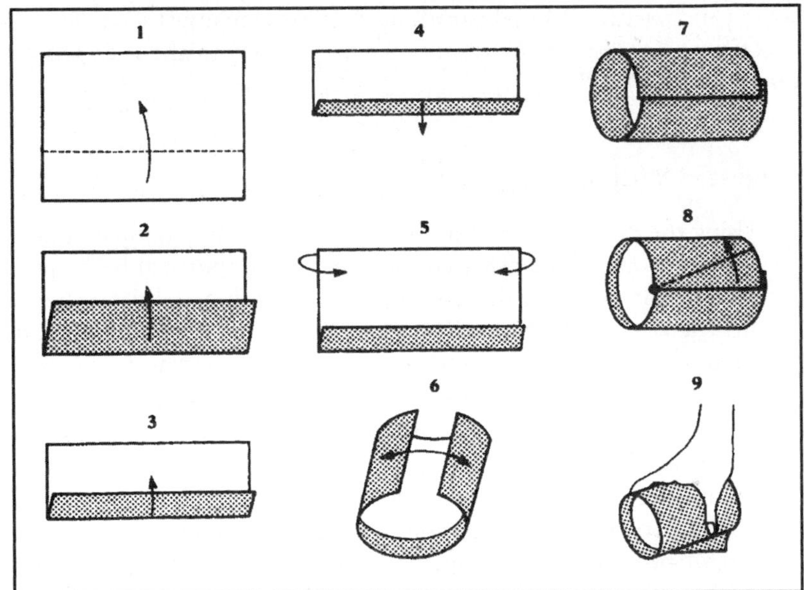

The Spider and the Wasp

■ Alexander Petrunkevitch

Alexander Petrunkevitch (1875–1964) was a Russian-born arachnologist and professor at Yale University for many years. He began his college studies in Russia but left for political reasons and finished his education at the University of Freiberg in Germany, where he also met his future American-born wife. As the leading expert of his time in spider biology, taxonomy, and fossils, he named and described more than a hundred spiders never known before to science, conducted studies on spider fossils, and ran experiments on live spiders in his lab at Yale. He published his first important work, The Index Catalogue of Spiders of North, Central, and South America, *in 1911. Petrunkevitch continued to conduct research after his retirement in 1945, at which time he also produced most of his publications. Petrunkevitch was also widely recognized for his accomplished translations of English and Russian poetry. Petrunkevitch received many awards during his lifetime, among them being elected to the National Academy of Science in 1954. He was also the first winner of the Yale Peabody Museum's Addison Emery Verrill Medal, given to distinguished naturalists and scholars of natural history.*

In this essay, first published in Scientific American *in 1954, Petrunkevitch describes the way in which nature pits the "intelligence" of digger wasps against the "instincts" of tarantula spiders.*

Reflecting on What You Know

Have you ever spent time examining the activities of spiders or other small and seemingly insignificant critters? What insights did you gain from your observations? Why might it be important for scientists to examine such creatures and the processes that characterize their lives?

In the feeding and safeguarding of their progeny insects and spiders exhibit some interesting analogies to reasoning and some crass examples of blind instinct. The case I propose to describe here is that of the tarantula spiders and their archenemy, the digger wasps of the genus 1

Pepsis. It is a classic example of what looks like intelligence pitted against instinct—a strange situation in which the victim, though fully able to defend itself, submits unwittingly to its destruction.

Most tarantulas live in the tropics, but several species occur in the temperate zone and a few are common in the southern United States. Some varieties are large and have powerful fangs with which they can inflict a deep wound. These formidable-looking spiders do not, however, attack man; you can hold one in your hand, if you are gentle, without being bitten. Their bite is dangerous only to insects and small mammals such as mice; for man it is no worse than a hornet's sting. 2

Tarantulas customarily live in deep cylindrical burrows, from which they emerge at dusk and into which they retire at dawn. Mature males wander about after dark in search of females and occasionally stray into houses. After mating, the male dies in a few weeks, but a female lives much longer and can mate several years in succession. In a Paris museum is a tropical specimen which is said to have been living in captivity for twenty-five years. 3

A fertilized female tarantula lays from two hundred to four hundred eggs at a time; thus it is possible for a single tarantula to produce several thousand young. She takes no care of them beyond weaving a cocoon of silk to enclose the eggs. After they hatch, the young walk away, find convenient places in which to dig their burrows, and spend the rest of their lives in solitude. The eyesight of tarantulas is poor, being limited to a sensing of change in the intensity of light and to the perception of moving objects. They apparently have little or no sense of hearing, for a hungry tarantula will pay no attention to a loudly chirping cricket placed in its cage unless the insect happens to touch one of its legs. 4

But all spiders, and especially hairy ones, have an extremely delicate sense of touch. Laboratory experiments prove that tarantulas can distinguish three types of touch: pressure against the body wall, stroking of the body hair, and riffling of certain very fine hairs on the legs called trichobothria. Pressure against the body, by the finger or the end of a pencil, causes the tarantula to move off slowly for a short distance. The touch excites no defensive response unless the approach is from above where the spider can see the motion, in which case it rises on its hind legs, lifts its front legs, opens its fangs and holds this threatening posture as long as the object continues to move. 5

The entire body of a tarantula, especially its legs, is thickly clothed with hair. Some of it is short and wooly, some long and stiff. Touching 6 this body hair produces one of two distinct reactions. When the spider is hungry, it responds with an immediate and swift attack. At the touch of a cricket's antennae the tarantula seizes the insect so swiftly that a motion picture taken at the rate of sixty-four frames per second shows only the result and not the process of capture. But when the spider is not hungry, the stimulation of its hairs merely causes it to shake the touched limb. An insect can walk under its hairy belly unharmed.

The trichobothria, very fine hairs growing from disklike membranes on the legs, are sensitive only to air movement. A light breeze makes them vibrate slowly, without disturbing the common hair. When one blows gently on the trichobothria, the tarantula reacts with a quick jerk of its four front legs. If the front and hind legs are stimulated at the same time, the spider makes a sudden jump. This reaction is quite independent of the state of its appetite. 7

These three tactile responses—to pressure on the body wall, to moving of the common hair, and to flexing of the trichobothria—are so different from one another that there is no possibility of confusing them. They serve the tarantula adequately for most of its needs and enable it to avoid most annoyances and dangers. But they fail the spider completely when it meets its deadly enemy, the digger wasp *Pepsis*. 8

These solitary wasps are beautiful and formidable creatures. Most species are either a deep shiny blue all over, or deep blue with rusty wings. The largest have a wingspan of about four inches. They live on nectar. When excited, they give off a pungent odor—a warning that they are ready to attack. The sting is much worse than that of a bee or common wasp, and the pain and swelling last longer. In the adult stage the wasp lives only a few months. The female produces but a few eggs, one at a time at intervals of two or three days. For each egg the mother must provide one adult tarantula, alive but paralyzed. The mother wasp attaches the egg to the paralyzed spider's abdomen. Upon hatching from the egg, the larva is many hundreds of times smaller than its living but helpless victim. It eats no other food and drinks no water. By the time it has finished its single gargantuan meal and become ready for wasphood, nothing remains of the tarantula but its indigestible chitinous skeleton. 9

The mother wasp goes tarantula-hunting when the egg in her ovary is almost ready to be laid. Flying low over the ground late on a sunny afternoon, the wasp looks for its victim or for the mouth of a tarantula burrow, a round hole edged by a bit of silk. The sex of the spider makes no difference, but the mother is highly discriminating as 10 to species. Each species of *Pepsis* requires a certain species of tarantula, and the wasp will not attack the wrong species. In a cage with a tarantula which is not its normal prey, the wasp avoids the spider and is usually killed by it in the night.

Yet when a wasp finds the correct species, it is the other way about. To identify the species the wasp apparently must explore the spider with her antennae. The tarantula shows an amazing tolerance to this exploration. The wasp crawls under it and walks over it without evoking any hostile response. The molestation is so great and so persistent that the tarantula often rises on all eight legs, as if it were on stilts. It may stand this way for several minutes. Meanwhile the wasp, having satisfied itself that the victim is of the right species, moves off a few inches to dig the spider's grave. Working vigorously with legs and jaws, it excavates a hole eight to ten inches deep with a diameter slightly larger than the spider's girth. Now and again the wasp pops out of the hole to make sure that the spider is still there. 11

When the grave is finished, the wasp returns to the tarantula to complete her ghastly enterprise. First she feels it all over once more with her antennae. Then her behavior becomes more aggressive. She bends her abdomen, protruding her sting, and searches for the soft membrane at the point where the spider's legs join its body—the only spot where she can penetrate the horny skeleton. From time to time, as the exasperated spider slowly shifts ground, the wasp turns on her back and slides along with the aid of her wings, trying to get under the tarantula for a shot at the vital spot. During all this maneuvering, which can last for several minutes, the tarantula makes no move to save itself. Finally the wasp corners it against some obstruction and grasps one of its legs in her powerful jaws. Now at last the harassed spider tries a desperate but vain defense. The two contestants roll over and over on the ground. It is a terrifying sight and the outcome is always the same. The wasp finally manages to thrust her sting into the soft spot and holds it there for a few seconds while she pumps in the poison. Almost immediately the tarantula falls paralyzed on its back. Its legs stop twitching; its heart stops beating. Yet it is not dead, as is shown by the fact that if taken from the wasp it can be restored to some sensitivity by being kept in a moist chamber for several months. 12

After paralyzing the tarantula, the wasp cleans herself by dragging her body along the ground and rubbing her feet, sucks the drop of blood oozing from the wound in the spider's abdomen, then grabs a leg of the flabby, helpless animal in her jaws and drags it down to the 13 bottom of the grave. She stays there for many minutes, sometimes for several hours, and what she does all that time in the dark we do not know. Eventually she lays her egg and attaches it to the side of the spider's abdomen with a sticky secretion. Then she emerges, fills the grave with soil carried bit by bit in her jaws, and finally tramples the ground all around to hide any trace of the grave from prowlers. Then she flies away, leaving her descendant safely started in life.

In all this the behavior of the wasp evidently is qualitatively different from that of the spider. The wasp acts like an intelligent animal. This is not to say that instinct plays no part or that she reasons as man does. But her actions are to the point; they are not automatic and can be modified to fit the situation. We do not know for certain how she identifies the tarantula—probably it is by some olfactory or chemo-tactile sense—but she does it purposefully and does not blindly tackle a wrong species. 14

On the other hand, the tarantula's behavior shows only confusion. Evidently the wasp's pawing gives it no pleasure, for it tries to move away. That the wasp is not simulating sexual stimulation is certain because male and female tarantulas react in the same way to its advances. That the spider is not anesthetized by some odorless secretion is easily shown by blowing lightly at the tarantula and making it jump suddenly. What, then, makes the tarantula behave as stupidly as it does? 15

No clear, simple answer is available. Possibly the stimulation by the wasp's antennae is masked by a heavier pressure on the spider's body, so that it reacts as when prodded by a pencil. But the explanation may be much more complex. Initiative in attack is not in the nature of tarantulas; most species fight only when cornered so that escape is impossible. Their inherited patterns of behavior apparently prompt them to avoid problems rather than attack them. For example, spiders always weave their webs in three dimensions, and when a spider finds that there is insufficient space to attach certain threads in the third dimension, it leaves the place and seeks another, instead of finishing the web in a single plane. This urge to escape seems to arise under all circumstances, in all phases of life, and to take the place of reasoning. For a spider to change the pattern of its web is as impossible as for an inexperienced man to build a bridge across a chasm obstructing his way. 16

In a way the instinctive urge to escape is not only easier but often more efficient than reasoning. The tarantula does exactly what is most efficient in all cases except in an encounter with a ruthless and determined 17 attacker dependent for the existence of her own species on killing as many tarantulas as she can lay eggs. Perhaps in this case the spider follows its usual pattern of trying to escape, instead of seizing and killing the wasp, because it is not aware of its danger. In any case, the survival of the tarantula species as a whole is protected by the fact that the spider is much more fertile than the wasp.

Thinking Critically about This Reading

In your own words, describe the process that the mother wasp follows when she hunts a tarantula.

Questions for Study and Discussion

1. What is Petrunkevitch's purpose in this essay? Where is his purpose revealed? (Glossary: *Purpose*)
2. The author contrasts the behavior of the tarantula with that of the wasp. What significant differences does he note? How do these differences relate to his overall purpose in the essay?
3. Petrunkevitch describes the way that the wasp hunts the tarantula to use it as food for its young. How does the explanation of this process relate to his overall purpose in this essay?
4. How has the author organized his essay? Before answering this question, you may find it helpful to outline the essay.
5. In paragraphs 10 through 13, Petrunkevitch describes what happens when the wasp encounters the tarantula. How has Petrunkevitch organized his description of this particular process? What transitional or linking devices does he use to give coherence to his description of the process? (Glossary: *Transitions*)

Classroom Activity Using Process Analysis

In her best-selling memoir of her life in Italy, *Under the Tuscan Sun,* Frances Mayes shares a number of her favorite recipes, including one for lemon cake. As you read her directions below, imagine yourself making this cake. Then answer these questions: Do you find her recipe interesting to read? How clear are her directions? Which parts of the recipe need clarification? Is it necessary to be familiar with the world of baking to read or appreciate Mayes's recipe? Explain.

Lemon Cake

A family import, this Southern cake is one I've made a hundred times. Thin slices seem at home here with summer strawberries and cherries or winter pears. . . .

Cream together 1 cup of sweet butter and 2 cups of sugar. Beat in 3 eggs, one at a time. The mixture should be light. Mix together 3 cups of flour, 1 teaspoon of baking powder, 1/4 teaspoon of salt, and incorporate this with the butter mixture alternately with 1 cup buttermilk. (In Italy, I use one cup of cream since buttermilk is not available.) Begin and end with the flour mixture. Add 3 tablespoons of lemon juice and the grated zest of the lemon. Bake in a nonstick tube pan at 300° for 50 minutes. Test for doneness with a toothpick. The cake can be glazed with 1/4 cup of soft butter into which 1-1/2 cups of powdered sugar and 3 tablespoons of lemon juice have been beaten. Decorate with tiny curls of lemon rind.

Suggested Writing Assignments

1. Using Petrunkevitch's essay as a model, write an essay in which you describe and explain a recurring natural process—for example, seed germination, bird migration, pollination, hibernation, an eclipse, or digestion.
2. In his essay, Petrunkevitch examines the interdependent relationship between the tarantula and the digger wasp. What other interdependent relationships have you observed in your own experiences of the natural world? Write an essay in which you explore one of these relationships. What do such relationships seem to tell us about life itself?

chapter **17**

Definition

Definition allows you to communicate precisely what you want to say. At its most basic level, you will frequently need to define key words. Your reader needs to know just what you mean when you use unfamiliar words (such as *accoutrement*), words that are open to various interpretations (such as *liberal*), or familiar words that are used in a particular sense. Important terms that are not defined or that are defined inaccurately confuse readers and hamper communication.

Consider the opening paragraph from a student essay titled "Secular Mantras":

> Remember *The Little Engine That Could*? That's the story about the tiny locomotive that hauled the train over the mountain when the big, rugged locomotives wouldn't. Remember how the Little Engine strained and heaved and chugged, "I think I can—I think I can—I think I can" until she reached the top of the mountain? That's a perfect example of a secular mantra in action. You probably have used a secular mantra (pronounce it "mantruh") already today. It's any word or group of words that helps you use your energy when you consciously repeat it to yourself. You must understand two qualities about secular mantras to be able to recognize one.
>
> –Keith Eldred, student

Eldred engages his readers with the story of the Little Engine and then uses that example to lead into a definition of *secular mantra*. He concludes the paragraph with a sentence that tells readers what is coming next.

There are three basic ways to define a word, and each is useful in its own way. The first method is to give a *synonym*—that is, use a word that has nearly the same meaning as the word you wish to define (*face* for *countenance*, *nervousness* for *anxiety*). No two words have exactly the same meaning, but you can nevertheless pair an unfamiliar word with a familiar one and thereby clarify your meaning.

Another way to define a word quickly, often within a single sentence, is to give a *formal definition*—that is, place the term in a general class and then distinguish it from other members of that class by describing its particular characteristics. For example:

Word	*Class*	*Characteristics*
A watch	is a mechanical device	that is used for telling time and is usually carried or worn.
Semantics	is an area of linguistics	that is concerned with the study of the meaning of words.

The third method of defining a word is to give an *extended definition*—that is, to use one or more paragraphs (or even an entire essay) to define a new or difficult term or to rescue a controversial word from misconceptions that may obscure its meaning. In an essay-length extended definition, you provide your readers with information about the meaning of a single word, a concept, or an object. You must consider what your readers already know, or think they know, about your topic. Are there popular misconceptions that need to be corrected? Are some aspects of the topic seldom considered? Have particular experiences helped you understand the topic? You can use synonyms or formal definitions in an extended definition, but you must convince readers to accept your particular understanding of it.

In the following four-paragraph sequence, the writers provide an extended definition of *freedom*, an important but elusive concept:

> Choosing between negative alternatives often seems like no choice at all. Take the case of a woman trying to decide whether to stay married to her inconsiderate, incompetent husband, or get a divorce. She doesn't want to stay with him, but she feels divorce is a sign of failure and will stigmatize her socially. Or think of the decision faced by many young men [more than forty] years ago, when they were forced to choose between leaving their country and family or being sent to Vietnam.
>
> When we face decisions involving only alternatives we see as negatives, we feel so little freedom that we twist and turn searching for another choice with some positive characteristics.
>
> Freedom is a popular word. Individuals talk about how they feel free with one person and not with another, or how their bosses

> encourage or discourage freedom on the job. We hear about civil wars and revolutions being fought for greater freedom, with both sides righteously making the claim. The feeling of freedom is so important that people say they're ready to die for it, and supposedly have.
>
> Still, most people have trouble coming up with a precise definition of freedom. They give answers describing specific situations—"Freedom means doing what I want to do, not what the Government wants me to do," or "Freedom means not having my mother tell me when to come home from a party"—rather than a general definition covering many situations. The idea they seem to be expressing is that freedom is associated with making decisions, and that other people sometimes limit the number of alternatives from which they can select.
>
> –Jerald M. Jellison and John H. Harvey

Another term that illustrates the need for extended definition is *obscene*. What is obscene? Books that are banned in one school system are considered perfectly acceptable in another. Movies that are shown in one town cannot be shown in a neighboring town. The meaning of *obscene* has been clouded by contrasting personal opinions as well as by conflicting social norms. Therefore, if you use the term *obscene* (and especially if you tackle the issue of obscenity itself), you must define clearly and thoroughly what you mean by that term—that is, you have to give an extended definition. There are a number of methods you might use to develop such a definition. You could define *obscene* by explaining what it does not mean. You could also make your meaning clear by narrating an experience, by comparing and contrasting it to related terms (such as *pornographic* or *exotic*), by citing specific examples, or by classifying the various types of obscenity. Any of these methods could provide an effective definition.

What Is Crime?

Lawrence M. Friedman

Born in 1930 in Chicago, Lawrence M. Friedman is currently the Marion Rice Kirkwood Professor of Law at Stanford University. He earned his undergraduate degree in 1948 and his law degree in 1951, both from the University of Chicago. After serving a two-year stint in the military, he practiced law in Chicago before embarking on his long and distinguished teaching and writing career. He taught law at St. Louis University and the University of Wisconsin before settling at Stanford in 1968. An expert on the history of American law, Friedman is perhaps best known for his A History of American Law *(1973) and its sequel,* American Law in the Twentieth Century *(2002). His other books include* The Republic of Choice: Law, Authority, and Culture *(1990),* The Horizontal Society *(1999), and* Law in America: A Short History *(2002). In 2003, he wrote* Legal Culture in the Age of Globalization: Latin America and Latin Europe *with Rogelio Perez Perdomo. Currently he is president of the American Society for Legal History.*

The following selection is taken from the introduction to Crime and Punishment in American History *(1993), a book in which Friedman traces the response to crime throughout U.S. history. Here he explains what it takes for a certain behavior or act to be considered a crime.*

Reflecting on What You Know

How would you answer the question "What is crime?" For you, what makes some acts criminal and others not? Explain.

There is no real answer to the question, What is crime? There are popular ideas about crime: crime is bad behavior, antisocial behavior, blameworthy acts, and the like. But in a very basic sense, crime is a *legal* concept: what makes some conduct criminal, and other conduct not, is the fact that some, but not others, are "against the law."* 1

*Most criminologists, but not all, would agree with this general formulation; for an exception see Michael R. Gottfredson and Travis Hirschi, *A General Theory of Crime* (1990). [Friedman's note]

Crimes, then, are forbidden acts. But they are forbidden in a special way. We are not supposed to break contracts, drive carelessly, slander people, or infringe copyrights; but these are not (usually) criminal acts. The distinction between a *civil* and a *criminal* case is fundamental in our legal system. A civil case has a life cycle entirely different from that of a criminal case. If I slander somebody, I might be dragged into court, and I might have to open my checkbook and pay damages; but I cannot be put in prison or executed, and if I lose the case, I do not get a criminal "record." Also, in a slander case (or a negligence case, or a copyright-infringement case), the injured party pays for, runs, and manages the case herself. He or she makes the decisions and hires the lawyers. The case is entirely voluntary. Nobody forces anybody to sue. I can have a good claim, a valid claim, and simply forget it, if I want. 2

In a criminal case, in theory at least, society is the victim, along with the "real" victim—the person robbed or assaulted or cheated. The crime may be punished without the victim's approval (though, practically speaking, the complaining witness often has a crucial role to play). In "victimless crimes" (gambling, drug dealing, certain sex offenses), there is nobody to complain; both parties are equally guilty (or innocent). Here the machine most definitely has a mind of its own. In criminal cases, moreover, the state pays the bills. It should be pointed out, however, that the further back in history one goes, the more this pat[1] distinction between "civil" and "criminal" tends to blur. In some older cultures, the line between private vengeance and public prosecution was indistinct or completely absent. Even in our own history, we shall see some evidence that the cleavage between "public" and "private" enforcement was not always deep and pervasive. 3

All sorts of nasty acts and evil deeds are not against the law, and thus not crimes. These include most of the daily events that anger or irritate us, even those we might consider totally outrageous. Ordinary lying is not a crime; cheating on a wife or husband is not a crime in most states (at one time it was, almost everywhere); charging a huge markup at a restaurant or store is not, in general, a crime; psychological abuse is (mostly) not a crime. 4

Before some act can be isolated and labeled as a crime, there must be a special, solemn, social, and *political* decision. In our society, Congress, a state legislature, or a city government has to pass a law or enact an 5

[1]*pat:* seemingly precise.

ordinance adding the behavior to the list of crimes. Then this behavior, like a bottle of poison, carries the proper label and can be turned over to the heavy artillery of law for possible enforcement.

We repeat: crime is a *legal* concept. This point, however, can lead to a misunderstanding. The law, in a sense, "creates" the crimes it punishes; but what creates criminal law? Behind the law, and above it, enveloping it, is society; before the law made the crime a crime, some aspect of social reality transformed the behavior, culturally speaking, into a crime; and it is the social context that gives the act, and the legal responses, their real meaning. Justice is supposed to be blind, which is to say impartial. This may or may not be so, but justice is blind in one fundamental sense: justice is an abstraction.[2] It cannot see or act on its own. It cannot generate its own norms, principles, and rules. Everything depends on society. Behind every *legal* judgment of criminality is a more powerful, more basic *social* judgment; a judgment that this behavior, whatever it is, deserves to be outlawed and punished. 6

Thinking Critically about This Reading

What does Friedman mean when he states, "Behind every *legal* judgment of criminality is a more powerful, more basic *social* judgment; a judgment that this behavior, whatever it is, deserves to be outlawed and punished" (paragraph 6)? According to Friedman, what must happen before any offensive behavior can be deemed criminal?

Questions for Study and Discussion

1. What general definition of *crime* do most criminologists agree on, according to Friedman?
2. What are the major differences between a criminal case and a civil case? Why does Friedman make this distinction? Explain.
3. In what sense is society the "victim" in a criminal case (3)? Do you believe that it is important for society to join with the "real victim" in prosecuting the criminal case? Explain.
4. Friedman states that "all sorts of nasty acts and evil deeds are not against the law, and thus not crimes" (4). What examples does he

[2]*abstraction:* a theoretical concept.

provide to illustrate this point? (Glossary: *Example*) Do any of his examples surprise you? Explain.

5. What does Friedman mean by "crime is a *legal* concept" (1)? Why do you think he repeats that statement in paragraph 6? According to the writer, what misunderstanding can the statement lead to?

Classroom Activity Using Definition

Define one of the following terms formally by putting it in a class and then differentiating it from other words in the class. (See p. 433.)

potato chips	tenor saxophone	sociology	Monopoly (the game)
love	physical therapy	chickadee	Buddhism

Suggested Writing Assignments

1. Write an essay recounting a time when you were the victim of somebody's outrageous behavior. What were the circumstances of the incident? How did you respond at the time? What action, if any, did you take at a later time? According to Friedman's definition, was the behavior criminal?
2. Some of the most pressing social issues in American life today are further complicated by imprecise definitions of critical terms. Various medical cases, for example, have brought worldwide attention to the legal and medical definitions of the word *death*. Debates continue about the meanings of other controversial words. Using one of the following controversial terms or another of your choosing, write an essay in which you discuss its definition and the problems that are associated with defining it.

minority (ethnic)	theft	equality
monopoly (business)	lying	success
morality	addiction	pornography
cheating	life	marriage

The Company Man

■ Ellen Goodman

Ellen Goodman was born in Boston in 1941. After graduating cum laude *from Radcliffe College in 1963, she worked as a reporter and researcher for* Newsweek. *In 1967, she began working at the* Boston Globe *and since 1974 has been a full-time columnist. Her regular column, "At Large," is syndicated by the* Washington Post*'s Writer's Group and appears in nearly four hundred newspapers across the country. In addition, her writing has appeared in* McCall's, Harper's Bazaar, *and* Family Circle, *and her commentaries have been broadcast on radio and television. Several collections of Goodman's columns have been published as books, including* Close to Home *(1979),* At Large *(1981),* Keeping in Touch *(1985),* Value Judgments *(1995),* Making Sense *(1999), and* Paper Trail: Common Sense in Uncommon Times *(2004).*

In "The Company Man," taken from Close to Home, *Goodman defines* workaholic *by offering a poignant example.*

Reflecting on What You Know

Many jobs have regular hours, but some—like journalism, medicine, and high-level management—are less predictable and may require far more time. Think about your career goals. Do you think that you will emphasize your work life more than your home life? How much time beyond the standard thirty-five work hours per week are you willing to spend to advance your career or support your family? Has this issue influenced your choice of career in any way, or do you anticipate that it will? Explain.

He worked himself to death, finally and precisely, at 3:00 a.m. Sunday morning. 1

The obituary didn't say that, of course. It said that he died of a coronary thrombosis—I think that was it—but everyone among his friends and acquaintances knew it instantly. He was a perfect 2

Type A, a workaholic, a classic, they said to each other and shook their heads—and thought for five or ten minutes about the way they lived.

3 This man who worked himself to death finally and precisely at 3:00 a.m. Sunday morning—on his day off—was fifty-one years old and a vice-president. He was, however, one of six vice-presidents, and one of three who might conceivably—if the president died or retired soon enough—have moved to the top spot. Phil knew that.

4 He worked six days a week, five of them until eight or nine at night, during a time when his own company had begun the four-day week for everyone but the executives. He worked like the Important People. He had no outside "extracurricular interests," unless, of course, you think about a monthly golf game that way. To Phil, it was work. He always ate egg salad sandwiches at his desk. He was, of course, overweight, by twenty or twenty-five pounds. He thought it was okay, though, because he didn't smoke.

5 On Saturdays, Phil wore a sports jacket to the office instead of a suit, because it was the weekend.

6 He had a lot of people working for him, maybe sixty, and most of them liked him most of the time. Three of them will be seriously considered for his job. The obituary didn't mention that.

7 But it did list his "survivors" quite accurately. He is survived by his wife, Helen, forty-eight years old, a good woman of no particular marketable skills, who worked in an office before marrying and mothering. She had, according to her daughter, given up trying to compete with his work years ago, when the children were small. A company friend said, "I know how much you will miss him." And she answered, "I already have."

8 "Missing him all these years," she must have given up part of herself which had cared too much for the man. She would be "well taken care of."

9 His "dearly beloved" eldest of the "dearly beloved" children is a hard-working executive in a manufacturing firm down South. In the day and a half before the funeral, he went around the neighborhood researching his father, asking the neighbors what he was like. They were embarrassed.

10 His second child is a girl, who is twenty-four and newly married. She lives near her mother and they are close, but whenever she was alone with her father, in a car driving somewhere, they had nothing to say to each other.

The youngest is twenty, a boy, a high-school graduate who has spent the last couple of years, like a lot of his friends, doing enough odd jobs to stay in grass and food. He was the one who tried to grab at his father, and tried to mean enough to him to keep the man at home. He was his father's favorite. Over the last two years, Phil stayed up nights worrying about the boy. 11

The boy once said, "My father and I only board here." 12

At the funeral, the sixty-year-old company president told the forty-eight-year-old widow that the fifty-one-year-old deceased had meant much to the company and would be missed and would be hard to replace. The widow didn't look him in the eye. She was afraid he would read her bitterness and, after all, she would need him to straighten out the finances—the stock options and all that. 13

Phil was overweight and nervous and worked too hard. If he wasn't at the office, he was worried about it. Phil was a Type A, a heart-attack natural. You could have picked him out in a minute from a lineup. 14

So when he finally worked himself to death, at precisely 3:00 a.m. Sunday morning, no one was really surprised. 15

By 5:00 p.m. the afternoon of the funeral, the company president had begun, discreetly of course, with care and taste, to make inquiries about his replacement. One of three men. He asked around: "Who's been working the hardest?" 16

Thinking Critically about This Reading

What is the significance of Phil's youngest son's statement, "My father and I only board here" (paragraph 12)? What does it convey about Phil's relationship with his family?

Questions for Study and Discussion

1. After reading Goodman's essay, how would you define *company man*? As you define the term, consider what such a man is not, as well as what he is. Is *company man* synonymous with *workaholic*? Explain.
2. In paragraph 4, Goodman says that Phil worked like "the Important People." How would you define that term in the context of the essay?

3. What is Goodman's purpose? (Glossary: *Purpose*) Explain.
4. Do you think Goodman's unemotional tone is appropriate for her purpose? (Glossary: *Tone; Purpose*) Why or why not?
5. Goodman repeats the day and time that Phil worked himself to death. Why are those facts important enough to bear repetition? What about them is ironic? (Glossary: *Irony*)

Classroom Activity Using Definition

The connotation of the term *workaholic* depends on the context. For Phil's employers—and at his workplace in general—the term had a positive connotation. For those who knew Phil outside the workplace, it had a negative one. Choose one of the terms below, and provide two definitions, one positive and one negative, that could apply to the term in different contexts.

go-getter | overachiever
party animal | mover and shaker

Suggested Writing Assignments

1. A procrastinator—a person who continually puts off responsibilities—is very different from a workaholic. Write an essay, modeled on Goodman's, using an extended example to define this personality type.
2. One issue that Goodman does not raise is how a person becomes a workaholic. Write an essay in which you speculate about how someone might develop workaholism. How does a desirable trait like a strong work ethic begin to affect someone adversely? How might workaholism be avoided?
3. The cartoon on page 443 depicts one "businessdog" talking with another about job benefits. What is your reaction to the idea that a company will put workers "to sleep at its own expense"? What insights does the cartoon give you into Goodman's essay about work in the corporate world? Write an essay in which you describe the ideal employee-management relationship. For support, use examples from Goodman's essay, the cartoon, or your own work experiences and observations.

"And when the time comes the company will put you to sleep at its own expense."

A Nincompoop

■ Anton Chekhov

One of Russia's most beloved and respected writers, Anton Chekhov (1860–1904) was born in Taganrog on the Sea of Azov in the south of Russia. He started writing short stories at the University of Moscow when he was a medical student. Soon after graduation in 1884, Chekhov embarked on his career as a writer, first as a freelance journalist and writer of humorous sketches and later as a playwright. His early one-act plays, including most notably The Bear *(1888) and* The Wedding *(1889), met with critical acclaim. But his full-length plays earned his lasting fame.* Uncle Vanya *(1899),* Three Sisters *(1901), and* The Cherry Orchard *(1904) are among the masterworks of modern theater. Ill health forced Chekhov to spend much of his later years in the mild southern climate of Yalta in the Crimea, where he met with the Russian greats Maxim Gorky and Leo Tolstoy. Chekhov died at the age of forty-four shortly after completing* The Cherry Orchard.

In the short story "A Nincompoop," he tells the story of a gentleman who teaches his children's governess a "cruel lesson" with a powerful message. As you read, notice how Chekhov reveals what a nincompoop is without actually defining the word.

Reflecting on What You Know

When did you first become aware of class distinctions? What did it feel like to discover that some people treated each other differently based on social class? Have other people ever tried to take advantage of you or make you feel less than adequate? Briefly describe the circumstances. Did you protest the other person's treatment of you? If not, why were you unable to express your feelings about what was happening to you?

A few days ago I asked my children's governess, Julia Vassilyevna, to come into my study. 1

"Sit down, Julia Vassilyevna," I said. "Let's settle our accounts. Although you most likely need some money, you stand on ceremony 2

and won't ask for it yourself. Now then, we agreed on thirty rubles
a month . . ."

"Forty." 3

"No, thirty. I made a note of it. I always pay the governess thirty. 4
Now then, you've been here two months, so . . ."

"Two months and five days." 5

"Exactly two months. I made a specific note of it. That means 6
you have sixty rubles coming to you. Subtract nine Sundays . . . you
know you didn't work with Kolya on Sundays, you only took walks.
And three holidays . . ."

Julia Vassilyevna flushed a deep red and picked at the flounce of 7
her dress, but—not a word.

"Three holidays, therefore take off twelve rubles. Four days Kolya 8
was sick and there were no lessons, as you were occupied only with
Vanya. Three days you had a toothache and my wife gave you permission not to work after lunch. Twelve and seven—nineteen. Subtract . . .
that leaves . . . hmm . . . forty-one rubles. Correct?"

Julia Vassilyevna's left eye reddened and filled with moisture. Her 9
chin trembled; she coughed nervously and blew her nose, but—not a
word.

"Around New Year's you broke a teacup and saucer: take off two 10
rubles. The cup cost more, it was an heirloom, but—let it go. When
didn't I take a loss! Then, due to your neglect, Kolya climbed a tree
and tore his jacket: take away ten. Also due to your heedlessness the
maid stole Vanya's shoes. You ought to watch everything! You get
paid for it. So, that means five more rubles off. The tenth of January I
gave you ten rubles . . ."

"You didn't," whispered Julia Vassilyevna. 11

"But I made a note of it." 12

"Well . . . all right." 13

"Take twenty-seven from forty-one—that leaves fourteen." 14

Both eyes filled with tears. Perspiration appeared on the thin, pretty 15
little nose. Poor girl!

"Only once was I given any money," she said in a trembling voice, 16
"and that was by your wife. Three rubles, nothing more."

"Really? You see now, and I didn't make a note of it! Take three 17
from fourteen . . . leaves eleven. Here's your money, my dear. Three,
three, three, one and one. Here it is!"

I handed her eleven rubles. She took them and with trembling 18
fingers stuffed them into her pocket.

"*Merci,*" she whispered. 19

I jumped up and started pacing the room. I was overcome with anger. 20

"For what, this—'*merci*'?" I asked. 21

"For the money." 22

"But you know I've cheated you—robbed you! I have actually stolen from you! *Why* this '*merci*'?" 23

"In my other places they didn't give me anything at all." 24

"They didn't give you anything? No wonder! I played a little joke on you, a cruel lesson, just to teach you . . . I'm going to give you the entire eighty rubles! Here they are in an envelope all ready for you . . . Is it really possible to be so spineless? Why don't you protest? Why be silent? Is it possible in this world to be without teeth and claws—to be such a nincompoop?" 25

She smiled crookedly and I read in her expression: "It is possible." 26

I asked her pardon for the cruel lesson and, to her great surprise, gave her the eighty rubles. She murmured her little "*merci*" several times and went out. I looked after her and thought: "How easy it is to crush the weak in this world!" 27

Thinking Critically about This Reading

The narrator confesses to Julia that he "played a little joke on you, a cruel lesson, just to teach you" (paragraph 25). What was cruel about the lesson, and what do you suppose he intended to teach his young governess? What does this cruel lesson reveal about the narrator's feelings toward Julia? Toward the poor and powerless? Explain.

Questions for Study and Discussion

1. What kind of man is the narrator of this story? How do you feel about him at the beginning of the story? Do your feelings change by the story's end?
2. What do we know about Julia Vassilyevna? In what ways, if any, does she change during the course of the story?
3. According to the narrator, what is a nincompoop? Do you agree, or does *nincompoop* mean something else for you?
4. Chekhov's story is a classic example of the writer's dictum, "Show, don't tell." Explain how Chekhov shows us what a nincompoop is instead of telling us.

5. What does dialogue contribute to this story? (Glossary: *Dialogue*) How would the story be different if there were no dialogue?
6. Chekhov has the employer narrate this story. How would the story be different if he had chosen Julia as the narrator?
7. From time to time—almost as an aside—the narrator provides a description of Julia's physical reactions to his words during his meeting with her. Why is it important for the narrator to provide this information to readers?

Classroom Activity Using Definition

Definitions often depend on perspective, as Chekhov illustrates in his story with the word *nincompoop*. Discuss with your classmates other words or terms (such as *competition, happiness, wealth, success, ethnicity, superstar, failure, poverty, luxury*) whose definitions depend on one's perspective. Choose several of these words, and write brief definitions for them from your perspective. Share your definitions with your classmates, and discuss any differences in perspective you can identify in your definitions.

Suggested Writing Assignments

1. Using Chekhov's story as a model, write a narrative in which you define *friend, jerk, survivor, procrastinator, boss, workaholic, hero, soul mate, nemesis,* or a character type of your own choosing. Be careful to show your definition and not to tell it.
2. In the final paragraph of this story, the narrator muses to himself, "How easy it is to crush the weak in this world!" Does this story offer any insights about how to stop the exploitation of the poor by the rich and powerful? Or do we live in a dog-cat-dog world in which everyone must have "teeth and claws" (25)? How does one teach the weak to protest and speak up for themselves? Or should the powerful assume some responsibility to look after the weak and protect them? Write an essay in which you present your views about how society should treat "the weak in this world."

chapter **18**

Division and Classification

A writer practices **division** by separating a class of things or ideas into categories following a clear principle or basis. In the following paragraph, journalist Robert MacNeil establishes categories of speech according to their level of formality:

> It fascinates me how differently we all speak in different circumstances. We have levels of formality, as in our clothing. There are very formal occasions, often requiring written English: the job application or the letter to the editor—the darksuit, serious-tie language, with everything pressed and the lint brushed off. There is our less formal out-in-the-world language—a more comfortable suit, but still respectable. There is language for close friends in the evenings, on weekends—bluejeans-and-sweat-shirt language, when it's good to get the tie off. There is family language, even more relaxed, full of grammatical short cuts, family slang, echoes of old jokes that have become intimate shorthand—the language of pajamas and uncombed hair. Finally, there is the languagc with no clothes on; the talk of couples—murmurs, sighs, grunts—language at its least self-conscious, open, vulnerable, and primitive.
>
> –Robert MacNeil

With **classification,** on the other hand, a writer groups individual objects or ideas into already established categories. Division and classification can operate separately but often accompany one another. Here, for example, is a passage about levers in which the writer first discusses generally how levers work. In the second paragraph, the writer uses division to establish three categories of levers and then uses classification to group individual levers into those categories:

> Every lever has one fixed point called the "fulcrum" and is acted on by two forces—the "effort" (exertion of hand muscles) and the "weight" (object's resistance). Levers work according to a

> simple formula: the effort (how hard you push or pull) multiplied by its distance from the fulcrum (effort arm) equals the weight multiplied by its distance from the fulcrum (weight arm). Thus two pounds of effort exerted at a distance of four feet from the fulcrum will raise eight pounds located one foot from the fulcrum.
>
> There are three types of levers, conventionally called "first kind," "second kind," and "third kind." Levers of the first kind have the fulcrum located between the effort and the weight. Examples are a pump handle, an oar, a crowbar, a weighing balance, a pair of scissors, and a pair of pliers. Levers of the second kind have the weight in the middle and magnify the effort. Examples are the handcar crank and doors. Levers of the third kind, such as a power shovel or a baseball batter's forearm, have the effort in the middle and always magnify the distance.

The following paragraph introduces a classification of the kinds of decisions one has to make when purchasing a mobile phone:

> When you buy a mobile phone you have a great number of options in phone technology and business offerings from which to choose; for example, plan type, coverage, minutes, data usage, voice communications, battery life, design, size, and weight. In just the area of design alone, there are even more options, each with its own advantages and disadvantages: flip, candy-bar, clamshell, slider, and swivel or twist open (with single or dual screens) styles.
>
> –Freddy Chessa, student

In writing, division and classification are affected directly by the writer's practical purpose—what the writer wants to explain or prove. That purpose determines the class of things or ideas being divided and classified. For instance, a writer might divide television programs according to their audiences (adults, families, or children) and then classify individual programs into each category to show that television stations value certain audiences more than others. A writer who is concerned about violence in television programming would divide programs into those with and without fights and murders and then would classify several programs into those categories. Other writers with different purposes might divide television programs differently (by the day and time of broadcast, for example, or by the number of women featured in prominent roles) and then would classify individual programs accordingly.

Another example may help clarify how division and classification work hand in hand in writing. Suppose a sociologist wants to determine whether income level influences voting behavior in a particular neighborhood. The sociologist chooses as her subject the fifteen families living on Maple Street. Her goal then becomes to group these families in a way that is relevant to her purpose. She knows that she wants to divide the neighborhood in two ways—according to (1) income level (low, middle, and high) and (2) voting behavior (voters and nonvoters). However, her process of division won't be complete until she can classify the fifteen families into her five groupings.

In confidential interviews with each family, the sociologist learns what the family's income is and whether any member of the household voted in a state or federal election in the last four years. Based on this information, she classifies each family according to her established categories and at the same time divides the neighborhood into the subclasses that are crucial to her study. Her work leads her to construct a diagram of her divisions and classifications.

The diagram on page 451 allows the sociologist to visualize her division and classification system and its essential components—subject, basis or principle of division, subclasses or categories, and conclusion. Her ultimate conclusion depends on her ability to work back and forth among divisions, subclasses, and the actual families to be classified.

The following guidelines can help you use division and classification in your writing:

1. *Identify a clear purpose, and use a principle of division that is appropriate to that purpose.* If you want to examine the common characteristics of four-year athletic scholarship recipients at your college or university, you might consider the following principles of division—program of study, sport, place of origin, or gender. In this case it would not be useful to divide students on the basis of their favorite type of music because that seems irrelevant to your purpose.
2. *Divide your subject into unique categories.* An item can belong to only one category. For example, don't divide students as men, women, and athletes.
3. *Make your division and classification complete.* Your categories should account for all items in a subject class. In dividing students on the basis of geographic origin, for example, don't consider only the United States because such a division does not account for foreign students. For your classification to be complete, every student must be placed in one of the established categories.

Purpose: To group fifteen families according to income and voting behavior and to study the relationships between the two.

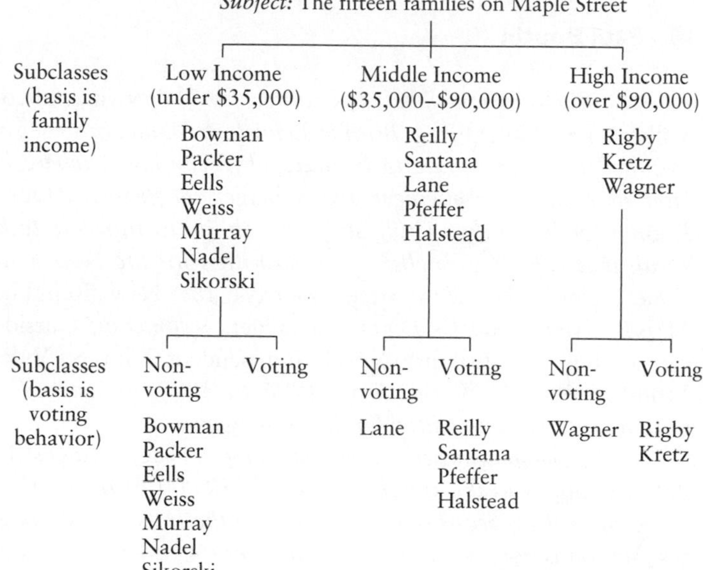

Conclusion: On Maple Street, there seems to be a relationship between income level and voting behavior: the low-income families are nonvoters.

4. *State the conclusion that your division and classification lead you to draw.* For example, after conducting your division and classification of athletic scholarship recipients, you might conclude that the majority of male athletes with athletic scholarships come from the western United States.

You Are What You Search

Paul Boutin

Paul Boutin is a journalist and writer for Valleywag: Silicon Valley's Tech Gossip Rag. *Born in Lewiston, Maine, in 1961, he attended the Massachusetts Institute of Technology, where he later worked as an engineer and manager on Project Athena. Known for his lively writing style and ability to translate tech-speak into everyday English, he has written for the* New York Times, Slate, *the* Wall Street Journal, *the* New Republic, *MSNBC.com,* Reader's Digest, Engadget, *Salon.com,* Outside, Cargo, Business 2.0, InfoWorld, Independent Film & Video Monthly, *and* PC World. *From 1996 to 2007, he worked as both a writer and an editor for* Wired *magazine.*

In the following article, published online in Slate *on August 11, 2006, Boutin uses the search records of 650,000 AOL members to examine the reasons that people search the Internet. Although his division is not a scientific study, it relies on his experience and that of others (such as his editors at* Slate*) who are accustomed to examining large volumes of data. Rather than simply provide a collection of random personal search sequences, he grouped the searches in a way that was meaningful to* Slate's *nontechnical readership and human-interest focus.*

Reflecting on What You Know

Reflect on how you usually use the Internet to search for information. Make a list of the five subject categories you look for most often, and place them in descending order of frequency. What does the list say about your interests and about you in general?

AOL researchers recently [2006] published the search logs of about 650,000 members—a total of 36,389,629 individual searches. AOL's search nerds intended the files to be an academic resource but didn't consider that users might be peeved to see their private queries become a research tool. Last weekend, the Internet service provider tried to pull back the data, but by that point it had leaked all over the Web. If you've ever wanted to see what other people type into search boxes, now's your chance. 1

The search records don't include users' names, but each search is tagged with a number that's tied to a specific AOL account. The *New York Times* quickly sussed out that AOL searcher No. 4417749 was sixty-two-year-old Thelma Arnold. Indeed, Arnold has a "dog who urinates on everything," just as she'd typed into the search box. Valleywag has become one of many clearinghouses for funny, bizarre, and painful user profiles. The searches of AOL user No. 672368, for example, morphed over several weeks from "you're pregnant he doesn't want the baby" to "foods to eat when pregnant" to "abortion clinics charlotte nc" to "can christians be forgiven for abortion." 2

While these case studies are good voyeuristic fodder, snooping through one user's life barely scratches the surface of this data trove. The startup company I work for, Splunk, makes software to search computer-generated log files. AOL's 36 million log entries might look like an Orwellian nightmare to you, but for us it's a user transaction case study to die for. Using the third-party site splunkd.com, I've parsed the AOL data to create a typology of AOL Search users. Which of the seven types of searcher are you? 3

The Pornhound. Big surprise, there are millions of searches for mind-bendingly kinky stuff. User No. 927 is already an Internet legend. When I clicked Splunk's "Show Events by Time" button, though, I found that porn searchers vary not only by *what* they search for, but *when* they search for it. Some users are on a quest for pornography at all hours, seeking little else from AOL. Another subgroup, including No. 927, search only within reliable time slots. The data doesn't list each user's time zone, but 11 p.m. Eastern and 11 p.m. Pacific appear to be prime time for porn on AOL's servers. My favorite plots show hours of G-rated searches before the user switches gears—what I call the Avenue Q Theory of Internet usage. User No. 190827 goes from "talking parrots jokes" and "poems about a red rose" before midnight to multiple clicks for "sexy dogs and hot girls" a half hour later. An important related discovery: nobody knows how to spell "bestiality." 4

The Manhunter. The person who searches for other people. Again, I used Splunk's "Show Events by Time" function to plot name searches by date and time. Surprisingly, I didn't uncover many long-term stalkers. Most of the data showed bursts of searches for a specific name only once, all within an hour or a day, and then never again. Maybe these folks are background-checking job candidates, maybe they're looking up the new cutie at the office, or maybe they just miss 5 old friends. Most of the names in AOL's logs are too ambiguous to pinpoint to a single person in the real world, so don't get too tweaked if you find your own name and hometown in there. I've got it much worse. There are 36 million searches here, but none of them are for me.

The Shopper. The user who hits "treo 700" thirty-seven times in three days. Here, the data didn't confirm my biases. I'd expected to find window shoppers who searched for Porsche Cayman pages every weekend. But AOL's logs reveal that searches for "coupons" are a lot more common. My favorite specimen is the guy who mostly looked up food brands like Dole, Wendy's, Red Lobster, and Turkey Hill, with an occasional break for "asian movie stars." How much more American could America Online get? 6

The Obsessive. The guy who searches for the same thing over and over and over. Looking at the search words themselves can obfuscate a more general long-term pattern—A, A, A, A, B, A, A, C, A, D, A—that suggests a user who can't let go of one topic, whether it's Judaism, real estate, or Macs. Obsessives are most likely to craft advanced search terms like "craven randy fanfic-wes" and "pfeffern**sse." 7

The Omnivore. Many users aren't obsessive—they're just online a lot. My taxonomy fails them, because their search terms, while frequent, show little repetition or regularity. Still, I can spot a few subcategories. There are the trivia buffs who searched "imdb" hundreds of times in three months and the nostalgia surfers on the hunt for "pat benatar helter skelter lyrics." 8

The Newbie. They just figured out how to turn on the computer. User No. 12792510 is one of many who confuses AOL's search box with its browser address window—he keeps searching for "www.google." Other AOLers type their searches without spaces between the words ("newcaddillacdeville") as if they were 1990s-era AOL keywords. 9

The Basket Case. In college I had to write a version of the classic ELIZA program, a pretend therapist who only responds to your problems ("I am sad") with more questions ("Why do you say you are sad?"). AOL Search, it seems, serves the same purpose for a lot of users. I stumbled across queries like "i hate my job" and "why am i so ugly?" For me, one log entry stands above the rest: "i hurt when i think too much i love roadtrips i hate my weight i fear being alone for the rest of my life." Me too, 3696023. Me too. 10

If you want to try sifting through the AOL data, install the latest Firefox browser or use Internet Explorer 6. Then go to splunkd.com and click on one of the sites on the "Mirror List." If you're behind a firewall, the URLs with numbers in them ("www.ocs.net:8000") might not work. Once you click, wait a minute for the Splunk interface to load itself into your browser. You should see a search box at the top and something like "36,389,577 events indexed" below it. 11

To search AOL records, type something into the search box. As you type, a panel will appear that lists the number of possible results for what you've typed so far, such as "slate (2766)." That's a good way to quickly see how many searches for a particular word are in AOL's logs. 12

After typing a word or two, click the ">" button at the right to run your search. The results page looks like a cross between Google and a nuclear reactor console—a hip, stylish Web 2.0 reactor, of course. For help with the interface, click on "Cheat Sheet" at the upper right. You can also pop open the Splunk Assistant in the lower right corner for as-you-go hints. If all else fails, read the manual. Yes, "Splunk" is a pun on "spelunking," as in data mining. 13

The format of each search log entry is: user number, search term, time stamp. If the user clicked on one of their search results, there are two more fields: the results rank and the URL of the link they clicked. The results are easier to read if you find Splunk's Preferences menu and turn off Show Event Meta Data—you're not troubleshooting a denial of service attack. 14

Thinking Critically about This Reading

Do you think that AOL should have saved the search logs of 650,000 of its members, making it possible for computer sleuths to attach searchers' names to search queries? Google, which makes billions of dollars by analyzing Web search data, saves search logs and names for eighteen months and then deletes them. Do you think it's right that Google saves this information for any length of time? Explain.

Questions for Study and Discussion

1. What is Boutin's purpose in this essay? (Glossary: *Purpose*)
2. What does the author's "typology of AOL Search users" (paragraph 3) reveal about AOL's data? How, if at all, do you fit into his typology?

3. Why does Boutin think that the time of day that users search for certain types of information is worth noting? What might time slots reveal about users' thought patterns?
4. What humor does Boutin find in his analysis? Does his humor add or detract from his analysis? Explain.
5. What surprises do you find in Boutin's typology? In the examples that he uses to illustrate each type of user? Explain.

Classroom Activity Using Division and Classification

Be prepared to discuss in class why you believe that division and classification are important ways of thinking about everyday life. Give examples of how you use the two complementary strategies when you use a computer search engine, shop for music CDs on the Web, select items in your local supermarket, or look for textbooks in your college bookstore.

Suggested Writing Assignments

1. Write an essay in which you divide and classify your friends, relatives, classmates, and teachers based on why they use computers. What types of activities do they pursue (such as gaming, numerical analysis, music, gambling, instant messaging, e-mailing, word processing, researching, YouTubing, and editing photographs)? How much time do they spend on these tasks? Make a comprehensive list of activities, and ask people how much time they spend with each one. Be sure to have a clear thesis and purpose for your essay. What do you want your readers to learn from your research about the way computers are used today?
2. Write an essay on the types of automobiles that are on the market today. Some cars have traditional styles, some appeal to active lifestyles (vans, off-road vehicles, convertibles, sports cars), and some are energy-efficient (subcompacts, hybrids, alternative energy users). For your essay, examine the automobile market, determine a principle of division for it, and classify the cars so that a buyer will have a better idea of what's available and will best suit his or her needs.

3. Consider any of the following topics for an essay of classification. You may find it helpful to review the guidelines for using division and classification on pages 448–51.

   movies
   college instructors
   country music
   newspapers
   pets
   students

Friends, Good Friends—and Such Good Friends

■ **Judith Viorst**

Judith Viorst was born in Newark, New Jersey, in 1931 and attended Rutgers University. She has published several volumes of light verse and collections of prose, as well as many articles in popular magazines. Her numerous children's books include the perennial favorite Alexander and the Terrible, Horrible, No Good, Very Bad Day *(1972). Her recent books for adults include* Necessary Losses: The Loves, Illusions, Dependencies, and Impossible Expectations That All of Us Have to Give Up in Order to Grow *(1997),* Imperfect Control: Our Lifelong Struggles with Power and Surrender *(1998),* Suddenly Sixty: And Other Shocks of Late Life *(2000),* Grown-Up Marriage: What We Know, Wish We Had Known, and Still Need to Know about Being Married *(2002), and* I'm Too Young to Be Seventy: And Other Delusions *(2005).*

The following selection appeared in Viorst's regular column in Redbook *in 1977. In it she analyzes and classifies the various types of friends that a person can have. As you read, assess the validity of her analysis by trying to place your own friends into her categories. Determine also whether the categories themselves are mutually exclusive.*

Reflecting on What You Know

Think about your friends. Do you regard them all in the same light? Would you group them in any way? On what basis would you group them?

Women are friends, I once would have said, when they totally love and support and trust each other, and bare to each other the secrets of their souls, and run—no questions asked—to help each other, and tell harsh truths to each other (no, you can't wear that dress unless you lose ten pounds first) when harsh truths must be told. 1

Women are friends, I once would have said, when they share the same affection for Ingmar Bergman,[1] plus train rides, cats, warm rain, charades, Camus,[2] and hate with equal ardor Newark[3] and Brussels sprouts and Lawrence Welk[4] and camping. 2

In other words, I once would have said that a friend is a friend all the way, but now I believe that's a narrow point of view. For the friendships I have and the friendships I see are conducted at many levels of intensity, serve many different functions, meet different needs, and range from those as all-the-way as the friendship of the soul sisters mentioned above to that of the most nonchalant and casual playmates. 3

Consider these varieties of friendship: 4

1. Convenience friends. These are women with whom, if our paths weren't crossing all the time, we'd have no particular reason to be friends: a next-door neighbor, a woman in our car pool, the mother of one of our children's closest friends, or maybe some mommy with whom we serve juice and cookies each week at the Glenwood Co-op Nursery. 5

Convenience friends are convenient indeed. They'll lend us their cups and silverware for a party. They'll drive our kids to soccer when we're sick. They'll take us to pick up our car when we need a lift to the garage. They'll even take our cats when we go on vacation. As we will for them. 6

But we don't, with convenience friends, ever come too close or tell too much; we maintain our public face and emotional distance. "Which means," says Elaine, "that I'll talk about being overweight but not about being depressed. Which means I'll admit being mad but not blind with rage. Which means that I might say that we're pinched this month but never that I'm worried sick over money." 7

But which doesn't mean that there isn't sufficient value to be found in these friendships of mutual aid, in convenience friends. 8

2. Special-interest friends. These friendships aren't intimate, and they needn't involve kids or silverware or cats. Their value lies in some interest jointly shared. And so we may have an office friend or a yoga friend or a tennis friend or a friend from the Women's Democratic Club. 9

---

[1]*Ingmar Bergman* (1918–2007): Swedish film writer and director.

[2]*Albert Camus* (1913–1960): French novelist, essayist, and playwright.

[3]*Newark:* a city in northeastern New Jersey.

[4]*Lawrence Welk* (1903–1992): American band leader and accordion player whose *The Lawrence Welk Show* aired on television in 1955–1971.

"I've got one woman friend," says Joyce, "who likes, as I do, to take psychology courses. Which makes it nice for me—and nice for her. It's fun to go with someone you know and it's fun to discuss what you've learned, driving back from the classes." And for the most part, she says, that's all they discuss. 10

"I'd say that what we're doing is *doing* together, not being together," Suzanne says of her Tuesday-doubles friends. "It's mainly a tennis relationship, but we play together well. And I guess we all need to have a couple of playmates." 11

I agree. 12

My playmate is a shopping friend, a woman of marvelous taste, a woman who knows exactly *where* to buy *what,* and furthermore is a woman who always knows beyond a doubt what one ought to be buying. I don't have the time to keep up with what's new in eyeshadow, hemlines, and shoes and whether the smock look is in or finished already. But since (oh, shame!) I care a lot about eyeshadow, hemlines, and shoes, and since I don't *want* to wear smocks if the smock look is finished, I'm very glad to have a shopping friend. 13

3. Historical friends. We all have a friend who knew us when . . . maybe way back in Miss Meltzer's second grade, when our family lived in that three-room flat in Brooklyn, when our dad was out of work for seven months, when our brother Allie got in that fight where they had to call the police, when our sister married the endodontist[5] from Yonkers,[6] and when, the morning after we lost our virginity, she was the first, the only, friend we told. 14

The years have gone by and we've gone separate ways and we've little in common now, but we're still an intimate part of each other's past. And so whenever we go to Detroit we always go to visit this friend of our girlhood. Who knows how we looked before our teeth were straightened. Who knows how we talked before our voice got un-Brooklyned. Who knows what we ate before we learned about artichokes. And who, by her presence, puts us in touch with an earlier part of ourself, a part of ourself it's important never to lose. 15

"What this friend means to me and what I mean to her," says Grace, "is having a sister without sibling rivalry. We know the texture of each other's lives. She remembers my grandmother's cabbage 16

[5]*endodontist:* a dentist who specializes in diseases of the teeth and gums.
[6]*Yonkers:* a city in southeastern New York, just north of New York City.

soup. I remember the way her uncle played the piano. There's simply no other friend who remembers those things."

4. Crossroads friends. Like historical friends, our crossroads friends are important for *what was*—for the friendship we shared at a crucial, now past, time of life. A time, perhaps, when we roomed in college together; or worked as eager young singles in the Big City together; or went together, as my friend Elizabeth and I did, through pregnancy, birth, and that scary first year of new motherhood. 17

Crossroads friends forge powerful links, links strong enough to endure with not much more contact than once-a-year letters at Christmas. And out of respect for those crossroad years, for those dramas and dreams we once shared, we will always be friends. 18

5. Cross-generational friends. Historical friends and crossroads friends seem to maintain a special kind of intimacy—dormant but always ready to be revived—and though we may rarely meet, whenever we do connect, it's personal and intense. Another kind of intimacy exists in the friendships that form across generations in what one woman calls her daughter-mother and her mother-daughter relationships. 19

Evelyn's friend is her mother's age—"but I share so much more than I ever could with my mother"—a woman she talks to of music, of books, and of life. "What I get from her is the benefit of her experience. What she gets—and enjoys—from me is a youthful perspective. It's a pleasure for both of us." 20

I have in my own life a precious friend, a woman of sixty-five who has lived very hard, who is wise, who listens well; who has been where I am and can help me understand it; and who represents not only an ultimate ideal mother to me but also the person I'd like to be when I grow up. 21

In our daughter role we tend to do more than our share of self-revelation; in our mother role we tend to receive what's revealed. It's another kind of pleasure—playing wise mother to a questing younger person. It's another very lovely kind of friendship. 22

6. Part-of-a-couple friends. Some of the women we call our friends we never see alone—we see them as part of a couple at couples' parties. And though we share interests in many things and respect each other's views, we aren't moved to deepen the relationship. Whatever the reason, a lack of time or—and this is more likely—a lack of chemistry, our friendship remains in the context of a group. But the fact that our feeling on seeing each other is always, "I'm *so* glad she's 23

here" and the fact that we spend half the evening talking together says that this too, in its own way, counts as a friendship.

(Other part-of-a-couple friends are the friends that came with the marriage, and some of these are friends we could live without. But sometimes, alas, she married our husband's best friend; and sometimes, alas, she *is* our husband's best friend. And so we find ourself dealing with her, somewhat against our will, in a spirit of what I'll call *reluctant* friendship.) 24

7. Men who are friends. I wanted to write just of women friends, but the women I've talked to won't let me—they say I must mention man–woman friendships too. For these friendships can be just as close and as dear as those that we form with women. Listen to Lucy's description of one such friendship: 25

"We've found we have things to talk about that are different from what he talks about with my husband and different from what I talk about with his wife. So sometimes we call on the phone or meet for lunch. There are similar intellectual interests—we always pass on to each other the books that we love—but there's also something tender and caring too." 26

In a couple of crises, Lucy says, "he offered himself for talking and for helping. And when someone died in his family he wanted me there. The sexual, flirty part of our friendship is very small, but *some*—just enough to make it fun and different." She thinks—and I agree—that the sexual part, though small, is always *some,* is always there when a man and a woman are friends. 27

It's only in the past few years that I've made friends with men, in the sense of a friendship that's *mine,* not just part of two couples. And achieving with them the ease and the trust I've found with women friends has value indeed. Under the dryer at home last week, putting on mascara and rouge, I comfortably sat and talked with a fellow named Peter. Peter, I finally decided, could handle the shock of me minus mascara under the dryer. Because we care for each other. Because we're friends. 28

8. There are medium friends, and pretty good friends, and very good friends indeed, and these friendships are defined by their level of intimacy. And what we'll reveal at each of these levels of intimacy is calibrated with care. We might tell a medium friend, for example, that yesterday we had a fight with our husband. And we might tell a pretty good friend that this fight with our husband made us so mad that we slept on the couch. And we might tell a very good friend that 29

the reason we got so mad in that fight that we slept on the couch had something to do with that girl that works in his office. But it's only to our very best friends that we're willing to tell all, to tell what's going on with that girl in his office.

The best of friends, I still believe, totally love and support and 30
trust each other, and bare to each other the secrets of their souls, and run—no questions asked—to help each other, and tell harsh truths to each other when they must be told.

But we needn't agree about everything (only twelve-year-old girl 31
friends agree about *everything*) to tolerate each other's point of view. To accept without judgment. To give and to take without ever keeping score. And to *be* there, as I am for them and as they are for me, to comfort our sorrows, to celebrate our joys.

Thinking Critically about This Reading

The third type of friend Viorst writes about is the "historical friend." Why is it important to have a friend who "puts us in touch with an earlier part of ourself" (paragraph 15)?

Questions for Study and Discussion

1. In her opening paragraph, Viorst explains how she once would have defined *friendship*. Why does she now think differently?
2. What is Viorst's purpose? (Glossary: *Purpose*) Why is division and classification an appropriate strategy for her to use?
3. Into what categories does Viorst divide her friends?
4. What principles of division does Viorst use to establish her categories of friends? Where does she state these principles?
5. Discuss the ways in which Viorst makes her categories distinct and memorable.
6. What is Viorst's tone? (Glossary: *Tone*) In what ways is her tone appropriate for both her audience and subject matter? (Glossary: *Audience*) Explain.

Classroom Activity Using Division and Classification

The following drawing is a basic exercise in classification. By determining the features that the figures have in common, establish the general class to which they all belong. Next, establish subclasses by

a
b
c
d
e
f
g
h
i
j
k
l
m
n
o

determining the distinctive features that distinguish one subclass from another. Finally, place each figure in an appropriate subclass within your classification system. You may wish to compare your classification system with those developed by other members of your class and to discuss any differences that exist.

Suggested Writing Assignments

1. Review the categories of friends that Viorst establishes in her essay. Do the categories apply to your friends? What new categories would you create? Write an essay in which you explain the types of friends in your life.
2. Music can be classified into many different types (such as jazz, country, pop, rock, hard rock, alternative, classical, big band, hip-hop, and so on). Each of these large classifications has a lot of variety within it. Write an essay in which you identify your favorite type of music as well as at least three subclassifications of that music. Explain the characteristics of each category, using two or three artists as examples.
3. In her essay Viorst focuses on the types of friendships between women. (Glossary: *Focus*) What about friendships between men, one of which is represented in the cartoon on page 466? What statement does the cartoon make about the nature of men's friendships? In what ways do they differ from women's friendships? (Glossary: *Comparison and Contrast*) Using Viorst's essay as a model, write an essay in which you divide and classify the friendships that you have observed men to have.

A friend will give up his life for you.
A *real* friend will help you move.

Doubts about Doublespeak

■ William Lutz

William Lutz is a professor of English at Rutgers University–Camden and was the editor of the Quarterly Review of Doublespeak *for fourteen years. Born in Racine, Wisconsin, in 1940, Lutz is best known for* Doublespeak: From Revenue Enhancement to Terminal Living *(1990) and* The New Doublespeak: Why No One Knows What Anyone's Saying Anymore *(1996). His most recent book,* Doublespeak Defined: Cut through the Bull**** and Get to the Point, *was published in 1999. (The term* doublespeak *was coined by George Orwell in his novel* Nineteen Eighty-Four. *It refers to speech or writing that presents two or more contradictory ideas in a way that deceives an unsuspecting audience.) As chair of the National Council of Teachers of English's Committee on Public Doublespeak, Lutz has been a watchdog of public officials who use language to "mislead, distort, deceive, inflate, circumvent, and obfuscate." Each year, the committee presents the Orwell Awards to recognize outrageous uses of doublespeak in government and business.*

The following essay first appeared in the July 1993 issue of State Government News. *As you read, notice how Lutz organizes his essay by naming and defining four categories of doublespeak, describing each one's function or consequences, and giving examples of each type. This organizational pattern is simple, practical, and easy to follow.*

Reflecting on What You Know

Imagine that you work for a manufacturing plant in your town and that your boss has just told you that you are on the list of people who will be "dehired" or that you are part of a program of "negative employee retention." What would you think was happening to you? Would you be happy about it? What would you think of the language that your boss used to describe your situation?

During the past year, we learned that we can shop at a "unique retail biosphere" instead of a farmers' market, where we can buy items made of "synthetic glass" instead of plastic, or purchase a "high velocity, multipurpose air circulator," or electric fan. A "waste-water conveyance facility" may "exceed the odor threshold" from time to time due to the presence of "regulated human nutrients," but that is not to be confused with a sewage plant that stinks up the neighborhood with sewage sludge. Nor should we confuse a "resource development park" with a dump. Thus does doublespeak continue to spread. 1

Doublespeak is language which pretends to communicate but doesn't. It is language which makes the bad seem good, the negative seem positive, the unpleasant seem attractive, or at least tolerable. It is language which avoids, shifts, or denies responsibility; language which is at variance with its real or purported meaning. It is language which conceals or prevents thought. 2

Doublespeak is all around us. We are asked to check our packages at the desk "for our convenience" when it's not for our convenience at all but for someone else's convenience. We see advertisements for "preowned," "experienced," or "previously distinguished" cars, not used cars, and for "genuine imitation leather," "virgin vinyl," or "real counterfeit diamonds." Television offers not reruns but "encore telecasts." There are no slums or ghettos, just the "inner city" or "substandard housing" where the "disadvantaged" or "economically nonaffluent" live and where there might be a problem with "substance abuse." Nonprofit organizations don't make a profit, they have "negative deficits" or experience "revenue excesses." With doublespeak it's not dying but "terminal living" or "negative patient care outcome." 3

There are four kinds of doublespeak. The first kind is the euphemism, a word or phrase designed to avoid a harsh or distasteful reality. Used to mislead or deceive, the euphemism becomes doublespeak. In 1984 the U.S. State Department's annual reports on the status of human rights around the world ceased using the word "killing." Instead the State Department used the phrase "unlawful or arbitrary deprivation of life," thus avoiding the embarrassing situation of government-sanctioned killing in countries supported by the United States. 4

A second kind of doublespeak is jargon, the specialized language of a trade, profession, or similar group, such as doctors, lawyers, plumbers, or car mechanics. Legitimately used, jargon allows members of a group to communicate with each other clearly, efficiently, and quickly. Lawyers and tax accountants speak to each other of an 5 "involuntary conversion" of property, a legal term that means the loss or destruction of property through theft, accident, or condemnation. But when lawyers or tax accountants use unfamiliar terms to speak to others, then the jargon becomes doublespeak.

In 1978 a commercial 727 crashed on takeoff, killing three passengers, injuring twenty-one others, and destroying the airplane. The insured value of the airplane was greater than its book value, so the airline made a profit of $1.7 million, creating two problems: the airline didn't want to talk about one of its airplanes crashing, yet it had to account for that $1.7 million profit in its annual report to its stockholders. The airline solved both problems by inserting a footnote in its annual report which explained that the $1.7 million was due to "the involuntary conversion of a 727." 6

A third kind of doublespeak is gobbledygook or bureaucratese. Such doublespeak is simply a matter of overwhelming the audience with words—the more the better. Alan Greenspan, a polished practitioner of bureaucratese, once testified before a Senate committee that "it is a tricky problem to find the particular calibration in timing that would be appropriate to stem the acceleration in risk premiums created by falling incomes without prematurely aborting the decline in the inflation-generated risk premiums." 7

The fourth kind of doublespeak is inflated language, which is designed to make the ordinary seem extraordinary, to make everyday things seem impressive, to give an air of importance to people or situations, to make the simple seem complex. Thus do car mechanics become "automotive internists," elevator operators become "members of the vertical transportation corps," grocery store checkout clerks become "career associate scanning professionals," and smelling something becomes "organoleptic analysis." 8

Doublespeak is not the product of careless language or sloppy thinking. Quite the opposite. Doublespeak is language carefully designed and constructed to appear to communicate when in fact it doesn't. It is language designed not to lead but mislead. Thus, it's not a tax increase but "revenue enhancement" or "tax-base broadening." So how can you complain about higher taxes? Those aren't useless, billion dollar pork barrel projects; they're really "congressional projects of national significance," so don't complain about wasteful government spending. That isn't the Mafia in Atlantic City; those are just "members of a career-offender cartel," so don't worry about the influence of organized crime in the city. 9

New doublespeak is created every day. The Environmental Protection Agency once called acid rain "poorly-buffered precipitation," then dropped that term in favor of "atmospheric deposition of anthropogenically-derived acidic substances," but recently decided that acid rain should be called "wet deposition." The Pentagon, which has in the past given us such classic doublespeak as "hexiform rotatable surface compression unit" for steel nut, just published a pamphlet warning soldiers that exposure to nerve gas will lead to "immediate permanent incapacitation." That's almost as good as the Pentagon's official term "servicing the target," meaning to kill the enemy. Meanwhile, the Department of Energy wants to establish a "monitored retrievable storage site," a place once known as a dump for spent nuclear fuel. 10

Bad economic times give rise to lots of new doublespeak designed to avoid some very unpleasant economic realities. As the "contained depression" continues so does the corporate policy of making up even more new terms to avoid the simple, and easily understandable, term "layoff." So it is that corporations "reposition," "restructure," "reshape," or "realign" the company and "reduce duplication" through "release of resources" that involves a "permanent downsizing" or a "payroll adjustment" that results in a number of employees being "involuntarily terminated." 11

Other countries regularly contribute to doublespeak. In Japan, where baldness is called "hair disadvantaged," the economy is undergoing a "severe adjustment process," while in Canada there is an "involuntary downward development" of the work force. For some government agencies in Canada, wastepaper baskets have become "user friendly, space effective, flexible, deskside sortation units." Politicians in Canada may engage in "reality augmentation," but they never lie. As part of their new freedom, the people of Moscow can visit "intimacy salons," or sex shops as they're known in other countries. When dealing with the bureaucracy in Russia, people know that they should show officials "normal gratitude," or give them a bribe. 12

The worst doublespeak is the doublespeak of death. It is the language, wrote George Orwell in 1946, that is "largely the defense of the indefensible . . . designed to make lies sound truthful and murder respectable, and to give an appearance of solidity to pure wind." In the doublespeak of death, Orwell continued, "defenseless villages are bombarded from the air, the inhabitants driven out into the countryside, the cattle machine-gunned, the huts set on fire with incendiary bullets. This is called pacification. Millions of peasants are robbed of 13 their farms and sent trudging along the roads with no more than they can carry. This is called transfer of population or rectification of frontiers." Today, in a country once called Yugoslavia, this is called "ethnic cleansing."[1]

It's easy to laugh off doublespeak. After all, we all know what's going on, so what's the harm? But we don't always know what's going on, and when that happens, doublespeak accomplishes its ends. It alters our perception of reality. It deprives us of the tools we need to develop, advance, and preserve our society, our culture, our civilization. It breeds suspicion, cynicism, distrust, and, ultimately, hostility. It delivers us into the hands of those who do not have our interests at heart. As Samuel Johnson[2] noted in eighteenth-century England, even the devils in hell do not lie to one another, since the society of hell could not subsist without the truth, any more than any other society. 14

Thinking Critically about This Reading

According to Lutz, doublespeak "alters our perception of reality. . . . It breeds suspicion, cynicism, distrust, and, ultimately, hostility" (paragraph 14). What is Lutz's plan for combating doublespeak and its negative effects?

Questions for Study and Discussion

1. What is Lutz's thesis? (Glossary: *Thesis*)
2. The author divides doublespeak into four categories. What are they?
3. For what purpose has Lutz used division and classification? (Glossary: *Purpose*)
4. Why might Lutz have ordered the categories as he has? (Glossary: *Organization*)
5. Are Lutz's illustrative examples good ones? (Glossary: *Example*) Why or why not? Should he have used fewer examples? More examples? Explain.

[1]*"ethnic cleansing":* Lutz is referring to the breakup of the Federal Republic of Yugoslavia in the Balkan region of southeastern Europe in the early 1990s and the 1992–1995 genocide centered in the cities of Sarajevo and Srebrenica.
[2]*Samuel Johnson* (1709–1784): an important English writer.

6. Could the order of Lutz's first two paragraphs be reversed? (Glossary: *Beginnings and Endings*) What would be gained or lost if they were?
7. Reread Lutz's last paragraph, where he makes some serious claims about the importance of doublespeak. Is such seriousness on his part justified by what he has written about doublespeak in the body of his essay? Why or why not?

Classroom Activity Using Division and Classification

Examine the following lists of hobbies, books, and buildings. Determine at least three principles that could be used to divide the items listed in each group. Finally, classify the items in each group according to one of the principles you have established.

Hobbies

watching sports on TV	surfing the Web
stamp collecting	hiking
scuba diving	dancing

Books

The Adventures of Huckleberry Finn	*Guinness Book of World Records*
American Heritage Dictionary	*To Kill a Mockingbird*
The Joy of Cooking	*Gone with the Wind*

Buildings

Empire State Building	Taj Mahal
White House	Library of Congress
The Alamo	Buckingham Palace

Suggested Writing Assignments

1. Write an essay in which you consider the effects of doublespeak. Is it always a form of lying? Is it harmful to our society, and if

so, how? How can we measure its effects? Be sure to cite instances of doublespeak that are not included in Lutz's essay. You can uncover these through your reading, Web browsing, or library research.

2. College is a time of stress for many students. In an essay, use division and classification to discuss the different kinds of pressure students experience at your school.

chapter **19**

Comparison and Contrast

A **comparison** points out the ways that two or more people, places, or things are alike. A **contrast** points out how they differ. The subjects of a comparison or contrast should be in the same class or general category; if they have nothing in common, there is no good reason for setting them side by side.

The function of any comparison or contrast is to clarify and explain. The writer's purpose may be simply to inform or to make readers aware of similarities or differences that are interesting and significant in themselves. Or the writer may explain something unfamiliar by comparing it with something very familiar, perhaps explaining the game of squash by comparing it with tennis. Finally, the writer can point out the superiority of one thing by contrasting it with another—for example, showing that one product is the best by contrasting it with all its competitors.

As a writer, you have two main options for organizing a comparison or contrast: the subject-by-subject pattern or the point-by-point pattern. For a short essay comparing and contrasting the cities of Atlanta, Georgia, and Seattle, Washington, as vacation destinations, you would probably follow the *subject-by-subject* pattern of organization. With this pattern, you first discuss the points you wish to make about one city and then discuss the corresponding points for the other city. An outline of the body of your essay might look like this:

Subject-by-Subject Pattern

I. Atlanta
   A. Climate
   B. Public transportation
   C. Tourist attractions (museums, zoos, theme parks)
   D. Accommodations

II. Seattle
   A. Climate
   B. Public transportation
   C. Tourist attractions (museums, zoos, theme parks)
   D. Accommodations

The subject-by-subject pattern presents a unified discussion of each city by emphasizing the cities and not the four points of comparison. Because these points are relatively few, readers should easily remember what was said about Atlanta's climate when you later discuss Seattle's climate and should be able to make the appropriate connections between them.

For a somewhat longer essay comparing and contrasting solar energy and wind energy, however, you should consider the *point-by-point* pattern of organization. With this pattern, your essay is organized according to the various points of comparison. Discussion alternates between solar and wind energy for each point of comparison. An outline of the body of your essay might look like this:

Point-by-Point Pattern

I. Installation expenses
   A. Solar
   B. Wind
II. Efficiency
   A. Solar
   B. Wind
III. Operating costs
   A. Solar
   B. Wind
IV. Convenience
   A. Solar
   B. Wind
V. Maintenance
   A. Solar
   B. Wind
VI. Safety
   A. Solar
   B. Wind

With the point-by-point pattern, the writer makes immediate comparisons between solar and wind energy so that readers can consider each of the similarities and differences separately.

Each organizational pattern has its advantages. In general, the subject-by-subject pattern is useful in short essays where few points are to be considered, and the point-by-point pattern is preferable in long essays where numerous points are under consideration.

A good essay of comparison and contrast tells readers something significant that they do not already know—that is, it must do more than merely point out the obvious. As a rule, therefore, writers tend to draw contrasts between things that are usually perceived as being similar or comparisons between things usually perceived as being different. In fact, comparison and contrast often go together. For example, an essay about Minneapolis and St. Paul might begin by showing how much they are alike but end with a series of contrasts revealing how much they differ. A consumer magazine might report the contrasting claims made by six car manufacturers and then go on to demonstrate that the cars all actually do much the same thing in the same way.

The following student essay about hunting and photography explores the increasing popularity of photographic safaris. After first pointing out the obvious differences between hunting with a gun and hunting with a camera, the writer focuses on the similarities between the two activities that make many hunters "willing to trade their guns for cameras." Notice how she successfully uses the subject-by-subject organizational plan in the body of her essay to explore three key similarities between hunters and photographers.

Guns and Cameras

The hunter has a deep interest in the apparatus he uses to kill his prey. He carries various types of guns, different kinds of ammunition, and special sights and telescopes to increase his chances of success. He knows the mechanics of his guns and understands how and why they work. This fascination with the hardware of his sport is practical—it helps him achieve his goal—but it frequently becomes an end, almost a hobby in itself.

Not until the very end of the long process of stalking an animal does a game hunter use his gun. First he enters into the animal's world. He studies his prey, its habitat, its daily habits, its watering holes and feeding areas, its migration patterns, its enemies and allies, its diet and food chain. Eventually the hunter himself becomes animal-like, instinctively sensing the habits and moves of his prey. Of course, this instinct gives the hunter a better chance of killing the animal; he knows where and when he will get the best shot. But it gives him more than that. Hunting is not just pulling the trigger and killing the prey. Much of it is a multifaceted and ritualistic identification with nature.

After the kill, the hunter can do a number of things with his trophy. He can sell the meat or eat it himself. He can hang the animal's head on the wall or lay its hide on the floor or even sell these objects. But any of these uses is a luxury, and its cost is high. An animal has been destroyed; a life has been eliminated.

Like the hunter, the photographer has a great interest in the tools he uses. He carries various types of cameras, lenses, and film to help him get the picture he wants. He understands the way cameras work, the uses of telephoto and micro lenses, and often the technical procedures of printing and developing. Of course, the time and interest a photographer invests in these mechanical aspects of his art allow him to capture and produce the image he wants. But as with the hunter, these mechanics can and often do become fascinating in themselves.

The wildlife photographer also needs to stalk his "prey" with knowledge and skill in order to get an accurate "shot." Like the hunter, he has to understand the animal's patterns, characteristics, and habitat; he must become animal-like in order to succeed. And like the hunter's, his pursuit is much more prolonged and complicated than the shot itself. The stalking processes are almost identical and give many of the same satisfactions.

The successful photographer also has something tangible to show for his efforts. A still picture of an animal can be displayed in a home, a gallery, a shop; it can be printed in a publication, as a postcard, or as a poster. In fact, a single photograph can be used in all these ways at once; it can be reproduced countless times. And despite all these ways of using his "trophies," the photographer continues to preserve his prey.

–Barbara Bowman, student

Analogy is a special form of comparison. When a subject is unobservable, complex, or abstract—when it is so unfamiliar that readers may have trouble understanding it—**analogy** can be effective. By pointing out certain similarities between a difficult subject and a more familiar or concrete subject, writers can help their readers grasp a difficult subject. Unlike a true comparison, though, which analyzes items that belong to the same class (breeds of dogs or types of engines), analogy pairs things from different classes that have nothing in common except through the imagination of the writer. In addition, whereas comparison seeks to illuminate specific features of both subjects, the primary purpose of analogy is to clarify the one subject that is complex or unfamiliar. For example, to explore the similarities (and differences) between short stories and novels (two forms of fiction), you probably would choose comparison. Short stories and novels belong to the same class (fiction), and your purpose is to reveal something about both. If, however, your purpose is to explain the craft of fiction writing, you might note its similarities to the craft of carpentry. Then you would be drawing an analogy because the two subjects clearly belong to different classes. Carpentry is the more concrete subject and the one more people will have direct experience with. If you use your imagination, you will easily see many ways that the tangible work of the carpenter can be used to help readers understand the abstract work of the novelist.

Depending on its purpose, an analogy can be made in a sentence or in several paragraphs to clarify a particular aspect of the larger topic being discussed, as in the following example, or it can provide the organizational strategy for an entire essay:

> It has long struck me that the familiar metaphor of "climbing the ladder" for describing the ascent to success or fulfillment in any field is inappropriate and misleading. There are no ladders that lead to success, although there may be some escalators for those lucky enough to follow in a family's fortunes.
>
> A ladder proceeds vertically, rung by rung, with each rung evenly spaced, and with the whole apparatus leaning against a relatively flat and even surface. A child can climb a ladder as easily as an adult, and perhaps with a surer footing.
>
> Making the ascent in one's vocation or profession is far less like ladder climbing than mountain climbing, and here the analogy is a very real one. Going up a mountain requires a variety of skills, and includes a diversity of dangers, that are in no way involved in mounting a ladder.
>
> Young people starting out should be told this, both to dampen their expectations and to allay their disappointments. A mountain is rough and precipitous, with uncertain footing and a predictable number of falls and scrapes, and sometimes one has to take the long way around to reach the shortest distance.
>
> –Sydney J. Harris

Two Ways of Seeing a River

■ Mark Twain

Samuel L. Clemens (1835–1910), who wrote under the pen name of Mark Twain, was born in Florida, Missouri, and raised in Hannibal, Missouri. He wrote the novels Tom Sawyer *(1876),* The Prince and the Pauper *(1882),* Huckleberry Finn *(1884), and* A Connecticut Yankee in King Arthur's Court *(1889), as well as many other works of fiction and nonfiction. One of America's most popular writers, Twain is generally regarded as the most important practitioner of the realistic school of writing, a style that emphasizes observable details.*

The following passage is taken from Life on the Mississippi *(1883), Twain's study of the great river and his account of his early experiences learning to be a river steamboat pilot. As you read the passage, notice how Twain makes use of figurative language in describing two quite different ways of seeing the Mississippi River.*

Reflecting on What You Know

As we age and gain experience, our interpretation of the same memory—or how we view the same scene—can change. For example, the way that we view our own appearance changes all the time, and photos from our childhood or teenage years may surprise us in the decades that follow. Perhaps something we found amusing in our younger days may make us feel uncomfortable or embarrassed now, or the house we grew up in later seems smaller or less appealing. Write about a memory that has changed for you over the years. How does your interpretation of it now contrast with how you experienced it at the time?

Now when I had mastered the language of this water and had come to know every trifling feature that bordered the great river as familiarly as I knew the letters of the alphabet, I had made a valuable acquisition. But I had lost something, too. I had lost something which could never be restored to me while I lived. All the grace, the beauty, the poetry, had gone out of the majestic river! I still kept in mind a 1 certain wonderful sunset which I witnessed when steamboating was new to me. A broad expanse of the river was turned to blood; in the middle distance the red hue brightened into gold, through which a solitary log came floating, black and conspicuous; in one place a long, slanting mark lay sparkling upon the water; in another the surface was broken by boiling, tumbling rings that were as many-tinted as an opal;[1] where the ruddy flush was faintest was a smooth spot that was covered with graceful circles and radiating lines, ever so delicately traced; the shore on our left was densely wooded, and the somber shadow that fell from this forest was broken in one place by a long, ruffled trail that shone like silver; and high above the forest wall a clean-stemmed dead tree waved a single leafy bough that glowed like a flame in the unobstructed splendor that was flowing from the sun. There were graceful curves, reflected images, woody heights, soft distances, and over the whole scene, far and near, the dissolving lights drifted steadily, enriching it every passing moment with new marvels of coloring.

I stood like one bewitched. I drank it in, in a speechless rapture. The 2
world was new to me and I had never seen anything like this at home. But as I have said, a day came when I began to cease from noting the glories and the charms which the moon and the sun and the twilight wrought upon the river's face; another day came when I ceased altogether to note them. Then, if that sunset scene had been repeated, I should have looked upon it without rapture and should have commented upon it inwardly after this fashion: "This sun means that we are going to have wind tomorrow; that floating log means that the river is rising, small thanks to it; that slanting mark on the water refers to a bluff reef which is going to kill somebody's steamboat one of these nights, if it keeps on stretching out like that; those tumbling 'boils' show a dissolving bar and a changing channel there; the lines and circles in the slick water over yonder are a warning that that troublesome place is shoaling up dangerously; that silver streak in the shadow of the forest is the 'break' from a new snag and he has located himself in the very best place he could have found to fish for steamboats; that tall dead tree, with a single living branch, is not going to last long, and then how is a body ever going to get through this blind place at night without the friendly old landmark?"

No, the romance and beauty were all gone from the river. All the 3
value any feature of it had for me now was the amount of usefulness

[1]*opal:* a multicolored, iridescent gemstone.

it could furnish toward compassing the safe piloting of a steamboat. Since those days, I have pitied doctors from my heart. What does the lovely flush in a beauty's cheek mean to a doctor but a "break" that ripples above some deadly disease? Are not all her visible charms sown thick with what are to him the signs and symbols of hidden decay? Does he ever see her beauty at all, or doesn't he simply view her professionally and comment upon her unwholesome condition all to himself? And doesn't he sometimes wonder whether he has gained most or lost most by learning his trade?

Thinking Critically about This Reading

In the opening paragraph Twain exclaims, "All the grace, the beauty, the poetry, had gone out of the majestic river!" What is "the poetry," and why was it lost for him?

Questions for Study and Discussion

1. What method of organization does Twain use in this selection? (Glossary: *Organization*) What alternative methods might he have used? What would have been gained or lost?
2. Explain the analogy that Twain uses in paragraph 3. (Glossary: *Analogy*) What is his purpose in using this analogy?
3. Twain uses a number of similes and metaphors in this selection. (Glossary: *Figure of Speech*) Identify three of each, and explain what Twain is comparing in each case. What do these figures of speech add to Twain's writing?
4. Now that he has learned the trade of steamboating, does Twain feel he has "gained most or lost most" (3)? What has he gained, and what has he lost?
5. Twain points to a change of attitude he underwent as a result of seeing the river from a new perspective, that of a steamboat pilot. What role does knowledge play in Twain's inability to see the river as he once did?

Classroom Activity Using Comparison and Contrast

Compare two places that have the same purpose. For example, compare your college cafeteria with your dining room at home, or compare the classroom you are in now with another one on campus. Draw up a list of descriptive adjectives for each, and discuss them with your classmates. What do you like about each place? What do you dislike? What do you learn from comparing them? How important are your surroundings to you?

Suggested Writing Assignments

1. Twain's essay contrasts the perception of one person before and after acquiring a particular body of knowledge. Different people also usually perceive the same scene or event differently, even if they are experiencing it simultaneously. To use an example from Twain's writing, a poet and a doctor might perceive a rosy-cheeked young woman in entirely different ways. Write a comparison and contrast essay in which you show how two people with different experiences might perceive the same subject. It can be a case of profound difference (such as a musician and an electrician at the same pyrotechnic rock music concert) or more subtle (such as a novelist and a screenwriter seeing the same lovers' quarrel in a restaurant). Add a short postscript in which you explain your choice of subject-by-subject comparison or point-by-point comparison in your essay.
2. Learning how to drive a car may not be as involved as learning how to pilot a steamboat on the Mississippi River, but it has a tremendous impact on how we function and on how we perceive our surroundings. Write an essay about short trips you took as a passenger and as a driver. Compare and contrast your perceptions and actions. What is most important to you as a passenger? What is most important to you as a driver? How do your perceptions shift between the two roles? What changes in what you notice around you and in the way you notice it?
3. What perspective does the cartoon on page 483 give you on Twain's point about his different views of the Mississippi River? Is it possible for two people to have two completely different views of something? How might experience or perspective change how they view something? Write an essay modeled on Twain's in which you offer two different views of an event. You might consider a reporter's view compared with a victim's view, a teacher's view compared with a student's view, or a customer's view compared with a salesperson's view.

"By George, you're right! I thought there was something familiar about it."

Some Lessons from the Assembly Line

Andrew Braaksma

Andrew Braaksma was born in St. Joseph, Michigan, in 1985 and grew up in nearby Portage. He is a 2007 graduate of the University of Michigan with a major in history. While at Michigan, he was a writing tutor at the Sweetland Peer Tutoring Center and a coeditor of a satirical newspaper, the Every Three Weekly. *As he explains in his essay, he worked summers for a car manufacturer (Benteler Automotive Corporation) in Galesburg, Michigan. Currently, Braaksma is studying law at the University of Minnesota.*

Braaksma wrote "Some Lessons from the Assembly Line," which first appeared in the September 12, 2005, issue of Newsweek, *when he was a junior at Michigan. His essay was the winning entry in* Newsweek's *"back to school contest" that year. In contrasting his life as a factory worker with his life as a student, Braaksma comes away with a new appreciation for education.*

Reflecting on What You Know

Consider a summer job that you once had or a job that you now have while attending school. What do you think about the nature of the work you do at your job compared with the work you do as a student? What do you find fulfilling about your job and about your schoolwork?

Last June, as I stood behind the bright orange guard door of the machine, listening to the crackling hiss of the automatic welders, I thought about how different my life had been just a few weeks earlier. Then, I was writing an essay about French literature to complete my last exam of the spring semester at college. Now I stood in an automotive plant in southwest Michigan, making subassemblies for a car manufacturer. 1

I have worked as a temp in the factories surrounding my hometown every summer since I graduated from high school, but making the transition between school and full-time blue-collar work during the break 2 never gets any easier. For a student like me who considers any class before noon to be uncivilized, getting to a factory by six o'clock each morning, where rows of hulking, spark-showering machines have replaced the lush campus and cavernous lecture halls of college life, is torture. There my time is spent stamping, cutting, welding, moving or assembling parts, the rigid work schedules and quotas of the plant making days spent studying and watching *SportsCenter* seem like a million years ago.

I chose to do this work, rather than bus tables or fold sweatshirts 3
at the Gap, for the overtime pay and because living at home is infinitely cheaper than living on campus for the summer. My friends who take easier, part-time jobs never seem to understand why I'm so relieved to be back at school in the fall or that my summer vacation has been anything but a vacation.

There are few things as cocksure as a college student who has never 4
been out in the real world, and people my age always seem to overestimate the value of their time and knowledge. After a particularly exhausting string of twelve-hour days at a plastics factory, I remember being shocked at how small my check seemed. I couldn't believe how little I was taking home after all the hours I spent on the sweltering production floor. And all the classes in the world could not have prepared me for my battles with the machine I ran in the plant, which would jam whenever I absentmindedly put in a part backward or upside down.

As frustrating as the work can be, the most stressful thing about 5
blue-collar life is knowing your job could disappear overnight. Issues like downsizing and overseas relocation had always seemed distant to me until my coworkers at one factory told me that the unit I was working in would be shut down within six months and moved to Mexico, where people would work for sixty cents an hour.

Factory life has shown me what my future might have been like 6
had I never gone to college in the first place. For me, and probably many of my fellow students, higher education always seemed like a foregone conclusion: I never questioned if I was going to college, just where. No other options ever occurred to me.

After working twelve-hour shifts in a factory, the other options 7
have become brutally clear. When I'm back at the university, skipping classes and turning in lazy rewrites seems like a cop-out after seeing what I would be doing without school. All the advice and public-service announcements about the value of an education that used to sound trite now ring true.

These lessons I am learning, however valuable, are always tinged with a sense of guilt. Many people pass their lives in the places I briefly work, spending thirty years where I spend only two months at a time. When fall comes around, I get to go back to a sunny and beautiful campus, while work in the factories continues. At times I feel almost voyeuristic, like a tourist dropping in where other people make their livelihoods. My lessons about education are learned at the expense of those who weren't fortunate enough to receive one. "This job pays well, but it's hell on the body," said one coworker. "Study hard and keep reading," she added, nodding at the copy of Jack Kerouac's *On the Road* I had wedged into the space next to my machine so I could read discreetly when the line went down. 8

My experiences will stay with me long after I head back to school and spend my wages on books and beer. The things that factory work has taught me—how lucky I am to get an education, how to work hard, how easy it is to lose that work once you have it—are by no means earth-shattering. Everyone has to come to grips with them at some point. How and when I learned these lessons, however, has inspired me to make the most of my college years before I enter the real world for good. Until then, the summer months I spend in the factories will be long, tiring, and every bit as educational as a French-lit class. 9

Thinking Critically about This Reading

Is it really fair to compare doing full-time blue-collar work in the summer with being a college student? Would it be fairer to compare temporary summer work with full-time employment in one's chosen field? Explain.

Questions for Study and Discussion

1. Why did Braaksma choose to work summers in an automotive manufacturing plant? What were his other options?
2. In what ways is Braaksma's life as a blue-collar factory worker different from his life as a student?
3. What does the author mean when he says, "There are few things as cocksure as a college student who has never been out in the real world, and people my age always seem to overestimate the value of their time and knowledge" (paragraph 4)?

4. What does Braaksma see as the most stressful thing about "blue-collar life" (5)?
5. Braaksma admits that he sometimes feels "a sense of guilt" (8) when he reflects on his factory work. Where does this guilt come from?
6. In what ways does Braaksma consider his summer employment "every bit as educational as a French-lit class" (9)?

Classroom Activity Using Comparison and Contrast

Carefully read and analyze the following paragraph from Suzanne Britt's "That Lean and Hungry Look," an essay that first appeared in *Newsweek* and later became the basis for her book *Skinny People Are Dull and Crunchy Like Carrots* (1982). Then answer the questions that follow.

> Some people say the business about the jolly fat person is a myth, that all of us chubbies are neurotic, sick, sad people. I disagree. Fat people may not be chortling all day long, but they're a hell of a lot *nicer* than the wizened and shriveled. Thin people turn surly, mean, and hard at a young age because they never learn the value of a hot-fudge sundae for easing tension. Thin people don't like gooey soft things because they themselves are neither gooey nor soft. They are crunchy and dull, like carrots. They go straight to the heart of the matter while fat people let things stay all blurry and hazy and vague, the way things actually are. Thin people want to face the truth. Fat people know there is no truth. One of my thin friends is always staring at complex, unsolvable problems and saying, "The key thing is. . . ." Fat people never say that. They know there isn't any such thing as the key thing about anything.

What is the point of Britt's paragraph? How does she use comparison and contrast to make this point? How does Britt organize her paragraph?

Suggested Writing Assignments

1. Using Braaksma's essay as a model, write an essay in which you explore the lessons that you have learned from your temporary summer employment or part-time work during the school year. What do you look for in a summer or part-time job? Were the lessons that you learned something you expected from the job, or

did they come as a total surprise? You may find it helpful to review your response to the Reflecting on What You Know prompt for this selection before you begin to write.

2. Write an essay in which you compare and contrast a blue-collar summer job (such as a factory job like the one Braaksma had in an automotive factory, a fast-food restaurant job, or a sales job in a store) with another type of summer job (such as a counselor in a camp, an intern in an office, or a tutor for elementary or high school students). What did you find more interesting—the similarities or the differences between your two jobs? What life lessons does each job offer? What are the advantages and disadvantages of each?

Grant and Lee: A Study in Contrasts

■ Bruce Catton

Bruce Catton (1899–1978) was born in Petoskey, Michigan, and attended Oberlin College. Early in his career, Catton worked as a reporter for various newspapers, among them the Cleveland Plain Dealer. *Having an interest in history, Catton became a leading authority on the Civil War and published a number of books on this subject, including* Mr. Lincoln's Army *(1951),* Glory Road *(1952),* A Stillness at Appomattox *(1953),* The Hallowed Ground *(1956),* The Coming Fury *(1961),* Never Call Retreat *(1966), and* Gettysburg: The Final Fury *(1974). Catton was awarded both the Pulitzer Prize and the National Book Award in 1954.*

The following selection was included in The American Story: The Age of Exploration to the Age of the Atom *(1956), a collection of historical essays edited by Earl Schenk Miers. In it, Catton considers "two great Americans, Grant and Lee—very different, yet under everything very much alike." As you read, pay attention to how Catton organizes his essay of comparison and contrast and how this organization helps readers follow Catton's thinking.*

Reflecting on What You Know

Do a brief freewrite about the Civil War generals Ulysses S. Grant and Robert E. Lee. What do you know about each man and his role in the war? What images do you have, and what stories have you heard about each one?

When Ulysses S. Grant[1] and Robert E. Lee[2] met in the parlor of a modest house at Appomattox Court House, Virginia, on April 9, 1865, to work out the terms for the surrender of Lee's Army of Northern 1

[1]*Ulysses S. Grant* (1822–1885): commander of the armies of the United States of America (the Union armies) during the late years (1864–1865) of the American Civil War and eighteenth president of the United States (1869–1877).

[2]*Robert E. Lee* (1807–1870): commander of the Army of Northern Virginia, the most successful of the armies of the Confederate States of America (the Confederacy) during the American Civil War (1861–1865).

Virginia, a great chapter in American life came to a close, and a great new chapter began.

These men were bringing the Civil War to its virtual finish. To be sure, other armies had yet to surrender, and for a few days the fugitive Confederate government[3] would struggle desperately and vainly, trying to find some way to go on living now that its chief support was gone. But in effect it was all over when Grant and Lee signed the papers. And the little room where they wrote out the terms was the scene of one of the poignant,[4] dramatic contrasts in American history. 2

They were two strong men, these oddly different generals, and they represented the strengths of two conflicting currents that, through them, had come into final collision. 3

Back of Robert E. Lee was the notion that the old aristocratic concept might somehow survive and be dominant in American life. 4

Lee was tidewater Virginia, and in his background were family, culture, and tradition . . . the age of chivalry[5] transplanted to a New World which was making its own legends and its own myths. He embodied a way of life that had come down through the age of knighthood and the English country squire. America was a land that was beginning all over again, dedicated to nothing much more complicated than the rather hazy belief that all men had equal rights and should have an equal chance in the world. In such a land Lee stood for the feeling that it was somehow of advantage to human society to have a pronounced inequality in the social structure. There should be a leisure class, backed by ownership of land; in turn, society itself should be keyed to the land as the chief source of wealth and influence. It would bring forth (according to this ideal) a class of men with a strong sense of obligation to the community; men who lived not to gain advantage for themselves, but to meet the solemn obligations which had been laid on them by the very fact that they were privileged. From them the country would get its leadership; to them it could look for the higher values—of thought, of conduct, of personal deportment—to give it strength and virtue. 5

Lee embodied the noblest elements of this aristocratic ideal. Through him, the landed nobility justified itself. For four years, the 6

[3]*Confederate government:* the Confederate States of America, which was the government of eleven Southern states that seceded from the Union during the Civil War.

[4]*poignant:* touching; emotional.

[5]*chivalry:* values of courtesy, valor, and civility that are associated with medieval knights.

Southern states had fought a desperate war to uphold the ideals for which Lee stood. In the end, it almost seemed as if the Confederacy fought for Lee; as if he himself was the Confederacy . . . the best thing that the way of life for which the Confederacy stood could ever have to offer. He had passed into legend before Appomattox.[6] Thousands of tired, underfed, poorly clothed Confederate soldiers, long since past the simple enthusiasm of the early days of the struggle, somehow considered Lee the symbol of everything for which they had been willing to die. But they could not quite put this feeling into words. If the Lost Cause, sanctified by so much heroism and so many deaths, had a living justification, its justification was General Lee.

Grant, the son of a tanner on the Western frontier, was everything Lee was not. He had come up the hard way and embodied nothing in particular except the eternal toughness and sinewy[7] fiber of the men who grew up beyond the mountains. He was one of a body of men who owed reverence and obeisance[8] to no one, who were self-reliant to a fault, who cared hardly anything for the past but who had a sharp eye for the future. 7

These frontier men were the precise opposite of the tidewater aristocrats. Back of them, in the great surge that had taken people over the Alleghenies and into the opening Western country, there was a deep, implicit dissatisfaction with a past that had settled into grooves. They stood for democracy, not from any reasoned conclusion about the proper ordering of human society, but simply because they had grown up in the middle of democracy and knew how it worked. Their society might have privileges, but they would be privileges each man had won for himself. Forms and patterns meant nothing. No man was born to anything, except perhaps to a chance to show how far he could rise. Life was competition. 8

Yet along with this feeling had come a deep sense of belonging to a national community. The Westerner who developed a farm, opened a shop, or set up in business as a trader, could hope to prosper only as his own community prospered—and his community ran from the Atlantic to the Pacific and from Canada down to Mexico. If the land was settled, with towns and highways and accessible markets, he could better 9

[6]*Appomattox:* a town in Virginia, site of the courthouse where the Confederate forces surrendered on April 9, 1865.

[7]*sinewy:* strong; tough.

[8]*obeisance:* deference; homage.

himself. He saw his fate in terms of the nation's own destiny. As its horizons expanded, so did his. He had, in other words, an acute dollars-and-cents stake in the continued growth and development of his country.

10 And that, perhaps, is where the contrast between Grant and Lee becomes most striking. The Virginia aristocrat, inevitably, saw himself in relation to his own region. He lived in a static society which could endure almost anything except change. Instinctively, his first loyalty would go to the locality in which that society existed. He would fight to the limit of endurance to defend it, because in defending it he was defending everything that gave his own life its deepest meaning.

11 The Westerner, on the other hand, would fight with an equal tenacity[9] for the broader concept of society. He fought so because everything he lived by was tied to growth, expansion, and a constantly widening horizon. What he lived by would survive or fall with the nation itself. He could not possibly stand by unmoved in the face of an attempt to destroy the Union.[10] He would combat it with everything he had, because he could only see it as an effort to cut the ground out from under his feet.

12 So Grant and Lee were in complete contrast, representing two diametrically opposed elements in American life. Grant was the modern man emerging; beyond him, ready to come on the stage, was the great age of steel and machinery, of crowded cities and a restless burgeoning vitality. Lee might have ridden down from the old age of chivalry, lance in hand, silken banner fluttering over his head. Each man was the perfect champion of his cause, drawing both his strengths and his weaknesses from the people he led.

13 Yet it was not all contrast, after all. Different as they were—in background, in personality, in underlying aspiration—these two great soldiers had much in common. Under everything else, they were marvelous fighters. Furthermore, their fighting qualities were really very much alike.

14 Each man had, to begin with, the great virtue of utter tenacity and fidelity. Grant fought his way down the Mississippi Valley in spite of acute personal discouragement and profound military handicaps. Lee hung on in the trenches at Petersburg after hope itself had died. In each man there was an indomitable quality . . . the born fighter's refusal to give up as long as he can still remain on his feet and lift his two fists.

15 Daring and resourcefulness they had, too; the ability to think faster and move faster than the enemy. These were the qualities which gave

[9]*tenacity:* persistence; stubbornness.
[10]*Union:* the federal government of the United States.

Lee the dazzling campaigns of Second Manassas and Chancellorsville and won Vicksburg[11] for Grant.

Lastly, and perhaps greatest of all, there was the ability, at the end, to turn quickly from war to peace once the fighting was over. Out of the way these two men behaved at Appomattox came the possibility of a peace of reconciliation. It was a possibility not wholly realized, in the years to come, but which did, in the end, help the two sections to become one nation again . . . after a war whose bitterness might have seemed to make such a reunion wholly impossible. No part of either man's life became him more than the part he played in their brief meeting in the McLean house[12] at Appomattox. Their behavior there put all succeeding generations of Americans in their debt. Two great Americans, Grant and Lee—very different, yet under everything very much alike. Their encounter at Appomattox was one of the great moments of American history. 16

Thinking Critically about This Reading

What do you think Catton means when he claims that Grant was "the modern man emerging" (paragraph 12)? How does he support this statement?

Questions for Study and Discussion

1. In paragraphs 10–12, Catton discusses what he considers to be the most striking contrast between Grant and Lee. What is that difference?
2. List the similarities that Catton sees between Grant and Lee. What similarity does Catton believe is most important? Why?
3. What would have been lost had Catton compared Grant and Lee before contrasting them? Would anything have been gained?
4. How does Catton organize the body of his essay—paragraphs 3–16? (Glossary: *Organization*) You may find it helpful in answering this question to summarize the point of comparison in each paragraph and label it as being concerned with Lee, Grant, or both.

---

[11]*Second Manassas, Chancellorsville, Vicksburg:* significant battles during the American Civil War.

[12]*McLean house:* the building of the Appomattox Court House in which Lee formally surrendered to Grant.

5. What attitudes and ideas does Catton describe to support the view that tidewater Virginia was a throwback to the "age of chivalry" (5)? (Glossary: *Attitude*)
6. Catton constructs clear transitions between paragraphs. (Glossary: *Transition*) Identify the transitional devices he uses. How do they help you read the essay?

Classroom Activity Using Comparison and Contrast

In preparation for writing an essay of comparison and contrast on two world leaders (or popular singers, actors, or sports figures), write out answers to the following questions:

Who could I compare and contrast?
What is my purpose?
Are their similarities or differences more interesting?
What specific points should I discuss?
What organizational pattern will best suit my purpose: subject-by-subject or point-by-point?

Suggested Writing Assignments

1. Using your answers to the Classroom Activity (above) as your starting point, write an essay in which you compare and contrast any two world leaders (or popular singers, actors, or sports figures).
2. Select one of the following topics, and write an essay of comparison and contrast:

two cities	two sections of the town you live in
two friends	two books by the same author
two cars	two ways to heat a home
two restaurants	two teachers
two mountains	two brands of pizza

Fahrenheit 59: What a Child's Fever Might Tell Us about Climate Change

■ Audrey Schulman

Novelist Audrey Schulman was born in Montreal, Quebec, Canada, in 1963. She attended Sarah Lawrence College from 1981 to 1983 and graduated from Barnard College in 1985. Schulman has worked as a scriptwriter, a computer consultant, and an Internet Web site designer while developing her skills as a writer. In her first novel, The Cage *(1995), Schulman tells the story of a young female photographer who is sent to the wilds of northern Canada to study polar bears. She followed this with* Swimming with Jonah *(1999) and* A House Named Brazil *(2000). Her articles on global climate change and severe climatic events have appeared in* E Magazine, Conservation Matters, Ms., *and* Grist.

In "Fahrenheit 59," first published in the January–February 2007 issue of Orion *magazine, Schulman explores the inner workings of climate change. As you read, pay attention to how she uses a vivid analogy (her son's body and its ability to deal with temperature changes and illness) to explain how the earth deals with the complexities of climate change.*

Reflecting on What You Know

How concerned are you about climate changes or global warming? What, if anything, do you think needs to be done? Have you personally made any lifestyle changes as a result of your concerns? If so, describe what you have done.

Yesterday afternoon, my six-year-old son practiced swimming with me. Delighted with the water and my attention, Corey stayed in for forty minutes. Despite the water's chill, I knew if I took his temperature it would be close to 98.6° Fahrenheit. For an hour afterward he ran through the humid July heat, playing tag with his cousins, his hair damp with sweat. Still, a reading would have shown his body to be within a degree or two of 98.6°. 1

This stability is a product of homeostasis. A holy word for biologists, *homeostasis* refers to an organism's ability to maintain its ideal temperature and chemistry. 2

Each species has its own preferred level of warmth, but among most mammals the possible range is surprisingly narrow, generally between 97° and 103°F. Each body's temperature works to optimize the function of its enzymes, which are critical to its every chemical interaction. Too cold, and these catalysts slow down. Too hot, and they break down entirely. 3

Such homeostatic regulation depends on a mechanism known as negative feedback: a response that maintains a system's balance. Yesterday, for example, when Corey ran in the hot sun, his cheeks got rosy as more blood moved to the surface, maximizing heat loss off his skin. No, his body said to his increasing temperature. 4

It turns out that our bodies' homeostasis can provide an analogy with which to understand the complexities of climate change—and the human response to it. Over geological time, the biosphere uses negative feedbacks in a way that maintains a stable global average temperature. When the earth's oceans heat up past a certain point, for example, hurricanes (which thrive only on warm water) increase their intensity, leaving a trail of stirred-up nutrients. The food creates a massive bloom of phytoplankton, which suck in enough of the greenhouse gas carbon dioxide to start cooling the global climate. 5

Conversely, when temperatures fall too low, vast quantities of methane are released into the atmosphere, possibly in part because ice sheets build up, lowering sea levels and exposing coastal methane hydrates. As a greenhouse gas twenty times more powerful than carbon dioxide, the methane warms the biosphere quickly. 6

Through a large array of negative feedbacks like these, the biosphere has managed to maintain a relatively stable temperature, despite massive volcanic eruptions of greenhouse gasses and orbital and solar irregularities. To earth-based organisms, the fluctuations may have seemed severe, allowing ice sheets to roll in or crocodiles to paddle across the Arctic. But through its self-corrections, the biosphere has remained habitable. 7

According to New York University biology professor Tyler Volk, the sun's temperature has increased 30 percent over the course of earth's history, which would have increased temperatures about one hundred degrees were it not for the cooling effect of phytoplankton and other life. And scientists calculate that the earth would be a frigid 8 fifty to sixty degrees colder without any greenhouse gases. Over the last million years, the biosphere has remained within about eighteen degrees of 59°F.

Humanity's intemperate carbon emissions, however, have severely tested these negative feedbacks. Since 1900 alone, the earth has warmed more than a full degree—one-fifth the entire temperature range over the past ten thousand years. The earth is now within two degrees of its warmest levels in one million years. 9

The increased heat dries up the soil faster and pumps water vapor into the clouds, exaggerating the severity of drought, then rain. Gentle summer days turn into baking onslaughts, temperate-zone drizzles become tropical monsoons, tropical diseases and pests have whole new latitudes to conquer, and temperate-zone animals and plants are fleeing toward the poles. The increased heat has also warmed the oceans, causing hurricanes to grow in intensity. 10

And when a situation becomes extreme enough, biological systems can abandon their attempts at moderation. Corey crawled into bed with me in the middle of last night, saying his head hurt. His hands and face felt hot. Touching his ribs I could feel his heart racing. Ill with the flu, his body no longer fought to maintain its normal temperature. Instead it was using positive feedbacks, reactions that amplify a change, to create a fever. Holding him close in bed, I could feel his muscles violently shivering, creating heat and more heat. Within an hour of the first symptoms, his temperature was 102°. 11

Positive feedbacks can also shift the earth's climate quickly, with the kind of results seen in the latest global warming news. As ice sheets melt near the poles, for example, the water slips through the crevasses to the rock below. At some point the water pools up enough to raise the glacier just a fraction, greasing its slide into the ocean. James Hansen of the Goddard Institute, whose science has been uncannily accurate since he alerted Congress in 1988 to signs of human-induced climate change, points out that this phenomenon can cause millennia-old ice sheets to disappear with an explosive splash. At that point, white ice no longer reflects sunlight into space. Instead, dark water draws the sunlight in as heat, accelerating the rise in the earth's temperature. Yes, the water says, yes. 12

The thaw of the Siberian permafrost may provide another example of a positive feedback. Roughly 400,000 megatons of dead plant matter that has never finished decaying because it has been frozen, the permafrost is now thawing more rapidly than expected, according to 13 recent reports. Because all this plant flesh is wet—under snow that's now melting—the decay is engineered by anaerobic bacteria, which metabolize the plants straight into methane, that muscular greenhouse gas. Once truly underway, this release of methane would dwarf any effect humans have on climate change. There'd be no more discussion of Energy Star appliances or raising the emission standards of cars. The rising temperatures would effectively no longer be powered by us, or subject to our influences. The system would take over.

As medical researchers have discovered in the past decade, our bodies give us fevers for a specific reason: certain antibodies and other infection-fighting agents function optimally at 100°F or higher. When Corey's body detected the presence of overly aggressive microbes, it turned its thermostat up high. His hypothalamus made his muscles shiver, minimized the blood flow to his skin, conserved heat in his gut. For a little while, his body could withstand a high temperature while the immune system brought out its heavy artillery. Overall this strategy tends to work well: Corey slept straight through the day, and, late in the afternoon, he sat up, skinnier and ferociously thirsty, but healthy again. Research shows, however, that while the feverish response may preserve the human organism as a whole, some of the immune system's agents have side effects: their activity can kill many "innocent" nonaggressive cells. 14

We should take note. It may seem a poetic stretch to say the earth itself ever sickens or has a fever. Seen from a distance, the earth itself does not become more or less "healthy"—just more or less populated with life. But as seen from the ground, the view is rather different. If our planet's feedback systems switch over from negative to positive and the biosphere heats up fast, the earth will certainly seem feverishly ill to a number of species, many of which will not survive. 15

In terms of our planetary climate, it's easy to guess which species is playing the role of overly aggressive microbe. But we do have a choice. Some human cultures, through their agriculture and hunting, have respected and adapted to ecological limits. We have the ability to shape our destiny—to be microbial attackers, or humble cells inside a living body. 16

Thinking Critically about This Reading

In her final paragraph Schulman says that "it's easy to guess which species is playing the role of the overly aggressive microbe." In terms of her analogy, in what ways can human beings be considered "overly aggressive microbes"? Does this analogy help you understand what is happening to our planetary climate? Explain.

Questions for Study and Discussion

1. Schulman opens her essay with a description of her son Corey swimming for forty minutes and later running about for an hour with cousins in the July heat. What point about the human body does she make here?
2. What is homeostasis? How does it work in humans? Why is it an important concept to understand?
3. What is negative feedback? How does the author use her son Corey to explain this concept?
4. According to Schulman, how has the biosphere used negative feedbacks to maintain a relatively constant temperature over time?
5. Schulman states that "the earth is now within two degrees of its warmest levels in one million years" (9). What happens when the earth gets warmer? Why does the earth react in this way?
6. How does Schulman use her son's fever to explain what is happening with the earth's climate today? Does her analogy help you to understand climate change? Explain.

Classroom Activity Using Comparison and Contrast

After reviewing the discussion of analogy in the introduction to this chapter (pp. 477–78) and Schulman's analogy in this essay, create an analogy to explain one of the following:

your relationship with one of your parents or with a relative

the essence of a game that you enjoy

a scientific principle or idea

an activity such as writing, painting, or composing music

Share your analogies with other members of your class, and discuss how well they work.

Suggested Writing Assignments

1. Write an essay in which you develop one of the analogies that you created for the Classroom Activity for this selection (above). Or use Schulman's essay as a model to create an analogy to explain a complex idea or concept.

2. Schulman concludes that "Some human cultures, through their agriculture and hunting, have respected and adapted to ecological limits. We have the ability to shape our destiny—to be microbial attackers, or humble cells inside a living body" (16). Which choice do you think Schulman recommends? Write an essay in which you propose measures that could be taken on your college campus to make it more climate-friendly. What energy-saving measures are already being taken? What can be done to control carbon dioxide emissions? What measures do you think would have the greatest effect? You may find it helpful to review your response to the Reflecting on What You Know prompt for this selection before you start writing.

chapter **20**

Cause and Effect

Every time you answer a question that asks *why,* you engage in the process of *causal analysis*—that is, you try to determine a *cause* or series of causes for a particular *effect.* When you answer a question that asks *what if,* you try to determine what *effect* will result from a particular *cause.* You will have many opportunities to use **cause-and-effect analysis** in the writing you will do in college. For example, in history you might be asked to determine the causes for the 1991 breakup of the former Soviet Union; in political science you might be asked to determine the critical issues in the 2008 presidential election; in sociology you might be asked to analyze the effects that the AIDS epidemic has had on sexual-behavior patterns among Americans; and in economics you might be asked to predict what will happen to our country if we enact large tax cuts.

Fascinated by the effects that private real estate development was having on his neighborhood, a student writer decided to find out what was happening in the older sections of cities across the country. In his first paragraph, Kevin Cunningham describes three possible effects (or fates) of a city's aging. In his second paragraph, he singles out one effect, redevelopment, and discusses in detail the impact it has had on Hoboken, New Jersey.

Effect: decay

Effect: urban renewal

Effect: redevelopment

Effects of redevelopment

One of three fates awaits the aging neighborhood. Decay may continue until the neighborhood becomes a slum. It may face urban renewal, with old buildings being razed and ugly new apartment houses taking their place. Or it may undergo redevelopment, in which government encourages the upgrading of existing housing stock by offering low-interest loans or outright grants; thus, the original character of the neighborhood may be retained or restored, allowing the city to keep part of its identity.

> An example of redevelopment at its best is Hoboken, New Jersey. In the early 1970s Hoboken was a dying city, with rundown housing and many abandoned buildings. However, low-interest loans enabled some younger residents to refurbish their homes, and soon the area began to show signs of renewed vigor. Even outsiders moved in and rebuilt some of the abandoned houses. Today, whole blocks have been restored, and neighborhood life is active again. The city does well, too, because property values are higher and so are property taxes.
>
> –Kevin Cunningham, student

Determining causes and effects is usually a complex process. One reason for this is that *immediate causes* are readily apparent (because they are closest to the effect) and *ultimate causes* are not as apparent (because they are somewhat removed and even hidden). Furthermore, ultimate causes may bring about effects that themselves become immediate causes, thus creating a *causal chain*. Consider the following causal chain: Sally, a computer salesperson, prepared extensively for a meeting with an important client (ultimate cause), impressed the client (immediate cause), and made a very large sale (effect). The chain did not stop there: the large sale caused her to be promoted by her employer (effect). For a detailed example of a causal chain, read Barry Commoner's analysis of the near disaster at the Three Mile Island nuclear facility in Chapter 5 (pp. 115–16).

A second reason causal analysis can be complex is that an effect may have several possible or actual causes and a cause may have several possible or actual effects. An upset stomach may be caused by eating spoiled food, but it may also be caused by overeating, flu, allergy, nervousness, pregnancy, or any combination of factors. Similarly, the high cost of electricity may have multiple effects—higher profits for utility companies, fewer sales of electrical appliances, higher prices for other products, and the development of alternative sources of energy.

Sound reasoning and logic are present in all good writing, but they are central to any causal analysis. Writers of believable causal analysis examine their material objectively and develop their essays carefully. They examine methodically all causes and effects and evaluate them. They are convinced by their own examination of the material but are not afraid to admit that other causes and effects might exist.

Above all, they do not let their own prejudices interfere with the logic of their analyses and presentations.

Because people are accustomed to thinking of causes with their effects, they sometimes commit an error in logic known as the "after this, therefore because of this" fallacy (in Latin, *post hoc, ergo propter hoc*). This **logical fallacy** leads people to believe that one event somehow caused a second event, just because the second event followed the first—that is, they sometimes make causal connections that are not proven. For example, if students perform better after a free breakfast program is instituted at their school, one cannot assume that the improvement was caused by the breakfast program. There could be any number of other causes for this effect, and a responsible writer would analyze and consider them all before suggesting the cause.

Why We Crave Horror Movies

■ **Stephen King**

Stephen King's name is synonymous with horror stories. Born in 1947, King is a 1970 graduate of the University of Maine. He worked as a janitor in a knitting mill, a laundry worker, and a high school English teacher before he struck it big with his writing. Many consider King to be the most successful writer of modern horror fiction today. To date, he has written dozens of novels, collections of short stories and novellas, and screenplays, among other works. His books have sold well over 250 million copies worldwide, and many of his novels have been made into popular motion pictures, including Stand by Me, Misery, The Green Mile, *and* Dreamcatcher. *His books, starting with* Carrie *in 1974, include* Salem's Lot *(1975),* The Shining *(1977),* The Dead Zone *(1979),* Christine *(1983),* Pet Sematary *(1983),* The Dark Half *(1989),* The Girl Who Loved Tom Gordon *(1999),* From a Buick 8 *(2002),* The Colorado Kid *(2005),* Cell *(2006),* Lisey's Story *(2006),* Duma Key *(2008), and* Everything's Eventual: Five Dark Tales *(2002), a collection of short stories. Other works of his include* Danse Macabre *(1980), a nonfiction look at horror in the media, and* On Writing: A Memoir of the Craft *(2000). The widespread popularity of horror books and films attests to the fact that many people share King's fascination with the macabre.*

In the following selection, originally published in Playboy *in 1982, a variation on "The Horror Movie as Junk Food" chapter in* Danse Macabre, *King analyzes the reasons we flock to good horror movies.*

Reflecting on What You Know

What movies have you seen recently? Do you prefer watching any particular kind of movie—comedy, drama, science fiction, or horror, for example—more than others? How do you explain your preference?

I think that we're all mentally ill; those of us outside the asylums only hide it a little better—and maybe not all that much better, after all. 1

We've all known people who talk to themselves, people who sometimes squinch their faces into horrible grimaces when they believe no one is watching, people who have some hysterical fear—of snakes, the dark, the tight place, the long drop . . . and, of course, those final worms and grubs that are waiting so patiently underground.

When we pay our four or five bucks and seat ourselves at tenth-row center in a theater showing a horror movie, we are daring the nightmare. 2

Why? Some of the reasons are simple and obvious. To show that we can, that we are not afraid, that we can ride this roller coaster. Which is not to say that a really good horror movie may not surprise a scream out of us at some point, the way we may scream when a roller coaster twists through a complete 360 or plows through a lake at the bottom of the drop. And horror movies, like roller coasters, have always been the special province of the young; by the time one turns forty or fifty, one's appetite for double twists or 360-degree loops may be considerably depleted. 3

We also go to reestablish our feelings of essential normality; the horror movie is innately conservative, even reactionary. Freda Jackson as the horrible melting woman in *Die, Monster, Die!* confirms for us that no matter how far we may be removed from the beauty of a Robert Redford or a Diana Ross, we are still light-years from true ugliness. 4

And we go to have fun. 5

Ah, but this is where the ground starts to slope away, isn't it? Because this is a very peculiar sort of fun, indeed. The fun comes from seeing others menaced—sometimes killed. One critic has suggested that if pro football has become the voyeur's[1] version of combat, then the horror film has become the modern version of the public lynching. 6

It is true that the mythic, "fairy-tale" horror film intends to take away the shades of gray. . . . It urges us to put away our more civilized and adult penchant for analysis and to become children again, seeing things in pure blacks and whites. It may be that horror movies provide psychic relief on this level because this invitation to lapse into simplicity, irrationality, and even outright madness is extended so rarely. We are told we may allow our emotions a free rein . . . or no rein at all. 7

[1] *voyeur:* one who observes from a distance.

If we are all insane, then sanity becomes a matter of degree. If your insanity leads you to carve up women like Jack the Ripper or the Cleveland Torso Murderer,[2] we clap you away in the funny farm (but neither of those two amateur-night surgeons was ever caught, heh-heh-heh); if, on the other hand, your insanity leads you only to talk to yourself when you're under stress or to pick your nose on your morning bus, then you are left alone to go about your business . . . though it is doubtful that you will ever be invited to the best parties. 8

The potential lyncher is in almost all of us (excluding saints, past and present; but then, most saints have been crazy in their own ways), and every now and then, he has to be let loose to scream and roll around in the grass. Our emotions and our fears form their own body, and we recognize that it demands its own exercise to maintain proper muscle tone. Certain of these emotional muscles are accepted—even exalted—in civilized society; they are, of course, the emotions that tend to maintain the status quo of civilization itself. Love, friendship, loyalty, kindness—these are all the emotions that we applaud, emotions that have been immortalized in the couplets of Hallmark cards and in the verses (I don't dare call it poetry) of Leonard Nimoy.[3] 9

When we exhibit these emotions, society showers us with positive reinforcement; we learn this even before we get out of diapers. When, as children, we hug our rotten little puke of a sister and give her a kiss, all the aunts and uncles smile and twit and cry, "Isn't he the sweetest little thing?" Such coveted treats as chocolate-covered graham crackers often follow. But if we deliberately slam the rotten little puke of a sister's fingers in the door, sanctions follow—angry remonstrance from parents, aunts, and uncles; instead of a chocolate-covered graham cracker, a spanking. 10

But anticivilization emotions don't go away, and they demand periodic exercise. We have such "sick" jokes as, "What's the difference between a truckload of bowling balls and a truckload of dead babies?" (You can't unload a truckload of bowling balls with a pitchfork . . . a joke, by the way, that I heard originally from a ten-year-old.) Such a joke may surprise a laugh or a grin out of us even as we recoil, a possibility that confirms the thesis: if we share a brotherhood of 11

---

[2]*Jack the Ripper or the Cleveland Torso Murderer:* serial murderers who were active in the 1880s and the 1930s, respectively.

[3]*Leonard Nimoy* (b. 1931): an actor famous for playing Mr. Spock on the U.S. television series *Star Trek,* which aired in 1966–1969.

man, then we also share an insanity of man. None of which is intended as a defense of either the sick joke or insanity but merely as an explanation of why the best horror films, like the best fairy tales, manage to be reactionary, anarchistic,[4] and revolutionary all at the same time.

The mythic horror movie, like the sick joke, has a dirty job to do. It deliberately appeals to all that is worst in us. It is morbidity unchained, our most base instincts let free, our nastiest fantasies realized . . . and it all happens, fittingly enough, in the dark. For those reasons, good liberals often shy away from horror films. For myself, I like to see the most aggressive of them—*Dawn of the Dead,* for instance—as lifting a trap door in the civilized forebrain and throwing a basket of raw meat to the hungry alligators swimming around in that subterranean river beneath. 12

Why bother? Because it keeps them from getting out, man. It keeps them down there and me up here. It was Lennon and McCartney who said that all you need is love, and I would agree with that. 13

As long as you keep the gators fed. 14

Thinking Critically about This Reading

What does King mean when he states that "the horror movie is innately conservative, even reactionary" (paragraph 4)?

Questions for Study and Discussion

1. What, according to King, causes people to crave horror movies? What other reasons can you add to King's list?
2. Identify the analogy King uses in paragraph 3, and explain how it works. (Glossary: *Analogy*)
3. What emotions does society applaud? Why? Which ones does King label "anticivilization emotions" (11)?
4. In what ways is a horror movie like a sick joke? What is the "dirty job" or effect that the two have in common (12)?
5. King starts his essay with the attention-grabbing sentence, "I think that we're all mentally ill." How does he develop this idea of

[4]*anarchistic:* against any authority; anarchy.

insanity in his essay? What does King mean when he says, "The potential lyncher is in almost all of us" (9)? How does King's last line relate to the theme of mental illness?

6. What is King's tone? (Glossary: *Tone*) Point to particular words or sentences that lead you to this conclusion.

Classroom Activity Using Cause and Effect

Use the following test, developed by William V. Haney, to determine your ability to analyze accurately evidence that is presented to you. After completing Haney's test, discuss your answers with other members of your class.

THE UNCRITICAL INFERENCE TEST

Directions

1. You will read a brief story. Assume that all of the information presented in the story is definitely accurate and true. Read the story carefully. You may refer back to the story whenever you wish.
2. You will then read statements about the story. Answer them in numerical order. *Do not go back* to fill in answers or to change answers. This will only distort your test score.
3. After you read each statement carefully, determine whether the statement is:
   a. "T"—meaning: On the basis of the information presented in the story the statement is *definitely true.*
   b. "F"—meaning: On the basis of the information presented in the story the statement is *definitely false.*
   c. "?"—The statement *may* be true (or false) but on the basis of the information presented in the story you cannot be definitely certain. (If any part of the statement is doubtful, mark the statement "?".)
4. Indicate your answer by circling either "T" or "F" or "?" opposite the statement.

The Story

Babe Smith has been killed. Police have rounded up six suspects, all of whom are known gangsters. All of them are known to have been near the scene of the killing at the approximate time that it occurred. All had substantial motives for wanting Smith killed. However, one of these suspected gangsters, Slinky Sam, has positively been cleared of guilt.

Statements about the Story

1. Slinky Sam is known to have been near the scene of the killing of Babe Smith.	T	F	?
2. All six of the rounded-up gangsters were known to have been near the scene of the murder.	T	F	?
3. Only Slinky Sam has been cleared of guilt.	T	F	?
4. All six of the rounded-up suspects were near the scene of Smith's killing at the approximate time that it took place.	T	F	?
5. The police do not know who killed Smith.	T	F	?
6. All six suspects are known to have been near the scene of the foul deed.	T	F	?
7. Smith's murderer did not confess of his own free will.	T	F	?
8. Slinky Sam was not cleared of guilt.	T	F	?
9. It is known that the six suspects were in the vicinity of the cold-blooded assassination.	T	F	?

Suggested Writing Assignments

1. Write an essay in which you analyze, in light of King's remarks about the causes of our cravings for horror movies, a horror movie you've seen. In what ways did the movie satisfy your "anticivilization emotions" (11)? How did you feel before going to the theater? How did you feel when leaving?
2. Write an essay in which you analyze the most significant reasons or causes for your going to college. You may wish to discuss such matters as your high school experiences, people and events that influenced your decision, and your goals in college as well as in later life.
3. In the film still on page 510 from Alfred Hitchcock's 1960 thriller *Psycho*, Marion Crane (Janet Leigh) screams in terror as Norman Bates (Anthony Perkins) opens the shower curtain and she realizes he is about to kill her with a large kitchen knife. For many viewers, this scene is iconographic—an unforgettable symbol of the essence of terror. For many others, different scenes of terror, actual or artistically represented, have become similarly powerful. Write an essay examining a situation or scene that terrifies you and examining the causes of your fright.

Why and When We Speak Spanish in Public

Myriam Marquez

An award-winning columnist for the Orlando Sentinel, *Myriam Marquez was born in Havana, Cuba, in 1954 and grew up in South Florida. After graduating from the University of Maryland in 1983 with a degree in journalism and a minor in political science, she worked for United Press International in Washington, D.C., and in Maryland, covering the Maryland legislature as statehouse bureau chief. Marquez joined the editorial board of the* Sentinel *in 1987 and, since 1990, has been writing three weekly columns. Her commentaries focus on state and national politics, the human condition, civil liberties, and issues important to women and Hispanics. The Florida Society of Newspaper Editors awarded her its highest award for commentary in 2003.*

Marquez grew up bilingual and recognizes that English is the "common language" in America but knows that being American has little if anything to do with what language one speaks. In this article, which first appeared in the Orlando Sentinel *on July 5, 1999, Marquez explains why she and her parents continue to speak Spanish when they are together, even though they have lived in the United States for forty years.*

Reflecting on What You Know

When you are in public and hear people around you speaking a foreign language, what is your immediate reaction? Are you intrigued? Do you feel uncomfortable? How do you regard people who speak a language other than English in public? Why?

When I'm shopping with my mother or standing in line with my stepdad to order fast food or anywhere else we might be together, we're going to speak to one another in Spanish. 1

That may appear rude to those who don't understand Spanish and overhear us in public places. 2

Those around us may get the impression that we're talking about them. They may wonder why we would insist on speaking in a foreign tongue, especially if they knew that my family has lived in the United States for forty years and that my parents do understand English and speak it, albeit with difficulty and a heavy accent. 3

Let me explain why we haven't adopted English as our official family language. For me and most of the bilingual people I know, it's a matter of respect for our parents and comfort in our cultural roots. 4

It's not meant to be rude to others. It's not meant to alienate anyone or to Balkanize[1] America. 5

It's certainly not meant to be un-American—what constitutes an "American" being defined by English speakers from North America. 6

Being an American has very little to do with what language we use during our free time in a free country. From its inception,[2] this country was careful not to promote a government-mandated official language. 7

We understand that English is the common language of this country and the one most often heard in international business circles from Peru to Norway. We know that, to get ahead here, one must learn English. 8

But that ought not mean that somehow we must stop speaking in our native tongue whenever we're in a public area, as if we were ashamed of who we are, where we're from. As if talking in Spanish—or any other language, for that matter—is some sort of litmus test[3] used to gauge American patriotism. 9

Throughout this nation's history, most immigrants—whether from Poland or Finland or Italy or wherever else—kept their language through the first generation and, often, the second. I suspect that they spoke among themselves in their native tongue—in public. Pennsylvania even provided voting ballots written in German during much of the 1800s for those who weren't fluent in English. 10

In this century, Latin American immigrants and others have fought for this country in U.S.-led wars. They have participated fully in this nation's democracy by voting, holding political office, and paying taxes. And they have watched their children and grandchildren become so "American" that they resist speaking in Spanish. 11

---

[1]*Balkanize:* to divide a region or territory into small, often hostile units.
[2]*inception:* the beginning of something.
[3]*litmus test:* a test that uses a single indicator to prompt a decision.

You know what's rude? 12

When there are two or more people who are bilingual and another person who speaks only English and the bilingual folks all of a sudden start speaking Spanish, which effectively leaves out the English-only speaker. I don't tolerate that. 13

One thing's for sure. If I'm ever in a public place with my mom or dad and bump into an acquaintance who doesn't speak Spanish, I will switch to English and introduce that person to my parents. They will respond in English, and do so with respect. 14

Thinking Critically about This Reading

Marquez states that "being an American has very little to do with what language we use during our free time in a free country" (paragraph 7). What activities does Marquez suggest truly make someone an American?

Questions for Study and Discussion

1. What is Marquez's thesis? (Glossary: *Thesis*)
2. Against what ideas does she seem to be arguing? How do you know?
3. Writers are often advised not to begin a paragraph with the word *but*. Why do you think Marquez ignores this rule in paragraph 9?
4. Is this essay one of causes, effects, or both? What details lead you to this conclusion?
5. Do you agree with Marquez that our patriotism should not be gauged by whether we speak English in public? Or do you think that people living in this country ought to affirm their patriotism by speaking only English in public? Explain.

Classroom Activity Using Cause and Effect

Develop a causal chain in which you examine the ramifications of an action you took in the past. Identify each part in the chain. For example, you decided you wanted to do well in a course (ultimate cause), so you got started on a research project early (immediate cause), which enabled you to write several drafts of your paper (immediate cause), which earned you an A for the project (effect), which earned you an excellent grade for the class (effect), which enabled you to take the advanced seminar you wanted (effect).

Suggested Writing Assignments

1. Marquez's essay is set against the backdrop of a larger language-based controversy currently taking place in the United States called the English-only movement. Research the controversy in your school library or on the Internet, and write a cause-and-effect essay exploring why the movement began and what is keeping it alive.
2. There is often more than one cause for an event. List at least six possible causes for one of the following events:

   an upset victory in a competition
   a change in your major
   an injury you suffered
   a quarrel with a friend

   Examine your list, and identify the causes that seem most probable. Which of these are immediate causes, and which are ultimate causes? Using this material, write a short cause-and-effect essay on one of the topics.

Stuck on the Couch

■ Sanjay Gupta

Sanjay Gupta is a practicing neurosurgeon at Grady Memorial Hospital in Atlanta, Georgia, is CNN's chief medical correspondent, and occasionally can be seen on the CBS Evening News with Katie Couric *and on* Anderson Cooper 360. *An American of Indian descent, Gupta grew up in Novi, Michigan, and received both his undergraduate and medical degrees at the University of Michigan in Ann Arbor. As an embedded correspondent in the Iraq war in 2003, he witnessed the first surgical operation that was performed in the war and operated on a wounded Marine twice pronounced dead on the battlefield. Criticized for switching roles from correspondent to surgeon, Gupta said in* Newsweek *magazine, "Medically and morally, it was the right thing to do." Author of numerous scholarly articles on neurosurgery, Gupta has also published* Chasing Life: New Discoveries in the Search for Immortality to Help You Age Less Today *(2007) for general audiences.*

In "Stuck on the Couch," first published in Time *on February 22, 2008, Gupta attempts to answer the puzzling question of why we don't exercise more when all the evidence supports the medical benefits of being active.*

Reflecting on What You Know

If you exercise regularly, you have also probably experienced periods of inactivity. What were your reasons for failing to maintain a regular exercise schedule?

As a doctor, I can give you a lot of useful advice about how to get healthy and stay that way, but one thing you don't need me to tell you is that exercise is good for you. By this point, it's not news to anyone that staying active can benefit the heart, the waistline, even the mind. Still, there's a real disconnect between what we know and what we do. More than 60 percent of American adults do not exercise regularly, and many are content to admit they don't exercise at all. More than 72 million are obese, and almost every one of them would 1 like to shed the extra pounds. So if exercise is such a good idea, why don't more people do it?

The most paradoxical part of our sedentary nature is that we don't 2
start out that way. Even as I write this, I am watching my two-year-old run around in circles. In the last paragraph alone, she has made six circumnavigations of the house. Kids seem to be born in constant motion, but along the way that behavior gets hijacked.

According to kinesiologist Steven Bray at McMaster University in 3
Ontario, the slowdown occurs for many of us at around the time we start college. Bray followed 127 subjects and found that on the whole, first-year college students participate in significantly less exercise than they did just one year before. Academic demands and lack of organized sports are certainly part of the problem. A bigger part may be a curious human tendency to look at life changes as an occasion to blow up the old rules and not create new ones in their place. This is especially so when it comes to staying fit. "College is the first big transition in life," Bray says. "And it becomes an excuse not to exercise."

That's a pattern we repeat over and over. The demands of a new 4
job usually mean less time at the gym or on the jogging track. How about a new marriage? How many times have we seen newlyweds looking a lot plumper in first-anniversary photos than they did in the wedding pictures? And whatever exercise resolve that married couples have left can be wiped out when a new baby comes along. "A lot of people don't like to exercise," says Bray, "so it's the first thing to go when you get the opportunity to rearrange your schedule."

In a recent issue of *Observer*, the magazine of the Association for 5
Psychological Science, Ian Herbert, a journalist and triathlete, reported on numerous other studies that explain why we fall off the exercise wagon. Research by psychologist Roy Baumeister at Florida State University, for example, suggests that self-control is like a psychological muscle—one that can simply become exhausted. Spend your day trying to maintain your composure with a willful toddler or a demanding boss, and you may not have enough discipline left later to stick to your fitness routine. If that routine involves a diet, things can get even more complicated, as the effort you make to resist having a Snickers in the afternoon depletes your resolve to work out in the evening. "The more you use the self-control muscle," Herbert says, "the more tired it gets."

Not having a clearly defined exercise plan can hurt too. Investi- 6
gators at Berlin's Free University found that people who set general goals, like "I will exercise in my free time," did a far worse job of sticking to that plan than did people who made a firm commitment, like "I will

walk to my friend's house and back every Monday, Wednesday, and Friday."

Even something that ought to help—having a personal trainer—can hurt over time. Research at the University of Saskatchewan shows that while a trainer may ensure that we stick to a fitness program, our resolve melts away once the training sessions end. In these cases, we become so dependent on someone else to monitor our progress that we never develop what psychologists call the self-efficacy to follow a plan on our own. 7

The good news is, there are solutions to all of these problems. Baumeister thinks the self-control muscle may be strengthened and trained—sometimes beginning with exercises as simple as remembering to sit straighter or drink enough water. Specific workout plans, like scheduling a gym visit with friends, can turn a general desire to exercise into a firm commitment. Trying to do without a trainer, or at least tapering off slowly when you quit, can help you learn to be accountable only to you. We may never again have the stamina of a two-year-old, but recapturing even a little of our early-life energy can make our later lives a whole lot healthier. 8

Thinking Critically about This Reading

How helpful do you find Gupta's reasons for why we stop exercising? Do you think that knowing why you stop will help you get started again and maintain your commitment? Explain.

Questions for Study and Discussion

1. What is Gupta's purpose in this essay? (Glossary: *Purpose*)
2. Why do so many "first-year college students participate in significantly less exercise than they did just one year before," according to kinesiologist Steven Bray (paragraph 3)?
3. Gupta quotes journalist and triathlete Ian Herbert in paragraph 5 as saying, "The more you use the self-control muscle, . . . the more tired it gets." What is "the self-control muscle," and what does he mean?
4. What has research shown about the benefits of a personal trainer over time? What suggestion does Gupta make about using a personal trainer?
5. What suggestions does the author offer for sticking with an exercise program?

6. Is Gupta's tone in this essay appropriate for his subject and audience, or do you think that he should be more forceful in his approach? (Glossary: *Tone*)

Classroom Activity Using Cause and Effect

In preparation for writing a cause-and-effect essay, list four effects (two on society and two on personal behavior) for one of the following items—television, cell phones, e-mail, microwave ovens, DVD technology, the Internet, or an item of your choice. For example, the automobile could be said to have had the following effects:

Society

A national highway system developed that is based on asphalt roads.
The petroleum and insurance industries expanded in size and influence.

Personal Behavior

People with cars can live far from public transportation.
Suburban and rural drivers walk less than urban dwellers.

Suggested Writing Assignments

1. Write an essay in which you assess the effects of the Internet. What do the relatively new capabilities of search engines allow us to do now that people could not do a few years ago? Also consider negative effects that the ability to search the Internet has caused.
2. One way to think of ourselves is in terms of the influences that have caused us to be who we are. Write an essay in which you discuss two or three of the most important influences in your life. You may wish to consider the following areas as you plan your essay:

books or movies	coaches
parents	ethnic background
clergy	neighborhoods
teachers	friends
heroes	youth organizations

Forty Acres and a Gap in Wealth

■ **Henry Louis Gates Jr.**

The preeminent African American scholar of our time, Henry Louis Gates Jr. is the W. E. B. Du Bois Professor of the Humanities, chair of Afro-American studies, and director of the W. E. B. Du Bois Institute of Afro-American Research at Harvard University. Among his impressive list of publications are Figures in Black: Words, Signs, and the "Racial" Self *(1987),* The Signifying Monkey: A Theory of Afro-American Literary Criticism *(1988),* Loose Canons: Notes on Culture Wars *(1992),* The Future of the Race *(1997),* Thirteen Ways of Looking at a Black Man *(1999), and* Mr. Jefferson and Miss Wheatley *(2003). His* Colored People: A Memoir *(1994) recollects in a wonderful prose style his youth growing up in Piedmont, West Virginia, and his emerging sexual and racial awareness. In 2009 Gates will publish his eagerly awaited history,* In Search of Our Roots: How 19 Extraordinary African Americans Reclaimed Their Past. *Born in 1950, Gates graduated from Yale and took his advanced degrees at Clare College at the University of Cambridge. He has been honored with a MacArthur Foundation Fellowship, inclusion in* Time *magazine's "Twenty-five Most Influential Americans" list, a National Humanities Medal, and election to the American Academy of Arts and Letters.*

In "What's in a Name?," found on pages 361–64 of this book, Gates tells the story of his first encounter with the language of prejudice used by white people to refer to African Americans. In the following selection, published in the New York Times *on November 18, 2007, Gates gives another reason why there is an "increasingly entrenched inequality" between poor and middle-class African Americans and suggests what might be done about it.*

Reflecting on What You Know

Do you or your parents own a home? If you do, what significance does ownership have for you? If no one in your family owns a home, do you aspire to home ownership? Why or why not?

1 Last week, the Pew Research Center published the astonishing finding that 37 percent of African Americans polled felt that "blacks today can no longer be thought of as a single race" because of a widening class divide. From Frederick Douglass to the Rev. Dr. Martin Luther King Jr., perhaps the most fundamental assumption in the history of the black community has been that Americans of African descent, the descendants of the slaves, either because of shared culture or shared oppression, constitute "a mighty race," as Marcus Garvey often put it.

2 "By a ratio of 2 to 1," the report says, "blacks say that the values of poor and middle-class blacks have grown more dissimilar over the past decade. In contrast, most blacks say that the values of blacks and whites have grown more alike."

3 The message here is that it is time to examine the differences between black families on either side of the divide for clues about how to address an increasingly entrenched inequality. We can't afford to wait any longer to address the causes of persistent poverty among most black families.

4 This class divide was predicted long ago, and nobody wanted to listen. At a conference marking the fortieth anniversary of Daniel Patrick Moynihan's infamous report on the problems of the black family, I asked the conservative scholar James Q. Wilson and the liberal scholar William Julius Wilson if ours was the generation presiding over an irreversible, self-perpetuating class divide within the African American community.

5 "I have to believe that this is not the case," the liberal Wilson responded with willed optimism. "Why go on with this work otherwise?" The conservative Wilson nodded. Yet, no one could imagine how to close the gap.

6 In 1965, when Moynihan published his report, suggesting that the out-of-wedlock birthrate and the number of families headed by single mothers, both about 24 percent, pointed to dissolution of the social fabric of the black community, black scholars and liberals dismissed it. They attacked its author as a right-wing bigot. Now we'd give just about anything to have those statistics back. Today, 69 percent of black babies are born out of wedlock, while 45 percent of black households with children are headed by women.

How did this happen? As many theories flourish as pundits—from slavery and segregation to the decline of factory jobs, crack cocaine, draconian drug laws, and outsourcing. But nobody knows for sure. 7

I have been studying the family trees of twenty successful African Americans, people in fields ranging from entertainment and sports (Oprah Winfrey, the track star Jackie Joyner-Kersee) to space travel and medicine (the astronaut Mae Jemison and Ben Carson, a pediatric neurosurgeon). And I've seen an astonishing pattern: fifteen of the twenty descend from at least one line of former slaves who managed to obtain property by 1920—a time when only 25 percent of all African American families owned property. 8

Ten years after slavery ended, Constantine Winfrey, Oprah's great-grandfather, bartered eight bales of cleaned cotton (four thousand pounds) that he picked on his own time for eighty acres of prime bottomland in Mississippi. (He also learned to read and write while picking all that cotton.) 9

Sometimes the government helped: Whoopi Goldberg's great-great-grandparents received their land through the Southern Homestead Act. "So my family got its forty acres and a mule," she exclaimed when I showed her the deed, referring to the rumor that freed slaves would receive land that had been owned by their masters. 10

Well, perhaps not the mule, but 104 acres in Florida. If there is a meaningful correlation between the success of accomplished African Americans today and their ancestors' property ownership, we can only imagine how different black-white relations would be had "forty acres and a mule" really been official government policy in the Reconstruction South. 11

The historical basis for the gap between the black middle class and underclass shows that ending discrimination, by itself, would not eradicate black poverty and dysfunction. We also need intervention to promulgate a middle-class ethic of success among the poor, while expanding opportunities for economic betterment. 12

Perhaps Margaret Thatcher, of all people, suggested a program that might help. In the 1980s, she turned 1.5 million residents of public housing projects in Britain into homeowners. It was certainly the most liberal thing Mrs. Thatcher did, and perhaps progressives should borrow a leaf from her playbook. 13

The telltale fact is that the biggest gap in black prosperity isn't in income, but in wealth. According to a study by the economist Edward 14

N. Wolff, the median net worth of non-Hispanic black households in 2004 was only $11,800—less than 10 percent that of non-Hispanic white households, $118,300. Perhaps a bold and innovative approach to the problem of black poverty—one floated during the Civil War but never fully put into practice—would be to look at ways to turn tenants into homeowners. Sadly, in the wake of the subprime mortgage debacle, an enormous number of houses are being repossessed. But for the black poor, real progress may come only once they have an ownership stake in American society.

People who own property feel a sense of ownership in their future and their society. They study, save, work, strive, and vote. And people trapped in a culture of tenancy do not. 15

The sad truth is that the civil rights movement cannot be reborn until we identify the causes of black suffering, some of them self-inflicted. Why can't black leaders organize rallies around responsible sexuality, birth within marriage, parents reading to their children, and students staying in school and doing homework? Imagine Al Sharpton and Jesse Jackson distributing free copies of Virginia Hamilton's collection of folktales *The People Could Fly* or Dr. Seuss, and demanding that black parents sign pledges to read to their children. What would it take to make inner-city schools havens of learning? 16

John Kenneth Galbraith once told me that the first step in reversing the economic inequalities that blacks face is greater voter participation, and I think he was right. Politicians will not put forth programs aimed at the problems of poor blacks while their turnout remains so low. 17

If the correlation between land ownership and success of African Americans argues that the chasm between classes in the black community is partly the result of social forces set in motion by the dismal failure of forty acres and a mule, then we must act decisively. If we do not, ours will be remembered as the generation that presided over a permanent class divide, a slow but inevitable process that began with the failure to give property to the people who had once been defined as property. 18

Thinking Critically about This Reading

What did Margaret Thatcher do for people living in public housing projects in England? What effect might her actions have had? Do you think her model is a good one for our government to pursue? Why or why not?

Questions for Study and Discussion

1. What does Gates mean by "a widening class divide" (paragraph 1) in the African American community?
2. What causes were put forth in the past by Daniel Patrick Moynihan and others for this class divide?
3. What does Gates see as the difference between income and wealth? Why does he think the distinction is an important one?
4. What does Gates think may be a cause for the class divide? On what evidence does he base his claim? (Glossary: *Evidence*)
5. Why does Gates think that "ending discrimination, by itself, would not eradicate black poverty and dysfunction" (12)?
6. What effect does Gates think that greater voter participation would have on the inequality divide in the African American community? Do you agree? Why or why not?

Classroom Activity Using Cause and Effect

Determining causes and effects requires careful thought, and establishing a causal chain of events can help clarify complex issues. Consider the following example involving pollution and environmental stewardship:

Ultimate Cause	Industrial smokestack emissions
Immediate Cause	Smoke and acid rain damage
Effect	Clean air legislation
Effect	Improved air quality and forest growth

Develop a causal chain for each of the four following cause-and-effect pairs. Then create a new pair (for example, develop a causal chain for vacation/anxiety). Be prepared to discuss your answer with the class.

fire drill/fear	party/excitement
giving a speech/anxiety	vacation/relaxation

Suggested Writing Assignments

1. Gates writes in paragraph 13, "In the 1980s, [Margaret Thatcher] turned 1.5 million residents of public housing projects in Britain into homeowners." What would it take to do the same here in

the United States? Construct several causal chains of actions that could be taken by business, education, and local, state, and national government agencies that might get the job done. Choose one causal chain, and write an argument in which you advocate for home ownership programs for low-income Americans.

2. Write an essay about a recent achievement (your own or someone else's) or about an important achievement in your community. Before beginning to write the essay, list the causes of the achievement and its effects. Also explain how you selected the main cause of the causal chain that led to the achievement.

chapter **21**

Argument

The word **argument** probably brings to mind a verbal disagreement of the sort that nearly everyone has participated in. Such disputes are satisfying when you convert someone to your point of view. More often, though, verbal arguments are inconclusive and frustrating because you might fail to make your position understood or feel that your opponent has been stubborn and unreasonable. Because verbal arguments generally arise spontaneously, they cannot be thoughtfully planned or researched. Indeed, it is often not until later that the convincing piece of evidence or the forcefully phrased assertion finally comes to mind.

Also known as **argumentation**, written arguments share common goals with spoken ones: they attempt to convince a reader to agree with a particular point of view, to make a particular decision, or to pursue a particular course of action. Written arguments, however, involve the presentation of well-chosen evidence and the artful control of language. Writers of arguments must imagine their probable audience and predict the sorts of objections that may be raised. Writers must choose in advance a specific, sufficiently detailed thesis or proposition. There is a greater need to be organized, to choose the most effective types of evidence from all that is available, and to determine the strategies of rhetoric, language, and style that will best suit the argument's subject, purpose, and thesis and ensure its effect on the intended audience. In the end, such work can be far more satisfying than spontaneous oral argument.

Most people who specialize in the study of arguments identify two essential categories—persuasion and logic. *Persuasive appeals* are directed at readers' emotions, at their subconscious, even at their biases and prejudices. These appeals involve diction, slanting, figurative language, analogy, rhythmic patterns of speech, and the establishment of a tone that will encourage a positive response. Persuasion very often attempts to get the audience to take action. Examples of persuasive argument are found in the exaggerated claims of advertisers and the speech making of political and social activists.

Logical appeals, on the other hand, are directed primarily at the audience's intellectual faculties, understanding, and knowledge. Such appeals depend on the reasoned movement from assertion to evidence to conclusion and on an almost mathematical system of proof and counterproof. Logical argument, unlike persuasion, does not normally impel its audience to action. Logical argument is commonly found in scientific or philosophical articles, in legal decisions, and in technical proposals.

Most arguments are neither purely persuasive nor purely logical. A well-written newspaper editorial, for example, will present a logical arrangement of assertions and evidence, but it will also employ striking diction and other persuasive patterns of language to reinforce its effectiveness. Thus the kinds of appeals that a writer emphasizes depend on the nature of the topic, the thesis or proposition of the argument, the writer's purpose, the various kinds of support (evidence, opinions, examples, facts, statistics) offered, and a thoughtful consideration of the audience. Knowing the differences between persuasive and logical appeals is essential in learning both to read and to write arguments.

True arguments make assertions about which there is a legitimate and recognized difference of opinion. Readers probably do not need to be convinced that falling in love is a beautiful and intense experience, that crime rates should be reduced, or that computers are changing the world; most everyone would agree with such assertions. But not everyone would agree that women experience love more intensely than men, that the death penalty reduces the incidence of crime, or that computers are changing the world for the worse; these assertions are arguable and admit of differing perspectives. Similarly, a leading heart specialist might argue in a popular magazine that too many doctors are advising patients to have pacemakers implanted when the devices are not necessary; the editorial writer for a small-town newspaper could write urging that a local agency supplying food to poor families be given a larger percentage of the town's budget; in a long and complex book, a foreign-policy specialist might attempt to prove that the current administration exhibits no consistent policy in its relationship with other countries and that the Department of State needs to be overhauled. No matter what its forum or its structure, an argument has as its chief purpose the detailed setting forth of a particular point of view and the rebuttal of any opposing views.

Argumentation frequently utilizes the other rhetorical strategies covered in Chapters 13 to 20. In your efforts to argue convincingly, you may find it necessary to define, to compare and contrast, to analyze causes and effects, to classify, to describe, or to narrate. Nevertheless, it is the writer's attempt to convince, not explain, that is of primary importance in an argumentative essay. In this respect, it is helpful to keep in mind that there are two basic patterns of thinking and presenting our thoughts that are followed in argumentation—**induction** and **deduction.**

Inductive reasoning, the more common type of reasoning, moves from a set of specific examples to a general statement. In doing so, the writer makes an *inductive leap* from the evidence to the generalization. For example, after examining enrollment statistics, we can conclude that students do not like to take courses offered early in the morning or late in the afternoon.

Deductive reasoning, in contrast, moves from a general statement to a specific conclusion. It works on the model of the **syllogism,** a three-part argument that consists of a major premise, a minor premise, and a conclusion, as in the following example:

a. All women are mortal. *(Major premise)*
b. Jeanne is a woman. *(Minor premise)*
c. Jeanne is mortal. *(Conclusion)*

A syllogism will fail to work if either of the premises is untrue:

a. All living creatures are mammals. *(Major premise)*
b. A butterfly is a living creature. *(Minor premise)*
c. A butterfly is a mammal. *(Conclusion)*

The problem is immediately apparent. The major premise is false: many living creatures are not mammals, and a butterfly happens to be one of the nonmammals. Consequently, the conclusion is invalid.

WRITING ARGUMENTS

Writing an argument is a challenging assignment that can be very rewarding. By nature, an argument must be carefully reasoned and thoughtfully structured to have maximum effect. Allow yourself, therefore, enough time to think about your thesis, to gather the evidence you need, and to draft, revise, edit, and proofread your essay. Fuzzy thinking, confused expression, and poor organization will be immediately evident to your reader and will diminish your chances for completing the assignment successfully. The following seven steps will remind you of some key features of arguments and help you sequence your activities as you research and write.

1. Determine the Thesis or Proposition

Begin by deciding on a topic that interests you and that has some significant differences of opinion or some points that you have questions about. Find out what's in the news about your topic, what people are saying about it, and what authors and instructors are emphasizing as important intellectual arguments. As you pursue your research, consider what assertion or assertions you can make about the topic you choose. The more specific that you make this thesis or proposition, the more directed your research can become and the more focused your ultimate argument will be. Don't hesitate to modify or even reject an initial thesis as your research warrants.

A thesis can be placed anywhere in an argument, but while learning to write arguments, you should place the statement of your controlling idea near the beginning of your composition. Explain the importance of the thesis, and make clear to your reader that you share a common concern or interest in this issue. State your central assertion directly in your first or second paragraph so that your reader will have no doubt or confusion about your position. You may also wish to lead off with a striking piece of evidence to capture your reader's interest.

2. Take Account of Your Audience

In no other type of writing is the question of audience more important than in argumentation. The tone you establish, the type of diction you choose, the kinds of evidence you select to buttress your assertions, and the organizational pattern you follow can influence your audience to trust you and believe your assertions. If you judge the nature of your audience accurately, respect its knowledge of the subject, and correctly envision whether it is likely to be hostile, neutral, complacent, or receptive, you will be able to tailor the various aspects of your argument appropriately. (For more on audience, refer to the discussion of ethos, pathos, and logos on pp. 531–32.)

3. Gather the Necessary Supporting Evidence

For each point of your argument, be sure to provide appropriate and sufficient evidence—verifiable facts and statistics, illustrative examples and narratives, or quotations from authorities. Don't overwhelm your reader with evidence, but don't skimp either. Demonstrate your command of the topic and control of the thesis by choosing carefully from all the evidence at your disposal.

4. Settle on an Organizational Pattern

Once you think you have sufficient evidence to make your assertion convincing, consider how best to organize your argument. To some extent, your organization will depend on your method of reasoning—inductive, deductive, or a combination of the two. For example, is it necessary to establish a major premise before moving on to discuss a minor premise? Should most of your evidence precede your direct statement of an assertion or follow it? Will induction work better with the particular audience you have targeted? As you present your primary points, you may find it effective to move from least important to most important or from most familiar to least familiar. A scratch outline can help, but often a writer's most crucial revisions in an argument involve rearranging its components into a sharper, more coherent order. Often it is difficult to tell what that order should be until the revision stage of the writing process.

5. Consider Refutations to Your Argument

As you proceed with your argument, you may wish to take into account well-known and significant opposing arguments. To ignore opposing views would be to suggest to your readers any one of the following: you don't know about the opposing views, you know about them and are obviously and unfairly weighting the arguments in your favor, or you know about them and have no reasonable answers for them. Grant the validity of opposing arguments or refute them, but respect your reader's intelligence by addressing the objections to your assertion. Your readers will in turn respect you for doing so.

6. Avoid Faulty Reasoning

Have someone read your argument for errors in judgment and for faulty reasoning. Sometimes others can see easily what you can't see because you are so intimately tied to your assertion. These errors are typically called **logical fallacies.** Review the Logical Fallacies box on page 530, making sure that you have not committed any of these errors in reasoning.

Logical Fallacies

Oversimplification: A drastically simple solution to what is clearly a complex problem: *We have a balance-of-trade deficit because foreigners make better products than we do.*

Hasty generalization: In inductive reasoning, a generalization that is based on too little evidence or on evidence that is not representative: *My grandparents eat bran flakes for breakfast, just as most older folks do.*

Post hoc, ergo propter hoc: "After this, therefore because of this." Confusing chance or coincidence with causation. The fact that one event comes after another does not necessarily mean that the first event caused the second: *I went to the hockey game last night. The next thing I knew I had a cold.*

Begging the question: Assuming in a premise something that needs to be proven: *Lying is wrong because people should always tell the truth.*

False analogy: Making a misleading analogy between logically unconnected ideas: *If we can clone mammals, we should be able to find a cure for cancer.*

Either/or thinking: Seeing only two alternatives when there may in fact be other possibilities: *Either you love your job, or you hate it.*

Non sequitur: "It does not follow." An inference or conclusion that is not clearly related to the established premises or evidence: *She is very sincere. She must know what she's talking about.*

7. Conclude Forcefully

In the conclusion of your essay, be sure to restate your position in new language, at least briefly. Besides persuading your reader to accept your point of view, you may also want to encourage some specific course of action. Above all, your conclusion should not introduce new information that may surprise your reader. It should seem to follow naturally, almost seamlessly, from the series of points that you have carefully established in the body of the essay. Don't overstate your case, but at the same time don't qualify your conclusion with the use of too many words or phrases like *I think, in my opinion, maybe, sometimes,* and *probably*. These words can make you sound indecisive and fuzzy-headed rather than rational and sensible.

THINKING CRITICALLY ABOUT ARGUMENT

Take a Stand

Even though you have chosen a topic, gathered information about it, and established a thesis statement or proposition, you need to take a stand—to fully commit yourself to your beliefs and ideas about the issue before you. Your writing will show if you attempt to work with a thesis that you have not clearly thought through or are confused about or if you take a position you do not fully believe in or care about. Your willingness to research, to dig up evidence, to find the most effective organizational pattern for your material, to construct strong paragraphs and sentences, and to find just the right diction to convey your argument is a direct reflection of just how strongly you take a stand and how much you believe in that stand. With a strong stand, you can argue vigorously and convincingly.

Consider Ethos, Pathos, and Logos

Classical thinkers believed that there are three key components in all rhetorical communication—the *speaker* (or writer) who comments on a *subject* to an *audience*. For purposes of discussion, we can isolate each of these entities, but in actual rhetorical situations they are inseparable, and each inextricably influences the other two. The ancients also recognized the importance of three elements of argumentation—ethos, which is related to the speaker/writer; logos, which is related to the subject; and pathos, which is related to the audience.

Ethos (the Greek word for "character") has to do with the authority, credibility, and, to a certain extent, morals of the speaker/writer. The classical rhetoricians believed that it was important for the speaker/writer to be credible and to argue for a worthwhile cause. Putting one's argumentative skills in the service of a questionable cause was simply not acceptable. But how does one establish credibility? Sometimes it is gained through achievements outside the rhetorical arena—that is, the speaker has had experience with an issue, has argued the subject before, and has been judged to be honest and sincere. In the case of your own writing, establishing such credentials is not always possible, so you will need to be more concerned than usual with presenting your argument reasonably, sincerely, and in language untainted by excessive emotionalism. Finally, you should always respect your audience in your writing.

Logos (Greek for "word") is related to the subject and is the effective presentation of the argument itself. Is the thesis or claim worthwhile? Is it logical, consistent, and well buttressed by supporting evidence? Is the evidence itself factual, reliable, and convincing? Finally, is the argument so thoughtfully organized and clearly presented that it will affect the audience? This aspect of argumentation is at once the most difficult to accomplish and the most rewarding.

Pathos (Greek for "emotion") has most to do with the audience. How does the speaker/writer present an argument to maximize its appeal for a given audience? One way is through artful and strategic use of well-crafted language. Certain buzzwords, slanted diction, or loaded language may become either rallying cries or causes of resentment in an argument. Remember that audiences can range from friendly and sympathetic to hostile and resistant, with a myriad of possibilities in between. A friendly audience will welcome new information and support your position; a hostile audience will look for flaws in your logic and examples of dishonest manipulation. Caution, subtlety, and critical thinking must be applied to an uncommitted audience.

The Declaration of Independence

■ Thomas Jefferson

President, governor, statesman, lawyer, architect, philosopher, and writer, Thomas Jefferson (1743–1826) is one of the most important figures in U.S. history. He was born in Albemarle County, Virginia, in 1743 and attended the College of William and Mary. After being admitted to law practice in 1767, he began a long and illustrious career of public service to the colonies and, later, the new republic. In 1809, after two terms as president, Jefferson retired to Monticello, a home he had designed and helped build. Ten years later, he founded the University of Virginia. Jefferson died at Monticello on July 4, 1826, the fiftieth anniversary of the signing of the Declaration of Independence.

Jefferson drafted the Declaration in 1776. Although it was revised by Benjamin Franklin and his colleagues at the Continental Congress, the declaration retains in its sound logic and forceful, direct style the unmistakable qualities of Jefferson's prose.

Reflecting on What You Know

In your mind, what is the meaning of democracy? Where do your ideas about democracy come from?

When in the course of human events, it becomes necessary for one people to dissolve the political bands which have connected them with another, and to assume among the Powers of the earth, the separate and equal station to which the Laws of Nature and of Nature's God entitle them, a decent respect to the opinions of mankind requires that they should declare the causes which impel them to the separation. 1

We hold these truths to be self-evident, that all men are created equal, that they are endowed by their Creator with certain unalienable Rights, that among these are Life, Liberty and the pursuit of Happiness. That to secure these rights, Governments are instituted among Men deriving their just powers from the consent of the governed. That 2 whenever any Form of Government becomes destructive of these ends, it is the Right of the People to alter or to abolish it, and to institute new Government, laying its foundation on such principles and organizing its powers in such form, as to them shall seem most likely to effect their Safety and Happiness. Prudence, indeed, will dictate that Governments long established should not be changed for light and transient[1] causes; and accordingly all experience hath shown, that mankind are more disposed to suffer, while evils are sufferable, than to right themselves by abolishing the forms to which they are accustomed. But when a long train of abuses and usurpations pursuing invariably the same Object evinces a design to reduce them under absolute Despotism, it is their right, it is their duty, to throw off such government, and to provide new Guards for their future security. Such has been the patient sufferance of these Colonies; and such is now the necessity which constrains them to alter their former Systems of Government. The history of the present King of Great Britain[2] is a history of repeated injuries and usurpations, all having in direct object the establishment of an absolute Tyranny over these States. To prove this, let Facts be submitted to a candid world.

He has refused his Assent to Laws, the most wholesome and nec- 3
essary for the public good.

He has forbidden his Governors to pass Laws of immediate and 4
pressing importance, unless suspended in their operation till his Assent should be obtained; and when so suspended, he has utterly neglected to attend to them.

He has refused to pass other Laws for the accommodation of large 5
districts of people, unless those people would relinquish the right of Representation in the Legislature, a right inestimable to them and formidable to tyrants only.

He has called together legislative bodies at places unusual, uncom- 6
fortable, and distant from the depository of their Public Records, for the sole purpose of fatiguing them into compliance with his measures.

He has dissolved Representative Houses repeatedly, for opposing 7
with manly firmness his invasions on the rights of the people.

He has refused for a long time, after such dissolutions, to cause 8
others to be elected; whereby the Legislative Powers, incapable of

[1]*transient:* not lasting; not permanent.

[2]*King of Great Britain:* King George III (1738–1820), who ruled the British empire from 1760 to 1820.

Annihilation, have returned to the People at large for their exercise; the State remaining in the mean time exposed to all the dangers of invasion from without, and convulsions within.

He has endeavoured to prevent the population of these States; for 9 that purpose obstructing the Laws of Naturalization of Foreigners; refusing to pass others to encourage their migration hither, and raising the conditions of new Appropriations of Lands.

He has obstructed the Administration of Justice, by refusing his 10 Assent to Laws for establishing Judiciary Powers.

He has made Judges dependent on his Will alone, for the tenure of 11 their offices, and the amount and payment of their salaries.

He has erected a multitude of New Offices, and sent hither swarms 12 of Officers to harass our People, and eat out their substance.

He has kept among us, in time of peace, Standing Armies without 13 the Consent of our Legislature.

He has affected to render the Military independent of and superior 14 to the Civil Power.

He has combined with others to subject us to jurisdictions foreign 15 to our constitution, and unacknowledged by our laws; giving his Assent to their acts of pretended Legislation:

For quartering large bodies of armed troops among us: 16

For protecting them, by a mock Trial, from Punishment for 17 any Murders which they should commit on the Inhabitants of these States:

For cutting off our Trade with all parts of the world: 18

For imposing Taxes on us without our Consent: 19

For depriving us in many cases, of the benefits of Trial by Jury: 20

For transporting us beyond Seas to be tried for pretended offenses: 21

For abolishing the free System of English Laws in a Neighbouring 22 Province, establishing therein an Arbitrary government, and enlarging its boundaries so as to render it at once an example and fit instrument for introducing the same absolute rule into these Colonies:

For taking away our Charters, abolishing our most valuable Laws, 23 and altering fundamentally the Forms of our Governments:

For suspending our own Legislatures, and declaring themselves 24 invested with Power to legislate for us in all cases whatsoever.

He has abdicated Government here, by declaring us out of his 25 Protection and waging War against us.

He has plundered our seas, ravaged our Coasts, burnt our towns 26 and destroyed the Lives of our people.

He is at this time transporting large Armies of foreign Mercenaries 27
to compleat works of death, desolation and tyranny, already begun with circumstances of Cruelty & perfidy scarcely paralleled in the most barbarous ages, and totally unworthy the Head of a civilized nation.

He has constrained our fellow Citizens taken Captive on the high 28
Seas to bear Arms against their Country, to become the executioners of their friends and Brethren, or to fall themselves by their Hands.

He has excited domestic insurrections amongst us, and has endeav- 29
oured to bring on the inhabitants of our frontiers, the merciless Indian Savages, whose known rule of warfare, is an undistinguished destruction of all ages, sexes and conditions.

In every stage of these Oppressions We Have Petitioned for Redress 30
in the most humble terms: Our repeated petitions have been answered only by repeated injury. A Prince, whose character is thus marked by every act which may define a Tyrant, is unfit to be the ruler of a free People.

Nor have We been wanting in attention to our British brethren. We 31
have warned them from time to time of attempts by their legislature to extend an unwarrantable jurisdiction over us. We have reminded them of the circumstances of our emigration and settlement here. We have appealed to their native justice and magnanimity[3] and we have conjured them by the ties of our common kindred to disavow these usurpations, which would inevitably interrupt our connections and correspondence. They too have been deaf to the voice of justice and of consanguinity. We must, therefore acquiesce[4] in the necessity, which denounces our Separation, and hold them, as we hold the rest of mankind, Enemies in War, in Peace Friends.

We, therefore, the Representatives of the United States of America, 32
in General Congress, Assembled, appealing to the Supreme Judge of the world for the rectitude of our intentions, do, in the Name, and by Authority of the good People of these Colonies, solemnly publish and declare, That these United Colonies are, and of Right ought to be Free and Independent States; that they are Absolved from all Allegiance to the British Crown, and that all political connection between them and the State of Great Britain, is and ought to be totally dissolved; and that as Free and Independent States, they have full power to levy War,

[3]*magnanimity:* quality of being calm, generous, upstanding.
[4]*acquiesce:* comply; accept.

conclude Peace, contract Alliances, establish Commerce, and to do all other Acts and Things which Independent States may of right do. And for the support of this Declaration, with a firm reliance on the protection of Divine Providence, we mutually pledge to each other our lives, our Fortunes and our sacred Honor.

Thinking Critically about This Reading

What, according to the Declaration of Independence, is the purpose of government?

Questions for Study and Discussion

1. In paragraph 2, Jefferson presents certain "self-evident" truths. What are these truths, and how are they related to his argument? Do you consider them self-evident?
2. The Declaration of Independence is a deductive argument; it can, therefore, be presented in the form of a syllogism. (Glossary: *Syllogism*) What are the major premise, the minor premise, and the conclusion of Jefferson's argument?
3. The list of charges against the king is given as evidence in support of Jefferson's minor premise. (Glossary: *Evidence*) Does he offer any evidence in support of his major premise?
4. How does Jefferson refute the possible charge that the colonists should have tried to solve their problems by less drastic means?
5. Where in the Declaration does Jefferson use parallel structure? (Glossary: *Parallelism*) What does he achieve by using it?
6. While the basic structure of the Declaration reflects sound deductive reasoning, Jefferson's language, particularly when he lists the charges against the king, tends to be emotional. (Glossary: *Diction*) Identify as many examples of this emotional language as you can, and discuss possible reasons for why Jefferson uses this kind of language.

Classroom Activity Using Argument

Choose one of the following controversial subjects, and think about how you would write an argument for or against it. Write three sentences that summarize three important points, two based on logic and one based on persuasion/emotion. Then write one sentence that acknowledges the opposing point of view. For example, if you were to argue for stricter enforcement of a leash law and waste pickup ordinance for dog owners in your town, you might write the following:

Logic	Dogs allowed to run free can be a menace to joggers and local wildlife.
Logic	Dog waste poses a health risk, particularly in areas where children play.
Emotion	How would you feel if you hit an unleashed dog with your car?
Counterargument	Dogs need fresh air and exercise, too.

Gun control
Tobacco restrictions
Cutting taxes and social programs
Paying college athletes
Assisted suicide for the terminally ill
Widespread legalization of gambling

Suggested Writing Assignments

1. The issue of human rights is often discussed. Review the arguments for and against our country's active and outspoken promotion of the human rights issue as reported in the press. Then write an argument of your own in favor of a continued strong human rights policy on the part of our nation's leaders.
2. Using one of the subjects listed below, develop a thesis, and then write an essay in which you argue in support of that thesis:

Minimum wage	Welfare
Social Security	Separation of church and state
Capital punishment	First Amendment rights
Erosion of individual rights	

I Have a Dream

■ Martin Luther King Jr.

Civil rights leader Martin Luther King Jr. (1929–1968) was the son of a Baptist minister in Atlanta, Georgia. Ordained at the age of eighteen, King went on to earn academic degrees from Morehouse College, Crozer Theological Seminary, Boston University, and Chicago Theological Seminary. He came to prominence in 1955 in Montgomery, Alabama, when he led a successful boycott against the city's segregated bus system. The first president of the Southern Christian Leadership Conference, King became the leading spokesman for the civil rights movement during the 1950s and 1960s, espousing a consistent philosophy of nonviolent resistance to racial injustice. He also championed women's rights and protested the Vietnam War. Named Time *magazine's Man of the Year in 1963, King was awarded the Nobel Peace Prize in 1964. King was assassinated in April 1968 after speaking at a rally in Memphis, Tennessee.*

"I Have a Dream," the keynote address for the March on Washington in 1963, has become one of the most renowned and recognized speeches of the past century. Note how King uses allusions and parallelism to give life to his argument.

Reflecting on What You Know

Most Americans have seen film clips of King delivering the "I Have a Dream" speech. What do you know of the speech? What do you know of the events and conditions under which King presented it over forty-five years ago?

Five score years ago, a great American, in whose symbolic shadow we stand, signed the Emancipation Proclamation.[1] This momentous decree came as a great beacon light of hope to millions of Negro slaves 1

[1]*Emancipation Proclamation:* a decree enacted by Abraham Lincoln (1809–1865) in 1863 that freed the slaves in the southern states.

who had been seared in the flames of withering injustice. It came as a joyous daybreak to end the long night of captivity.

But one hundred years later, we must face the tragic fact that the Negro is still not free. One hundred years later, the life of the Negro is still sadly crippled by the manacles of segregation and the chains of discrimination. One hundred years later, the Negro lives on a lonely island of poverty in the midst of a vast ocean of material prosperity. One hundred years later, the Negro is still languishing in the corners of American society and finds himself an exile in his own land. So we have come here today to dramatize an appalling condition. 2

In a sense we have come to our nation's Capitol to cash a check. When the architects of our republic wrote the magnificent words of the Constitution and the Declaration of Independence, they were signing a promissory note to which every American was to fall heir. This note was a promise that all men would be guaranteed the unalienable rights of life, liberty, and the pursuit of happiness. 3

It is obvious today that America has defaulted on this promissory note insofar as her citizens of color are concerned. Instead of honoring this sacred obligation, America has given the Negro people a bad check; a check which has come back marked "insufficient funds." But we refuse to believe that the bank of justice is bankrupt. We refuse to believe that there are insufficient funds in the great vaults of opportunity of this nation. So we have come to cash this check—a check that will give us upon demand the riches of freedom and the security of justice. We have also come to this hallowed spot to remind America of the fierce urgency of *now*. This is no time to engage in the luxury of cooling off or to take the tranquilizing drug of gradualism. *Now* is the time to make real the promises of Democracy. *Now* is the time to rise from the dark and desolate valley of segregation to the sunlit path of racial justice. *Now* is the time to open the doors of opportunity to all of God's children. *Now* is the time to lift our nation from the quicksands of racial injustice to the solid rock of brotherhood. 4

It would be fatal for the nation to overlook the urgency of the moment and to underestimate the determination of the Negro. This sweltering summer of the Negro's legitimate discontent will not pass until there is an invigorating autumn of freedom and equality. 1963 is not an end, but a beginning. Those who hope that the Negro needed to blow off steam and will now be content will have a rude awakening if the nation returns to business as usual. There will be neither rest nor tranquility in America until the Negro is granted his citizenship 5 rights. The whirlwinds of revolt will continue to shake the foundations of our nation until the bright day of justice emerges.

But there is something I must say to my people who stand on the 6
warm threshold which leads into the palace of justice. In the process of gaining our rightful place we must not be guilty of wrongful deeds. Let us not seek to satisfy our thirst for freedom by drinking from the cup of bitterness and hatred. We must forever conduct our struggle on the high plane of dignity and discipline. We must not allow our creative protest to degenerate into physical violence. Again and again we must rise to the majestic heights of meeting physical force with soul force. The marvelous new militancy which has engulfed the Negro community must not lead us to a distrust of all white people, for many of our white brothers, as evidenced by their presence here today, have come to realize that their destiny is tied up with our destiny and their freedom is inextricably bound to our freedom. We cannot walk alone.

And as we walk, we must make the pledge that we shall march 7
ahead. We cannot turn back. There are those who are asking the devotees of civil rights, "When will you be satisfied?" We can never be satisfied as long as the Negro is the victim of the unspeakable horrors of police brutality. We can never be satisfied as long as our bodies, heavy with the fatigue of travel, cannot gain lodging in the motels of the highways and the hotels of the cities. We cannot be satisfied as long as the Negro's basic mobility is from a smaller ghetto to a larger one. We can never be satisfied as long as a Negro in Mississippi cannot vote and a Negro in New York believes he has nothing for which to vote. No, no, we are not satisfied, and we will not be satisfied until justice rolls down like waters and righteousness like a mighty stream.

I am not unmindful that some of you have come here out of great 8
trials and tribulations. Some of you have come fresh from narrow jail cells. Some of you have come from areas where your quest for freedom left you battered by the storms of persecution and staggered by the winds of police brutality. You have been the veterans of creative suffering. Continue to work with the faith that unearned suffering is redemptive.

Go back to Mississippi, go back to Alabama, go back to South 9
Carolina, go back to Georgia, go back to Louisiana, go back to the slums and ghettoes of our northern cities, knowing that somehow this situation can and will be changed. Let us not wallow in the valley of despair.

I say to you today, my friends, that in spite of the difficulties and 10
frustrations of the moment I still have a dream. It is a dream deeply rooted in the American dream.

I have a dream that one day this nation will rise up and live out the true meaning of its creed: "We hold these truths to be self-evident; that all men are created equal."[2] 11

I have a dream that one day on the red hills of Georgia the sons of former slaves and the sons of former slaveowners will be able to sit down together at the table of brotherhood. 12

I have a dream that the state of Mississippi, a desert state sweltering with the heat of injustice and oppression, will be transformed into an oasis of freedom and justice. 13

I have a dream that my four little children will one day live in a nation where they will not be judged by the color of their skin but by the content of their character. 14

I have a dream today. 15

I have a dream that the state of Alabama, whose governor's[3] lips are presently dripping with the words of interposition and nullification,[4] will be transformed into a situation where little black boys and black girls will be able to join hands with little white boys and white girls and walk together as sisters and brothers. 16

I have a dream today. 17

I have a dream that one day every valley shall be exalted, every hill and mountain shall be made low, the rough places will be made plain, and the crooked places will be made straight, and the glory of the Lord shall be revealed, and all flesh shall see it together. 18

This is our hope. This is the faith with which I return to the South. With this faith we will be able to hew out of the mountain of despair a stone of hope. With this faith we will be able to transform the jangling discords of our nation into a beautiful symphony of brotherhood. With this faith we will be able to work together, to pray together, to struggle together, to go to jail together, to stand up for freedom together, knowing that we will be free one day. 19

This will be the day when all of God's children will be able to sing with new meaning. 20

---

[2]*"We hold . . . created equal":* a phrase from the Declaration of Independence by Thomas Jefferson (1743–1826) (see p. 533).

[3]*Alabama . . . governor:* George Wallace (1919–1998), a segregationist in 1963 who later changed his views and received integrated political support.

[4]*nullification:* a state's refusal to recognize or enforce within its borders U.S. federal law.

My country, 'tis of thee
Sweet land of liberty,
Of thee I sing:
Land where my fathers died,
Land of the pilgrims' pride,
From every mountainside
Let freedom ring.

And if America is to be a great nation this must become true. So let freedom ring from the prodigious hilltops of New Hampshire. Let freedom ring from the mighty mountains of New York. Let freedom ring from the heightening Alleghenies of Pennsylvania! 21

Let freedom ring from the snowcapped Rockies of Colorado! 22

Let freedom ring from the curvaceous peaks of California! 23

But not only that; let freedom ring from Stone Mountain of Georgia! 24

Let freedom ring from Lookout Mountain of Tennessee! 25

Let freedom ring from every hill and molehill of Mississippi. From every mountainside, let freedom ring. 26

When we let freedom ring, when we let it ring from every village and every hamlet, from every state and every city, we will be able to speed up that day when all of God's children, black men and white men, Jews and Gentiles, Protestants and Catholics, will be able to join hands and sing in the words of the old Negro spiritual, "Free at last! free at last! thank God almighty, we are free at last!" 27

Thinking Critically about This Reading

What does King mean when he says that "in the process of gaining our rightful place [in society] we must not be guilty of wrongful deeds" (paragraph 6)? Why is this issue so important to him?

Questions for Study and Discussion

1. What is King's thesis? (Glossary: *Thesis*) How has America "defaulted" on its promise?
2. King delivered his speech to two audiences—the huge audience that listened to him in person and another, larger audience. (Glossary: *Audience*) What is that larger audience? How does King's speech catch the audience's attention and deliver his point?

3. Examine the speech to determine how King organizes his presentation. (Glossary: *Organization*) What are the main sections of the speech, and what is the purpose of each? How does the organization serve King's overall purpose? (Glossary: *Purpose*)
4. King uses parallel constructions and repetitions throughout his speech. (Glossary: *Parallelism*) Identify the phrases and words that he emphasizes. Explain what these techniques add to the persuasiveness of his argument.
5. Explain King's choice for the title. (Glossary: *Title*) Why is the title particularly appropriate given the context in which the speech was delivered? What other titles might he have used?

Classroom Activity Using Argument

Write a paragraph that argues that people should compliment one another more. Use *one* of the following quotes to support your argument:

> "Compliments are the high point of a person's day," said self-help author Melodie Bronson. "Without compliments, anyone's life is sure to be much more difficult."

> "Compliments have been proven to lower blood pressure and increase endorphin production to the brain," said Dr. Ruth West of the Holistic Medicine Committee. "A compliment a day may lengthen your life span by as much as a year."

> "Compliments are a special way people communicate with each other," said Bill Goodbody, therapist at the Good Feeling Institute. "Ninety percent of our patients report happier relationships or marriages after they begin compliment therapy."

Explain why you chose the quote you did. How did you integrate it into your paragraph?

Suggested Writing Assignments

1. King's language is powerful, and his imagery is vivid, but the effectiveness of any speech depends partially on its delivery. If read in monotone, King's use of repetition and parallel language would sound almost redundant rather than inspiring. (Glossary: *Parallelism*) Keeping presentation in mind, write a short speech

that argues a point of view about which you feel strongly. Using King's speech as a model, incorporate imagery, repetition, and metaphor to communicate your point. (Glossary: *Figure of Speech*) Read your speech aloud to a friend to see how it flows and how effective your use of language is. Refine your presentation—both your text and how you deliver it—before presenting the speech in class.

2. Using King's assessment of the condition of African Americans in 1963 as a foundation, research the changes that have occurred in the years following King's speech. How have laws changed? How have demographics changed? Present your information in an essay that assesses what still needs to be done to fulfill King's dream for America. Where do we still fall short of the racial equality envisioned by King? What are the prospects for the future?

Building Baby from the Genes Up

■ **Ronald M. Green**

Ronald M. Green is Eunice and Julian Cohen Professor of Ethics and Human Values and director of the Ethics Institute at Dartmouth College. A graduate of Brown University, he received his PhD in religious ethics from Harvard University in 1973. In 1996 and 1997, Green was the founding director of the Office of Genome Ethics at the National Human Genome Research Institute of the National Institutes of Health. He is the author of seven books and more than 125 articles in theoretical and applied ethics. Green has served as an officer on major professional boards and societies as well as on the editorial boards of several journals in his fields of interest. In 1980, he received the Dartmouth Distinguished Teaching Award, voted on by the entire graduating class. Green's most recent book, Babies by Design: The Ethics of Genetic Choice, *was published in 2007. He makes his home in Norwich, Vermont.*

In the following article published in the Washington Post *on April 13, 2008, Green writes that he'd like to shake up some people's certainty that human genetic tampering is a bad idea.*

Reflecting on What You Know

Should we attempt to tamper with the human genome to improve on nature? If you think we should or should not, on what information and evidence do you base your opinion?

The two British couples no doubt thought that their appeal for medical help in conceiving a child was entirely reasonable. Over several generations, many female members of their families had died of breast cancer. One or both spouses in each couple had probably inherited the genetic mutations for the disease, and they wanted to use in-vitro fertilization and preimplantation genetic diagnosis (PGD) to select only the healthy embryos for implantation. Their goal was to eradicate breast cancer from their family lines once and for all. 1

In the United States, this combination of reproductive and genetic medicine—what one scientist has dubbed "reprogenetics"—remains largely unregulated, but Britain has a formal agency, the Human Fertilization and Embryology Authority (HFEA), that must approve all requests for PGD. In July 2007, after considerable deliberation, the HFEA approved the procedure for both families. The concern was not about the use of PGD to avoid genetic disease, since embryo screening for serious disorders is commonplace now on both sides of the Atlantic. What troubled the HFEA was the fact that an embryo carrying the cancer mutation could go on to live for forty or fifty years before ever developing cancer, and there was a chance it might never develop. Did this warrant selecting and discarding embryos? To its critics, the HFEA, in approving this request, crossed a bright line separating legitimate medical genetics from the quest for "the perfect baby." 2

Like it or not, that decision is a sign of things to come—and not necessarily a bad sign. Since the completion of the Human Genome Project in 2003, our understanding of the genetic bases of human disease and non-disease traits has been growing almost exponentially. The National Institutes of Health has initiated a quest for the "$1,000 genome," a ten-year program to develop machines that could identify all the genetic letters in anyone's genome at low cost (it took more than $3 billion to sequence the first human genome). With this technology, which some believe may be just four or five years away, we could not only scan an individual's—or embryo's—genome; we could also rapidly compare thousands of people and pinpoint those DNA sequences or combinations that underlie the variations that contribute to our biological differences. 3

With knowledge comes power. If we understand the genetic causes of obesity, for example, we can intervene by means of embryo selection to produce a child with a reduced genetic likelihood of getting fat. Eventually, without discarding embryos at all, we could use gene-targeting techniques to tweak fetal DNA sequences. No child would have to face a lifetime of dieting or experience the health and cosmetic problems associated with obesity. The same is true for cognitive problems such as dyslexia. Geneticists have already identified some of the mutations that contribute to this disorder. Why should a child struggle with reading difficulties when we could alter the genes responsible for the problem? 4

Many people are horrified at the thought of such uses of genetics, seeing echoes of the 1997 science fiction film *Gattaca*, which depicted a 5 world where parents choose their children's traits. Human weakness has been eliminated through genetic engineering, and the few parents who opt for a "natural" conception run the risk of producing offspring—"invalids" or "degenerates"—who become members of a despised underclass. *Gattaca*'s world is clean and efficient, but its eugenic obsessions have all but extinguished human love and compassion.

These fears aren't limited to fiction. Over the past few years, many bioethicists have spoken out against genetic manipulations. The critics tend to voice at least four major concerns. First, they worry about the effect of genetic selection on parenting. Will our ability to choose our children's biological inheritance lead parents to replace unconditional love with a consumerist mentality that seeks perfection? 6

Second, they ask whether gene manipulations will diminish our freedom by making us creatures of our genes or our parents' whims. In his book *Enough,* the techno-critic Bill McKibben asks: if I am a world-class runner, but my parents inserted the "Sweatworks2010 GenePack" in my genome, can I really feel pride in my accomplishments? Worse, if I refuse to use my costly genetic endowments, will I face relentless pressure to live up to my parents' expectations? 7

Third, many critics fear that reproductive genetics will widen our social divisions as the affluent "buy" more competitive abilities for their offspring. Will we eventually see "speciation," the emergence of two or more human populations so different that they no longer even breed with one another? Will we re-create the horrors of eugenics that led, in Europe, Asia, and the United States, to the sterilization of tens of thousands of people declared to be "unfit" and that in Nazi Germany paved the way for the Holocaust? 8

Finally, some worry about the religious implications of this technology. Does it amount to a forbidden and prideful "playing God"? 9

To many, the answers to these questions are clear. Not long ago, when I asked a large class at Dartmouth Medical School whether they thought that we should move in the direction of human genetic engineering, more than 80 percent said no. This squares with public opinion polls that show a similar degree of opposition. Nevertheless, "babies by design" are probably in our future—but I think that the critics' concerns may be less troublesome than they first appear. 10

Will critical scrutiny replace parental love? Not likely. Even today, parents who hope for a healthy child but have one born with disabilities tend to love that child ferociously. The very intensity of parental love is the best protection against its erosion by genetic technologies. Will a child somehow feel less free because parents have helped select 11 his or her traits? The fact is that a child is already remarkably influenced by the genes she inherits. The difference is that we haven't taken control of the process. Yet.

Knowing more about our genes may actually increase our freedom by helping us understand the biological obstacles—and opportunities—we have to work with. Take the case of Tiger Woods. His father, Earl, is said to have handed him a golf club when he was still in the playpen. Earl probably also gave Tiger the genes for some of the traits that help make him a champion golfer. Genes and upbringing worked together to inspire excellence. Does Tiger feel less free because of his inherited abilities? Did he feel pressured by his parents? I doubt it. Of course, his story could have gone the other way, with overbearing parents forcing a child into their mold. But the problem in that case wouldn't be genetics, but bad parenting. 12

Granted, the social effects of reproductive genetics are worrisome. The risks of producing a "genobility," genetic overlords ruling a vast genetic underclass, are real. But genetics could also become a tool for reducing the class divide. Will we see the day when perhaps all youngsters are genetically vaccinated against dyslexia? And how might this contribute to everyone's social betterment? 13

As for the question of intruding on God's domain, the answer is less clear than the critics believe. The use of genetic medicine to cure or prevent disease is widely accepted by religious traditions, even those that oppose discarding embryos. Speaking in 1982 at the Pontifical Academy of Sciences, Pope John Paul II observed that modern biological research "can ameliorate the condition of those who are affected by chromosomic diseases," and he lauded this as helping to cure "the smallest and weakest of human beings . . . during their intrauterine life or in the period immediately after birth." For Catholicism and some other traditions, it is one thing to cure disease, but another to create children who are faster runners, longer-lived, or smarter. 14

But why should we think that the human genome is a once-and-for-all-finished, untamperable product? All of the biblically derived faiths permit human beings to improve on nature using technology, from agriculture to aviation. Why not improve our genome? I have no doubt that most people considering these questions for the first time are certain that human genetic improvement is a bad idea, but I'd like to shake up that certainty. 15

Genomic science is racing toward a future in which foreseeable improvements include reduced susceptibility to a host of diseases, increased life span, better cognitive functioning, and maybe even cosmetic 16 enhancements such as whiter, straighter teeth. Yes, genetic orthodontics may be in our future. The challenge is to see that we don't also unleash the demons of discrimination and oppression. Although I acknowledge the risks, I believe that we can and will incorporate gene technology into the ongoing human adventure.

Thinking Critically about This Reading

In paragraph 2, Green discusses the trouble that the Human Fertilization and Embryology Authority (HFEA) in Great Britain had in making a decision regarding the two couples who had breast cancer in their genetic histories. What distinguished the case that HFEA was examining from others where genetic screening was commonplace?

Questions for Study and Discussion

1. What is Green's thesis in this essay? (Glossary: *Thesis*) Where does he state his thesis?
2. What are some of the diseases and disabilities that scientists may be capable of eliminating through gene-targeting techniques?
3. What are the reasons that many people object to genetic manipulations? How has Green answered those criticisms?
4. How do major religions and their leaders regard genetic manipulation?
5. What does Green mean when he writes in paragraph 16, "The challenge is to see that we don't also unleash the demons of discrimination and oppression"?
6. According to his biography, Green does not have any scientific degrees or practical experience in genetic manipulation. Why does he think he is qualified to speak on the issue?
7. Green cites only a few authorities. Does that fact help or hinder his argument or have no real effect on it? Explain.
8. For what audience do you think Green is writing? (Glossary: *Audience*) On what evidence do you base your evaluation?

Classroom Activity Using Argument

Discuss in class whether Green's argument is inductive, deductive, or a combination of both models of argumentation.

Suggested Writing Assignments

1. If you are against genetic manipulation, research the matter further, and write an argument putting forth your own findings and thoughts on the issue.
2. Find an editorial in a local or national newspaper that presents a view on an issue that you disagree with. Bring the editorial to class, reread and study it for a few minutes, and then write a brief letter to the editor of the newspaper arguing against its position on the issue. Your letter should be brief; short letters have a much better chance of being published than long ones. During a subsequent class, form groups of two or three students to share your letters and to comment on the effectiveness of each other's arguments. Revise your letter, and consider sending it to the newspaper for possible publication.

In Praise of the F Word

■ Mary Sherry

Mary Sherry was born in Bay City, Michigan, and received her bachelor's degree from Rosary College in River Forest, Illinois. She owns her own research and publishing company specializing in information for economic and development organizations. Sherry also teaches in adult-literacy programs and has written essays on educational problems for various newspapers, including the Wall Street Journal *and* Newsday.

In the following essay, originally published in Newsweek *in 1991, Sherry takes a provocative stance—that the threat of flunking is a "positive teaching tool." She believes students would be better off if they had a "healthy fear of failure," and she marshals a series of logical appeals to both clarify and support her argument.*

Reflecting on What You Know

Comment on what you see as the relationship between learning and grades. Do teachers and students pay too much attention to grades at the expense of learning? Or are grades not seen as important enough?

Tens of thousands of eighteen-year-olds will graduate this year and be handed meaningless diplomas. These diplomas won't look any different from those awarded their luckier classmates. Their validity will be questioned only when their employers discover that these graduates are semiliterate. 1

Eventually a fortunate few will find their way into educational-repair shops—adult-literacy programs, such as the one where I teach basic grammar and writing. There, high-school graduates and high-school dropouts pursuing graduate-equivalency certificates will learn the skills they should have learned in school. They will also discover they have been cheated by our educational system. 2

As I teach, I learn a lot about our schools. Early in each session I ask my students to write about an unpleasant experience they had in school. No writers' block here! "I wish someone would have made me 3 stop doing drugs and made me study." "I liked to party and no one seemed to care." "I was a good kid and didn't cause any trouble, so they just passed me along even though I didn't read well and couldn't write." And so on.

I am your basic do-gooder, and prior to teaching this class I blamed 4
the poor academic skills our kids have today on drugs, divorce, and other impediments to concentration necessary for doing well in school. But, as I rediscover each time I walk into the classroom, before a teacher can expect students to concentrate, he has to get their attention, no matter what distractions may be at hand. There are many ways to do this, and they have much to do with teaching style. However, if style alone won't do it, there is another way to show who holds the winning hand in the classroom. That is to reveal the trump card[1] of failure.

I will never forget a teacher who played that card to get the atten- 5
tion of one of my children. Our youngest, a world-class charmer, did little to develop his intellectual talents but always got by. Until Mrs. Stifter.

Our son was a high-school senior when he had her for English. 6
"He sits in the back of the room talking to his friends," she told me. "Why don't you move him to the front row?" I urged, believing the embarrassment would get him to settle down. Mrs. Stifter looked at me steely-eyed over her glasses. "I don't move seniors," she said. "I flunk them." I was flustered. Our son's academic life flashed before my eyes. No teacher had ever threatened him with that before. I regained my composure and managed to say that I thought she was right. By the time I got home I was feeling pretty good about this. It was a radical approach for these times, but, well, why not? "She's going to flunk you," I told my son. I did not discuss it any further. Suddenly English became a priority in his life. He finished out the semester with an A.

I know one example doesn't make a case, but at night I see a 7
parade of students who are angry and resentful for having been passed along until they could no longer even pretend to keep up. Of average intelligence or better, they eventually quit school, concluding they were too dumb to finish. "I should have been held back" is a comment I hear frequently. Even sadder are those students who are high-school graduates who say to me after a few weeks of class, "I don't know how I ever got a high-school diploma."

---

[1]*trump card:* a secret weapon; hidden advantage.

Passing students who have not mastered the work cheats them and the employers who expect graduates to have basic skills. We excuse this dishonest behavior by saying kids can't learn if they come from terrible environments. No one seems to stop to think that—no matter what environments they come from—most kids don't put school first on their list unless they perceive something is at stake. They'd rather be sailing. 8

Many students I see at night could give expert testimony on unemployment, chemical dependency, abusive relationships. In spite of these difficulties, they have decided to make education a priority. They are motivated by the desire for a better job or the need to hang on to the one they've got. They have a healthy fear of failure. 9

People of all ages can rise above their problems, but they need to have a reason to do so. Young people generally don't have the maturity to value education in the same way my adult students value it. But fear of failure, whether economic or academic, can motivate both. 10

Flunking as a regular policy has just as much merit today as it did two generations ago. We must review the threat of flunking and see it as it really is—a positive teaching tool. It is an expression of confidence by both teachers and parents that the students have the ability to learn the material presented to them. However, making it work again would take a dedicated, caring conspiracy between teachers and parents. It would mean facing the tough reality that passing kids who haven't learned the material—while it might save them grief for the short term—dooms them to long-term illiteracy. It would mean that teachers would have to follow through on their threats, and parents would have to stand behind them, knowing their children's best interests are indeed at stake. This means no more doing Scott's assignments for him because he might fail. No more passing Jodi because she's such a nice kid. 11

This is a policy that worked in the past and can work today. A wise teacher, with the support of his parents, gave our son the opportunity to succeed—or fail. It's time we return this choice to all students. 12

Thinking Critically about This Reading

According to Sherry, "We must review the threat of flunking and see it as it really is—a positive teaching tool. It is an expression of confidence by both teachers and parents that the students have the ability to learn the material presented to them" (paragraph 11). How can flunking students be "an expression of confidence" in them?

Questions for Study and Discussion

1. What is Sherry's *thesis?* (Glossary: *Thesis*) What evidence does she use to support her argument?
2. Sherry uses dismissive terms to characterize objections to flunking—*cheats* and *excuses*. In your opinion, does she do enough to acknowledge the other side of the argument? Explain.
3. What is the "F word" discussed in the essay? Does referring to it as the "F word" increase the effectiveness of the essay? Why?
4. Who is Sherry's audience? (Glossary: *Audience*) Is it receptive to the "F word"? Explain your answer.
5. In what way is Sherry qualified to comment on the potential benefits of flunking students? Do you think her induction is accurate?

Classroom Activity Using Argument

A first-year composition student, Marco Schmidt, is preparing to write an essay in which he will argue that music should be a required course for all public high school students. He has compiled the following pieces of evidence:

- Informal interviews with four classmates. Three of the classmates stated that they would have enjoyed and benefited from taking a music course in high school, and the fourth stated that she would not have been interested in taking music.
- An article from a professional journal for teachers comparing the study habits of students who were involved in music and those who were not. The author, a psychologist, found that students who play an instrument or sing regularly have better study habits than students who do not.
- A brief article from a national newsmagazine praising an inner-city high school's experimental curriculum, in which music classes play a prominent part.
- The personal Web site of a high school music teacher who posts information about the successes and achievements of her former students.

Discuss these pieces of evidence with your classmates. Which are most convincing? Which provide the least support for Marco's argument?

Why? What other types of evidence might Marco find to support his argument?

Suggested Writing Assignments

1. Write an essay in which you argue against Sherry's thesis. (Glossary: *Thesis*) In what ways is flunking bad for students? Are there techniques more positive than a "fear of failure" that can be used to motivate students?
2. Think of something that involves short-term pain or sacrifice but that can be beneficial in the long run. For example, exercising requires exertion, but it may help prevent health problems. Studying and writing papers when you'd rather be having fun or even sleeping may seem painful, but earning a college degree leads to personal growth and development. Even if the benefits are obvious, imagine a skeptical audience, and write an argument in favor of the short-term sacrifice over the long-term consequences of avoiding it. (Glossary: *Audience*)

Don't Eat the Flan

■ Greg Critser

Greg Critser was born in 1954 and lives in Pasadena, California, where he writes regularly for USA Today *and the* Los Angeles Times *on issues of nutrition, health, and medicine. An authority on the subject of food politics, Critser has been interviewed by PBS and other media, and his writing on obesity earned him a James Beard nomination for best feature writing in 1999. Embarrassed by a passing motorist who shouted "Watch it, fatso," Critser went on a diet and lost forty pounds. In the process, he discovered that in America weight is a class issue—fat and poor often go together. In exposing the heavy truths about American obesity, Critser gives our bloated nation a wake-up call. His books include* Fat Land: How Americans Became the Fattest People in the World *(2003) and* Generation Rx: How Prescription Drugs Are Altering American Lives, Minds, and Bodies *(2005).*

In the following essay, which first appeared in the February 3, 2003, issue of Forbes, *Critser explains that in doing the research for* Fat Land *he could not find any present-day connection between the sin of gluttony and our national problem with obesity. He argues, therefore, that we should reintroduce moral authority in fighting obesity, a tactic that has worked well in our fight against unsafe sex and smoking.*

Reflecting on What You Know

Most health reports indicate that obesity continues to rise in America toward epidemic proportions. What do you think has gone wrong? What do you think needs to be done? What incentives are needed to encourage change?

By now you have likely seen nearly every imaginable headline about obesity in America. You've seen the ominous statistical ones: "Nearly two-thirds of all Americans now overweight, study says." Or 1 the sensational ones: "Two N.Y. teens sue McDonald's for making them fat." Or the medical ones: "Adult-onset diabetes now soars among children."

But one obesity headline you will not see is the one that deals with morality. Specifically, it is the one that might read like this: "Sixth deadly sin at root of obesity epidemic, researchers say." This is because gluttony,[1] perhaps alone among humanity's vices, has become the first media non-sin. 2

I first got a whiff of this transformation a few years ago while working on a book about obesity. Looking for a book about food and morality, I asked a clerk in the religious bookstore at the Fuller Seminary in Pasadena where I might find one on gluttony. 3

"Hmm," he pondered. "Maybe you'd want to look under eating disorders." 4

"But I'm not looking for a medical book. I'm looking for something about gluttony—you know, one of the seven deadly sins." I was sure he'd point me to Aquinas, Dante or at least a nice long shelf on sin. But he didn't. 5

"Oh, why didn't you say so?" the young man said, now quite serious. "If we have anything like that, it'll be over in self-help." 6

I then made inquiries about interviewing a professor who might be an expert on sin. I was told there was no one at this conservative seminary who had anything to say on the subject. 7

What might be called the "therapization" of gluttony is hardly limited to the sphere of conventional religion. Of much greater import is the legitimizing of gluttony in medicine and public health. For at least two decades any suggestion that morality—or even parental admonition[2]—be used to fight the curse of overeating has been greeted like Ted Bundy at a Girl Scout convention. Behind this lies the notion, widely propounded[3] by parenting gurus, that food should never become a dinner-table battle. 8

The operative notion here is simple: Telling people to not eat too much food is counterproductive. Worse, it leads to "stigmatization," which can lead to eating disorders, low self-esteem, and bad body image. Though the consequences of being overweight, numerous and well documented, are dangerous, little if any evidence supports the notion that 9

[1]*gluttony:* excessive eating or drinking.
[2]*admonition:* cautionary advice or warning.
[3]*propounded:* put forth; supported.

it is dangerous to stigmatize unhealthy behavior. Nevertheless, suggest to an "obesity counselor" that people should be counseled against gluttony and nine out of ten times you will be admonished as a veritable child abuser.

That's too bad, because it eliminates a fundamental—and proven— 10
public health tactic. In the campaigns against unsafe sex and smoking, stigmatizing unhealthy behaviors proved highly effective in reducing risk.

Worse, this absence of moral authority in the realm of food leaves 11
children—everyone, really—vulnerable to the one force in American life that has no problem making absolute claims: food advertisers, who spend billions teaching kids how to bug their parents into feeding them high-fat, high-sugar foods. Combine that with the lingering (albeit debunked) 1980s dogma—that "kids know when kids are full"—and you get, as one nutritionist-parent forcefully told me, the idea that "kids have the right to make bad nutritional decisions."

You would have a hard time selling that to the one Western nation 12
that apparently avoided the obesity epidemic: France. The French intentionally created a culture of dietary restraint in the early 20th century, through a state-sponsored program known as *puériculture*. Reacting to early cases of childhood obesity, health activists wrote parenting manuals, conducted workshops and published books. Their advice: Parents must control the dinner table; all portions should be moderate; desserts were for holidays. Eating too much food was a bad thing.

And therein lies at least part of the explanation for the legendary 13
leanness of the very confident French: They were taught as children not to overeat. And they didn't even have to look in the self-help section for the advice.

Thinking Critically about This Reading

What does Critser mean by "gluttony, perhaps alone among humanity's vices, has become the first media non-sin" (paragraph 2)? What evidence does he provide to support this claim?

Questions for Study and Discussion

1. What is Critser's argument in this essay? How convincing do you find it?
2. What do you think of people who sue fast-food companies such as McDonald's for making them fat? Who is most responsible in

these cases—the fast-food companies or the people who choose to eat there? Explain.

3. How have the French fought off obesity, according to Critser? Are you convinced of the cause-and-effect relationship that Critser points to between the *puériculture* the French established in the early twentieth century and their "legendary leanness" (13)? (Glossary: *Cause and Effect*) Might there be other reasons for their leanness?
4. What does Critser mean by the "'therapization' of gluttony" (8)? Why do you suppose he places the word in quotation marks?
5. What are the "seven deadly sins" (5)? Are they all now as much out of favor as gluttony, in your estimation? Explain.
6. What is the meaning of the word *flan* in Critser's title? (Glossary: *Title*) How effective is the title in your opinion?

Classroom Activity Using Argument

Identify the fallacy in each of the following statements. (For more information on logical fallacies, see the box on p. 530.)

a. Oversimplification
b. Hasty generalization
c. *Post hoc, ergo propter hoc*
d. Begging the question
e. False analogy
f. Either/or thinking
g. *Non sequitur*

1. America: Love it or leave it! ______
2. Two of my best friends who are overweight don't exercise at all. Overweight people are simply not getting enough exercise. ______
3. If we use less gasoline, the price of gasoline will fall. ______
4. Life is precious because we want to protect it at all costs. ______
5. Randy is a good mechanic so he'll be a good race car driver. ______
6. Susan drank hot lemonade and her cold went away. ______
7. Students do poorly in college because they do too much surfing on the Web. ______
8. If we can eliminate pollution, we can cure cancer. ______
9. Such actions are illegal because they are prohibited by law. ______
10. Every time I have something important to do on my computer it crashes. ______

11. We should either raise taxes or cut social programs. ______
12. Education ought to be managed just as a good business is managed. ______

Suggested Writing Assignments

1. Have you ever been criticized for being too heavy or too thin? Have you ever tried to lose or gain weight? Was it difficult? What were the ups and downs? What did you learn from the experience? Did criticism about your weight help or hinder your efforts? Write an essay, based on your own experiences, in which you argue for or against a particular approach to maintaining a healthy weight.
2. As Critser points out, "food advertisers . . . spend billions teaching kids how to bug their parents into feeding them high-fat, high-sugar foods" (11). Write an essay in which you argue that food advertising has a negative influence on children and what they eat. Be sure to support your claim by offering evidence that children in general are vulnerable to advertising and, in particular, to claims made about food.
3. Write an essay in which you argue that a lack of exercise is at the root of the obesity epidemic. How have "indoor media," such as video games, the Internet, and television, contributed to children's physical inactivity? What effect has slashed physical education programs in schools had on children's health? (Glossary: *Cause and Effect*) Conduct library and Internet research to find evidence—facts, figures, and expert testimony—that supports your argument. (Glossary: *Evidence*) To begin your research online, go to **bedfordstmartins.com/models** and click on "Argument Links."

Supersize Me: It's Time to Stop Blaming Fat People for Their Size

■ **Alison Motluk**

Alison Motluk was born in Hamilton, Ontario, where she went to public school before receiving her BA from the University of Toronto. The creator of two radio documentaries, See, If You Can Hear This *and* Synaesthesia, *Motluk has written numerous articles for* New Scientist *magazine where she covers science policy.*

In the following essay, first published in New Scientist *on October 30, 2004, Motluk argues that instead of blaming people for being overweight, health officials have turned their attention to what has been termed our "obesogenic" environment, a new set of conditions that has made it much easier in the last few decades for people to gain weight.*

Reflecting on What You Know

What kind of physical activities were part of your childhood experience? In general, are you more, less, or about as active as you were as a child? What, if anything, has changed about you, your interests, or your environment to affect your activity as you have aged? Explain.

Whether it is undertakers introducing a new range of extra-large coffins or airlines planning to charge passengers by the kilo,[1] these days our expanding waistlines are rarely out of the news. It is hard to ignore the fact that body shape has changed dramatically over the past few decades. 1

In 1992 about 13 percent of Americans were clinically obese. Only ten years later that figure had rocketed to 22 percent, and in the three fattest states, Alabama, Mississippi, and West Virginia, it was over 2

[1]*kilo:* kilogram; a metric unit of weight equal to 2.2 pounds.

25 percent. As the UK, Australia, and many other Western countries follow the U.S. lead, the epidemic of obesity is now seen as one of the developed world's biggest public-health problems.

It is tempting to blame fat people for the state they're in. But health officials have recently begun to focus on a different culprit: the so-called "obesogenic" environment. In the United States, goes the argument, the prevailing culture actually promotes obesity, making an unhealthy lifestyle the default option. 3

Take diet. "Calorie-dense foods are far more readily available than ever before," says Martin Binks, a psychologist at Duke University's Diet and Fitness Center in Durham, North Carolina. Thanks to widespread affluence and agricultural subsidies, food in the United States is cheap and plentiful. Because fewer households have a stay-at-home parent to prepare meals from scratch, families increasingly turn to highly processed convenience foods, takeouts, or fast-food restaurants. Half the average American food budget goes on food eaten outside the home, much of which is high-fat. 4

Another insidious[2] influence on the American diet has been the gradual increase in portion sizes. "You eat more," says Judith Stern, a nutritionist and physician at the University of California at Davis, "even if you don't finish it." Restaurants and processed-food manufacturers can boost their profits by ratcheting up portion size and charging a little more because the price of food ingredients is so low relative to other costs such as packaging and transport. The original 1960s McDonald's meal of a hamburger, fries, and a twelve-ounce Coke contained about 590 calories. But today, a quarter-pounder with cheese and supersized fries and Coke—a meal that some kids consider an after-school snack—racks up a whopping 1550 calories. That's about three-quarters of the recommended daily calorie intake for an average woman. 5

The supersized diet is becoming the norm just as activity levels are dropping to an all-time low. "There's a great deal less access to physical activity than ever before in history," says Binks. The problem starts young. One-third of U.S. secondary-school students fail to get enough physical activity and over a tenth get none at all, according to recent figures from the Centers for Disease Control in Atlanta, Georgia. "The average child doesn't have any physical activity in school any more," says Binks. Many schools no longer even have breaks, let alone 6

---

[2]*insidious:* working harmfully in a subtle manner.

structured physical education, he says. "Physical activity is put on the back burner in favor of test results."

And thanks to the way that most U.S. towns and cities are designed, it is becoming increasingly difficult to get anywhere without driving. "We have suburbs without sidewalks," laments Stern. 7

Ironically, the U.S.'s obesogenic environment is one that societies through the ages have dreamed of: tasty, cheap food in abundance and barely a lick of hard work to be done. Who would have thought that it would one day hasten our demise? 8

Thinking Critically about This Reading

What does Motluk mean when she writes, "Ironically, the U.S.'s obesogenic environment is one that societies through the ages have dreamed of: tasty, cheap food in abundance and barely a lick of hard work to be done" (paragraph 8)? Explain the irony.

Questions for Study and Discussion

1. Motluk argues that health officials are beginning to blame our "obesogenic" environment for the obesity gripping our society (3). What is the "obesogenic" environment, and what are its components, according to Motluk?
2. Motluk concedes, "It is tempting to blame fat people for the state they're in" (3). Why doesn't she elaborate on this concession or put more blame on people's eating habits for their obesity?
3. What kinds of proof does Motluk offer for her claim that portion sizes have increased? (Glossary: *Evidence*)
4. Is obesity a problem that Americans alone face? Explain.
5. What solutions, if any, does Motluk propose to lessen the harmful effects of our "obesogenic" environment?

Classroom Activity Using Argument

In "Supersize Me," Motluk argues that it is "Time to Stop Blaming Fat People for Their Size." Through classroom discussion explore ways in which we can lessen the prejudice against those who are overweight by shedding light on the causes of obesity that go beyond personal eating habits.

Suggested Writing Assignments

1. Write an essay in which you argue for ways to counter the "obesogenic" environment. What can individuals, families, support groups, dietitians, schools, advertisers, food producers, and policy makers do to lessen the harmful trends that Motluk points out?
2. In an essay, argue that the federal government should make it mandatory for every school child to participate in some form of daily exercise in school. What objections would you anticipate arising as a result of such a mandate, and what counterarguments would you offer in defense of your proposal? After sharing your argument with your classmates, considering their advice, and revising your argument accordingly, send it to your congressional representatives for their consideration.
3. Write an essay in which you argue that obesity is both a serious health problem and a major economic concern. Conduct library and Internet research on the estimated costs of obesity to the insurance and healthcare industries, employers, and individuals. What effects do these costs have on the economy? (Glossary: *Cause and Effect*) To begin your research online, go to **bedfordstmartins.com/models** and click on "Argument Links."

Condemn the Crime, Not the Person

■ **June Tangney**

*Psychology educator and researcher June Tangney was born in Buffalo, New York, in 1958. After graduating from the State University of New York at Buffalo in 1979, she attended the University of California–Los Angeles, where she earned a master's degree in 1981 and a doctorate in 1985. Tangney taught briefly at Bryn Mawr College and held a research position at the Regional Center for Infants and Young Children in Rockville, Maryland. Since 1988 she has been a professor of psychology at George Mason University, where she was recognized with a Teaching Excellence Award. She is a coauthor of two books—*Self-Conscious Emotions: The Psychology of Shame, Guilt, Embarrassment, and Pride *(1995), with Kurt W. Fisher, and* Shame and Guilt *(2002), with Rhonda L. Dearing—and an associate editor at the journal* Self and Identity.

In the following essay, first published in the Boston Globe *on August 5, 2001, Tangney argues against the use of public humiliation as punishment. She bases her position on recent scientific evidence, much of which comes from her own work on shame and guilt.*

Reflecting on What You Know

For you, what is the difference between *shame* and *guilt*? Provide an example from your own experience to illustrate your understanding of each concept.

As the costs of incarceration mount and evidence of its failure as a deterrent grows, judges understandably have begun to search for creative alternatives to traditional sentences. One recent trend is the use of "shaming" sentences—sanctions explicitly designed to induce feelings of shame. 1

Judges across the country are sentencing offenders to parade around in public carrying signs broadcasting their crimes, to post signs on their front lawns warning neighbors of their vices, and to display "drunk driver" bumper stickers on their cars. 2

A number of social commentators have urged America to embrace public shaming and stigmatization as cheaper and effective alternatives for curbing a broad range of nonviolent crimes. Punishments aimed at public humiliation certainly appeal to our sense of moral righteousness. They do indeed appear fiscally attractive when contrasted with the escalating costs of incarceration. 3

But recent scientific evidence suggests that such attempts at social control are misguided. Rather than fostering constructive change, shame often makes a bad situation worse. 4

The crux[1] of the matter lies in the distinction between shame and guilt. Recent research has shown that shame and guilt are distinct emotions with very different implications for subsequent moral and interpersonal behavior. Feelings of shame involve a painful focus on the self—the humiliating sense that "I am a bad person." 5

Such humiliation is typically accompanied by a sense of shrinking, of being small, worthless, and powerless, and by a sense of being exposed. Ironically, research has shown that such painful and debilitating feelings of shame do not motivate constructive changes in behavior. 6

Shamed individuals are no less likely to repeat their transgressions (often more so), and they are no more likely to attempt reparation[2] (often less so). Instead, because shame is so intolerable, people in the midst of the experience often resort to any one of a number of defensive tactics. 7

They may seek to hide or escape the shameful feeling, denying responsibility. They may seek to shift the blame outside, holding others responsible for their dilemma. And not infrequently, they become irrationally angry with others, sometimes resorting to overtly aggressive and destructive actions. In short, shame serves to escalate the very destructive patterns of behavior we aim to curb. 8

Contrast this with feelings of guilt which involve a focus on a specific behavior—the sense that "I did a bad thing" rather than "I am a bad person." 9

[1]*crux:* the essential or deciding point.
[2]*reparation:* a making of amends; repayment.

Feelings of guilt involve a sense of tension, remorse, and regret over 10
the "bad thing done."

Research has shown that this sense of tension and regret typically 11
motivates reparative action (confessing, apologizing, or somehow repairing the damage done) without engendering[3] all the defensive and retaliative responses that are the hallmark of shame.

Most important, feelings of guilt are much more likely to foster 12
constructive changes in future behavior because what is at issue is not a bad, defective self, but a bad, defective behavior. And, as anyone knows, it is easier to change a bad behavior (drunken driving, slumlording, thievery) than to change a bad, defective self.

How can we foster constructive feelings of guilt among America's 13
offenders? Well, one way is to force offenders to focus on the negative consequences of their behavior, particularly on the painful negative consequences for others.

Community service sentences can do much to promote constructive 14
guilt when they are tailored to the nature of the crime. What is needed are imposed activities that underscore the tangible destruction caused by the offense and that provide a path to redemption by ameliorating[4] similar human misery.

Drunk drivers, for example, could be sentenced to help clear sites 15
of road accidents and to assist with campaigns to reduce drunken driving. Slumlords could be sentenced to assist with nuts and bolts repairs in low-income housing units. In this way, offenders are forced to see, first-hand, the potential or actual destructiveness of their infractions and they become actively involved in constructive solutions.

Some critics have rejected community service as an alternative to 16
incarceration, suggesting that such community-based sentences somehow cheapen an otherwise honorable volunteer activity while at the same time not adequately underscoring the criminal's disgrace.

Scientific research, however, clearly indicates that public shaming 17
and humiliation is not the path of choice. Such efforts are doomed to provoke all sorts of unintended negative consequences.

In contrast, thoughtfully constructed guilt-oriented community ser- 18
vice sentences are more likely to foster changes in offenders' future behaviors, while contributing to the larger societal good. My guess is

---

[3]*engendering:* causing or producing.

[4]*ameliorating:* improving or making better.

that any honorable community service volunteer would welcome such constructive changes.

Thinking Critically about This Reading

Tangney states that "a number of social commentators have urged America to embrace public shaming and stigmatization as cheaper and effective alternatives for curbing a broad range of nonviolent crimes" (paragraph 3). What evidence does she present to counter these arguments?

Questions for Study and Discussion

1. What is a "shaming" sentence (1)? According to Tangney, why do judges use such sentences in place of more traditional ones?
2. What is Tangney's position on using sentences intended to shame offenders? Briefly state her thesis in your own words. (Glossary: *Thesis*)
3. What for Tangney is the key difference between *shame* and *guilt*? Why does she believe that guilt works better than shame as a form of punishment?
4. Paragraph 13 begins with a rhetorical question: "How can we foster constructive feelings of guilt among America's offenders?" (Glossary: *Rhetorical Question*) How does Tangney answer this question? What suggestions would you add to her solution?
5. How does Tangney counter the critics of community service? Do you find her counterarguments convincing? Why or why not?

Classroom Activity Using Argument

The effectiveness of a writer's argument depends in large part on the writer's awareness of audience. For example, a writer arguing that there is too much violence portrayed on television might present different kinds of evidence, reasoning, and diction for different audiences, such as parents, lawmakers, or television producers and writers.

Review several of the argument essays you have read in this chapter. In your opinion, for what primary audience is each essay intended? List the evidence you use to determine your answers. (Glossary: *Evidence*)

Suggested Writing Assignments

1. Write an essay in which you tell the story of a childhood punishment that you received or witnessed. (Glossary: *Narration*) How did you feel about the punishment? Was it justified? Appropriate? Effective? Why or why not? In retrospect, did the punishment shame or humiliate you, or did it bring out feelings of guilt? What did you learn from this experience? Before starting to write, read or review Dick Gregory's "Shame" (pp. 278–82).
2. According to Tangney, "as the costs of incarceration mount and evidence of its failure as a deterrent grows, judges understandably have begun to search for creative alternatives to traditional sentences" (1). Ideally, knowing what the punishment will be should deter people from doing the wrong thing in the first place, but do punishments really act as deterrents? Are certain punishments more effective as deterrents than others? What are the deterrent benefits of both shame and guilt punishments? Conduct library and Internet research to answer these questions, and then report your findings and conclusions in an essay. To begin your research online, go to **bedfordstmartins.com/models** and click on "Argument Links."

Shame Is Worth a Try

■ **Dan M. Kahan**

Dan M. Kahan was born in 1963 and graduated from Middlebury College in 1986 and Harvard Law School in 1989, where he served as president of the Harvard Law Review. *He clerked for Judge Harry Edwards of the U.S. Court of Appeals for the District of Columbia circuit in 1989–1990 and for Justice Thurgood Marshall of the U.S. Supreme Court in 1990–1991. After practicing law for two years in Washington, D.C., Kahan launched his teaching career, first at the University of Chicago Law School and later at Yale Law School, where since 2003 he has been the Elizabeth K. Dollard Professor of Law. His teaching and research interests include criminal law, risk perception, punishment, and evidence. Kahan, who has written widely in legal journals on current social issues including gun control, is the co-author, with Tracey Meares, of* Urgent Times: Policing and Rights in Inner-City Communities *(1999). From 2005 to 2006, he was deputy dean of Yale Law School.*

In the following essay, first published in the Boston Globe *on August 5, 2001, Kahan argues in favor of the use of shame as a punishment that is "an effective, cheap, and humane alternative to imprisonment."*

Reflecting on What You Know

Think about the times you were punished as a child. Who punished you—parents, teachers, or other authority figures? What kinds of bad behavior were you punished for? What type of punishment worked best to deter you from behaving badly later on? Explain.

Is shame an appropriate criminal punishment? Many courts and legislators around the country think so. Steal from your employer in Wisconsin and you might be ordered to wear a sandwich board proclaiming your offense. Drive drunk in Florida or Texas and you might be required to place a conspicuous "DUI" bumper sticker to your car. 1

Refuse to make your child-support payments in Virginia and you will find that your vehicle has been immobilized with an appropriately colored boot (pink if the abandoned child is a girl, blue if a boy).

Many experts, however, are skeptical of these new shaming punishments. Some question their effectiveness as a deterrent. Others worry that the new punishments are demeaning and cruel. 2

Who's right? As is usually the case, both sides have their points. But what the shame proponents seem to be getting, and the critics ignoring, is the potential of shame as an effective, cheap, and humane alternative to imprisonment. 3

There's obviously no alternative to imprisonment for murderers, rapists, and other violent criminals. But they make up less than half the American prison population. 4

Liberal and conservative reformers alike have long believed that the remainder can be effectively punished with less severe "alternative sanctions," like fines and community service. These sanctions are much cheaper than jail. They also allow the offender to continue earning an income so he can compensate his victim, meet his child-support obligations, and the like. 5

Nevertheless, courts and legislators have resisted alternative sanctions—not so much because they won't work, but because they fail to express appropriate moral condemnation of crime. Fines seem to say that offenders may buy the privilege of breaking the law; and we can't very well condemn someone for purchasing what we are willing to sell. 6

Nor do we condemn offenders to educate the retarded, install smoke detectors in nursing homes, restore dilapidated low income housing, and the like. Indeed, saying that such community service is punishment for criminals insults both those who perform such services voluntarily and those whom the services are supposed to benefit. 7

There's no confusion about the law's intent to condemn, however, when judges resort to public shaming. As a result, judges, legislators, and the public at large generally do accept shame as a morally appropriate punishment for drunken driving, nonaggravated assaults, embezzlement,[1] small-scale drug distribution, larceny,[2] toxic waste dumping, perjury, and a host of other offenses that ordinarily would result in a short jail term. 8

---

[1]*embezzlement:* stealing money or goods entrusted to one's care.

[2]*larceny:* theft.

The critics' anxieties about shame, moreover, seem overstated. Clearly, shame hurts. People value their reputations for both emotional and financial reasons. In fact, a series of studies by Harold Grasmick, a sociologist at the University of Oklahoma, suggests that the prospect of public disgrace exerts greater pressure to comply with the law than does the threat of imprisonment and other formal punishments. 9

There's every reason to believe, then, that shaming penalties will be an effective deterrent, at least for nonviolent crimes. Indeed, preliminary reports suggest that certain shaming punishments, including those directed at dead beat dads, are extraordinarily effective. 10

At the same time, shame clearly doesn't hurt as much as imprisonment. Individuals who go to jail end up just as disgraced as those who are shamed, and lose their liberty to boot. Those who've served prison time are also a lot less likely to regain the respect and trust of their law-abiding neighbors—essential ingredients of rehabilitation. Given all this, it's hard to see shame as cruel. 11

Consider the case of a Florida mother sentenced to take out a newspaper ad proclaiming "I purchased marijuana with my kids in the car." 12

The prospect that her neighbors would see the ad surely caused her substantial embarrassment. But the alternative was a jail sentence, which would not only have humiliated her more but could also have caused her to lose custody of her children. Not surprisingly, the woman voluntarily accepted the shaming sanction in lieu of[3] jail time, as nearly all offenders do. 13

Shame, like any other type of criminal punishment, can definitely be abused. Some forms of it, like the public floggings imposed by authoritarian states abroad, are pointlessly degrading. 14

In addition, using shame as a supplement rather than a substitute for imprisonment only makes punishment more expensive for society and destructive for the offender. Accordingly, requiring sex offenders to register with local authorities is harder to defend than are other types of shaming punishments, which are true substitutes for jail. 15

These legitimate points, however, are a reason to insist that shaming be carried out appropriately, not to oppose it across the board. 16

In short, shame is cheap and effective and frees up scarce prison space for the more serious offenses. Why not at least give it a try? 17

---

[3]*in lieu of:* in place of; instead of.

Thinking Critically about This Reading

What does Kahan mean when he states that "requiring sex offenders to register with local authorities is harder to defend than are other types of shaming punishments" (paragraph 15)?

Questions for Study and Discussion

1. What is Kahan's thesis? (Glossary: *Thesis*) Where does he state it most clearly?
2. What examples of shaming punishments does Kahan provide? For you, do these punishments seem to fit the crime? Explain.
3. How does Kahan handle the opposition argument that public shaming is cruel?
4. According to Kahan, why have courts and legislators resisted alternative punishments such as fines and community service?
5. What evidence does Kahan present to show that shaming punishments work? (Glossary: *Evidence*)
6. How convincing is Kahan's argument? What is the strongest part of his argument? The weakest part? Explain.

Classroom Activity Using Argument

Can killing ever be justified? If so, under what circumstances? Have six members of the class, three on each side of the question, volunteer to hold a debate. Team members should assign themselves different aspects of their position and then do library and Internet research to develop ideas and evidence. The teams should be allowed equal time to present their assertions and the evidence they have to support them. Finally, the rest of the class should be prepared to discuss the effectiveness of the presentations on both sides of the question.

Suggested Writing Assignments

1. Write an essay in which you argue your position on the issue of using public shaming as a punishment. Is public shaming appropriate for some or all offenses that would otherwise result in a short jail term? Explain. Support your argument with evidence from Kahan's essay, June Tangney's "Condemn the Crime, Not the

Person" (pp. 566–69), the cartoon on page 107, and your own experiences and observations. (Glossary: *Evidence*) You may find it helpful to review your journal response for this selection.

2. Identify several current problems at your college or university involving violations of campus rules for parking, cheating on exams, plagiarizing papers, recycling waste, using drugs or alcohol, defacing school property, and so on. Select *one* problem, and write a proposal to treat violators with a shaming punishment of your own design. Address your proposal to your school's student government organization or administration office.
3. What is your position on the issue of whether convicted sex offenders should be required to register with local authorities? Should registration be required even though they have already served their sentences in prison? Should people have the right to know the identity of any sex offenders living in their neighborhoods, or is this an invasion of privacy? Conduct library and Internet research on the subject of sex offender registration, and write an essay arguing for or against such measures. To begin your research online, go to **bedfordstmartins.com/models** and click on "Argument Links."

Need Transplant Donors? Pay Them

■ Virginia Postrel

Virginia Postrel was born in 1960 and is a political and cultural writer who is best known for her two nonfiction books, The Future and Its Enemies *and* The Substance of Style. *A Phi Beta Kappa graduate of Princeton University in literature, Postrel began her writing career as a reporter for* Inc. *and the* Wall Street Journal *before becoming an editor at* Reason: Free Minds and Free Markets, *a print and online magazine. She now writes the monthly column "Commerce & Culture" for the* Atlantic *and contributes columns to* Forbes *four times a year. An opponent of federal bans on payment of "any valuable consideration" to organ donors, Postrel donated a kidney in 2006 to her friend Sally Satel, a psychiatrist and research fellow at the American Enterprise Institute. She frequently speaks on the subject of organ donation to business, academic, design, and technology groups.*

In the following article, which appeared in the June 10, 2006, issue of the Los Angeles Times, *Postrel argues for a solution to the problems of a broken transplant system in this country and of an ever-increasing number of patients who are unable to get transplants.*

Reflecting on What You Know

Are you aware of the need for donated organs? Have you ever considered giving an organ to someone in need? What factors would influence your decision?

When Kaiser Permanente forced kidney patients to transfer from the UC Davis and UC San Francisco transplant centers to its own fledgling program, it shortened their lives—and created a scandal. 1

But the Kaiser story represents much more than a single health maintenance organization's bad decisions. It reveals a fundamentally broken transplant system, a system that spends its time coping with an ever-growing, life-threatening organ shortage rather than finding ways to reduce or end it. 2

More than 66,000 Americans are languishing on the national waiting list for kidneys—ten times the number of kidneys transplanted from deceased donors each year. And the list keeps growing, with a queue of more than 100,000 expected by 2010. 3

Kidney patients literally live or die by where they are on the waiting list. While getting progressively sicker, they must spend several hours at least three times a week hooked up to a dialysis machine, the kidney-disease equivalent of an iron lung (it prolongs your life but imposes a physically debilitating prison sentence). 4

Increasing the supply of deceased donors, while desirable, is difficult—organ donors have to die healthy and in exactly the right circumstances. But even if every eligible cadaver were harvested, it wouldn't fill the gap. We need more kidney donors, lots more. And they need to be alive. 5

Unfortunately, our laws and culture discourage healthy people from donating organs, as I learned this spring when I gave a kidney to a friend. 6

My parents were appalled. My doctor told me, "You know you can change your mind." Many people couldn't understand why I didn't at least wait until my friend had been on dialysis for a while. 7

This pervasive attitude not only pressures donors to back out, it shapes policies that deter them. Some transplant centers require intrusive, demeaning psychological probes that scare people off. Some bioethicists suspect that donors suffer from a mental disorder, as opposed to being motivated by benevolence or religious conviction. 8

The scrutiny is particularly nasty when healthy people want to give their organs to strangers—not truly unknown people, mind you, but patients they have gotten to know through Internet sites or press coverage. 9

Many transplant centers flatly refuse "directed donations" to specific strangers. Some argue that it's "unfair" for patients to jump the queue with personal initiative and an appealing story; others insist that such donors aren't to be trusted (they must be either criminal or crazy). Posters at livingdonorsonline.org warn givers to never even mention the Internet, lest their good intentions be thwarted. 10

Sandra Grijalva, a San Francisco woman with polycystic kidney disease, asked Kaiser officials if she could find a donor online—after having one of her friends disqualified because of high blood pressure. "They said absolutely not," she says. The donor, Kaiser maintained, might someday try to extort money. (So might your cousin, but at least you'd be alive.) 11

Instead of dire possibilities, consider a cold reality: without tens of thousands of new living donors, most of the people on that very long waiting list are going to suffer and die on dialysis. The transplant community's top priority should be increasing the supply of willing donors. 12

The most obvious way to increase the supply of any scarce commodity—paying more for it—is illegal. Federal law blocks transplant centers, patients, and insurers from compensating donors in an above-board process, with full legal and medical protections. The growing and inevitable "transplant tourism" industry, and even shadier organ brokers, are the kidney equivalents of back-alley abortionists. 13

Legalized financial incentives would encourage more people to volunteer their organs. Donors would probably still be relatively rare, just as surrogate mothers are. Many, like me, would still help out without payment, just as some people get paid for giving blood or fighting fires while others do it for free. 14

Paying donors need not hurt the poor, any more than paying dialysis centers does. Compensation could, in fact, help low-income Americans, who are disproportionately likely to suffer from kidney disease. A one-year tax holiday for donors would nudge rich people to help. A pool to make up for lost wages (legal, but rare today) would enable many otherwise willing friends and relatives to contribute. 15

But even talking about incentives is taboo to some self-styled patient advocates. On Monday, the American Enterprise Institute will hold a conference in Washington on incentive-based transplant reforms. (It's organized by my kidney recipient, a physician and health-policy scholar at the institute.) When the National Kidney Foundation heard about the conference, its chief executive, John Davis, complained to the institute's president, "We don't see how an AEI forum would contribute substantively to debate on this issue." 16

Davis's group adamantly opposes donor compensation, lobbying against even experimental programs and small tax credits. It's as though the National Parkinson Foundation opposed stem cell research, or thought researchers should work for free. 17

Even a limited market in kidneys would transfer power from the rationing establishment to kidney patients and supportive communities. It would give patients more options. Grijalva, who works with developmentally disabled seniors, would welcome the shift. 18

"My biggest fear and my biggest feeling," she says, "is that I'm totally out of control, that these people have the control, and they are making all the decisions, and I have absolutely no input whatsoever." 19

Thinking Critically about This Reading

Why do you suppose there is heated opposition to allowing people to acquire organs in foreign countries, through the Internet, and from family and friends or to pay for them? Is it simply resistance to "jumping the queue" or the fear of extortion, as was explained to Postrel? Why do you think that health maintenance organizations object when patients try to find transplant donors by themselves?

Questions for Study and Discussion

1. What is Postrel's purpose in this essay? (Glossary: *Purpose*)
2. What makes the climate difficult for those wishing to donate organs?
3. Why do some transplant centers reject "directed donations"?
4. What does Postrel mean when she writes in paragraph 13, "The growing and inevitable 'transplant tourism' industry, and even shadier organ brokers, are the kidney equivalents of back-alley abortionists"?
5. What solutions to the organ shortages that she describes does Postrel put forth? Do they sound reasonable to you?
6. Postrel mentions some counterarguments to her suggestions that we should pay or give tax credits to organ donors and that patients should be able to search for them on the Internet or enlist the aid of acquaintances or friends in obtaining organs. What are those counterarguments? Do they seem reasonable to you? Explain.

Classroom Activity Using Argument

Deductive reasoning works on the model of the syllogism. After reviewing the material on syllogisms in the chapter introduction (p. 527), analyze the following syllogisms. Which work well, and which do not?

1. All of my CDs have blue lettering on them.
   I saw the new Youssou N'Dour CD the other day.
   The new Youssou N'Dour CD has blue lettering on it.
2. I have never lost a tennis match.
   I played a tennis match yesterday.
   I won my tennis match yesterday.
3. Surfers all want to catch the perfect wave.
   Jenny is a surfer.
   Jenny wants to catch the perfect wave.
4. Writers enjoy reading books.
   Bill enjoys reading books.
   Bill is a writer.
5. Cotton candy is an incredibly sticky kind of candy.
   Amy ate some incredibly sticky candy.
   Amy ate cotton candy.

Write two effective syllogisms of your own.

Suggested Writing Assignments

1. Write an essay in which you argue that people need to know more about the controversies surrounding organ transplants—to be better informed about organ shortages, about ways that the shortages can be reduced or eliminated, and about their own position on the issue. What can the government and the media do to inform the public about the shortage of donors and the many people who are waiting for organs? What can individuals do to better inform themselves?
2. If you think it is right, argue against paying for organ transplants or seeking help from friends or acquaintances to acquire a needed organ. What kinds of evidence will you need to build an effective argument? Where might you find such information? How will you present counterarguments such as those Postrel has presented and attempt to dismiss them?

A Moral Solution to the Organ Shortage

■ **Alexander Tabarrok**

Alexander Tabarrok is a Canadian economist and an associate professor of economics at George Mason University in Virginia. He was born in 1966, received his PhD in 1994 from George Mason University, and has taught at the University of Virginia and at Ball State University. Tabarrok is the research director for the Independent Institute, a think tank based in California, and assistant editor of the Independent Review. *Among the books he has edited for the Independent Institute are* Entrepreneurial Economics: Bright Ideas from the Dismal Science *(2002),* The Voluntary City: Choice, Community, and Civil Society *(2002), and* Changing the Guard: Private Prisons and the Control of Crime *(2002).*

In the following article, published as a Newsroom essay at the Independent Institute in February 2001, Tabarrok argues for a new way of relieving the acute shortage of donor organs.

Reflecting on What You Know

Have you registered with your state donor agency or indicated your permission on your driver's license to allow your organs to be harvested when you die? If you have, what persuaded you that it was a good idea? If you have not, what persuaded you that it was not something you wanted done?

Thousands of people will die this year while they wait helplessly for an organ transplant. Tragically, these deaths could be avoided if only more people signed their organ donor cards. Yet every year the organ shortage tends to become worse as medical technology increases the number of potential beneficiaries while social apathy and fear keep the number of donors relatively constant. Today, roughly 60,000 people are waiting for organ transplants, while less than 10,000 will become donors. Despite a prominent advertising campaign with Michael Jordan as spokesperson, and a national campaign of pastors, rabbis, and other clergy supporting donation, the supply of donors remains far below that necessary to save everyone on the waiting list. 1

Nobel Prize–winning economist Gary Becker has suggested that one possible solution to the crisis is to increase the incentive to donate organs by paying donors. One system, for example, would let organ procurement organizations pay the funeral expenses of organ donors. 2

Economists argue that anytime the price of a good or service is held below its market demand, a shortage develops. Just as government-mandated rent controls imposed in New York and other cities have led to a shortage of housing, government rules that outlaw buying or selling organs on the open market hold the price of organs at zero and make an organ shortage inevitable. Lift the restrictions, Becker and others say, and the shortage will end. 3

To some, this analysis may sound shocking, but these ideas are now so familiar to economists that at least one well-known textbook—Pindyck and Rubinfeld's *Microeconomics*—uses the organ shortage to illustrate the effect of price controls more generally. Nonetheless, many people may still be uncomfortable with the idea of human organs for sale. And for better or worse, few politicians are likely to take up the banner of laissez-faire when it comes to human organs. Fortunately, there is another possible solution. 4

I propose that the United Network for Organ Sharing (UNOS) consider restricting organ transplants to those who previously agreed to be organ donors; in short, a "no-give no-take" rule. While it is understandable that some people may have misgivings about becoming donors for personal or religious reasons, why should someone who was not willing to give an organ be allowed to take an organ? 5

Signing your organ donor card should be thought of as entry into a club, the club of potential organ recipients. Current UNOS policy is that organs are a "national resource." This is wrong. Organs should be the resource of potential organ donors, and signing an organ donor card should be tantamount to buying insurance. Being willing to give up an organ, should it no longer be of use to you, is the premium to be paid for the right to receive someone else's organ if one of yours fails. 6

How would the "no-give no-take" rule work in practice? Anyone could sign an organ donor card at any time and be registered as a potential donor. Most people would sign their cards when they receive their driver's license, as occurs today. Children would be automatically eligible to receive organs until the age of sixteen, when they would have the option of signing their card. To prevent someone from signing after learning they were in need, there would be a mandatory waiting period of at least one year before the right to receive an organ took effect. 7

Organs are now allocated on the basis of a point system in which medical need, the probability that the transplant would be effective, and the length of time already spent on the waiting list all play a role. A modest version of the "no-give no-take" rule could be implemented by stating that, henceforth, points should also be awarded for previously having signed one's organ donor card. 8

While this change may result in some people losing the chance to receive a transplant, far more people will be able to be served because there will be many more potential organ donors. If enough people sign their donor cards, this plan could even produce a surplus of organs. 9

What is needed to end the shortage of human organs, and to save the thousands of individuals who die because of the shortage, is a rethinking of the moral basis of organ collection and donation. Organs should not be owned by the nation as a whole, but rather by you and me and every other potential organ donor. We may still disagree on whether organs should be commodities traded on the open market, but few could argue with the notion that those who are willing to give should be the first to receive. 10

Thinking Critically about This Reading

Should human organs be treated as a commodity like all other material goods? Would creating a marketplace for human organs address the shortfall in supply? What's good about the idea? What's not good about it?

Questions for Study and Discussion

1. What do you think Tabarrok means by the use of the word *moral* in his title?
2. In your opinion, would the "no-give no-take" (paragraph 5) policy work in practice? Why or why not?
3. Might there be good reasons for wanting an organ but not giving one? Explain.
4. Have you been aware of the national campaign to encourage people to sign donor cards? Is it an effective advertising campaign, in your opinion? Why do you think that it has not worked well?
5. Comment on Tabarrok's style. Are his attitude toward his subject and his tone with his audience appropriate, in your opinion? Explain. (Glossary: *Attitude; Tone*)

Classroom Activity Using Argument

One strategy for developing a strong argument that most people find convincing is illustration. An array of examples, both brief and extended, has a remarkable ability to convince readers of the truth of a proposition. Although it is possible to argue a case with one specific example that is both appropriate and representative, most writers find that a varied set of examples often makes a more convincing case. Therefore, it is important to identify your examples before starting to write.

As an exercise in argumentation, choose one of the following position statements and make a list of at least four examples to illustrate the position:

Capital punishment is an ineffective deterrent to crime.

A lot of work needs to be done to make us energy independent.

Most children's television programs are marked by many incidents of violence.

If asked, most people will contribute their time, effort, and money to a charitable cause.

Suggested Writing Assignments

1. Write a letter to the director of the United Network for Organ Sharing (UNOS) in which you explain that you think that Tabarrok's idea for organ sharing is a good one for various reasons. Use the statistics published on the UNOS site, and refer to the ideas that Virginia Postrel has presented in her essay "Need Transplant Donors? Pay Them" (pp. 576–79). If you have a family member or a friend who is waiting for an organ, consider describing their situation as a firsthand example of the crisis. Above all, show respect, and be mindful of your tone in attempting to persuade UNOS officials of your views.
2. When Tabarrok published his article in 2001, 60,000 people were waiting for organ transplants. As of July 15, 2008, that number had risen to 99,294, with fewer than 10,000 transplants having taken place. What ideas do you have for alleviating the short supply of donor organs? Might something be done among college students that has not already been tried? What more can doctors, healthcare workers, and clergy do? Write an essay arguing for your proposal.

Hiding in Plain Sight

■ Heather Rogers

Heather Rogers is a documentary filmmaker, journalist, and author of Gone Tomorrow: The Hidden Life of Garbage *(2005). The theme of her 2002 documentary and later book are the same: our mass production of goods and the consumerism associated with it have created a garbage-disposal problem of staggering dimensions. Her documentary has been shown in numerous venues around the globe, and* Library Journal *has said that parts of her book "read like a thriller." Rogers has published in the* Nation, Utne Reader, Z Magazine, Brooklyn Rail, Punk Planet, *and* Art and Design. *She makes her home in Brooklyn, New York.*

In the following excerpt adapted from Gone Tomorrow, *Rogers describes how garbage is collected, processed, and then buried in a major commercial waste dumping site in Pennsylvania as a way to argue against the unnecessary production of materials.*

Reflecting on What You Know

Do you ever think about the role that you play in producing and disposing of garbage? Do you know where the garbage that you personally generate every day ends up? Does it matter to you? Why or why not?

In the dark chill of early morning, heavy steel garbage trucks chug and creep along neighborhood collection routes. A worker empties the contents of each household's waste bin into the truck's rear compaction unit. Hydraulic compressors scoop up and crush the dross, cramming it into the enclosed hull. When the rig is full, the collector heads to a garbage depot called a "transfer station" to unload. From there the rejectamenta is taken to a recycling center, an incinerator, or, most often, to what's called a "sanitary landfill." 1

Land dumping has long been the favored disposal method in the United States thanks to the relative low cost of burial, and North 2

America's abundant supply of unused acreage. Although the great majority of our castoffs go to landfills, they are places the public is not meant to see. Today's garbage graveyards are sequestered, guarded, veiled. They are also high-tech, and, increasingly, located in rural areas that receive much of their rubbish from urban centers that no longer bury their own wastes.

There's a reason landfills are tucked away, on the edge of town, in otherwise untraveled terrain, camouflaged by hydroseeded, neatly tiered slopes. If people saw what happened to their waste, lived with the stench, witnessed the scale of destruction, they might start asking difficult questions. Waste Management Inc., the largest rubbish handling corporation in the world, operates its Geological Reclamation Operations and Waste Systems (GROWS) landfill just outside Morrisville, Pennsylvania—in the docile river valley near where Washington momentously crossed the Delaware leading his troops into Trenton in 1776. Sitting atop the landfill's three-hundred-foot-high butte composed entirely of garbage, the logic of our society's unrestrained consuming and wasting quickly unravels. 3

Up here is where the dumping takes place; it is referred to as the fill's "working face." Clusters of trailer trucks, yellow earthmovers, compacting machines, steamrollers, and water tankers populate this bizarre, thirty-acre nightmare. Churning in slow motion through the surreal landscape, these machines are remaking the earth in the image of garbage. Scores of seagulls hover overhead then suddenly drop into the rotting piles. The ground underfoot is torn from the metal treads of the equipment. Potato chip wrappers, tattered plastic bags, and old shoes poke through the dirt as if floating to the surface. The smell is sickly and sour. 4

The aptly named GROWS landfill is part of Waste Management Inc.'s (WMI) six-thousand-acre garbage treatment complex, which includes a second landfill, an incinerator, and a state-mandated leaf composting lot. GROWS is one of a new breed of waste burial sites referred to as "mega-fills." These high-tech, high-capacity dumps are comprised of a series of earth covered "cells" that can be ten to one-hundred acres across and up to hundreds of feet deep—or tall, as is the case at GROWS. (One Virginia whopper has disposal capacity equivalent to the length of one thousand football fields and the height of the Washington Monument.) As of 2002, GROWS was the single largest recipient of New York City's garbage in Pennsylvania, a state that is the country's biggest depository for exported waste. 5

WMI's Delaware-side operation sits on land that has long served the interests of industry. Overlooking a rambling, mostly decommissioned U.S. Steel factory, WMI now occupies the former grounds of the Warner Company. In the previous century, Warner surface mined the area for gravel and sand, much of which was shipped to its cement factory in Philadelphia. The area has since been converted into a reverse mine of sorts; instead of extraction, workers dump, pack, and fill the earth with almost 40 million pounds of municipal wastes daily. 6

Back on top of the GROWS landfill, twenty-ton dump trucks gather at the low end of the working face, where they discharge their fetid cargo. Several feet up a dirt bank, a string of large trailers are being detached from semi trucks. In rapid succession each container is tipped almost vertical by a giant hydraulic lift and, within seconds, twenty-four tons of putrescence cascades down into the day's menacing valley of trash. In the middle of the dumping is a "landfill compactor"—which looks like a bulldozer on steroids with mammoth metal spiked wheels—that pitches back and forth, its fifty tons crushing the detritus into the earth. A smaller vehicle called a "track loader" maneuvers on tank treads, channeling the castoffs from kitchens and offices into the compactor's path. The place runs like a well-oiled machine, with only a handful of workers orchestrating the burial. 7

Get a few hundred yards from the landfill's working face and it's hard to smell the rot or see the debris. The place is kept tidy with the help of thirty-five-foot tall fencing made of "litter netting" that surrounds the perimeter of the site's two landfills. As a backup measure, teams of "paper pickers" constantly patrol the area retrieving discards carried off by the wind. Small misting machines dot fence tops, roads, and hillsides, spraying a fine, invisible chemical-water mixture into the air, which binds with odor molecules and pulls them to the ground. 8

In new state-of-the-art landfills, the cells that contain the trash are built on top of what is called a "liner." The liner is a giant underground bladder intended to prevent contamination of groundwater by collecting leachate—liquid wastes and the rainwater that seeps through buried trash—and channeling it to nearby water treatment facilities. WMI's two Morrisville landfills leach on average 100,000 gallons daily. If this toxic stew contaminated the site's groundwater it would be devastating. 9

Once a cell is filled, which might take years, it is closed off or "capped." The capping process entails covering the garbage with several feet of dirt, which gets graded, then packed by steamrollers. After that, layers of clay-embedded fabric, synthetic mesh, and plastic sheeting are 10 draped across the top of the cell and joined with the bottom liner (which is made of the same materials) to encapsulate all those outmoded appliances, dirty diapers, and discarded wrappers.

Today's landfill regulations, ranging from liner construction to post-capping oversight, mean that disposal areas like WMI's GROWS are potentially less dangerous than the dumps of previous generations. But the fact remains that these systems are short-term solutions to the garbage problem. While they may not seem toxic now, all those underground cells packed with plastics, solvents, paints, batteries, and other hazardous materials will someday have to be treated since the liners won't last forever. Most liners are expected to last somewhere between thirty and fifty years. That time frame just happens to coincide with the post-closure liability private landfill operators are subject to; thirty years after a site is shuttered, its owner is no longer responsible for contamination, the public is. 11

There is a palpable tension at waste treatment facilities, as though at any minute the visitor will uncover some illegal activity. But what's most striking at these places isn't what they might be hiding; it's what's in plain view. The lavish resources dedicated to destroying used commodities and making that obliteration acceptable, even "green," is what's so astounding. Each landfill (not to mention garbage collection systems, transfer stations, recycling centers, and incinerators) is an expensive, complex operation that uses the latest methods developed and perfected at laboratories, universities, and corporate campuses across the globe. 12

The more state-of-the-art, the more "environmentally responsible" the operation, the more the repressed question pushes to the surface: what if we didn't have so much trash to get rid of? 13

Thinking Critically about This Reading

In her final sentence Rogers writes, "What if we didn't have so much trash to get rid of?" Why do you suppose we have this problem? Are we overpackaging our consumer goods? If so, why? What might be some of the other reasons we generate so much trash?

Questions for Study and Discussion

1. What is Rogers's purpose in this essay? (Glossary: *Purpose*)
2. What is Rogers's thesis? (Glossary: *Thesis*)

3. Does the author argue using induction or deduction or a combination of both? (Glossary: *Induction; Deduction*) Why do you suppose that she uses the type of argument she does?
4. Why is Waste Management Inc.'s GROWS landfill only a short-term solution? Who will ultimately have to deal with the garbage?
5. Cite at least a half dozen examples of where Rogers uses emotionally charged language to highlight what is in the landfill that she describes. (Glossary: *Diction*) How does her diction help to support her argument? Why in paragraph 1 do you think that Rogers placed the term "sanitary landfill" in quotation marks?
6. What is the "leachate" that Rogers discusses in paragraph 9? Why is it potentially dangerous?

Classroom Activity Using Argument

In a classroom discussion, determine whether Rogers make use of ethos, pathos, or logos or some combination of the three types in her argument.

Suggested Writing Assignments

1. Some have suggested that humans may psychologically take delight in throwing things away. Because we live in a society that overproduces products, the tendency to discard has gained acceptance and is on the increase. For example, about 80 percent of U.S. products are used once and then thrown away. Seek out information on the Web or in your school library to test the validity of the idea that we have a psychological tendency to discard and, if it exists, to determine how prevalent it is. Write an essay based on your findings that either supports the idea or argues against it.
2. One aspect of our throwaway society that most people have encountered is the disposal of electronics products. For two days each year, the Small Dog computer company in Vermont runs a collection service for outdated small electronic products. The photograph on page 590 shows what they collected in two days.

   Write an essay or an op-ed article for your local newspaper in which you argue that your campus or community can run a similar program. Make sure that you explain the need for the program.

Photo by Liz Rosa.

Also mention that the responsibility for the proper disposal of computer and electronic products (some of which contain dangerous substances) rests with both the consumer and also with those who produce, distribute, sell, and service these products. You can find out more about Small Dog's recycling program at http://images.smalldog.com/pressroom/PR_2008_ewaste_national.pdf.

On Dumpster Diving

■ **Lars Eighner**

Born in Texas in 1948, Lars Eighner attended the University of Texas at Austin. After graduation, he launched a career writing essays and fiction. A volume of his short stories, Bayou Boy and Other Stories, *was published in 1985. Eighner became homeless in 1988 when he left his job as an attendant at a mental hospital. He has written two novels,* Pawn to Queen Four *(1995) and* Whispered in the Dark *(1996), and a collection of essays,* Gay Cosmos *(1995).*

The following selection, which appeared in the Utne Reader *in 1995, is an abridged version of an essay that first appeared in* Threepenny Review. *The piece eventually became part of Eighner's startling account of the three years that he spent as a homeless person,* Travels with Lizbeth *(1993). The essay recounts how Eighner lived virtually hand-to-mouth and scavenged in Dumpsters to stay alive. In describing how he supported himself on throwaways, Eighner makes a poignant argument against the excessive waste that our society generates—overpackaging, thoughtless food waste, blind consumerism, and the lost economic value of what we nonchalantly toss in the trash.*

Reflecting on What You Know

Do you ever think about what you throw away? Might we find some psychological gratification in rejecting objects and removing them from our sight? Is there really an "away"? Are we not simply moving objects from one place to another? Have you ever thrown away something that was perfectly good?

I began Dumpster diving about a year before I became homeless. 1

I prefer the term *scavenging.* I have heard people, evidently mean- 2
ing to be polite, use the word *foraging,* but I prefer to reserve that word for gathering nuts and berries and such, which I also do, according to the season and opportunity.

I like the frankness of the word *scavenging.* I live from the refuse 3
of others. I am a scavenger. I think it a sound and honorable niche,

although if I could I would naturally prefer to live the comfortable consumer life, perhaps—and only perhaps—as a slightly less wasteful consumer owing to what I have learned as a scavenger.

Except for jeans, all my clothes come from Dumpsters. Boom boxes, candles, bedding, toilet paper, medicine, books, a typewriter, a virgin male love doll, coins sometimes amounting to many dollars: all came from Dumpsters. And, yes, I eat from Dumpsters, too. 4

There is a predictable series of stages that a person goes through in learning to scavenge. At first the new scavenger is filled with disgust and self-loathing. He is ashamed of being seen. 5

This stage passes with experience. The scavenger finds a pair of running shoes that fit and look and smell brand-new. He finds a pocket calculator in perfect working order. He finds pristine ice cream, still frozen, more than he can eat or keep. He begins to understand: people do throw away perfectly good stuff, a lot of perfectly good stuff. 6

At this stage he may become lost and never recover. All the Dumpster divers I have known come to the point of trying to acquire everything they touch. Why not take it, they reason, it is all free. This is, of course, hopeless, and most divers come to realize that they must restrict themselves to items of relatively immediate utility. 7

The finding of objects is becoming something of an urban art. Even respectable, employed people will sometimes find something tempting sticking out of a Dumpster or standing beside one. Quite a number of people, not all of them of the bohemian[1] type, are willing to brag that they found this or that piece in the trash. 8

But eating from Dumpsters is the thing that separates the dilettanti[2] from the professionals. Eating safely involves three principles: using the senses and common sense to evaluate the condition of the found materials; knowing the Dumpsters of a given area and checking them regularly; and seeking always to answer the question "Why was this discarded?" 9

Yet perfectly good food can be found in Dumpsters. Canned goods, for example, turn up fairly often in the Dumpsters I frequent. I also have few qualms about dry foods such as crackers, cookies, cereal, chips, and pasta if they are free of visible contaminants and still dry and crisp. Raw fruits and vegetables with intact skins seem perfectly 10

---

[1]*bohemian:* nonconformist; eccentric.

[2]*dilettanti:* amateurs; dabblers, not experts.

safe to me, excluding, of course, the obviously rotten. Many are discarded for minor imperfections that can be pared away.

A typical discard is a half jar of peanut butter—though nonorganic peanut butter does not require refrigeration and is unlikely to spoil in any reasonable time. One of my favorite finds is yogurt—often discarded, still sealed, when the expiration date has passed—because it will keep for several days, even in warm weather. 11

No matter how careful I am I still get dysentery[3] at least once a month, oftener in warm weather. I do not want to paint too romantic a picture. Dumpster diving has serious drawbacks as a way of life. 12

I find from the experience of scavenging two rather deep lessons. The first is to take what I can use and let the rest go. I have come to think that there is no value in the abstract. A thing I cannot use or make useful, perhaps by trading, has no value, however fine or rare it may be. 13

The second lesson is the transience of material being. I do not suppose that ideas are immortal, but certainly they are longer-lived than material objects. 14

The things I find in Dumpsters, the love letters and rag dolls of so many lives, remind me of this lesson. Now I hardly pick up a thing without envisioning the time I will cast it away. This, I think, is a healthy state of mind. Almost everything I have now has already been cast out at least once, proving that what I own is valueless to someone. 15

I find that my desire to grab for the gaudy bauble has been largely sated. I think this is an attitude I share with the very wealthy—we both know there is plenty more where whatever we have came from. Between us are the rat-race millions who have confounded their selves with the objects they grasp and who nightly scavenge the cable channels for they know not what. 16

I am sorry for them. 17

Thinking Critically about This Reading

Is Eighner's implicit statement regarding our throwaway society ironic? (Glossary: *Irony*) Doesn't he throw away things? Or is he a person who is thoughtful about what he takes possession of in the first place? Explain.

---

[3]*dysentery:* severe diarrhea caused by an infection.

Questions for Study and Discussion

1. What is Eighner's purpose in this essay? (Glossary: *Purpose*) What implicit argument does he make?
2. What is "Dumpster diving"? Why does Eighner use the word "scavenging" rather than "foraging" or "Dumpster diving"? What do these three terms mean to him? What does his discussion of these three terms early in the essay tell you about Eighner?
3. What two lessons does Eighner learn from scavenging? Why are they important to him? In what ways has scavenging benefited Eighner? In what ways has it harmed him?
4. If you have read Heather Rogers's essay "Hiding in Plain Sight" (pp. 585–88), what relationship do you see between Eighner's experiences and Rogers's visit to the Pennsylvania waste disposal site?
5. Explain Eighner's last two paragraphs. What does he mean in writing that between the attitudes of the wealthy and himself as a scavenger "are the rat-race millions who have confounded their selves with the objects they grasp" (16)?
6. Assess Eighner's attitude toward his subject and himself. (Glossary: *Attitude*) Is he confounded by what he finds in Dumpsters? Is he proud of what he does? Is he upset with himself? Does he approach his subject with a matter-of-fact attitude? Is he a realist?
7. How do you respond to Eighner's Dumpster diving practices? Are you shocked? Bemused? Accepting? Challenged?

Classroom Activity Using Argument

In a classroom discussion, share ideas about what to buy, what to keep, what to use, what to neglect, and what to throw away. What principles, if any, guide you and the other members of your class in making such decisions? Has your attitude toward ownership of material objects changed over time? If so, how? What principles would you like to work toward?

Suggested Writing Assignments

1. How important are material objects to you? Eighner emphasizes the transience of material objects and thinks that all of us delude ourselves with the objects we strive to acquire. Is there anything

wrong with desiring material goods? Write an essay in which you react to Eighner's position on materialism.

2. In paragraph 3, Eighner states that he "live[s] from the refuse of others." How do his confession and the following cartoon affect you? Do you agree with the cartoon's central idea—that "we've . . . become a throwaway society"? If so, how? How do Eighner's accounts of homelessness and Dumpster diving make you feel about your own consumerism and trash habits? Write an essay in which you examine the things you throw away in a single day. What items did you get rid of? Why? Could those items be used by someone else? Have you ever felt guilty about throwing something away? If so, what was it and why?

"We've certainly become a throwaway society."

appendix

Writing a Research Paper

The research paper is an important part of a college education—and for good reason. In writing a research paper, you acquire a number of indispensable skills that you can adapt to other college assignments and to situations after graduation.

The real value of writing a research paper, however, goes beyond acquiring basic skills; it is a unique hands-on learning experience. The purpose of a research paper is not to present a collection of quotations that show you can report what others have said about your topic. Rather, your goal is to analyze, evaluate, and synthesize the materials you research—and thereby learn how to do so with any topic. You learn how to view the results of research from your own perspective and to arrive at an informed opinion of a topic.

Writing a researched essay is not very different from the other writing you will be doing in your college writing course. You will find yourself drawing heavily on what you learned from the four student papers in the first two chapters of this text. First you determine what you want to write about. Then you decide on a purpose, consider your audience, develop a thesis, collect your evidence, write a first draft, revise and edit, and prepare a final copy. What differentiates the research paper from other kinds of papers is your use of outside sources and how you acknowledge them.

In this appendix, you will learn some valuable research techniques, including how to:

- Establish a realistic schedule for your research project
- Conduct research on the Internet using directory and keyword searches
- Evaluate print and Internet sources
- Analyze print and Internet sources
- Develop a working bibliography

- Take useful notes
- Summarize, paraphrase, and quote your sources
- Acknowledge your sources using Modern Language Association (MLA) style in-text citations and a list of works cited

Your library research will involve working with both print and electronic sources. In both cases, however, the process is essentially the same. Your aim is to select the most appropriate sources for your research from the many that are available on your topic.

A research project easily spans several weeks. To avoid losing track of time and finding yourself facing an impossible deadline at the last moment, establish a realistic schedule for completing key tasks. By thinking of the research paper as a multistaged process, you avoid becoming overwhelmed by the size of the whole undertaking.

Your schedule should allow at least a few days to accommodate unforeseen needs and delays. Use the following template, which lists the essential steps in writing a research paper, to plan your own research schedule.

Research Paper Schedule

Task	Completion Date
1. Choose a research topic, and pose a worthwhile question.	___/___/___
2. Locate print and electronic sources.	___/___/___
3. Develop a working bibliography.	___/___/___
4. Evaluate and analyze your sources.	___/___/___
5. Read your sources, taking complete and accurate notes.	___/___/___
6. Develop a preliminary thesis, and make a working outline.	___/___/___
7. Write a draft of your paper, including sources that you have summarized, paraphrased, and quoted.	___/___/___
8. Visit your college writing center for help with your revision.	___/___/___
9. Decide on a final thesis, and modify your outline.	___/___/___
10. Revise your paper, and properly cite all borrowed materials.	___/___/___
11. Prepare a list of works cited.	___/___/___
12. Prepare the final manuscript, and proofread.	___/___/___
13. Submit your research paper.	___/___/___

USING PRINT AND ONLINE SOURCES

In most cases, you should use print sources (books, newspapers, journals, magazines, encyclopedias, pamphlets, brochures, and government documents) as your primary tools for research. Print sources, unlike many Internet sources, are often reviewed by experts in the field before they are published, are generally overseen by a reputable publishing company or organization, and are examined by editors and fact checkers for accuracy and reliability. Unless you are instructed otherwise, you should try to use print sources in your research.

The best place to start any search for print and online sources is your college library's home page. There you will find links to the computerized catalog of book holdings, online reference works, periodical databases, electronic journals, and a list of full-text databases. You'll also find links for subject study guides and for help conducting your research.

To find print sources, search through your library's reference works, electronic catalog, periodical indexes, and other databases to generate a preliminary listing of books, magazine and newspaper articles, public documents and reports, and other sources that may be

Library Home Page

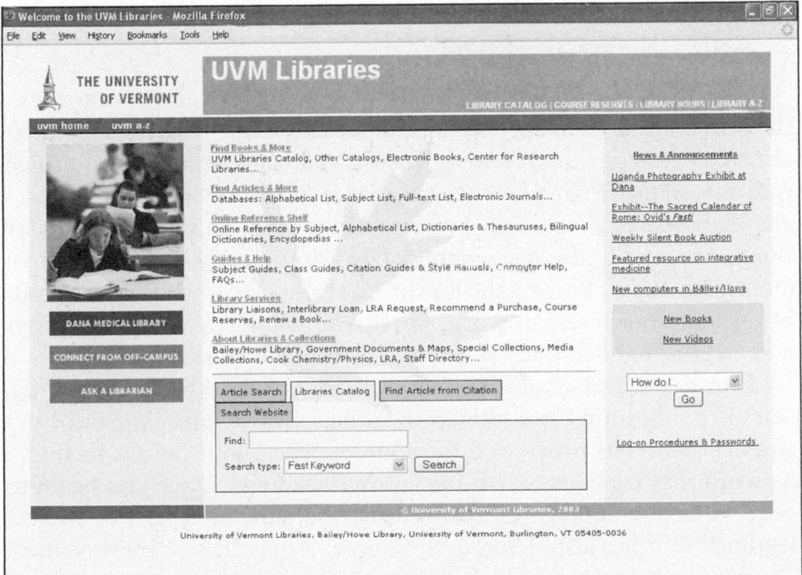

helpful in exploring your topic. At this early stage, it is better to err on the side of listing too many sources, so that later on, you will not have to relocate sources you discarded too hastily.

You will find that Internet sources can be informative and valuable additions to your research. The Internet is especially useful in providing recent data, stories, and reports. For example, you might find a just-published article from a university laboratory or a news story in your local newspaper's online archives. Generally, however, both print and Internet sources should be used. Print sources are generally published under the guidance of a publisher or an organization, but practically anyone with access to a computer and an Internet connection can place text and pictures online. No governing body checks Web sites' content for accuracy. The Internet offers both carefully maintained resources and much unreliable information. It is your responsibility to determine whether a given Internet source should be trusted.

If you need more instruction on conducting Internet searches, go to your campus computer center, or consult one of the many books written for Internet beginners. You can also access valuable information for searching the Internet at Diana Hacker's Research and Documentation Online at **bedfordstmartins.com/resdoc.**

USING KEYWORD SEARCHES TO LOCATE INFORMATION IN THE LIBRARY AND ON THE INTERNET

Use a keyword search to start your search for sources about your topic. The search might be in an electronic database, in the library's computerized catalog, or on the Internet. To use your time efficiently, you will want to conduct a keyword search that is likely to yield solid sources and leads for your research project. As obvious or simple as it may sound, you need to use meaningful keywords to start a successful search about your topic. You might find it helpful to list potential keywords throughout your research work. Often you will discover combinations of keywords that will lead you directly to the sources that you need.

Databases and library catalogs index sources by author, title, year of publication, and subject headings (which are assigned by a cataloger who has previewed the source). The object here is to find a keyword that matches one of the subject headings. Once you begin to locate sources that are on your topic, be sure to note the subject headings that are listed for each source. You can use these subject

Computer Catalog Screen: Complete Record for a Book

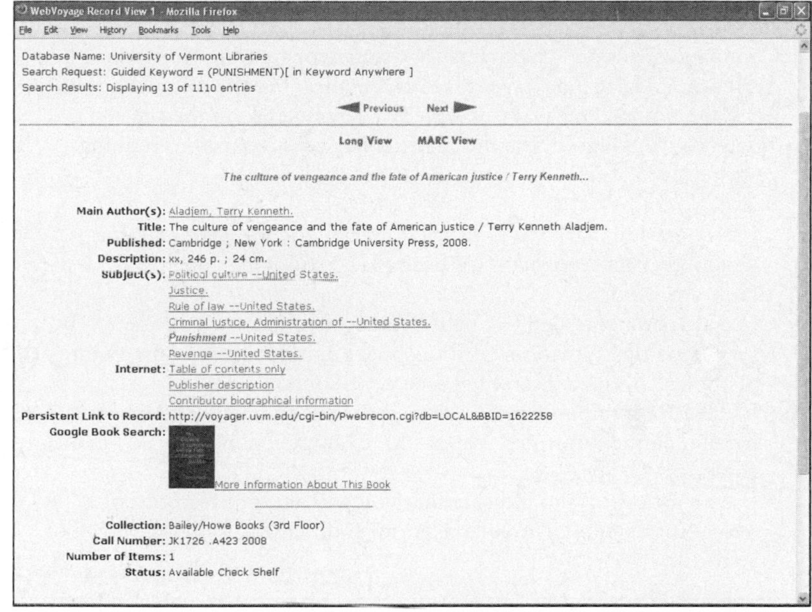

headings as keywords to lead you to additional book sources. They also can lead you to articles in periodicals that are gathered in full-text databases (like *Info Trac, LexisNexis, Expanded Academic ASAP,* or *JSTOR*) to which your library subscribes. Notice the additional subject headings on the computer catalog for a book above.

Web searches are less structured. When you type in a keyword in the "Search" box on a search engine's home page, the search engine electronically scans Web sites to match your keyword to titles and texts. On the Web, the quality of the search terms (the keywords) is determined by the relevance of the hits on the first page that comes up. A search on the Internet might yield a million hits, but the search engine's algorithm puts the best sources up front. After you scan the first couple of pages of results, you can decide whether these sites seem on topic. If they seem off topic, you will need to refine your search terms to narrow or broaden your search. It is always a good idea to look for search tips on the help screens or advanced search instructions for the search engine you are using before initiating a keyword search.

Refining Keyword Searches on the Web

Command terms and characters vary somewhat among electronic databases and popular Internet search engines, but the following functions are almost universally accepted. You can click on the site's "Help" or "Advanced Search" links to ask questions about refining your keyword search.

- Use quotation marks or parentheses when you are searching for words in exact sequence—for example, "whooping cough"; (Supreme Court).
- Use AND or a plus sign (+) between words to narrow your search by specifying that all words need to appear in a document—for example, tobacco AND cancer; Shakespeare + sonnet.
- Use NOT or a minus sign (−) between words to narrow your search by eliminating unwanted words—for example, monopoly NOT game; cowboys – Dallas.
- Use an asterisk (*) to indicate that you will accept variations of a term—for example, "food label*" for food labels, food labeling, and so forth.

USING SUBJECT DIRECTORIES TO DEFINE AND DEVELOP YOUR RESEARCH TOPIC

You can browse through the subject directories on the home pages of search engines and look for interesting subjects and topics. Subject directories are also helpful if you have a topic but need an exact research question or if you want to know if you'll be able to supplement your research work with enough print sources. Once you choose a subject area in the directory, you can select specialized subdirectories and eventually arrive at a list of sites that are closely related to your topic.

At this stage in a Web search, students commonly ask, "How can I tell if I'm looking in the right place?" There is no simple answer to this question. If more than one subject area sounds plausible, you will have to dig more deeply into each of their subdirectories, using logic and the process of elimination to determine which one is likely to produce the best leads for your topic. In most cases, it takes just one or two clicks to figure out whether you're searching in the right subject area. If you click on a subject area and the topics in its subdirectories do not relate to your research topic, try a different subject area. As you browse through various subject directories and subdirectories, keep a running list of keywords that are associated with your topic so that you can use them in subsequent keyword searches.

EVALUATING YOUR PRINT AND ONLINE SOURCES

You will not have to spend much time in the library to realize that you cannot read every print and online source that appears relevant. Given the abundance of print and Internet sources, the key to successful research is identifying those books, articles, Web sites, and other online sources that will help you most. You must evaluate your potential sources to determine which materials you will read, which you will skim, and which you will simply eliminate. The following box lists strategies for identifying promising sources.

Strategies for Evaluating Print and Online Sources

Evaluating a Book

- Read the dust jacket or cover copy for insights into the book's coverage, its currency, and the author's expertise.
- Scan the table of contents, and identify any promising chapters.
- Read the author's preface, looking for his or her thesis and purpose.
- Check the index for key words or key phrases related to your research topic.
- Read the opening and concluding paragraphs of any promising chapters. If you are unsure about its usefulness, skim the whole chapter.
- Does the author have a discernible bias?

Evaluating an Article

- What do you know about the journal or magazine that has published the article? Scholarly journals (*American Economic Review*, *Journal of Marriage and the Family*, the *Wilson Quarterly*) publish articles that are written by authorities who have conducted original research. Research essays always cite their sources in footnotes or bibliographies. Popular news and general-interest magazines (*National Geographic*, *Smithsonian*, *Time Magazine*, and *Ebony*), on the other hand, publish informative, entertaining, and easy-to-read articles that are written by editorial staff or freelance writers. Popular essays sometimes cite sources but often do not.

- What is the reputation of the journal or magazine? Determine the publisher or sponsor. Is it an academic institution, a commercial enterprise, or an individual? Does the publisher or publication have a reputation for accuracy and objectivity?
- Who are the readers of this journal or magazine?
- What are the author's credentials?
- Consider the title or headline of the article, the opening paragraph or two, and the conclusion. Does the source appear to be too general or too technical for your needs and audience?
- For articles in journals, read the abstract (a summary of the main points), if there is one.
- Examine any photographs, charts, graphs, or other illustrations that accompany the article. Determine how useful they might be for your research purposes.

Evaluating a Web Site

- Consider the type of Web site. Is this site a personal blog or professional publication? Often the URL, especially the top-level domain name, can give you a clue about the kinds of information provided and the type of organization behind the site. Common suffixes include:

  .com — business, commercial, or personal
  .edu — educational institution
  .gov — government sponsored
  .net — various types of networks
  .org — nonprofit organization, but also some commercial or personal

  Be advised that *.org* is not regulated like *.edu* and *.gov*, for example. Most nonprofits use *.org*, but many commercial and personal sites do as well.
- Examine the home page of the site. Does the content appear to be related to your research topic?
- Is there an "About" link on the home page that takes you to background information on the site's sponsor? Is there a mission statement, history, or statement of philosophy? Can you verify if the site is official—actually sanctioned by the organization or company?
- Identify the author of the site. What are the author's qualifications for writing on this subject?
- Is a print equivalent available? Is the Web version more or less extensive than the print version?
- When was the site last updated? Is the content current enough for your purposes?

You can also find sources on the Internet itself that offer useful guidelines for evaluating electronic sources. One excellent example was created by reference librarians at the Wolfgram Memorial Library of Widener University. Google *Wolfgram evaluate web pages.* For additional guidance, go to **bedfordstmartins.com/rewriting** and click on "Evaluating Online Sources Tutorial."

On the basis of your evaluation, select the most promising books, articles, and Web sites to pursue in depth for your research project.

ANALYZING YOUR PRINT AND ONLINE SOURCES

Before beginning to take notes, analyze your sources for their relevance, bias, overall argument, and reliability in helping you explore your topic. Look for the writers' main ideas, key examples, strongest arguments, and conclusions. Read critically: it is easy to become absorbed in sources that support your beliefs, but always seek out several sources with opposing viewpoints, if only to test your own position. Look for information about the authors themselves—information that will help you determine their authority and perspective or bias on the issues. You should also know the reputation and special interests of book publishers and magazines because you are likely to get different views—conservative, liberal, international, feminist—on the same topic, depending on the publication you read. Use the accompanying checklist to help analyze your print and online sources.

Checklist for Analyzing Print and Online Sources

- What is the writer's thesis or claim?
- How does the writer support this thesis? Does the evidence seem reasonable and ample, or is it mainly anecdotal?
- Does the writer consider opposing viewpoints?
- Does the writer have any obvious political or religious biases? Is the writer associated with a special-interest group such as Planned Parenthood, Greenpeace, Amnesty International, or the National Rifle Association?
- Is the writer an expert on the subject? Do other writers mention this author in their work?
- Does the publisher or publication have a reputation for accuracy and objectivity?

- Is important information documented in footnotes or links so that it can be verified or corroborated in other sources?
- Is the author's purpose to inform? Or is it to argue for a particular position or action?
- Do the writer's thesis and purpose clearly relate to your topic?
- Does the source appear to be too general or too technical for your needs and audience?
- Does the source reflect current thinking and research in the field?

DEVELOPING A WORKING BIBLIOGRAPHY

As you discover books, journal and magazine articles, newspaper stories, and Web sites that you think might be helpful for writing your paper, you need to start maintaining a record of important information about each source. This record, called a *working bibliography,* will enable you to know where sources are located when it comes time to consult and acknowledge them in your paper and list of works cited (see pp. 615–21). In all likelihood, your working bibliography will contain more sources than you actually consult and include in your list of works cited.

You may find it easy to make a separate bibliography card, using a 3 × 5 index card, for each work that you think might be helpful to your research. As your collection of cards grows, alphabetize them by the authors' last names. By using a separate card for each book, article, or Web site, you can continually edit your working bibliography, dropping sources that do not prove helpful and adding new ones.

With the computerization of most library resources, you can copy bibliographic information from the library computer catalog and periodical indexes or from the Internet and paste it into a document on your computer. Then you can edit, add, delete, and search these sources throughout the research process. You also can track your project online with the Bedford Bibliographer (**bedfordstmartins.com/bibliographer**). The advantage of copying and pasting over writing on index cards is accuracy, especially in punctuation, spelling, and capitalization.

Checklist for a Working Bibliography

For Books

Library call number
Names of all authors, editors, and translators
Title and subtitle
Publication data:
  Place of publication (city and state)
  Publisher's name
  Date of publication
Edition number (if not the first) and volume number (if applicable)

For Periodical Articles

Names of all authors
Name and subtitle of article
Title of journal, magazine, or newspaper
Publication data:
  Volume number and issue number
  Date of issue
  Page numbers

For Internet Sources

Names of all authors, editors, compilers, or sponsoring agents
Title and subtitle of the document
Title of the longer work to which the document belongs (if applicable)
Title of the site or discussion list name
Author, editor, or compiler of the Web site or online database
Date of release, online posting, or latest revision
Name and vendor of database or name of online service or network
Medium (online, CD-ROM, etc.)
Format of online source (Web page, e-mail, etc.)
Date of access
Electronic address (URL or network path)

For Other Sources

Name of author, government agency, organization, company, recording artist, personality, etc.
Title of the work

Format (pamphlet, unpublished diary, interview, television broadcast, etc.)
Publication or production data:
Name of publisher or producer
Date of publication, production, or release
Identifying codes or numbers (if applicable)

TAKING NOTES

As you gather and sort your source materials, you'll want to record the information that you consider most pertinent to your topic. As you read, take notes. You're looking for ideas, facts, opinions, statistics, examples, and other evidence that you think will be useful as you write your paper. As you work through books and articles, look for recurring themes, and notice where writers are in agreement and where they differ. Try to remember that the effectiveness of your paper is largely determined by the quality—not necessarily the quantity—of your notes. Your purpose is not to present a collection of quotes that show you've read all the material and know what others have said about your topic. Your goal is to analyze, evaluate, and synthesize the information you collect—in other words, to enter into the discussion of the issues and thereby take ownership of your topic. You want to view the results of your research from your own perspective and arrive at an informed opinion of your topic.

Now for some practical advice on taking notes: First, be systematic in your note taking. As a rule, write one note on a card and include the author's full name, the complete title of the source, and a page number indicating the origin of the note. Use cards of uniform size, preferably 4 × 6 cards because they are large enough to accommodate even a long note on a single card and yet small enough to be easily handled and conveniently carried. Following this system will also help you when you get to the planning and writing stage because you will be able to sequence your notes according to the plan you envision for your paper. Furthermore, should you decide to alter your organizational plan, you can easily reorder your cards to reflect your revisions. You can, of course, do note taking on your computer as well, which makes it easy for you to reorder your notes. An added advantage of the computer is that the Copy and Paste features let you move notes and their citations directly into your essay.

Second, try not to take too many notes. One good way to control your note taking is to ask yourself, "How exactly does this material help prove or disprove my thesis?" Try to envision where in your paper you could use the information. If it does not seem relevant to your thesis, don't bother to take a note.

Once you decide to take a note, you must decide whether to summarize, paraphrase, or quote directly. The approach you take should be determined by the content of the passage and the way you plan to use it in your paper. All the examples in the following discussion are taken from essays in *Models for Writers.*

Summary

When you *summarize* material from one of your sources, you capture in condensed form the essential idea of a passage, an article, or an entire chapter. Summaries are particularly useful when you are working with lengthy, detailed arguments or long passages of narrative or descriptive background information in which the details are not germane to the overall thrust of your paper. You simply want to capture the essence of the passage because you are confident that your readers will readily understand the point being made or do not need to be convinced about its validity. Because you are distilling information, a summary is always shorter than the original; often a chapter or more can be reduced to a paragraph, or several paragraphs to a sentence or two. Remember, in writing a summary you should use your own words.

Consider the following paragraphs, in which Richard Lederer compares big words with small words in some detail:

> When you speak and write, there is no law that says you have to use big words. Short words are as good as long ones, and short, old words—like *sun* and *grass* and *home*—are best of all. A lot of small words, more than you might think, can meet your needs with a strength, grace, and charm that large words do not have.
>
> Big words can make the way dark for those who read what you write and hear what you say. Small words cast their clear light on big things—night and day, love and hate, war and peace, and life and death. Big words at times seem strange to the eye and ear

> and the mind and the heart. Small words are the ones we seem to have known from the time we were born, like the hearth fire that warms the home.
>
> –Richard Lederer, "The Case for Short Words," pages 284–85

A student wishing to capture the gist of Lederer's point without repeating his detailed contrast created the accompanying summary note card.

Summary Note Card

Short Words

Lederer favors short words for their clarity, familiarity, durability, and overall usefulness.

Lederer, "The Case for Short Words," 284–85

Paraphrase

When you *paraphrase* material from a source, you restate the information in your own words instead of quoting directly. Unlike a summary, which gives a brief overview of the essential information in the original, a paraphrase seeks to maintain the same level of detail as the original to aid readers in understanding or believing the information presented. A paraphrase presents the original information in approximately the same number of words but with different wording. To put it another way, your paraphrase should closely parallel the presentation of ideas in the original, but it should not use the same words or sentence structure as the original. Even though you are using your own words in a paraphrase, it's important to remember that you are borrowing ideas and therefore must acknowledge the source of these ideas with a citation.

How would you paraphrase the following passage from "The Ways of Meeting Oppression" by Martin Luther King Jr.?

> If the American Negro and other victims of oppression succumb to the temptation of using violence in the struggle for freedom, future generations will be the recipients of a desolate night of bitterness, and our chief legacy to them will be an endless reign of meaningless chaos. Violence is not the way.
>
> –Martin Luther King Jr., "The Ways of Meeting Oppression," page 134

See the accompanying note card for an example of how one student paraphrased the passage.

Paraphrase Note Card

Non-Violence

African Americans and other oppressed peoples must not resort to taking up arms against their oppressors because to do so would lead the country into an era of turmoil and confusion. Armed confrontation will not yield the desired results.

Martin Luther King Jr.,
"The Ways of Meeting Oppression," 134

In most cases, it is best to summarize or paraphrase material—which by definition means using your own words—instead of quoting verbatim (word for word). Capturing an idea in your own words demonstrates that you have thought about and understood what your source is saying.

Direct Quotation

When you *quote* a source directly, you copy the words of your source exactly, putting all quoted material in quotation marks. When you make a quotation note card, check the passage carefully for accuracy, including punctuation and capitalization. Be selective about what you choose to quote. Reserve direct quotation for important ideas stated memorably, for especially clear explanations by authorities, and for arguments by proponents of a particular position in their own words.

Consider the accompanying direct quotation note card. It quotes a passage from William Zinsser's "Simplicity," on page 174 in this text, emphasizing the importance—and rarity—of clear, concise writing.

Direct Quotation Note Card

Wordiness

"Clutter is the disease of American writing. We are a society strangling in unnecessary words, circular constructions, pompous frills, and meaningless jargon."

William Zinsser, "Simplicity," 174

On occasion you'll find a long, useful passage with some memorable wording in it. Avoid the temptation to quote the whole passage; instead, try combining summary or paraphrase with direct quotation. Consider the following paragraph from Abe Whaley's essay "Once Unique, Soon a Place Like Any Other":

> Though native Appalachians like me are gradually being outnumbered by newcomers, we remain tied to the land in a way outsiders will never understand. It provides for us physically, socially, spiritually, and emotionally. Without it, we lose our cultural identity and, ultimately, ourselves. This is not a new fight; it has raged in these mountains for generations as our land has been exploited again and again. For too long, we have suffered the effects of clear-cutting, strip mining, and unscrupulous land grabs by timber companies, coal companies, and even the federal government. Developers are simply the latest to try their hand at making a buck.
>
> –Abe Whaley, "Once Unique, Soon a Place Like Any Other," page 182

In the accompanying quotation and summary note card, notice how the student is careful to put quotation marks around all words borrowed directly.

Quotation and Summary Note Card

Sense of Place and Personal Identity

Even though outsiders have flooded in, "we remain tied to the land in a way outsiders will never understand. It provides for us physically, socially, spiritually, and emotionally. Without it, we lose our cultural identity and, ultimately, ourselves." Over the years greedy business types have ravaged our land, leaving us and the once beautiful mountains scarred forever.

Abe Whaley, "Once Unique, Soon a Place Like Any Other," 182

Notes from Internet Sources

Working from the computer screen or from a printout, you can take notes from the Internet just as you would from print sources. You will need to decide whether to summarize, paraphrase, or quote directly the information you wish to borrow. Copy the material into a separate document by using your mouse to highlight the portion of the text you want to save and then using the Copy and Paste features to add it to your research notes. For a complete discussion of how to integrate your outside sources into your paper and how to avoid plagiarism, see Chapter 10, Writing with Sources.

DOCUMENTING SOURCES

Whenever you summarize, paraphrase, or quote a person's thoughts and ideas and whenever you use facts or statistics that are not commonly known or believed, you must properly acknowledge the source of your information. If you do not properly acknowledge ideas and information created by someone else, you are guilty of *plagiarism*, of using someone else's material but making it look as if it were your own (see pages 247–51). You must document the source of your information whenever you do the following:

- Quote a source word-for-word
- Refer to information and ideas from another source that you present in your own words as either a paraphrase or a summary
- Cite statistics, tables, charts, or graphs

You do not need to document these types of information:

- Your own observations, experiences, and ideas
- Factual information available in a number of reference works (known as "common knowledge")
- Proverbs, sayings, and familiar quotations

A reference to the source of your borrowed information is called a *citation*. There are many systems for making citations, and your citations must consistently follow one of these systems. The documentation style recommended by the Modern Language Association is commonly used in English and the humanities and is the style used throughout this book. Another common system is the American Psychological Association (APA) style, which is generally used in the social sciences. Your instructor will probably tell you which style to use. For more information on documentation styles, consult the appropriate manual or handbook, or go to Diana Hacker's Research and Documentation Online at **bedfordstmartins.com/resdoc**.

There are two components of documentation. *In-text citations* are placed in the body of your paper, and the *list of works cited* provides complete publication data for your in-text citations and is placed at the end of your paper. Both of these components are necessary for complete documentation.

In-Text Citations

In-text citations, also known as *parenthetical citations*, give the reader citation information immediately, at the point at which it is most meaningful. Rather than having to find a footnote or an endnote, the reader sees the citation as a part of the writer's text.

Most in-text citations consist of only the author's last name and a page reference. Usually the author's name is given in an introductory or signal phrase at the beginning of the borrowed material, and the page reference is given in parentheses at the end. If the author's name is not given at the beginning, put it in parentheses along with the page reference. When you borrow material from two or more works by the same author, you must include the title of the work in the signal phrase or parenthetically at the end. (See pages 264 and 266 for examples.) The parenthetical reference signals the end of the borrowed material and directs your readers to the list of works cited should they want to pursue a particular source. Treat electronic sources as you do print sources, keeping in mind that some electronic sources use paragraph numbers instead of page numbers. Consider the following examples of in-text citations, which are from student Bonnie Sherman's paper titled "Should Shame Be Used as Punishment?"

In-Text Citations (MLA Style)

The use of "shaming" punishments as alternatives to traditional sentences of jail time has sparked a heated debate in the world of criminal justice. Many believe that such punishments—designed to humiliate offenders—are unusually cruel and should be abandoned. Psychology professor June Tangney argues that "shame serves to escalate the very destructive patterns of behavior we aim to curb" (567). In contrast, one law school professor believes that "the critics' anxieties about shame . . . seem overstated" and cites a recent study showing "that the prospect of public disgrace exerts greater pressure to comply with the law than does the threat of imprisonment" (Kahan 573).

List of Works Cited (MLA Style)

Kahan, Dan M. "Shame Is Worth a Try." *Models for Writers.* 10th ed. Eds. Alfred Rosa and Paul Eschholz. Boston: Bedford, 2010. 571–73. Print.

Tangney, June. "Condemn the Crime, Not the Person." *Models for Writers.* 10th ed. Eds. Alfred Rosa and Paul Eschholz. Boston: Bedford, 2010. 566–69. Print.

List of Works Cited

In this section, you will find general MLA guidelines for creating a works cited list followed by sample entries that cover the citation situations you will encounter most often. Make sure that you follow the formats as they appear on the following pages. If you would like to compile your list of works cited online, go to **bedfordstmartins.com/bibliographer.**

General Guidelines

- Begin the works cited list on a new page following the last page of text. Center the title "Works Cited" at the top of the page.
- Organize the list alphabetically by authors' last names. If a source has no author, alphabetize the entry using the first major word of the title.
- Double-space within and between entries.
- Begin each entry at the left margin. If the entry is longer than one line, indent the second and subsequent lines five spaces or one-half inch.
- Do not number entries.

Books

BOOK BY ONE AUTHOR

List the author's last name first, followed by a comma and the first name. Italicize the title. Follow with the city of publication and a shortened version of the publisher's name—for example, *Houghton* for *Houghton Mifflin,* or *Cambridge UP* for *Cambridge University Press.* Next add the date of publication. End by indicating that the source is a printed one.

Nathan, Rebekah. *My Freshman Year: What a Professor Learned by Becoming a Student.* Ithaca: Cornell UP, 2005. Print.

BOOK BY TWO OR THREE AUTHORS

List the first author (following the order on the title page) in the same way as for a single-author book; list subsequent authors, first name first, in the order in which they appear on the title page.

Drew, Ned, and Paul Sternberger. *By Its Cover: Modern American Book Cover Design.* New York: Princeton Architectural P, 2004. Print.

BOOK BY FOUR OR MORE AUTHORS

List the first author in the same way as for a single-author book, followed by a comma and the abbreviation *et al.* ("and others").

Beardsley, John, et al. *Gee's Bend: The Women and Their Quilts*. Atlanta: Tinwood, 2002. Print.

Or you may list the first author in the same way as for a single-author book, followed by a comma and then the names of all subsequent authors, first name first, in the order in which they appear on the title page. (Note, however, that if you choose this method your in-text citations must list each author's last name, matching the corresponding entry on your works cited page.)

Beardsley, John, William Arnett, Paul Arnett, Jane Livingston, and Alvia J. Wardlaw. *Gee's Bend: The Women and Their Quilts.* Atlanta: Tinwood, 2002. Print.

TWO OR MORE SOURCES BY THE SAME AUTHOR

List two or more sources by the same author in alphabetical order by title. List the first source by the author's name. After the first source, in place of the author's name substitute three unspaced hyphens followed by a period.

Quart, Alissa. *Branded: The Buying and Selling of Teenagers.* New York: Perseus, 2003. Print.

---. "Welcome to (Company Name Here) High (TM)." *New York Times* 1 July 2003, late ed.: A19. Print.

REVISED EDITION

Phillipson, David W. *African Archeology.* 3rd ed. New York: Cambridge UP, 2005. Print.

EDITED BOOK

Wollstonecraft, Mary. *The Collected Letters of Mary Wollstonecraft.* Ed. Janet Todd. New York: Penguin, 2004. Print.

TRANSLATION

Basho, Matsuo. *Basho's Journey: The Literary Prose of Matsuo Basho.* Trans. David Landis Barnhill. Albany: State U of New York P, 2005. Print.

ANTHOLOGY

Eggers, Dave, ed. *The Best American Nonrequired Reading, 2002.* New York: Houghton, 2002. Print.

SELECTION FROM AN ANTHOLOGY

Smith, Seaton. "'Jiving' with Your Teen." *The Best American Nonrequired Reading, 2002.* Ed. Dave Eggers. New York: Houghton, 2002. 88-94. Print.

SECTION OR CHAPTER FROM A BOOK

Kurlansky, Mark. "The Hapsburg Pickle." *Salt: A World History*. New York: Walker, 2002. 234-310. Print.

Periodicals

ARTICLE IN A JOURNAL WITH CONTINUOUS PAGINATION THROUGHOUT AN ANNUAL VOLUME

Some journals paginate issues continuously, by volume; that is, the page numbers in one issue pick up where the previous issue left off. For these journals, the year of publication, in parentheses, follows the volume number.

Kramer-Moore, Daniela, and Michael Moore. "Pardon Me for Breathing: Seven Types of Apology." *ETC: A Review of General Semantics* 60 (2003): 160-69. Print.

ARTICLE IN A JOURNAL WITH SEPARATE PAGINATION IN EACH ISSUE

Some journals paginate by issue; that is, each issue begins with page 1. For these journals, follow the volume number with a period and the issue number. Then give the year of publication in parentheses.

McGlone, Matthew S. "Quoted Out of Context: Contextomy and Its Consequences." *Journal of Communication* 55.2 (2005): 330–46. Print.

ARTICLE IN A MONTHLY MAGAZINE

List the author or authors the same way as for books. List the article's title in quotation marks, followed by the publication's title, italicized. Abbreviate all months except May, June, and July. If an article in a magazine or newspaper is not printed on consecutive pages—for example, an article might begin on page 45 and then skip to 48—include only the first page, followed by a plus sign.

Kaiser, Charles. "Civil Marriage, Civil Rights." *Advocate* Mar. 2004: 72. Print.

ARTICLE IN A WEEKLY OR BIWEEKLY MAGAZINE

Quittner, Josh. "Who Will Rule the New Internet?" *Time* 16 June 2008: 47-50. Print.

ARTICLE IN A NEWSPAPER

If the newspaper lists an edition, add a comma after the date and specify the edition.

Wheeler, Ginger. "Weighing in on Chubby Kids: Smart Strategies to Curb Obesity." *Chicago Tribune* 9 Mar. 2004, final ed.: C11+. Print.

EDITORIAL (SIGNED/UNSIGNED)

Jackson, Derrick Z. "The Winner: Hypocrisy." Editorial. *Boston Globe* 6 Feb. 2004, late ed.: A19. Print.

"A Real Schedule for Ground Zero." Editorial. *New York Times* 18 June 2008, national ed.: A22. Print.

LETTER TO THE EDITOR

Liu, Penny. Letter. *New York Times* 17 Jan. 2004, late ed.: A14. Print.

Internet Sources

Citations for Internet sources follow the same rules as citations for print sources, but several additional pieces of information are required to cite an Internet source—the date of electronic publication (if available), and the date you accessed the source. Additionally, citations for different types of Internet sources require different types of information, so be sure to review the models that follow.

ENTIRE WEB SITE (SCHOLARLY PROJECT, INFORMATION DATABASE, OR PROFESSIONAL WEB SITE)

List the site's title first, italicized, followed by the editor, compiler, or person responsible for maintaining or updating the site, if known. Next, include the date of the site's last update, if known; the name of the sponsoring organization, if known; a notation that you accessed the site via the Web; and the date you accessed the site.

BBC: Religion and Ethics. British Broadcasting Corporation, 2008. Web. 29 Sept. 2008.

The Victorian Web. Ed. George P. Landow. 19 Apr. 2006. Brown U. Web. 10 Jan. 2008.

SHORT WORK FROM A WEB SITE

"Designer Babies." *BBC: Religion and Ethics.* British Broadcasting Corporation, 2008. Web. 29 May 2008.

Wojtczak, Helena. "The Women's Social and Political Union." *The Victorian Web*. Ed. George P. Landow. 19 Apr. 2006. Brown U. Web. 10 Jan. 2008.

PERSONAL HOME PAGE

Budbill, David. Home page. 1 June 2008. Web. 20 Aug. 2008.

ONLINE BOOK

Whitman, Walt. *Leaves of Grass*. 1900. Ed. Steven van Leeuwen. 2004. *Bartleby.com: Great Books Online*. Web. 1 Sept. 2005.

SECTION OR CHAPTER FROM AN ONLINE BOOK

Whitman, Walt. "Crossing Brooklyn Ferry." *Leaves of Grass*. 1900. Ed. Steven van Leeuwen. 2004. *Bartleby.com: Great Books Online*. Web. 1 Sept. 2005.

ARTICLE IN AN ONLINE SCHOLARLY JOURNAL

Drury, Nevill. "How Can I Teach Peace When the Book Only Covers War?" *Online Journal of Peace and Conflict Resolution* 5.1 (2003: n. page). Web. 18 Mar. 2008.

ARTICLE IN AN ONLINE MAGAZINE

Engber, Daniel. "How Do You Measure Sea Level?" *Slate*. Newsweek Interactive Co., 29 Aug. 2005. Web. 1 Sept. 2008.

ARTICLE IN AN ONLINE NEWSPAPER

Bhatt, Sanjay. "Got Game? Foundation Promotes Chess as Classroom Learning Tool." *Seattle Times Online*. Seattle Times Co., 15 Mar. 2004. Web. 31 Aug. 2008.

ARTICLE IN AN ONLINE REFERENCE WORK

"Chili Pepper." *Encyclopedia Britannica*. 2008. *Encyclopedia Britannica Online*. Web. 19 June 2008.

ARTICLE FROM A LIBRARY SUBSCRIPTION SERVICE

Follow the guidelines for citing an article from a print periodical. Complete the citation by providing the name of the database, italicized, if known; the name of the subscription service; medium of access; and date of your access.

Strimel, Courtney B. "The Politics of Terror: Rereading *Harry Potter*." *Children's Literature in Education* Mar. 2004: 35-53. *Academic Search Premier*. Web. 22 Feb. 2008.

E-MAIL MESSAGE

Bohjalian, Christopher. "Re: Preview *Skeletons at the Feast*—Coming May 6, 2008." Message to Paul Eschholz. 18 Mar. 2008. E-mail.

ONLINE POSTING

Weiss, Larry. "Old Fat Hamlet?" *Shaksper: The Global Electronic Shakespeare Conf.* 18 Aug. 2005. Web. 15 Nov. 2008.

Other Nonprint Sources

TELEVISION OR RADIO PROGRAM

"Everyone's Waiting." *Six Feet Under*. Dir. Alan Ball. Perf. Peter Krause, Michael C. Hall, Frances Conroy, and Lauren Ambrose. Writ. Alan Ball. HBO. 21 Aug. 2005. Television.

FILM OR VIDEO RECORDING

Million Dollar Baby. Dir. Clint Eastwood. Perf. Clint Eastwood, Hilary Swank, and Morgan Freeman. Warner, 2004. DVD.

PERSONAL INTERVIEW

Kozalek, Mark. Personal interview. 22 Jan. 2008.

LECTURE

England, Paula. "Gender and Inequality: Trends and Causes." President's Distinguished Lecture Series. U of Vermont Memorial Lounge, Burlington. 22 Mar. 2004. Lecture.

Glossary of Useful Terms

Abstract *See Concrete/Abstract.*

Allusion An allusion is a passing reference to a familiar person, place, or thing, often drawn from history, the Bible, mythology, or literature. An allusion is an economical way for a writer to capture the essence of an idea, atmosphere, emotion, or historical era, as in "The scandal was his Watergate" or "He saw himself as a modern Job" or "The campaign ended not with a bang but a whimper." An allusion should be familiar to the reader; if it is not, it will add nothing to the meaning.

Analogy Analogy is a special form of comparison in which the writer explains something unfamiliar by comparing it to something familiar: "A transmission line is simply a pipeline for electricity. In the case of a water pipeline, more water will flow through the pipe as water pressure increases. The same is true of electricity in a transmission line."

Anecdote An anecdote is a short narrative about an amusing or interesting event. Writers often use anecdotes to begin essays as well as to illustrate certain points.

Argumentation To argue is to attempt to persuade the reader to agree with a point of view, to make a given decision, or to pursue a particular course of action. There are two basic types of argumentation: logical and persuasive. See the introduction to Chapter 21 (pp. 525–32) for a detailed discussion of argumentation.

Attitude A writer's attitude reflects his or her opinion of a subject. The writer can think very positively or very negatively about a subject or have an attitude that falls somewhere in between. See also *Tone.*

Audience An audience is the intended readership for a piece of writing. For example, the readers of a national weekly newsmagazine come from all walks of life and have diverse interests, opinions, and educational backgrounds. In contrast, the readership for an organic chemistry journal is made up of people whose interests and education are quite similar. The essays in *Models for Writers* are intended for general readers, intelligent people who may lack specific information about the subject being discussed.

Beginnings and Endings A beginning is the sentence, group of sentences, or section that introduces an essay. Good beginnings usually identify the thesis or controlling idea, attempt to interest readers, and establish a tone.

An ending is the sentence or group of sentences that brings an essay to a close. Good endings are purposeful and well planned. They can be a summary, a concluding example, an anecdote, or a quotation. Endings satisfy readers when they are the natural outgrowths of the essays themselves and give readers a sense of finality or completion. Good essays do not simply stop; they conclude. See the introduction to Chapter 6 (pp. 137–45) for a detailed discussion of beginnings and endings.

Cause and Effect Cause-and-effect analysis explains the reasons for an occurrence or the consequences of an action. See the introduction to Chapter 20 (pp. 501–3) for a detailed discussion of cause and effect.

Classification See *Division and Classification.*

Cliché A cliché is an expression that has become ineffective through overuse. Expressions such as *quick as a flash, jump for joy,* and *slow as molasses* are clichés. Writers normally avoid such trite expressions and seek instead to express themselves in fresh and forceful language. See also *Diction.*

Coherence Coherence is a quality of good writing that results when all sentences, paragraphs, and longer divisions of an essay are naturally connected. Coherent writing is achieved through (1) a logical sequence of ideas (arranged in chronological order, spatial order, order of importance, or some other appropriate order), (2) the purposeful repetition of key words and ideas, (3) a pace suitable for your topic and your reader, and (4) the use of transitional words and expressions. Coherence should not be confused with unity. (See *Unity.*) See also *Transition.*

Colloquial Expression A colloquial expression is an expression that is characteristic of or appropriate to spoken language or to writing that seeks the effect of spoken language. Colloquial expressions are informal, as *chem, gym, come up with, be at wit's end, won't,* and *photo* illustrate. Thus, colloquial expressions are acceptable in formal writing only if they are used purposefully. See also *Diction.*

Combined Strategies By combining rhetorical strategies, writers are able to develop their ideas in interesting ways. For example, in writing a cause-and-effect essay about a major oil spill, the writer might want to describe the damage that the spill caused, as well as explain the cleanup process step by step.

Comparison and Contrast Comparison and contrast is used to point out the similarities and differences between two or more subjects in the same class or category. The function of any comparison and contrast is to clarify—to reach some conclusion about the items being compared and contrasted. See the introduction to Chapter 19 (pp. 474–78) for a detailed discussion of comparison and contrast.

Conclusions See *Beginnings and Endings.*

Concrete/Abstract A concrete word names a specific object, person, place, or action that can be directly perceived by the senses: *car, bread, building, book, John F. Kennedy, Chicago,* or *hiking.* An abstract word, in contrast, refers to general qualities, conditions, ideas, actions, or relationships that cannot be directly perceived by the senses: *bravery, dedication, excellence, anxiety, stress, thinking,* or *hatred.* See the introduction to Chapter 11 (pp. 273–77) for more on abstract and concrete words.

Connotation/Denotation Both connotation and denotation refer to the meanings of words. Denotation is the dictionary meaning of a word, the literal meaning. Connotation, on the other hand, is the implied or suggested meaning of a word. For example, the denotation of *lamb* is "a young sheep." The connotations of *lamb* are numerous: *gentle, docile, weak, peaceful, blessed, sacrificial, blood, spring, frisky, pure, innocent,* and so on. See the introduction to Chapter 11 (pp. 273–77) for more on connotation and denotation.

Controlling Idea See *Thesis.*

Coordination Coordination is the joining of grammatical constructions of the same rank (e.g., words, phrases, clauses) to indicate that they are of equal importance. For example, "*They ate hot dogs,* and *we ate hamburgers.*" See the introduction to Chapter 9 (pp. 217–21) for more on coordination. See also *Subordination.*

Deduction Deduction is the process of reasoning from stated premises to a conclusion that follows necessarily. This form of reasoning moves from the general to the specific. See the introduction to Chapter 21 (pp. 525–32) for a discussion of deductive reasoning and its role in argumentation. See also *Syllogism.*

Definition Definition is a rhetorical pattern. Definition is a statement of the meaning of a word. A definition may be either brief or extended, part of an essay or an entire essay itself. See the introduction to Chapter 17 (pp. 432–34) for a detailed discussion of definition.

Denotation See *Connotation/Denotation.*

Description Description tells how a person, place, or thing is perceived by the five senses. See the introduction to Chapter 15 (pp. 387–88) for a detailed discussion of description.

Details Details are the small elements that collectively contribute to the overall impression of a person, place, thing, or idea. For example, in the sentence "The *organic, whole-grain* dog biscuits were *reddish brown, beef flavored,* and in the *shape of a bone*" the italicized words are details.

Dialogue Dialogue is the conversation of two or more people as represented in writing. Dialogue is what people say directly to one another.

Diction Diction refers to a writer's choice and use of words. Good diction is precise and appropriate: The words mean exactly what the writer intends, and the words are well suited to the writer's subject, intended audience, and purpose in writing. The word-conscious writer knows that there are differences among *aged, old,* and *elderly; blue, navy,* and *azure;* and *disturbed, angry,* and *irritated.* Furthermore, this writer knows in which situation to use each word. See the introduction to Chapter 11 (pp. 273–77) for a detailed discussion of diction. See also *Cliché; Colloquial Expression; Connotation/Denotation; Jargon; Slang.*

Division and Classification Division and classification are rhetorical patterns used by the writer first to establish categories and then to arrange or sort people, places, or things into these categories according to their different characteristics, thus making them more manageable for the writer and more understandable and meaningful for the reader. See the introduction to Chapter 18 (pp. 448–51) for a detailed discussion of division and classification.

Dominant Impression A dominant impression is the single mood, atmosphere, or quality a writer emphasizes in a piece of descriptive writing. The dominant impression is created through the careful selection of details and is, of course, influenced by the writer's subject, audience, and purpose. See the introduction to Chapter 15 (pp. 387–88) for more on dominant impression.

Emphasis Emphasis is the placement of important ideas and words within sentences and longer units of writing so that they have the greatest impact. In general, what comes at the end has the most impact, and at the beginning nearly as much; what comes in the middle gets the least emphasis.

Endings See *Beginnings and Endings.*

Evaluation An evaluation of a piece of writing is an assessment of its effectiveness or merit. In evaluating a piece of writing, one should ask the following questions: What is the writer's purpose? Is it a worthwhile purpose? Does the writer achieve the purpose? Is the writer's information sufficient and accurate? What are the strengths of the essay? What are its weaknesses? Depending on the type of writing and the purpose, more specific questions can also be asked. For example, with an argument one could ask: Does the writer follow the principles of logical thinking? Is the writer's evidence sufficient and convincing?

Evidence Evidence is the information on which a judgment or argument is based or by which proof or probability is established. Evidence usually takes the form of statistics, facts, names, examples or illustrations, and opinions of authorities.

Example An example illustrates a larger idea or represents something of which it is a part. An example is a basic means of developing or clarifying an idea. Furthermore, examples enable writers to show and not simply to tell readers what they mean. See the introduction to Chapter 13 (pp. 325–28) for more on example.

Facts Facts are pieces of information presented as having objective reality—that is, having actual existence. For example, water boils at 212°F, Katherine Hepburn died in 2003, and the USSR no longer exists—these are all facts.

Fallacy See *Logical Fallacy.*

Figure of Speech A figure of speech is a brief, imaginative comparison that highlights the similarities between things that are basically dissimilar. Figures of speech make writing vivid, interesting, and memorable. The most common figures of speech are:

Simile: An explicit comparison introduced by *like* or *as.* "The fighter's hands were like stone."

Metaphor: An implied comparison that makes one thing the equivalent of another. "All the world's a stage."

Personification: A special kind of figure of speech in which human traits are assigned to ideas or objects. "The engine coughed and then stopped."

See the introduction to Chapter 12 (pp. 303–4) for a detailed discussion of figurative language.

Focus Focus is the limitation that a writer gives his or her subject. The writer's task is to select a manageable topic given the constraints of time, space, and purpose. For example, within the general subject of sports, a writer could focus on government support of amateur athletes or narrow the focus further to government support of Olympic athletes.

General See *Specific/General.*

Idiom An idiom is a word or phrase that is used habitually with special meaning. The meaning of an idiom is not always readily apparent to nonnative speakers of that language. For example, *catch cold, hold a job, make up your mind,* and *give them a hand* are all idioms in English.

Illustration Illustration is the use of examples to explain, elucidate, or corroborate. Writers rely heavily on illustration to make their ideas both clear and concrete. See the introduction to Chapter 13 (pp. 325–28) for a detailed discussion of illustration.

Induction Induction is the process of reasoning to a conclusion about all members of a class through an examination of only a few members of the class. This form of reasoning moves from the particular to the general. See the introduction to Chapter 21 (pp. 525–32) for a discussion of inductive reasoning and its role in argumentation.

Inductive Leap An inductive leap is the point at which a writer of an argument, having presented sufficient evidence, moves to a generalization or conclusion. See also *Induction.*

Introduction See *Beginnings and Endings.*

Irony Irony is the use of words to suggest something different from their literal meaning. For example, when Jonathan Swift suggested in "A Modest Proposal" that Ireland's problems could be solved if the people of Ireland fattened their babies and sold them to the English landlords for food, he meant that almost any other solution would be preferable. A writer can use irony to establish a special relationship with the reader and to add an extra dimension or twist to the meaning. See the introduction to Chapter 11 (pp. 273–77) for more on irony.

Jargon Jargon, or technical language, is the special vocabulary of a trade, profession, or group. Doctors, construction workers, lawyers, and teachers, for example, all have a specialized vocabulary that they use on the job. See also *Diction.*

Logical Fallacy A logical fallacy is an error in reasoning that renders an argument invalid. See the introduction to Chapter 21 (pp. 525–32) for a discussion of common logical fallacies.

Metaphor See *Figure of Speech.*

Narration To narrate is to tell a story, to tell what happened. While narration is most often used in fiction, it is also important in expository writing, either by itself or in conjunction with other types of prose. See the introduction to Chapter 14 (pp. 357–60) for a detailed discussion of narration.

Opinion An opinion is a belief or conclusion, which may or may not be substantiated by positive knowledge or proof. (If not substantiated, an opinion is a prejudice.) Even when based on evidence and sound reasoning, an opinion is personal and can be changed and is therefore less persuasive than facts and arguments.

Organization Organization is the pattern or order that the writer imposes on his or her material. Some often-used patterns of organization include time order, space order, and order of importance. See the introduction to Chapter 5 (pp. 114–18) for a detailed discussion of organization.

Paradox A paradox is a seemingly contradictory statement that is nonetheless true. For example, "We little know what we have until we lose it" is a paradoxical statement.

Paragraph The paragraph, the single most important unit of thought in an essay, is a series of closely related sentences. These sentences adequately develop the central or controlling idea of the paragraph. This central idea, usually stated in a topic sentence, is necessarily related to the purpose of the whole composition. A well-written paragraph has several distinguishing characteristics: a clearly stated or implied topic sentence, adequate development, unity, coherence, and an appropriate organizational strategy. See the introduction to Chapter 7 (pp. 169–72) for a detailed discussion of paragraphs.

Parallelism Parallel structure is the repetition of word order or grammatical form either within a single sentence or in several sentences that develop the same central idea. As a rhetorical device, parallelism can aid coherence and add emphasis. Franklin Roosevelt's statement "I see one-third of a nation ill-housed, ill-clad, and ill-nourished" illustrates effective parallelism. See the introduction to Chapter 9 (pp. 217–21) for more on parallelism.

Personification See *Figure of Speech.*

Persuasion Persuasion, or persuasive argument, is an attempt to convince readers to agree with a point of view, to make a decision, or to pursue a particular course of action. Persuasion appeals strongly to the emotions, whereas logical argument does not.

Point of View Point of view refers to the grammatical person in an essay. For example, the first-person point of view uses the pronoun *I* and is commonly found in autobiography and the personal essay; the third-person point of view uses the pronouns *he, she,* or *it* and is commonly found in objective writing. See the introduction to Chapter 14 (pp. 357–60) for a discussion of point of view in narration.

Process Analysis Process analysis is a rhetorical strategy used to explain how something works or to give step-by-step directions for doing something. See the introduction to Chapter 16 (pp. 407–10) for a detailed discussion of process analysis.

Purpose Purpose is what the writer wants to accomplish in a particular piece of writing. Purposeful writing seeks to *tell* (narration), to *describe* (description), to *explain* (process analysis, definition, classification, comparison and contrast, and cause and effect), or to *convince* (argumentation).

Rhetorical Question A rhetorical question is asked for its rhetorical effect but requires no answer from the reader. "When will nuclear proliferation end?" is such a question. Writers use rhetorical questions to introduce topics they plan to discuss or to emphasize important points. See the introduction to Chapter 6 (pp. 137–45) for another example.

Sentence A sentence is a grammatical unit that expresses a complete thought. It consists of at least a subject (a noun) and a predicate (a verb). See the introduction to Chapter 9 (pp. 217–21) for a detailed discussion of effective sentences.

Simile See *Figure of Speech*.

Slang Slang is the unconventional, informal language of particular subgroups in our culture. Slang terms, such as *bummed, sweat, dark,* and *cool,* are acceptable in formal writing only if used selectively for specific purposes.

Specific/General General words name groups or classes of objects, qualities, or actions. Specific words, on the other hand, name individual objects, qualities, or actions within a class or group. To some extent the terms *general* and *specific* are relative. For example, *clothing* is a class of things. *Shirt,* however, is more specific than *clothing* but more general than *T-shirt*. See also *Diction*.

Strategy A strategy is a means by which a writer achieves his or her purpose. Strategy includes the many rhetorical decisions that the writer makes about organization, paragraph structure, sentence structure, and diction. In terms of the whole essay, strategy refers to the principal rhetorical mode that a writer uses. If, for example, a writer wishes to explain how to make chocolate chip cookies, the most effective strategy would be process analysis. If it is the writer's purpose to analyze why sales of American cars have declined in recent years, the most effective strategy would be cause-and-effect analysis.

Style Style is the individual manner in which a writer expresses his or her ideas. Style is created by the author's particular choice of words, construction of sentences, and arrangement of ideas.

Subordination Subordination is the use of grammatical constructions to make one part of a sentence dependent on, rather than equal to, another. For example, the italicized clause in the following sentence is subordinate: "They all cheered *when I finished the race.*" See the introduction to Chapter 9 (pp. 217–21) for more on subordination. See also *Coordination.*

Supporting Evidence See *Evidence.*

Syllogism A syllogism is an argument that utilizes deductive reasoning and consists of a major premise, a minor premise, and a conclusion:

All trees that lose leaves are deciduous. (*Major premise*)
Maple trees lose their leaves. (*Minor premise*)
Therefore, maple trees are deciduous. (*Conclusion*)

See pages 525–32 in Chapter 21 for more on syllogisms. See also *Deduction.*

Symbol A symbol is a person, place, or thing that represents something beyond itself. For example, the bald eagle is a symbol of the United States, and the maple leaf, a symbol of Canada.

Syntax Syntax refers to the way in which words are arranged to form phrases, clauses, and sentences, as well as to the grammatical relationship among the words themselves.

Technical Language See *Jargon.*

Thesis The thesis, also known as the controlling idea, is the main idea of an essay. It may sometimes be implied rather than stated directly. See the introduction to Chapter 3 (pp. 73–75) for more on the thesis statement.

Title A title is a word or phrase set off at the beginning of an essay to identify the subject, to state the main idea of the essay, or to attract the reader's attention. A title may be explicit or suggestive. A subtitle, when used, explains or restricts the meaning of the main title.

Tone Tone is the manner in which a writer relates to an audience, the "tone of voice" used to address readers. Tone may be friendly, serious, distant, angry, humorous, cheerful, bitter, cynical, enthusiastic, morbid, resentful, warm, playful, and so forth. A particular tone results from a writer's diction, sentence structure, purpose, and attitude toward the subject. See the introduction to Chapter 11 (pp. 273–77) for several examples that display different tones.

Topic Sentence The topic sentence states the central idea of a paragraph and thus limits the content of the paragraph. Although the topic sentence normally appears at the beginning of the paragraph, it may appear at any other point, particularly if the writer is trying to create a special effect. Not all paragraphs contain topic sentences. See also *Paragraph*.

Transition A transition is a word or phrase that links sentences, paragraphs, and larger units of a composition to achieve coherence. Transitions include parallelism, pronoun references, conjunctions, and the repetition of key ideas, as well as the many conventional transitional expressions such as *moreover, on the other hand, in addition, in contrast,* and *therefore.* See the introduction to Chapter 8 (pp. 192–95) for a detailed discussion of transitions. See also *Coherence.*

Unity Unity is that quality of oneness in an essay that results when all the words, sentences, and paragraphs contribute to the thesis. The elements of a unified essay do not distract the reader. Instead, they all harmoniously support a single idea or purpose. See the introduction to Chapter 4 (pp. 94–97) for a detailed discussion of unity.

Verb Verbs can be classified as either strong verbs (*scream, pierce, gush, ravage,* and *amble*) or weak verbs (*be, has, get,* and *do*). Writers prefer to use strong verbs to make their writing more specific, more descriptive, and more action filled.

Voice Verbs can be classified as being in either the active or the passive voice. In the *active voice,* the doer of the action is the grammatical subject. In the *passive voice,* the receiver of the action is the subject:

Active: Glenda questioned all of the children.
Passive: All of the children were questioned by Glenda.

Acknowledgments

Diane Ackerman. "Watching a Night Launch of the Space Shuttle." From *A Natural History of the Senses.* Copyright © 1990 by Diane Ackerman. Used by permission of Random House, Inc.

Maya Angelou. "Momma, the Dentist, and Me." From *I Know Why the Caged Bird Sings.* Copyright © 1969 and renewed 1997 by Maya Angelou. Used by permission of Random House, Inc.

Isaac Asimov. "What Is Intelligence, Anyway?" Published by the permission of the Isaac Asimov Estate, c/o Ralph M. Vicinanza Ltd, via Trident Media Group, LLC. All rights reserved.

Russell Baker. "Becoming a Writer." Excerpt from Chapter 2 of *Growing Up.* Copyright © 1982 by Russell Baker. Reprinted with the permission of Don Congdon Associates, Inc.

Sharon Begley. "Praise the Humble Dung Beetle." From *Newsweek,* June 9, 2008. Copyright © 2008 by Newsweek, Inc. All rights reserved. Used by permission and protected by the Copyright Laws of the United States. The printing, copying, redistribution, or retransmission of the Material without express written permission is prohibited. www.newsweek.com.

Buzz Bissinger. "Faster, Higher, Stronger, No Longer." From the *New York Times,* April 13, 2008. Copyright © 2008 by The New York Times Company. All rights reserved. Used by permission and protected by the Copyright Laws of the United States. The printing, copying, redistribution, or retransmission of the Material without express written permission is prohibited. www.nytimes.com.

Paul Boutin. "You Are What You Search." From *Slate,* August 11, 2006. Reprinted by permission of United Media. All rights reserved.

Andrew Braaksma. "Some Lessons from the Assembly Line." Originally titled "My Turn," from *Newsweek,* September 12, 2005. Reprinted by permission of the author.

Steve Brody. "How I Got Smart." From the *New York Times,* September 21, 1986. Originally titled "Love, with Knowledge Aforethought." Copyright © 1986 by The New York Times Company. All rights reserved. Used by permission and protected by the Copyright Laws of the United States. The printing, copying, redistribution, or retransmission of the Material without express written permission is prohibited.

Rachel Carson. "Fable for Tomorrow." From *Silent Spring.* Copyright © 1962 by Rachel L. Carson. Copyright © renewed 1990 by Roger Christie. Used by permission of Houghton Mifflin Harcourt Publishing Company. All rights reserved.

Bruce Catton. "Grant and Lee: A Study in Contrasts." From the *American Story,* edited by Earl Schenk Miers. Copyright © by the U.S. Capitol Historical Society. All rights reserved. Reprinted with the permission of the U.S. Capitol Historical Society.

Anton Chekhov. "A Nincompoop." Translated by Ann Dunnigan, from *Anton Chekhov: Selected Stories.* Copyright © 1960 by Ann Dunnigan. Used by permission of Dutton Signet, a division of Penguin Group (USA) Inc.

Sandra Cisneros. "My Name." From *The House on Mango Street.* Copyright © 1984 by Sandra Cisneros. Published by Vintage Books, a division of Random House, Inc., and in hardcover by Alfred A. Knopf in 1994. Reprinted by permission of Susan Bergholz Literary Services, New York, NY, and Lamy, NM. All rights reserved.

James Lincoln Collier. "Anxiety: Challenge by Another Name." From *Reader's Digest,* December 1986. Reprinted with the permission of the author.

Greg Critser. "Don't Eat the Flan." From *Forbes,* February 3, 2003. Reprinted with the permission of the author.

Meghan Daum. "My House: Plain and Fantasy." From *Metropolitan Home,* September/October 2001. Copyright © 2001 by Meghan Daum. Reprinted with the permission of the author.

Lars Eighner. "On Dumpster Diving." From *Travels with Lizbeth.* Copyright © 1993 by Lars Eighner. Reprinted with the permission of St. Martin's Press, LLC.

Lawrence M. Friedman. "What Is Crime?" From *Crime and Punishment in American History.* Copyright © 1993 by Lawrence M. Friedman. Reprinted with the permission of Basic Books, a member of Perseus Books Group, LLC.

Thomas L. Friedman. "My Favorite Teacher." From the *New York Times,* January 9, 2001. Copyright © 2001 by The New York Times Company. All rights reserved. Used by permission and protected by the Copyright Laws of the United States. The printing, copying, redistribution, or retransmission of the Material without express written permission is prohibited. www.nytimes.com.

Martin Gansberg. "Thirty-Eight Who Saw Murder Didn't Call Police." From the *New York Times,* March 17, 1964. Copyright © 1964 by The New York Times Company. All rights reserved. Used by permission and protected by the Copyright Laws of the United States. The printing, copying, redistribution, or retransmission of the Material without express written permission is prohibited. www.nytimes.com.

Henry Louis Gates Jr. "Forty Acres and a Gap in Wealth." From the *New York Times,* November 18, 2007. Copyright © 2007 by The New York Times Company. All rights reserved. Used by permission and protected by the Copyright Laws of the United States. The printing, copying, redistribution, or retransmission of the Material without express written permission is prohibited. www.nytimes.com. "What's in a Name?" From *Dissent,* Volume 36, No. 4, Fall 1989. Reprinted with the permission of the Foundation for the Study of Independent Social Ideas.

Nancy Gibbs. "The Magic of the Family Meal." From *Time,* June 12, 2006. Copyright © 2006 by Time, Inc. Reprinted with permission of Time via Copyright Clearance Center.

Bernard Gladstone. "How to Build a Fire in a Fireplace." From *The New York Times Complete Manual of Home Repair.* Copyright © 1978 by Bernard Gladstone. Used by permission of Times Books, a division of Random House, Inc.

Malcolm Gladwell. "No Mercy." From the *New Yorker,* September 4, 2006. Copyright © 2006 by Malcolm Gladwell. Reprinted with the permission of the author.

Natalie Goldberg. "Be Specific." From *Writing Down the Bones: Freeing the Writer Within.* Copyright © 1986 by Natalie Goldberg. Reprinted by arrangement with Shambhala Publications, Inc., Boston, MA. www.shambhala.com.

Ellen Goodman. "The Company Man." From *Value Judgments.* Copyright © 1993 by Ellen Goodman. Reprinted with the permission of International Creative Management, Inc.

Ronald M. Green. "Building Baby from the Genes Up." Originally published in the *Washington Post,* April 13, 2008. Reprinted by permission.

Dick Gregory. "Shame." From *Nigger: An Autobiography.* Copyright © 1964 by Dick Gregory Enterprises, Inc. Used by permission of Dutton, a division of Penguin Group (USA) Inc.

Sanjay Gupta. "Stuck on the Couch." From *Time,* February 21, 2008. Copyright © 2008 by Time, Inc. Reprinted with permission of Time via Copyright Clearance Center.

Gilbert Highet. "Subway Station." From *Talents and Geniuses: The Pleasures of Appreciation.* Copyright © 1957 by Gilbert Highet. Reprinted by permission of Curtis Brown Ltd.

Oscar Hijuelos. "Memories of New York City Snow." From *Metropolis Found: New York Is Book Country 25th Anniversary Collection* (New York: New York Is Book Country, 2003). Copyright © 2003 by Oscar Hijuelos. Reprinted with the permission of The Jennifer Lyons Literary Agency, LLC, for the author.

Langston Hughes. "Salvation." From *The Big Sea: An Autobiography.* Copyright 1940 by Langston Hughes, renewed © 1968 by Arna Bontemps and George Houston Bass. Reprinted by permission of Hill and Wang, a division of Farrar, Straus & Giroux, LLC.

Bill Husted. "Constitution." Copyright © 2003 by *Atlanta Journal-Constitution.* Reproduced with permission of *Atlanta Journal-Constitution* in the format Textbook via Copyright Clearance Center.

Barbara Huttmann. "A Crime of Compassion." Originally published in *Newsweek,* August 8, 1983. Copyright © 1983 by Barbara Huttmann. Reprinted with the permission of the author.

Jake Jamieson. "The English-Only Movement: Can America Proscribe Language with a Clear Conscience?" Reprinted with the permission of the author.

Dan M. Kahan. "Shame Is Worth a Try." From the *Boston Globe,* August 5, 2001. Copyright © 2001 by Dan M. Kahan. Reprinted with the permission of the author.

Michael T. Kaufman. "Of My Friend Hector and My Achilles Heel." From the *New York Times,* November 11, 1992. Copyright © 1992 by The New York Times Company. All rights reserved. Used by permission and protected by the Copyright Laws of the United States. The printing, copying, redistribution, or retransmission of the Material without express written permission is prohibited.

Martin Luther King Jr. "I Have a Dream." Copyright © 1963 by Dr. Martin Luther King Jr., copyright renewed 1991 by Coretta Scott King. Reprinted by arrangement with the Heirs to the Estate of Martin Luther King Jr., c/o Writer's House as agent for the proprietor, New York, NY. "The Ways of Meeting Oppression." From *Stride toward Freedom: The Montgomery Story*. Copyright © 1958 by Dr. Martin Luther King Jr. Copyright © 1986 by Coretta Scott King.

Stephen King. "Why We Crave Horror Movies." From *Playboy*, 1982. Copyright © by Stephen King. Reprinted with permission. All rights reserved.

Richard Lederer. "The Case for Short Words." From *The Miracle of Language*. Copyright © 1991 by Richard Lederer. Reprinted with the permission of Pocket Books, a division of Simon & Schuster Adult Publishing Group.

William Lutz. "Doubts about Doublespeak." From *State Government News*, July 1993. Copyright © 1993 by William Lutz. Reprinted with the permission of the author.

Myriam Marquez. "Why and When We Speak Spanish in Public." From *Orlando Sentinel*, June 28, 1998. Copyright © 1999 by the *Orlando Sentinel*. Reprinted with the permission of the publisher.

Frances Mayes. Recipe for "Lemon Cake." From *Under the Tuscan Sun: At Home in Italy*. Copyright © 1996 by Frances Mayes. Used with permission of Chronicle Books, LLC, San Francisco. Visit ChronicleBooks.com.

Cherokee Paul McDonald. "A View from the Bridge." From *Sun-Sentinel* (Fort Lauderdale, FL), February 12, 1989. Reprinted with the permission of the Author. All rights reserved.

Paul W. Merrill. "The Principles of Poor Writing." From the *Scientific Monthly*, January 1947. Copyright © 1947 by American Association for the Advancement of Sciences. Reprinted with permission.

Alison Motluk. "Supersize Me: It's Time to Stop Blaming Fat People for Their Size." From *New Scientist*, October 30, 2004. Copyright © 2004. Reprinted with the permission of *New Scientist*.

Bharati Mukherjee. "Two Ways to Belong in America." From the *New York Times*, 1996. Copyright © 1996 by The New York Times Company. All rights reserved. Used by permission and protected by the Copyright Laws of the United States. The printing, copying, redistribution, or retransmission of the Material without express written permission is prohibited. www.nytimes.com.

Gloria Naylor. "The Meanings of a Word." From the *New York Times*, February 20, 1986. Copyright © 1986 by Gloria Naylor. Reprinted with the permission of SLL/Sterling Lord Literistic, Inc.

George Orwell. "A Hanging." From *Shooting an Elephant and Other Essays*. Copyright 1950 by Sonia Brownell Orwell and renewed © 1978 by Pitt-Rivers. Reprinted by permission of Houghton Mifflin Harcourt Publishing Company.

Gregory Pence. "Let's Think outside the Box of Bad Clichés." From *Newsweek*, August 6, 2007. Copyright © 2007 by Newsweek, Inc. All rights reserved. Used by permission and protected by the Copyright Laws of the United States. The printing, copying, redistribution, or retransmission of the Material without express written permission is prohibited. www.newsweek.com.

Alexander Petrunkevitch. "The Spider and the Wasp." From *Scientific American*, August 1952. Copyright 1952 and renewed © 1980 by Scientific American, Inc. Reprinted with the permission of *Scientific American*.

Steven Pinker. "In Defense of Dangerous Ideas." From *What Is Your Dangerous Idea? Today's Leading Thinkers on the Unthinkable*, edited by John Brockman. Copyright © 2007 by Edge Foundation, Inc. Reprinted with the permission of HarperCollins Publishers.

Virginia Postrel. "Need Transplant Donors? Pay Them." From the *Los Angeles Times*, June 10, 2006. Reprinted by permission of Tribune Media Services.

Robert Ramirez. "The Barrio." Original title, "The Woolen Serape," from *Pain and Promise: The Chicano Today*, edited by Edward Simmens (New York: New American Library, 1972). Reprinted with the permission of the author.

David Raymond. "On Being 17, Bright, and Unable to Read." From the *New York Times*, April 25, 1976. Copyright © 1976 by The New York Times Company. Used by permission and protected by the Copyright Laws of the United States. The printing, copying, redistribution, or retransmission of the Material without express written permission is prohibited. www.nytimes.com.

Heather Rogers. "Hiding in Plain Sight." From *Gone Tomorrow: The Hidden Life of Garbage*. Copyright © 2005 by Heather Rogers. Reprinted with the permission of The New Press.

Mike Rose. "I Just Wanna Be Average." From *Lives on the Boundary: Struggles and Achievements of America's Underprepared*. Copyright © 1989 by Mike Rose. Reprinted with the permission of The Free Press, a division of Simon & Schuster, Inc. All rights reserved.

Carl T. Rowan. "Unforgettable Miss Bessie." From *Reader's Digest,* March 1985. Copyright © 1985 by The Reader's Digest Association, Inc. Reprinted with permission from *Reader's Digest.*

Ruth Russell. "The Wounds That Can't Be Stitched Up." From *Newsweek,* December 20, 1999. Copyright © 1999 by Newsweek, Inc. Used by permission and protected by the Copyright Laws of the United States. The printing, copying, redistribution, or retransmission of the Material without express written permission is prohibited. www.newsweek.com.

Audrey Schulman. "Fahrenheit 59: What a Child's Fever Might Tell Us about Climate Change." Originally published in *Orion,* January/February 2007. Reprinted by permission of the author.

David Sedaris. "Me Talk Pretty One Day." From *Me Talk Pretty One Day*. Copyright © 2000 by David Sedaris. Reprinted by permission of Little, Brown & Company.

Tiffany Sharples. "Young Love." From *Time,* January 17, 2008. Copyright © 2008 by Time, Inc. Reprinted by permission of Time via Copyright Clearance Center.

Mary Sherry. "In Praise of the F Word." From *Newsweek,* May 6, 1991. Copyright © 1991 by Mary Sherry. Reprinted with the permission of the author.

Gary Soto. "The Jacket." From *The Effects of Knut Hamsun on a Fresno Boy: Recollections and Short Essays*. Copyright © 1983, 2000 by Gary Soto. Reprinted with the permission of Persea Books, Inc. (New York).

Alexander Tabarrok. "A Moral Solution to the Organ Shortage." From The Independent Institute, February 19, 2001. Copyright © 2001. Reprinted with permission from The Independent Institute, 100 Swan Way, Oakland, CA 94621-1428, USA, www.independent.org.

June Tangney. "Condemn the Crime, Not the Person." From the *Boston Globe,* August 5, 2001. Copyright © 2001 by June Tangney. Reprinted with the permission of the author.

University of Vermont. Screenshots of UVM Libraries' Web pages, http://library.uvm.edu. Used by permission of the University of Vermont Libraries.

Judith Viorst. "Friends, Good Friends—and Such Good Friends." From *Redbook,* 1977. Copyright © 1977 by Judith Viorst. Reprinted with the permission of Lescher & Lescher, Ltd.

Sarah Vowell. "Pop-A-Shot." From *The Partly Cloudy Patriot*. Copyright © 2002 by Sarah Vowell. Reprinted with the permission of Simon & Schuster, Inc. All rights reserved.

Alice Walker. "Childhood." From *Dream Me Home Safely: Writers on Growing Up in America*, edited by Marian Wright Edelman, published by Houghton Mifflin Company. Copyright © 2003 by Alice Walker. Reprinted with the permission of The Wendy Weil Agency, Inc.

Linton Weeks. "Burdens of the Modern Beast." From the *Washington Post*, February 8, 2006. Copyright © 2006 by The Washington Post Writers Group. Used by permission and protected by the Copyright Laws of the United States. The printing, copying, redistribution, or retransmission of the Material without express written permission is prohibited. www.washingtonpost.com.

Eudora Welty. "The Corner Store." Original title, "The Little Store." From *The Eye of the Story: Selected Essays and Reviews*. Copyright © 1975 by Eudora Welty. Used by permission of Random House, Inc.

Abe Whaley. "Once Unique, Soon a Place Like Any Other." From *Newsweek,* November 14, 2005. Copyright © 2005 by Newsweek, Inc. Used by permission and protected by the Copyright Laws of the United States. The printing, copying, redistribution, or retransmission of the Material without express written permission is prohibited. www.newsweek.com.

William Zinsser. "Simplicity." From *On Writing Well,* Sixth Edition (New York: HarperCollins Publishers, 1994). Copyright © 1976, 1980, 1985, 1988, 1990, 1994, 1998, 2001, 2006 by William K. Zinsser. Reprinted by permission of the author.

Index